American Muse

American Muse

The Life and Times of William Schuman

Joseph W. Polisi

AMADEUS
PRESS

An Imprint of Hal Leonard Corporation
New York

Published in 2008 by Amadeus Press
An Imprint of Hal Leonard Corporation
7777 West Bluemound Road, Milwaukee, WI 53213

Trade Book Division Editorial Offices
19 West 21st Street, New York, NY 10010

Printed in the United States of America

Book design by Donald Giordano

Library of Congress Cataloging-in-Publication Data

Polisi, Joseph.
  American muse : the life and times of William Schuman / Joseph W. Polisi.
      p. cm.
  Includes bibliographical references and index.
  ISBN 978-1-57467-173-5
  1. Schuman, William, 1910-1992. 2. Composers--United States--Biography. I. Title.

  ML410.S386P65 2008
  780.92--dc22
  [B]
                                                2008039386

www.amadeuspress.com

To my beloved wife
Elizabeth Marlowe Polisi

Contents

Acknowledgments

My first discussion concerning a biography of William Schuman took place with Bill's wife, Frankie, soon after his death in February 1992. Frankie said that she wanted a story of Bill's life presented only in his own words. It could be done, she believed: Bill had worked on no fewer than five oral histories during his later years, the most detailed ones overseen by Vivian Perlis in 1977 and Heidi Waleson from 1990 to 1992.

Frankie also emphatically stated that she did not want a musicological study that would analyze her husband's life through a revisionist or psychological lens, nor did she want a theoretical analysis of his music such as she had read in recent biographies of composers she had known.

As a friend, I tried to help Frankie find an author who would be willing to write about Bill's life following Frankie's parameters, but we did not succeed. In an effort to move the project forward, I wrote two exploratory chapters based on Frankie's preferred format: one dealing with Bill's early years as a composer and another regarding his relationship with John D. Rockefeller 3rd.

I quickly realized that writing an honest and complete biography of Bill could not be accomplished using only material from the oral histories. Sadly, Frankie died before I could share with her my expanded chapters, which used Bill's letters and other sources to accurately present a full picture of his extraordinary life.

Tony and Andie Schuman, Bill and Frankie's children, however, eventually did see the chapters and encouraged me to undertake the full biography, providing me access to valuable research materials that had not been available before. To both of them I wish to express my unending gratitude for their many helpful suggestions after reading the final text and for their permission to use materials that are in their private possession in the Schuman Family Archives. Other family members to whom I am indebted are Judith Israel Gutmann and Henry Heilbrunn, Bill's niece and his first cousin once removed, for their willingness to answer genealogical questions and for providing valuable information and materials relating to the Schuman and Heilbrunn families. I also thank John Israel, Bill's nephew, for his helpful comments on the first several chapters.

Since I wrote the entire biography on 8 ½" by 14" legal pads—writing on a keyboard has never brought out the best in me—I needed to have my words transcribed to digital form. This arduous task was realized by my superb and highly intelligent assistant, Mary Belanger. I will quickly add that transcribing was only one of many tasks she undertook in the realization of the final manuscript. She also functioned as an insightful researcher and a meticulous editor. For her diligence, determination, and good-spirited work, I extend my deepest gratitude.

Sincere thanks also go to my editor, Barbara Norton, for her perceptive and sensitive work on my manuscript, which helped clarify my thoughts and made the entire volume more concise and focused. Her editorial precision and musical knowledge added immeasurably to the flow and contents of the book. My gratitude goes as well to John Cerullo, Amadeus Press publisher, and to Carol Flannery, Amadeus's editorial director, and all their colleagues at Amadeus for their generous support in bringing to life this second volume of mine under their aegis.

Wei-Chieh Lin, a talented composer and Juilliard doctoral student, helped enormously by transcribing all the musical examples found in the book's appendix. I also thank Lisa Robinson, senior writer for special projects and proposals of Juilliard's Development Office, who holds a doctorate in music theory from Yale, for her important assistance with analysis of the works in the book's appendix and for her help with the musical examples. In addition, I owe much gratitude to Don Giordano, Juilliard's director of creative services, who so expertly designed this book and who was tremendously helpful in evaluating and digitally scanning the book's photographs. And I thank the recent Juilliard doctoral recipient and gifted pianist Aaron Wunsch for the many articles and reviews he so accommodatingly researched.

Several good friends were kind enough to read my manuscript and provide insightful comments, a great many of which I have incorporated in the text. My colleague Ara Guzelimian, Juilliard's provost and dean, graciously offered numerous valuable suggestions that made the overall text more clear and engaging. Bruce MacCombie, composer and Juilliard's former dean, provided me with, in particular, excellent advice about Schuman's interactions with his publishers, as well as on the analyses in the appendix. Kenneth S. Davidson, Nathan Leventhal, and Martin E. Segal were also kind enough to provide very helpful suggestions.

I owe a great debt of gratitude to Jane Gottlieb, Juilliard's vice president for library and information resources, for providing me with wise counsel and precise information concerning numerous bibliographical queries over the years, as well as for making available to me Schuman's bound scores, housed in Juilliard's Lila Acheson Wallace Library. Her colleague Jeni Dahmus, Juilliard's archivist, was also extremely accommodating in helping me to research Schuman's presidency at Juilliard through the School's holdings of his presidential papers and photographs. Thanks go as well to Juilliard's library staff members Sandra Czajkowski, Robert Sherrane, Alan Klein, and Patricia Thomson.

The most voluminous source of all things Schuman is found in the American Music Collection of the Music Division of the New York Public Library at Lincoln Center, where all of Schuman's papers are held. Since Schuman was clearly inclined to save every scrap of paper he ever acquired—from a parking ticket to correspondence with artistic luminaries—his papers are a cornucopia of valuable information that provide significant insight into how this extraordinary person approached his life. My gratitude goes to Jacqueline Z. Davis, the Barbara G. and Lawrence A. Fleischman Executive Director, New York Public Library for the Performing Arts, Dorothy and Lewis B. Cullman Center, for allowing me access to the great institution she leads. The Schuman Papers are overseen by a dedicated and talented staff headed by George E. Boziwick, chief of the Music Division of the New York Public Library for the Performing Arts, whose knowledge and generosity of spirit assisted me in my research. In addition, Paul Friedman, special collections assistant in the Music Division of the New York Public Library at Lincoln Center, also was of great assistance to me in my research there.

I owe a special debt of gratitude to Heidi Waleson and Vivian Perlis for creating two illuminating Schuman oral histories, which provided invaluable details concerning his life. I thank them for their permission to quote extensively from their works. In addition, I also wish to thank David Wright and William Zinsser for granting me permission to use materials from their Schuman oral history projects. The work of K. Gary Adams in his book *William Schuman: A Bio-Bibliography* was also enormously helpful in confirming dates and searching out articles relating to Schuman's life.

For research into Schuman's Lincoln Center years, I wish to thank Judith Johnson, director of Information Services at Lincoln Center for the

Performing Arts, for providing me access to Lincoln Center board minutes, photos, and clipping files, and a Lincoln Center—sponsored oral history series realized by Sharon Zane involving interviews of Schuman, Edgar Young, and Schuyler Chapin. Thanks also go to Reynold Levy, president of Lincoln Center, and Lesley Friedman Rosenthal, vice president, general counsel and secretary of Lincoln Center, for permission to view this information. In addition, my thanks go to Barbara Haws, archivist/historian, and Richard C. Wandel, associate archivist of the New York Philharmonic, for providing me access to information regarding Schuman premieres with the orchestra, as well as to sound recordings of selected live performances.

Schuman's manuscript scores are housed in Washington, D.C., at the Library of Congress. My gratitude goes to Susan H. Vita, chief of the Music Division of the Library of Congress, for allowing me to view these manuscripts. Schuman had only two principal publishers during his classical compositional career. I would like to thank G. Schirmer, Inc., and the Theodore Presser Company for providing permission to reprint excerpts from ten Schuman scores appearing in the appendix of the book.

Since certain of Schuman's compositions were either withdrawn or never commercially recorded, I turned to various sound archives to experience the music beyond the printed score. For providing me with access to archival recordings, I wish to thank Robert Taibbi, director of Juilliard's Recording Department; Sarah Velez, curator of the Rodgers and Hammerstein Archives of Recorded Sound of the New York Public Library at Lincoln Center; Gary Galo, audio engineer of the Crane School of Music, State University of New York, Potsdam; and David Hunter, music librarian and curator of the Historical Recordings Collections of the Fine Arts Library of the University of Texas at Austin.

In my effort to learn of the environment in which Schuman lived I am very appreciative of being welcomed as a researcher by the New-York Historical Society, in particular the vice president and library director, Jean W. Ashton, and the Print Room reference librarian, Susan E. Kriete, who assisted me in reviewing photographs of New York City at the time of Schuman's youth; by the American Jewish Historical Society; by the Sarah Lawrence College Library and by Abby Lester, archivist of the college; by the Delaware Symphony Orchestra and by Holly J. Grasso, music librarian and education/operations associate; by the New Rochelle Public Library and Barbara Davis, community relations coordinator; and by Bridget P. Carr, archivist of the Boston Symphony Orchestra.

During my research and writing I was ably supported in the activities of my "day job" as president of Juilliard by my executive assistant, Martha Sterner. Thanks also go to my former assistant Sharon Hayes Sachs for her work on the early chapters of the book and to recent Juilliard doctoral recipient Yelena Grinberg for her research assistance in its beginning phases. My gratitude goes, as well, to the staff of Shenorock #39 for their work in making my writing environment as supportive as possible during the summer months.

This book could not have been realized without the love and encouragement of my wife, Elizabeth Marlowe Polisi, to whom this book is dedicated. She was patient and supportive of me during the many hours I spent bringing this volume to fruition. Elizabeth and my children provided me with the motivation and energy to approach this deeply gratifying project.

The monogram that appears above and is used as a divider throughout the text is taken from the back of a gold watch owned by William Schuman and given to the author by Frankie Schuman at the time of her husband's death.

All dates of compositions in the text refer to their premieres unless otherwise indicated.

Please refer to the official William Schuman website www.williamschuman.org for current discography and listing of compostions.

For additional information regarding this book, visit www.schuman_americanmuse.com.

Prologue

There they stood on the red carpet. He, beaming with a broad and satisfied smile, crisply attired in white tie and tailcoat, an American Academy rosette adorning his left lapel; she, with a slightly incredulous stare, lips tightly pursed, dressed in an elegant dove gray Vera Maxwell gown, grasping white gloves in her left hand, her lace wrap gently obscuring her pearl necklace. Behind them was the façade of a $46 million edifice fitted with gold banisters, red carpets, crystal chandeliers, and mammoth Chagall murals looking out on a spacious fountain plaza. Society ladies, dressed in haute-couture designs and bedecked with furs, jewels of various shapes, sizes, and colors, and the occasional tiara mingled with Rockefellers, Whitneys, Vanderbilts, government officials, ambassadors, tycoons.

The date: September 16, 1966. The occasion: the inauguration of the Metropolitan Opera House at Lincoln Center. The couple: Bill and Frankie Schuman. The moment: the height of William Schuman's power as the most prominent arts leader in America.

The story of how William Schuman rose to prominence is one deeply rooted in America of the twentieth century, where a person could rise to dizzying heights with intelligence, talent, determination, and grit—all in full supply for the brilliant and driven Schuman. His middle-class roots instilled in him a lifelong industriousness and desire for advancement. Born into a German Jewish middle class family living on the Upper West Side of Manhattan, Schuman had parents who could not even have imagined attending a gala performance of the sort that had now become the daily fare of their accomplished son.

William Schuman's life spanned most of the twentieth century. He saw the United States evolve from an isolated, protectionist nation to a superpower. He was instrumental in shaping how America perceived and supported the performing arts in schools and concert halls throughout the nation. Schuman guided the future of two august artistic institutions through his leadership of the Juilliard School of Music and the fledgling Lincoln

Center for the Performing Arts. In both cases, he left a legacy of innovation and accomplishment that flourishes into the twenty-first century. A commentator wrote at the end of Schuman's life that although he "never achieved the kind of name recognition that was enjoyed by his friends and colleagues Leonard Bernstein and Aaron Copland, [Schuman] probably had a stronger and more durable effect on American musical life."

During the demanding times that he led distinguished arts organizations, Schuman lived a separate and equally committed life as a composer of over one hundred works for solo instruments, chamber ensembles, ballet and opera companies, choruses, and symphony orchestras. Innovative in his art, he utilized texts from Walt Whitman to the Sears, Roebuck catalog in his choral works, juxtaposed unorthodox assemblages of musical elements, and developed his own compositional vocabulary at a time when the "serious" composer was being pushed toward an embrace of dodecaphony. His passion to compose was a leitmotif of his frenetic life. Never was any other pursuit permitted to dilute his intense drive to create new music. Schuman saw his music as an integral part of his persona: "Whatever meaning my life has is to be found in the music itself."

William Schuman's life crisscrossed the various strata of American society. He composed songs for dance bands, analyzed the curve ball of an aspiring rookie pitcher on the baseball field, and interacted with some of the most prominent political and financial leaders of his time. In many ways he was the first artist-administrator who had to address the demands of the modern arts world, keeping budgets balanced on the one hand and high artistic standards inviolate on the other. However, Schuman's deeply held belief that artistic endeavors should always take precedence over financial exigencies turned out to be a fundamental miscalculation of his Lincoln Center presidency.

Once described as "a radical with conservative ideas," Schuman was a complex man. He could be gleeful, playful, entrepreneurial, aggressive, visionary, and self-assured, as well as introspective, arrogant, vulnerable, self-righteous, and naive. He interacted with many of the artistic giants of the twentieth century, yet his musical education was to a great degree self-directed. He made the fateful decision to become a composer of concert music in 1930 and, amazingly, had his Second Symphony performed by the Boston Symphony Orchestra only nine years later. He was prone to impetuous decisions, highly talented, a brilliant public speaker, and a bit vain.

William Schuman's extraordinary life as a composer and arts leader reflects his role as an artistic catalyst within the fertile and constantly evolving environment of America of the twentieth century. A passionate champion of his country, Schuman once wrote, "It seems to me that the . . . development of American artists in all media—music, visual arts, letters—has been truly remarkable. . . . I believe [American artists] . . . have been a complete success. They have been as diverse as the democracy that gave them birth, and their achievements have found world acceptance."

Schuman's dear friend Leonard Bernstein elegantly summed up the man and his music in an often-noted encomium:

> I have rarely met a composer who is so faithfully mirrored in his music; the man is the music. We are all familiar with the attributes generally ascribed to his compositions: vitality, optimism, enthusiasm, long lyrical line, rhythmic impetuosity, bristling counterpoint, brilliant textures, dynamic tension. But what is not so often remarked is what I treasure most: the human qualities that flow directly from the man into the works—compassion, fidelity, insight, and total honesty. Compassion is the keynote; it is the mark of a man, and, for me, the mark of this man's music.

Through both his music and his visionary leadership, Schuman was an authentic American muse who helped make his nation a leader in performing arts and arts education in the twenty-first century. His legacy manifests the profound impact that talent, tough leadership, and determination can have on the arts, in a nation and around the world.

CHAPTER 1

The Fiddle and Baseball

Seen through the lens of the father-and-son photographers George P. and James S. Hall, New York City at the turn of the twentieth century looked surprisingly like the Paris of Eugène Atget's historic photographs. The cityscapes were punctuated by mansard roofs and exquisitely appointed gardens, with women in long frilly skirts carrying parasols and men in bowler hats holding canes. These remarkable photographs showed elaborate statuary and flowing flags on elegant homes made of stone and brick embellished with ornate metal gratings and multiple chimneys, complex iron structures and fanciful arcades supporting elevated trains, and crowded produce and flower markets frequented by the city's multicultural population.

But on the city's wide boulevards, new buildings were taking shape next to the elegant homes. These structures, with their modern, angular shapes, had a grandeur and mass that were anathema to the delicate Parisian aesthetic. Pushing aside the elegance of the past, they embodied a brash new era in a new world.

There was another side to America's largest city: tenements in the Lower East Side, immigrants making their way along Hester Street, new arrivals on Ellis Island. And the nation that protected and nurtured this bustling center of humanity was a country filled with hopes and dreams born of idealism, determination, and optimism. It was a place where success could be realized through hard work, education, and grit. The city at the center of this limitless energy could only be New York.

At the turn of the century New York's church steeples were being replaced by the tallest buildings in the entire country, and new approaches to technology and transportation were heralded by such engineering wonders as the Brooklyn Bridge, the Flatiron Building, and Pennsylvania Station. In 1900 the city's 3,437,202 inhabitants numbered more than the total population of all but six U.S. states. In population New York was the largest city in the nation, twice the size of Chicago, and of the world's great cities it was second only to London—especially after 1898, when it consolidated its government and added Brooklyn, Queens, the Bronx, and Staten Island to Manhattan. More than a third of all Americans were immigrants, most of them German and Irish born, followed by Italians and Eastern European Jews.

As the twentieth century burst forth, the city's population moved northward from its center near City Hall toward farmlands above 59th Street. By 1879 elevated train tracks had sprung up along 2nd, 3rd, 6th, and 9th Avenues, allowing New Yorkers to travel by train up to 110th Street. At the same time "apartment houses" sprang up, commodious buildings capable of housing numerous families in multi-room flats. One of the first and most luxurious, located at Central Park West and 72nd Street, was commissioned by Edward S. Clark, president of the Singer Sewing Machine Company, and in the view of most New Yorkers was proof of Clark's folly: "The building was so far out of town . . . that it might as well be out West somewhere, and they began to call it the Dakota," a name that stuck. It is now one of the most sought-after residences in Manhattan.

By 1910 New York City's population was close to five million people, almost half of them living in Manhattan. About 41 percent of New Yorkers were foreign born, and about one in eight lived in tenements south of 14th Street. It was in this booming urban center that William Howard ("Billy") Schuman was born on August 4, 1910, and here he would live almost all his life, the embodiment of his native city's boldness, focus, and energy.

Only five days after Billy's birth, New York's mayor, William Gaynor, narrowly escaped assassination while boarding the *SS Kaiser Wilhelm* on the way to Europe. At the end of the summer marauding white gangs were beating up blacks in race riots. The average employee worked more than fifty-six hours and earned less than $15 a week. That fall Gimbels opened on Greeley Square between 32nd and 33rd Streets—just a block south of its main rival, Macy's. The magnificent Pennsylvania Station was ready for passengers the same year, and the Ziegfeld Follies and Victor Herbert's *Naughty Marietta* were playing on Broadway.

Schuman's heritage was rooted in the wave of German Jews who journeyed to the New World in the second half of the nineteenth century. From 1880 to 1914 hundreds of thousands of immigrants came to the United States in hopes of finding a new life. Assimilation into their new home— Americanization—was for them paramount. After 1840 German Jews predominated among the Jewish population in their new country, and it was they who shaped American Jewish society, its institutions and manners, which all other U.S. Jewish populations eventually embraced.

Between 1830 and 1880 approximately ten million people immigrated to the United States. Of these, the 200,000 or so German Jews made up just a small fraction relative to the 3 million Germans, 2.7 million Irish, almost 1 million English, and less than half a million Scandinavians. Although the number of German Jewish immigrants to the United States dwindled between 1880 and 1914, they were replaced by a large number of Eastern European and Russian Jews; as a result, by 1914 there were 2.5 million Jews in the United States, up tenfold from the number just a third of a century earlier. Of these, about 1 million lived in New York City. German Jews in New York City were scattered throughout Manhattan at this time. Most, and the poorest, were in a section of the Lower East Side known as Kleindeutschland. There was another, smaller Jewish enclave with greater financial resources in Chelsea, in an area clustered around 7th Avenue and 19th Street.

Unlike the Sephardic Jews who had come from Spain and Portugal during the American colonial period, German American Jews embraced the importance of individual freedom. In the United States they were able, even entitled, to break away from community-based restraints. These new Americans took very seriously their newfound freedom, not only in politics and economics, but also in culture and religion.

Middle-class German American Jews at the turn of the twentieth century often exhibited a deep-seated desire to assimilate into American culture, and William Schuman's family was no exception:

> Jews labored to absorb American social tastes and habits. While moral codes applied equally to all classes, manners varied according to socioeconomic status. . . . Jews looked beyond their [community's] teachings and adopted the criteria for proper behavior set by those whose acceptance they craved—the upper middle class. . . . The American Jew['s] patriotism was unimpeachable . . . [He] kept his Jewish interests within the confines of his community and never called attention unnecessarily to his Jewishness politically or in other public fashion.

The more-established German American Jews often looked down on the new Eastern European and Russian Jewish immigrants, fearing that these recent Jewish arrivals would incite American anti-Semitism. Once again, assimilation into American society was advanced by German American Jewish leaders as the solution: "These newcomers must be turned into useful American citizens or they will upset our position before the community."

The most secure route immigrants could take to becoming "useful American citizens" was education. In the first three decades of the twentieth century the main road to higher education for New York Jews led to City College, located after 1907 at Convent Avenue and 137th Street in Upper Manhattan. Essentially tuition free and with an admissions policy based on merit, the college had an enrollment that was 85 percent Jewish. Numerous City College Jewish alumni became admired and successful business persons, legal scholars, and teachers.

Billy Schuman's parents, Samuel and Rachel, embodied the values that characterized immigrant families in New York City at the beginning of the twentieth century, with their optimistic belief that the future was bright for anyone who worked hard and was determined to succeed. Second-generation German American Jews, they "believed in education and never buying anything unless you had the money in hand." According to family lore, Billy's paternal grandfather, Moritz (Morris) Schuhmann, the son of a jeweler to King Ludwig II of Bavaria, arrived in New Orleans from Munich after the Civil War. He later traveled north up the Mississippi to a large German-speaking community that had settled in and around Cincinnati, Ohio. In Cincinnati he opened a shop that sold clothing and furs. Eventually Morris moved to New York City, where he met his wife, Rosa (born Kramer). Their three children, Sophie, Samuel, and Henry, were all born in New York City in the late 1860s and early 1870s. An entrepreneur, Morris helped develop the idea of cold storage for furs and also ran an employment agency. In addition, he occasionally played the flute during reel changes at Edison movies. Morris died in 1914, when Billy was only four, but Billy's older sister, Audrey, remembered her paternal grandfather as whimsical, imaginative, and playful.

Sam was a veteran of the Spanish-American War, and although too old to fight in 1917 when the United States entered World War I, he was intensely patriotic, a trait he instilled in his son. During the war he even changed the spelling of the family name to make it look and sound less German. Sam marched for many years in holiday parades up Riverside Drive. His patriotism led him to name his first son after the sitting president, William Howard Taft.

Billy inherited from his father a joie de vivre and sense of optimism that would stay with him his entire life. Sam's granddaughter Judith Israel Gutmann described him as happy and outgoing—a man who sang popular songs all the time, even in a hospital bed. Sam also had lofty values. Recalled his son: "He always said that the greatest callings in life were teacher, doctor, or minister, not necessarily in that order." Sam progressed from office boy—and the only Jew—at Oberly and Newell, printers and lithographers in downtown Manhattan, to the firm's vice president and general manager, a position that enabled him to support his family quite comfortably, even during the Depression. Schuman's mother, Rachel ("Ray," born Heilbrunn in 1882), was listed in the 1900 U.S. census as a "type-writer." She was very musical and could play tunes on the piano that she had just heard at a Broadway show. In contrast to the outgoing and sociable Sam, Ray was quiet and restrained.

Schuman's maternal grandfather, Louis Heilbrunn, the second of five surviving children of Moses and Hannah (born Stern) Heilbrunn, was born on February 26, 1852, in the town of Netra, northeast of Frankfurt and due west of Leipzig. Louis emigrated to America and New York City in 1869, followed by his parents in 1876. He married Julia (born Kahn in 1849) in 1873. A native of Alsace-Lorraine and equally fluent in French and German, Julia was a warm and gentle person who was admired and loved by her children and grandchildren.

In 1883 both Louis and Julia became naturalized American citizens. The Heilbrunns had five surviving children, all born in New York City: Elizabeth (born in 1877), Jennie (born in 1879 or 1880), Rachel (born in 1882), Hattie (born in 1887), and Henry (born in 1889). Rachel married Samuel Schuman in New York City on June 11, 1906, and three children were born during the next nine years: Audrey Hazel in 1907, William Howard in 1910, and Robert Monroe in 1915.

Where Sam Schuman was ebullient and talkative, Ray was self-contained and reserved. In her more upbeat moments, Ray was cheerful, dancing and playing the piano. Schuman recalled hearing her described during those periods as *ausgelassen* (relaxed or carefree). But she was often ill and endured frequent bouts of depression. Schuman remembered, "My mother was a woman of astonishingly strong character who, beginning at about the time I was nine years old (1919) through to her death when I was 37 (1947), gallantly suffered a series of difficult and devastating illnesses."

Schuman's remembrances of his father were of a man with a gentle nature, a happy demeanor, and considerable self-control. He viewed his father and his philosophy as "a combination of Walt Whitman and the Chamber of Commerce." Sam also, however, loved to gamble. During Sam and Ray's honeymoon at Niagara Falls in 1906, Sam lost all his money at the races and had to wire his employer to send him more. He promised his new wife he would abstain from this vice from then on, and in order to stay on the straight and narrow he would work all day on Saturdays.

Billy scarcely remembered his maternal grandmother, Julia, although he was told by his parents that she favored her French and not her German roots. But he had fond memories of his maternal grandfather, Louis Heilbrunn. "Grandpa Hy" was a butcher and owned a horse exchange and stables called Heilbrunn and Kahn at 60th Street and West End Avenue, close to the railroad tracks, where livestock were unloaded. He supplied horses for delivery wagons, catering especially to the milk trade. He also owned a great deal of real estate in Manhattan, Queens, and New Jersey. Family lore recounts that Louis was given the opportunity to buy the land where Manhattan's Columbus Circle is now located, but he turned it down, saying he didn't want to buy a property fit only for a goat farm.

During Billy's early childhood, Louis and Julia lived on 71st Street, very close to the Hudson River, where Louis would frequently take the night boat to transact business north of the city. Known for his earthiness and thrift (a trait he would pass on to his grandson), Louis insisted that a fixed percentage of his weekly business revenue be put into savings, no matter how bad earnings might be. Billy and his grandfather's close and playful relationship can be seen in a statement written by Hy in his own hand on April 10, 1916:

Dear Partner

The cow you and me bought last Friday for sixty dollars I sold this morning and I Enclose check for your part of the provid [profit].

1220 lbs 7 ½		91.50
less Expenses		1.50
		90.00
I Paid Cash		60 —
	Provid	30.00
Check Enclosed for your half		15.00

so you can see you where [sic] mistaken when you said she was worth forty dollars.

Respectfully your
Partner.
Louis Heilbrunn

Grandpa Hy once observed presciently of his little grandson, "That boy is only interested in two things: the fiddle and baseball." Hy also introduced Billy to live musical performances, frequently taking him to Saturday matinees at the Riverside Theatre at 96th Street and Broadway. It was there that Billy first saw a vaudeville show. Seeing singers and actors in a live performance had a lifelong impact on him.

One family member recalled a typical Saturday for the Heilbrunn and Schuman families when Billy was a young boy:

> Temple in the morning at Shaaray Teflia at 160 W. 82nd St. followed by lunch. Then trolley from 112th St. to 96th St and Broadway to Riverside Theatre. The group would then walk up Broadway to 112th St. to Louis' [Heilbrunn] apartment [605 W. 112th St] where a meal was prepared by Hattie [Billy's maternal aunt]. They would gather around the piano played by Rachel.

Around 1910 Louis Heilbrunn, wishing to live in the "country," moved to Englewood, New Jersey. Sam, Ray, and their children followed soon thereafter, along with Billy's aunt and uncle, Lizzie and Sam Sonn, and their family. Billy entered the Cleveland Public School kindergarten and was occasionally brought to school in town on the handlebars of his older cousin Howard's bicycle. On July 4, 1915, Schuman's grandmother Julia died of cancer. Schuman retained vivid memories of himself at age five being held up by his grandfather to see his grandmother in her coffin.

Owing to Sam's desire to assimilate into American society and his disdain for organized religion, the Schuman children often followed the traditions of their neighbors. Recalled Schuman: "We put on shows, made lemonade, and especially had marvelous Christmas mornings. Santa Claus was imaginative in his benefactions to us both, and it was a source of never-ending delight to us that my father's stocking was always filled with coal." It was in Englewood that Billy first became extremely close to his sister, Audrey, and they remained so throughout their lives.

One of the joys of Billy's early life was going to his grandfather's stables in Manhattan by horse and buggy from Englewood to the Fort Lee ferry, north of 125th Street. Years later Schuman remembered his grandfather telling him that the horse business would continue no matter what happened with the automobile. The Heilbrunn stable, however, closed when Hy died in 1930.

The Schumans led a rather peripatetic yet comfortable existence for most of Billy's childhood and adolescence. The family lived in nearly a dozen different homes and the children attended public schools. Their parents were able to afford the $300 needed each year for Audrey and Billy to attend summer camp. Recalled Schuman:

> We lived in Far Rockaway for a while, in Englewood, New Jersey and at a number of different addresses in the Columbia University area. . . . Englewood was beautiful and rural, but also uncomfortable. I think we were the only Jews in town, with the exception of the tailor, and Audrey and I were subjected to anti-Semitic comments from other schoolchildren.

According to Schuman, his father hated all religion and thought Jews should assimilate entirely into American society. He frequently ate pork when the family dined out, though it was never served at home: Schuman's mother was an observant Jew and attended Reform temple every Saturday, accompanied only rarely by his father. His mother's belief that religion would be important to her son was probably a case of wishful thinking, for in later years he rarely showed evidence of being influenced by the Jewish religion or its culture.

The most permanent Schuman residence during Billy's teenage years was at 605 West 112th Street, where the entire clan would gather on weekend nights. In fact, at times many members of the extended family lived in the building. Schuman later recalled having "sings" around the piano every Sunday night, with his mother playing the accompaniment and Billy starring as the lead singer in such semi-classics as "Hanging Apples on the Lilac Tree."

Sam Schuman's sister and her husband, Sophie and Louis Wertheim, had both died of cancer within a short time of each other when Audrey and Billy were teenagers, leaving three daughters. The extended Wertheim family had all become practicing Catholics, except for Louis, who retained his Jewish faith. When Sophie and Louis died, Sam Schuman could afford to take in only the eldest daughter, Ruth. He appealed to his brother Henry, a physician, to take one of the girls, but he refused. Finally, Sam approached members of the Wertheim family and was told that they would support the younger girls, Adele and Eleanor, but only if they were placed in Catholic foster care. As a result, Sam placed the girls in a Catholic orphanage. Ruth became a big sister to the Schuman children and shared a room with Audrey, who was three years younger; the two girls became lifelong friends. In a note to Sam at the time of Ray's death in 1947, Ruth expressed her lifelong appreciation for being welcomed into the Schuman family:

> As the years have passed since I made my home with you I have understood more and more the unselfish devotion of Aunt Ray's sacrifice, and yours too, in welcoming me into your household. . . . [I hope] that you will find a measure of comfort in the memories of the splendid life you and Aunt Ray have had together.

Billy's paternal grandmother, Rosa Kramer Schuhmann, also lived in the Schuman apartment. Billy had glowing memories of her. She had been born near Eisenach, Germany, around 1840. Partially blind, she would recite Schiller and Goethe by memory to Billy for hours. Her mellifluous German remained one of his most vivid memories of childhood: "The fantastic sounds are still in my ears, their special highs and lows in her inimitable and uninhibited manner." The occasional friction between Ray and Rosa—disagreements in which Sam never intervened—did not detract from Schuman's happy childhood.

The Schumans (who in their politics were Democratic Party centrists) provided a strong moral grounding for their children. In particular, they instilled in Billy a lasting and broad-based inquisitiveness. Schuman often saw himself as "a part of many different worlds" in which a variety of people and pursuits came together. Perhaps most important, his parents nurtured in Billy a supreme self-confidence that some saw as arrogance but that would serve him well throughout his life.

Both Sam and Ray had gone to business school in New York, and like many middle-class families of the time, they made sure their children had all the benefits of a good education. That included piano and violin lessons, which Billy approached in a perfunctory manner. However, his intellect was stimulated by the extracurricular activities to which his parents exposed him. Almost every Friday night Ray and Sam went to lectures at the Institute of

Arts and Sciences of Columbia University, where programs dealing with issues of the day were presented at a cost of ten cents per admission. They would then return home and share the experience in great detail with Billy and Audrey. The elder Schumans also subscribed to modern dance concerts at Columbia and eventually shared the tickets with their older son.

Billy's younger brother, Robert, was born with a developmental disorder that eventually led to his institutionalization. Schuman and his family kept Robert's very existence from the public for seventy-one years, until, in 1986, a mention of Robert was included in Schuman's dedication of his composition *On Freedom's Ground.* Schuman recalled late in his life that Robert's "condition was not discussed, because no one talked about such things out of shame, and all my parents ever got by way of a medical diagnosis were flowery phrases like 'a rose that didn't blossom.' He lived at home with us until he was nine or ten years old." Judith Gutmann, Schuman's niece, believes that Robert left the household earlier, at the age of five, and she corroborates her conclusion through conversations she had with her mother, Audrey. Billy was very close to Robert early on and quickly noticed the cruel taunts that the neighborhood children directed at his brother. Robert often behaved in ways that made him a danger to himself and others—their father once had to rescue Robert from the roof of a garage, which he had climbed onto after jumping out a bedroom window. After doctors advised Sam and Ray that it would be best to remove him from the home, Robert was at first housed with families and then eventually institutionalized in hospitals in the New York City area. His parents told the other two children of Robert's departure as the family was walking along the Rockaway beach one day. Billy cried himself to sleep for many nights.

Yet Schuman visited his younger brother only once, when Robert was first enrolled in a special school. His parents, wanting to shield him from Robert's condition, did not let Billy accompany them when visiting Robert. Remembered Schuman: "Both my parents and my sister wanted, it would seem, to protect me from an encounter that they knew would be difficult. But for whatever reason, I never saw my brother again, and at the time of his death in 1950 [actually 1957] my sister and brother-in-law, Dr. James A. Brussel, who had been notified of his death, only called me after his cremation."

This curiously protective approach continued even after Schuman married. His daughter, Andrea (Andie), recalled:

My mother actually went to see him [Robert] just after they were married [1936]. . . . I think my father was "protected" from seeing

Robert, and then he just never did. . . . His mother [Ray] had relatively early onset Paget's disease [a debilitating bone disease], which left her fairly bent, but I don't know if this had anything to do with the decision to "place" Robert [outside the home].

Schuman's son, Anthony (Tony), remarked:

[The] attitude within the family was "let's not have any unpleasantness," a holdover from friction he [William] experienced in his own household growing up. I remember my mother talking about delivering dad's old clothes to his brother and being struck by how much Robert looked like dad. My mother always protected dad from confronting difficult emotional issues. "Let's not mess with genius" was the gist of her approach.

Audrey's daughter, Judith Israel Gutmann, has another recollection of encounters with Robert. She says she was told of Robert's existence around 1954, when she was sixteen, and that after Sam Schuman died in 1950, Bill and Audrey did in fact periodically visit Robert at the Willowbrook State Hospital on Staten Island, bringing candy, which Robert would devour. But he never spoke. Said Gutmann: "[Audrey and Bill] distanced themselves emotionally from Robert. They didn't seem to feel a sense of regret and they clearly adored him, so Robert must have created a trauma. [Bill and Audrey] just totally accepted their parents' approach to Robert and never questioned."

Robert's departure from the Schuman home and the tension between Ray and Rosa contradict Schuman's recollection of his childhood as a happy time. As an adult, Schuman took a stoic approach to many challenges and was often able to blot out disturbing or negative experiences in order to accomplish his goals. It is disconcerting to think that Schuman was capable of completely erasing his memories of and connections to his only brother, but that is what he clearly did. If Judith Gutmann's recollections of both Audrey and Bill visiting Robert in the early 1950s at Willowbrook State Hospital are correct, it is remarkable that Bill was able to sublimate those memories in oral histories dating from the 1970s to just before his death in 1992.

Despite the trauma of Robert's departure, the Schuman household held many joys for Billy. Although Sam and Ray were not great classical-music devotees, there was music in the household. Sam had the charming practice of playing the *William Tell Overture* on the pianola every morning before he left for work. And Ray sat at the piano on Sundays to sing songs, always concluding with Anton Rubinstein's *Melody in F*. Schuman recalled that "later on, with my newfound musical erudition, I realized that she played the *Melody in F* in C." Records on the Victrola of Enrico Caruso singing or Efrem Zimbalist playing the violin were also a constant in the home, and Sam and Ray would occasionally attend a light opera—never Wagner.

Audrey studied the piano and Billy the violin with a local teacher named Blanche Schwartz. Billy, in fact, showed the personal verve for which he would be known throughout his entire life when sister and brother were to play at an annual recital given by their teacher at Aeolian Hall on 57th Street. When the duo came onstage, Audrey got such a severe case of stage fright that during the introduction of Edward MacDowell's "To a Wild Rose" she was unable to move so much as a finger. Literally not missing a beat, Billy proceeded to perform unaccompanied. Commented an admiring relative in the audience: "That boy is going to be something someday."

When Billy was nine the family moved to Far Rockaway, where they lived in a rented home on Seneca Avenue. There he encountered for the first time what was to become one of his great passions: baseball. Throughout Schuman's life he often referred to baseball in allegorical terms, and he certainly saw the game as one of the foundations of the American experience.

Billy played with boys' clubs and in pick-up games. At this time the New York Giants, managed by John McGraw, with Christy Mathewson as their ace pitcher, dominated New York baseball—Babe Ruth and the Yankees would not take over the top position in town for a few years. Schuman was a lifelong Giants fan, and there is little doubt that Mathewson was his idol, as he was for most American boys Billy's age. Later, when Schuman lived near Columbia University, he remembered walking over to "South Field and watch[ing] Lou Gehrig, who was then a freshman [at Columbia] hitting the balls from 114th Street to 116th Street. Everybody knew he wouldn't stay in college very long."

Around 1921 the family moved once again, to West 107th Street in Manhattan, just east of Broadway and that much closer to the Polo Grounds, the Giants' home in Upper Manhattan. Billy enrolled in P.S. 165 and remembered having "the wonderful experience of being in the sixth grade under a remarkable teacher, Susan M. Squire. . . . Mis [sic] Squire interested me in learning." It was at this time that Billy met two people who would become lifelong friends: Edward B. Marks Jr., whose father was a music publisher, and Tony Ross, born Meyer Rosenthal, who became a successful actor on Broadway, most notably for originating the role of the gentleman caller in Tennessee Williams's play *The Glass Menagerie*. It was Meyer who told his new friend about Camp Cobbossee, a summer pastime that would turn out to be a pivotal early experience in Schuman's life.

Located in Winthrop, Maine, between Augusta and Lewiston, Camp Cobbossee was established in 1902. The camp allowed Billy to immerse himself in his equal passions of music and baseball, and he attended every summer but one from the time he was about twelve until he was eighteen (1922–29). Recalled Schuman: "I loved camp with the greatest passion. . . . I loved swimming, I loved track, I loved baseball, I loved the dramatics." The camp newspaper, the *Almanak*, reported one summer that "Billy Schuman yesterday accomplished a feat that many major league pitchers try but that very few succeed in doing. Namely, pitching and winning a double header."

It was at Camp Cobbossee that Billy and Eddie Marks became involved in music. At first they wrote only the songs for the Friday-night camp shows, but later they graduated to writing full-fledged productions, one of which even toured several small towns in Maine. Recalled Schuman, "The music reflected the discernible influence of Gilbert and Sullivan and Rodgers and Hart, the darlings of the day."

Billy indulged in "the entire spirit of camp life—its wonders and its horrors." One horror Schuman recalled many years later was "the sadism of fraternity initiations at night on a lonely island in the middle of Lake Cobbossee." As Schuman remembered, "In 1924, I was awarded the Camp Cobbossee All-Around Camper's Cup. . . . I think that once you've been given that honor, the Pulitzer Prize is nothing."

In a letter to his parents of July 7, 1922, Schuman showed that he was fundamentally a city boy—and a musician:

Dear Ma and Pa
 I just came back from a four mile *walk* to a little hick town. Please send up my music stand as I need it to practice. Camp is wonderful and I am trying out for the Junior team. . . .
With lots of love and kisses
O O O O O O O love X X X X X X X
Bill

The Cobbossee tradition continued for much of Schuman's life. He attended the camp's periodic reunions (one of which, held many years later, included no fewer than thirty campers), and his son, Tony, also became a camper in the mid-1950s.

Schuman was educated in the public schools of New York City. At P.S. 165, on 109th Street near Broadway, his parents bought Billy a three-quarter-size violin for $11 so he could play in the school orchestra. Billy later attended Speyer Experimental Junior High School for Boys, at 126th Street just off of Amsterdam Avenue, and George Washington High School, in Upper Manhattan. Speyer was what would now be called a magnet school for exceptional students. The curriculum was designed so that the student would complete the seventh and eighth grades and the freshman year of high school in two years. Schuman's academic work was below average, but he excelled in extracurricular activities: producing and acting in plays, playing baseball, and even joining the ninety-pound boxing team, where he lost every one of his matches. The Speyer experience not only allowed Schuman to prove his determination in the boxing ring, but also framed more of Schuman's lifelong traits: his playfulness, his glee, and his determination to challenge authority.

By his own admission, Schuman was a wild boy at Speyer. He was suspended for six months for replicating a Charlie Chaplin prank of pouring coffee into a bowl of sugar in the teachers' lunchroom, and he tried to get around the school tradition of Silent Tuesday during the changing of classes by creating "Schuman's Complicated Handshake," a series of moves that over time became progressively more complex. He excelled in English and civics, did badly in math, and wrote a play that was performed at Speyer. Entitled *College Chums*, it dealt with finding balance between one's studies and baseball: "The basic moral was the virtue of moderation, a virtue I have never since believed in or practiced," Schuman later said.

Considering the age of the author—Schuman was only in his early teens—the writing in the play is quite remarkable for its clarity of narrative and moral direction. The exceedingly short work ends with George, an athlete, and Sam, a "book worm," agreeing that

> Anything done to an excess is useless. Work and play are both essential. . . . let our motto be:

Don't work to excess,
Don't play to excess,
But follow a happy medium.

Though he held moderation in low esteem, Schuman's active life as a composer and an administrator did create for him that "happy medium." And by the time he graduated, he was voted "Best Orator" in the school yearbook, a harbinger of his talent in adult life for public speaking.

The larger community of George Washington High School provided Schuman with still more opportunities. He taught himself double bass and played in the school orchestra, which also allowed him to get out of his Latin class, held at the same time as orchestra rehearsals. Schuman recalled that his high school orchestra was one of nineteen invited to compete in a citywide contest. All the ensembles had to perform the overture to Carl Maria von Weber's *Oberon*. "At the contest it turned out that we were the only school to have a double bass, and I was therefore loaned as a participant to all the other 18 schools. My adoring parents sat through all 19 renditions."

Billy was a good but unmotivated student in high school. His only serious problem seemed to be in drawing, which he failed so consistently that his graduation was in question. Fortunately, he was able to persuade the school's principal that the weakness was not his, but the curriculum's. He finally prevailed and graduated in January 1928, demonstrating another lifelong trait: the ability to sway others to his point of view.

Schuman luxuriated in the New York City of the 1920s, traveling around Manhattan for a nickel on the subway and frequently attending shows on Broadway, with the added treat of lunch at Schrafft's for thirty-five cents. Schuman congregated with his friends in his neighborhood on the West Side, avoiding the East Side's elite society. On Sundays, friends would promenade on Broadway between 86th and 96th Streets. Boys and girls shared food and conversation at such innocent haunts as the Tiptoe Inn on the northwest corner of 86th Street or Childs Restaurant at Columbus Circle, where pancakes were a favorite. Because this was during Prohibition, Schuman and his pals drank "either beer or bathtub gin."

The one year that the young Schuman missed the pleasures of Camp Cobbossee was 1925, when, at the age of almost fifteen, he was chosen to spend a summer in France in a travel program Schuman recalled as being named "The Boys' Educational Tour of France." Cooperatively designed by the city of New York and the French government, it enabled a number of boys from the city schools—Schuman remembered J. Robert Oppenheimer, the future atomic scientist, being in the group—to travel at relatively low cost to France, where, seven years after the Armistice, they could observe firsthand the devastation that France had suffered during World War I.

With the support of his excited father and teary-eyed mother, Schuman left on the French ship *La Savoie*. His group toured several French cities, where they visited lycées and universities. The trip would have been an extraordinary one for any boy his age, but the impact of such a rich experience on a middle-class New York child was truly profound.

Before he left, though, Schuman's father took Billy to visit his uncle, Henry Schuhmann, a physician living in Brooklyn. Dr. Schuhmann gave his nephew a book bound in red and frighteningly entitled *The Boy's Venereal Peril*. Remembered Schuman, "No one could ever be the same again after having read that book."

On the trip Billy showed remarkable maturity and self-assurance for a fifteen-year-old. He wrote in his best penmanship to his father's Paris-based first cousin, Robert Schuhmann, to accept an invitation for a visit, because "it certainly would be a shame for me to leave Paris without seeing my father's first cousin. You can expect me at 12.30 July 16.th."

Whether because of Uncle Henry's reading selection, the impact of his travels, or normal teenage development, at the age of sixteen Schuman turned away from full-time socializing and started his first musical organization—a jazz ensemble called "Billy Schuman and his Alamo Society Orchestra." The band was hired for school dances and also played for local proms, bar mitzvahs, weddings, and so on. Schuman's recollection of how such a name came out of New York's West Side was fuzzy, but he did comment that "at the time, a lot of bands were called 'Society Orchestras,' which sounded fancy, and I wanted to add something to it that would give it a little extra glamour, and I thought 'Alamo' had a certain ring to it." Despite the name's exotic implications, though, "not one of [the band's] members was ever south of Jersey City."

Schuman was the leader on violin, an occasional banjo player, and also, as a baritone, the singer. The band, whose personnel fluctuated between six and twelve players depending on the job, obtained its orchestrations free from publishers. Its repertoire was a mix of Broadway and popular music—everything from Jerome Kern's *Showboat* to Rudy Vallee favorites. Fees were generally $5 per player, and Schuman served as the producer and contractor. The experience also gave Schuman his first opportunity to compose and arrange, self-taught skills that were, by his own admission, quite crude. Schuman's career as a bandleader ended when he was offered a permanent spot in another band that played at a second-floor Chinese restaurant; it would have paid him between $10 and $13 a night to play violin and sing. But because it would have meant leaving high school, he declined the opportunity, to his father's great joy.

Schuman's early music education was sporadic and often self-directed. His private lessons on violin and piano did not bring him to a high performance level for his age. His performing career was hampered by weakness in his hands and arms, a malady he first experienced at Camp Cobbossee. He suffered from a painful disorder of the thumb, wrist, and lower arm. Schuman would notice that, as he drew the bow across the strings of his violin, he couldn't provide the muscle control necessary to make the sound stable. He also experienced weakness in his arms when playing baseball or boxing. This physical problem affected Schuman his entire life, and he readily acknowledged that he had no digital dexterity whatsoever on the piano or violin. His penmanship suffered as well.

Although a career as a performer was clearly not in young Schuman's future, musical composition was, if not in the style with which he would be eventually associated. Billy Schuman's Alamo Society Orchestra required new musical material, and he naturally drifted toward songwriting. At first he collaborated with his friend Eddie Marks. In a letter to Marks of October 31, 1928, the eighteen-year-old Schuman showed the sarcasm and hipness that were already a major part of his persona:

> For C— sake if you do write lyrics write them in the day time. I've gotten at least five different tunes for the dam[n] thing and each one sounds more like Bye Bye Blackbird. Really Ed, I think it[']s [Marks' lyrics] pretty bad, but the tunes I wrote to it are much worse in comparison, so don't take it too much to heart.

Schuman closed his letter with a rakish handwritten postscript to Marks, who was a freshman at Dartmouth College: "See you [at] Thanksgiving. How are the women? Remember me to all the Jews."

However, it was when he met Frank Loesser that Schuman's work took a more serious direction. Loesser was a classmate of Schuman's at Speyer and went on to graduate from the elite Townsend Harris High School. Both boys lived on the Upper West Side in Manhattan during their high school years. Schuman remembered Loesser as a brilliant young man: "Frank didn't play any instruments, so I taught him to play the piano by translating the ukulele signs in sheet music, ubiquitous because most people played the ukulele." Loesser provided the lyrics and Schuman wrote the music. Together they created over forty popular songs, though none became a hit. Loesser would eventually become one of Broadway's most distinguished composers, with a number of songs to his credit as well as such hits as *Guys and Dolls*, *The Most Happy Fella*, and *How to Succeed in Business without Really Trying*.

In a remarkable and playful letter of April 10, 1948, to Vincent Persichetti, who was preparing a biography of Schuman at the time, Loesser provided several irreverent recollections of his friend:

> When I first met Bill we were both about eleven and he was much larger and stronger than I. He kept punching me all the time . . . [but] he never hurt me badly. . . . [When he played the piano for me] it was obvious from the first bar that this boy would have to become a composer or at least a conductor, as his piano playing was an abomination. . . . [He also played a violin for me] once again it was painfully clear that Bill Schuman had better not become an instrumentalist.

Loesser's concluding observation about his boyhood friend was a comment on Schuman's perseverance: "Once when we were about twelve, I dared him to eat six peanut butter sandwiches without drinking anything. He did it."

Although a budding composer, Schuman saw himself in retrospect as a "musical illiterate" who didn't even use staff paper to notate his songs. However, he set out to fill in the gaps in his knowledge by taking his orchestrations to professional bands on the West Side, which would play and critique his compositions in exchange for a carton of cigarettes.

Loesser and Schuman became Tin Pan Alley song pluggers for their material, but without much success. Describing their style as "straight out of Damon Runyon," Schuman recalled marching into a publisher's office and saying, "We've got a hell of a song for you," whereupon Loesser sat down and played the piano while Schuman sang. Considering the team's limited musical skills, it is little wonder that publishers did not jump at the material.

Finally, Leo Feist published one of the pair's songs, "In Love with the Memory of You." It immediately sank into oblivion. Schuman remarked, "As far as I know, it's the only flop he [Loesser] ever wrote." Royalties for the team ran to three cents per song, with a penny going to the publisher; clearly, money was not the main impetus behind the venture. The entrepreneurial Schuman even approached the very popular Rudy Vallee to try one of the team's songs. Because Vallee's band included a guitarist, which was not in Schuman's orchestration, Vallee said his band could not play the song. Schuman announced, "I'll have one for you in an hour," and then secretly begged the band's guitarist to sketch out the chords. In the end, Vallee did sing the song with the added guitar part, which had been provided at the reduced fee of only one pack of cigarettes.

In addition to their less-than-successful forays as songwriters, Schuman and Loesser also decided to write an operetta on the life of no less a personage than Leonardo da Vinci: "Frank's idea was that da Vinci was a great entrepreneur who hired people from all the various arts to work with him." The piece included interchanges between Christopher Columbus and Queen Isabella. The young team had indeed done their history homework, for although there is no record that da Vinci and Columbus ever met, they were contemporaries. The operetta was never completed, but Schuman resurrected a waltz melody from it for *On Freedom's Ground* (1986). When this work was premiered by the New York Philharmonic under Zubin Mehta, the maestro mentioned how he enjoyed the waltz. Schuman's reply must have shocked Mehta: "Do you know what the original lyrics were for that waltz? 'Here comes that drunken da Vinci again, all filled with highballs, stewed to the eyeballs.'"

Loesser eventually learned of an opportunity to work in Hollywood and asked Schuman to join him. Although he loved popular music, Schuman sensed that his real calling lay in so-called serious or concert music. Loesser's final words on Schuman's decision as he took off for Universal Studios were rational if not optimistic: "You'll never make a living at it." According to Schuman, "Over the years we maintained our friendship, although we rarely met. He sang me the entire score of 'Most Happy Fella' over the telephone, Hollywood to New Rochelle."

As serendipity would have it, a 78 rpm recording created around 1930 of Schuman on vocals and Loesser on piano still survives. Schuman's crisp diction, high baritone, and precise intonation and Loesser's rather plodding piano accompaniment are heard in two of their songs: "Doin' the Dishes" and "Where the Grass Grows Green." The song team's youthful enthusiasm overrides the rather mundane lyrics and conventional melodies. This rare recording allows the modern listener to hear a quality in Schuman's singing that is quite reminiscent of Fred Astaire's approach to crooning at the time.

In his mid- to late teens Schuman continued to live out the wildness that had surfaced at Speyer. An inveterate prankster, he and a friend rented a very small apartment at 20 West 72nd Street for partying purposes, and he was a founding member of UMPPA (United Musical Poker Players of America). Recalling the Roaring Twenties, Schuman reported that he "drank too much at night, bum gin, and . . . wore a dirty hat." He dated so many girls that his future "mother-in-law used to say she'd never met anybody around New York who didn't say: 'Oh yes, my daughter used to go out with Billy.'" Still latent within him, however, were the sensitivity and seriousness of purpose that were to send him in more productive directions.

Eventually the entire Schuman clan moved to 20 West 72nd Street, also known as the Hotel Franconia, a resident hotel with tiny kitchens. During Bill's early Teachers College years he lived there with his parents and sister in one apartment, with his Grandfather Hy and Aunt Hattie and Uncle Isadore Weisel in a second apartment and his Aunt Lizzie and her husband, Samuel Sonn, in a third.

Schuman often said that although he did not hear a symphony orchestra until he was nineteen, he had experienced much in other kinds of music. But in 1930, his sister and the New York Philharmonic stimulated an epiphany in Schuman's life that propelled him forever into the world of classical music.

Audrey had often invited her brother to share in her subscription to the Philharmonic, but Bill had always declined—too highbrow for his tastes, he thought. He finally accompanied her to hear the orchestra in Carnegie Hall on April 4, 1930, for a matinee performance. The program, conducted by the legendary Arturo Toscanini, included Robert Schumann's Third Symphony, Zoltán Kodály's *Summer Evening*, Bedřich Smetana's *Moldau*, and, as a tribute to Cosima Wagner, whose funeral was that day in Bayreuth, the "Trauermarsch" from Wagner's *Götterdämmerung*. Schuman's strongest impressions of the concert seemed to have been more visual than aural. He was amazed at the way this gigantic ensemble's string section bowed together. And he saw to his disbelief that the percussionist rarely played, in contrast to his own band, where the drummer played all the time.

Although the musical intricacy was still a mystery to Schuman, the total experience was overwhelming. As Schuman tells the story, he made an impulsive and almost instantaneous decision, presaging his lifelong penchant for deciding important matters very quickly: "I decided on the spot that this was my world; that I was going to be a musician."

At the time Schuman was enrolled at New York University, studying both at its uptown Liberal Arts College and at its School of Commerce at Washington Square. The day after the concert, he walked into the bursar's office at Washington Square, asked for a tuition refund, and promptly dropped out of school. He also quit his part-time job at the Paramount Advertising Agency, where he did copy editing on a candy account.

Deep in thought, he walked uptown all the way from 4th Street to the corner of 78th Street and West End Avenue. There he looked up and saw a sign that would change his life: "The Malkin Conservatory of Music."

Schuman entered the building and was immediately greeted by the school's receptionist, who must have been slightly taken aback by the young man's fervor: "I want to be a composer. What do I have to do?" The response was as matter-of-fact as a recipe: he would need to study harmony, $1 for a class, $3 for a private lesson.

The response from his family was no less remarkable, considering the difficult economic times. After Schuman explained that studying to be a composer was an intellectual experience, his father calmly agreed to his dramatically altered plans and even provided an allowance to support his studies. Nevertheless, Sam's practical side surfaced when he mused to Ray, "He is almost twenty. Even if he has talent, it is so late to begin. . . . Where has it been hiding itself all these years? All that jazz doesn't mean a thing. This is entirely different. Why should I let him make a failure of himself when he has everything in him that could make for success?"

The actual facts behind this remarkable tale, told by Schuman in numerous oral histories and interviews, suggest a slightly different sequence of events. There is no question that Arturo Toscanini did conduct the New York Philharmonic in a Friday concert beginning at 2:30 P.M. on April 4, 1930. However, according to Schuman's New York University School of Commerce transcript, he dropped out of school on April 3, 1929—one year earlier almost to the day than in his story. Schuman had entered New York University's undergraduate School of Commerce, Accounts and Finance in February 1928 for the spring term and earned grades in economics, law, and marketing that can only be described as abysmal. In March 1929 he was put on academic probation. He dropped all his courses on March 25 and April 3, 1929, definitively departing from NYU forever, according to his official transcript, which lists his "bachelor pad" address of 20 West 72nd Street, not his home address at 605 West 112th Street.

Curiously, the transcript also shows, in handwritten notations, requests for Schuman's transcript to be sent to the University of Georgia in May, the University of Maryland in June, and the University of Michigan and the University of Virginia in July 1929. It seems that the young Schuman was not totally committed to a compositional career in the summer of 1929.

The best-known "Malkin Conservatory of Music" in the annals of twentieth-century American music education was the institution founded in Boston in 1933 by the distinguished Russian cellist Joseph Malkin. This conservatory is historically prominent for Malkin's successful effort to bring Arnold Schoenberg to America to teach there, which he did for the academic year 1933–34.

However, Joseph Malkin's brother, Manfred, a pianist, had opened the first "Malkin Conservatory of Music" in New York City in 1913. Originally located at 131 West 122nd Street, coincidentally quite close to the Institute of Musical Art and eventually the Juilliard School of Music, the conservatory moved in the mid-1920s to a new location at 381 West End Avenue, at the corner of 78th Street.

On the second page of the conservatory's 1927–28 catalog are fourteen pithy statements about the school, explaining, in part, that the school "is dedicated to the establishment of a worthy standard of musicianship and the dissemination of artistic instruction"; "It offers every advantage for the systematic study of music under the trustworthy guidance of masters. . . . The director, Mr. Manfred Malkin, is exceptionally fitted for his position. He is a genuine artist, a brilliant pianist, and a sincere and most successful pedagogue"; and at the very bottom of the page: "It is a school with ideals."

Schuman recalled that the school "was sort of a fly-by-night conservatory with some very good people. A lot of people opened conservatories. You know—you paid the school and the school would keep a dollar . . . and [pay] the other two to the teacher."

Regardless of the exact chronology, there is no question that Toscanini's performance changed the course of Schuman's life. His first composition teacher at Malkin was Max Persin, a graduate of the Odessa Conservatory who had studied with Anton Arensky. Persin's students included Olin Downes, music critic of the *New York Times* from 1924 to 1955, and Samuel Chotzinoff, also a future music critic and general music director of NBC radio and television. According to the school catalog, "Mr. Persin's courses are so arranged as to develop the pupil from within, and to lead him step-wise to the highest goal in musical education, namely, musical expression."

Persin's style of teaching was eccentric but passionate. The $3 lesson was supposed to last an hour but usually extended for several, during which the young Schuman, surrounded by a cloud of smoke from his teacher's perpetually lit cigar, would become ravenously hungry. The harmony and structure of musical works were analyzed, from the chorales of J. S. Bach to the contemporary pieces of Ernest Bloch.

Schuman also studied counterpoint with Charles Trowbridge Haubiel, a faculty member at his old school, NYU, as well as at the Institute of Musical Art, the predecessor of the Juilliard School. A champion of American music, in 1935 he founded the Composers Press to support American composition. In contrast to Persin, with his flexible teaching approach, Haubiel was quite formal, requiring strict counterpoint exercises of his pupils, which Schuman undertook eagerly. Schuman recalled that Haubiel claimed "that he could trace his teachers back to Palestrina through [Joseph] Joachim. . . . In harmony I was really sort of self-taught by analysis and things. But in counterpoint with Haubiel . . . you end up doing fourteen individual parts, and you think everything is fine, and he'd say: 'Now, for next week do a clarinet obbligato over that.'" Schuman never admired Haubiel as a person and was troubled by his fascist inclinations during World War II. However, Schuman's music consistently included contrapuntal textures that became a compositional component of almost all his future works.

Schuman studied orchestration, primarily on his own, though he did take a few lessons from Adolf Schmid, who taught at the Juilliard Graduate Institute. In addition, he had occasional composition lessons, or rather critiques, with Roy Harris at his home in Princeton, New Jersey. In Flora Rheta Schreiber and Vincent Persichetti's 1954 biography of Schuman, Schreiber claims that "at the end of his [Schuman's] first summer with Harris at Juilliard [Summer School] Schuman earned three A-plusses. This was an auspicious beginning of a teacher-pupil relationship that was to last for two years." No transcripts are extant that document Schuman's enrollment in Harris's Juilliard Summer School classes, but it is certainly possible that he audited the courses.

Schuman was a non-matriculated student at the Institute of Musical Art of the Juilliard School of Music, studying piano and violin in the spring term of 1934 and piano for the entire academic year of 1934–35. This was his first contact with Juilliard, an institution that would be an integral part of much of Schuman's adult life. He enrolled in these courses through Teachers College. Schuman also attended the Juilliard Summer School in 1932, 1933, and 1936, studying orchestration, advanced theory, advanced conducting, brass instruments, and chorus, and during the 1932–33 academic year he played violin in an ensemble called the Special Supervisors' Orchestra under the direction of Adolf Schmid. At this time Schuman was also a devoted attendee of New York Philharmonic concerts, going to multiple performances of the same program and always arriving with scores in hand.

Of his comparatively late start as a serious music student, Schuman noted: "I was not a literate musician, but I knew I had innate musicality. . . . I didn't know the names of the chords, and I couldn't play it, but it didn't matter. I could hear. And because I was starting late, I was motivated to an almost fiendish degree." A desire to be a serious composer burned within him: "I hear[d] sounds in my head that I didn't understand. You know, wild sounds . . . and not knowing what they are doing, where they were going . . . and I knew that something was stirring within me." Aside from some brief tourist or summer study trips to Europe in the mid 1920s and early 1930s, Schuman did not formally study in Europe with a composition mentor in the manner of his contemporaries Aaron Copland, Roy Harris, Walter Piston, and Virgil Thomson, all of whom studied in France with Nadia Boulanger.

As the young Schuman became more immersed in his formal musical studies, his middle-class German Jewish values periodically surfaced. He took a part-time job at his father's printing business, Oberly and Newell, and made occasional forays back to Tin Pan Alley. The generous monthly stipend of $60 that he received from his father allowed Schuman "to lead a perfectly normal social life and buy Frank Loesser his dinners." Realizing he would need some way to earn a living, in 1933 he reluctantly entered Teachers College of Columbia University as a freshman. Impractical, entrepreneurial, impetuous, talented, articulate, and highly motivated, Schuman was philosophically in conflict with many of the college's educational approaches. Nevertheless, he graduated with a bachelor of science degree two years later and a master's in 1937.

In her biography Schreiber describes some personal attributes that manifested early and remained a part of Schuman throughout his entire life:

Schuman is relatively free of introspection and of psychic conflict. He was able to change the whole course of his life without wasting much energy in self-reproach or foreboding. But nonetheless the restlessness that spurred his ambition remains to deprive him of simple quietude. He cannot empty his mind of ideas and responsibilities and let a wise passivity fill it.

Although his parents supported Bill's educational and professional changes, they were also realistic. His father once told him, "The problem is in music you are up against genius . . . like Irving Berlin. . . . In business . . . you don't have to be very smart . . . to make a living. But in music you are not good unless you are at the top." With his innate talent, abundant self-confidence, and steely determination, William Schuman would come to embrace his father's challenge.

CHAPTER 2

Exploring the Arts

During a period of musical exploration and occasional self-doubt, William Schuman met the woman he would eventually marry, who would be a pillar of strength during their life together.

In 1931 Schuman was dating a young woman named Evelyn, and the relationship was serious enough that her mother thought an engagement announcement was imminent. Evelyn's mother had told Schuman that his musical studies were absurd—he should manage a garage where she knew of an opening.

Meanwhile the activities of UMPPA were flourishing, and girlfriends were welcome at their soirées. One member's girlfriend, Bea, attended Barnard College, on the Upper West Side, which had strict parietal hours and the punishments to back them up. In an effort to get around the college's restrictions, Bea would often stay on weekends at the Manhattan home of one of her classmates, Frances (Frankie) Prince. Bill and Frankie were introduced—according to family lore, by their friend Frank Loesser—at an UMPPA party in the fall of 1931. Schuman broke a date with Evelyn, invited Frankie to a Broadway performance of Eugene O'Neill's recently premiered play *Mourning Becomes Electra*, and then walked her home from Times Square to 96th Street—about two and a half miles. Sometime that evening he fell in love. He never dated Evelyn again.

Bill remembered his attraction to Frankie as "instantaneous and mutual." Frank Loesser told her that he was working with the man she would eventually marry, and that if Bill didn't marry her, he would. Like Bill, Frankie came from an Upper West Side German Jewish family, and she had a keen interest in classical music, far richer than Bill's. Frankie was three years younger than Bill, born on June 12, 1913. She had studied piano, and at home her mother frequently played the piano and her father, the violin. Bill felt that her family was more "worldly and sophisticated [than his]." His future father-in-law, Leonard Prince, was a moderately successful businessman who worked in a liquor and wine business on Grand Street in Lower Manhattan that had been owned by his father, Adolph. Leonard and Frankie's mother, Gertrude (born Rheinauer), owned a small vineyard in Penn Yan, New York, not far from Ithaca, which they sold during Prohibition to a "chemist" who turned out to be a bootlegger.

In later years Schuman was dismissive of his father-in-law's paucity of business acumen. Bill and Frankie's son, Tony, recalled that the family was "amused by his [Leonard's] failed business ventures (a rent-an-umbrella scheme that failed when people didn't return the umbrellas . . .). He was eventually bailed out by his brother Seymour ('Jim') who had a successful candy business built from sending care packages to GIs overseas during the War (WWII)."

After graduating from high school, Frankie was awarded a New York Regents Scholarship to Cornell, which she declined because she wanted to go to college out of state. Her parents insisted on her attending a single-sex school, so she enrolled in the North Carolina College for Women in Greensboro for a year, then transferred to Barnard, from which she graduated in 1933, at the precocious age of nineteen.

They had met during the depths of the Depression and had no money for a wedding. Frankie continued to live with her parents on 96th Street, and both she and Bill agreed that they would "keep company" until he found a job. This arrangement lasted for five years until they were finally married in 1936.

Schuman knew he wished to be a classical composer, but his practical, middle-class upbringing and his desire to marry Frankie led him to enroll at Teachers College of Columbia University, located at 120th Street and Broadway, where he could study to enter the teaching profession if his composing career did not flourish. Schuman wanted to pursue a degree in music and was permitted to place out of several required music courses through examination so that he could complete his bachelor of science degree in two years. He came to regret his haste, however. Throughout his lifetime he felt that this abbreviated course of study had left him inadequately grounded in music history.

Because Teachers College was a teacher training institution, Schuman was required to take many courses in the philosophy of education and related subjects, which were in direct conflict with his own fledgling theories of teaching. Schuman admitted to many "high and low points" in his Teachers

College experience. One course, called "Principles of Teaching," was his nadir. Schuman later remembered the professor lugubriously explaining, over a three-week period, the concept of "generalization" as a teaching tool. Schuman was only interested in how to specifically solve problems, and he found the teacher's approach to be onerous.

During his studies Schuman came to embrace the educational philosophy of John Dewey. He was intellectually motivated by a particularly strong course in the history of education, which analyzed past theories and practices. Fundamentally, Schuman saw the teaching of teachers as a highly suspect endeavor: "the ability to teach must be an inborn skill, an aptitude. How much of it can actually be taught I have never been certain."

Schuman's single most dramatic experience at Teachers College occurred in a lecture course entitled "The Arts in Education and Life," taught by Harold Rugg. (Rugg would go on to achieve a certain level of notoriety with the publication of a widely used high school social sciences textbook, *Man and His Changing World*, that was eventually attacked in the early 1940s for its disparaging view of the private enterprise system and the negative impact of advertising on the public.) One of the guest speakers in the class was Lilla Belle Pitts, a recipient of a bachelor of arts from Columbia University in 1935, who would eventually become one of the most respected music educators of the mid-twentieth century. According to Schuman, Pitts proffered the concept she had developed through experimentation that an effective way to teach children to listen to music was to have them visually depict through drawing what they had just heard. A brash and enraged Schuman jumped to his feet and announced, "Dr. Rugg, I absolutely—respectfully—disagree. I think that's just the wrong thing to do—you're taking away your attention from one art and putting it on another." The response from Dr. Rugg was peremptory: "Would the young man who just spoke be seated, and see me after class." At the end of class Rugg told him, "I just love what you said. Come to my house for lunch."

Not only did Schuman say things well, he also developed a strong writing style at Teachers College. Schuman reflected on his Jewish roots in a term paper dated 1933 and entitled "Richard Wagner Alias 'K. Freigedank.'" In the paper, he attacks Wagner's anti-Semitism, expressed in an essay entitled "Judaism in Music" written under the pen name "K. Freigedank" (K. Freethought) and published in 1850 in the *Neue Zeitschrift für Musik*. In it Wagner rails against the Jewish presence in the European art scene, contending that the Jew will always be, in language and in thought, an alien in European culture.

Schuman's rebuttal was well reasoned and well written:

> Hebrew is scarcely more the every day means of Jewish communication than is Latin to the Roman Catholic. . . . Most non-Jews who understand the temperament of Jews will comment on the extreme warmth and passion the Jew possesses; it is generally regarded as an innate quality. . . . How little Wagner understood the very essence of Jewish thought, the eternal love and passion for justice that burns within the true son of Israel!

He concluded the essay by aiming a barb at Wagner:

> In conclusion, I can only repeat my regard for him [Wagner] as musician and composer, and to express the thought that possibly his great musical talent borrowed from his other powers and made them weaker, such as would allow a treatise as unfounded as "Judaism in Music."

Despite his later dismissiveness of the influence of his Jewish heritage on his music or his psyche, the young Schuman felt a strong sense of pride in and identity with his Jewish roots.

Schuman felt no inhibitions about corresponding with some of the most important musical figures of his day. In a research paper entitled "On the Increased Use of Modes," written for a music education course and dated May 26, 1934, Schuman presented an eloquent argument that presaged a compositional approach he would embrace in later years. Stating that "the inadequacy of using our Major and Minor System exclusively has often been felt by composers," he went on to include original letters on the topic that he had solicited from his old counterpoint teacher, Charles Haubiel; the composer and director of the Eastman School of Music, Howard Hanson; the dean of the Yale School of Music, David Stanley Smith; and the distinguished composer, Randall Thompson, all of whom discussed their approach to the use of modes with considerable enthusiasm.

In another paper submitted in the next academic year entitled "'Prometheus' as Experience" (for which he received a grade of A-plus), Schuman and his co-author, Arthur P. Moor, approached their analysis of Alexander Scriabin's *Prometheus* by quoting from John Dewey, Cyril Scott, and Alfred J. Swan. Complaining that Scriabin's music was still (in 1935) not widely known, Schuman and Moor once again made a highly perceptive observation: "If the music of this modern giant [Scriabin] seems to be esoteric in appealing only to the tutored few, there is no cause for dismay. Great works of music often reach the hearts of men only after many hearings, indeed in some instances only after many generations."

Teachers College, for all its inadequacies in young Schuman's view, was important in the intellectual growth of a man who would eventually become one of the most influential arts educators in the twentieth century. His undergraduate experiences created the foundation upon which many of his innovative educational ideas were based:

> I saw that education in the wrong hands was a disastrous tool, and that the best minds were not necessarily going into education but into the academic world, and the academicians looked down on the pedagogical institutions (in some cases rightfully) and had no interest in teaching. That shocked me. I also became increasingly convinced the courses in "how to teach" were useless, and that what really counted was a full and passionate understanding of the subject to be taught in itself.

Schuman more or less pieced together a composition curriculum for himself, studying music with various teachers privately and at the Institute of Musical Art of the Juilliard School of Music, across Broadway. With the exception of his brief and perfunctory work at NYU, Teachers College was the only continuous, curriculum-based higher education Schuman ever had. However, his time there also imbued him with a fundamental distrust of the music teaching profession that later manifested itself in his iconoclastic approaches to the teaching of music at Sarah Lawrence, Juilliard, and Lincoln Center, as well as his fiery public tirades in the 1950s excoriating American music education.

In 1935, toward the end of Schuman's undergraduate career at Teachers College, he was accepted in a summer conducting program at the Salzburg Mozarteum. At the time, the tradition of American musicians studying in Europe was a strong one. In addition to his 1925 trip to France, Schuman also visited Europe with his parents, his sister, and a cousin in 1931. Schuman had a lifelong aversion to tourism. If he had something to do abroad, he was engaged in the process; otherwise he found foreign vacations a bore. However, while in Salzburg he was able to purchase many scores for future study, and he dined in Munich with members of his extended family.

Schuman had no intention of ever becoming a conductor, but he saw Salzburg as an opportunity to continue studying and composing. The conducting teacher was Bernhard Paumgartner, director of the Mozarteum and co-founder, with Max Reinhardt, of the Salzburg Festival. Schuman remembered Paumgartner as "a specialist in Mozart and women." The maestro often looked longingly at one woman or another in a theater box close to the stage as he conducted the "Haffner" Symphony. Schuman also had the privilege of hearing and seeing Arturo Toscanini, Bruno Walter, and Felix Weingartner in concert during that summer. Schuman never forgot Walter's interrupting a rehearsal to admonish his young charges, whom he evidently thought unprepared: "The score should be in the head; not the head in the score."

Schuman considered himself untalented as a conductor, but did value score analysis, which was integral to the conducting experience. There were many American students at the Mozarteum that summer, including the mezzo-soprano Risë Stevens. During the summer Schuman set about composing his Symphony No. 1, a work he eventually withdrew. Coincidentally, the Columbia Teachers College Choir also toured that summer to Salzburg, and the inclusion in their program of Schuman's "Chorale Canons" considerably enhanced his artistic stature in the eyes of his fellow students and the school's administrators.

The separation caused by the Salzburg stay was difficult for both Bill and Frankie, who would be married in March of 1936. Bill's many feelings and thoughts are openly expressed in a long and revealing letter to Frankie spanning August 14–17, 1935:

> Frankie, if I ever had any doubts that I was a composer—they are shattered once and for all—I'm not referring to the quality of my work (that is unimportant since the good will always live and the other die) but to my desire to create music and the abundance of ideas that are always in my head. . . .
>
> This summer has definitely proven to me that I dislike Opera with all my heart, soul and might. I was bored to death with practically every one but Fidelio and Falstaff but even for those two the orchestra was the main feature. Wagner is still a great composer

but I am losing the requisite patience to sit out a whole four hours for one hour of inspiration. . . .

I love you and every thought connected with you and the very thrilling future before us. Keep on loving me like you do and just see where it gets you—the more I receive the more I give and there is nothing I wouldn't give my dearest girl. Darling in two weeks from today we'll be together and in a very few hours after you read this we'll have met—oh my what a girl to have and love. Hold everything Frankie and prepare to be kissed.
Forever your,
Bill

During his Austrian stay, Schuman witnessed the ominous developments that would soon affect Europe and the world. After a rehearsal in which Schuman conducted the first movement of Brahms's Symphony No. 2, the orchestra's concertmaster invited him out for beer with his friends. Schuman and another American, Paul Apfelder, bicycled almost ten miles to a country inn, where they found not only their concertmaster friend, but also a large group of men seated at tables in a semicircle, all dressed in Nazi uniforms and greeting the newcomers with a lusty "Heil!" This was in 1935, before the *Anschluss*, and such attire was prohibited in Austria. Schuman had been warned that Nazi sympathies were strong in Austria and had been advised to indicate his religion on official forms as Protestant or Congregationalist.

Schuman sat down among the brownshirts and began to drink a great deal of *Weizenbier*, a country wheat beer topped with a slice of lemon. "One of the men on my right showed me a snapshot of himself with Hitler," he recalled, "and asked me whether I knew who that was, and I said I thought I had seen his picture in the papers, and I was very careful. I wanted to leave alive." Schuman's inherent charm prevailed: he sang a song in German that his Grandpa Hy had taught him, much to the delight of the inn's customers.

This harrowing experience stayed with Schuman and resurfaced when he was booked to leave Europe on a ship departing from Rotterdam, which required that he travel by rail through Germany. German soldiers were everywhere, and he was careful not to talk to anyone during the time it took to cross Germany.

Prior to Schuman's studies in Salzburg and the completion of his undergraduate degree work at Teachers College, he set about in the spring of 1935 to find a job for the ensuing fall so that he and Frankie could get married. The Teachers College Placement Bureau sent him to Nyack, New York, in the suburbs north of New York City, where Schuman was offered a position conducting the district's bands, orchestras, and choruses. The job fell considerably short of his aspirations, and he pledged to find something better before the fall arrived.

Schuman persevered. He went to the desk of the Teachers College reference librarian and asked for the catalogs of every college within a thirty-five- to fifty-mile radius of New York City. It made for some desperately boring reading. Eventually, though, he came across a catalog that "set [him] on fire." The Sarah Lawrence College catalog wrote of a new approach to higher education in which "education [would be] geared toward each individual" and "great concern [given] for the motivation of the student." Located in Bronxville, New York, just north of New York City, the college, for women only, had opened in 1928 and was considered quite exclusive.

With his typical impulsiveness, Schuman immediately telephoned the college and asked to speak with the president, Constance Warren. He was greeted by the imperious voice of Warren's assistant, Mary Milligan, who, upon learning that Schuman would soon be graduating from Teachers College and wanted a job as a music teacher, said, "I can tell you now that there are no openings in music . . . and I can't imagine that anyone graduating from Teachers College at Columbia would be interested in Sarah Lawrence, and vice versa."

Schuman was not to be put off by what seemed to be a wall of exceedingly tight security around Warren and obtained an appointment with her six weeks hence. Schuman remembered Constance Warren as "very much the old New England schoolmarm, tough and bright. I liked her very much, and we hit it off immediately." He was then sent to meet with Jerome Swinford at his New York apartment on lower Fifth Avenue. A voice teacher and member of the faculty advisory committee on appointments, he told Schuman again that there were no positions at the college but suggested he look into a music position at the Brooklyn Ethical Culture School, which had sought a recommended candidate from Sarah Lawrence.

Schuman agreed to be interviewed for the Brooklyn position and was asked to conduct elementary and more advanced ensembles. Schuman simply couldn't see himself at the Brooklyn school any more than he could at Nyack. Fortunately, he wasn't offered the position; the principal gently told him that he feared the young children would try to imitate his voice and sing an octave lower than they should. Years later he wrote to a friend, "After dining at the School on a cold baked potato I remember a depressed ride home on the IRT, and then a call from Sarah Lawrence." In a dramatic turnaround, Swinford had decided to invite the young composer to a meeting with the Sarah Lawrence appointments committee, which was exploring a new approach to the teaching of the arts. The program would eventually be funded by the Rockefeller Foundation. The committee met at the Vassar Club in the New Weston Hotel in Manhattan and included Warren; Beatrice Doerschuk, director of education and chair of the committee; the sociologist Helen Merrell Lynd, who with her husband, Robert Staughton Lynd, had written a milestone book entitled *Middletown: A Study in Contemporary American Culture;* Swinford; and Henry Ladd of the English department.

The members of the committee wished to know if Schuman was equipped to teach all the arts to freshmen. He responded with his characteristic mix of wit and nerve: "I said I definitely was not but I knew someone who was, and they said: 'Who is that?' [and] I said da Vinci." He then explained to them: "Nobody can possibly claim to be able to teach all the arts. The best one person can do is [to] fake them. But what I'd like to do is organize such a course, teach the music portion and some of the dance, and bring in other people to head the other disciplines."

The committee must have been able to see past their candidate's cockiness to his passion, because William Schuman was soon hired to teach "Exploring the Arts" at Sarah Lawrence College, beginning in the fall of 1935, for an annual salary of $2,400.

Having finally established gainful employment, Bill married Frankie on March 27, 1936. Although the couple at first intended the wedding to be at City Hall, Bill knew that his mother would be happier with a religious service. The ceremony and reception took place in the Prince family's apartment at 41 West 96th Street and included the couple's immediate families, along with one or two friends. The rabbi they found to officiate, who was about the same age as Bill, was Hyman Schachtel of the West End Synagogue; he was later chosen to lead Congregation Beth Israel in Houston, Texas, and on January 20, 1965, delivered the inaugural prayer for President Lyndon Johnson. Years later, Schuman wryly noted that Schachtel "must have known that he was destined for greatness because he delivered the words of the ceremony as though he were addressing Madison Square Garden, both in length (long) and tone (stentorian)."

After a wedding breakfast, the entire entourage walked to the West Side piers, where the newlyweds took a three o'clock ship to Virginia Beach for their honeymoon. Unfortunately, the groom became violently seasick on his wedding night, but he recovered in time for a memorable long-weekend honeymoon at the Club Hotel in Virginia Beach. The couple wanted to stay longer, but it was the Depression, and Frankie feared that she might jeopardize her job at the New York State Employment Bureau if she took too much time off. They returned from their honeymoon to settle into an apartment at 260 Riverside Drive.

The next year Frankie and Bill made up for their short honeymoon by spending an idyllic summer in France, with a short visit to London as well. In late June the Schumans met Bill's French cousins, the Schuhmanns, in Paris. Monsieur and Madame were already retired. Their son, Pierre, was a university student and planned to visit America in August. Schuman wrote to his parents that their conversation "included talk of the Jews. The situation in France is becoming more acute and for the first time they are made aware of the fact they are Jews. In French society no difference has been made between French Jews and other Frenchmen but the situation now seems to be growing more in the direction of separation."

The Schumans then traveled to Talloires on Lac d'Annecy, one of the most beautiful regions in all of France, where they spent the month of July relaxing and, on Bill's part, composing. Schuman followed a disciplined regimen: "My work schedule calls for five hours each day and I have been following it religiously since our arrival. As a result I have completed the orchestration of my Prelude and already started on the Fugue which I hope to complete in another six or seven days. After that I plan to start on a String Quartet." (The Prelude and Fugue for orchestra was never publicly performed and was withdrawn by Schuman; the String Quartet No. 2 was premiered in 1938.)

The anti-Semitism the Schuhmanns had described to him did not seem to dampen Schuman's enthusiasm for the French attitude toward life: "The thing I like best about France is the freedom and lack of Germanic disciplin[e]. No one really cares what you do and all things are regarded as private." Ultimately, though, his evaluation of the French was equivocal: "If one carried over the French culture into one's own work the product would be of surface value and skin deep like the French. However, I find this atmosphere conducive to thinking, working and playing."

Schuman's recollections of his Sarah Lawrence years, which stretched from 1935 to 1945, clearly delineate a love-hate relationship with the college and its people. Coming from the social and ethnic milieu of Manhattan's West Side, Schuman was thrust into a world completely new to him:

> Sarah Lawrence students were a breed apart. The daughters of the elite, not of the professional classes, but of corporate CEO's, they had been washed with the finest lotions all their lives, had had the best nannies, and were exceedingly polite. They were also famous for being beautiful. They weren't the best students in the world; some of them were not really at college level. But many of them were good, and highly motivated—after all, they didn't *have* to do this.

Schuman remembered that Warren attempted to address the issue of diversity on campus by asking him if he thought Sarah Lawrence "should drop its quota on the number of Jewish students admitted to the School." His response reflected his father's belief in assimilating all religions and cultures into American society and his own equivocal stance on the issue: "I told her that she should persuade all the private colleges to do it together, otherwise Sarah Lawrence would become an entirely Jewish school."

Schuman found the faculty to be an extraordinary group. It included the Lynds, the poet Genevieve Taggard, the great mythologist Joseph Campbell, and René d'Harnoncourt, who taught art history and eventually became the long-serving director of the Museum of Modern Art. The teaching environment also mirrored what Schuman would eventually experience at Juilliard, where "everyone was a professional, did what they taught, and taught out of conviction. Sarah Lawrence wasn't caught up with methods and formal lesson plans; you taught the way you wanted to teach." Eventually, though, Schuman came to feel he was being exploited by the amount of time he needed to spend with individual students through the college's mentoring, or donning, system, in which the faculty members had to write highly detailed reports on the progress of each "donee." Although he admitted that such intensive faculty-student contact could be useful, he ultimately saw it as "wasteful of time."

Schuman's first class in "Exploring the Arts" came with an added challenge. Doerschuk, the director of education, asked if the new teacher would mind having a few visitors. "Not at all," Schuman gulped. He then learned that the visitors were an evaluative committee from the course's funder, the Rockefeller Foundation. They included Edmund Ezra Day, director of social sciences for the foundation and eventually (beginning in 1937) president of Cornell University. Schuman recalled, "The music studio was in an old stable. I climbed to the second floor, ducked into the men's room and told myself, 'Now, the first thing is straighten your tie, and the second thing is to make sure your fly is buttoned. Then put some cold water on your face and just go down there and do it.'"

The fledgling teacher did it, and did it well. His approach to the course demonstrated his lifelong strategy of problem solving. Instead of devising a careful lesson plan, Schuman guided the students toward an enormous universe and asked them to find their own way, much as he had done in his own musical studies. Sending his students to the college's record library, he asked them to seek out compositions that they liked: "See if you can find things that intrigue you. Spend hours in that library." His aim was to teach his students the art of what he called "penetrative listening," and he claimed that his initiated students "could read scores as a visual aid without being able to read music." Ironically, Schuman later pointed out with pride that he could get his Sarah Lawrence students to "graph a melody" by listening to a symphony's principal theme and then charting what they heard. Apparently he had forgotten his outburst in Rugg's symposium at Teachers College against the Pitts method of asking students to draw what they heard.

Schuman set about to truly enrich the cultural environment at the college by inviting such luminaries as Aaron Copland, Roy Harris, Antony Tudor, and Frank Loesser to speak. During his ten years at Sarah Lawrence Schuman developed his public speaking skills as well, a hallmark of his persona in future years. Unexpectedly, he also became a choral conductor of significant achievement.

Around 1938 Schuman was asked to substitute at a performance at nearby Scarsdale High School for the college choir conductor, who was indisposed. Schuman had studied orchestral conducting during his Salzburg summer and had taken the advanced conducting class at the Juilliard Summer School in 1933. Although he never considered himself a strong practitioner on the podium, he jumped into the task with his usual enthusiasm. Under Schuman the Sarah Lawrence Chorus had considerable success, presenting concerts to entertain the troops during World War II and joint concerts with the all-male choruses of several other universities and colleges, among them Harvard, Columbia, Williams, and Amherst. It became so popular that it began to be referred to as the "Sarah Lawrence football team." The ensemble was even asked to sing with the Boston Symphony Orchestra (BSO) under Serge Koussevitzky on February 13 and 14, 1943, performing Debussy's *La demoiselle élue* with the soloists Marcelle Denya, soprano, and Jennie Tourel, contralto. Schuman recalled that the maestro prefaced his invitation by saying, "William, I hear [that] you have a chorus of 55 virgins." Replied Schuman, "Well, I do have a chorus of young ladies. I can't vouch for their virginity, but they sing very well."

In addition to conducting, Schuman also composed for the ensemble: an arrangement of the popular *Orchestra Song* (1939); *Prelude* for women's voices (1939), based on a text by Thomas Wolfe; *Holiday Song* (1942), with words by Genevieve Taggard; and *Requiescat* (1942), in memory of his fellow faculty member Henry Ladd. (Schuman arranged all the works for mixed chorus, as well.) Schuman remarked, "I was always conscious that I wrote simpler music for the chorus . . . because I think the chorus is more effective when the materials are simpler."

Schuman taught for nine of his ten years at Sarah Lawrence College, having taken a leave of absence on a Guggenheim Fellowship to compose during the academic year 1939–40. He claimed to have "loved six of the ten unequivocally." His teaching methods, based on wide-ranging explorations of musical masterworks ideally taught by professional practitioners, not only formed the foundation of his teaching reforms at Juilliard, but were also the basis for his master's thesis at Teachers College; the degree was conferred in 1937.

However, Schuman eventually soured on the intensive one-on-one commitment of the donning system, and he was bored by the daily practice of teaching familiar courses. After teaching a class for which he had not prepared with seeming ease and success, he "realized that one could become a campus bum: you could just live on what you had prepared in the past." Schuman knew that he wished to have a life in education but not as a classroom teacher: "I wanted to teach teachers and do other things that had an aspect of education." First, though, he had to establish himself as a composer.

CHAPTER 3

If He Fails He Will Fail
on a Grand Scale

Although Schuman expended a good deal of effort on his Sarah Lawrence teaching responsibilities, his passion was clearly composition. He made a tentative beginning at age sixteen with a tango for violin called "Fate" that was eventually set to lyrics by his childhood friend Eddie Marks (he had of course composed many songs with both Marks and Frank Loesser). Schuman's first real compositional effort can be traced to a setting of Edna St. Vincent Millay's poem "God's World," a three-minute work for voice and piano written in 1932 at the beginning of his formal music studies. Toward the end of his life Schuman commented on this piece: "I remember playing it for Lenny [Bernstein], and when I got to the end of it he groaned, 'Prithee, no bird call, Oh, no!' It's a very young piece, and a juvenile taste and I'm always hoping nobody will find it, but every once in a while they do. I admit, I still love the poem, because it's simple and it's what it is."

The year 1932 also saw Schuman's first experiment in orchestral writing, "Potpourri," never publicly performed and later withdrawn. These efforts were followed in 1933 by a choral work, "Chorale Canons" (eventually renamed *Four Canonic Choruses*), based on texts by Millay, Countée Cullen, Carl Sandburg, and Tennyson and premiered by the Teachers College A Cappella Choir. The choir eventually took the piece on tour to Europe and to Salzburg in 1935 at the same time Schuman was studying conducting there.

The Teachers College choral concert was the first time Schuman heard his own work successfully performed. He was struck by "how wonderful it was to hear . . . mere symbols turned into this excellent presentation of my concept. On the other hand I learned . . . that there is an enormous difference between what a composer may have in mind and what the result of the reading of his score might be."

Schuman's compositional roots, however, were firmly in the sound of the symphony orchestra. Composing a work for full orchestra, with all the complexity inherent in the process, held few inhibitions for a composer whose education was as self-directed as his. The musical setbacks that Schuman experienced in his earlier years might well have played out in a less public way had he received his musical education in a more formal institutional setting. Nevertheless, there was clearly an intense fire burning in the young Schuman that allowed him to survive the debacles of his earliest works.

Schuman's First Symphony, for eighteen players, was influenced by modern dance performances he had seen at Columbia. Entitled "Choreographic," much of it was completed in the summer of 1935 while he was studying in Salzburg. Schuman regarded the work as a flawed "experiment." He eventually withdrew it, but not before submitting it to Columbia University's Bearns Prize jury in 1936. Daniel Gregory Mason, the music department's chairman, viewed the work as "overly modernistic and experimental," in contrast to the previously submitted "Chorale Canons," which Mason found worthy but, at only eight minutes in duration, too short.

While preparing to teach a course in orchestration at Teachers College, Schuman happened to hear Roy Harris's *Symphony 1933*, which impressed him so much that he decided to seek Harris out as a teacher. Schuman was on a quest to master a more sophisticated level of composition, and Harris was one of two composers who would become Schuman's lifelong friends and mentors; the other was Aaron Copland. In the mid-1930s Harris and Copland, along with Howard Hanson and Walter Piston, were the acknowledged leaders in the field of American composition. Although both Copland and Harris were only in their mid-thirties, each composer had a uniquely pervasive influence on the style and eventual performance of American works that no composer, with the exception of Leonard Bernstein, has held in the United States since.

Roy Harris was born, he was always fond of pointing out, on Lincoln's birthday in Lincoln County, Nebraska. (I'm sure he made up the whole thing.) He delighted in playing the role of the rough-hewn, backwoods country boy, truck farmer, and baseball player who made it in the highest realm of culture because he was "of the people" and his music was not "arty." Aaron Copland was the opposite: Brooklyn born of a Jewish family, brought up in a household of department store merchants. He made no claims to anything except his desire to be a composer, and always said he was surprised that anyone of his background should grow up wishing to be a composer of serious music. . . . I got to know them both very well over the years. I witnessed the emergence of Aaron as the pre-eminent American composer of his time, and the decline in the position of Harris.

During the summer of 1936 Harris was teaching at the Juilliard Summer School at Broadway and 122nd Street, two streets north of Teachers College. Schuman sought him out and expressed his admiration for *Symphony 1933*. He asked if he could attend his classes, to which Harris quickly agreed. When Schuman showed him the First Symphony, Harris warned him, "You're not going to be happy with it at all when you hear it." As the summer drew to a close, Harris, who was then teaching at Westminster Choir College in Princeton, New Jersey, agreed to review Schuman's work from time to time.

Harris had an enormous musical influence on the young Schuman. It was while working with Harris that Schuman first heard compositions from the Renaissance period, analyzed Stravinsky's *Rite of Spring*, and learned how new harmonic devices worked, especially polytonality, the simultaneous use of multiple keys. Schuman's early settings of Walt Whitman were inspired by Harris's *Song for Occupations*, a choral work based on Whitman's poem.

Schuman was to realize after his student years that Harris's pride in his status as one of America's most important composers of the 1930s was a greater detriment to him than it had seemed at the time. Schuman believed that Harris "spent more time promoting his music than writing it . . . because I think he wasted his energies that way, and the great originality his music had when I first knew of it was ultimately undermined by his failure to develop technically":

> In his "Third Symphony," for example, his most famous work, he seemed to me to be already taming the ruggedness that had so excited me in "Symphony 1933." That may have been in part because it was originally written as a violin concerto for Jascha Heifetz. Heifetz decided he didn't want to continue with it, so Roy turned it into a symphony. The piece is very smooth, especially the middle section, appropriate for a violin concerto. Roy was obsessed with being a success in the wrong way. He once had a job with a government agency, and used his position to send out a letter soliciting the names of "the first three American composers," and thereafter advertised himself as "America's number one composer."

Harris's foibles included a particular aversion to picking up tabs at restaurants and absconding with half of Schuman's shirts during a stay at the Schuman apartment. Harris's wife was a popular piano teacher at Juilliard. Born Beulah Duffy, soon after their marriage she changed her name, at her husband's urging, to Johana—in honor of J. S. Bach. Harris's influence over her extended even to her taste in attire, which changed from flamboyant dresses to heavy tweed suits much like Harris's own.

In the volatile ideological climate of the mid-1930s, the young Schuman found Harris's politics highly suspect. Schuman recalled that Harris once stated that "'nothing will ever happen to Jews in America, they're too powerful.' He was perfectly serious about this, though I don't think he really was a fascist—his comments all came out of Spengler and Schopenauer and other German philosophers." This curious right-wing position was not borne out in Harris's future activities: he often championed liberal causes such as the Musicians Committee to Aid Spanish Democracy (an activity he would need to defend during the McCarthy era) and, still later, minority rights.

Personality and politics aside, Harris's influence made its mark on Schuman's early compositions, as Schuman himself recognized. In particular, Harris's "emphasis on the importance of melody and the free development of melody feeding on its own potential was a new thought to me, and I would write purely melodic conversations." Harris's deep commitment to American musical populism also had a distinct influence on the young Schuman. Throughout their compositional careers, both Harris and Schuman had an affinity for creating works for patriotic occasions, arrangements of folk materials, and pieces for student performers.

In an article on Schuman's seventieth birthday, a critic for the *New York Times* wrote:

Mr. Schuman's music recalls Harris's in its direct emotionality and its refusal to embrace the complexity and chromatic density that have marked American composers influenced by Schoenberg and Webern. Yet at the same time his music also holds itself free from the eccentricities of experimental music, being full of American directness in its vibrant rhythms and brilliant orchestrations.

Harris was helpful in furthering Schuman's career through his position as a judge of a choral contest supported by the Works Progress Administration Federal Music Project in 1938. The contest was presented in cooperation with the publishing firm Carl Fischer, the Columbia Phonograph Company, and the Columbia Broadcasting System. The judges included Harris, Howard Hanson, Harold Morris, Lee Orean Smith, and Lehman Engel. The award letter to Schuman made clear that his music was considered superior to that of some soon-to-be-distinguished composers: "The names [of the winners] are listed in accordance to the wishes of the Committee *as to their importance:* William Schuman, Armin Loos, David Diamond, John Vincent, Elliott Carter" (emphasis added).

In Schuman's later years he looked kindly upon Harris's music:

> In my mind, Roy Harris is one of the most original minds ever to appear in music. He is greatly underestimated as a composer even today [1967]. The reason for this is that his technique never advanced in terms equal to his fantastic talent. . . . It is rather absurd that everybody discovers Charles Ives and lets Roy Harris wither on the vine. Ives was a great originator but he is vastly overrated in every way except as an originator.

Schuman was finally able to hear his First Symphony when the Composers' Forum Laboratory, created by the Works Progress Administration, invited him to present an entire concert of his work, although Schuman had asked the project's director, Ashley Pettis, only for a reading of the symphony. The concert took place on October 21, 1936, and included, in addition to the symphony, Schuman's First String Quartet and the "Chorale Canons."

The young composer did not view the concert as a great success, owing in great part to the fact that he did not consider the Gotham Symphony Orchestra, under the direction of Jules Werner, up to the task of playing the symphony. He also realized that Harris was quite correct about the technical and structural problems of the work. Lehman Engel's Madrigal Singers garnered greater success with the "Chorale Canons" for mixed chorus. Schuman eventually withdrew both the symphony and the string quartet.

These performances gave Schuman his first taste of the cruelty occasionally inflicted by seasoned musicians on young composers. The members of the New String Quartet, who performed the premiere of the First String Quartet (including first violinist Maurice Eisenberg and violist Sidney Cohen), laughed a great deal, seemingly about the music, throughout the rehearsals. Schuman was deeply hurt but did not allow himself to be deterred by the quartet's scornful reaction.

On the positive side of this experience was Schuman's discovery of his ability as an extemporaneous speaker:

> In those early days, the composer appeared as a speaker at the Composers' Forum concerts, and answered questions about his music from the public. The unsympathetic reception of the symphony and string quartet was balanced not only by the success of the choral music, but also by my public speaking, a talent I was to go on using. I believe it was also the first and last time any of my cousins and aunts ever came to hear music I had written. The family survived.

Early in their marriage Bill and Frankie were comfortably settled at 17 Springdale Road in Larchmont, a home his mother had helped them buy. But after the couple moved to the Westchester suburbs to be closer to Sarah Lawrence and owing in part to Schuman's increasing teaching duties there, he had little opportunity for contact with other composers. One exception was Aaron Copland. Copland's loft, on Manhattan's West Side where Lincoln Center now stands, was a gathering place for young composers. Copland was known for his generosity of spirit toward other composers and often used his influence to find performance opportunities for composer friends. The two first met at a gathering in Copland's apartment at which Copland played a recording of his new opera for children, *The Second Hurricane.*

Schuman saw Copland as a "just man . . . possessed of a brilliantly analytical mind" who tirelessly pursued his artistic ideals. Yet although he was close to Copland professionally, in those early days Schuman never saw himself as Copland's trusted friend:

> I was never part of Aaron's inner circle, in part because of my disinclination to be in any circle, but also because I was not homosexual. Many of the homosexual composers flocked to Aaron, and their influence, and that of homosexual musicians was very strong at that time. Aaron certainly never discussed his homosexuality with me; he was an extremely private person. . . . Aaron never made me feel excluded, but the atmosphere around him was not entirely welcoming.

Nevertheless, as a young composer Schuman was frequently the object of Copland's generosity. Although he never considered himself a student of Copland's, he would frequently bring him scores for evaluation:

> The remarkable thing about him as a teacher was that he didn't try to make a lot of little Coplands, in the way that Hindemith tried to make little Hindemiths and often succeeded. Copland tried to understand what you were about. Over the years, Frankie, Aaron and I became close friends. We visited him several times up at Tanglewood where he taught composition each summer and in Hollywood, where he wrote the music for *Of Mice and Men*. He used our house in Larchmont for a few months while we were in New York and wrote his Piano Sonata there.

Despite his limited access to his composer colleagues at this time, Schuman did have an enlightening encounter with one of the twentieth century's musical giants: Igor Stravinsky. In 1937, during a dinner party at the home of a Sarah Lawrence colleague, Schuman made the acquaintance of Paul Stassevitch, a well-known violinist and conductor of contemporary music. Both the camaraderie and the libations were abundant, and the two jousted with each other on musical topics as the evening progressed and the cognac flowed.

The next morning Schuman was awakened by a headache and a phone call. On the other end was a Russian-accented voice inquiring, "Schuman? Igor Stravinsky here." The hung-over young composer was in no mood for jokes and told the caller to "cut the crap and leave me alone." After a brief pause, the voice of the violinist Samuel Dushkin came on the line to explain that Stassevitch, Schuman's drinking buddy of the night before, had recommended him to provide publisher's corrections for Stravinsky's new ballet score, *Jeu de cartes*, which would be premiered with choreography by George Balanchine in 1937 at the Metropolitan Opera during a Stravinsky festival. Said Dushkin, "Stassevitch says you're the only composer in New York who can do this, and Stravinsky would like to engage you."

Later in the morning Schuman went to Stravinsky's hotel on Park Avenue and was greeted by "horrific sounds" coming from one of the rooms. The source turned out to be a less-than-stellar rehearsal for an upcoming performance of Stravinsky and Dushkin's nationwide tour of duo recitals. Stravinsky, clothed in what seemed to be mink-lined slippers and a bathrobe, welcomed his guest, explained what he needed, and asked Schuman what his fee would be. Having been warned of Stravinsky's miserly ways, Schuman bid high, asking for $300. Stravinsky blanched and responded, "Mais, je suis pauvre [But I'm poor]," and turned his pockets out. Schuman responded in his best schoolboy French, "Mais, je suis marié [But I'm married]." After a bit more playful discussion, the fee was set at $250, and the great Russian composer sealed the deal with an embrace.

Stravinsky then handed the sole copy of *Jeu de cartes* to Schuman, who was so terrified that the treasure would be lost or stolen that he kept it during the daytime in the comptroller's office safe at Sarah Lawrence and at night in his home refrigerator (for security and conservation purposes).

Although Schuman saw Roy Harris as his musical mentor, it was Aaron Copland who put Schuman on the map as one of the best of a new generation of American composers. In 1938 Copland was part of a panel charged with choosing a new American work that would be presented within the context of fund-raising activities for the republican government in Spain, where the civil war was raging. The other judges included Roy Harris (who excused himself when he recognized Schuman's musical notation), Roger Sessions (who voted against the symphony, but who later spent an entire day with Schuman analyzing the work and making suggestions for its improvement), Bernard Wagenaar, Horace Grenell, and Wallingford Riegger.

The prize was awarded to Schuman for his Symphony No. 2, an eighteen-minute work in one movement that had been completed in 1937. The intended performance and publication of the symphony as part of the prize never came to pass, but Copland demonstrated his commitment to the work by attending its first performance on May 25, 1938, by the Greenwich Orchestra conducted by Edgar Schenkman. Like the ensemble that performed Schuman's First Symphony, this orchestra was supported through the Works Progress Administration. The players were uneven in quality, "a few excellent, many mediocre, and a number who clearly never achieved the level of perfection required to play any standard symphonic music."

Irritated by the substandard performance and moved by his own enthusiasm for Schuman's choral work *Pioneers* (based on a text by Whitman and premiered by the Westminster Festival Chorus only two days before the Second Symphony's first performance), Copland set about giving an enormous—and career-altering—boost to Schuman's composing career. He wrote enthusiastically: "Schuman is, so far as I am concerned, the musical find of the year. There is nothing puny or miniature about this young man's talent. If he fails he will fail on a grand scale. . . . From the testimony of this piece [*Pioneers*] alone, it seems to me that Schuman is a composer who is going places."

Copland also contacted Serge Koussevitzky, music director of the BSO and the preeminent supporter of new American music at the time, about the symphony. Copland sent a penny postcard to Schuman with instructions to send the score of the Second Symphony to Koussevitzky as soon as possible. Not wanting to gamble that Koussevitzky might reject the score, Schuman also submitted it to Howard Barlow, conductor of CBS's Sunday afternoon radio program *Everybody's Music*. To his amazement, Schuman received a telephone call from Davidson Taylor, head of the CBS music department, saying that Maestro Barlow liked the symphony and wished to perform it on an upcoming program.

The classical master of the radio at the time was Arturo Toscanini, conductor of the NBC Symphony, which began nationwide broadcasts in 1937. Toscanini was not known as a champion of American music. Occasionally he would program American composers, as he did on November 5, 1938, when two works by Samuel Barber—*Essay No. 1* for orchestra and the Adagio for Strings—were performed. Goddard Lieberson, who was later to become one of the major classical-record producers of the twentieth century but at the time was a composer whose works also were performed by WPA ensembles, commented that it was so surprising to hear Toscanini conduct American music that it reinforced the shock of Orson Welles's infamous broadcast of *War of the Worlds*, which had aired the week before.

In 1938 CBS radio was more committed to the performance of new American music than either NBC or the Mutual Broadcasting System. In the mid-1930s Mutual presented a series, *Let's Make Music*, in which Roy and Johana Harris were involved. That program had evolved from the Composers' Forum Laboratory, the WPA unit that presented Schuman's first two symphonies. By 1938 Barlow had been conducting new commissioned American works on CBS for two years. Not only had the network agreed to broadcast six commissioned works by such composers as Quincy Porter, Robert Russell Bennett, and Vittorio Giannini, but it actively sought other works, including Schuman's Symphony No. 2, Paul Creston's Partita, and Charles Jones's Suite.

Schuman immediately called Copland with the news of the pending CBS performance. Copland advised Schuman to charge CBS for performing the symphony. When Schuman informed Taylor that he would require a $25 fee, the CBS executive was taken aback. In his view, the extraordinary public exposure the broadcast would provide Schuman's music would counterbalance the need for a fee. Taylor first told him he might lose the broadcast and then made a counter-offer of $15, but the young composer stuck to his guns, and Taylor finally agreed to the full fee.

Schuman considered his Symphony No. 2 a flawed work, difficult to listen to "probably because it grew out of a basically intellectual idea rather than being centered in a musical one":

> My intellectual idea was that painters always had a blank canvas with which to start, and wouldn't it be interesting to create the blank canvas in sound, and then present the music against this blank canvas. I decided that I would write a symphony on the note of C, either sounding or implied. The work began with alternating trumpets that sounded the note of C. This went on for about five or six minutes, and underneath that constant sound came the music. . . . This gave the effect of a Tibetan trumpet call played by a man who never went out of breath.

Schuman's approach here seems heavily rooted in Harris's concept of compositional form, which he called "autogenesis." Harris saw a "melody or harmonic design flower[ing] from a seed motive . . . [giving the] effect of gradual, organic growth." Elsewhere Schuman described the artistic problem with his "intellectual" concept:

> What I didn't know, in my inexperience, was that the audience was going crazy with that note that wouldn't go away.

The composer's attempts at economy drove the last nail into the coffin:

> To exacerbate the problem, I had also written the piece at a very slow tempo, not only because I heard it that way, but also because the slower the tempo, the fewer the pages, and the lower the copying costs.

Schuman's greatest fears about the work were unfortunately realized. After the broadcast on September 11, 1938, a heavy volume of complaints poured into CBS's mailbags. One came from a farmer in Iowa, who wrote,

"That so-called symphony has given me a headache that I haven't been able to get rid of for three days with aspirin." Unexpectedly, Taylor was thrilled with the audience reaction—any reaction would do, apparently—and decided to program it again in two or three weeks.

The saga of the flawed symphony continued when Copland's penny-postcard advice resulted in a letter from John Burk, the Boston Symphony's program annotator, informing him that Koussevitzky had scheduled the Symphony No. 2 for performances beginning on February 17, 1939. Schuman was invited to meet the maestro when the orchestra was next in New York. Both Copland and Harris went with Bill and Frankie to the New York concert. Recalled Schuman:

> When we went backstage afterwards, Koussevitsky, elegant and caped—a *boulevardier* and peasant all in one—looked at me and said with his heavily Russian-accented English, "I vill play, but no two Schumans. You must change the name." I thought about suggesting that I change my name to Schumansky or to Koussevitsky, but Providence told me to shut up, and I only smiled. He never mentioned it again.

In preparation for the February performance, Schuman was invited to rehearsals in Boston. He was to stay in the Alumni Suite at Harvard's Elliot House. Two Harvard students were sent to greet Schuman at the train station: I. Bernard Cohen, a teaching fellow who later became a distinguished scholar in the history of science, and a junior by the name of Leonard Bernstein.

> Lenny was 20 when I met him. If the expression "star caliber" didn't exist, one would have had to invent it for him. It didn't matter that he was young and gauche, he was the real thing—knowledgeable, sophisticated, and tremendously exciting. He had great energy that could be completely chaotic, yet you were always aware of his extraordinary mind. . . . Lenny took me right back to Elliot House, where we got some food and beer, and started looking at my score. We went on from that to discuss everything from Sibelius to Gilbert and Sullivan, poetry and the Bible, and a lifelong friendship was born.

Many years later, at a sixtieth-birthday celebration for Bernstein in Washington, D.C., in 1978, Schuman remarked again on his first meeting with the brilliant Bernstein: "What now is wise, was then precocious; what now is erudition was then promise; what now is mastery was then technique; what now is wit, charm, brilliance, is now—wit, charm, brilliance."

Schuman was given access during the day to Cohen's room (as well as his supply of sherry and macaroons, which had been placed on the piano). There he worked on a composition for mixed chorus and orchestra entitled *Prologue* that was eventually premiered in New York City on May 7, 1939, at a Composers' Forum Laboratory concert at Carnegie Hall featuring works by Schuman, Harris, Copland, Paul Nordoff, and Walter Piston. Noel Straus wrote in the *New York Times* that the Prologue, based on a poem of Genevieve Taggard

> concerning the opening of "tomorrow's door[,]" was splendidly sung by the youthful members of the assisting chorus [chorus of the High School of Music and Art], possessed the most positive and straightforward ideas of any of the composers represented. . . . Mr. Schuman is forging to the front among native composers of the day.

It was Bernstein who, as a favor to Schuman, anonymously transcribed the orchestral part for piano for future publication. Schuman recalled at the time that Bernstein had told him "he was very excited about his upcoming production of Marc Blitzstein's *The Cradle Will Rock*," which he presented in Cambridge. Bernstein and Blitzstein became good friends as a result.

At the end of their first Elliot House encounter, Bernstein asked if he could borrow the score of Schuman's Symphony No. 2, and the composer agreed to part with his creation overnight. Anxiety over the upcoming rehearsal kept him awake, and by 7:00 A.M. he was already on his way to Symphony Hall for the 10:00 A.M. rehearsal. First, though, he needed to retrieve his score. He found Bernstein asleep in his dormitory room. Opening his eyes long enough to hand Schuman the score, Bernstein murmured drowsily, "Good morning, Sibelius." (Bernstein resurrected this criticism in an article that appeared a few years later in *Modern Music*, in which he claimed that it was unjustified to view Schuman's music as "only inferior Harris, combined with inferior Hindemith, touched up more recently with inferior Copland, and *even Sibelius as some say*" [emphasis added].) Bernstein's comment was a backhanded compliment if ever there was one, and as he trudged off to the rehearsal, Schuman was crushed by this unexpected critique of his compositional style from his brilliant new friend.

At Symphony Hall Schuman finally had the opportunity to hear one of his works rehearsed and performed by a truly great orchestra. Koussevitzky greeted the young composer with typical flair at the stage door and introduced him to Jesús Maria Sanromá, known to everyone as Choo-Choo. For many years the official pianist of the BSO, he actively sought out new music to perform. Sanromá wisely cautioned Schuman not to "say anything critical in front of the orchestra."

The rehearsal went smoothly. Koussevitzky periodically made comments and offered suggestions. These included adding an organ part, an idea Schuman politely rejected.

Before the first performance, Koussevitzky sealed a professional friendship that would endure until the conductor's death in 1951. As Schuman recalled, Koussevitzky said, "'This work with the 'pooblic' will be no 'succès.' But with me it is a 'succès.' You must hear a great orchestra and conductor play your music, and I want you to write something more for me, and everything you write I will play.' Young composers hear statements like that in their dreams, not in life."

Koussevitzky was also a practical man, so he advised Schuman not to come onstage at the end of the symphony, as was ordinarily done, but rather to walk down the aisle to the front of the podium. At the conclusion of the work, as anticipated, applause was light, and silence and hissing prevailed, with the exception of periodic loud "bravos" from the balcony, generated by Bernstein and his Harvard friends. Capping this tragicomic experience was a request from a member of the audience:

> I walked up, took my little bow and when I came back, to a bit of buzzing in the audience, the man sitting behind me, who had been among the most fervent of the hissers, asked for my autograph. Frankie said my reaction was right out of Noel Coward: I said "Sir, considering your mixed reaction, I do not know whether it's more pretentious of you to ask me to sign, or for me to sign" and with that I sat down.

Frankie and Bill decided to escape and went to a local movie theater, where a Jesse James movie starring Tyrone Power and Henry Fonda was playing. Schuman was also evicted from Elliot House: women, even wives, could not stay in the building. One last insult was yet to be added to their injury: they found a room in "a hotel called the Hemenway just down the block from Symphony Hall. We moved in there Friday night and found that it was a whorehouse, plain and simple. So we got out of there the next day and found what we could with the little money we had."

A recording of a broadcast of the Symphony No. 2 housed in the Historical Recordings Collection of the Fine Arts Library of the University of Texas at Austin, with Howard Barlow conducting the CBS Symphony Orchestra, presents an interesting opportunity to hear a withdrawn Schuman work. The mood of the symphony is austere and ominous. The first section stretches for about eight minutes, with very little melodic or harmonic variation. The work's relentless intensity, combined with the dark and forbidding musical motives and the paucity of musical material, present a lugubrious texture and a significant aesthetic challenge for any uninitiated listener.

Over the next few days after the BSO performance uniformly negative critical reviews began coming in. The *Boston Globe* wrote that the work "is technically unconventional. He [Schuman] sets great store by the use of a sustained note (C) which is, as he says, 'stated or implied' through the whole piece. . . . In a phrase, it may justly be termed an interesting intellectual experiment but not a work of inspired art." Warren Storey Smith of the *Boston Post* seemed to be the most distraught critic present: "When in the course of the single movement this pedal tone [C], mostly carried by a trumpet, is dropped, the listener experiences a blessed sense of relief, as when a dentist removes his drill, and the music for a moment seems actually to get somewhere."

There were two or three positive comments linked to the symphony, however. According to the reviewer for the *Boston Transcript*, "The young composer clearly knew what he wanted to say and how to say it . . . and what he had to say was worth saying." Bernstein commented in *Modern Music* that

the Schuman Symphony . . . was for the most part a joy to hear. A first impression is one of formidable structure, direct, clear, unified, and innocent of padding. The theme is angular in character, probably because of the abundance of tritonic figures. These tritones, in fact, used throughout the piece give it its general melodic feeling. . . . The theme undergoes augmentation, diminution, inversion, reharmonization (very effectively), fugato, canon, and all the rest. The total effect is one of accumulation of matter, building to a startling climax at the end.

However, he took exception to the exceedingly slow tempo (larghissimo), which broke the "connectivity of the melodic line."

Goddard Lieberson also saw a "marked development" throughout the symphony, "especially when one remembers some of the inchoate representations on his first Composers' Forum Concert." Yet he saw the work as hampered by the "too constant reiteration of the original material." Schuman's parents and sister attended the Saturday performance. Afterward Schuman's father congratulated his son. The composer retorted, "'Now, wait a minute, Dad, you don't mean to tell me you liked that music.' He said, 'No, I'm congratulating you because I'm still your friend, and if you're going to write music like that you're going to need a lot of friends.'"

Such negative responses were naturally devastating to Schuman. He attempted to dissuade Howard Barlow from subsequently programming his Symphony No. 2 with the Baltimore Symphony, but to no avail. Once again the reviews were devastating. One critic wrote "that the music was a great study in mass psychology, for he had felt that if it had gone on for one more minute the audience would have been on the stage en masse to stop the proceedings." The work's many problems led Schuman eventually to withdraw it.

Still, one of the great orchestras of the world had played his symphony, and the legendary Serge Koussevitzky had committed himself and his orchestra to performing subsequent works. Schuman had also learned an important compositional lesson regarding the need for greater structural and technical focus. Most important, he now felt he was a composer, able to write from his heart and his mind no matter what the audience response. His passionate need to express himself through music was in full bloom.

CHAPTER 4

I Wanted to Run
Before I Could Creep

Schuman was determined to continue his career as a composer, no matter what the critical response. He emerged from his Symphony No. 2 experiences with only a few bruises. Financially supported by his teaching at Sarah Lawrence and enjoying the support of such major figures as Copland, Harris, and, especially, Koussevitzky, for Schuman the late 1930s marked the beginning of an amazing period of compositional productivity and success.

In the fall of 1939 Koussevitzky decided to give "two special concerts in honor of the American composer." The BSO was justly proud of its support of American music. The program books of these concerts included a long list of works by American composers performed since 1924, when Koussevitzky began his twenty-five-year leadership of the orchestra. This festival took place nine days before the formal opening of the BSO's 1939–40 season. The Boston event seems, curiously enough, to have been in response to the orchestra's inability, owing to its non-union status, to participate in a similarly themed series of concerts in New York, sponsored by and celebrating the twenty-fifth anniversary of the American Society of Composers, Authors and Publishers (ASCAP). The Boston concerts were presented free to the public for the first time in the orchestra's fifty-nine-year history, and the orchestra's box office was swamped with people wanting to attend.

Roy Harris was Koussevitzky's advisor on the project. Schuman approached his friend and mentor about composing an "American Festival Overture." Said Harris, "Koussevitzky is never going to agree to perform something by you after the disaster he had with your Second Symphony." However, Harris was not aware that Koussevitzky had told Schuman he would welcome the opportunity to perform other new works by the young composer. Despite their friendship, Schuman felt that "unlike Aaron, he [Harris] never showed any particular interest in promoting me or my music, which was odd (though thoroughly in keeping with his personality), considering that he knew me far better than Aaron did."

Harris was eventually persuaded that Schuman's non-commissioned piece would work for the concert series. Schuman based the opening of the overture on a surprisingly American concept: he explained to Harris that he remembered calling his neighborhood friends together as a young boy by yelling "Wee-Awk-Eee." "I want to open this overture with 'Wee-Awk-Eee' on a minor third, and develop it in a very energetic, celebratory style . . . [which would eventually lead to] a non-academic fugue which would again start out with the minor third." After Schuman sang the fugue subject to the older composer—while Harris was shaving at home in New Jersey, according to one story—he was surprised when Harris responded, "Great, that's a wonderful theme. I'll see what I can do."

Koussevitzky finally authorized Schuman to write the piece, although with no guarantee that it would be performed. Schuman composed most of the overture in the summer of 1939 at the vacation home of Frankie's aunt and uncle, Amy and Walter Charak, at Menemsha, in Chilmark on Martha's Vineyard. After reviewing the score, the conductor invited Bill and Frankie to lunch at his home in Brookline, Massachusetts, to discuss the new work. Schuman recalled that Koussevitzky "was very hospitable but his table manners were appalling—at one point, he actually spat on his plate."

The overture was premiered at the second of the two special concerts on the afternoon of Friday, October 6, 1939, in a program that included Gershwin's Concerto in F (with Abram Chasins as soloist), Harris's Third Symphony, and Randall Thompson's Second Symphony. Schuman was not pleased with the conclusion of his overture and wanted to rework it, especially because it was scheduled to be performed again in New York City—the first performance by a major orchestra in his hometown. Schuman recalled the original ending as having "pages that were filled with consecutive fourths . . . melodic fourths, and I recognized that it just wasn't right."

Koussevitzky's response to Schuman's dilemma was touching in its sensitivity: he agreed to let Schuman write a new ending for the overture. He would rehearse it in a special session in New York just prior to the concert, which was to be given at Carnegie Hall on November 25, 1939, as part of a program that included works by the American composers Edward Burlingame Hill (Violin Concerto), John Alden Carpenter (*Skyscrapers: A Ballet of Modern American Life*), and Howard Hanson (Symphony No. 3).

This was not the first time Koussevitzky had demonstrated such generosity toward a young composer. He had premiered Harris's Third Symphony on February 24, 1939. Although the work was considered a success at its first reading, Koussevitzky felt that its ending was too abrupt. His concern led Harris to create "the quite extraordinary coda that really makes the Symphony work," said Schuman. "Koussevitzky had great instincts and could put his finger on the few crucial points that made all the difference. His approach was not intellectual, but his instinctive judging of the qualities of immediate sound was of enormous help to a composer."

Schuman's new ending was performed to great acclaim. A work of unending musical energy, it embodied his youthful bravado and inherent American optimism. The composer wrote a short program note for the world premiere in Boston:

The first three notes of this piece will be recognized by some listeners as the "call to play" of boyhood days. In New York City it is yelled on the syllables, "Wee-Awk-Eee" to get the gang together for a game or a festive occasion of some sort. This call very naturally suggested itself for a piece of music being composed for a very festive occasion. From this it should not be inferred that the Overture is program music. In fact, the idea for the music came to mind before the origin of the theme was recalled. The development of this bit of "folk material," then, is along purely musical lines.

The first section of the work is concerned with the material discussed above and the ideas growing out of it. This music leads to a transition section and the subsequent announcement by the violas of a fugue subject. The entire middle section is given over to this fugue. The orchestration is at first for strings alone, later for wood winds alone and finally, as the Fugue is brought to fruition, by the strings and wood winds in combination. This climax leads to the final section of the work, which consists of opening materials paraphrased and the introduction of new subsidiary ideas. The tempo of the work, save the last measures, is fast.

Elliott Carter, writing in *Modern Music*, observed that the overture

has vitality and conviction behind it. Schuman's gift is undeniable, though so far his musical material has shown a tendency to be slight.

Olin Downes of the *New York Times* commented:

This overture is a lusty piece, full of vitality, and fearless. It is the poorest composed piece of yesterday's program, but far from the least in ideas and creative urge. The harmonic style may not be what the composer will show when he has become completely himself, and more skilled than he is today in the arts of instrumentation and development. But the piece is full of spirit and talent . . . there is wit and imagination in this music.

Leonard Bernstein also waxed enthusiastic about the overture and its energy:

[There is] an energetic drive, a vigor of propulsion which seizes the listener by the hair, whirls him through space, and sets him down at will. This involves a buoyancy and lust-for-life which I find (at the risk of being called old-fashioned and artificially nationalistic) wholly American. To help me make my point I wish I could somehow perform the *American Festival Overture* on these pages for each reader, to prove that Young America exists, acts, and speaks in this music.

American Festival Overture became Schuman's first successful work and went far toward helping him overcome the sense of failure he had known with his Second Symphony.

See the appendix for further discussion of *American Festival Overture*.

Schuman saw his successes of 1939 as a turning point in his life as a composer. The Symphony No. 2; the *Prologue* for chorus and orchestra, first performed on May 7, 1939, in New York City by the "Federal Symphony Orchestra and Chorus of the New York City High School of Music and Art," conducted by Alexander Richter; and the String Quartet No. 2 of 1938 all spurred Paul Rosenfeld to write an article linking Schuman to both Copland and Harris, two of the most prominent American composers of the time. Rosenfeld began the segment on Schuman by praising his *Prologue* and the widely dismissed Second Symphony. He then focused on the Second String Quartet:

[The quartet] . . . revealed . . . the modernity of his style. It is entirely a melodic one. The harmonic consistency is unusually distinguished, the counterpoint is very openly spaced. The Quartet's melodic lines were noticeably long: the middle movement indeed is a piece of beautifully sustained song pervaded by a sensuousness not invariably to be found in modern music.

Rosenfeld was no less enthusiastic about the Second Symphony:

In the Second Symphony his structural style has energy and grandeur. The effects are large and ample, the feeling is elevated. Again the instrumentation is strikingly fresh, plainly that of a musician with a new sonority. The raucous and sensuous sound reflects the world of mechanism and industrial techniques; its closer parallels are in Varèse and Chavez; but it is clear and firm in its own way. . . . The Symphony testifies to the presence of something primitive in the composer's feeling, a fierceness and an earthiness.

Schuman's String Quartet No. 3 received mixed reviews from the critics but still garnered praise. It was premiered on February 27, 1940, in Town Hall, by the Coolidge Quartet, and had been commissioned in a first-time joint venture by Town Hall and the League of Composers: "Olin Downes found energy and assurance in the part-writing but was unable to predict whether [these] were more than part of an experimental phase."

Francis D. Perkins in the *New York Herald Tribune* praised the work:

[Schuman's] new quartet is marked by notable instrumental craftsmanship. The introduction is distinguished by long-breathed, meditative lyricism; the musical ideas themselves, as well as their subtly colored harmonic investiture, had an exceptional poetic appeal. The sonority and transparency of the scoring spoke well for the composer's ability to make thorough use of the tonal resources of his chosen medium.

Irving Kolodin in the *New York Sun* noted that

the fugue . . . was abstruse and over-complex with little variety. Similarly the intermezzo and the rondo finale with variations, were juiceless and lacking in thematic distinction.

Schuman eventually used material from the last movement of the Third Quartet in the finale of his Fourth Symphony.

In fact, both the Second and Third Quartets exhibit many of the compositional characteristics that would be evident in Schuman's subsequent symphonies and works for dance: movements based on baroque forms such as the passacaglia and fugue, which appear in both the Second Quartet and Part I of the Third Symphony; complex rhythmic textures; harmonic structures that create piquant dissonances; polychords that combine major and minor triads; and an overall structural unity, something that was lacking in his earlier works. What is most remarkable about the String Quartets Nos. 2 and 3 is their musical sophistication. Schuman had only begun his formal music studies less than a decade earlier. He clearly believed that he was developing a new voice, one distinct from Harris's. Now Koussevitzky, in a profoundly perceptive piece of advice, told Schuman in no uncertain terms that he had to forge his own creative path: "You have to learn to hate Roy Harris."

The *American Festival Overture* success not only reinforced the young composer's confidence, but also made him even more determined to compose for large orchestral forces: "[Because] I had very unconventional training . . . I really learned how to be a composer by composing symphonies. I didn't fool around. I wanted to run before I could creep." Schuman's Third Symphony, one of his great works, was a manifestation of this momentum. Although not commissioned by Koussevitzky and the BSO, Schuman dedicated the work to the maestro who had championed his compositions with such consistent enthusiasm.

The demands placed on Schuman by his teaching duties at Sarah Lawrence led him to apply for a Guggenheim Fellowship and a leave from the college, both of which he received in 1939. The fellowship—$2,500—was almost equivalent to his annual salary. For the first time in his life, Schuman was a full-time composer. This newfound freedom to compose seemed to be a double-edged sword for Schuman. Although progress on the symphony went well, he also missed the camaraderie of his teaching days: "In some respects, the days were *too* long. I wrote the Third Symphony in less than a year, and when I finished it, early one January morning in 1941, I told myself 'well, I don't know what else to do, so I'd better start my Fourth Symphony.'"

This uneasiness with being *only* a composer was a leitmotif throughout Schuman's life. As the president of the Juilliard School of Music and then of Lincoln Center for the Performing Arts, Schuman was happiest and at his most creative when he could easily jump from being a composer to working as an administrator. As a result, Schuman asked the Guggenheim fellowship administration to make an exception and allow him to teach or conduct while he completed his fellowship. He told Henry Allen Moe, president of the foundation: "This has nothing to do with money, but I can't just be a composer. I'll go out of my mind, and my publisher will go broke trying to put out everything I produce. I need to do something else as well." Moe agreed and allowed Schuman to continue working part-time at Sarah Lawrence. He even renewed the fellowship for a second year.

The late 1930s and early 1940s were for Schuman a time of exceptional creativity and productivity. His routine usually involved composing for about three hours every morning, time dedicated in particular to sketching and developing new ideas. Then, after a walk, he would turn for the rest of the day to more mundane endeavors such as proofreading or orchestration. Schuman always contended that if a person was a true composer, the music would inevitably be written no matter what might be the circumstances of employment or available commissions. Although he wrote for long hours, he also prided himself on being an efficient composer—a trait that permitted him to follow both of his career paths.

Schuman did not compose at the piano, but he did have a drafting board adjacent to it where "he frequently banged out . . . chords," according to his son, Tony. Explained Schuman, "When I go to the piano, I waste a lot of time, because I have fun improvising. For me, just sitting and thinking is a very pure exercise, and I love writing music that way. Occasionally, if I'm not sure of a sound, I go over to the piano and try it out."

Prior to the important premiere of the Third Symphony, Schuman made public his proletarian inclinations with the first performance of his work entitled *This Is Our Time: Secular Cantata No. 1,* for chorus and orchestra. The text was by Genevieve Taggard, whose Marxist and socialist affiliations were widely known. The work was performed at Lewisohn Stadium in Upper Manhattan on July 4, 1940, by the People's Philharmonic Chorus and the New York Philharmonic, conducted by Alexander Smallens. The chorus was "made up of iron workers, painters, carpenters, workers in shoe factories, housewives and white-collar workers. . . . Schuman wrote: 'Music which the layman can perform is essential if we hope to reach a wide audience.'"

Taggard's text for the cantata is certainly proletarian in spirit but mild in terms of Marxist rhetoric. Rather, her words embrace the romance of hard work and the need for all to band together to achieve new initiatives in America. The five movements, entitled "Celebration," "Work," "Foundations," "Questions," and "Fanfares," deal with such themes as "Celebrate our time," "The idle are the sad," and a traditional American barn-raising.

The Third Symphony was premiered on October 17, 1941, by Koussevitzky and the BSO, with Leonard Bernstein assisting the conductor in its preparation. Both the composer and the conductors soon agreed that the original manuscript needed significant cuts and adjustments. Recalled Schuman:

> In writing the symphony I had discovered the interval of the fourth, so I had pages built on that interval. It was a youthful excess and I caught it myself . . . the need for other cuts became obvious in rehearsal. In the toccata I had a virtuoso section for the double basses that sounded terrible . . . on the first reading Koussevitzky looked up at me, shook his head, and out it went.

In retrospect, it is possible that the cuts made by the composer, Koussevitzky, and Bernstein might have been precipitous. In 2005 Leonard Slatkin and the National Symphony Orchestra restored some of the cut material, which in the opinion of informed listeners made the symphony much stronger.

Schuman did not accept all of Koussevitzky's suggestions. With the debacle of the Second Symphony perhaps still lurking in the conductor's memory, he proposed that the performance only include the second half of the symphony. Schuman politely rejected that notion. However, Koussevitzky was quite solicitous of the young composer. In a letter to Frankie dated three days before the world premiere of the Third Symphony, Schuman wrote that during a rehearsal, "as the Passacaglia was drawing to a close Kousse turns to me and says—exact quotes 'Bravo Schuman these pages are truly wonderful.'" Frankie had been able to travel to Boston to be with her husband during rehearsals for the symphony, and their time together was deeply meaningful for Schuman: "Yesterday with you was too too you know what—a man in love with his wife—how dull . . . all the boys say Frankie's the nuts. Flatterererer."

The Third Symphony is in two parts: the first consists of a passacaglia and fugue, and the second, a chorale and toccata. Schuman did not use these baroque forms strictly, but only as suggestions in developing each movement.

Audience reaction to the Third Symphony was very positive, much to Koussevitzky's joy. Bernstein also embraced the new work with great enthusiasm and subsequently recorded it twice, calling it "my symphony." Its New York premiere was scheduled for a Friday matinee performance on November 22, 1941, preceded by Ravel's suite *Le tombeau de Couperin* and followed after intermission by Tchaikovsky's Sixth Symphony. Schuman had hoped for a premiere on the evening before, when he anticipated a more "sophisticated audience." George Judd, the manager of the BSO, gave some valuable advice to the composer by taking him to a peephole backstage that looked out at the audience: "Young man . . . tell me how many empty seats you see." None, replied Schuman. Judd then delivered his eminently practical assessment: "That, my friend, is a great audience."

After the first New York performance Olin Downes wrote, "It is a symphony which for this chronicler takes the position of the best work by an American of the rising generation." The December 6 *New Yorker* crowed that "young Mr. Schuman is the composer of the hour by virtue of the popular and critical success of his Third Symphony." Many years later Winthrop Sargeant wrote in the same magazine: "This Third Symphony is, in my opinion, by far the finest that Mr. Schuman has written. It shows evidences of that rare ingredient of contemporary symphonic music—talent—and it has the virtues of clarity and coherence."

Not only was the work a popular success, but it garnered Schuman in 1942 the first New York Music Critics Circle Award. The young composer expressed total disdain for the honor. His arrogance in protesting the awarding of the prize opens a window into the psyche of this up-and-coming American composer. In a recollection that appeared in most of the oral histories Schuman participated in over the years, he told of inviting the composers Paul Creston and Norman Dello Joio, who were also candidates for the award, to lunch at the Russian Tea Room on West 57th Street, where he proposed that they all declare their lack of interest in receiving anything in the way of recognition from a critic: "Now, look boys, the last thing we want is for the critics to give us a prize. Let's denounce the whole idea . . . let's just say we won't accept any critics' prizes: it's bad enough to have to submit to criticism." When Creston and Dello Joio refused to go along with such a divisive scheme, Schuman said: "All right, remember I warned you. I'm going to win it because mine is the best piece."

Such reckless language within the close-knit and highly sensitive world of classical music seems nothing short of an attempt at professional suicide on Schuman's part. Yet his self-confidence and his desire to push the envelope were evident as early as his years in Speyer Experimental School for Boys, then at Juilliard and particularly at Lincoln Center many years later, when his pugnacity would not be looked upon so benignly as it had been by Olin Downes, the chairman of the award committee. In any event, Schuman's rhetoric quickly cooled and he decided to accept the award.

See the appendix for further discussion of the Third Symphony.

A Guggenheim grant in hand, Schuman decided to create another symphonic work. Thanks to Koussevitzky's success with the Third Symphony, Artur Rodzinski and the Cleveland Orchestra requested the right to perform Schuman's next new work, which was the Symphony No. 4. At the time, the country's most respected conductors were competing for compositions from the next "new talent." Eugene Ormandy of the Philadelphia Orchestra also sought out Schuman for a new work.

Frankie and Bill traveled to Cleveland in January 1942 to attend the rehearsals and performances of his Symphony No. 4. Schuman remembered Rodzinski as eccentric, an impression reinforced by the widespread belief that he carried a concealed handgun with him at all times.

Although Schuman did not recall having extensive discussions with Rodzinski, he did know that the conductor wanted to repeat the success that Koussevitzky had enjoyed with the Symphony No. 3. The premiere of the Fourth Symphony took place on January 22, 1942, and a post-concert reception was given at the home of Frank Loesser's older half-brother, Arthur, a concert pianist, teacher, and writer.

Arthur viewed the new work positively:

> The Symphony is the work of a remarkable musical mind, of predominantly intellectual bent; the composer has great skill in the arts of counterpoint and thematic manipulation, and is animated by a passion for logic and unity. The Symphony is an essay in pure design; its three movements are a consistent evolution of an elaborate structure from the same one or two germinal motives . . . the entire work arouses admiration, gives a feeling of strength and inspires a desire for re-hearing.

At the reception Rodzinski and Loesser became involved in an animated discussion of Scarlatti, ignoring the young composer: "It wasn't personal, it was just the way the things were. . . . Composers were salesmen, not customers, and very few conductors treated you very pleasantly. Some of them were outright rude."

Schuman again encountered this dismissive attitude from Ormandy's performances of the Symphony No. 4 in Philadelphia on April 4 and 6, 1942, and in Carnegie Hall on April 7. Ormandy, concerned that too much "noise" was coming from the percussion section, wanted the composer to revise the work; as he explained, "My audiences can't take anything like that." Schuman's remembrance of the exchange between himself and Ormandy shows that the composer's self-confidence was on the upswing. He told the conductor:

> "Well, Mr. Ormandy, I need that there, and if I thought it was a good suggestion I would certainly consider it." He replied, "Don't you want me to have a big success with the Fourth the way Koussevitzky had with the Third?" And I said, "Yes, but I have a counter-proposal. Let's you and me have a grand failure." Ormandy was furious and yelled, "What are you saying to me?"

Schuman hit a sore spot when he reminded Ormandy of his days as a conductor at the Capitol Theater in New York City, where the resident orchestra accompanied films and attractions: "Ormandy was *not* pleased to be reminded of this; he shouted, 'You have the nerve to come in here and mention that?'"

Despite the personal friction between the two, the Ormandy performances of Schuman's Fourth Symphony were a success, and according to the composer, the "audiences [liked] the music very much, better than they had in Cleveland, though Rodzinski did it well." Many critics commented that they had never known two new symphonies by one American composer to be performed in one season. Ormandy later became one of Schuman's greatest supporters, performing new and established works with the Philadelphia Orchestra throughout his tenure.

Critical views of the new symphony were unenthusiastic. Olin Downes found the symphony "disappointing and by no means as strong a work as the preceding symphony." He added insult to injury by spelling Schuman with two *n*s throughout the review.

Virgil Thomson's thoughts on the work were poisonous and condescending:

> I found it [the Fourth Symphony] vague and more than a little diffuse. Its musical thought flows without hinderance [sic], but it assumes its

precise form with great difficulty. . . . He writes pleasant little exercises in free counterpoint that go along nicely but that lack definition. . . . He reminds me not a little of Theodore Dreiser. I should like to put him to work writing incidental music for plays or doing ballet scores. I fancy the necessity of making music say something briefly and clearly and simply might be a valuable experience for him. He has an agreeable kind of boisterousness, also, that should be fun to dance to.

Schuman himself remarked about the Fourth Symphony, "I think it's quite a different work from the Third Symphony in every way. It was for me at that time a forward-moving work, I think principally because of the second movement."

Although one hears in the symphony's first and third movements the now-familiar brashness and "muscularity" with which Schuman would always be identified, his compositional approach toward the second movement was different, though he had also used it in the chorale in Part II of the Third Symphony. The intensely moving and elongated melody of the Fourth Symphony's second movement presages Schuman's approach, seen frequently in his later works, of developing a melodic line over an extended period. In addition, his masterful orchestration, also a hallmark of subsequent compositions, utilizes woodwind, brass, and string choirs in highly effective juxtapositions throughout the movement. And in one of his first borrowings of material from a previously composed work, a practice he would embrace enthusiastically toward the end of his life, Schuman used the musical material from the last movement of his Third String Quartet as the basis for the symphony's last movement.

In late 1941 Schuman composed his first work for band, entitled *Newsreel, in Five Shots*. Schuman had always loved the sounds of bands: "I wanted to write music that could be performed by kids, because I love kids . . . but I got better at it after [*Newsreel*] because [it's] too difficult to play in terms of musical content." Another reason Schuman enjoyed band writing was that "it makes you feel like a citizen. Bands want new pieces. Unlike most symphony orchestras, who do new music on sufferance, bands love to do it."

In the 1930s and early 1940s the newsreel was an integral part of any moviegoing experience. It presented short snippets of the news of the day, both serious and whimsical: "[I] thought how amusing it would be to imagine these events and write music to go with them, so I did. . . . It was great fun to do—kind of a joke. Lukas Foss loves that piece. . . . He never played anything of any importance that I wrote, but he loved that."

Newsreel was premiered in 1942 by the Pennsylvania State College Band under the direction of George S. Howard. Written in five movements whose titles depict various topics in a newsreel ("Horse Race," "Fashion Show," "Tribal Dance," "Monkeys at the Zoo," and "Parade"), the piece became a favorite with bands around the United States and eventually was even played by junior high school bands.

During this busy and successful time for Schuman the world was thrust into the cataclysm of World War II. Schuman, who at the time was in his very early thirties, was swept up in the patriotic fervor. He had always had a deep love for all that America stood for, and, like most men of his generation, he wanted to fight for his country. Unfortunately, a congenital physical malady, progressive muscular atrophy (PMA), which Schuman described as a "form of dystrophy," made him unfit to serve. PMA is one of a group of motor neuron disorders that includes amyotrophic lateral sclerosis (ALS, also known as Lou Gehrig's disease), primary lateral sclerosis, and post-polio syndrome, among others:

> In most people who have one of these disorders, the cause is unknown.
> . . . In all of these disorders, motor nerves in the spinal cord or brain
> progressively deteriorate, causing muscle weakness that can progress
> to paralysis. However, in each disorder, a different part of the nervous
> system is affected. Consequently, each disorder primarily affects
> different muscles and different parts of the body. . . . [Progressive
> muscular atrophy] is similar to amyotrophic lateral sclerosis, but it
> progresses more slowly, . . . and muscle weakness is less severe. . . .
> Many people with this disorder survive 25 years or longer.

Both Schuman children recalled discussions of their father's health as an ongoing litany of vaguely diagnosed maladies. The composer's daughter, Andie, spoke of an "atypical ALS" that may have caused his muscle weakness and a case of Charcot-Marie-Tooth disease, an inherited neurological disorder that often presents in adolescence whose symptoms include weakness and atrophy in the extremities, all leading to his "illegible handwriting and musical notation. . . . The problem was first medically evaluated shortly after [my parents] were married—they were told he had only a few years to live, which may have been why they waited so long to have Tony (8 years post-marriage)." Schuman was turned down by the Phoenix Mutual Life Insurance Company because of the condition, as seen in a letter dating from 1942: "Our medical department regrets to advise that your history of *progressive muscular atrophy* does not warrant further consideration of you as an insurable risk at this time" (emphasis added). PMA is incurable and can be fatal, but Schuman was able to live with it to the age of eighty-one. Nonetheless, it constantly threatened his physical well-being and affected his ability to write clearly and exercise vigorously.

Schuman, with his customary resourcefulness and optimism, tried to find a way to serve despite his uncertain health. He learned of a unit of the army called the Army Specialist Corps, which would provide "music advisers to the service commands." Members of this new corps "must be ineligible for drafting for combat service under Selective Service, and must have a specialty of value to some phase of military activity." Schuman had approached Harold Spivacke, chairman of the Sub-Committee on Music of the Joint Army and Navy Committee on Welfare and Recreation and chief of the Music Division of the Library of Congress, almost immediately after Pearl Harbor. Spivacke wrote to Schuman on December 27, 1941, and told him that owing to the recent attack, he would need more time to respond to Schuman's desire to join the armed forces.

Some months later Spivacke advised Schuman that he might, in fact, be taken into the Specialist Corps, which also required that all members be at least at the rank of captain. The strategy was to first enlist in the regular army and then eventually be transferred to the Corps. After consulting with a physician in Larchmont, who was dubious about Schuman's chances for success, Schuman went to his local draft board in Scarsdale for an interview. Because Schuman was under the impression at the time that the Specialist Corps would "only accept 4F men from the first draft," he went to his local draft board and was able to convince them to change his status from 3A to 4F. Schuman told Spivacke, "I feel that part of being patriotic is to continue to do creative work as long as it is humanly possible to do so. If, however, this can be coupled with a direct war job in music, I am prepared to offer my services."

Once again the news was negative, but a ray of light appeared when the board said that rules might change soon thanks to ever-greater demands for manpower. Schuman informed Constance Warren, Sarah Lawrence's president, of his impending induction and even bought a uniform at Brooks Brothers. This strategic move was based on the example of Frank Loesser, who, although only a private, had acquired a uniform from the renowned gentlemen's clothier.

In August 1942 Spivacke wrote to Schuman to say "that we are now prepared to offer your application to the Army for final consideration [and] should an appointment be offered you, [are] you prepared to accept it immediately, *without any reservations whatsoever?*" (emphasis added).

Unfortunately, Schuman's plan collapsed soon after his army physical at Fort Slocum, close to New Rochelle. He was advised through letters from the office of the director of the Special Service Division, dated September 21 and October 17, 1942, that "it is with considerable regret that, because your physical examination failed to meet the standard requirements, no waiver was recommended, and your application [for the Specialist Corps] is withdrawn from consideration."

As it turned out, Schuman was mistaken about the necessity to change his draft status to 4F: "The regulations drawn up for the Corps indicate that, subject to certain restrictions, 'the minimum physical requirements for appointment in the Corps will be the same as those . . . for limited military service (class 1-B standards).'" Schuman wrote to Spivacke the day he received the final letter from the Special Service Division:

> Since I cannot serve in the Specialist Corps I am trying to do what I can with my pen. The first work is a Cantata for Chorus and Orchestra [*A Free Song: Secular Cantata No. 2* for chorus and orchestra] which Koussevitzky will perform. It has wonderful words by Walt Whitman. If I've done my job well it can't help but be a moving patriotic affair.

Spivacke wrote back on October 20:

> I was surprised to hear that your application has received unfavorable action. . . . [I] presumed that it was moving along all right. You are correct in stating that your 4F status was frankly established from the start, but in all 4F cases it is up to the Surgeon General whether or not the man is fit for the duty in question.

Schuman was crushed by the news. However, in a discussion with Carl Engel, his publisher at Schirmer's, he received some wise advice: "Write a piece of music. Take it out in music." The resulting work, written almost at the same time as *A Free Song*, was originally entitled *Prayer, 1943*, and was premiered by Fritz Reiner and the Pittsburgh Symphony on February 26, 1943. The title was later changed to *Prayer in a Time of War*. Schuman also composed a brief piano work, "Three-Score Set," in honor of Engel's sixtieth birthday in 1943. The composer later borrowed some material from this work for use in his Fifth Symphony.

Prayer in a Time of War had its New York premiere on March 25, 1943, with the New York Philharmonic, conducted again by Fritz Reiner. It was also performed by Leopold Stokowski and the NBC Symphony Orchestra on a national broadcast in December 1943, at the height of U.S. patriotic fervor during the war. Stokowski invited the composer to a rehearsal, asked for Schuman's comments, and then, remarkably, asked Schuman to take the podium to rectify a tempo problem Schuman had pointed out to the maestro. Summoning his experiences in Salzburg eight years earlier, Schuman conducted the great orchestra and was given a bravo and a round of applause from the musicians. Stokowski returned to the podium from the radio control room, said thank you, and never made another comment. The eventual performance, with Stokowski conducting, retained all the correct tempi.

The only memory Schuman had of contributing to the war effort was his performances with the Sarah Lawrence Chorus at military bases and hospitals: "When I walked out on stage with all these beautiful young girls, the girls got whistles and I got very good applause. My applause was mostly envy."

In an episode that reveals a glimmer of Schuman's personality and politics at the time, Schuman received a letter in February 1942 from a Mrs. Robert A. Schmid, who complained that the Sarah Lawrence Chorus was performing Aaron Copland's *An Immorality* (for three-voice women's choir, soprano solo, and piano) with text taken from the poem "Lustra" by Ezra Pound, whose fascist sympathies many Americans despised. (This work is often paired with another Copland choral work from 1925 entitled *The House on the Hill*, with text by Edward Arlington Robinson. The works became known as *Two Choruses*.) Schuman explained to Mrs. Schmid that Copland's work "proved a very meaty and novel addition to the repertory of modern choral music" and that Pound's poem had been written back in 1916. Schuman concluded the letter with a powerful statement on his view of the confluence of art and politics:

Don't you agree that we must be very careful these days not to let our hatred for all the brutality and retrogression for which Fascism stands confuse our judgment of matters in art. May I say personally that if the Duce himself were a fine composer I would still want to see him shot but in the meantime I would perform his music.

Schuman showed his response to Copland, who observed: "I thought your replique admirable, though I must say I'm rather relieved that the Duce doesn't compose anything. What will happen when somebody discovers all the anti-Semitic references in Chopin's letters??"

During the war Schuman also composed the music for the film *Steeltown* (1944), commissioned by the United States Office of War Information.

Eventually the pain of his army rejection passed, and Schuman continued his frenetic pace as both a composer and teacher at Sarah Lawrence. An important evening concert was dedicated solely to Schuman's music in New York City's Town Hall on January 13, 1943. The concert was produced by Kenneth Klein as the first of three Music Forums. Klein's wife, Rosalyn Tureck, would perform Schuman's Concerto for Piano and Small Orchestra, accompanied by Daniel Saidenberg conducting the Saidenberg Little Symphony. The composer also had a few choral pieces he wished to be heard, especially *Holiday Song*, with text by his friend Genevieve Taggard.

The format of the Music Forum included not only a performance of music by the featured composer, but also a post-performance discussion and analysis of the music during which the audience was invited to comment and ask questions. Schuman needed a particularly thick skin to survive the event, described in a 1943 article in *Musical America* by Ronald F. Eyer.

The performance included Schuman's *Prelude* for voices, the Choral Etude, *Four Canonic Choruses*, the *Holiday Song*, and *Requiescat*, followed by the premiere of the Piano Concerto. Tureck, no shrinking violet, also decided to perform a *second* concerto—J. S. Bach's Keyboard Concerto in F Minor—for reasons that can only be attributed to her considerable ego. Although Schuman commented that he was pleased to "have a fellow like Bach on the same program with me," Eyer wrote that "Bach had his trials, but it is doubtful whether he ever was put under a microscope and mercilessly dissected by his interpreters, critics, colleagues in full view of the public as Mr. Schuman was on this occasion."

Joining Schuman for this "dissection" were all the performers and Virgil Thomson, music critic of the *New York Herald-Tribune*. Klein chaired the discussion. Thomson "sought out resemblances between the current composer and his name-sake, Robert Schumann. He also suggested that Mr. Schuman is orchestral minded in his choral writing." Finally, a woman in the balcony "wanted to know why Mr. Schuman wrote music at all." That seemed to rouse the young composer from a "reticent and monosyllabic" state and he became "fluently vocal," saying "I feel I have to write music, so I write it."

The forum also included a query to Virgil Thomson as to whether Schuman's concerto was "atonal or polytonal," to which the critic and composer playfully answered, "No." Tureck then awkwardly attempted to define a melody by stating that "any succession of notes is a melody provided they—the notes—are not repeated." Eyer ended his article with the bemused observation that "whether or not anything of value was accomplished by this essay in musical vivisection is hard to say."

Dissatisfied with Hugh Ross's Schola Cantorum—the New York chorus of choice at the time—for the Music Forum performance, Schuman asked in the fall of 1942, "Isn't there some new chorus around in New York that's really exciting?" The response was a suggestion to meet "a fellow who conducted the Fred Waring Glee Club and also had his own group [called the Collegiate Chorale]. His name was Robert Shaw."

Shaw invited Schuman to hear the Collegiate Chorale in rehearsal working on a Brahms motet and a Negro spiritual. After the rehearsal, over hot chocolate at a local automat, Schuman critiqued the work of the man who was to become America's most respected choral conductor of the twentieth century:

> Number one, the chorus is marvelous and you're a better choral conductor than I could be in a thousand years and I want you to conduct [the Town Hall concert]. But having said that, I have to tell you that you're absolutely ignorant. You don't know a thing about music. Your whole performance of the Brahms was absurd; it was almost a caricature. . . . Have you ever heard the Eroica Symphony?

Shaw hadn't. So on November 21, 1942, he, Bill, and Frankie sat in a box in Carnegie Hall to listen as Koussevitzky conducted the BSO in Beethoven's

Third Symphony. Recalled Schuman: "As the 'Eroica' started unfolding, he sat there with tears rolling down his cheeks. He had never heard music like that."

Through Schuman's contacts Shaw began studying with George Szell, who began with the analysis of Bach chorales. Said Schuman: "Shaw lasted four lessons. The wonderful irony of it is that Bob spent ten years as Szell's assistant later on."

Shaw returned the favor by eventually putting Schuman in contact with the great Broadway producer Billy Rose. Rose was producing an elaborate revue entitled "The Seven Lively Arts." It included a new ballet by Stravinsky eventually entitled *Scènes de ballet*, with choreography by George Balanchine, new songs by Cole Porter, roles for the comedians Bert Lahr and Beatrice Lilly, and a performance by Benny Goodman and his band. Schuman first met Rose when the producer wanted the composer to set a poem that he had found in the *Nation* magazine called "The Ballad of Free Enterprise." Although Schuman rejected the commission, he met with Rose anyway at the producer's instigation: "Rose was a vulgarian of the worst sort. He decided that in order to get ahead in the world you had to be a secretary to a famous man, so he became a secretary to Bernard Baruch. . . . He also married Fannie Brice."

Rose laid out his plan for the revue, with its cornucopia of luminaries, and then countered Schuman's rejection of the choral work by inviting him to compose an orchestral piece to be played onstage. If Schuman agreed, Rose was ready to offer him $1,000 for the work. Rose continued, "That's an advance. If I like the score that you're doing, I'm going to commission you for another thousand dollars to do incidental music for *Henry VIII* that I'm going to put on, directed by Margaret Webster and Laird Krieger [a movie star at the time] playing Henry." Schuman was also entrusted with finding a conductor for the revue. After Alexander Smallens was rejected as being "too rich" for Rose's blood, Schuman contacted Maurice Abravanel, who was interested in the project.

The revue went to tryouts in Philadelphia before its opening in New York, scheduled awkwardly on December 7, 1944—the third anniversary of the Pearl Harbor attack. Alicia Markova and Anton Dolin were the dancers for the Stravinsky work. Rose was concerned about the orchestration, so Schuman said he would find out more about it from Robert Russell Bennett, who was arranging the Cole Porter songs.

The news was not good for Rose. Stravinsky's orchestration added about eleven woodwind players to the revue's basic orchestra, which enlarged the weekly payroll considerably. Rose wanted to cut the length and reduce the orchestra by having Schuman arrange the woodwind parts for four saxophones. Rose approached the problem with his typical gusto: "You're going to earn another thousand bucks tonight, Baby," he told Schuman. He continued, "Will four saxophones make as much sound as eleven woodwinds?" "Probably even more," replied Schuman.

Rose was decisive. "That settles it. . . . I'm wiring Stravinsky that you're going to re-orchestrate it. Can you do it overnight?" Schuman's sheepish "yes" was followed by an incredulous question: "Do you think I would have the temerity to rewrite Stravinsky?"

In a final effort to move the project forward Rose sent a telegram to Stravinsky: "Your ballet colossal success. Can be even greater success if you'll agree to certain cuts and reduction in orchestration." Replied Stravinsky: "Thank you for your telegram. Quite content with colossal success."

Schuman was saddened to see that his piece for the revue, *Side Show* (eventually renamed *Circus Overture*), was dropped after three performances and that his advance for *Henry VIII* was never honored. However, Schuman was able to take two of his compositional ideas from the *Henry VIII* "commission" to develop the beautiful song "Orpheus with His Lute," for voice and piano, with text by Shakespeare, and a Te Deum for a cappella mixed chorus, both published in 1944. Rose continued to be a friend of Schuman, but the composer's brief foray into show business convinced him that was a field he did not care to explore further.

In the midst of Schuman's compositional and educational activities, he enjoyed a singular honor as the first recipient of a Pulitzer Prize in composition. The jury, composed of the conductor Chalmers Clifton, who had become aware of Schuman's music through his position as director of the Works Progress Administration Federal Music Project; the composer Quincy Porter; and the conductor Alfred Wallenstein, announced their decision on May 3, 1943. The prize was to be awarded for *A Free Song: Secular Cantata No. 2*, written soon after Schuman learned he would not be allowed to serve in the armed forces.

Schuman had become fascinated with Walt Whitman's poetry when he first heard Roy Harris's a cappella work *A Song for Occupations*, with text by Whitman. Schuman created the title *A Free Song* and

changed the "I's" to "we's" because I felt more comfortable saying "we." I suppose that's why I wrote so little solo vocal music: you can't

really write romantic vocal music unless you're willing to say "I."
I have no trouble doing it in popular music. I think of Whitman as a
poet of ideas, not of form, so I always felt quite free to change and
juxtapose his words.

A Free Song, written for a full mixed chorus and orchestra, is divided
into two parts: Part I, with "Long, too long, America" and "Look down,
fair moon"; and Part II, "Song of the Banner." It is a work that engenders
a good deal of patriotic feeling. The first part presents the horrors of war:
"pour softly down on faces ghastly, swollen, purple. . . . On the dead on
their backs with their arms tossed wide." The second features a
triumphantly animated choral part. It first trumpets the text "O, a new
song, a free song" and concludes:

> We hear and see not strips of cloth alone,
> We hear again the tramp of armies,
> We hear the drums beat and the trumpets blowing,
> A new song, a free song,
> We hear the jubilant shouts of millions of men,
> we hear Liberty!

The patriotic theme and stirring conclusion of the work resonated in an
America deeply committed to the war effort.

Schuman described the experience of hearing the wonderful news of the
prize for the first time:

> I was so surprised. . . . I had finished the chorus rehearsal at Sarah
> Lawrence. I was driving home from Bronxville to Larchmont.
> Leonard Bernstein and Henry Simon—the . . . critic and publisher—
> were coming for dinner, and on the way home I turned on the radio,
> and . . . it said "Now for the first time in the history of the Pulitzer
> Prize, there is an award given for music." . . . They announced my
> name. . . . When I got home everybody had been calling. It had been
> in the afternoon papers . . . and my students at Sarah Lawrence were
> furious with me. They said "You can't tell us you didn't know this
> afternoon. You didn't tell us!"

> Later that day I got a telegram from Nicholas Murray Butler, the
> President of Columbia University, misspelling the name of the piece

and my name, and the next morning it was announced that [this] year the prize was reduced from a thousand dollars to five hundred.

Actually, it seems that Schuman heard the wonderful news, not on his car radio, but on his home radio. In an interview with the Sarah Lawrence College student newspaper—the *Campus*—which appeared on May 5, 1943, only two days after the announcement, it was reported that "he [Schuman] first learned of the honor while listening to the radio at his home." Schuman told the student interviewer: "I was eager to hear about the fighting in Tunisia . . . and tuned in on the radio. I recognized the Boston accent of Quincy Howe. He announced the news of the Pulitzer winners and my name was among them. Naturally it was exciting." Other 1943 Pulitzers went to Thornton Wilder for his drama *The Skin of Our Teeth*, Robert Frost for his volume of poetry *A Witness Tree*, and Upton Sinclair for his novel *Dragon's Teeth*.

Schuman capped the banner year of 1943 with the premiere of his Symphony for Strings, commissioned by the Koussevitzky Music Foundation and dedicated to Nataliya Koussevitzky, the conductor's wife, who had died in 1942. The foundation would go on to commission some of the seminal works of the twentieth century, including Bartók's Concerto for Orchestra, Copland's Symphony No. 3, Britten's *Peter Grimes*, and Messiaen's *Turangalîla-symphonie*.

Schuman decided to avoid any comparison with earlier Fifth Symphonies by naming the work Symphony for Strings. It was premiered by Koussevitzky and the BSO on November 12, 1943. Schuman's recollection of the symphony's genesis was that he "had a great desire to write a piece for string orchestra. Koussevitzky said . . . 'good piece for strings is always welcome.' I remember [driving for] miles in Westchester, singing the opening theme to myself, to get it absolutely right." The Symphony for Strings is a work of great imagination, pathos, and driving energy. It and the Third were to become Schuman's most popular symphonies.

See the appendix for further discussion of the Symphony for Strings.

During this prodigiously productive compositional period, Schuman became intrigued with the hymns and anthems of the American composer William

Billings (1746–1800). Interestingly, it was also at this time that Aaron Copland enjoyed great success with his ballet *Appalachian Spring* (1943–44), written for Martha Graham, in which he used a Shaker melody as the basis of a set of variations.

"I became sufficiently intrigued with the music [of Billings] to perform it rather widely [with chorus]," Schuman said. He examined the original manuscripts in the New York Public Library and found that Billings "had feelings which I recognized as being wholly akin to my own." The result was the *William Billings Overture*, a set of variations on Billings's melodies, including "Be Glad Then, America," "When Jesus Wept," and the anthem and marching song "Chester." It was premiered on February 17, 1944, by Artur Rodzinski and the New York Philharmonic. Eventually withdrawn by the composer, it nonetheless resurfaced in 1956 as the foundation for one of Schuman's most popular works, *New England Triptych*.

Schuman was also asked to write a variation as part of a compilation entitled *Variations on a Theme of Eugene Goossens* in honor of Goossens and the Cincinnati Symphony Orchestra. Goossens was quite succinct with Schuman: "I am asking you to write Variation 7. I would like it to be in C Major, treated as fugato or canonically throughout, but not vigorous—subject of course to your reaction to the theme which I have devised and a copy of which you will find enclosed." The variation, of only a few minutes' duration, was performed in Cincinnati on March 23, 1945, but was never published and remains a *pièce d'occasion*.

Although his successes as a serious composer continued, after nine years of presenting essentially the same material, his patience with teaching at Sarah Lawrence was wearing thin. In addition, Frankie and Bill celebrated the birth of their first child, Anthony William, on December 22, 1943, while they lived in Larchmont. Schuman "always wanted a family" and was "wild about children." The long delay in starting their family seemed to have been based not only on his mysterious lifelong illness, but also on concerns about the added financial burden on an up-and-coming composer.

The opportunity for a career change came in May 1944 when Carl Engel, director of publications and president at G. Schirmer, Schuman's publisher, died. Engel had been both Schuman's friend and a trusted professional partner. He was instrumental in guiding Schuman through the difficult days after his rejection from the armed forces in 1942.

Koussevitzky recommended Schuman for the prestigious position of director of publications at G. Schirmer, but Schuman was reticent to apply for the job, saying, "Well, I don't know. I'm not a business man, Serge." Koussevitzky replied, "Through the night you will become a business man." Schuman soon was offered the job at a considerable jump in pay, from his $4,500 at Sarah Lawrence to $10,000 at G. Schirmer. In addition, he was given a contract for at least three years, a resounding vote of confidence for Schuman. He was to work part-time at the publishing house until he had completed his academic obligations at Sarah Lawrence.

His greatest regret in leaving the college was the loss of his chorus directorship, which he was asked to continue—but Schuman eventually came to believe it was important to make a complete break: "After a while, it was a kind of self-indulgence, because I wasn't going to add anything to the experience of the chorus, nor to my own experience. So I gave it up."

Schuman had first approached G. Schirmer in 1932 to publish his "Chorale Canons," but the work was rejected. However, a few years later Schirmer agreed to publish his *Prologue*. Said Carl Engel: "I am not sure I understood it all, but I was intrigued by it. Welcome to the house." After the success of the Third Symphony Engel arranged a monthly stipend for Schuman so the composer could teach less and compose more. Schuman submitted several choral works for publication in 1942, including *Requiescat*, *Holiday Song*, and the once-rejected "Chorale Canons," which Engel suggested renaming *Four Canonic Choruses*. Schuman was also asked to give Schirmer the right of first refusal on all subsequent compositions, a proposal Schuman accepted with alacrity.

Schuman had accepted the Schirmer position on the premise that he would have complete control over what would be published. He set about reviewing past publications and bringing new composers under contract. Schuman saw Schirmer as publishing only two types of music: "There was music we thought we could sell, regardless of its quality, and music of high quality regardless of its commercial value":

> In my mind, publishing was a romantic pursuit. If I had ever given it much thought, I undoubtedly would have realized that if the publisher did not make a profit, he would soon be out of business. . . . Too, I was impressed with the great number of works of artistic worth but of no economic value that are also issued by . . . responsible and imaginative publishers.

His first composer contract was with Roger Sessions, whose Second Symphony Schirmer published. Schuman also tried to recruit the talented, eccentric, and difficult David Diamond at a lunch at the Lotos Club on East 66th Street. "Your music isn't being published, and I want Schirmer to do it," Schuman told Diamond. "Let's start with some small choral pieces and songs rather than the big pieces." Diamond erupted. "Fuck you!" he screamed. "'You *would* pick the commercial things!' and he stormed out," Schuman remembered.

In addition, it was not long before Schuman began to have disagreements with the owner and president of the firm, Gustave Schirmer: "Mr. Gustave Schirmer knew nothing about music, and whatever interest he had in it was limited to sales reports. His principal preoccupation, especially at Christmastime, was to go out onto the floor of the store himself and sell music boxes, or in later years, television sets." Schirmer challenged Schuman regarding the financial viability of publishing Sessions's Second Symphony, wanting to know how many copies would be sold. Three hundred at maximum, replied Schuman, and then added that all three hundred would be distinguished members of the music profession, and therefore Schirmer would have to send them complimentary copies.

Schuman's generous compensation at the firm and a subsequent six-year term as special consultant on publications after his departure in the fall of 1945 held considerable allure for the young composer and teacher: "At Schirmer's I not only left the economic realm of the teacher [but] for the rest of my professional life enjoyed the higher brackets of executive pay commensurate with the undertaking that I led." However, his new position left Schuman feeling "trapped. . . . Mr. Schirmer was a straight out and out commercial man, and dealing with him I felt degraded. And I was sorry that I got myself into this fix."

CHAPTER 5

Maestro in Play Clothes

From Schuman's earliest years at Camp Cobbossee, he exhibited a natural ability to lead that was never inhibited by a lack of experience or a too-slight acquaintance with the requirements for a specific professional pursuit. Buoyed by his native intelligence and a sense of confidence provided by his caring parents, there was no challenge he was unwilling to address.

So it was with the complex demands of heading a prestigious music conservatory. In 1945, when Schuman accepted the position of president of the Juilliard School of Music, it was located on 122nd Street with Broadway on the east and Claremont Avenue on the west. Juilliard's physical plant was a combination of the Institute of Musical Art's first building on the site, dedicated by New Jersey's governor, Woodrow Wilson, in 1910, and the taller building to the north, built in 1931 to accommodate the combined student body of the institute and the Juilliard Graduate School, which moved to Morningside Heights in the same year.

By 1945 the graduates of the Institute of Musical Art and the Juilliard Graduate School were or would soon become some of the best-known American-educated musicians of the day. They included Henry D. Brant (composer), Alvin Brehm (double bassist), Margaret Butterly Pardee (violinist), Norman Dello Joio (composer), Bernard Greenhouse (cellist), Alan Greenspan (clarinetist and future chairman of the Federal Reserve), Robert Mann (violinist), Harvey Shapiro (cellist), Risë Stevens (mezzo-soprano), William Vacchiano (trumpeter), and Zvi Zeitlin (violinist), to name only a few. It was these and others who helped to realize Frank Damrosch's mission, beginning in 1905, of developing a music conservatory in America that would replicate the best of European musical traditions.

When World War II ended in August, the Juilliard School of Music was positioned not only to educate the returning GIs who were anxious to move on with their lives, but also to welcome and educate the uprooted and bruised European, and eventually Asian, musicians in their late teens and twenties whose musical educations had been interrupted by the upheaval of the war. Juilliard would also benefit from the political and economic stature of the United States, which, along with the Soviet Union, was to become a superpower, wielding enormous influence throughout the globe.

Schuman first heard of the Juilliard presidential search through James P. Warburg, a member of the Juilliard board, whose father had been one of the founding directors of the Institute of Musical Art. Schuman was at this time very unhappy with his position at G. Schirmer and had nothing but contempt for the firm's owner. Still, when Warburg phoned Schuman at his home in Larchmont about the position, the composer minced no words in giving his opinions of Juilliard's curriculum and especially its approach to new music:

> I have such mixed feelings about the Juilliard School. I admire many of the instrumental teachers. I don't know much about the voice faculty. . . . I have doubts about it . . . but I think the teaching of theory and composition is terrible. You never play new music and I think it's a stuffy institution. So I really don't see much point in coming.

He didn't want to even speak with the search committee. (With the exception of his determined approach to President Warren at Sarah Lawrence, Schuman recalled, he was a reluctant candidate for every professional position he attained.)

"Don't be so tough," Warburg told Schuman. "Since you care so deeply about music and have strong convictions about Juilliard, don't you think you have a responsibility to give the Board the benefit of your observations?" The composer grudgingly acquiesced: "I would do so if it were clearly understood that I was not coming as a candidate."

Schuman met with the presidential search committee at the Broad Street Club, across from the New York Stock Exchange, where they enjoyed lunch and a discussion in a private dining room overlooking New York harbor. One can imagine the not-quite-thirty-five-year-old firebrand of a composer jousting with these senior businessmen who oversaw not only a music school, but also the Juilliard Musical Foundation, which supported the School as well as music programs throughout the country with an endowment of about $12 million in 1945. Schuman's creativity and agile intellect must have been beguiling, even if his youth was a major concern for these conservative board members.

Schuman was already known, by reputation at least, to certain key members of the board. Warburg, though he had never met Schuman before, knew of his teaching and choral conducting successes through his daughter, Kay, who sang in the Sarah Lawrence chorus. Schuman was revered as a teacher at the college, and there is little doubt that Kay reported Schuman's legendary teaching ability to her father. In addition, as Schuman was to learn after his appointment, Warburg was a dedicated advocate of the Sarah Lawrence approach to higher education, an educational philosophy viewed by Schuman as having fertile possibilities within the Juilliard environment.

Another prominent member of the Juilliard board was John Erskine, the distinguished writer and Columbia University teacher, who had served as president of the Juilliard Graduate School from 1928 to 1937. Erskine had been impressed with Schuman's ballet music for *Undertow* of 1945, choreographed by Antony Tudor; their first personal encounter took place at a fund-raising dinner at the New School in the spring of 1945, where a forum on new music involving a panel discussion with Aaron Copland, the conductor Erich Leinsdorf, Erskine, and Schuman had been created as the evening's "entertainment." Schuman recalled, "To my great surprise the chairman called on me first and said that I was entitled, as each of the other speakers would be, to an introductory statement not to exceed ten minutes." He declined, so Erskine spoke first.

Erskine first asserted that music that didn't communicate was not music at all. He then playfully contended that modern music had two problems: "The first was that it wasn't heard; the second that it was heard." He also noted that modern music had no melody.

At that Schuman leaped to his feet. He asked to have his original ten minutes back to respond to Erskine, then declared that he would never contest Erskine's words in any field "except that of music, which was the field of my professional competence and clearly not his." This strikingly impolitic statement must have jarred Erskine, who had often performed with orchestras in New York and thought of himself as a professional-level pianist. Schuman then went on to speak on his view of melody, embellishing his talk by singing excerpts from works of Paul Hindemith, Arnold Schoenberg, and assorted American composers. Schuman recalled that the forum conversation was actually quite "jolly," with Erskine approaching Schuman at the end of the talk and saying, "I loved the way you came after me tonight. I wasn't always an old fuddy-duddy. We must have lunch one day." The intensity of the meeting, however, seems better reflected in Copland's advice to Frankie: "You must do something. Bill simply can't get up and speak that way."

The interview with the presidential search committee was animated and substantive, with Schuman discussing his views of Juilliard's current faculty and curriculum. He made scathing comments on its teaching of music theory and composition, which he found "incompetent and without any relationship whatsoever to the study of music." Thanks to his experience at Sarah Lawrence, as well as his work as a composer and publisher, Schuman felt quite confident he knew how to lead Juilliard in a more positive direction. The discussion was only hypothetical, though; he was not, he reemphasized, a candidate for the position.

Schuman's insistence on his non-candidacy began to weaken after he was asked to meet with a senior member of the board, John M. Perry, who was Augustus Juilliard's trust attorney from the firm Rathbone, Perry, Kelley & Drye (now known as Kelley Drye & Warren). A positive view of Schuman by Perry would be tantamount to an offer. Perry and Schuman must have had a meeting of the minds, because Warburg called Schuman and advised him that the board wished to invite him to be the fourth president of the Juilliard School of Music.

Privately, Schuman did not believe that the Juilliard board would agree to the "revolution" he had in mind. He also told Warburg in no uncertain terms that he could not accept the invitation if the Juilliard faculty had tenure, which it did not. Schuman's stance on tenure was one he and his colleagues had consistently expressed at Sarah Lawrence. A tenured faculty would have stood in the way of the rapid changes Schuman envisioned for Juilliard.

By the time the formal invitation was issued in August 1945, Schuman, realizing the great opportunities this new appointment held for him, had gone from a reluctant to an eager candidate. Warburg capped the invitation with a disarming—if slightly ominous—remark: "Now that it is all settled, I promised to give you a message from Mr. Perry. Mr. Perry says to tell you for the Directors that your appointment will either be the greatest thing that's happened to the Juilliard School or the most colossal mistake of our collective lives."

In 1945 the board of the Juilliard School of Music included, in addition to Erskine, Warburg, and Perry, the former president, Ernest Hutcheson; Edward Johnson, the general manager of the Metropolitan Opera Company; Henry S. Drinker, a lawyer and translator of Bach's vocal texts; and three attorneys—Parker McCollester, Allen Wardwell, and Franklin B. Benkard. The dean of the Juilliard Graduate School was Oscar Wagner, and the dean of the Institute of Musical Art and director of the Juilliard Summer School was George A. Wedge.

Press accounts of Schuman's appointment ranged from enthusiasm to doubts about the direction in which Schuman would take the institution.

Schuman told *Time*, "It's like Westbrook Pegler taking over *PM*."* The *Time* reporter commented, "Actually it was more like a *New Republic* editor taking over the *Saturday Evening Post*."

In the *Time* article Schuman spoke of his aspirations for his new school and its students. He wanted to add courses in sociology and race relations to the Juilliard curriculum, for they would

> make responsible adults of musicians. . . . Right now, when we need musical leaders in every community, we are concerned only with training virtuosi for a nonexistent market. Musical education has to be ventilated. We must develop educated people who are musicians in order to develop music.

This idea of providing musicians with a broad education, rather than just technical training, became the centerpiece of Schuman's educational philosophy.

In the *New York Times* Schuman presented another agenda, saying that American musicians of the future must take their art to the "hinterland" in order to develop the appreciation of music in smaller communities:

> Our large music centers suffer from an over-supply of musicians of all kinds, while our hinterland remains comparatively barren. . . . If our professional schools recognize the challenge in this situation, the coming generation of American musicians will have not only technical proficiency but a realization of its responsibility toward the cultural advance of the country.

Newsweek's story on Schuman's appointment was much more jocular in tone. Entitled "Maestro in Play Clothes," the article rather offhandedly observed that "Unlike his distinguished and dignified predecessors, John Erskine and Ernest Hutcheson, he [Schuman] is addicted to loud sports jackets and other Esquire-ish attire. . . . Schuman doesn't even act the part. He is both infectiously enthusiastic and practical, a type usually not associated with the austerity of academic music."

---

* Schuman was referring to the American columnist Westbrook Pegler (1894–1969), an intense critic of the Roosevelt administration during the war who was viewed as a conservative and right-wing thinker. *PM* was a newspaper founded in 1940 by the liberal editor Ralph Ingersoll as an alternative publication to the conservative New York newspapers of the time. *PM* was an outspoken supporter of FDR.

A later description provides a snapshot of how the new president was viewed by the outside world: as both talented and abrasive. In his 1954 biography, Schuman was described as someone whom artists "resent . . . strongly. To them he seems *too* well-adjusted to be an artist at all. His integration strikes them as sterility, his ability to get along with people of different types, as Philistinism."

One of the first persons to learn of the appointment was Mark Schubart, whom Schuman had wanted to hire while he was still at G. Schirmer. During a summer lunch Schuman asked Schubart to guess who the next president of Juilliard might be. Schubart was surprised by the news. Ultimately Schuman invited him to come to Juilliard so that he could "do some useful work." Subsequently Schubart, who had not studied beyond high school and had never expressed any interest whatsoever in academic institutions, had a long and successful career as Juilliard's dean and then as founder of the Lincoln Center Institute.

Over the years Schuman and Schubart developed a mutual taste for sardonic and witty exchanges that were a source of great delight to friends within earshot of their gibes. In a letter to Schuman in 1962, Schubart poked fun at the kinds of communications received by heads of arts institutions:

> I am 43 years old and very much interested in music. My flute teacher has asked me to write an article about music, so would you please answer the following questions for me:
>
> (1) What is the history of music?
> (2) Why is some good and some not good?
> (3) Who are the 78 greatest composers, and what is their life story?

Some years later Schuman sent a thank-you note disguised as a letter of corporate complaint to Schubart's life partner, Martin Rapp, for a jar of homemade marmalade:

> It is . . . painful for me to tell you that your organization has a problem with quality control. . . . It is this kind of laxity that has caused the continual trouble with American companies, much to the advantage of the Japanese. . . .

To close on a hopeful note, I have found that combining . . . three marmalades . . . with peanut butter, ginger, oil and dehydrated corn flakes, plus one small can of Portuguese sardines, produces a marmalade that approaches the ideal, which in all candor we all know is Smucker's.

Though he had already accepted the position at Juilliard, Schuman still had a multi-year contract with G. Schirmer. Gustave Schirmer released him on the condition that he stay on as the firm's top editorial consultant, a post Schuman held until 1951. In the meantime, Schuman agreed to work full-time at G. Schirmer until October 1945 to ease the firm through its leadership transition. But his mind was clearly on the future, for he took to carrying a small notebook in which he could jot down what he thought needed to be done at Juilliard. It filled up quickly.

The absence of faculty tenure at Juilliard allowed Schuman to carry out certain curricular changes immediately, especially in the area of music theory: "I explained to the Juilliard Board that I believed the principal changes and appointments to the faculty could probably be achieved during my second year and that after that time I would not expect extensive changes in faculty and administration except for natural causes." Although Schuman believed that faculty changes could be made in a sensitive way, the loss of a Juilliard appointment must have been exceedingly difficult for all affected faculty members. In a time when age discrimination legislation was still decades away, the young president had a free hand to make whatever changes he wished.

Schuman's little notebook contained some big concepts. First on his list was hiring the best composers as faculty members in a new approach to the teaching of composition and especially music theory that would soon become known as the "Literature and Materials of Music." Second, he would create a resident string quartet whose members would function as both teachers and performers—an initiative that led to the creation of the Juilliard String Quartet.

On October 1 William Schuman entered Juilliard as the School's fourth president. Hutcheson returned full-time to the piano faculty. Schuman had mixed feelings about his predecessor: "Hutcheson was always the gentleman. I am sure he would have quite happily slit my throat. . . . He was a very weak president."

Hutcheson had made the somewhat unorthodox decision several years earlier to place his secretary and her desk next to him in his private office. When Schuman told his assistant that she would now have to work in the outer office, she took offense and decided to give notice. She calmed down and returned to the job, though, after some gentle coaxing from her new boss.

Schuman's second presidential request was to meet with the School's controller, William J. Bergold. His secretary informed him (from her new office) "that this was an extraordinary request since the Controller did not normally come to the office unless the budget was being discussed." Clearly the new president was being tested, but he prevailed with a healthy mix of charm and determination.

Throughout Schuman's tenure as president of Juilliard, he wrote detailed reports to his board that were distributed prior to each meeting, in a continuation of a tradition established by Erskine during his presidency. Schuman also maintained the quaint tradition of presenting these reports in the third person. He recalled that it was all "very elegant. 'The President requests' or 'the President wishes to report that. . . .' Very stuffy, very objective."

In the last report Schuman made to the School's board of directors as president on December 15, 1961, he provided, under the heading "Recapitulation," a list of what he felt were his most important accomplishments during his tenure of sixteen years. The first paragraph of this section of the report provides a rich and succinct view of the Schuman years at Juilliard:

> Since the President assumed office in 1945 he has submitted over 100 reports to the Directors of which this is the last. In perusing these reports a number of projects and developments of the School during his tenure were vividly recalled: the amalgamation of the Institute of Musical Art and the Juilliard Graduate School into a single institution; the inauguration of a Placement Bureau under professional management; a series of Juilliard broadcasts, recordings and telecasts; special Carnegie Hall concerts, one in which the Juilliard Chorus and Orchestra were conducted by the late Serge Koussevitzky in a performance of Beethoven's Ninth Symphony; festivals honoring Ernest Bloch, Paul Hindemith, Aaron Copland, a Festival of French Music and a Festival of British Music; the establishment of a Department of Dance; a series of commissions to composers and choreographers; the 50th Anniversary celebration of the School in the form of a Festival of American Music; the

development of the Department of Academic Studies from an enrollment of less than 6 per cent to well over 70 per cent of the student body; the beginning of an organized fund raising effort and the publication of the Juilliard Review; the negotiations that led ultimately to the pending move of the School to Lincoln Center with the projected addition of a Division of Drama; a European tour of the Juilliard Orchestra; the establishment of the Juilliard program in the Literature and Materials of Music and the publication by W. W. Norton and Company, of THE JUILLIARD REPORT ON TEACHING THE LITERATURE AND MATERIALS OF MUSIC; the establishment of the Juilliard String Quartet; productions of symphonic, operatic, chamber music and dance works, many of which were première performances; the training of a host of brilliant young performing musicians, among whom are Leontyne Price, Van Cliburn, John Browning.

These "vividly recalled" highlights, of course, present the most prominent elements of a presidential tenure at Juilliard that can only be classified as transformative. Taking a known but unfocused institution at the end of World War II that housed both the elite Juilliard Graduate School and the more plebeian Institute of Musical Art, Schuman led the School to new levels of national and international prominence. By the end of his presidency, the efforts he had begun back in the 1950s to bring Juilliard to Lincoln Center had placed the School at the center of the New York arts scene.

Known as an affable and decisive administrator, Schuman's term at Juilliard must be considered his most productive and successful years, both as an arts administrator and as a creative force on the American arts scene. Quick to delegate to a highly capable staff, he was known to arrive at the School at around noon so that he could dedicate the morning to composing at home. He also decided that he would not teach during his time as president. Schuman committed himself fully to the day-to-day tasks that take up most of administrators' time: issues relating to trustees, faculty, students, budget, enrollment, endowment management, building conditions, pensions (which he studied in great depth early in his tenure)—all the myriad elements of a complex modern institution of higher learning.

In the early years of Schuman's presidency, the enrollment of the School he inherited was influenced by historical and organizational phenomena. From 1945 till about 1950 Juilliard and other institutions of higher learning in America needed to accommodate the waves of returning World War II veterans who were making use of the GI Bill to start or complete their college education.

The Institute of Musical Art (IMA), founded by Frank Damrosch in 1905, and the Juilliard Graduate School, created in 1924 after Augustus Juilliard's death in 1919, had inhabited two large buildings at 120 and 130 Claremont Avenue. The Juilliard School of Music was created after the two institutions were combined in 1926. However, although they shared a common board of directors and a president, at the time of Schuman's arrival as president they retained their individual identities and functioned in disparate ways. The institutions had grown from distinctly different roots: the Institute of Musical Art enrolled students at different levels of musical ability, while the Juilliard Graduate School, supported by the endowment of the Juilliard Musical Foundation (JMF), was much more selective in its admission standards. Furthermore, the Graduate School provided all its students full tuition scholarships, for which the Institute students were ineligible. The JMF also provided the essential budgetary component of covering the so-called deficit the School ran after tuition income was received. In the fiscal year ending June 30, 1945, for example, the JMF had provided $350,000, or 45 percent of the total budgeted revenue for the year, on expenses of $778,780.

Almost immediately Schuman set out to merge the two institutions in order to develop greater administrative efficiency, create a unified curriculum, and raise artistic standards. Schuman's first official communication as president with his board set the tone for his entire tenure:

> The end of the war has brought with it a period of re-evaluation in many phases of American life, including that of music education. Because of the psychological atmosphere of the times, we have before us the opportunity for constructive, positive change. The professional musician of tomorrow who is under our guidance today, must continue to observe the highest standards. But he must be equipped to practice his art in conjunction with, and fully conscious of the realities and necessities of contemporary musical life.

Schuman then presented his proposed reorganization, central to which was the merger of the Institute of Musical Art with the Juilliard Graduate

School. He pointed out that "this report assumes that the matter up for discussion [merger] is no longer whether the two schools should merge but when and how."

Schuman found the merger "one of the most difficult things he had to do" as president:

> Practically anyone could go to the Institute, which had hundreds of students. . . . The Graduate School was selective, and offered only "solo" instruments, voice, and composition. All 150 or so students in the Graduate School had scholarships—including the granddaughter of J. P. Morgan. The teachers in the Graduate School got enormous sums of money, while teachers at the Institute were very poorly paid. I equalized the pay scales, and instituted the policy that any student could apply for financial aid, based on need.

Schuman persevered in the face of strong opposition from the Graduate School faculty: "I pointed out that it was ridiculous to have two schools. You had to have the courage to make one." Fortunately, Schuman's board supported its president.

The offerings for the newly amalgamated Juilliard School of Music would include the diploma, bachelor of science, post-graduate diploma, and master of science degrees. The BS was extended to five years of study, and the MS program required an additional year of study beyond the BS. A "special" category was also created for "exceptionally gifted students who, though obviously slated for a professional career, may not require or be able to assimilate the general curriculum."

In a burst of creative energy the young president presented a panoply of revisions for the School that would set it on a new course of excellence. Proposals included in the President's Report under the heading "Public Activities" involved a reworked orchestral program that would include "a nucleus of fifteen of the best professional first-desk men" who would help anchor a superb symphony orchestra for the School (this concept of professional musicians performing with students never came to fruition); an increased emphasis on choral singing and a Collegiate Chorale under Robert Shaw (who would also function as the School's choral director) as a resident ensemble through the School's extension department; greater attention to opera productions, with the goal of aiding the development of opera in cities and towns throughout the United States; and the enhancement of composition studies at Juilliard, with a concomitant commissioning program to create new works for educational as well as presentation purposes. Schuman emphasized that this program was important not only for Juilliard, but for the nation. He even prophetically pointed out the potential for the creation of drama and dance divisions at the School. He promised the directors, though, with typical dry wit, that he had no intention of starting a medical school.

Schuman reflected years later on his impulsive administrative style at the beginning of his tenure, which led to a number of missteps:

> I don't mean to imply as a young administrator I didn't make mistakes. Of course I did. But I gladly accept the mistakes that I made in terms of the things that were accomplished. I was sometimes too impatient making them [decisions]. . . . Don't be afraid of getting a young person. Get someone who is on fire with it, and let him make the mistakes, because at a certain time in your life you take chances and you are bold in a way that you can't be bold later on.

These initial efforts were complemented by a proposal to engage highly renowned conductors and composers to realize Juilliard's new goals, including Fritz Reiner, Pierre Monteux, Aaron Copland, and William Bergsma. In fact, only Bergsma spent any significant teaching time at Juilliard. George Wedge was removed from his deanship, though he continued in a less prestigious position as director of the summer school and special departments. Norman Lloyd, an important figure in many future curricular developments at the School, was given the preliminary title of director of student and faculty personnel and then director of education; and Mark Schubart, a future dean and Schuman's closest professional confidante, was hired away from his job as a music editor at the *New York Times* to become the director of public activities.

At the end of his reorganization proposal Schuman asked the directors to agree to these initiatives; the faculty, students, and the general public would then be informed of the changes, all at the same time, at some point in the future. Seeing such a thoroughgoing plan of action from the new president only three months after he started, Schuman's board must have realized that they had engaged an educational reformer of tremendous energy.

Schuman worked effectively with his board throughout his tenure, no small feat for any college president:

> It was a very small Board, and aside from Warburg, who was a brilliant, brilliant man, and Eddie Johnson, who was then head of the Metropolitan Opera, they were all lawyers. And that's what made it so easy for me, because lawyers are trained in grasping an abstraction, a concept, and I would just have to give them the concept of this change in [music] theory and they would understand it very quickly, whereas others might not be that fast . . . they were very supportive.

The enrollment statistics at the end of the 1945–46 academic year show 1,422 students in degree, diploma, special, and preparatory programs in the IMA and 151 students in the Juilliard Graduate School, for a total enrollment of 1,573. Of those, 1,309 students were enrolled in what would soon be called the "Regular School" (IMA and JGS enrollments combined), an exceedingly robust number for a music school in the mid-twentieth century.

By October 1948 Schuman realized that he could not develop the high standards he had proposed in 1945 unless the School's enrollment was lowered drastically. Schuman understood the financial impact of such a decrease but explained to his board of directors, as he would so often do, that excellence had to take precedence over financial issues:

> While it is true that the loss of tuition fees from a reduced student body will present a budgetary problem, especially in this time of inflation, it is, nevertheless, necessary to select students on a qualitative rather than a quantitative basis if those of questionable seriousness of purpose and musical potentialities are to be eliminated. Furthermore, budgetary planning must make this possible without reducing scholarship grants.

Following Schuman's directive, Juilliard enrolled 1,106 students in the regular school at the beginning of the 1948–49 academic year, a reduction of 230 students from the previous year. Not only were more rigorous standards applied to the admissions auditions, but for the first time, a significant reduction occurred in the number of military veterans entering the School. However, in

October 1948, in a total regular school (excluding extension and preparatory departments) population of 1,106, no fewer than 522 were veterans (47 percent).

By the 1949–50 academic year Schuman's strategy to decrease enrollment in order to enhance standards had brought the regular school tally to 947 students, yet the disparity in the distribution of instrumentalists enrolled varied wildly. Any serious music conservatory requires a critical mass of instrumentalists and singers to staff orchestral, opera, and chamber music activities. In addition, the size of every department must be sufficient to allow ample performance opportunities for all students in each department.

In the fall of 1949, when Schuman was trying to raise standards at Juilliard, the outsized instrumental departments included 63 clarinetists, 35 percussionists, 240 pianists, 23 trombonists, 63 trumpeters, and 196 singers. These instruments (excluding the pianists and singers) make up the core of a band, probably a reflection of the many veteran enrollees' musical experience. The paucity of violists (5) and cellists (18) raises the question of how student orchestras were formed, although at the time it was standard practice for all violinists (123) to play viola as well.

Schuman also needed to address the Juilliard Summer School, which had been in existence since 1932. Although the program functioned as a cash cow during the immediate postwar years, generating close to a $75,000 "profit" in 1946 and 1947 and enrolling over 2,000 students, the surplus of revenue over expenses dwindled quickly in ensuing years due to a significant drop-off in GI Bill–supported veterans and the growth of music festivals in non-urban centers, such as Tanglewood. In addition, it was next to impossible to engage first-rate teachers for the program. Finally, Schuman was concerned about the significantly lower standards of the summer program, a confused situation that "enabled students to represent themselves as Juilliard trained . . . [even though] these same students often would not have been accepted in the regular session of the School." (Ironically, Schuman himself had studied in the Juilliard summer school during his Teachers College years.) In 1953 the summer school was discontinued on Schuman's recommendation.

Geographically, Schuman expanded the reach of his School. In the fall of 1949 the student body included students from almost every state in the union and twenty-four countries; Israel was the best-represented country, with 14 students. The increased size of the international population was due in part to the insistence of Schuman, in diametric opposition to his predecessors, that Juilliard students represent the entire international community. The geopolitical position of the United States after World War II was also partly responsible for the School's demographic change; however, with the Korean War and the military draft that accompanied it, those same geopolitical forces caused Juilliard's overall student population to plummet to 698 musicians (plus 48 new dance students) in September 1951.

Although music enrollment continued to decrease until the mid to late 1950s, the number of musicians eventually stabilized in the low 600s by the time Schuman left office in 1961. However, the disparity of numbers within instrumental departments never really changed: clarinetists, pianists (243 in the 1959–60 academic year), trumpeters, and singers overpopulated the School, while only one viola major and three bassoonists were registered in the fall of 1961.

Early on in his Juilliard tenure, Schuman floated the notion that musicians of the future would need new educational experiences in music as well as nonmusical education. His strategy was to foster an atmosphere of what he called "constructive self-evaluation," in which the School created "a realistic relationship between craft and the world in which the craft is practiced, [with] its curriculum [going] beyond the narrow confines of technical skills":

> Music education must certainly bear much of the responsibility for the fact that few musicians today are adequately equipped in what a prominent conductor has described as "the common decencies of music." It is perhaps not an exaggeration to claim that the average musician, far from being an enlightened exponent of the noblest art, is little more than a skilled laborer.

Schuman then presented his concern, first addressed while he was a student at Teachers College and subsequently a faculty member at Sarah Lawrence, that there was almost no relationship between what the private instrumental teacher addressed in the studio and what was taught in the music theory classroom: "In the years ahead it is planned to restudy these relationships at Juilliard and to develop more effective means of producing musicians with an integrated knowledge of their art." With this rather demure introduction, Schuman presented to his board his revolutionary approach to the teaching of music history and music theory, which Schuman named "The Literature and Materials of Music" and which was known by future generations of Juilliard students as L&M.

Schuman linked his new approach to the teaching of music in the classroom for pre-professionals by first asking the studio faculty of the School to shake up their own approach to teaching. He called a meeting of all studio faculty and said, "I have a request for you. My request is that during the current year you discover and teach three pieces of music that you've never known before. I don't care what the music is—and I'm not saying what period the music should come from. My purpose is to get you thinking of music again."

Schuman was passionate about this new approach to teaching music theory and composition, along with other ancillary skills, to musicians. He had inherited a music theory and ear-training curriculum developed by the School's dean, George Wedge, and based on Wedge's text, *Advanced Ear-Training and Sight-Singing* (1922). Schuman noted that deleting the "Wedge system" at Juilliard had caused the sale of Wedge's book to drop precipitously—a book published by his former full-time employer, G. Schirmer.

Schuman shaped the curriculum with his colleague Norman Lloyd, a composer and pianist whom Schuman had first met at Sarah Lawrence when Lloyd accompanied dance classes. Lloyd was Juilliard's director of education in 1946. He and Schuman went off to Atlantic City and "worked like demons for ten or twelve hours a day and wrote up this curriculum. When we'd done enough for one day, we went to the movies and played a slot machine game at which he [Lloyd] excelled (I used to bet him and I always lost)."

Juilliard's first courses in L&M were offered at the beginning of the 1947–48 academic year. Schuman worked intensively at honing the L&M concept in New York City. He also took his show on the road, so to speak, meeting with educators and speaking to music organizations from Boston to San Francisco, including the Music Teachers National Association, the National Association of Schools of Music, and the American Musicological Society. Clearly Schuman saw this new way to teach music theory as a national issue, and he claimed that his audiences agreed with his vision:

> The outstanding impression of the trip was the great interest shown by so many musicians and teachers in the new approach to the teaching of music theory being developed at Juilliard. They expressed a growing

recognition of the failures of conventional theory instruction and a genuine desire for more enlightened teaching in this field.

Schuman's first public explanation of L&M appeared in the April 1948 issue of the *Musical Quarterly*. The article was just as much about Schuman's fundamental philosophy of how to teach young persons aspiring to be professional musicians as it was about L&M:

> It is essential that their education lead them beyond mere technical proficiency and insure intelligent and musicianly comprehension. Clearly, to produce musicians who approach this ideal, there must be a thorough and catholic training which will encompass a practical understanding of the entire historical and artistic range of musical creativeness.

Schuman went on to explain that the conventional way of teaching music theory was unsuccessful because it was essentially divorced from the music it analyzed. The Literature and Materials of Music program would revitalize the process, in Schuman's view, developing "virtuoso listeners" who would be able to understand the entire structure of a musical composition through intelligent and informed listening.

The curriculum would be taught primarily by composers, who in the 1947–48 academic year included William Bergsma, Vittorio Giannini, Richard Franko Goldman, Peter Mennin, Vincent Persichetti, and Robert Ward. Schuman had offered the existing music theory faculty the opportunity to teach this new approach, but, he remarked, "Most of them said they wouldn't have the slightest idea of how to teach something like that and did not apply, so I was able to bring in the composers I had in mind." This was a bit disingenuous: clearly Schuman wished to install prominent composers as teachers, and in his view the former Juilliard theory faculty members simply did not qualify.

The new president's first call went out to Vincent Persichetti, the distinguished composer, teacher, and pianist, who agreed to come to New York to meet with Schuman. On the train ride home to Philadelphia, though, Persichetti remembered something that "he thought might enlarge his salary in the new program. As soon as he got to the station, he sent off a telegram [to Schuman] saying, 'Forgot to tell you I have a doctorate in music.' [Schuman] wrote back, 'that will not be held against you.'"

The new curriculum was based on what Schuman called "organized flexibility," where each instructor had the autonomy to teach the topics as he or she saw fit. The autodidactic quality of Schuman's own education surfaced in L&M: "He [the student] must assume the responsibility for his own education. For only when the student understands this will it be possible for him to make genuine progress and develop within himself his own discipline."

Schuman's predilection for student self-direction had surfaced as early as a 1938 article in *Modern Music,* in which "he described how a student [at Sarah Lawrence] had proceeded naturally by cultivating her own interests of the moment rather than being forced to follow the accepted chronology of theory instruction." This article was Schuman's first public pronouncement that music instruction for both amateurs and pre-professionals was substandard: "There are many reasons why the present public is without aggressive and intelligent interest in the music it so apathetically absorbs. One of these, perhaps outstanding, is an obvious deficiency in the quality of its education."

In the article Schuman proudly notes that at Sarah Lawrence College "the arts play a very important role," and that the students involved in music classes are "trained in the technic of penetrative listening." He then presents the foundation upon which he would eventually develop the L&M program at Juilliard: "Theoretical subjects are not taught in the abstract. They are pursued because the materials present problems which require investigation." When Schuman is challenged by an anonymous student named Joan, who asks, "Why wasn't she using a text book with day to day steps of increasing complexity? Was she getting at the fundamentals?," Schuman answers that "the situation was definitely experimental, that the method would entail some blundering as well as exciting progress," a remarkably prescient comment considering how the L&M program eventually unfolded at Juilliard.

Included in the L&M concept was a teacher-training program, and in his 1948 *Musical Quarterly* article Schuman made his views known with characteristic bluntness: "If we are to raise the standards of music teaching, our professional schools must no longer steer the least talented students into teaching. . . . There is no reason to expect every professional musician to be a teacher but there is every reason to insist that every music teacher be a musician of professional caliber." He concluded with a call to arms:

> If what we are doing seems too "progressive" to some educators, I think the reason is not so much that it is daring but that education in the theory of music has for a long time been in need of thorough

rejuvenation. And, finally, the point of view to which we hold is not a system, but a way of musical life. . . . If young musicians can be imbued with a sense of real values, their chances for adjusted lives and useful careers are increased. And musicians recognizing these values need never sink to the banalities of tired professionalism; they will take pride in being part of music—an art that enriches the world beyond understanding.

A comprehensive description of L&M in Juilliard's 1952–53 catalog showed how broad the concept had become, having grown to encompass diverse topics from sight-singing to music history:

Study of the Literature and Materials of Music is based on music itself, from the Middle Ages to the present day, with emphasis on changing concepts of music in writing and performance. The work ranges— according to the student's needs, progress, and potentialities—from the rudiments of musical craft to advanced instruction in the techniques of composition, and is accomplished through classroom and individual instruction and discussion groups. The curriculum includes study and analysis of repertoire, development of writing and listening skills, reading assignments, music history, and integrated work adequate to the individual student's needs in such studies as orchestration, basic elements of conducting, notation, keyboard harmony, sight reading and sight singing, and elementary ensemble performance. Students requiring specialized work in a given area may be assigned to special courses or to other departmental personnel upon recommendation of the instructor.

By the winter of 1951 Schuman felt that, after four years, it was time to evaluate this new venture in the teaching of music theory. Schuman admitted that his vision of integrating the study of harmony, counterpoint, sight-singing, and music history into one course "has aroused great interest and controversy throughout music education circles both here and abroad and has found ardent supporters and severe critics." Schuman proposed the publication of a text that would eventually be entitled "The Juilliard Report on Teaching the Literature and Materials of Music." Most of the book was written by Richard Franko Goldman, with an introduction by Schuman; it was published by Norton in 1953.

The L&M concept was based on the ability and focus of the teacher in the classroom. Not only did the teacher have to approach a wide array of topics, but he or she also had to meticulously prepare class materials. As with any innovative program, the energy generated by this major curricular innovation began to wane as the practicality of the approach was tested.

One of the fundamental precepts of L&M, especially in its early years, was the insistence that active composers, not music theoreticians, teach the course. Because the first priority of any active composer has to be the creation of new music, the extraordinary demands of teaching L&M caused the quality of the classroom experience to be decidedly mixed by the 1951–52 academic year. In the winter of 1952 Schuman attempted to counter this downward trend by putting even more emphasis on the individual L&M teacher:

> [the] Literature and Materials instructor serves as the student's general adviser, and *plans the student's course of study with a view to facilitating the student's musical development in a well-rounded manner.* The student is expected to progress according to his abilities and application, and not mechanically on a year-to-year basis from one course to another. (Emphasis added)

Curiously, this approach resembled the teaching environment at Sarah Lawrence College, of which Schuman had become extremely critical by the end of his tenure there. Schuman's ideal of individualized interaction between faculty and students for the purpose of charting the progress of each music student at Juilliard—698 in the 1951–52 academic year—was not only a nightmare for registrars and teachers alike, but also highly cumbersome, and eventually the program returned to the conventional class periods known since time immemorial. What Schuman hoped to create at Juilliard through L&M was a pervasive spirit of encouraging young musicians to look beyond technical perfection in their own discipline and understand the larger world of the arts— in other words, the environment within which audiences experienced music. The L&M concept fought against the prevailing attitude of both teacher and student at Juilliard that unless the learning experience directly related to how to play an instrument better, there was no reason to participate.

Schuman said of L&M that

> when it worked, it worked wonderfully, but it didn't always work. It worked according to the varying intellects of the people who were

exposed to it. When Peter Mennin succeeded me as president at Juilliard, the L&M department became very weak, because he never really understood it. I had found out early that what Mennin really wanted was a chronological approach, and [he] didn't have a feel for the freedom of L&M.

Distinguished musicians and scholars often agreed with Schuman's approach. In a review, the American musicologist H. Wiley Hitchcock suggested that *The Juilliard Report* was a worthy and necessary read for any music teacher:

The program is courageous in its refusal to separate the world of musical training into narrow, water-tight compartments which prevent any "meaningful transfer of theoretical knowledge into practical performance." It is humanistic in its affirmation of the student's right to *learn* (find out) rather than to be *taught*. Humanistic, too, is its insistence that the student think of "an *art* of music that is larger and more enduring than (his) own interests in it."

John H. Lowell also extolled the virtues of the program, explaining that "the L. and M. curriculum constitutes about fifty percent of the student's total work for the bachelor of science degree or diploma course." Schuman had committed essentially all noninstrumental instruction and rehearsals to his new curricular initiative, but the key to the success of the program, Lowell pointed out, was the person who taught the class: "In the final analysis, the L. and M. curriculum works as well as it does because of the person who stands in front of the class—a good teacher."

In retrospect, the emphasis on the individual teacher as the primary source of information in as diverse an array of topics as harmony, counterpoint, music history, sight-reading and sight-singing, composition, and keyboard harmony, among others, turned out to be the fundamental flaw of the L&M concept. Exceptional teachers had to be found, and they had to maintain a high level of intensity from one year to the next; but the autonomy granted to each of them allowed them to focus on their own particular areas of interest, a practice that did not necessarily lend itself to handing off the student to a new teacher in the next year of study. In addition, owing to the extraordinary demands put on the individual teacher and the time-intensive component of integrating L&M into a curriculum, the program was not easily exportable to other schools and departments of music. An idealistic and highly innovative curricular modification created by Schuman's fertile imagination eventually settled back at Juilliard during the Mennin administration in the 1960s and 1970s to the traditional approach of having separate courses in music theory, music history, ear training, and orchestration. Its impact nationwide prompted administrators to reevaluate their music theory programs, but it never really succeeded in creating a revolution in the teaching of the subject, as Schuman had hoped. Yet the essential concept of educating the complete musician who must be a strong advocate for the arts in American society lives to this day at Juilliard.

In line with the comprehensive view that Schuman hoped to provide for Juilliard students on the world of music, he also gave great thought to the nonmusical education of the School's degree students. By the end of the 1951–52 academic year, Schuman reported to his board that "over the last seven years, matriculation in the Academic Division of the School has risen from approximately ten to approximately fifty per cent of the regularly enrolled students." All Juilliard students were admitted to the School, first and foremost, on the basis of the artistic audition, with high school grades being a secondary consideration, so Schuman was well aware of the diversity of academic ability within the student body.

C. Harold Gray was appointed to undertake a study of the academic department's future needs. At the time head of the English department at Rensselaer Polytechnic Institute in Troy, New York, Gray was an experienced educator and administrator who would eventually be appointed by Schuman as the new director of the division of general education at Juilliard to develop a non-artistic or liberal arts curriculum suited specifically for the young musician. Gray and his faculty colleagues set out to provide a broad palette of academic courses that stimulated the intellect and developed writing and analytical skills in the first two years of study and then provided elective studies in literature, history, acoustics, and the visual arts for ensuing years.

Schuman's belief that musicians of the future should be broadly educated generated considerable suspicion on the part of the performance faculty. Flora Rheta Schreiber wrote in 1954:

There was opposition, of course, based partly on the old guard's suspicion of young men in high places and partly on a frank skepticism as to the validity of any music study aside from actual performance. Even Erskine, Schuman's champion, felt during these early days that perhaps Schuman, acting with headlong recklessness, tended to make up his mind too quickly. Erskine's faith in Schuman never wavered, but he wished fervently that Schuman would proceed less precipitously.

During the Sarah Lawrence years, Frankie and Bill lived in a small home in Larchmont, at 91 Edgewood Avenue. By 1942 they had moved to 17 Springdale Road, also in Larchmont, where their son, Tony, was born.

Frankie and Bill had traveled by train to be present at the premiere of the Symphony for Strings by the Boston Symphony Orchestra conducted by Koussevitzky on November 12, 1943. Recalled Schuman:

> We had a long train ride up, and Frankie of course was very, very, very pregnant, and so we came into the green room . . . then he [Koussevitzky] said to her: "Eeet vill be a boy." . . . When I sent him a note that our son was born, he sent me a telegram which said DELIGHTED MADE RIGHT GUESS, PERFORMING YOUR SYMPHONY TONIGHT IN CAMBRIDGE HONOR OF YOUR FIRST-BORN.

Owing to the increased entertaining responsibilities of the Juilliard presidency, Frankie insisted that they purchase a new, larger home. Schuman's salary at Juilliard allowed them a very comfortable upper-middle-class lifestyle, so the Springdale Avenue home was sold and a larger home was purchased at 241 Elk Avenue in New Rochelle. The Schumans had two domestic employees, a cook and laundress named Florida Chapman, who lived in the house, and a butler/handyman and sometime chauffeur named Raymond, who was employed only occasionally and did not live with the Schumans. An outdoor pool and an indoor lap pool were eventually built so that Bill could swim year-round.

While living in the Elk Avenue house the Schumans adopted an infant girl born on April 30, 1949, whom they named Andrea (Andie):

> We didn't seem to be having a second child, and we didn't want to know anything about our daughter except whether she was

physically healthy and whether she seemed to [be] all put together in psychological terms as far as one could tell from an infant . . . from the word go there was absolutely never any difference in our feelings toward an adopted child as toward a natural child, and there isn't to this day. . . . It's your child, the child that you love.

The Schumans told Andie at an early age that she was adopted: "Frankie and I have often wondered whether we did the right thing because that was the advice the analyst and other experts give or gave at that time, and we are not at all sure that it is correct, that it would have been better [not to tell]."

In 1978 Andie set out, with the support of Frankie and Bill, to find her biological parents. Working with a New York organization that matched birth parents with children, she learned that her birth mother, Geraldine, was a visual artist living in Colorado. Andie and Geraldine have stayed in touch since they found each other.

Both Tony and Andie had happy recollections of their childhood years in New Rochelle. They remembered their father at that time as remote: he was at Juilliard during the day, attended concerts in the evening, and composed almost all day Saturday. According to Tony, "The study was off-limits, with Dad singing loudly and chords crashing on the piano. Mom was always fiercely protective of his work." Andie recalled that the most personal contact they had with their dad was when they would take leisurely walks around the block near their home; Schuman used a walking stick and promenaded in the style of his own father, who had told his son to walk with his arms thrown back. Sundays were dedicated to the family. They visited Manor Park in Larchmont and had hot dogs and ice cream at a local restaurant called Cook's.

Frankie once told a New Rochelle newspaper that "my first move after our marriage was being firm about a six-day, not a seven-day working week. He fought for a while, but when he discovered the delights of a day off—it's worked ever since." Frankie had worked for the Vocational Advisory Service of the City of New York from 1935 to 1949. She then became a full-time mother and also volunteered as a founding member of the Cerebral Palsy Association of Southern Westchester and a member and director of the Urban League of Westchester.

The Schuman children saw themselves in retrospect as leading a typical middle-class New York suburban life, with sandlot baseball, Cub Scouts, Brownies, and summer days at the beach on Glen Island. "Mom was mostly involved in our homework, since Dad was not a spectacularly good speller.

He would also sing songs to me from the 1920s just before bedtime," Tony recalled, and Frankie would read to Andie. Frankie served dinner at 7:30 P.M., later than most of their neighborhood friends. Andie remembered the dinner table as somewhat formal, with her father often asking, "Tell me what you did today."

Schuman's passion for baseball played out with his son through neighborhood pick-up games, but when Tony got older he asked his father not to participate in future games because of his weak throws and hits, caused by his muscular deficiencies. Only after he was an adult did Tony realize how hurt his father had been at being excluded from these games.

Tony and Andie considered their parents to be stoics in both practice and philosophy:

> Dad wouldn't talk about his feelings. Dad, in particular, always said [referring to familial squabbling], "Let's not have any unpleasantness." [Regarding his own physical health he would say], "No matter what condition I have, I'll come to terms with it." And the only thing he feared was mental deterioration, and fortunately both of them were blessed that that didn't happen. He also wouldn't have had a social life if my mother hadn't created it. He did not have a best friend, and he literally had nothing to do with the house; never went shopping. He was driven to write music and Mom understood that. The times when Dad was emotional . . . were when Mom was ill, and he'd say I really need your help here; you've got to pitch in.

Such times included Frankie's mastectomy in 1966, a detached retina in the 1970s, and a broken hip around 1990. In many ways, Schuman did have a best friend—Frankie.

In the 1950s and 1960s the Schuman family would spend a month every summer in Menemsha, where Frankie's aunt and uncle, Amy and Walter Charak, owned a beautiful home. They permitted Schuman to renovate a small cottage on the property and turn it into a three-bedroom cottage, although he never actually owned the house. Many of Schuman's compositions of this period were created at Menemsha. Sadly, when Amy's nephew Robert Prince inherited the entire Menemsha property at the time of his aunt's and uncle's deaths, around 1980, he refused to allow Schuman to take possession of the piano in the cottage, even though he had purchased it many years earlier and intended it for his grandson, Josh. Said Tony and Andie:

This was one of the great sadnesses in Mom's life. We were a family who didn't have these types of disagreements. Mom was an only child and was actually quite close to Bobby who was really Mom's only cousin since Amy and Walter had no children. Bobby sort of kidnapped Aunt Amy on her deathbed and would not allow my mother to talk to her. It was a horrible, horrible thing.

Like their own parents, Bill and Frankie did not have a religious home. Sam Schuman had always been in favor of complete assimilation into American society, rejecting the family's Jewish roots. Andie recalled that her mother "believed that religion was the source of all that was bad in the world." The Schuman children saw their family life as

secular in the extreme, a nonreligious household. No temple, zero observance, no bat/bar mitzvahs. There was a concern that we know that we were Jewish, but this had to do with the secular history of the Jewish people. . . . We had a Christmas tree, but no angel. We believed in Santa, and we also celebrated Easter with an egg hunt and a ham dinner.

Tony also recalled that "Dad was not Semitic in appearance, and he was party to a number of conversations where Jews were disparaged." Schuman himself experienced this prejudice when being considered for admission to the Century Association, a New York institution founded in 1847, that "derive[d] its name from the fact that 'one hundred gentlemen engaged or interested in Letters and the Fine Arts have been invited to join in forming the Association.'" Its stately headquarters at 7 West 43rd Street had been designed by McKim, Mead & White and completed in 1891. This landmark building played host to many artistic luminaries over the decades. When Schuman was first nominated and became a member in 1954, he was well aware of the restrictive policies of the association, which severely limited but did not totally prohibit Jews as members. Schuman recalled telling his nominator, Parker McCollester, a lawyer and member of the Juilliard board, that he "referred obliquely to Anti-Semitism by saying . . . that 'I don't want to become the Jackie Robinson of the Century [Association].'" The Century would eventually become one of Schuman's favorite clubs, along with the Lotos Club on East 66th Street.

Schuman's mother, Ray, died of Paget's disease and heart problems on September 3, 1947. Then, on October 11, 1949, just before Andie's adoption was finalized, Schuman's father was hit by an automobile as he was crossing 72nd Street near his home. Although he recovered from the accident (he died of colon cancer on November 29, 1950), he was hospitalized at Roosevelt Hospital for over eight months. Frankie asked Bill if they should proceed with the adoption, and he insisted that the process continue: "I remember it because it was so dramatic. There you thought one member of your family was about to die and you were about to acquire another one."

In the emergency room it became plain that despite his promise to his wife, Sam had never been able to kick his long-standing gambling habit: he told his son to remove a large wad of dollar bills from his stricken father's pocket, explaining that "he had had a good day at the track."

A tape recording was prepared on Thanksgiving Day of 1949 as a get-well gift to Sam, who was in the hospital. Included in the group gathered for dinner at the Schuman home in New Rochelle were Bill, Frankie, Tony, who announced that his new sister "was a very nice girl," and a crying infant Andie; Frankie's parents, Leonard and Gertie Prince; Bill's sister and brother-in-law, Audrey and Bert Israel; Bill's niece and nephew, Judith and John Israel; and even the Schumans' maid, Florida, all singing "McNally's Row of Flats." A second recording has Sam telling his family from the hospital that what he heard "will increase my chances of recovery tenfold" and then singing a verse of a Harrigan and Hart song, "Oh How I Love My Ada."* The recording shows the kind of gleeful enthusiasm and playful comments so characteristic of Schuman's entire extended family. This pervasive sense of optimism was an important element of William Schuman's persona, and it served him well in his future endeavors.

---

* Sound recordings provided to the author by Judith Israel Gutmann.

CHAPTER 6

In the End We Prevailed with a Broader View

Situated in New York City, the cultural capital of the United States—and, especially after World War II, perhaps the world as well—Schuman had access to many of the great artists and teachers of the time as president of Juilliard. In addition to appointing most of the principal players of the New York Philharmonic to the faculty, Schuman also sought out many great solo artists and pedagogues, among them the pianists Joseph Bloch, Sascha Gorodnitzki, William Kapell, and Beveridge Webster; the violinists Dorothy DeLay, Joseph Fuchs, and Oscar Shumsky; the violist William Primrose; the cellists Leonard Rose and Luigi Silva; the voice teacher Hans Heinz; the oboist Robert Bloom; and the clarinetist Daniel Bonade.

Schuman was a keen judge of teaching talent. He was also realistic about the basics a young artist needed from a teacher. Ivan Galamian was a distinguished violin pedagogue recommended to Schuman by Eugene Ormandy, who had known of Galamian's work at the Curtis Institute of Music in Philadelphia. Galamian told Schuman, "I have to tell you I don't know the difference between playing a scale in Stravinsky or Mozart. But if I see a faulty spiccato, I know that in eighteen months I can correct it." Schuman embraced the diversity of skills among his faculty: "Not everyone can have breadth of view; you had to have some narrow specialists—your 'ear, nose, and throat men.' Galamian was a technician, and we needed him."

Schuman first encountered the conductor and teacher Jean Morel while he was conducting *Pelléas et Mélisande* at the City Center in 1948 with the New York City Opera in a production featuring the legendary Maggie Teyte as Mélisande. After engaging him to conduct a concert in Juilliard's Festival of Contemporary French Music on November 30–December 3, 1948, Schuman attended Morel's rehearsals and offered him the position of Juilliard's principal conductor and teacher of conducting. Morel was taken aback: "But you haven't heard the concert." Schuman said, "I'm not interested in the concert. I'm interested in you as a teacher. The concert may be fine or it may not be fine, but where the education takes place is in these rehearsals."

Schuman reflected years later that he was never quite comfortable with Morel's approach to conducting: "His repertory was so limited. He couldn't play Brahms, Haydn or Mozart. He did the most wonderful *Don Juan* and a marvelous *Enigma Variations* and if [he] had his way, he would have played Franck and Saint-Saëns on every concert." However, he said, Morel "was a poor conductor for the public. Every time a real climax would come, he could never let anything go away. He would always put up his hand and bring it down, and he treated the musicians so badly." In earthier terms, Schuman would laughingly say that Morel never let the orchestra have an orgasm.

In addition to his faculty appointments, Schuman sought to create an American institution that would have an enormous impact in the United States and around the world on how chamber music was performed and experienced by audiences. The young president was very intent on creating a resident string quartet that would become an important part of the School and "that would stand for something specific: It would play all the standard literature with the sense of discovery that should apply to new music, and play new music with the reverence that should be applied to the classics." Schuman also wanted "an American string quartet that would achieve international stature."

Schuman found the first violinist of this quartet in Robert Mann, a recent graduate of Juilliard who had won the Naumburg Competition in 1941. Mann's passion for chamber music captivated Schuman. The new quartet also included Robert Koff, Mann's brother-in-law, as the second violinist, and Raphael Hillyer as the violist, released by Koussevitzky from his BSO contract at Schuman's behest. Schuman was looking for the fourth member of the quartet when Mann remarked to him, "I've got a wonderful cellist [Arthur Winograd]. We've been in the army together, and we were so starved for chamber music that we played the outer voices of quartets just to play some chamber music, with violin and cello. But he's not from Juilliard, he's Curtis." Schuman said that he didn't care where the man was educated and promptly hired Winograd.

The new quartet's birth was not entirely painless. A member of the School's board, John Perry, was concerned that the quartet might not be up to the standards of the Juilliard name. Schuman's response was direct: "Then we'll change the personnel, but we'll have a Juilliard Quartet." Even before the quartet made its formal New York debut at Town Hall on December 23, 1947, Juilliard scheduled about twenty professional engagements for the group, many of them at universities and colleges. Nor was the faculty enthralled with the new group. Some faculty members went so far as to question the quartet's musical values, especially when they performed the Beethoven string quartets according to the composer's metronome markings, which were viewed at the time as absurdly fast. In addition, the quartet's appearance onstage was not at the highest sartorial level. Said Schuman, "Although the Quartet played like angels, they looked like pigs—they dressed atrociously and their socks were always falling down." Schuman sent a note to Mann after one concert at which the quartet looked particularly unkempt: "Dear Bobby: Fight the Big Battles. Love, Bill."

Under the agreement with the Juilliard String Quartet, the ensemble was guaranteed an annual compensation of $6,000 granted directly through the Juilliard Musical Foundation for performances organized by the School. Any fees earned beyond that went directly to the members of the quartet. For example, in 1948–49, gross fees amounted to $12,150 from forty-eight engagements. Expenses were estimated at $4,200, leaving a balance of $7,950 to offset the $6,000 allocation; the $1,950 that remained was distributed to the quartet as extra income.

As part of the quartet's employment contract, they also coached chamber ensembles regularly and presented several concerts at the School, including lecture-concerts through the extension department on the quartets of Beethoven and Bartók. Importantly, it was not until the late 1980s that the members of the quartet were also invited to teach their individual instruments. Their earlier nonparticipation in private teaching was likely related to their demanding touring schedule, which took them away from New York for several weeks at a time.

What was quite remarkable about Schuman's financial and artistic model for the creation of the Juilliard String Quartet was that the Juilliard name was made known throughout the nation, and eventually the world, based on the ensemble's extraordinary artistic excellence. At the same time, the quartet presented no financial burden for the institution, thanks to the Juilliard Musical Foundation grant and the supplementary money given to the quartet as their performance schedule grew. In the mid-1950s, as the quartet's engagements increased, it was decided that an artist manager outside of the School would oversee their engagements, although Juilliard retained the right to authorize all their contracts. In 1958 the quartet met with great success owing to triumphant performances in several European capitals sponsored by the United States International Cultural Exchange and UNESCO. In Budapest, only two years after the Soviet invasion of Hungary, the quartet won enthusiastic accolades: "The audience yelled so loudly for encores that the quartet gave an additional concert for students, who almost dismantled the hall with enthusiasm." The quartet at that time was made up of Mann, Isidore Cohen (second violin), Hillyer, and Claus Adam (cello).

The Juilliard String Quartet went on to become legendary. It set the standard for string quartets of the twentieth century, many of them formed or coached at Juilliard. Although all engagements of the ensemble were eventually made independent of the Juilliard administration, the ensemble remains the most visible entity to represent Juilliard outside of the School. Ever since the group was formed in 1946, Schuman's brilliant vision of a resident professional quartet has reflected positively on Juilliard.

The status quo was anathema to Schuman's leadership style. Seeing his presidency as an entrepreneurial position, in the 1951–52 academic year Schuman considerably expanded Juilliard's artistic agenda by inaugurating a dance division.

Schuman had always been a knowledgeable connoisseur of dance, dating back to his first compositions and his attendance at dance performances as a child with his parents. In addition, he had important artistic contacts with Antony Tudor and Martha Graham through his composition of *Undertow* (1945) for Tudor and *Night Journey* (1947) and *Judith* (1949) for Graham. Schuman felt strongly that the complementary elements of music and dance made the creation of a dance division in a music school the logical extension of Juilliard offerings.

As early as November 1945, Schuman had mentioned to his board the possibility of creating "a School of Theatre and Dance as part of Juilliard." In May 1950 he reported on a successful evening dedicated to modern dance, where choreographers and dancers collaborated with student composers and "also served as a means of exploring possibilities for future development in the field of the dance at Juilliard."

In February 1951 Schuman proposed to his board the creation of a Department of Dance at Juilliard. He laid out his argument in artistic terms:

> Dance . . . uses more music than any other [performing art] but is actually dependent on music for a large measure of its effectiveness

and for this reason it is hardly surprising that dance has always exerted a strong influence on music . . . it is important to the art of music that dancers have high musical standards.

In this country there is no school which offers a comprehensive education in the dance. Instruction is usually centered in the studio of a well-known modern dancer or school of ballet. What is studied, then, is not so much the art of the dance as a particular point of view, technique, or even cult. In music it would be comparable to one school teaching the works of only one composer. . . . Therefore, the need exists for instruction in dance based on a broad curriculum.

Schuman outlined a curriculum that would address a very wide range of dance traditions, from classical ballet to preclassical and modern forms. In addition, dancers would take L&M, just like the musicians, and would also immerse themselves in choreography and dance notation. At the time it was a revolutionary approach to the teaching of dance to young professionals. Juilliard's first Department of Dance brochure described the mission of the new venture as "train[ing] students to become expert dancers, choreographers, teachers, and, at the same time, develop[ing] in them penetrative musical insights."

Schuman appointed Martha Hill, a respected dance teacher and administrator, to lead this new effort. He then engaged perhaps the most distinguished dance faculty ever created in America: Martha Graham, Doris Humphrey, José Limón, Agnes de Mille, Jerome Robbins, and Antony Tudor. Ann Hutchinson would teach dance notation, and Louis Horst would be in charge of dance composition.

Support of dance at Juilliard was hardly universal. Several dance professionals told Schuman, "You want them all together [ballet and modern] because you are not a dancer, and you look at it theoretically as an artist and an administrator, but you don't understand the different physical needs, the different physical techniques."

Schuman persevered, asking both Martha Graham and Antony Tudor, "'Can I bring the two of you together under one roof without blowing it off?' And they couldn't have been nicer."

The first academic year of dance at Juilliard was 1951–52, with the School enrolling forty-five dancers divided almost equally between the diploma course and the bachelor of science degree. In April 1952 Martha Graham and her company presented an elaborate series of two separate programs performed three times each. Frederick Prausnitz conducted the Juilliard Orchestra. The first program included *Errand into the Maze*, with music by Gian Carlo Menotti and décor by Isamu Noguchi, and *Judith*, with music by Schuman and sets by Noguchi. On the second program were *Hérodiade*, with music by Paul Hindemith and décor by Noguchi, and *Triumph of St. Joan*, with music by Norman Dello Joio and sets by Frederick Kiesler. These exceptional concerts, involving extraordinary composers and designers with the Graham company, were both an artistic and a financial success: they raised enough money to allow the establishment of a scholarship fund for Juilliard's new dancers.

In the ensuing academic year the distinguished dancer and choreographer José Limón also gave a series of dance concerts to benefit dance scholarships. The performing arts profession clearly supported the teaching of dance in a music conservatory, with *Musical America* proclaiming: "Once again the Juilliard School of Music deserves the thanks of dance lovers. . . . By establishing a dance department and putting its resources at the disposal of leading contemporary artists the Juilliard School is contributing greatly to the security and progress of the art."

Juilliard dance students gave their first public performances on May 7 and 8, 1953. The program was designed to feel like a workshop as Hill and her faculty stepped gingerly into the competitive world of New York dance performance. Nevertheless, Juilliard had two extraordinary dance luminaries, Tudor and Humphrey, leading their young charges. In the first half of the concert Tudor presented a lecture-demonstration on techniques of ballet entitled "Let's Be Basic," followed by a work called *Exercise Piece* he had choreographed for twenty-six dancers. In the second half, Humphrey gave a lecture called "What Dances Are Made Of" that used a number of the students and then concluded with her *Song of the West*, with music by Schuman's former teacher, Roy Harris.

In the spring of 1955 Schuman and Hill created the Juilliard Dance Theater and engaged Doris Humphrey to be the artistic director. Funded by the B. de Rothschild Foundation for the Arts and Sciences, the new venture garnered high praise from Schuman, who reported that "the quality of the young dancers who performed was on a level comparable to the advanced student artists of the school in musical performance." However, the broad-based aesthetic in dance championed by Hill was, in many ways, its Achilles' heel. Hill and most of her faculty had a very open-minded approach to dance presentation. Their performances featured a mix of classical ballet and modern dance performed by dancers with a wide array of body types, a style and look contrary to the aesthetic of New York's reigning choreographer, George Balanchine. As a result, as the Department of Dance approached its tenth anniversary, there were decidedly mixed feelings in the profession and even within Juilliard about the quality of the School's dance presentations.

Schuman himself signaled his concern about the viability of the dance division in its new location when he reported to the board as early as May 1959 that because of projected cost overruns in the construction of the new Juilliard building at Lincoln Center, "the Division of Dance would have to be discontinued after the move to the Lincoln Center until funds were made available to provide for physical facilities and operational costs. The inauguration of the Division of Drama would be similarly postponed."

By June 1961 Schuman and Lincoln Center were still negotiating over how Juilliard's dance division would interact with the yet-to-be-named principal dance constituent. In a letter to Edgar Young, the acting president of Lincoln Center, Schuman made it crystal clear that Juilliard's dance program could not and should not be linked to the aesthetic of what would be Lincoln Center's dance company:

> I must say that the planning for dance education can[not] be any more dependent on the professional dance company at Lincoln Center than in the instance of drama training vis-à-vis the Lincoln Center Repertory Theater. . . . The degree to which we will be able to cooperate with the professional dance company will depend largely on the persons who operate this company and their attitude. . . . the training programs at Juilliard are not meant solely to serve the various constituents of the Center but also the country at large.

In December 1961, in his last President's Report to the board, Schuman took an equivocal stand concerning the viability of a dance program in Juilliard's Lincoln Center building:

> the problem for support for the *projected* Division of Dance for the School at Lincoln Center has yet to be solved. It is to be hoped that the Lincoln Center Fund for Education and Creative Artistic Advancement will assist in meeting the costs of this Division, at least during its early years. This is a subject which should be discussed during the coming year. (Emphasis added)

The saga of Juilliard dance at Lincoln Center grew to melodramatic proportions in the 1960s, when Schuman's successor, Peter Mennin, attempted to bring in Lincoln Kirstein and George Balanchine's School of American Ballet as the dance component of the Juilliard School. After a difficult birth, though, Juilliard's dance program grew and thrived at Lincoln Center, with a tighter focus on contemporary dance and a vibrant faculty and students interacting on a regular basis with the School's musicians and actors.

Throughout Schuman's tenure he was highly sensitive as to how to present Juilliard in its best light. He embraced the optimism and dynamism that marked the postwar years in the United States. Although the term "marketing" would have been considered déclassé for an educational institution in the mid-twentieth century, marketing is exactly what Schuman did to put forward his educational and artistic philosophy, as well as to begin establishing Juilliard as the leading institution of its type in America.

Schuman, recognizing the power of artistic excellence in shaping the image of his School, instituted a series of what he called "public activities." These included special festivals focusing on the music of Bloch, Hindemith, and Stravinsky; concerts presented at the School and in Carnegie Hall with leading conductors such as Koussevitzky, Monteux, and others; world premieres of works by leading composers and American premieres of such operas as Richard Strauss's *Capriccio* and Benjamin Britten's adaptation of *The Beggar's Opera*; the creation of the *Juilliard Review*, a scholarly journal intended as a vehicle to promote the School; and the celebration of the successes of recent graduates such as Leontyne Price, Van Cliburn, and John Browning.

Schuman also publicly embraced the concept that America needed to win the cold war. In a Juilliard convocation speech of 1950 Schuman said:

> Music has a stake in the ideological struggle that is in progress in the world today. The dictators have always understood this and have cunningly harnessed the talents of composers and performers to suit their own objectives. For they realize that music, like other arts, is a useful tool in the propagation of their ideologies. However . . . this willful misuse of artistic forces has never succeeded. For when the artist is enslaved, he ceases to be an artist. Musicians are no longer insulated from the struggles of the world.

Later in the 1950s and into the early 1960s, Schuman would put his ideas into action as a member of the United States Information Agency's (USIA) Advisory Committee on Cultural Information and as chair of a music advisory panel to the USIA. The committee included his old friend Harold Spivacke, head of the music division of the Library of Congress, as well as David Ritchie Robertson, director of the Oberlin Conservatory, and John Stuart Wilson, jazz critic of the *New York Times.*

In his 1958 Juilliard commencement address, Schuman declared that the American government should approach the support of the arts with the same intensity it did other endeavors: "We must look to them [members of Congress] to initiate a review of our present Federal arts program which will ensure . . . the same efficiency of organization and consistency of policy which characterize our most successful endeavors." He went on to urge that the federal government create "a single Government agency which, with the aid of civilian experts, would be responsible for the selection and exploitation of all the artistic attractions we export," presaging the creation of the National Endowment for the Arts in 1965.

Schuman was ahead of his peers in bringing his message to the public by utilizing the media of the time: not only radio and print, but also the newer television and long-playing records. As early as 1947 Juilliard presented Friday evening radio broadcasts of music from 8:30 to 10 P.M. on WNYC featuring students, faculty, and various ensembles, with announcers selected from the student body—a highly innovative move.

Schuman negotiated with the United States Department of State in 1951 to have a film (which was never realized) made about the School. He also worked with the nascent entity of public television by exploring the possibility of making up to thirty films dealing primarily with the Literature and Materials program (also never realized). He established a program for Juilliard performers with the NBC television affiliate in New York entitled *Recital Hall* that featured students and faculty such as the Juilliard String Quartet, Oscar Shumsky, Beveridge Webster, Malcolm Frager, Marcel Grandjany, John Corigliano Sr., Julius Baker, and a recently graduated pianist named John Browning.

However, Schuman's most elaborate effort to make the Juilliard School of Music better-known around the world was an extraordinary tour by the Juilliard Orchestra to Europe encompassing fifty-three days with twenty-five separate concerts performed before approximately 50,000 people. Jean Morel conducted all but six concerts, which were conducted by Frederick Prausnitz.

The tour was initiated through an invitation in the spring of 1957 by Marcel Cuvelier, Secretary-General of the Fédération Internationale des Jeunesses Musicales and also Secretary-General of UNESCO's International Music Council, to perform in the Festival of Youth Orchestras scheduled for the Brussels Exposition (World's Fair) on July 13–21, 1958. (Perhaps not coincidentally, Martha Hill's husband, Thurston Davies, was at the time the head of the United States Pavilion at the Brussels World's Fair.) Schuman seized on the opportunity and quickly set about finding other venues where the orchestra could perform. The International Cultural Exchange Service, a government agency administered by the American National Theatre and Academy (ANTA), supervised the tour from the American side and requested that the ensemble perform in the Balbec Festival in Lebanon as well as concerts in Egypt. Although these Middle Eastern concerts never came to pass, clearly ANTA put a great deal of faith in Juilliard to deliver a high-quality artistic product in America's intense cultural competition with the Soviet Union.

Since the federal government provided funding only for the orchestra's transportation, Schuman had to cobble together financial resources to support this mammoth excursion. As of one month before the tour commenced, a bit over $11,000 had been raised, principally from the Martha Baird Rockefeller Aid to Music Program ($5,000) and the Rodgers and Hammerstein Foundation ($3,000), leaving the venture $3,200 short, this amount to be absorbed by general Juilliard funds.

And what a venture it was. The Juilliard Orchestra performed in England, Belgium, Germany, Denmark, Austria, and Italy in many famous halls, including the Royal Festival Hall (London), the Main Auditorium of the Brussels World Fair, the Great Hall of the Mozarteum (Salzburg). There was also a special live broadcast on Danish state radio. The female personnel of the orchestra were attired in specially designed ensembles created by the legendary fashion designer Vera Maxwell, who "manufactured [the clothes] in her own plant, donating the entire wardrobe." Another financial contribution paid for the men's concert attire.

Bill hated to fly, so in late June 1958 he, Frankie, Tony, and Andie sailed to Europe first-class on the *SS America*. They periodically made contact with the touring Juilliard Orchestra—in London on July 3, at the Brussels Exposition on July 16, and in Rome for the concerts there on August 9 and 10. Otherwise, they experienced a traditional nineteenth-century-style European Grand Tour, with visits to Paris, Amsterdam,

Lucerne, Venice, and San Remo. They returned from Le Havre on the *SS United States* on August 14.

Tony was fourteen and Andie nine at the time of the tour, and they always retained vivid and happy memories of the extraordinary excursion. Not only were they seeing the world outside of New Rochelle for the first time, but they were also able to be with their parents almost constantly, which was quite different from the way they lived back home. Tony recollected the time he and his father attempted to have their camera repaired in Le Touquet. Tony used his best schoolboy French to communicate with the shopkeeper, but it was Dad who saved the day by simply saying, "Mal de Kodak."

Another benefit accrued to Schuman during the trip, because the Philadelphia Orchestra was also touring at this time. Eugene Ormandy programmed Schuman's *Credendum* in Moscow and Leningrad and then at the Brussels Exposition on July 2, two weeks before the arrival of the Juilliard Orchestra.

The trip was also special for Frankie. A few years earlier, in September 1952, Bill had gone to Venice, where he was the American representative at a UNESCO Arts Conference, but Frankie had stayed in New Rochelle. Both parents had been worried about leaving eight-year-old Tony and three-year-old Andie at home. In a candid letter to Leonard Bernstein, Frankie confided, "I am also terribly let-down. I keep thinking about it and coming up with nothing. If Bill is going to be uneasy all the time we're gone, it will not be possible for me to feel secure and enjoy the trip—and if he thinks I'll be in his way, it will lessen his efficiency." Six years later, with the children old enough to travel, the whole family had a memorable time.

The Juilliard Orchestra's repertoire would make any professional orchestra turn collectively pale. Considering the young age of the Juilliard musicians, it seems quite remarkable that they were able to address these major symphonic works without simply coming apart at the seams. Rehearsals were scheduled morning, noon, and night for three weeks prior to the tour departure. The enormity of the repertoire was due to the orchestra having to play at least five concerts in the same venue at the Brussels Fair. Reproduced below is the table listing all the works presented and the number of times each was performed during the tour.

JUILLIARD ORCHESTRA TOUR: REPERTORY

Composer		*Times performed*
Samuel Barber	Second Essay for Orchestra	1
	Overture "The School for Scandal"	6
Ludwig van Beethoven	Overture to "Egmont"	3
	Symphony No. 3 in E-flat ("Eroica")	3
Hector Berlioz	"Le Carneval Romain" Overture	8
Aaron Copland	"Appalachian Spring"	4
Edward Elgar	Variations on an Original Theme ("Enigma")	5
César Franck	Symphony in D Minor	8
Gustav Mahler	Adagietto from Symphony No. 5 in C-sharp Minor	1
Walter Piston	Symphony No. 4	7
Serge Prokofieff	Symphony No. 5	1
Maurice Ravel	"Daphnis et Chloe," Suite No. 2	5
	"La Valse"	5
Ottorino Respighi	"Fountains of Rome"	5
Nicolai Rimsky-Korsakoff	"Tsar Saltan" Suite	2
Robert Schumann	Overture to "Genoveva"	2
William Schuman	"New England Triptych," Three Pieces for Orchestra after William Billings	1
	Symphony for Strings	4
Richard Strauss	"Don Juan," Symphonic Poem	6
Igor Stravinsky	"L'Oiseau de feu"	5
Carl Maria von Weber	Overture to "Der Freischütz"	5

Critical reports in European newspapers were universally admiring. London's *Evening Standard* trumpeted in a headline "Students Play like Masters." The *New Statesman* reported that the technical level of the orchestra was astounding "and should prompt some serious self-appraisal among our own schools: when has anything remotely comparable been heard at either the Royal Academy or the Royal College [London]." France's *La Cité* acclaimed "a world reputation perfectly justified." Declared the *Frankfurter Allgemeine Zeitung*: "Freshness, optimism and vitality . . . the ideal of perfection of American orchestras seems assured with such young reserves, with such vitamin food." And Schuman relished a telling remark from the critic for the *Südwestdeutsche Rundschau*, obviously writing in a country divided by politics and ideology: "These musical messengers from the United States have done more for their country than would ever be possible for politicians. Their great art fashioned a firm bond from human being to human being and from country to country!" The camaraderie and good spirit of the tour lasted for many years amongst the participants, many of whom met for a fiftieth-anniversary reunion in 2008.

Ninety-two players were listed in the orchestra's personnel roster, including eleven former students "who were invited to replace members of the Orchestra who were unable to make the trip." The president of the National Association of Schools of Music (NASM) at the time, the University of Texas's E. William Doty, who was a member of a panel asked to choose the American youth orchestra that would perform in Brussels, questioned before the tour took place whether there were enough registered students at Juilliard to staff a full symphonic orchestra. Implicit in Doty's query was the suspicion that Juilliard would be using ringers to staff the orchestra, thus calling into question its status as a student ensemble.

Although the panel ultimately chose Juilliard for the tour, Schuman insisted that Doty write a letter "which states unequivocally his recognition of having made erroneous statements about the orchestra of the Juilliard School. . . . On the receipt of such letter I will consider the matter closed."

No letter arrived from Doty that satisfied Schuman. Juilliard therefore resigned from the NASM on April 30, 1959, and the resignation was accepted with regret in November. Doty's accusations were clearly offensive to Schuman, but, in retrospect, Schuman seems to have overreacted considering the numerous efforts that the other NASM officers made to quiet the conflict. To this day Juilliard has not rejoined NASM.

With the tour, Schuman and the Juilliard School of Music realized a colossal public-relations coup. The great acclaim garnered by this orchestral tour catapulted Schuman's School to new heights of visibility and celebrity around the world. It was not the orchestra alone, though, that pushed Juilliard into the limelight around this time: the School had a major international achievement with the triumph of Van Cliburn, a Juilliard alumnus, in the first International Tchaikovsky Competition in Moscow in April 1958.

Cliburn's achievement in Moscow was seen as a political triumph as well as an artistic one. It came at the height of the cold war and six months after Sputnik I, the world's first man-made satellite in space, had been successfully launched by the Soviet Union. In an extraordinary moment, a tall young pianist from Kilgore, Texas, had reenergized America's pride and confidence in itself. Senators Lyndon Johnson and William Fulbright read into the Congressional Record the importance of Cliburn's win and he was deluged with appearance offers flowing through Juilliard, including a spot on *The Steve Allen Show* and concerts around the country. Cliburn's beloved teacher, Rosina Lhévinne, was euphoric over the win (though she was momentarily hurt that her star pupil had not contacted her immediately after the contest). He returned to a tumultuous ticker-tape parade in New York usually reserved for victorious soldiers or champion athletes. Never had a classical artist been showered with such adoration.

Juilliard's dean, Mark Schubart, accompanied Cliburn to the competition. In a playful and gossipy letter to Schubart dated April 17, 1958, the president of Juilliard reported to his dean on the reaction back home to Cliburn's triumph:

Dear Mark:

The great advantage that you now enjoy over me is that my letters are dictated and typed by an expert, while yours are written in a semi-conspiratorial manner underneath your trenchcoat on bumpy planes. Still in all, I gather that you feel that you have had the most fantastic experience of your life and that you consider that's saying a good deal. . . .

Just as we must await your return to hear a real accounting of what has taken place so too must we wait to tell you in any reasonably adequate fashion the stir that has been created by Van's triumph. . . . The biggest problem of all, of course, is to keep Rosina on the ground. At the moment she is having a picture taken with her current crop of students for Life Magazine. The room is, of course, the very room in which she taught the great Van Cliburn. Incidentally, can you get any good rates in Europe on the engraving of Van Cliburn plaques. I am planning several for the outside of the building and am even thinking of taking one home to New Rochelle. Now that I have replaced you—temporarily, let me assure you—as Rosina's principal adviser, I can only report that I am having a third telephone put in at home for her exclusive use. Today is one of those typical Juilliard days interspersed with telephone calls from Rosina Lhevinne, the writing of Directors reports, the visits to the office of new-born babes, and lots and lots of other things, but somehow always returning to Van.

. . . Rosina is crushed and I am afraid hurt by the fact that Van has not been in touch with her since the contest.

. . . Everybody suddenly gets the brilliant idea that Van would be a great soloist for Brussels. . . .

Have you decided to take my advice and come home a few days later, traveling by boat? If you do fly home and reach here in time you might want to come to Washington with me on May 5. On May 6 I must appear before a Senate Committee as I wish to speak in opposition to a certain bill having to do with broadcasting and recording. However, I will go down a day before and may speak with Senator Wiley in answer to his request for additional ways in which music can be used as an international weapon. His query was ". . . your reactions as to further ways and means by which we can, through music, help to overcome the barrier of the Iron Curtain, and other barriers throughout the world." I told him in essence of your effective work which resulted in Van Cliburn's triumph and this may be an important wedge in getting our Government to do something.

Schuman had always had an interest in American music education at the primary and secondary levels, although his view of the landscape was always from above. His works for band were often performed by pre-college ensembles, but there is no evidence that Schuman became substantively involved in developing changes in primary- and secondary-school music curricula during his time at Juilliard.

Nevertheless, Schuman had no qualms about aiming some highly focused critical barbs at the American music educational establishment, embodied most prominently in its nationwide organization, the Music

Educators National Conference (MENC). Schuman was invited by the group to address the afternoon general session of the conference on April 17, 1956, during its biennial meeting in St. Louis. This was the first stop on a three-week speaking tour that would take him to the University of Minnesota, the University of Washington, UCLA, and the University of Iowa.

Entitling his talk "The Responsibility of Music Education to Music," Schuman pulled no punches in a speech to the delegates that many must have seen as rhetorical overkill or even downright condescension. Setting the stage for a barrage of criticism, he began, "Because I recognize your shortcomings as well as your noble achievements, I have chosen to be your fond critic. In short, then, do not expect compliments from me."

Schuman presented a litany of concerns about the state of pre-college music education in America that included his belief that most of the music-making in America's schools was mediocre; that music teachers were essentially deficient as musicians and most were not even interested in music; that American music teachers had virtually no interest in new music; and that most music programs used "cheap and tawdry materials in the schools when ample art music exists—both of the past and present—which is not too demanding technically." He made no substantive suggestions to remedy the problems he had highlighted except to state, "My purpose in bringing this situation to your attention is the hope that you will do something about it."

Perhaps in an effort to exit the hall alive, Schuman concluded with a typically charming quip "attributed to Johannes Brahms when leaving a distinguished gathering, 'If there is anyone here I have neglected to insult, I apologize.'" This deliberate broadside on Schuman's part seems mean-spirited. The delegates he was addressing were all practicing music teachers who toiled in a field that often received little financial or moral support from school boards, which frequently squeezed music instruction into the curriculum only under duress.

Considering the take-no-prisoners tone, reaction to Schuman's St. Louis speech was muted and respectful, but it was also voluminous. *Music Educators Journal*, the principal publication of MENC, printed three separate responses in three different issues. One writer acknowledged that some of Schuman's arguments were not new and were possibly even justified, but then questioned, "What, in terms of public education, is meant by an acceptable standard of performance, musical equipment, mediocrity, or contemporary?" Curiously, the article then went on to undercut any future argument on the question of standards by quoting Lord Chesterton, who allegedly said that "everything

Looking south toward the Flatiron Building,
c. 1905. (Photo by George P. Hall.
Collection of The New-York Historical
Society, negative no. 73465.)

Billy with his maternal grandfather,
Louis Heilbrunn, 1913.
(Schuman Family Archives.)

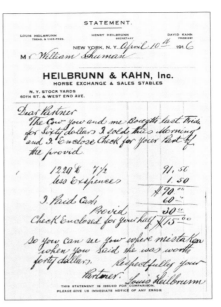

Invoice dated April 10, 1916, from Louis Heilbrunn to Billy for the sale of a cow. (Schuman Family Archives.)

Audrey and Billy, Englewood, New Jersey, 1914. (Schuman Family Archives.)

Robert, Audrey, and Billy, 1919. (Family collection of Judith Israel Gutmann.)

At Camp Cobbossee, c. 1925. Bill is seated
third from left. (Schuman Family Archives.)

Bill at seventeen.
(Photo by Chidnoff.
Schuman Family
Archives.)

In Bellagio, Italy,
fall 1931. *Left to
right:* Ray, Audrey,
Sam, and Bill
Schuman. (Schuman
Family Archives.)

Sheet music for "Lovesick," 1930.
Words by Edward B. Marks Jr.;
music by William H. Schuman.
(Schuman Family Archives.)

Sheet music for "Waitin' for the Moon,"
1932. Words and music by William H.
Schuman. (Schuman Family Archives.)

Aboard a coastal steamer to Virginia Beach on Bill and Frankie's wedding day, March 27, 1936. *Left to right:* Frankie, Ray, Sam, Bill, Gertrude Prince (Frankie's mother), Audrey, Leonard Prince (Frankie's father), and Bert Israel (Audrey's husband). (Schuman Family Archives.)

Schuman teaching a class at Sarah Lawrence College, 1940. (Schuman Family Archives.)

Serge Koussevitzky
(left) and Schuman
after a performance
by the Boston
Symphony Orchestra,
c. October 6, 1944.
(Juilliard School
Archives.)

Frankie and Bill,
November 1944.
(Schuman Family
Archives.)

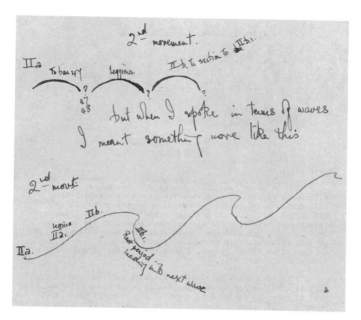

Illustration by Antony Tudor in a letter to Schuman, January 7, 1945.
(Antony Tudor Ballet Trust. Music Division, The New York Public
Library for the Performing Arts, Astor, Lenox and Tilden Foundations.)

Mark Schubart during his tenure as Juilliard's dean, 1949–62.
(Impact Photos, Inc. Juilliard School Archives.)

The Juilliard School, May 1952. *Left to right, standing:* Samuel Barber and Aaron Copland; *seated:* Virgil Thomson, Gian Carlo Menotti, and Schuman. (Photo by John Stewart. Juilliard School Archives.)

The Juilliard String Quartet, 1953. *Left to right:* Raphael Hillyer, Robert Mann, Arthur Winograd, and Robert Koff. (Photo by Balon. Juilliard School Archives.)

that is worth doing is worth doing badly, so long as it represents a joyous effort and remains unpretentious." The writer did show a little gumption when he conceded that charging that the average music educator is not sincerely interested in music "is at once . . . grave and serious." However, other published articles on Schuman's speech were mostly conciliatory. One writer asserted that the talk "stirred up so much thought and discussion [that] is probably an excellent thing for the health of school music."

Schuman was also a critic of requiring music teachers to take courses outside of their field, such as the psychology of education or educational philosophy, in order to obtain teacher certification. In an interview for the *International Musician*, a publication of the American Federation of Musicians, he stated, "If school administrators training teachers once understand that performance and composition constitute the stuff of education, then maybe they'll concentrate on these basic things and cut out 300,000 hours of extrinsic nonsense." Schuman evidently still nurtured a festering resentment of the curriculum he was required to follow at Teachers College in the 1930s. Schuman's comments, coming as they did from the president of a great music conservatory that produced extraordinary performers, reflected the ongoing friction between pre-college music educators and professional musicians.

In late 1955 Schuman had begun to develop a strategy that would solidify Juilliard's position as one of the preeminent schools of its type in New York City, the nation, and around the world and guarantee his legacy as a visionary leader who ensured the School's future excellence: he began the process that would bring Juilliard to Lincoln Center. Schuman reported to his board that during the summer of 1955 Dean Schubart and he had been meeting with Edgar B. Young in the offices of John D. Rockefeller 3rd to explore how "musical training" could be incorporated in a new Center for the Performing Arts in New York City and how Juilliard could be part of that process.

Schuman claimed that he himself had first raised the idea of Juilliard's being at Lincoln Center: "I brought the idea to them, because I knew they wanted to have an educational arm at Lincoln Center but they were considering a university. . . . I said 'You have to have a professional school, and you have to have the leading professional school, and that's Juilliard.'"

By early spring of 1956 considerable detail had been added to the newly proposed arts center at Lincoln Square, located on Broadway between 62nd and 66th Streets. Robert Moses, in his role as chairman of New York City's Slum Clearance Committee, had "ordained" that "the scythe of progress must move north" after completing the previous slum clearance project at what was then called the New York Coliseum below West 60th Street. "It was New York City's biggest Title I project, covering 53 acres as originally planned."* The clearance was the city's most complicated, but the heart of the program was the creation of Lincoln Center, which would eventually gentrify the clearance area.

Both Schuman and the Lincoln Center committee were quick to point out that should Juilliard become part of the arts complex, the School would continue to function as an autonomous unit, eventually to be termed a constituent. Rockefeller's exploratory committee, which developed the arts-complex concept, advised Schuman that any "educational facilities included in Lincoln Square would be limited to the *highest professional plane*" (emphasis added). It was to be termed "Advanced Study," meaning that in all likelihood Juilliard would have to discontinue its preparatory and extension programs. In 1956 the School had 635 students enrolled in the regular division, 571 in the preparatory department, and 159 in the extension department. The loss of approximately 730 paying (albeit part-time) students was not an insignificant financial issue for Juilliard.

Therefore, Schuman proposed a future downsizing of Juilliard to 400 students, including 50 exceptionally gifted students of elementary- and high-school age. He contended that only two departments would be significantly affected by the move downtown: the piano department would be reduced from 199 students to 90, and the voice department, from 128 singers to 80. Although the Juilliard building at Lincoln Center would be eventually designed for a student population of 400, the enrollment for the School never dropped that low; the School had to enroll many more students than that in order to create a critical mass of musicians to perform the various symphonic and chamber music concerts, operas, and dance concerts that were part of the Juilliard tradition. In addition, the School could not absorb the precipitous drop in tuition dollars that would ensue from lower enrollment, which amounted to an annual figure of $300,000 in 1957. A residence hall was also planned for the new Juilliard building, a goal that was realized only in 1990, twenty-one years after the move from Claremont Avenue.

Rockefeller's committee also discussed having professional education in both dance *and* drama taught by Juilliard at Lincoln Center. Assuming

---

* The Title I projects were generated by the federal Urban Renewal or Slum Clearance Program of 1949, intended to provide affordable housing for the poor. Unfortunately, the programs tended to destroy established neighborhoods, displacing thousands of families.

that Juilliard would receive a subsidy to support a new drama division, Schuman wrote in 1956:

> It is the President's conviction that a single school embracing the fields of music, dance, and drama would be desirable not only from the economic point of view but, more importantly, because of the inter-relationships of these fields and the enrichment to students working in close artistic collaboration with allied arts.

Juilliard's board was not particularly quick to embrace this complex and problematic initiative. After all, the School's budget was comparatively stable, its physical plant had been progressively refurbished annually, and its reputation could not be higher. But Schuman was a visionary, and he understood that the educational institution based in this new arts center in the heart of New York City would have all the resources to be the preeminent school of its type in the nation and perhaps the world. Schuman concluded in his board report that concentrating on a smaller school that would support the most gifted young performing artists was the direction to take for the future: "There does not exist a single music school in the United States today which caters to the needs of only the most highly talented young musicians and provides this select group with a broad education in music and academic studies." He believed Juilliard had to be that school.

Years later, Schuman recalled: "They [the board] didn't quite see it the way I saw it, as an opportunity for the School. But eventually they came around." However subdued Schuman was in his recollection of his efforts to bring the board around to his thinking, it seems highly likely, considering the conservative fiduciary views of a board composed mostly of lawyers, that it took a great deal of persuasion to convince them of the importance of this venture. That the board eventually supported this momentous change is evidence of its confidence in and respect for its president.

The road to Lincoln Center for Schuman and Juilliard was not as smooth as initially anticipated. By the fall of 1956 Juilliard's place as the educational entity at the Center was being evaluated by Charles Dollard, former president of the Carnegie Corporation of New York, who had been appointed by Rockefeller to research this important issue. In subsequent meetings with Rockefeller and his colleagues in late 1956, the original concept of an educational program only for "advanced study" now had Schuman suggesting to his board that the best enrollment number for Juilliard at Lincoln Center was 200. In addition, Schuman also tried to persuade the board that the School could meet the costs of the move by assuming that additional income would be available through the Juilliard Musical Foundation from the sale of the old Juilliard building at 122nd Street.

Furthermore, he claimed that they could "reduce present expenditures for building maintenance and general administrative services." This was either a desperate attempt to convince his board members that the School could remain solvent or the result of a catastrophically incorrect analysis from the Lincoln Center architects and engineers. In fact, the eventual annual cost of running the new Juilliard building was approximately three to four times that of the old building.

A major impediment to Schuman's plan to bring Juilliard to Lincoln Center surfaced some time between December 1956 and February 1957 when Rockefeller and his advisors told the president that Juilliard's focus might be too narrow to allow an alliance with the precepts of the new arts center. In fact, Young, Rockefeller's right-hand man in these matters, had been having parallel discussions with Columbia University regarding its interest in bringing a performing arts education program to the Center. However, according to Jack Beeson, a faculty member of Columbia's music department from 1945 to 1995 (and its chair from 1968 to 1972), Douglas Moore, a distinguished composer and the chairman of the department in 1956, believed that Columbia was not the right institution for Lincoln Center and eventually told Rockefeller he could not accept the invitation: "Rockefeller spoke to Douglas Moore about [Columbia] being the music education portion of Lincoln Center. Moore was negative because, although they had a small and robust graduate program, the undergraduates were not performers, and they wouldn't want to travel down to 65th Street to take classes at Lincoln Center." Beeson also remembered that he told Schuman several years later at a bar that "Juilliard was the second choice [for Lincoln Center], and Bill bristled and said, 'I don't believe you.'"

In fact, Schuman *was* told that Juilliard would not be the educational institution at Lincoln Center. At the end of a dinner party in the fall of 1956 at John D. Rockefeller 3rd's residence at Beekman Place, after the ladies and gentlemen had been separated in nineteenth-century fashion for coffee and, in the case of the men, cigars, Schuman was told by David Keiser, then president of the New York Philharmonic, a member of Juilliard's board of directors, and a trustee of the Juilliard Musical Foundation, who would eventually become Juilliard's board chairman in 1971, "I am sorry, Bill, but we just can't take the School." Schuman responded, "I am very disappointed, and I think you are making an enormous mistake because no other school has the accomplishment to look to that Juilliard has."

The choice of Columbia University's music department as the educational constituent of Lincoln Center would have been a wrongheaded one, for its main focus was historical musicology, not performance. Perhaps Rockefeller and his colleagues felt more comfortable inviting an established Ivy League institution to participate in their new venture, as opposed to a music school that focused only on performance. In any event, Columbia's lack of interest made the issue moot.

In the end, Juilliard was invited to become the educational component of Lincoln Center for the Performing Arts, joining the Metropolitan Opera Association and the New York Philharmonic-Symphony Society as charter members of this revolutionary new venture. The official announcement of the agreement appeared on February 7, 1957. Schuman informed the School's faculty and administrative staff on the evening of February 5 and the students the next day.

The faculty meeting announcing this momentous and historic decision was called for 5:00 P.M. and lasted an hour. Schuman, speaking in precise, clipped tones, began by providing some history behind the decision to move Juilliard to Lincoln Center. He then presented the two basic issues entailed by the move. The School would become an institution of "advanced training" at Lincoln Center, and a drama program would be added to Juilliard's music and dance programs. Schuman had been assured, he said, that Lincoln Center would provide financial support for both the dance and drama divisions (a promise that was only partially kept). In addition, the move might happen as early as the 1960–61 academic year, although the opening might be extended to 1962–63. As it turned out, that prediction was off by several years: the new Juilliard building opened on October 26, 1969. Schuman also restated his belief that the new building would be more economical to operate, therefore freeing money to put toward programming and scholarship assistance to ensure that "no student [would be] denied a Juilliard education due to financial problems."

The faculty had a number of questions for Schuman, most of them focused on the elimination of the preparatory department and the significant reduction in enrollment. Schuman attempted to defuse the preparatory-department issue by noting that efforts were under way to transfer it to another institution. He admitted that these decisions were "painful," but then went on to say that the planned move was predicated on the need for Juilliard to show how it

> can help the arts in America. . . . Juilliard never lacked the courage to move and to change. We've never hesitated to make moves for the best interest of the arts we love so well. . . . We respect the academic life but we don't respect academic bookkeeping. We're interested in talent. . . . We look for students who can become leading practitioners in the arts.

The question-and-answer session was sedate, considering the monumental changes that were proposed for Juilliard and the concomitant job losses that would most likely come from the downsizing. One questioner asked why Juilliard had agreed to embrace the concept of "advanced training." Schuman responded, "By backing the horses that we think are going to win and by giving them all our resources, those will be most likely to succeed. . . . By keeping the other divisions we dilute our energies and resources."

The faculty's worries about how to deal with a much smaller student population turned out to be unfounded: the enrollment in 1969 was roughly the same as in 1957, and the School actually *increased* in size during the early Lincoln Center years. The loss of the preparatory department became a non-issue with the creation of a pre-college division at Lincoln Center. It was also clear that in early 1957 the design of the new Juilliard building had not even begun; Schuman said he was not yet sure whether Juilliard would have its own performance hall or use the performance venues of the new arts center. The excitement and deep concerns generated by Schuman's announcement of the move reverberated for many years throughout Juilliard.

Rockefeller issued a press release in which he emphasized that Juilliard's move was a "milestone of major importance in the development of the Center," and Schuman rejoiced that education had become an integral part of the Lincoln Center concept:

> The interrelated activities in music, drama and dance, within a single professional school, will provide broad experience for the young performers and creative artists who will make up the student body. . . . Clearly, the School must develop in its students technical prowess to the highest possible degree, but it will also continue to direct the

student to a consideration of his art in terms of its broad cultural implications and responsibilities.

Another, seemingly unrelated issue was added to the mix about two years after the announcement when Schuman, in a speech at the High School of Music and Art on December 11, 1958, commemorating the birthday of the late Mayor Fiorello H. LaGuardia, suggested the merger of Music and Art High School, located at 135th Street and Convent Avenue (about 2,000 students), with the smaller High School of Performing Arts, at 120 West 46th Street (600 students). The newly merged high schools would be housed in a new building where the High School of Commerce stood, just west of the Juilliard School site on 65th Street.

Schuman's ultimate goal was for the discontinued Juilliard preparatory department of about 600 students to be the core of the student body of the new high school, tentatively to be called the Community School for Music, Drama and Dance. Juilliard could continue its work with pre–college age students and still comply with the regulations handed down by Lincoln Center to provide only "training of advanced students."

As noted earlier, Juilliard eventually ignored the Lincoln Center proviso and created a pre-college division. However, Schuman's idea of the merger of two arts high schools became a reality. Located on the southwest corner of 65th Street and Amsterdam Avenue (but with no formal relationship to the Juilliard School), the Fiorello H. LaGuardia High School of Music & Art and Performing Arts opened in 1984.

The members of the Juilliard board at the time who supported the historic decision to move to Lincoln Center were, besides Schuman himself, Franklin B. Benkard, Henry S. Drinker, John W. Drye Jr., Edward Johnson, David M. Keiser, Charles M. Spofford, James P. Warburg (chairman), and Edward R. Wardwell. The trustees of the Juilliard Musical Foundation, the source of all the School's endowment income at the time, were Drye (president), William S. Gray, Randolph C. Harrison, Robert A. Jones, Keiser, William L. Kleitz, and Spofford. The School would now be known simply as the Juilliard School.

Important grants were set in place as well to smooth Juilliard's transition to its new home, including a gift of $500,000 from the Carnegie Corporation of New York to "provide scholarships and other assistance to young artists in launching their professional careers."

The official groundbreaking ceremony for Lincoln Center for the Performing Arts took place on May 14, 1959, with President Dwight D.

Eisenhower in attendance. An enormous tent was erected to shield the performers from the elements. Leonard Bernstein was the master of ceremonies, with Leonard Warren singing the Prologue from *I Pagliacci*; Risë Stevens performing the Habañera from *Carmen*; and Bernstein conducting the New York Philharmonic in the *Egmont Overture*, the Hallelujah Chorus from *Messiah*, and John Philip Sousa's *Semper Fidelis* march. The speakers included Eisenhower, John D. Rockefeller 3rd, Robert Moses, Mayor Robert F. Wagner, and New York's lieutenant governor, Malcolm Wilson.

Representing Lincoln Center's constituent organizations were Schuman; Rudolf Bing of the Metropolitan Opera; George E. Judd Jr., of the New York Philharmonic; and Alfred Reginald Allen, director of operations for Lincoln Center. In an official photo, Schuman is shown smiling and Bing is looking glumly aside, reflecting the two men's future relationship. Eisenhower thanked the performing artists and then quipped, "If they can do this under a tent, why the square?"

As the Lincoln Center move loomed, Schuman's life at Juilliard became filled with the details of bringing the School to its new home. Schuman needed to negotiate a myriad of issues—financial, logistical, and governance—having to do with the project, but his final educational and artistic initiative as Juilliard's president was the creation of a drama division for the School.

By the winter of 1958 Schuman set about to meet with national leaders and to visit campuses across the country, not only to inspect various physical plants, but also to explore how drama was taught in America at the time. He had a good working knowledge of the art of dance, but he was less knowledgeable about drama (even though he was a great devotee of New York theater).

Schuman quickly found his primary drama advisor in the distinguished French director and educator Michel Saint-Denis, who was then the directeur général of the Centre Dramatique de l'Est in Strasbourg, France, and who had already met with John D. Rockefeller 3rd while Rockefeller was on an earlier fact-finding tour of Europe. Lee Strasberg, of the Actors Studio was also seriously considered to shape the Juilliard drama program, "but in the end we prevailed with a broader view, which St. Denis represented," said Schuman.

The Rockefeller Foundation provided a grant of about $5,000 to bring Saint-Denis to Juilliard from March through May 1958 to visit theater teaching centers in the United States and Canada and to lecture at Harvard's

American Shakespeare Festival Theatre. Schuman found Saint-Denis to be an extraordinary person, and much of his early enthusiasm for the new dramatic advisor had to do with Saint-Denis's nationality and his own love of many aspects of French culture, first expressed during his stay with Frankie in Talloires in the summer of 1937. Many years later Schuman would say:

> Anything you can say about the French, you're describing Michel St. Denis. . . . All the good things that are French I think he embodied. . . . He loved good food, he loved complicated abstractions, and he loved style—not in a superficial sense, of fashion, but real style in the sense of what's germane to a cultural projection at any given point in history.

By the fall of 1958 Saint-Denis's position was expanded, and he was given the title of chief consultant in planning the drama division. For six months, beginning in January 1959, Saint-Denis would work with the architect for the Juilliard building, Pietro Belluschi (dean of the School of Architecture and Planning at the Massachusetts Institute of Technology), on the design of the elements of the building related to drama, continue to study other drama programs around the country, and work to devise a budget.

Saint-Denis's fee was not to exceed $15,000, and it was with this comparatively small amount of money that a protracted series of negotiations began over how drama would be funded at Juilliard. Schuman had requested that Saint-Denis's fee be funded by Lincoln Center, but Rockefeller responded that "the Lincoln Center did not wish, as a matter of principle, to underwrite the expenses of constituent organizations." Finally, owing to what Rockefeller called Juilliard's "special problems" in bringing drama to the School, he agreed to split Saint-Denis's costs, with Juilliard board members Drye, Spofford, and Warburg supporting the other half. However, Schuman's concern went beyond the consulting fee, for it was his understanding that Lincoln Center would help subsidize the cost of the new drama division. This issue eventually caused great strain between Schuman, as the president of Lincoln Center, and his successor at Juilliard, Peter Mennin. John W. Drye, Juilliard's representative on the Lincoln Center board, reinforced Schuman's position in the spring of 1960.

The issue came to a head in April 1960 with an exchange of letters between Schuman, Rockefeller, and Drye. Schuman began by requesting in a letter to Rockefeller dated April 22, 1960, that Lincoln Center support the entire fee of $15,000 to pay for the Saint-Denis consultancy:

It is of utmost importance that Mr. Saint-Denis be brought back to the United States again next season. . . . As you know, we have all been most encouraged by the cordial and highly fruitful relationship which has developed between Saint-Denis and Robert Whitehead, and, more recently, Elia Kazan. Bob Whitehead feels that it would be desirable to have the initial phase of the drama training begin in the fall of 1961, so that Juilliard's Drama Division will be functioning by the time the repertory theatre begins operation in the season 1962–63.

Kazan and Whitehead represented the new leadership team of the Lincoln Center Theater, which began presenting plays in January 1964 as the Repertory Theater of Lincoln Center in a temporary building in Washington Square while a permanent home was under construction. The Vivian Beaumont Theater opened on October 21, 1965, and the Juilliard drama division finally opened in September 1968 in the International House across Claremont Avenue from the Juilliard School of Music building.

In a typically diplomatic yet emphatic letter, Rockefeller responded not to Schuman, but to Drye, on April 28, 1960, keeping the hierarchy intact of board member communicating to a peer, not to a staff person. Rockefeller recalled that the inclusion of a drama division for Juilliard at Lincoln Center was important to both institutions, "in other words, that the inclusion of Drama was not a concession on the part of the School to Lincoln Center." He conceded, however, that because the Juilliard Musical Foundation under the terms of Augustus Juilliard's will could fund only music studies, it was understood that new money needed to be found to support drama.

Rockefeller then made Lincoln Center's position clear on who would be responsible for what in the new arts complex:

My purpose in reviewing this background is in no way to attempt to relieve Lincoln Center from any responsibility concerning the Drama unit which it has under our agreement, but rather to stress once more the joint interest we have in it, and hence the joint effort which I feel we should make in connection with its financing. To me, if I may speak frankly, there is somewhat of a tendency on the part of the Juilliard School to approach the matter on the basis that they will be glad to accept and to run the Drama unit if Lincoln Center will assume all responsibilities as to the financing—both initial capital costs, as well as operational requirements. Because of the nature of

Lincoln Center and its relationship to its constituents, I feel it is quite reasonable for Lincoln Center to assume full responsibility for the capital needs. But, at the same time, I feel it is quite reasonable for us to consider that we are partners working towards the acquisition of the necessary funds for meeting the operational needs. It may well be that it is desirable for Lincoln Center to take the lead, but I do feel that the School has a responsibility to actively co-operate. . . . In any event, it would seem to me somewhat of a step backward if at this point Lincoln Center should take over the full payment of Mr. Saint-Denis salary. Having said this let me hasten to add that I was very pleased to see that the School was paying the full cost of the consultant in the field of the Dance.

After absorbing Rockefeller's decision, Schuman reminded his board of what the basic agreement was between Juilliard and Lincoln Center, dating back to Schuman's report to the board on December 7, 1956:

DRAMA AND DANCE The School's position in regard to education in the sister arts of drama and dance has remained unchanged during the periods of study and discussion of the Lincoln Center. It may be summarized as follows:

1. As a school of music, Juilliard has no obligation to embrace either the field of drama or that of dance. If separate facilities for a comprehensive education in the field of dance were established at the Center, and Juilliard were part of the Center, there would then be no reason for Juilliard to continue its present Department of Dance.

2. If Juilliard were asked by Mr. Rockefeller's Committee to expand its activities to include drama, dance, and the techniques of stage production, it would be willing to assume such responsibility, given requisite financial support.

In a letter to Maxwell D. Taylor, the president of Lincoln Center, Schuman presented anticipated deficits for a drama division in the 1964–65 academic year of $338,500 and for a dance division, of $204,000—gargantuan sums at the time.

Through most of the 1960–61 academic year, Schuman and his board negotiated both with Rockefeller and the Lincoln Center board, as well as with Whitehead and Kazan at Lincoln Center Theater. Curiously, the leadership of the Repertory Theater (as it was then called) had claimed that it was the theater, and not Juilliard, that had the responsibility for drama education at Lincoln Center. Schuman recalled:

> At one time they [Lincoln Center officials] wanted to have the drama division [Lincoln Center Theater] take on the education department of the Juilliard, and I objected to that strongly because I felt that Whitehead and Kazan were the heads of the Drama Theater, and even though they were splendid men, they had a professional view of how to run a theater without an educational view, which was very broad in concept. I didn't agree with that policy. . . . [It would be like] the Philharmonic [running] the Juilliard School. . . . It interfered with the primacy of the individual constituents.

In a strongly worded letter dated March 9, 1961, Schuman castigated Whitehead for reopening issues that had already been resolved:

> Adoption of your proposals for the structure and responsibility for the drama training program would preclude the autonomy of Juilliard as a constituent unit of Lincoln Center. Under your plan, other than providing clerical help and physical space, Juilliard would have little if any role in the school, and this arrangement is not acceptable to me, and, I am certain, would not be to my colleagues on the Juilliard Board.

This issue was resolved in June 1961, with the theater agreeing to defer to Juilliard in the area of drama education.

In addition, the Center's Committee on Education and Creative Artistic Advancement had developed a draft resolution on May 8, 1961, that was passed the next month. It authorized a grant of $1 million from Lincoln Center to Juilliard in support of a proposed drama program at the School. The grant clearly stated that this was the "maximum obligation of Lincoln Center to the Juilliard School for this purpose through the academic year ending June, 1966." However, an additional $1.5 million would be given to Juilliard for the drama program's continuation beyond 1966. The purpose of this second grant was "to provide a reasonable basis for the long-term planning of the Juilliard training program and to permit flexibility with respect to the use of Lincoln Center funds."

Lincoln Center made clear in the resolution that it had no responsibility to support drama at Juilliard beyond the promised $2.5 million. Although Schuman was appreciative of the Center's largesse and assumed that the Center and Juilliard would together attempt to raise more funds for the drama division, he told his board that "there is the possibility in this situation of creating a program for which no clear financial responsibility is established. *This problem needs resolution*" (emphasis added).

As Schuman's tenure as Juilliard's president drew to a close, he attempted to lock in Saint-Denis as the first director of the drama division for a period of at least two years. An associate director, specifically an American, would also be appointed and eventually succeed Saint-Denis. However, in the early winter of 1962 Saint-Denis turned down the offer, claiming that age (he was sixty-five) and long-term health problems prevented him from taking on such a large assignment. Instead, he accepted the position of general artistic advisor to the Royal Shakespeare Theatres in England, allowing him to stay closer to France and to continue his position there as inspector general of the French national theaters. Saint-Denis also disagreed with Schuman about the granting of academic degrees to young artists; as Schuman recalled his saying, "Giving that artist—I'm paraphrasing now—[a degree] was a bourgeois escape route."

It should also be noted that Saint-Denis's relationship with Whitehead and Kazan had soured considerably since their first meetings, primarily because of the theater's desire to create, beginning in the fall of 1962, its own training program for about thirty young actors, "some of whom will be selected to become members of the professional company when the Repertory Theatre opens in the season 1963–64," a scenario that was never fully realized. Theoretically, when Juilliard started its own drama program, the Repertory Theater training program would merge with Juilliard for the School to administer in the future. Saint-Denis did agree to serve as a consultant for the Juilliard drama division for short periods of time, as he eventually did in the mid to late 1960s in cooperation with John Houseman, who was appointed the first director of the division by Peter Mennin.

Schuman reminisced:

My successor, Peter Mennin, was not a great enthusiast about drama, and Houseman, according to his written testimony, his books, didn't feel he was getting the support that he should have had, and eventually left. I was disappointed, because I wanted the school to form a Juilliard Acting Company, the same as the Juilliard String

Quartet, and Peter didn't seem to cotton to that idea and eventually it became a separate company—The Acting Company. My wife, incidentally, formed the Board for them.

Remarkably, during this intense period of profoundly transformative change at Juilliard, Schuman lived another life as a composer. Juilliard provided an environment in which his musical imagination was allowed to flourish. To understand the man, one has also to comprehend his music. In his time at Juilliard, Schuman grew as an educational leader and an artistic force in America. His music of the same period mirrored the creativity and energy that was his lifelong hallmark.

CHAPTER 7

A Four-Minute Musical Essay on Fear

During the sixteen years that William Schuman headed the Juilliard School of Music, his artistic life as a composer continued to flourish. Schuman said on numerous occasions that he truly did not want his compositions regularly played at Juilliard. In many ways, Schuman saw his compositional life as distinct from his administrative life, and he enjoyed jumping back and forth, each activity feeding his desire for the other. On a few occasions during his tenure at both Juilliard and Lincoln Center, a supportive board member would advise Schuman that he should not feel a responsibility to compose when he was so busy running the school or the arts center. Schuman would always recount these anecdotes with a tone of exasperation. He did not compose, he explained, to achieve public or professional adulation, but only because he absolutely *had* to write music. Asking him to stop composing would be tantamount to asking him to stop breathing.

Schuman was an extremely disciplined person by nature. He therefore worked out a rigorous annual schedule of composition that set out a precise number of hours per year that he would devote to his art:

> I had determined that if I were able to devote between 800 and 1000 hours a year to composition, I would be able to write as much as I wished. I kept a diary detailing the number of hours I spent writing each day. It worked well: if I had no early appointments, for example, I would start writing first thing in the morning, at home, and go into the office later.

However, Schuman enjoyed procrastinating just as much as anyone else, admitting that with his composing, "it's always easier to do something else. Even if I am in the middle of a piece, I'll take any excuse not to do it, and I have to drive myself in composition."

Schuman focused on one piece from start to finish, much to the surprise of his colleague and friend Aaron Copland. According to Schuman, Copland would not approach a piece chronologically; that is, he often would jump from one section to another earlier or later in the developing work. Schuman, by contrast, primarily wrote a new work from beginning to end. Copland once asked Schuman, "Don't you sometimes find that there's a spot there where you wanted to accomplish something, and you put it aside to write the ending?" Replied Schuman, "I've never done that."

The administrative demands put upon Schuman from 1945 to 1968 did impinge on the number of compositions that he created, especially during his Lincoln Center presidency. The quantity of his compositions was in line with his philosophy of musical creativity. Referring to Paul Hindemith and Darius Milhaud as two composers who needed to write many hundreds of pages in order to realize their best works, Schuman also commented on Johann Sebastian Bach's total oeuvre as a mix: "I would say that 50% of it is wonderfully made, routine music of not great appeal, 25% is excellent, and 25% is of such astonishing beauty and depth of creative ability that you can find no way of explaining it."

In turn, Schuman admired the work of Copland but added that "quantitatively . . . it was not an amazing output." He drily observed that "the only writers who were always at their best were second-rate writers."

Although Schuman would regularly jot down musical ideas, his compositional approach was to start with a blank page and explore what would evolve from an initial musical idea: "I write consecutively. I rarely have [a] kind of bigger plan in mind, unless it's someplace in the back of my head. Rarely, only rarely." Another time he explained:

> The work proceeds because the creative mind is at work and the creative mind then begins to invent the beginning of a piece, and the creative mind, whether consciously or not consciously, is absolutely certain as to the tonal ambience and the emotional ambience of what's taking place. . . . You can't start a composition that starts with chaos. . . . Many composers do not feel this way, but I have to be absolutely certain of what I'm saying emotionally. . . . I don't find any satisfaction in music that intrigues me intellectually but doesn't reach me [emotionally].

In line with Schuman's compositional approach of writing "consecutively," he would also closely monitor the tempo markings of his work: "I am terribly conscious always of tempo . . . so much so that I sometimes keep a metronome going for an hour. I love to think against the pulse. . . . It's madness; it's a crazy thing to do. . . . And sometimes if I am writing a *larghissimo* I might have the pulse twice the speed or four times the speed." In many of his works he sets the tempo at the slowest possible mark on the metronome (quarter note = 40 beats per minute), which is a serious challenge for any performer. The Largo beginning of the withdrawn Second Symphony in fact caused numerous problems for performers and listeners alike owing to its extremely slow beginning tempo (half note = 30). In contrast, he also asked his performers to play at fast tempi that clearly challenged their technical abilities, as in the third movement of the Symphony for Strings, marked Presto (half note = 184).

Schuman purportedly composed in full score, a logical move given that the orchestrations of his larger works are often driven by the individual orchestral voices for which they are scored. Nathan Broder once commented on this approach:

> He [Schuman] does not write down his music and then orchestrate it, but composes directly in full score. (For this reason piano reductions of his orchestral music are even more than normally inadequate.) His orchestral colors are usually fresh and sharp, bold and clear, a favorite method being to treat the three main choirs— strings, wood-winds, and brasses—as separate blocks of color.

Schuman saw the creative musical process as closely linked to the development of literary works:

> I think the closest analogy I could make to writing a symphony is the writing of a novel. A novel is an extended work, which means an extended form, using characters invented by the author. . . . In music, I think the composer invents the characters or the situation, and he can develop that situation in any number of ways. The listener . . . must be convinced (intuitively if not consciously) that it all rings true, that these characters are there. Like a novel, the symphony is a complex situation, with multiple characters, and they interact one with each other and they produce the whole. How you get there is the art of composition itself.

From his earliest compositions to those written beyond his Juilliard years, Schuman's music was frequently characterized as "muscular" or "athletic," with an energy linked to the hustle and bustle of his native New York City and the youthful enthusiasm of twentieth-century America. In fact, the American composer Douglas Moore, best known for his opera *The Ballad of Baby Doe*, derisively referred to Schuman's work as "gymnasium music."

However, Schuman's compositions also possessed a profoundly introspective quality that as he matured seemed to become more and more integral to his oeuvre:

> In some recent performances, I was sorry to hear . . . part[s] rushed, when what I wanted was an oceanic calm. I suppose that so much of the . . . music was "muscular" that some performers felt I didn't want this side of my nature revealed in music. Frankie has always pointed out to me that I have lots of slow and very introspective music, which I hadn't realized.

Throughout Schuman's lifetime as a composer he was very fortunate to have his music performed by some of the finest musicians and ensembles, and he understood exceedingly well that the eventual impact of a new work, and what would enable the listener to engage with it, would ultimately be in the hands of the performer:

> A composer has both the advantage and the disadvantage of being revealed through a second party, namely the performer. . . . I would always prefer to have a very imaginative, interpretive artist, even though there are some distortions, provided they were deeply felt distortions, than I would have someone who would give a literal account and not bring anything to it. The older Bernstein got, the more liberties he took, and one can only be thankful for the excesses that were his. . . . Bernstein never distorted, although he did "Mahlerize" lots of performances in his later years. . . . I've had experiences where I have felt absolutely raped by some very well known performers, but that's a very rare occurrence. What was not so rare were mediocre performances.

Schuman's visibility and credibility as a composer were considerably heightened by two articles that appeared in prestigious scholarly journals in late 1944 and early 1945. Written by, respectively, Alfred Frankenstein and Nathan Broder, they were highly perceptive as well as very complimentary of the thirty-four-year-old composer's work.

Frankenstein's piece begins with two celebratory paragraphs:

> The evidence is accumulating on all sides and the conclusion is inevitable: William Schuman has caught the boat.
>
> In a certain, clearly apparent way, his recent commissions from Billy Rose for *The Seven Lively Arts and Henry VIII* might be regarded as the most important recognition Schuman has yet received. A man can win two Guggenheim fellowships, the annual award of the New York Music Critics' Circle, the Pulitzer Prize and a grant-in-aid from the Metropolitan Opera, all of which Schuman has done, and still not make much of a dent in the general consciousness of the citizenry. But if a Billy Rose show goes over, then he is definitely in with his fellow men.

Although the Rose venture was not a success for Schuman, Frankenstein is on the mark in his analysis of the composer's music, pointing out that "Schuman's choral music is more diatonic than his composition in other fields" and that his symphonic works are characterized by "ostinato rhythms and extended melodic lines." Frankenstein also emphasizes the spirit of Schuman's music:

> "Enthusiasm" is the word for Schuman, and his faults are the faults of enthusiasm. . . .
>
> Schuman's big instrumental pieces employ a far freer, subtler, more intricate and kaleidoscopically shifting tonal plan than his choral works. Here he is closer to Roy Harris. . . . Although he has much more rhythmic fire, variety and vivacity than Harris.

Broder's article dwells in greater depth on the technical aspects of Schuman's music up to that time. He observes that "despite its frequent irregularity and use of intervals commonly regarded as angular, his melody is all-pervasive and basically vocal." Furthermore,

Schuman's music in predominantly linear. The melodies are often combined in a contrapuntal texture that employs the time-honored devices of imitation, augmentation, diminution, and so on. The resulting harmonies are usually dissonant, by text-book standards. In the period from about 1937 to about 1941 Schuman was so fond of parallel fourths and fifths that their use became a mannerism. The later music employs such progressions less and less.

He also points to Schuman's frequent use of polychords as a harmonic device, as in the composer's slow movement of the Symphony for Strings.

More subjectively, he remarks that Schuman's music has as its most prominent traits "boldness, originality, freshness, resourcefulness, and intensity of feeling. The fast movements are full of an exuberant energy. There is little of what the average listener would be inclined to regard as grace or charm, but humor may be found." His penultimate reflection is an encomium of particular grace: "But what strikes the unbiased listener most of all in this music is its complete honesty and integrity, its deep seriousness—even at its gayest—, its unswerving fidelity to the highest aims. Schuman can be light and unpretentious but he is seldom trivial." Broder concludes, "His almost complete freedom from any recognizable influence of older composers is probably due to the strength and independence of his mind and to his having begun serious composition relatively late." Such a laudatory and perceptive analysis of Schuman's music stands out as a generous accolade for the young composer.

During Schuman's Juilliard years his music was interpreted through dance in his collaborations with two great choreographers of the twentieth century: Antony Tudor and Martha Graham. Schuman seemed to be attracted to modern dance in particular, perhaps because of his early memories of attending performances by avant-garde dance troupes at Columbia University with his parents. It is not by chance that one of his first works, written in 1934 (though later withdrawn), was entitled *Choreographic Poem for Seven Instruments.*

In 1944, his last year at Sarah Lawrence, Schuman received a telegram from Tudor proposing a collaboration. The British Tudor was respected in the United States for his complex, somber, and highly intellectualized movements on stage and for his piercing psychological insights in such works as *Jardin aux lilas* (1936, danced to Ernest Chausson's *Poème for Violin and Orchestra*); *Dark*

Elegies (1937, danced to Gustav Mahler's *Kindertotenlieder*); and *Pillar of Fire* (1942, danced to Arnold Schoenberg's *Verklärte Nacht*). Schuman recalled:

> I knew relatively little about him because I had been brought up on modern dance. That, as it turned out, was what he liked about me. He knew I was unfamiliar with ballet, and he thought this would be a very fresh idea. Tudor had never worked with a composer before. He did me the great honor of making me the first composer he ever commissioned, and also conferred upon me the dubious distinction of having been the last.

This collaboration between choreographer and composer is historically important because, as Schuman explained, he was the only composer to work with Tudor in creating a new ballet. All of Tudor's other creations were based on existing music. In addition, because Tudor was known as a "psychological choreographer," the correspondence between him and Schuman focuses a bright light on Tudor's thought process in developing a new work.

Although Tudor did not tell Schuman anything specific about the story line of the ballet or even its title in his detailed correspondence, he was quite explicit as to what he wanted in the music. Schuman recalled Tudor saying:

> "I need music which would be appropriate for a city in central Europe on a very misty night. You are taking a walk and the palms of your hands are moist. After you turn a corner, you look behind you before you proceed. This mood opens this work, and proceeds, atmospherically, with no melody, just sounds, interrupted by sudden outbursts, lasting for a second or two, going away, and occurring a little more frequently, reaching a climax. Then the most beautiful music, the most beautiful melody you could possibly write, which goes on for a while." For the last part, he said, "Can you write me a four-minute musical essay on fear?"

At the time Tudor was touring the United States with Ballet Theatre, so he communicated the details of the ballet primarily through Western Union telegrams, letters, and telephone calls. Tudor's writings to Schuman, sent from California, Missouri, Philadelphia, and New York, are remarkable for their imagination and elegant language, as well as for their psychological asides and jabs, devised to either motivate or intimidate the composer.

In Tudor's early letters to Schuman we see him just getting to know Schuman as a composer and a person. His breezy writing style reflected the intensely demanding and then playful approach he would take with Schuman over the next nine months. In his first letter, dated August 31, 1944, and postmarked "Hollywood," he reflected on the demands of their respective professions:

> It suddenly seems to me that the composer's life and that of the poor wretched choreographer-rehearser-supervisor have much more in common, speaking inartistically, than I had ever thought. I had the idea that you all relaxed in quiet nooks in the coun[t]ry, absorbed the sounds of the birds and the bees and the wind in the trees, and gaily composed when the spirit moved. None of those mundane horrors associated with ordinary laborers. You think I am lying about all this?

Tudor then goes on to describe in abstract terms the ballet he is envisioning, asking Schuman to create a musical environment in which "the emotional instability of our main figure is projected. We need here a feeling that is spatial, and almost cerebral, but holding in it all the unsatisfied romantic desires, that start off our tale of destruction." The letter is then put aside until September 9, when he closes it by disingenuously remarking, "It is impossible to write this subject in words. It is a thing of time and space and emotion." He finishes with a handwritten postscript that embodies the many facets of Tudor's complex personality with which Schuman had to contend:

> The other interpolated motifs we were using were to be a salvation army meeting and a brawl of singing drunken women. The period I see between "Sous les toits de Paris" and "Anna Christie"—But each of these takes me unpleasantly far away from the classic shape that I wanted—because with a scientific approach it should be classic and extrovert—not romantic. I am very worried.

One would think that, between Tudor's highly abstract approach and his willingness to explore so many psychological aspects, it should have been the composer who would be worried, but Schuman was willing to throw off caution and dive into Tudor's mysterious world.

Tudor's next detailed communication to Schuman came from Philadelphia on November 8, 1944. Tudor was evidently moving deeper into his work and produced a letter full of elegantly stated images that might have led Schuman to rethink his collaboration with the distinguished choreographer. One example shows the tone of Tudor's instructions to Schuman:

> After the melody had been softly disappearing down the street I would want to become conscious of some rather turgid undertones, echoing from out of the distances of hundreds of small misused alleys and cul-de-sacs. This should d[e]velop its[e]lf like a rising and falling tide of sound into some rather passionate, sensual material that is almost fully developed and then is let go, like the coloured balloons that a child looses, and you see the waving colours disappearing into the blue caught in the gust of a rather surprisingly strong wind.

After apologizing for being so visual, Tudor then shows his psychologically demanding side for the first time by asking a rather disturbing question of Schuman after hearing an unidentified work of his at Carnegie Hall:

> I was very excited by the music, but it lacked to me th[e] freedom that I think you now are able to give. It sounded very mental although I am very certain that you gave your full emotions to it. It just was very slightly aiming for effect maybe. And the effects were wonderful. But it just made me wonder if you loved people, or if you did but much preferred not to show it.

He then comments offhandedly, in a tone that is both playful and a little sadistic: "All of which does not concern us at this moment."

After another page of directions in which Schuman is asked to create in his score feelings of a "chill in the air" and the "odd feeling that come[s] from the flurries of dead leaves being blown in circles about the street," Tudor concludes the letter by writing, "Consolations to you for having received such an awful letter," and then his obligatory handwritten postscript, "But this is where we have to go to get there."

The next Tudor letter, dated January 7, 1945, and postmarked Wichita, Kansas, was the proverbial straw that broke Schuman's patience with his manipulative collaborator. Tudor explains to Schuman that he has "forebodings" with his own choreography as well as "little moments of disquiet on account of the music. Now, please keep calm, and, if necessary rebuke me as being an idiot in these matters and explain to me why." Tudor then picks apart, with great musical knowledge, each section of the work that he had received so far, even including a rather artful drawing of "waves" that matched his view of how the music should flow:

> Then when we get to 2b., which should be the meat of this wave it doesn't seem to me to get very far. The opening chords are beautiful, and the tutti holds out hopes and premonitions of great portent; the *piu mosso* begins to continue this, but the *rit poco a poco* and the *meno mosso* are not quite the fulfilment of the promise you had just given, and then the very broad section with the fff. chords, shouts a lot but [I] cannot be sure what it is saying for you, or if they are content to be exciting sounds.

Tudor's handwritten postscripts contained some of his most perverse moments. He ends this letter by describing a female character that Schuman must capture in music: "She is the kind who gives in completely and every time, she is weak, emotional and very oversexed. Love & greetings to you all. Antony."

On January 13, 1945, Schuman shot back a response beginning, "Your letter has been quite a shock to me," informing Tudor that he had been quite literal in attempting to follow his instructions, and explaining that he was very pleased with the results:

> Please don't despair until you've seen the whole and then not until I've given you one of my incompetent singing demonstrations at the piano.
> In contrast to your feelings I am just delighted with the progress of the work. I have slaved all of the Christmas holiday. . . . But because of my good feelings (because the music is right) your letter caused a minor depression. But now that I've told all I do feel better. Please write again.

Tudor took Schuman up on his request, sending another blistering letter from Los Angeles on February 21, 1945, chock full of suggestions and admonitions and including a frustrated comment that he was not getting the best from his composer: "You promised me the best music you had ever written, remember?" He then sarcastically suggested that if he could not do better, perhaps Schuman would consider "extract[ing] a movement from one of your more recent symphonies, if you could find one that might reasonably closely approach the atmosphere." He concludes in the fashion typical of the whole correspondence: "I expect to see you in two or three weeks, wearing an expression of divine relief, that the work is through, and that you know it to be the most beautiful work that you have ever composed, just like you promised."

Nonetheless, Schuman and Tudor eventually became good friends, and Tudor was one of the charter members of the Juilliard dance faculty in 1951. Schuman remembered Tudor as sarcastic and difficult with his dancers but not with him—a strange opinion, considering the letters. One scholar of the ballets of Tudor wrote that "Tudor had a diabolical and sardonic side that alienated many of his friends and dancers." Schuman also noted that Tudor "wouldn't have ever liked anyone's wife; plenty of homosexuals appreciate women, but he wasn't one of them."

The entire experience for Schuman must have been an intoxicating one, working with a distinguished choreographer like Tudor and having his music danced to by a first-class ensemble and soloists: "American composers wrote for them [Ballet Theatre], and the place was filled with youth and excitement and a variegated repertory." Just as he had had world-class orchestras perform his recent symphonic works, he now had the same level of performance in the dance ensemble of Ballet Theatre. Schuman's analysis of Tudor's output as a choreographer was perceptive; he found Tudor's work to have been influenced by Martha Graham, "but he made ballet out of it":

> To me, he [Tudor] is a more interesting choreographer than Balanchine, although Balanchine, to me, is *the* Stravinsky of choreographers. In almost every respect Stravinsky has a very different kind of depth from other composers. . . . If I were to make a comparison, I would think of Tudor as Beethoven and Balanchine as Poulenc or Ravel. . . . Not that Balanchine is superficial, but rather that I think of Tudor as the equivalent of a composer of development, and I think of Balanchine as one who is a composer of episodes and impressions. I don't think one is better than another, but I think they're very different and to me, the more interesting is Tudor.

Schuman realized what the story of the ballet was only at the dress rehearsal, where he learned that Tudor intended to depict a childbirth on stage at the beginning of the work: "He was terribly clever, because had he given me something precise, it might have sent me in a different direction altogether, and I might have written something much more mundane."

The ballet was named *Undertow* and was premiered in New York at the Metropolitan Opera House on April 10, 1945, by Ballet Theatre, the orchestra conducted by Antal Doráti. The story of the ballet involved murder and rape, and Tudor had requested that the score be through-composed, with no individual sections. Remarkably, Tudor's abstract yet detailed instructions led Schuman to realize in music just what the choreographer had envisioned. In one scene, Schuman had been told to write highly contrapuntal music, which, it turned out, was to accompany a gang rape on stage. He had used the music earlier in a foundry scene for *Steeltown*.

Tudor wrote in the program notes for the premiere that the ballet "concerns itself with the emotional development of a transgressor. The choreographic action depicts a series of related happenings, the psychological implications of which result in an inevitable murder":

> The hero is seen at various stages, beginning with his babyhood when he is neglected by his mother who leaves him hungry while she seeks the embrace of her husband. . . . [In a large city the boy] encounters prostitutes, street-urchins, an innocent young girl, a gay bridal couple, carousing dypsomaniacs [*sic*] and a visiting mission worker whose friendship and care he seeks.
>
> [After murdering a "lascivious woman"] he is apprehended for this crime [and] his soul is purged by the tremendous relief that is his at the realization that he will no longer be called upon to endure the anguish of being a misfit and an outcast among his fellow men.

All the characters in this large ballet, with the exception of the Transgressor, have Greek or Roman names—Cybele, Volupia, Medusa. One scholar of Tudor's work sees *Undertow* as a ballet that brings forth, more than ever before, the choreographer's desire to delve into the human psyche and the results of a twentieth century filled with war and horrors:

> The characters in *Undertow* are reminiscent of the personalities in expressionist dramas by Wedekind or Capek. As in their expressionist plays, Tudor's message paints a bleak, futile picture; all the incidents lead to one, usually violent, ending. One could ask if Tudor might have seen Kurt Weill's operas or Alben [*sic*] Berg's *Lulu*, whose scripts describe the evil and decadent impact of postwar city life (Berlin during the Weimar Republic) as well as the driving force of fate.

A disturbing scenario in any age, the story line must have been extraordinarily challenging for an audience in 1945.

The premiere of the ballet was overseen by the great impresario Sol Hurok. Schuman was distressed by the small size of the string section of the orchestra and asked Hurok for more players in order to generate a richer sound. Hurok responded, "It's a dance audience. They're not going to know. Forget about it." Eventually Tudor and Schuman hired sixteen extra string players at their own expense, much to the delight of Doráti.

According to Schuman, the score was well received, but Tudor's choreography was ahead of its time and was only appreciated by sophisticated dance audiences. The cast included Alicia Alonso, Hugh Laing, and Nana Gollner, "who was seven months pregnant, so that the opening birth scene had a special zip when she did it. . . . I was tremendously impressed, as a composer, that writing for virtuoso dancers was similar to the way you would write for instrumentalists. Watching a dancer fulfill the music, to movements made up by somebody else, is a great theatrical experience." Looking back at the experience in 1963, Schuman remarked, "I must regard it as one of the most productive and satisfying artistic experiences of my career."

Schuman received a highly detailed and perceptive analysis of *Undertow* from Virgil Thomson, who had already been one of Schuman's most severe critics. Thomson had suggested to Schuman in a 1942 review of the Fourth Symphony that his compositional style was appropriate for the theater, and *Undertow* provided him that opportunity.

Thomson began by positing that *Undertow* would live on as a concert piece even if Tudor's choreography disappeared, and that active American composers had done some of "their most striking work in the theater." Thomson complained that American concert compositions were "weak in specific expressivity partly because our American training in composition is formalistic, seeking chiefly abstract perfection, even at the expense of direct speech."

Presenting Schuman as "a pure product of the American musical scene," with all its faults, Thomson then skillfully dissected Schuman's compositions in a way that must have been just as instructive as it was galling for the young composer:

His workmanship is skillful, individual, striking. His expressivity has always been tenuous, timid, conventional. His serious works have shown a respectable seriousness of attitude without much private or particular passion, while his gayer ones have expressed either a standard American cheerfulness or the comforting bumptiousness of middle-quality comic-strip humor. He has written easily, abundantly and, in a technical sense, well; but his music has been, on the whole, reticent, has communicated to the public little about himself or about anything else.

However, Thomson saw a major epiphany for Schuman in the score of *Undertow*:

> Schuman turns out to be not at all the composer of small expressive range and assumed monumental proportions that his concert music has long led one to consider him, but a man of high, of spectacular expressive gifts who has been constricted by the elegant abstractions of the American concert style—and a little bit, too, perhaps, by his youth. . . . The theater gives him elbow room. His mind can move around in it.

Such a candid and occasionally scathing critique of his compositions must have taken Schuman aback, but the depth of Thomson's intelligence and perception cannot be denied. Schuman often told the author that he was not affected by criticism of his compositions, but in candid moments he would admit how painful such criticism could be. We have no way of knowing the direct result of Thomson's words on Schuman, except to note that he freely collaborated on other theatrical works in ensuing years. Schuman, in conversation with the author in later years, never expressed admiration for either Thomson's criticism or his music.

An orchestral score of *Undertow* for concert use was also produced. It was premiered on November 29, 1945, by the Los Angeles Philharmonic, conducted by Alfred Wallenstein.

Although Schuman never worked on a creative collaboration with Tudor again, his artistic association with Martha Graham was more fruitful. Schuman was introduced to Graham through the actress Katharine Cornell, who admired Schuman's music. In 1947 she was playing on Broadway in Shakespeare's *Antony and Cleopatra*. Backstage after the play, Schuman met Graham for the first time and, in typically dramatic style, staring with her deep-set eyes, she said, the composer later recalled, "'Mr. Schuman, your music *moves* me.' It was so intense that I wanted to run from the hall and scream, 'Mama!'"

Schuman was familiar with Graham's work, although he was not enthusiastic about some of the composers who had worked with her in the past, including Louis Horst and Lehman Engel. Graham also choreographed to the music of many distinguished contemporary composers, including Barber, Bartók, Copland, Cowell, Dello Joio, Diamond, Hindemith, Menotti, and Schoenberg, to name only a few. Schuman greatly admired her choreography and her innovative approach to dance: "Agnes de Mille used to say about Martha, 'She created a whole theatre. She really did, [including] the costumes and sculptures. It's as though the Kabuki or the Noh theatre in Japan had never existed before.'"

Schuman found Graham to be an "astonishing woman" and certainly believed that she was one of the greatest American artists of the twentieth century, an individual who was "a curious mix of sensitivity and self-centeredness." Schuman also understood that his music was eventually touched by her: "I was influenced tonally by her aesthetic, if not necessarily consciously. I noticed that other composers seemed to be too. . . . You couldn't not be. The subject matter of these works is so Graham-ish . . . the dark side and the fast side is very prominent."

The official invitation from Graham came to Schuman while he was vacationing in Martha's Vineyard in the summer of 1946. She explained in some detail that she had conceived of a work featuring the folk singer Susan Reed, a well-known entertainer of the time who was renowned for her "beautiful singing voice" and for her performance of "traditional folk songs from many countries." Graham continued in a postscript that she also was thinking about a work based on the Oedipus myth, but from the point of view of Jocasta "at that instant when [a typical Martha phrase] she recognized her dual destiny as mother and lover," Schuman said. It was that afterthought that grabbed Schuman's attention and would be the subject of Graham's and Schuman's first collaboration. The music was commissioned by the Elizabeth Sprague Coolidge Foundation, which also eventually supported the composition of Schuman's Fourth String Quartet and provided a grant for Graham's involvement in the premiere of the collaboration.

Based on his experience with Tudor, Schuman expected to receive from Graham a description of what type of music was needed and when it would appear in the dance. However, Graham provided the composer with a script that detailed every section and character of the dance. Said Schuman:

I wanted to know from her precisely what emotional climate, sound climate, she wanted me to create. Because I figured that the role of the composer was to give her the tonal ambience that would promote her needs as a choreographer and a dancer. Therefore, I needed her to be quite precise with me, and she was not accustomed to that.

Graham was not accustomed to such prodding from a composer, but she embraced it enthusiastically. Schuman made use of his knowledge of Jocasta's story to work with Graham on developing the composition a section at a time. He recalled that his experience with Tudor, whom he found very organized, was more efficient than his work with Graham, who, although she frequently produced extraordinary work, seemed to manifest a sort of distracted organization: "She would be backstage sewing a costume while the audience was waiting for the curtain to go up."

Nevertheless, Graham's passion for the topic, her extraordinary intelligence, and her elegant writing style provided Schuman with another rich palette for his composition. Graham understood music well and was delighted to work with Schuman and especially to choreograph the Jocasta story. On August 30, 1946, she wrote to Schuman: "I can hear your power and rich dark tragic sense musically. Of course it is all in my imagination. But I think I can feel on my skin what you will write."

In a letter of October 28, 1946, Graham included a detailed script for the story that was meant to guide Schuman in his composing. As opposed to Tudor's directions, which often had the consistency of clouds, Graham's were quite structured, with a description of each character in the dance and a presentation of sixteen scenes or episodes from beginning to end. She also made it clear in this letter that she was a flexible collaborator who looked forward to the give-and-take between the two creators: "It [the music] will have such a life of its own that the action will have to go with it. That has been my experience and I am not rigid in any sense when it comes to changing when it seems to indicate it in the musical life of the piece."

After floating various titles for the work, none of which she liked, including "As was the Deed," "Malignant Stars," "Storm of Sorrows," and "The Riddles Mystery," she wrote:

I do know that it is serious and strange and I think it can be very moving. I should like to keep it as moving without making it morbid as I possibly can. I know that I often sin on that side. I feel this character will be different from any other I have done because she is of heroic stature. The dream can be her weakness and very beautiful and tragic, I think.

Graham's description of the action of the "Dance for Jocasta," in the fourth section of the script, was passionately eloquent:

DANCE FOR JOCASTA:
This begins in the same formal almost ritualistic vein as the CHORUS. It is an acknowledgement of their presence, an acquiescence to their statement. It contains the courtesy of a great queen. But it is as though she were dancing before children. She is wooden like a doll. Her movements have the precision, the premeditated quality of a hypnotized being, performing precisely what she has been taught.
Suddenly she breaks.
She awakes into pain.
It is not an intellectual thing, this anguish, but is pain which has bitten deep into the bones and sinews. So deep that she is unaware of what it is. Something is feeding on her heart. She has lost her honor as a woman.
She ceases to be the queen and becomes a woman beseiged [sic] by memories.
The dance ends as she pitches to the floor, lost.
The CHORUS catches her in their arms. She lies across the knees of several of them like a child sobbing in its sleep.

The resulting ballet, *Night Journey*, was premiered on May 3, 1947, by the Graham Company, conducted by Louis Horst, during a symposium on music criticism hosted by Harvard University. Graham created *Night Journey* for herself as Jocasta, Erick Hawkins as Oedipus, Mark Ryder as the seer, and a chorus of six women. The décor, by Isamu Noguchi, consisted of "a metal bed shaped like the reclining figures of a man and woman." The three-day symposium was itself a groundbreaking event, bringing together music critics, scholars, performers, and composers of the likes of Archibald Davison, Olin Downes, Alfred Frankenstein, Otto Kinkeldey, Olga Samaroff, Roger Sessions, and Virgil Thomson. An earlier symposium concert on the second night had featured Robert Shaw and the Collegiate Choir performing works by Hindemith, Copland, and Gian Francesco Malipiero. *Night Journey* was presented at the theatrically inadequate auditorium of the Cambridge High and Latin School, along with Carlos Chávez's *Dark Meadow*.

Schuman recalled that Horst, who was also romantically linked to Graham for twenty years, was particularly rude to the orchestra members, many of whom were in the Boston Symphony Orchestra. Horst

> screamed at them [the orchestra] as though they were a bunch of hacks.
> . . . He was horrible that way. He wasn't horrible at all as a person.
> He was a very jolly, considerate and dedicated man. But I'll always
> remember [him as] a terrible conductor. A good rehearsal pianist and
> routine composer, you know. He wrote a lot of stuff for Martha.

Schuman felt that *Night Journey* would eventually be the most successful of the four collaborations he would have with Graham. Although notorious for her temperamental flare-ups, Graham was particularly solicitous of Schuman, even acknowledging at one point that it was her choreography and not his music that was a problem in a certain section. Schuman eventually shortened the work for performance in the concert hall, crediting both Tudor and Graham for teaching him the difference between theater music, which requires the re-setting of characters on stage, and concert music. A note in the score to Schuman's concert version of the work, subtitled *Choreographic Poem for Fifteen Instruments* and premiered in 1981, describes the story:

> In *Night Journey*, Martha Graham's dramatization of this myth, it is
> not Oedipus but Jocasta who is the protagonist. The action turns
> upon that instant of Jocasta's death when she relives her destiny, sees
> with double insight the triumphal entry of Oedipus, their meeting,
> courtship, marriage, their years of intimacy which were darkly
> crossed by the blind seer, Tiresias, until at last the truth burst from
> him. The chorus of women who know the truth before the seer
> speaks it, vainly try to divert the prophecy from its cruel conclusion.

John Martin of the *New York Times* wrote of the Cambridge premiere that *Night Journey* was "not one of Miss Graham's more inspired works, though it has its effective moments. With so familiar a theme it is essential, for us . . . that there be something revelatory, some particular emotional evocation, to justify the retelling. This is not forthcoming in the present work, which leaves us substantially where it finds us."

Schuman soon decided to collaborate with Graham again, only pausing to compose his Sixth Symphony in 1948. The project, realized in 1949, was *Judith*, a work for solo dancer and orchestra, which Schuman conceived as the equivalent of an instrumental concerto with the dancer as soloist. Schuman recalled that Graham was reading the Apocrypha, texts of uncertain authenticity outside of the main body of the Bible, and that these influenced her thinking about the choreography.

The ancient story recounts how Judith, a beautiful Jewish widow, arranged to be admitted to the tent of Holofernes, who had cut off the water supply of the city of Bethulia, in the land of Israel. She plied him with wine and decapitated him. She then took the severed head,

> and went forth up the mountain . . . and said with a loud voice: "Behold the head of Holofernes . . . the Lord has smitten him by the hand of a woman . . . I will sing unto the Lord a new song." . . . The women . . . made a dance among them for her . . . and she took branches in her hand . . . and she went before all the people in the dance.

Unlike *Night Journey*, *Judith* presented a challenge for Graham because she was to perform the work as a solo on the apron of the stage in front of the Louisville Orchestra, which would be obscured by a scrim. She wrote to Schuman on June 14, 1949, six months before the premiere, that "this has been the most difficult assignment I have ever set myself." In this remarkable letter, which includes a description of the dramatic treatment, Graham releases all her insecurities and pours forth intellectual analyses of the human condition, with quotes from Dante, Plato, T. S. Eliot, the Books of Adam and Eve, St. Augustine, Hart Crane, and Joseph Campbell. She explains that she envisions the dance as a legend of rebirth:

> The thing which has been so difficult has been to make the limitations seem part of the for[e]ordained scheme of the work. This has to be a communication in terms of music, dance, staging and deep inner meaning. I do not want the staging to have the elements of novelty

about it. I want it to look as though it were an indispensable part of the unity. I have not wanted it to be just a dance in front of an orchestra for lack of better facilities. Also I have wnated [*sic*] the fact that it is to be a solo dance to be a part of the necessity. Mathiesson says "no experiment in art is valuable unless it is psychologically necessary."

Graham ends this section of the letter with a slight apology: "I know that I am trying to fight through to a simplicity at which I have not arrived yet. Perhaps this is confusing. I hope not." Schuman must have received this missive with some consternation.

In a subsequent letter, dated June 24, 1949, Graham seemed to have a clearer scenario for Schuman to study, confirming that the work

is still a legend of re-birth and involved with the passion of ordeal and the exaltation of the success of that ordeal. . . . It has definite dramatic development but is not a drama and it has definite aspects of the ritualistic about it as all matters of inner life have without being in the usual sense of the word religious.

In the action scenario included in this letter Graham suggested timings for the sections of the work and also reiterated an idea she had presented earlier of having several garments onstage that are worn to identify moods or topics, such as "Garment for Gladness," "Garment for Temptation," "Garment for Sorrow." In order to create this unique choreographic experience with Graham, Schuman needed to call on his considerable patience, skill, and intellectual acuity.

The work was commissioned and premiered by the Louisville Orchestra on January 4, 1950, conducted by Robert Whitney. According to Schuman, the performance was "sensational, electric. . . . The story in Louisville is that it saved the orchestra." Not only did the Louisville Orchestra tour to New York City with *Judith*, but it also recorded the work, including *Undertow* on the second side with Schuman himself conducting, the one and only instance of his leading an orchestra on a commercial recording release. Regrettably, according to Schuman, the quality of the recording was so poor it was unusable.

In a *New York Times* review that appeared almost exactly one year after the Louisville premiere, John Martin wrote of the December 29, 1950 New York performance that

> *Judith* was a vivid and striking experience. . . . Obviously she [Graham] could not dance continuously, and yet the theme must be sustained without a break of interest. . . . By placing two strikingly handsome sculptural pieces of décor by Isamu Noguchi at the extreme right and left of the stage, she deliberately emphasized the lateral as well as the spiritual distance between them. . . . For the essential breathing spaces between dances, there were some admirably conceived dramatic interludes which actually forwarded the composition.

Martin concludes once again, however, that "the composition as a whole probably does not rank among Miss Graham's top achievements."

Although the concept of solo dancer with orchestra was a novel one, it was not embraced by orchestras of the time, and Graham asked Schuman to arrange the work for a smaller ensemble of about fifteen instruments, similar to the instrumentation for the reduced *Night Journey*. Schuman did not comply with the request; he never liked the idea of a small-ensemble version of the work. However, he did create a concert version for orchestra that met with moderate success. A 1952 performance of *Judith* by the Los Angeles Philharmonic, conducted by Alfred Wallenstein, was praised for "his mastery of somber orchestral color and an extremely intricate rhythmical scheme . . . the orchestra won an unusual reaction from an audience not noted for its hospitality to novelty."

A listener in Andover, Connecticut, upon hearing a radio broadcast of the work, wrote to the Juilliard School of Music, not knowing that Schuman was both the composer of *Judith* and the president of the school. In her letter she asked, "Is this din and discord, entirely lacking in tone and rhythm, to be cultivated as the future music of America? . . . To cultivate this uproar as music in the name of music is [a] criminal attack on the human ear." Schuman's response displayed his signature wit and style:

> Through a curious twist of fate, the composer of the work about which you complained and the President of the School to whom you addressed the complaint happen to be the same person. May I say at once that I am most appreciative of the frank manner in which you expressed your disapproval of the composition "Judith." Certainly, any composer dislikes apathy and prefers strong expressions of approval and disapproval to indifference on the part of his listeners. It is a source of never-ending wonder to me that a single broadcast

of a new piece of music should bring letters as negative in tone as yours, and others equally positive. . . .

. . . Your reaction was nonetheless appreciated because you found the music so distasteful. You may be interested to know, for example, that thousands of records of this particular composition were sold last year and that the piece has been performed with outstanding success in Louisville, New York, Denver and Los Angeles. I merely mention this so that you are aware that a difference of opinion exists.

With every good wish to you, I am,

Faithfully,

Schuman's compositional style of this period was often based on dark, somber melodies shaped around expressive intervals of the seventh and larger, which gave his music a gripping intensity. Nevertheless, *Judith* had episodic moments of lively energy, with rapid sixteenth-note flourishes characteristic of the composer, although the work ultimately returned to the dark quality reflected in Graham's story line. (The term "flourish" is used by the author to describe a burst of rapid sixteenth notes irregularly interrupted by sixteenth rests, with the melodic interval typically being that of the second, although larger intervals are also employed.)

Eventually Graham dropped *Judith* from her repertoire, and the choreography was not preserved. Yet Graham praised Schuman's score generously: "*Judith* is going to be remembered because of your score; I can't reproduce it, and it's just one of those things that we have to let go that way. I feel terrible about it, and I'm the loser, but I just can't do it."

In 1984 Schuman asked Graham to re-create *Judith* as part of his seventy-fifth birthday celebration the next year, but she declined: "'Judith' was done in another period of my life when I was still essentially a soloist and I feel, much as I would like to, that it would be impossible for me to reconstruct it. It must remain for many who heard it a treasured memory and for those who did not an inspiration in the musical world." Graham consistently expressed great admiration for Schuman and his music: "I hold you in great esteem, both as a composer and as a man with whom I have worked so magically. You have contributed so unbelievably much to my life and I deeply treasure you."

After the initial success of *Judith*, the next collaboration between Schuman and Graham was not as fruitful. Schuman had been commissioned by Sigma Alpha Iota, an international music fraternity for women, to write a piano work to commemorate its fiftieth anniversary. The work was to be premiered in the late summer of 1953 in Chicago at the fraternity's annual convention, with Lillian Steuber, a well-regarded soloist who was a professor at the University of Southern California, as the pianist. In what might be viewed as either a playful gesture or a cloaked way of getting her attention for a new collaboration, Schuman asked Graham in the winter of 1953 to listen to the work and name it. Graham responded by saying that she wished to choreograph it in her upcoming spring season.

Schuman then had the awkward mission of explaining to the organization that an orchestral version choreographed by Graham was requested to take place *before* the piano-version premiere in August. Happily, Sigma Alpha Iota agreed to the change, and on May 17, 1953, a pit-orchestra version, entitled *Voyage for a Theater*, was performed in New York City at the Alvin Theater, conducted by Simon Sadoff, with choreography by Graham. The work, commissioned by the Katharine Cornell Foundation, has been described as "an erotic frolic with three men." As usual, Graham placed herself in the prominent, and only female role, although "the three men . . . were young enough to be her sons."

The piano version, called *Voyage: A Cycle of Five Pieces for Piano*, was premiered by Steuber in Chicago on August 18, 1953: "Martha gave me the overall title, and I gave each movement a very Graham-ish name—Anticipation, Caprice, Realization, Decision, Retrospection—and had great fun doing it." Schuman eventually withdrew the chamber-orchestra version, *Voyage for a Theater*, but he did resurrect the work one more time in a composition he entitled *Voyage for Orchestra*, which was commissioned by the Eastman School of Music and premiered in Rochester, New York, on October 27, 1972, with Gustav Meier conducting the Eastman Philharmonia. Later Schuman recalled that once Graham presented *Voyage for a Theater* on the same program with *Night Journey*:

By chance, I was sitting across the aisle from Lenny and Felicia Bernstein, and Lenny said to me, "*Night Journey* is marvelous theatre, but the other one doesn't work." He was absolutely right. It didn't work, for two reasons: the choreography and the concept were weak, and the music didn't help it a lot. It was not a very strong score.

The last collaboration between Graham and Schuman reflected their long professional and personal friendship. According to Schuman, a festive dinner party was given to celebrate Graham's seventieth birthday in 1964. As Graham rose to acknowledge her friends, she said, "I'm going to ask Bill publicly for a birthday present. I want a new score." Schuman immediately agreed, and that was the genesis of *The Witch of Endor*.

After the party, Schuman approached Graham. Saying that they had been friends since *Night Journey*, he told her he was going to say something that would be difficult for her to hear. After acknowledging her legacy as a great dancer, he stated, "'but you'll really go down in history as a great choreographer. . . . And just as baseball players have to retire when their physical attributes change, you've got to face up to the fact that you mustn't choreograph a role for yourself.' She said, 'You're absolutely right, I'm not going to do it.'" Unfortunately, she reneged on her promise and created a large role for herself, which Schuman felt she was unable to realize.

As opposed to the abstract scenarios Graham provided for *Night Journey* and *Judith*, *The Witch of Endor*'s story is taken from the Old Testament's First Book of Samuel. In it, Saul asks the Witch of Endor to summon Samuel, Saul's teacher, from the dead. The witch is not aware that Saul is the king, and when the ghost appears standing on his feet, she realizes that she is in the presence of royalty because "when summoned[,] ghosts or spirits stood on their heads, unless in the presence of the great—and then, on their feet." Realizing she has been deceived by Saul, who has decreed the death of all prophets, she is afraid for her life, but then Samuel appears, condemns Saul to death, and declares David the new king. Samuel disappears and the "Witch beckons to fate—which is to foretell fate."

Schuman immediately set to work and completed the score in only four months. *The Witch of Endor* was premiered on November 2, 1965, in New York at the 54th Street Theatre, with Robert Irving conducting and décor by Ming Cho Lee. It was not a great critical success. It shared the program with Graham and Copland's masterpiece *Appalachian Spring*. Rosalyn Krokover wrote in *High Fidelity/Musical America* that the piece

> probably will not be considered one of Graham's greater works. Characterizations are not yet fully drawn (indeed, the choreographer's

portrayal of the title role appeared barely sketched in) and the symbolism is unnecessarily abstruse. . . . But the music . . . did not help matters. Scored mostly for percussion and winds, it moved relentlessly along in a narrow dynamic range, desperately avoiding anything resembling a melodic line.

Clive Barnes in the *New York Times* wrote that *The Witch of Endor* was

a work of great psychological complexity, whose strands are not always as neatly, or more important, as clearly placed, as they might have been. . . . William Schuman's specially commissioned, slightly dry, slightly somber, score was rather less [effective]. The perhaps deliberately sparse melodic invention, occasionally masked by oppressively sustained chords, did not always match the ballet's purple tragedy.

In order to facilitate the process of choreographing the ballet, Schuman and Graham had received a grant from the Ford Foundation to make a sound recording of the work. Years later, Columbia Records called Schuman to inquire if he would release the recording for commercial sale, but Schuman demurred, based on the quality of the recording and what he felt was a weak score.

In retrospect, Schuman was most satisfied with the scores to *Night Journey* and *Judith*. He opined that

Judith works better without the dance than *Night Journey* does; *Night Journey* is really a dramatic piece that needs the dance. It doesn't have the general appeal of something like *Appalachian Spring.* Writing for Graham for a full orchestra rather than for her pit band was also a more satisfying experience, because the pit band was a bastard arrangement, neither chamber music nor orchestra.

Concluded Schuman, the inveterate baseball fan: "So out of our four ballets, we batted .500, which is not too bad."

CHAPTER 8

Writing Music Is Something Wonderful

Schuman's dance compositions for Tudor and Graham are truly symphonic in scope. His Juilliard years had made him more and more comfortable with the larger forms that would become his compositional hallmark. However, Schuman retained his affinity for shorter choral works, one firmly established during his Sarah Lawrence days. His Te Deum, for a cappella mixed chorus, was premiered in April 1945 in Cambridge, Massachusetts, by the Harvard Glee Club and Sarah Lawrence Chorus, conducted by G. Wallace Woodworth. It was the product of the never-realized Billy Rose production of Shakespeare's *Henry VIII* that also generated Schuman's beautiful song for voice and piano "Orpheus with His Lute."

Around this time Schuman also composed an a cappella work for male chorus, "Truth Shall Deliver," for the Yale Glee Club, conducted by the legendary Marshall Bartholomew, with a text adapted from Chaucer by Marion Farquhar. Although the official premiere took place in Bronxville, New York, on December 7, 1946, "trial" performances were given with the Yale Glee Club at the Princeton and Harvard football concerts of November 15 and 22, 1946, respectively. Both works are about four minutes in duration.

Schuman and Frankie had befriended Farquhar when she was already quite elderly. Schuman admired her enormously, particularly her translations; he had commissioned her to translate several songs into English while he was director of publications at G. Schirmer. Farquhar also had an important influence on both Bill and Frankie "in the sense that she was the first 'lady,' in quotes, that we have ever known, really. And we were such raw kids. . . . she even taught me how to walk on a stage. . . . She was wonderfully critical in a constructive way," Schuman recalled.

Schuman felt that Chaucer's "Ballad of Good Advice" would be an excellent choral text. Farquhar's adaptation from Middle English subsequently became "Truth Shall Deliver." Farquhar also introduced Schuman to numerous musical rounds, which he eventually used in his viola

Concerto on Old English Rounds (1974), his *Amaryllis: Variations for String Trio* (1964), and the string orchestra work *Amaryllis* of 1976.

When Schuman last saw Farquhar, on a Lincoln Center trip to the West Coast, he was confronted with a woman who was in the last stages of dementia (she eventually died on March 14, 1965). Schuman approached the auto in which Farquhar was sitting, and a friend, Frederick Hart, said:

> "Marion, this is Bill, Bill Schuman, your old friend." Nothing. An absolutely frozen face. And so I said: "Marion, remember when you taught me 'Amaryllis,' that wonderful round?" And I started to sing "Amaryllis," and the tears came in the eyes and a smile on the face. . . . No one else had gotten through, and I got through because this brought it all back.

After the arduous process of working with Tudor on *Undertow* in 1945 and with Graham on *Night Journey* in 1947, Schuman returned to his first love with the creation of his Sixth Symphony. Its somber quality was no doubt due in part to the darkness in both the Tudor and Graham works, though this may not have been a deliberate choice on the part of the composer.

Commissioned by the Dallas Symphony Orchestra League, the Sixth Symphony was completed on December 31, 1948, and given its premiere by the Dallas Symphony Orchestra, Antal Doráti conducting, on February 27, 1949, in Dallas, Texas. The work, approximately twenty-eight minutes long, is in one movement composed of six parts marked Largo, Moderato con moto, Leggieramente, Adagio, Allegro risoluto–Presto, and Larghissimo. The Largo, in 3/2 with a metronome marking of half note = 40, once again reflected Schuman's fascination with exceedingly slow tempi. Doráti provided the following program note for the Dallas premiere:

> The first and last parts (the word "movement" is avoided advisedly), namely the largo and larghissimo provide a frame for the work; or rather, to use an architectural analogy, have a similar function as the two piers of a bridge—to hold and support the span of the whole structure. The sequence and character of the four middle parts (moderato con moto—leggieramente—adagio—allegro risoluto, presto) bear a trace of the "classical" symphony form—a fast opening

followed by a scherzo, adagio and finale (the presto in this case taking the place of a "stretta"). But beyond this above outlined sequence, the Symphony follows an order and strong logic of its own.

It has to be said here that to this writer the construction of the work seems fundamentally new; pointing more to the future than leaning on the past. At the same time, it is put forth with extreme assurance and clarity, void of any trait or feeling of experimentation.

Schuman was not at all satisfied with the Dallas performance: "the work did not receive a truly representative performance; witness the fact that it took some 36 minutes to play, rather than the approximately 27½ minutes correct duration. . . . The players in the Orchestra were for the most part of considerably less than outstanding ability." In fact, Schuman seemed quite bruised by the Dallas premiere, reminiscent of the performance of his Symphony No. 2 in Boston in 1939. He wrote that the Dallas audience "found the Symphony utterly without appeal. In fact, some were so incensed over the work that they questioned whether they should even complete payment of the commission."

The work was next performed in September 1951 in Copenhagen by the Danish Radio Orchestra, conducted by Eugene Ormandy. Ormandy became a champion of the work and brought it to Philadelphia in November 1951. Schuman was still smarting from the Dallas reaction when he was asked to speak at an open dress rehearsal of the work on November 8, prior to the next afternoon's Philadelphia premiere, to members of the women's committees of the Philadelphia Orchestra.

The Philadelphians played the work so well at the rehearsal that the composer was "deeply shaken by the performance." Charming and erudite, yet still somewhat defensive, Schuman then began in his masterly speaking style with a disclaimer for his talk: "I firmly believe that the fortunes of a piece of music cannot rest upon the erudition of a composer's verbal description." The best way to summarize his experience in Dallas, he continued disarmingly, was "to say that the good people of Texas did not question my sincerity—only my sanity." Schuman then, in a quick change of tone, began to expound his beliefs as to how a new work should be heard. He hoped that an audience would begin to "understand" a new work: "By understanding I do not mean to imply in any sense technical understanding. By understanding I mean that at each point in the course of listening there is absence of aural chaos and realization of the presence of coherent musical expression." (This statement harks back to the "penetrative listening" concept Schuman had first presented at Sarah Lawrence College, a tool he was now teaching at Juilliard.) Schuman concluded, "What I am trying to say is that this symphony really sounds the way I want it to sound, that I am well aware that hearing it for the first time presents formidable problems with which I am most sympathetic, but which I do not have the power to change."

The Sixth Symphony has been called craggy, dark, and emotionally impenetrable, but it stands as one of Schuman's finest works for its structural cohesion and musical intensity. It also represents a new maturity in Schuman's approach to his compositions. Perhaps this was due to his intense musical collaborations with two brilliant and dramatic choreographers who explored the human experience in a way Schuman had not known before.

Writing in 1963 after a performance of the Sixth Symphony by Ormandy and the Philadelphia Orchestra, two critics provided succinct and perceptive views of the work. Edwin H. Schloss wrote in the *Philadelphia Inquirer*, "The Symphony is beautifully written—superlative in craftsmanship," and Elliott W. Galkin of the *Baltimore Sun* commented, "Here is a sincere and serious work, a craggy composition in a style that is individual in its romanticized neo-classicism. It is a composition tightly wrought in its rhythmic impulses and astringent in its harmonies." Karl F. Miller, media librarian and curator of the Historical Music Recordings Collection of the University of Texas at Austin, wrote several months after Schuman's death that the Sixth Symphony represents "one of the most profound expressions in 20th Century orchestral literature ... it has been described as an orchestral requiem for this century. ... The Sixth Symphony struck me as a reflection on the horror of the war just passed."

Schuman recalled that

the Sixth Symphony ... is the one that composers all like. I don't know why that is. It's very different from most of my works. The opening is much more chamber music-like than symphonic; it starts in a very gradual way. It took me months to get started, and I had a very difficult time writing it. I couldn't think of anything that pleased me. ... I suppose there might be some of *Undertow* in the Sixth Symphony, but I really don't know, because I don't think it's possible, even for a composer who wishes to be objective, to be objective. You can be objective only by describing extraneous features.

On another occasion he remarked:

I think it does make a natural bridge between [Symphonies No.] Five and Seven, Eight, Nine and Ten. . . . At least Seven, Eight and Nine I tend to think of together.

The Sixth Symphony's dense and contemplative aura does in fact make it a kind of compositional bridge from his earlier to his later works. Many years later the composer Christopher Rouse wrote that the Sixth Symphony represented a "stylistic crossroads" for Schuman, with its "previously untapped seriousness and depth of expression":

The Sixth Symphony could hardly be considered optimistic. Its slower sections remain lyrical, but the lyricism is now less relaxed, more intense. . . . Though still conceived tonally, the harmony is more chromatic and dissonant . . . the rhythm generally more syncopated and nervous. Schuman's sense of melody has also undergone a metamorphosis; his themes in the Symphony No. 6 are substantially more chromatic than in earlier works. . . . All in all, this symphony is not only immensely satisfying in itself but is also a focal point within its composer's entire output.

The seriousness and depth Rouse referred to are quite evident, however, in Schuman's score to *Night Journey*, which predates the Sixth Symphony by two years. One would also expect *Undertow* of 1945 to musically embody a dark seriousness, as well, based on the horrific human experiences depicted by Tudor in the ballet. But Schuman's score for this work is light in orchestral texture, melodic line, and harmonic density compared with the somberness of *Night Journey*. Yet Rouse is quite correct that, from the time of the Sixth Symphony, with occasional exceptions such as *New England Triptych*, *The Mighty Casey*, the Variations on "America," and selected choral works, Schuman's compositional tone grew darker and darker.

Rouse first began corresponding with Schuman when he was barely a teenager. In 1969, at the end of his sophomore year at Oberlin, Rouse wrote an engaging and rather plucky letter to Schuman, stating, "I just thought it was about time I wrote again just so you wouldn't forget me." He goes on to explain that he periodically goes on "conversion kicks" where he selects a composer he admires and whose music is not well known and attempts to "convert" listeners to the particular composer:

During April and May, you were my conversion composer, and I'm happy to report that the results were most gratifying. Very few people were highly critical of your pieces (these were usually strict twelve-toners and so forth), and no one found nothing at all to like in your music. However, most people were unabashedly enthusiastic. The favorites were your Third and Eighth Symphonies, with Judith and the Sixth Symphony running close seconds.

If Schuman felt that his Sixth Symphony was very different from what he had composed before, his Violin Concerto represented his longest process of composition and editing, stretching from 1946 to 1959. By the late 1940s Schuman had become one of the most sought-after and distinguished American composers of his time. Up to then he had written only one work for soloist and orchestra, the Piano Concerto of 1943. Therefore, when he was approached by the well-known violinist, Samuel Dushkin, to compose a concerto, he accepted with enthusiasm.

Dushkin had a very distinguished record of first performances of violin works, including Stravinsky's Violin Concerto, *Duo concertant*, and *Suite italienne*. Schuman had first met Dushkin at Stravinsky's hotel suite many years earlier when the young composer had been entrusted with the manuscript to Stravinsky's *Jeu de cartes*. Regrettably, Schuman no longer remembered that the violin playing he had heard at the hotel room door was shockingly bad.

Dushkin commissioned Schuman to write the concerto in 1946, with the expectation that the composer's champion, Serge Koussevitzky, would eventually perform it with the Boston Symphony Orchestra. The completed score was sent to Koussevitzky for his review around the same time Dushkin had invited Schuman to come to New York's Town Hall to hear him play.

Unfortunately, the quality of Dushkin's playing had not improved. Koussevitzky stepped in: "I vill play, but not with Dushkin. You must tell Dushkin." Schuman was in a horribly awkward position, because Dushkin had already paid for the concerto and he had exclusive rights to it for three years. Koussevitzky could not be bothered by these legal niceties: "I don't care what your agreement is. Take it away from him. We'll give it to Isaac Stern and play it with the Boston Symphony."

Schuman decided to confront Dushkin after attending a concert with him at the Museum of Modern Art at which Koussevitzky was honored. As they settled in for drinks at the Plaza Hotel—Dushkin ordered a cognac in a stemmed glass—Schuman said, "Listen, Sam, this is the most difficult moment of my life in personal relationships, and it will be for you, too, but I can't go on with the Violin Concerto. I know you were a great performer at one time, but no one is going to play it, and this is what I have to tell you."

Dushkin's response was intense and immediate. In a moment of white-hot anger, he snapped the stem of his glass in two. Although Dushkin was not cut, Schuman remembered that the experience was *"just terrible . . . it was one of the saddest things in my life. I still don't know whether I was right or wrong."*

One would have thought that the relationship between Schuman and Dushkin would have been acrimonious from that time forward. But upon the death of Schuman's mother in September 1947, he received a gracious letter of condolence from Dushkin's wife, Louise. In addition, in January 1951 Dushkin wrote a personal and warm letter on the death of Schuman's father the prior November. In a final rapprochement, Schuman wrote Dushkin at the time of the premiere of the final version of the concerto in 1959: "I thought about you this summer during the period of preparation and performance of the Concerto in Aspen. I cannot help but feel that somehow you would have been pleased. Maybe this is wishful thinking on my part."

When the three years had passed—Dushkin had held on to the concerto for the period of contractual exclusivity—the work was scheduled for performance with the Boston Symphony Orchestra under its new conductor, Charles Munch, with Isaac Stern as soloist. According to Schuman, "Munch loved the work and said it was one of the great concertos of our time." In Schuman's view, though, Stern did not grasp the intellectual underpinnings of the work and therefore didn't present the concerto in its best light. Schuman was troubled by

the inability of certain performers who are only conventional literature performers to come to grips with a new piece on its own terms, so he [Stern] never understood it except superficially. He always thought the opening, which he used to sing, was frenetic, even though I wanted that to be broadly romantic . . . he would never play it that way.

Critical reaction was generally positive. One writer considered it "fiendishly difficult, although Stern's art conquered all with seeming ease . . . Undoubtedly the concerto is a skillful, intelligent and forceful piece of work.

Yet judging by the audience's reaction, it is not destined for early public acceptance." Another saw the concerto as

> a study of the individual, as represented by the solo violin, to maintain his integrity and balance . . . in the face of a harsh and often overbearing surrounding milieu. That milieu seemed to be the large, twentieth century city. Mr. Schuman is too sophisticated a musician . . . to be interested in reproducing the common noises of the city. But surely some of the sounds of the second movement must have been suggested by tugboat whistles and one got the impression of factory whistles in the finale.

Time wrote whimsically that Charles Munch found the work

> "horribly difficult" but it also "exploited the orchestra very adroitly, used the modern language" effectively, and altogether it was "très intéressant." Pudgy violinist Isaac Stern agreed. He had "worked and worked until the music was part of me." When his fiddling was finished he grinned up into the balcony of Symphony Hall, then hammed his exit offstage, staggering as if brutally exhausted [after the rehearsal].

Schuman was troubled by problems in the concerto itself and began to revise large sections of the second movement soon after the Boston premiere on February 10, 1950. The revised work was reintroduced in a performance with Stern and the Juilliard Orchestra, Jean Morel conducting, on February 24, 1956. Once again Schuman felt changes were needed. This time he added a new introduction and several other changes to the second movement. This third and final version of the concerto was presented on August 9, 1959, at the Aspen Music Festival in Colorado with Roman Totenberg as the soloist and Izler Solomon conducting. Schuman, finally satisfied with the piece, was thrilled by the Aspen performance and the audience response.

The reworking was a unique experience for Schuman, who called the process "very unusual." From inception to the final version, Schuman's Violin Concerto took close to fourteen years to come to fruition.

In light of the numerous changes made in the Violin Concerto, it is interesting to note the composer's view of such changes in the manuscript. Schuman once commented that all of his manuscripts, which are held by the Library of Congress, can be most unreliable [for study purposes] because when I make changes, I never go back and make the changes in the manuscript . . . so that any errors that are in the manuscripts are still in the manuscript . . . I don't make cuts that I've made, I don't put in additions. I am just so happy to be rid of it, of the manuscript itself, physically.

See the appendix for further discussion of the Violin Concerto.

Perhaps the most beloved work, as well as the most frequently performed original composition, in Schuman's oeuvre is the *New England Triptych*. Based on hymns of the Revolutionary War era by William Billings, it is an audience favorite thanks to its accessibility and energy. Here, unlike in earlier works such as the Tudor and Graham ballets, as well as the Sixth Symphony, in the *Triptych* Schuman allowed his exuberance, patriotism, and joie de vivre to come forward, as if he had consciously thrown off the highly intellectual and compositionally erudite style of previous works.

The work came to life through a request from Andre Kostelanetz, a well-known conductor of the mid-twentieth century famous for his pops concerts. In February 1954 Kostelanetz wrote to Schuman to tell him that the conductor's recently instituted Saturday evening concerts with the New York Philharmonic had been a success and would be continuing into the next season, since they were "bringing to Carnegie Hall a new and most enthusiastic audience." He then outlined the parameters of the requested work:

1. The rehearsal time for these concerts is very limited—actually about one and a half rehearsals.
2. The composition should be in a light vein with a ready appeal for many people, and should run about eight to ten minutes in length.
3. I would like to suggest that the work might be of a programmatic nature, with an American background.
4. It would be necessary to have the composition completed about the end of summer or in the early fall [of 1954].

Schuman was interested. Kostelanetz, a frequent guest conductor with orchestras throughout the United States, had said he would perform the new work often in other cities. However, the originally proposed commission fee of $1,000 was not to Schuman's liking. The composer eventually agreed to a fee of $1,500 and the promise that Kostelanetz would try to record the work, although that could not be guaranteed.

The composition of the work was delayed when Schuman came down with a case of infectious hepatitis in June 1954. He was bedridden for most of the summer, making it unlikely that he could deliver the piece for a November performance. Schuman asked Kostelanetz if he wished to retract the commission, but Kostelanetz quickly replied that there was no rush—the work could be performed in the following season.

Almost ten months passed before Schuman could report progress on the commission, writing to Kostelanetz that "at present it is my intention to compose a work called 'Sleepy Hollow Legend,' the spirit of which will be indicated in a program note quoting passages from Washington Irving's famous story 'The Legend of Sleepy Hollow.'" Schuman had also suggested a set of variations based on Victor Herbert's song "In Old New York," but Kostelanetz was cool to the idea.

Work on the composition had been further interrupted by a request from the Department of State to compose a special work for a UNESCO conference to be held in Cincinnati, Ohio, in November 1955. The work was entitled *Credendum*. Upon Schuman's request, Schuman's old friend Harold Spivacke, chief of the music division of the Library of Congress from 1937 to 1972, spoke with Kostelanetz to request permission to defer the original commission. Kostelanetz graciously agreed. Schuman finally said that he hoped to have the piece to the conductor by the summer of 1956.

The seemingly ill-fated commission was then confronted with yet another challenge, this time from Kostelanetz:

Regarding your idea of a work based on the "Legend of Sleepy Hollow," I am sure it is excellent. However, here is the predicament.

Ferde Grofé has written the "Hudson River Suite" . . . , which I conducted extensively this summer. The composition had national publicity including Time, Life, and Newsweek, and I am recording it this week. It seems to me that the subject matter for your proposed composition is too close to the one that Grofé has just written. Possibly you could substitute another idea. What do you think? Please give me your opinion about this matter.

Schuman took four months to rethink the commission. Finally, in December, the composer outlined his new idea in a detailed letter to Kostelanetz. Although the proposed title, "Spirit of '76—Three Pieces for Orchestra after William Billings," did not survive, the structure and content of the piece had now come alive in Schuman's fertile brain:

> Every [sic] since you decided that you could not spend your musical life conducting Hudson River pieces and that therefore I should come up with something different from "Sleepy Hollow" I have been plagued, undoubtedly by the ghost of Ichabod Crane. Don't be frightened—I have not changed my mind about the wisdom of your suggesting a theme other than the Hudson. Now I have a wonderful idea which I hope will please you. Here's the story:
>
> Beginning some years ago as part of my professional activities I conducted choral groups and the music of America's first professional composer—William Billings—came to my attention. I have been a Billings' [sic] fan ever since, finding in his crude utterances sentiments of great vigor which find in me a responsive chord. Some years ago I wrote an overture based on certain themes of his called, not unnaturally, "William Billings Overture." The first performance of this work was given by the Philharmonic under Rodzinski and it has been performed by a number of organizations since that time, yet I have never published the work because I have never been satisfied with it. I have finally determined to withdraw this composition with a view some day of re-writing it. Now, however, I wish to do a wholly new Billings composition which while employing some of the music I had used in the overture will be entirely new in concept and not an overture at all. What I plan is as follows: Some general title such as "Spirit of '76"—Three Pieces for Orchestra after William Billings:
>
> 1. "Be Glad Then America"
> 2. "When Jesus Wept"
> 3. "Chester"
>
> The first piece (words for the three pieces on which the music is based should be printed in the program book) would be a vigorous allegro of approximately 2 ½ to 3 minutes; the second piece would be based on "When Jesus Wept"—which is one of the most beautiful melodies I know and is in the form of a round. It would be scored for

solo oboe (possibly bassoon, also) and strings. I feel confident that this will make a beautiful adagio of 3 ½ to 4 minutes. The final movement "Chester" would be based on the song of that name which was the rallying song of the American Revolution. The movement would open with a subdued choral statement of "Chester" soon giving way to a spirited treatment and gradually building up to a climax in which the fast music would be pitted against the return of the hymn. This movement I should also judge would be approximately 3 to 4 minutes in length. I am very excited about the possibility of doing these three pieces for I believe that I can write the kind of work you commissioned without compromise and at the same time supplying a link of sentiment which will help you with the pop audience.

Kostelanetz enthusiastically accepted the new idea and scheduled the work for performance in the fall of 1956. The finished score arrived for Kostelanetz's review on July 11, 1956, with the new title of "New England Triptych," and he was thrilled with the results.

A final twist in the arduous path to *Triptych* occurred when, after studying the work, Kostelanetz told Schuman, "I'm too nervous to do it in New York for the first time. We could do it in Miami because I have an engagement there the week before. Would you come to Miami with me?" Schuman agreed. *New England Triptych* was finally premiered on October 26, 1956, in Miami, with Andre Kostelanetz conducting the University of Miami Symphony Orchestra; this was followed by a performance on November 3 by the New York Philharmonic, again conducted by Kostelanetz.

The work garnered considerable critical praise. Alfred Frankenstein of the *San Francisco Chronicle* wrote, "Billings and Schuman are both noteworthy for their infectious exuberance and enthusiasm. . . . Schuman's handling of Billings' material is, of course, dynamic, positive and creative rather than merely reflective, affirming the unity of American musical culture." In the *Los Angeles Times*, Albert Goldberg declared that "*New England Triptych* . . . impressed as a work of so much substance and vitality that it will very likely find its way into the permanent repertoire . . . it is a resoundingly successful example of skillful orchestration."

Although a recording of the *New England Triptych* was not made until early 1959, Kostelanetz traveled America with the work to great acclaim, and it has been performed by numerous orchestras ever since. The work's popularity brought new celebrity to Schuman. The second movement, "When Jesus Wept," was specifically requested to be played by the United States Marine Orchestra at President Gerald Ford's funeral on January 2, 2007, during a prelude to the ceremony. However, Schuman eventually resented its popularity, calling it his C sharp minor prelude—an allusion to the popularity of Rachmaninoff's composition of that title, which was played frequently in Schuman's youth.

Schuman also recalled being asked,

> "Why don't you write another *New England Triptych*? Don't you want another success?" I always say I would love another success, but I didn't write the piece to make it a success, it just happened to turn out to be successful. Writing music is really divided into two basic elements: the art of writing music, and the profession of being a composer. The profession of being a composer is an absurdity—it's not a profession, it's an indulgence. But writing music is something wonderful.

With Schuman's attraction to the sound of concert bands, it made sense for him to arrange this most accessible and original work of Americana for such an ensemble. The first band arrangement was titled *Chester Overture* and premiered by the University of Louisville Band in January 1957, only about two months after the first performance of the original *Triptych*. *When Jesus Wept: Prelude for Band* was premiered on June 18, 1958, by the Goldman Band in New York City, with Schuman's friend Richard Franko Goldman conducting.

Schuman points out in the *When Jesus Wept* score that "this Prelude is intended to serve as an introduction to the composer's *Chester*, Overture for Band . . . When performed together there should be no more than a momentary pause between the Prelude and the Overture."

Triptych's first movement, "Be Glad Then, America," finally appeared in a band arrangement in 1975, allowing the entire *New England Triptych* to be played by concert band.

See the appendix for further discussion of *New England Triptych*.

The work that interrupted the composition of *Triptych* was *Credendum: Article of Faith*, composed during the summer of 1955 as a commission from the United States National Commission for the United Nations Educational, Scientific and Cultural Organization (UNESCO) through the U.S. Department of State. It was the first time a department of the American government had commissioned a symphonic composition.

Schuman already had ties to the State Department. In 1952 the department had appointed him as the United States' musical representative at that September's International Conference of Creative Artists in Venice, sponsored by UNESCO. His letters to Frankie throughout the conference move from initial disdain to eventual enthusiasm. Schuman wrote on Monday, September 21, 1952:

> Suffice it to say that *nothing* [triple-underscored] is done right. The first plenary session had to be called off because the acoustics in the hall (a new one—not the Ducal Palace) were so bad no one could hear.
>
> The problem of presenting America to the European intellectual is a very important but difficult one. . . . They [European composers] don't believe in us as even potential artists. They are not interested in learning.

On Tuesday:

> I must tell you . . . that I did it—I made a major statement on music education and it was one of those beautiful times when the thoughts boiled over and the words flowed with ease—I was congratulated by Ibert, Honegger, Malipiero among others. . . . I'm no longer scared because I found that I can do it.

And on Wednesday:

> The conference grows more and more fantastic. I have, without egotism, become a leader in the composer's group. I get on well with the famous ones and speak on a friendly basis to the others as well. . . . It is exhausting but very important. It is not funny—a state department official said "We're at war" and he's not wrong.

Later in the decade Schuman would be a key member of an Advisory Committee to the United States Information Agency (USIA) and would exchange voluminous correspondence with David S. Cooper, chief of USIA's music program in the mid-1950s. In the late 1950s Cooper became dean of the Peabody Institute. Schuman stirred up considerable controversy when it came to choosing Cooper's replacement at USIA. The tension between Schuman and the agency staff was reflected in a letter dated October 10, 1959, to

Schuman from Cooper concerning the appointment of Angelo Eagon as Cooper's replacement:

> They planned to appoint him [Eagon] with or without your concurrence. By happy coincidence you endorsed him. Had you not endorsed him . . . there was considerable thought of asking you to resign from the advisory committee. The reason, of course, is obvious. You are a troublemaker who upsets well-oiled bureaucratic machines by insisting upon standards, upon professional competence and a well thought out program which would utilize an important art in an effective manner.

Credendum, written for large orchestra, is in three sections, played without pause: Declaration (Moderato con fuoco), Chorale (Lento), and Finale (Presto). It was premiered on November 4, 1955, by the Cincinnati Symphony Orchestra, Thor Johnson conducting, at a special concert in Cincinnati honoring the Fifth National Conference of the United States National Commission for UNESCO.

Schuman was honored to receive this unique commission, for it reinforced his conviction that the federal government should have a role in the arts. In his brief explanation of the work, he explained that "The first movement, *Declaration*, is scored for wind instruments and percussion" primarily, and that "the musical materials of this movement are 'oratorical' in nature." He continued, "In the second movement, *Chorale*, the chorale melody is first heard in the string section . . . where it is developed at some length." The chorale is taken up by the brass "while the strings begin filigree of a contrasting nature. The music gains in intensity and the woodwinds join in the figurations set against the chorale," moving to a quiet ending. Then "the *Finale* opens with scherzo-like material given to the strings[,] bassoons, and bass clarinet," which is developed through the cellos and eventually the violins. Finally, "as the music gains momentum, a vigorous subject derived from the melody originally heard in the 'celli is announced and developed contrapuntally, [ultimately leading] to a return to the Chorale. . . . The work ends with the music of the *Declaration* now paraphrased and leading to a peroration."

After the performance in Cincinnati, Eugene Ormandy and the Philadelphia Orchestra performed the *Credendum* on numerous occasions in the United States and around the world. The work was also recorded by Ormandy and Philadelphia on Columbia Records.

Schuman could have designated the *Credendum* a symphony owing to its length—about eighteen minutes—but, the composer remarked, "I wasn't trying to build up a large number of symphonies." He later elaborated, "It does not have as many complex elements in it as I have in my symphonies. The Fifth Symphony (1943) [Symphony for Strings] is more multi-character than the *Credendum*."

Schuman's motivation to compose the work was his idealized view of the UNESCO mission:

> I was so enamored of UNESCO. I was so naïve. I thought UNESCO was going to be one of the saviors of the world because [of] its intercultural nature, and its promotion of free exchange of materials. Before UNESCO you couldn't send a record to Europe or get a record from Europe. The title [*Credendum*] was a political statement, but it had nothing to do with the piece itself.

Schuman also said he had an "extramusical idea [with *Credendum*] which I will call a declaration, and I sought a suitable musical environment for the materials. The wind band and percussion of the orchestra for the first movement was a natural choice. Strings would have spoiled it."

The critical response to *Credendum* was quite favorable. Oliver Daniel wrote in the *Saturday Review* that "the work is important: it is broad and sweeping in both scope and content." Paul Henry Lang's tongue was squarely in his cheek when he began:

> Last night's concert of the Philadelphia Orchestra presented a work [*Credendum*] that has shattered all existing American traditions, violated the old and prudent doctrine of avoiding entangling alliances, and probably trampled the unwritten law against using tax money to subsidize long-hairs: William Schuman's "Credendum" was commissioned by a department of the United States Government! All honor to the perpetrator of this deed, but above all to the composer.

Paul Hume called *Credendum* "music of immense beauty, built with sure knowledge into a work of convincing power."

Credendum was written while Schuman was giving significant thought to *New England Triptych*, so it is intriguing to note how different the two pieces are. Whereas *Triptych* is clarity incarnate in its use of harmonic, melodic, and orchestral materials, *Credendum* is an exceptionally dense work of triple-forte brass chords and long, convoluted string melodies. Although Schuman was always known for his "muscular" writing, *Credendum*'s opening salvo in the brass and percussion, and the conclusion of the work—with crescendoing forte chords in the brass accompanied by clangorous outbursts of chimes, steel plate, tam-tam, and xylophone—drive this work to the edge of good taste.

By the mid- to late 1940s Schuman's compositional catalog was growing significantly, paralleling the growth of his reputation as one of America's most important composers. His popular songs were the first of his works to be professionally published by the Edward B. Marks Music Company in the early 1930s. Marks went on in 1932 to publish Schuman's first "classical" work, "God's World" for voice and piano, based on a text of Edna St. Vincent Millay.

Although Schuman had a few works overseen by other publishers during the 1930s, including Carl Fischer, Boosey & Hawkes, and J. & W. Chester for European publishing rights to the a cappella choral work *Pioneers*, by the early 1940s, Schuman and his music were firmly ensconced in the G. Schirmer family of composers. Not only was G. Schirmer one of the most prominent publishers of the time, but Schuman also felt a personal loyalty to Carl Engel, Schirmer's director of publications, for his friendship and support after Schuman was rejected for military service during World War II.

After World War II, as Schuman's reputation began to grow and his new presidency of the Juilliard School of Music provided him a prestigious administrative and financial base, his lifelong impatience with matters and individuals that did not meet his professional or personal standards began to surface with G. Schirmer. Schuman was clearly upset with his publisher in 1946 when he was told that a performance of his band work *Newsreel* was being held up because new performance copies could not be made owing to "lack of paper." Schuman shot back a brief letter to Nathan Broder of the Schirmer publications department: "As one not wholly unfamiliar with the workings of G. Schirmer, your 'lack of paper' line sounds very much like one of your form 'exigencies, etc.' lines. For shame."

By 1952, with his reputation growing in America's music world, Schuman decided to renegotiate his contract with Schirmer and to move his licensing agreement from ASCAP to Broadcast Music, Inc. (BMI). American composers of so-called classical or concert music are paid fees for the public performances of their work in concert halls or through the media based on their affiliation with either ASCAP or BMI. These agencies license the music and track the performances of compositions, then receive fees from the presenting entities, a percentage of which is paid to the composers. Most music publishers have at least two imprints that are affiliated with either ASCAP or BMI. The composer receives royalties, as well, from the publisher when the printed music is either sold to consumers or rented for a performance.

In 1952 Schuman wanted to have his music licensed through BMI, but he was not sure that Schirmer would agree to the change. BMI, unlike ASCAP, had begun giving financial guarantees to certain composers, no matter what music was performed during a given year. Schuman wished to take advantage of BMI's policy, and in the summer of 1952 BMI offered him a seven-year contract beginning on January 1, 1953, that provided for an annual guarantee of $7,000. In addition, Schuman was asked to act as a consultant to BMI on "matters affecting our general program for the overall promotion and exploitation of American Contemporary Serious Music" for a five-year period at the rate of another $7,000 annually. The total annual fee of $14,000 was a considerable amount at the time.

Schuman was not only pleased to realize the affiliation with BMI, but he was also gratified to learn that he could stay with G. Schirmer as his publisher. He wrote to BMI's vice president, Robert Burton: "Today I stopped in to see Mr. Schirmer and was delighted to find that he has had a change of heart over my affiliation with BMI. He now feels that he would like to continue to publish me and has expressed his willingness to do so through an affiliation with BMI." In the same letter he said that he had considered moving to Associated Music Publishers, but this would no longer be necessary.

When the new contracts between G. Schirmer and BMI came into effect on January 1, 1953, Schuman worked with his attorney, Abraham Friedman, to create a partnership called Howard Music Company that would act as the entity through which royalties and licensing fees would be paid in the new agreements. Frankie and Bill were the co-partners in this new venture, and the company would hold the copyright on any newly composed works. Howard Music was created to comply with Schuman's desire to have BMI as his licensing agent, and G. Schirmer agreed to be the "agent" for Howard "for the publication of your [Schuman's] works."

Unfortunately, this new and seemingly positive relationship between Schuman and G. Schirmer began to unravel only a year after the new agreement had been signed. In September 1954 Schuman began a long and acrimonious correspondence with G. Schirmer's director of publications, H. W. (Hans) Heinsheimer, concerning his belief that G. Schirmer was not adequately supporting the distribution and performance of his compositions. Schuman exploded in a four-page letter to Heinsheimer:

> There is no use in my making believe that I'm not very disturbed by my conversations last week with both you and Nat [Nathan Broder of G. Schirmer] for truly I am. . . . It is difficult because for years I had the idealistic notion that my allegiance to the firm was a two way street. You, better than anyone else, know that I was prepared to give up the BMI contract if it meant that I couldn't stay with G. S[chirmer]. Don't think that it wasn't painfully clear to me that Mr. S[chirmer] was willing . . . without a qualm, to have me leave the firm after so many years of happy ([Carl] Engel's regime and my own) association and a sizeable catalog. . . . I would like you to know personally and for your own consideration the things I want at Schirmer's. If you feel that I can't have them I shall ask Mr. S. to release me from my new contract (Howard Music Co.) and the privilege of buying back the unpublished works and the materials. Let's not bother to speculate whether he'll agree or not suffice it to say that that is one bridge I have no fear of crossing should I come to it.

Schuman went on to angrily demand that G. Schirmer make a "special effort" to promote his music. "Why have a publisher if he cannot exploit your music with consistent energy and a display of conviction whether real or simulated?" Schuman wrote.

Schuman also questioned Heinsheimer's commitment to the substance of his music and its eventual recording: "I have a realistic understanding of the commercial value of my music at the present time and I realize too that your admiration and estimate of its worth is strictly qualified. . . . Schirmer has never lifted a finger to get a work of mine recorded but I can recall at least one instance where the publisher lost me backing." The letter ended with a halfhearted effort at some level of reconciliation:

> I wish a peaceful as well as productive relationship with my publisher. . . . Frankly I have had to "handle" you as much as you have had to "handle" me and that's going some. Well relax—we can't fool each other for I will put up with no nonsense from you and you

have my word, that if we can start all this afresh, I'll be an angel as long as the publisher too wears at least half a halo.

For the next several months Heinsheimer and Schuman sparred over an endless list of issues, from rental availability for the *William Billings Overture* to cover art for Schuman's opera, *The Mighty Casey*. Throughout this period, Schuman continually pressed Schirmer for more active support of his music, expressing frustration about the distribution of his new piano piece "Voyage" and the critical failure of G. Schirmer's recently published biography of him.

By February 1955 the breach between Schuman and Heinsheimer seemed irreparable. In a note to his file Schuman recalled that during a telephone call of February 10, 1955, he told Heinsheimer that he

> had had enough and was going to leave Schirmer's. He [Heinsheimer] said he too had had enough and thought that I had treated him badly—that he was just as important to music as I was and more important to Schirmer's. In reply I said that the matter was simply that he had no conviction about my music and obviously a dislike of me personally so that I could no longer feel that Schirmer's was the right publisher for my works. . . . I feel relieved because I want no further association with this man.

Heinsheimer attempted to repair the situation, but in vain. Schuman met with Gustave Schirmer and Heinsheimer in the spring of 1955 to advise them that he wished to be relieved of his contractual obligation to G. Schirmer. In September Schuman noted that "now Heinsheimer is being very, very nice and quite obviously wants me to remain. My decision is a hard one to make. He remains the same, a bully—But there is not a really first rate publisher for serious music in NYC. What to do?"

Although Schuman had a few conversations with Associated Music Publishers, he ultimately decided to sign a long-term contract in mid-January 1956 with the Theodore Presser Company of Bryn Mawr, Pennsylvania. Schirmer relieved the Howard Music Company (representing Schuman) of its contractual obligations to G. Schirmer, and the long-term relationship between Schuman and G. Schirmer came to an end on the last day of 1955.

In negotiations with the president of Presser, Arthur A. Hauser, Schuman was given a ten-year contract that not only guaranteed an annual payment of $5,000 independent of royalties, but also stipulated that Presser would "use its best efforts to exploit all musical works of Composer . . . [and] further agrees that it will solicit each year the major conductors of orchestras in the United States with respect to Composer's major works." Schuman's music would be published through Presser's BMI subsidiary, Merion Music, and the Howard Music Company would no longer exist. Presser would be Schuman's publisher for the rest of his life.

The intensity with which Schuman demanded corporate support from Schirmer points to the focused and self-assured nature of this driven composer and administrator. By 1956 Schuman had a deep and overriding belief in his talent as a composer and in his stature as a major player in his country's artistic life. His abiding drive to succeed often pushed his professional relationships to the edge of dissolution, and his firm belief that his actions were correct, no matter what advice he might receive to the contrary, would eventually cause considerable problems for him in his future years at Lincoln Center.

In 1958 Schuman was approached by the Edward B. Marks Corporation to renew the copyright on two songs he had written in the early 1930s with his friend Eddie Marks, "Lovesick" and "Waitin' for the Moon." The letter came from the company's president, Herbert E. Marks, Eddie's brother, who signed the letter, "Your avaricious publisher and loving friend." There was an amusing postscript as well: "Remember 'Paper Doll?' What would have happened if that hadn't been renewed just in time!" That old song had been turned into a pops classic in the 1950s.

With characteristic chutzpah, Schuman treated his and Marks's old songs as if they had been perpetually performed during the past thirty years and asked for an advance for them. Herbert Marks responded, "Giving you an advance on songs which have not earned a penny in many, many years would be, in my opinion, just as wrong as bending over backwards because I've always been so very fond of you." Schuman then suggested that "Waitin' for the Moon" could "make a successful piece in [a] rock and roll arrangement. It lends itself to this type treatment."

This comic saga went on for several months. Finally, in February 1960, Herbert Marks wrote: "I must confess, a faint glimmer of a smile crosses my face when I note that the President of Ju[i]lliard is concerned about a song

'Waitin' For The Moon.'" Schuman quickly responded: "I am amused that you were amused that as President of Juilliard I should be concerned about WAITIN' FOR THE MOON. The truth of the matter is that among my large catalog of works I have no stepchildren." Suffice it to say that no Schuman song was ever turned into a rock-and-roll classic.

Between 1950 and 1962 Schuman was at the height of his compositional powers in both quality and quantity. Between the premiere of *Judith* in January 1950 and the first performance of *A Song of Orpheus* in February 1962 he produced eighteen major works or arrangements. These works included *George Washington Bridge* for concert band (premiere: July 30, 1950, by the Interlochen National Music Camp Band); the String Quartet No. 4 (premiere: October 28, 1950, in Washington, D.C., by the Hungarian Quartet); *The Mighty Casey*, an opera in three scenes (premiere: May 4, 1953, by the Hartt College of Music Opera Theater, Hartford, Connecticut), as well as an arrangement of choruses from *Casey* for mixed chorus and piano four hands; *Voyage: A Cycle of Five Pieces for Piano* (premiere: August 18, 1953, Chicago, Illinois); *Voyage for a Theater* (premiere: May 17, 1953, choreographed by Martha Graham, New York City—withdrawn by the composer); *Credendum: Article of Faith* (premiere: November 4, 1955, Cincinnati, Ohio); *Chester Overture* (premiere: January 1957, by the University of Louisville Band); *Five Rounds on Famous Words* for a cappella mixed chorus or women's chorus (1956), a witty treatment of the words "Health" (Early to bed and early to rise), "Thrift" (He that goes a-borrowing, goes a-sorrowing), "Caution" (Look, look, look, Look before you leap!), "Beauty" (All that glitters isn't gold), and a fifth round added in 1969, "Haste" (Make Haste Slowly); *The Lord Has a Child* for mixed women's chorus and piano, on text by Langston Hughes (1957); *New England Triptych* (premiere: October 26, 1956, University of Miami Symphony Orchestra); and *Carols of Death* for mixed a cappella chorus, with text by Walt Whitman (first performed on March 20, 1959, by the Laurentian Singers of St. Lawrence University in Canton, New York). The three movements, entitled "The Last Invocation," "The Unknown Region," and "To All, To Each," express a mournful, yet hopeful view of death, with the text of the last movement peacefully depicting the most feared of human experiences: "Come, come, come lovely and soothing death." Schuman said that the three Whitman poems used in this work "haunted me for years, because I think they're absolutely beautiful, and I never could find the music that I felt was right to go with them. . . . People who know and like my choral music, such as Bob Shaw, think this is the best I've done."

Schuman was without doubt one of the most important American choral composers of the twentieth century. Robert Sabin, writing in a comprehensive survey of choral music, succinctly outlined the reasons for Schuman's lofty reputation in this genre:

> If one were asked point-blank to name the most original and forceful of twentieth-century American choral composers thus far, the choice would fall inevitably upon William Schuman. For he has revolutionized the style and technique of choral writing not merely for professionals but for amateurs, and his choral music is unmistakably American in spirit and texture. Like Emerson's essays, like Whitman's poetry, Schuman's music reveals the ideas and conceptions and visions and experiences that make the United States what it is.

During this time Schuman also composed *Three Piano Moods* (premiere: December 2, 1958, by Joel Rosen, in Athens, Greece); *When Jesus Wept* (premiere: June 18, 1958, in New York City by the Goldman Band, Richard Franko Goldman conducting); *The Earth Is Born*, a film score commissioned by Time-Life in 1959; Symphony No. 7 (premiere: October 21, 1960, in Boston by the Boston Symphony Orchestra, Charles Munch conducting); and *A Song of Orpheus* (premiere: February 17, 1962, in Indianapolis, Indiana, by Leonard Rose, soloist, with the Indianapolis Symphony Orchestra).

George Washington Bridge has always been a favorite of band directors for its high energy. Schuman once said that he loved bridges and "drove past the George Washington Bridge every day, going to and from Sarah Lawrence. I walked across it once about 3:00 in the morning, all alone . . . I still think it's a magnificent bridge. Bridges and railroads I like a lot; tunnels give me claustrophobia."

Schuman's 1957 choral work *The Lord Has a Child* is brief (at about three minutes) and simple, based on Langston Hughes's spiritual text: "The Lord has a child / That child I know is me / Even when I'm not all I ought to be." As the composer remarked, he used the work, originally for piano and voice, in many guises: "Later I did a choral version of it and in 1990, a version for chorus and brass quintet for the Greenwich Choral Society. I did a nine-minute band version, called *American Hymn*, and it also became a 26-minute orchestral piece, *American Hymn*, for the St. Louis Symphony and Leonard Slatkin." A version for brass quintet was also premiered in 1981.

The Fourth String Quartet was commissioned by the Elizabeth Sprague Coolidge Foundation in honor of the 150th anniversary of the founding of the Library of Congress. It was first performed during the eleventh Festival of Chamber Music at the Library of Congress on October 28, 1950, by the Hungarian String Quartet (Zoltán Székely and Alexandre Moskowsky, violins; Dénes Koromzay, viola; and Vilmos Palotai, cello), along with quartets by Beethoven and Schubert.

The quartet was composed at Menemsha, Martha's Vineyard, in record time between June 26 and August 3, 1950. Schuman had injured his leg in a Sunday pick-up softball game on a field in Chilmark and was laid up for most of the summer with a ruptured blood vessel; the forced inactivity allowed him to devote more time to composing. Schuman's Third Quartet had been premiered in 1940, a decade earlier, and his return to this important genre was a significant compositional milestone.

The work is in four movements: Adagio—Allegro con fuoco—Andante—Presto, Prestissimo. Aaron Copland wrote that it

> is one of Schuman's most mature works. . . . In some ways it is typical of the composer, in others it seems to be composed from a new premise. . . . I cannot remember another work of Schuman that strikes so somber a note. . . . a more tentative expressivity has taken over; a darker, more forbidding tone that seems far different from the basically optimistic—sometimes boyishly optimistic—tone of his earlier music. . . . Schuman has always had a strong structural sense, but he has not always succeeded in filling out his forms with music all the way. . . . This quartet has no such blemish. . . . Even a cultivated audience will be put off by a certain hermetic quality at its core. But it is just this hermetic quality—this somewhat forbidding and recalcitrant aspect—that presages an enlargement of the capacities of the William Schuman we already know.

Olin Downes wrote in the *New York Times* the day after the premiere of the Fourth Quartet that Schuman's new score was

> ultra-modern and . . . presents more difficulties of technique, intonation than Beethoven and Schubert together, rhythm with equally impressive authority . . . it is a score of a highly progressive composer who is well acquainted with the modern literature of music, knowing his Bartók, Hindemith, Schoenberg and Berg as well; able to adapt their idioms at will to his own esthetic needs.

Schuman's writing for the string quartet is masterly, and the work contains many of Schuman's typical compositional "fingerprints": tempo extremes, from the exceedingly slow tempo of the first movement (quarter note = c. 50) to the blisteringly fast pace of the final Prestissimo (half note = c. 184); long melodic lines; extreme dynamic changes; syncopated dotted eighth–sixteenth note figures; a dense assemblage of polychords in the third movement; and a concluding G major chord. A work of considerable substance and density, it ranks as one of his most focused and intense compositions. Schuman later used materials from the slow third movement in the second movement of his Eighth Symphony.

See the appendix for further discussion of the Fourth String Quartet.

If the Fourth Quartet was "ultra-modern," Schuman's first opera was the exact opposite in tone, looking back to a simpler time both musically and socially. Schuman had a lifelong love affair with baseball. Like so many others, he saw the game as more than a sporting event. Baseball was about the suspension of time, intricate strategies, the heroism of the moment, and all that was good in the American spirit. Choosing baseball as the centerpiece of a musical work took Schuman back to the memories of his youth and his joyful days at Camp Cobbossee.

The Mighty Casey was set at the turn of the twentieth century in the imaginary town of Mudville, idealized in the classic poem by Ernest Lawrence Thayer (1863–1940). Thayer was a Harvard graduate and an editor of the college's famous humor magazine, the Harvard *Lampoon*. He eventually settled in San Francisco at the invitation of his college chum William Randolph Hearst, owner of the *San Francisco Examiner*, who invited him to write a weekly humor column for the paper. "Casey at the Bat" was printed in the *Examiner* on June 3, 1888.

This bit of doggerel might have fallen away quietly had it not been for the actor and singer William De Wolf Hopper, who recited the poem at a performance to delirious applause. Thayer's poem became a permanent piece of Hopper's repertoire, and the fame of "Casey" spread widely. In Hopper's memoirs he writes:

> There always is a chance that the Babe will strike out . . . the contrast between the terrible threat of his swing and the futility of the result is a banquet for the malicious, which includes us all . . . there are one or more Caseys in every league, bush or big, and there is no day in the playing season that this supreme tragedy, as stark as Aristophanes for the moment, does not befall on some field.

The author Walter Simmons has written that "perhaps the notion of a great hero failing at the moment of truth, in the presence of his peers, touches a particularly sensitive nerve in the American collective unconscious."

Schuman began work on his opera in 1951 and chose as his librettist Jeremy Gury, a New York advertising executive who was the creative director of the Ted Bates Company at that time. Gury immersed himself in developing the Thayer poem, adding a Watchman, who explains the simple narrative throughout the opera; a love interest in the character of Merry, who adores Casey and wants him to succeed but fears that success will take him away from Mudville and her forever; the opposing team's pitcher, Snedeker, and a catcher, Thatcher; a bumptious umpire, Buttenheiser; and assorted townspeople, hawkers, and team members. In an ironic twist, the only character who never utters a word in the entire eighty-minute work is the hero himself, Casey.

Gury was a demanding collaborator. The author remembers conversations with Schuman regarding the creation of *Casey* in which the composer said he rued the day he chose Gury as his librettist, complaining that Gury would move the opera in directions of no interest to Schuman. Yet in his last oral history Schuman remarked, "I had a wonderful time working with him [Gury]. He turned out an excellent libretto." Yet the relationship between composer and librettist was visibly chilly at the 1989 Glimmerglass performance. Gury was largely ignored by the public during the festivities, at which were performed for the first time *Casey* together with Schuman's second opera, *A Question of Taste*, with libretto by J. D. McClatchy.

Gury's extensive correspondence with Schuman on the creation of *Casey* reveals that the librettist did not share the composer's passion for their subject. In one letter Gury wrote:

> We can permit ourselves to be a bit serious with the girl [Merry] and her romance—but not with the game itself. The great charm of Casey is that it is so colossally, magnificently unimportant. . . .
>
> I know of your deep concern to avoid banality and to make Casey a fresh work from start to finish. Nevertheless baseball in general presents us with a vast complex of banalities; and small town, competitive baseball adds to that burden. . . .
>
> All of which goes to say that we are working on a subject that is ninety percent corn and that it is, in my opinion, somewhat incumbent upon us to serve it up in a souffle, enriched and seasoned.

Such clear disparagement and lack of sympathy for America's pastime must have irked the composer no end.

Even before the score was finished, Schuman instructed G. Schirmer's Hans W. Heinsheimer, the publications director, to contact as many popular outlets as possible for his new opera in the hope that it would be embraced by the American public like no other work of its kind. Heinsheimer first contacted Ford Frick, then president of the National League and later commissioner of baseball, to suggest that major league baseball purchase the rights to the opera for a certain time so that baseball could then make it available, as a public relations gesture, to colleges and communities around America. It was also hoped that the Louisville Orchestra, the ensemble that premiered *Judith* and that performed in the home of the "Louisville Slugger," would premier the work.

In a frustrated and comical letter from the Eurocentric and baseball-ignorant Heinsheimer of July 12, 1951, the publisher laments the direction of this venture:

> Frankly, this whole thing is taking a slant I dislike. Gury tells me that, after having spoken with me, [a meeting took place] with Frick, who is "a sweet man," and who told them (most sensibly, I think) that he and his people were concerned with baseball and not with operas. He suggested that they should go to see a man by the name of Binswanger, in Pittsburgh, who is a "music fan, writes the program notes for the Pittsburgh Symphony, *and* used to own the

Pirates. He would be your man! Now really! There must be a limit to just how far we will go. . . . I am all for the American way of Free Enterprise, and love money as much as the next man, but something tells me that ain't the way to make it.

Well, Bill, as Walt Whitman Gury says: "Keep Kool, Keep Kool, Keep Kool."

Undeterred by rejection from both organized baseball and the Louisville Orchestra, Gury's optimism continued unabated: "At this point Casey gives promise of reaching out far beyond the chic Menotti audiences and re-creating opera as a mass medium." The reference to Gian Carlo Menotti points to the fact that the idea of an opera on Broadway was not a new one. Several of Menotti's operas had realized success on both Broadway and on television. *Amahl and the Night Visitors* had become extremely popular since its premiere on television in 1951, and *The Medium* (1947) was televised in 1948. *The Medium*, as well as Menotti's operas *The Consul* (1950), *The Telephone* (1947), and *The Saint of Bleecker Street* (1954), had all realized a modicum of success on Broadway. Schuman had reason to hope that *Casey* would have a future in a Broadway house.

To that end, Heinsheimer was persuaded to contact the well-known Broadway producer Alfred de Liagre Jr. (known to everyone as Delly), in November 1951 to listen to Schuman's "new *musical*" (emphasis added) *The Mighty Casey* for possible production on Broadway. In addition, NBC television was approached about broadcasting the new opera. Sadly, Heinsheimer failed in this endeavor as well: "The news from NBC is not encouraging. Apparently the libretto has not met with great enthusiasm among the various members of the staff, and I don't think we can expect a performance there next season." Indiana University also turned down the premiere for the 1952–53 season. *The Mighty Casey* was finally premiered in less grand circumstances by the Hartt Opera Guild of the Hartt College of Music in Hartford, Connecticut, on May 4, 1953, conducted by Moshe Paranov in a double bill with Douglas Moore's *The Devil and Daniel Webster*.

Casey's story has a demoralizing coda. When CBS television agreed to air the opera on its highly respected Omnibus series on March 6, 1955, Schuman sent a short note to de Liagre asking him to view the broadcast: "I still think it should go on the stage. Why not consider this [the broadcast] a full dress audition and have your money boys alerted." The production included a cast of approximately fifty principals and choristers and was estimated by one trade journal to have cost about $50,000 to produce. Danny Scholl played

Casey, Elise Rhodes was Merry, and George Irving, the watchman. The orchestra was conducted by Samuel Krachmalnick. The Schumans invited friends to come watch the broadcast and even wrote a playful questionnaire for the guests with multiple-choice questions such as "It is my conviction that the melodic material in 'The Mighty Casey' is superior to that of a. Madama Butterfly b. Tristan and Isolde c. Minsky's."

The joviality of the moment died the day after the broadcast, when Schuman received a letter from de Liagre:

My dear Bill:

Wholesale, premeditated massacre—that's what it was. I can't remember, on screen or off, ever having seen a first rate work so completely horsed up and loused up in every department as yours and Jerry's [Gury] was yesterday afternoon.

If you decided to launch litigation against the Omnibus people, which I hope you will, you can count on me as a full time witness.

All the best.

Yours,

Delly

The *New York Times* was no kinder, stating that the opera "is essentially unfitting to Thayer's immortal, resounding lines. It is essentially unvocal. . . . Thematically it is composed in a quasi-modern style that is lacking in charm."

In a much later review of the work appearing in the same newspaper in 1990, John Rockwell continued the negative criticism, finding the opera "downright annoying, suggesting that Mr. Schuman has little real theatrical instinct," and bothered by having the Thayer poem "inflated into bloated sentimentality. 'The Mighty Casey' makes 'Our Town' look like social realism, 'A Field of Dreams' like a film noir."

Composing *Casey* was clearly an act of love for Schuman as well as a considerable commitment of composing time, and he had great hopes that it would be embraced by the profession and the public. The work features Schuman's vibrant orchestrations, dynamic rhythms (with the Schuman flourishes appearing in the overture), and a homey simplicity, which possess an inherent charm for anyone who does not require gritty reality in a musical event on the stage. Merry's aria ("Kiss me not goodbye") has great beauty and depth of emotion; Umpire Buttenheiser's dignified and witty plea for respect ("You will never, never find any umpire who is fairer") has genuine charm;

the chorus ("Hist'ry hangs on a slender thread") provides a creative mix of a witty text with a jaunty choral part, including collective hand-clapping; and the final choral lament ("Oh, somewhere in this favored land, the sun is shining bright") has real intensity and pathos.

Schuman commented:

> I wasn't looking for any models when I wrote *Casey*, because I thought *Casey* dictated its own terms. I was partly wrong in the way I treated *Casey*, however. When people hear the subject is baseball, they expect a score on the level of "Take me out to the ballgame." *Casey*, although it has lots of theatrical elements, is a very serious score, and its comment on baseball is very knowing and loving.

As Schuman suggested, if there is an inherent problem with *The Mighty Casey*, it probably lies in the proposition that it is too complex musically for the general public to embrace readily and may be too simplistic and cloying for opera cognoscenti, who view the work as dripping with sentimentality and less-than-profound musical treatment. Dramatically, the entire work hinges on one event, the result of which is already known by the audience, and the dramatic tension sags significantly as Casey's time at the plate is interrupted by lengthy solo and choral sections. In addition, the eighty-minute length is not enough for an entire evening, so it requires a companion work (which Schuman supplied in 1989 with *A Question of Taste*). The results for Schuman were sadly as disappointing as *Casey*'s last swing in Mudville.

Soon after *The Mighty Casey* was premiered in Hartford, Schuman attempted to create a new opera project based on Theodore Dreiser's *An American Tragedy*. Schuman wrote Lincoln Kirstein in July 1953 asking for his assistance not only in finding a librettist, but in obtaining Rockefeller Foundation money to commission and produce the proposed work. Schuman had obtained exclusive rights to the Dreiser novel for ten years. Kirstein expressed interest in the project and suggested Edwin Denby, the librettist for Copland's opera, *The Second Hurricane*, and Howard Sackler as possible librettists. The project, however, was never realized.

While Schuman was immersed in the details of bringing the Juilliard School of Music to Lincoln Center toward the end of his tenure as president of the

School, he was to create an extraordinary composition that projected an exceptional pathos.

Schuman's Symphony No. 7 was premiered in Boston, with Charles Munch conducting the Boston Symphony Orchestra, on October 21, 1960. The work was commissioned by the Serge Koussevitzky Music Foundation in the Library of Congress and the Boston Symphony Orchestra in celebration of the orchestra's seventy-fifth anniversary. (The work was premiered five years after the actual anniversary.) It is dedicated to the memory of Serge and Natalie Koussevitzky. Although his "symphony-like" *Credendum* was premiered in 1955, Schuman had not written a formal symphony since the premiere of the Sixth Symphony in 1949.

The Symphony No. 7 is written for a very large orchestra: double woodwinds, six horns, four trumpets, two tubas, piano, and a large percussion section. The composition is in four movements (designated Largo assai, Vigoroso, Cantabile intensamente, and Scherzando brioso) played without pause. The effect is a one-movement work of profound orchestral intensity, typical of Schuman's late symphonies.

Leonard Burkat, the Boston Symphony's music administrator at the time of the premiere, wrote in the program notes: "Especially noteworthy in the Seventh Symphony is a kind of choral writing for the orchestra. No matter how full the sound, no matter how active the music, how busy the texture, there are almost never more than two musical elements being presented at one time."

The chorale-like quality that Burkat mentions is manifested in the symphony's long first and third movements. They create a mammoth wall of sound, against which the shorter, up-tempo second and fourth movements seem like diversions. The first movement is marked Largo assai, with the slow Schumanesque tempo marking of eighth note = c. 69. What is so distinctive and striking about this movement is the excruciatingly anguished affect, its tension intensified by grating polychords and large, expressive leaps. One cannot help but wonder about Schuman's inner world as he created such troubled and tortured musical lines. This movement is remarkable for its dark intensity even when he inserts his "muscular" brass chords, which also magnify the feeling of foreboding.

This twelve-minute slow movement is interrupted by the composer's gleeful side. In the three-minute second movement we hear big, brassy syncopated chords and the standard array of rim-shots, timpani solos, and clanging chimes that are so prevalent in Schuman's work. However, before the reverberation of the brass has time to die away, the work turns doubly somber with a third movement at the exceedingly slow tempo of quarter note = c. 40. Below the tempo marking, Schuman writes in the score "Thoughtfully, deliberately, expressively." Scoring the movement for divisi strings that are often marked "Sonoro molto," Schuman creates a polychordal counterpoint of profound expression. The power and emotionality that Schuman develops in this movement presage a new stage in the expressiveness of the composer's musical language.

However, in what seems to be an effort to tell his listeners that things are not as bad as they seem, Schuman creates a final movement of brassy passages reminiscent of a Sousa band and a scene from *West Side Story*, complete with Schumanesque flourishes in the strings and winds and a clangorous explosion of triple-forte percussion. A dissonant twelve-note chord that sounds throughout the orchestra ultimately resolves in a final E-flat major chord, a type of ending often used by Schuman in his large orchestral works.

One would be tempted to see Schuman's Symphony No. 7 as a window into the composer's psyche as he turned fifty years old in 1960. At the height of his compositional career and just about to venture out to new administrative challenges (although he did not know it at that time), Schuman gives voice in this music to two opposing aspects of his persona: gleeful, playful, aggressive, and self-assured on the one hand; introspective, insecure, and vulnerable on the other. One can find a parallel here to Robert Schumann's *Carnaval*, with the exuberant Florestan and introspective Eusebius depicted in selected musical miniatures. Although he always presented a brave front in public, Schuman's private side was easily wounded by criticism of his music or his administrative decisions. The Seventh Symphony allows us to experience both sides of this complex and energetic man.

Critical response to the symphony was mildly positive, although most critics agreed that it was not an audience-friendly work. Paul Hume in the *Washington Post* wrote:

> the Seventh Symphony of William Schuman . . . is a piece of unmistakable power. It presents a new profile among contemporary American symphonies. Among the elements that can be discerned in that profile . . . are a vast and extraordinarily complex structure—a striking new field of sonorities achieved through the use of a large choir of woodwinds playing in a massed manner. These winds are deployed in a harmonic scheme that uses chords fashioned out of nearly all the notes of the diatonic scale at one time. . . . Schuman can

give us chords of high density without creating dissonances of undue harshness . . . there is everywhere the feeling of a work which Schuman has broken through into a new realm toward which he was moving, but without so marked a sense of achievement, in his *Credendum.*

Harold C. Schonberg in the *New York Times* commented:

Mr. Schuman has his own style of melody, and it's not to everybody's taste. In the slow movement, he aimed for a near-perpetual melodic line. . . . The harmonic dissonance that underpinned it sounded too tense and, even, rather dated. One kept thinking of the Nineteen Thirties when this kind of writing made such an impact. Somehow it does not seem to mean as much these days.

Winthrop Sargeant, writing in the *New Yorker* in December 1960, took a decidedly dyspeptic stance not only toward the Seventh Symphony, but also toward the process of bringing new musical compositions to the public:

The ceremony was familiar enough—that of launching a new symphony . . . by a well-known American composer. The audience applauded politely, and long enough to bring the composer to the stage. . . . Some of the audience probably reflected that Mr. Schuman is the head of the Juilliard School of Music . . . and that therefore what he had to say . . . should be considered worth listening to . . . [and other orchestras will perform it] . . . because Mr. Schuman, as head of the Juilliard School, is inevitably a dispenser of patronage in the form of teaching jobs and scholarships, and a valuable man to be on good terms with.

According to Tony Schuman, his father "was particularly stung by Sargeant's allegation that his music was performed because of his influence in the music world, and he considered a libel suit against Sargeant but was dissuaded from taking this course."

The last work Schuman composed before he left Juilliard was *A Song of Orpheus: Fantasy for Violoncello and Orchestra,* commissioned by the Ford Foundation for the great American cellist and pedagogue Leonard Rose. It was begun on September 25, 1960, and completed on July 4, 1961, and is dedicated to Frankie in celebration of their twenty-fifth wedding anniversary. The first performance took place in Indianapolis, Indiana, on February 17, 1962, with the Indianapolis Symphony Orchestra, conducted by Izler Solomon, and Leonard Rose as the soloist.

Schuman was fond of borrowing melodies to create new works that were not variations on a theme but rather elaborate transmogrifications of the melodic material. One need only look to the rounds provided by Marion Farquhar, selected sections of his 1958 *Three Piano Moods* as the basis for movements of his Seventh Symphony, and the Revolutionary War hymns for *New England Triptych*. But with *A Song of Orpheus* the melody comes from Schuman himself: he used his song "Orpheus with His Lute," composed in 1944 for the ill-fated Billy Rose production of Shakespeare's *Henry VIII*. Schuman's Juilliard colleague Vincent Persichetti had suggested that the song would make an excellent theme for a set of variations. Wrote Schuman in his program notes:

> His suggestion came to mind when I was searching for an idea for the work I had agreed to compose for Mr. Rose. Although the composition is not in the form of set variations, all of the music grows out of the melodic line of the song which is stated at the very beginning of the composition. . . . My aim in writing the fantasy for cello and orchestra . . . was to compose a piece which exploited that instrument, yet a piece where the other instruments needed the cello, and a work in which the cello could be heard at every moment. It is not a bravura piece in the conventional sense of the concerto; however it certainly exploits the instrument and challenges the soloist. . . .
>
> As I began to compose *Song of Orpheus*, I decided to open with a statement of the theme by the cello. I soon found myself enjoying the freedom to interrupt the song with harmonic statements, little things which gave atmosphere, and enjoying the business of interpreting the song in a different way than I had done before. . . . Certainly, *Song of Orpheus* is symphonic in form the same as *Credendum*. I did not call it a concerto because I think of it as a fantasy with a simpler approach.

The work received critical praise at its premiere. Henry Butler of the *Indianapolis Times* wrote: "He is writing allusively, not conclusively . . . his writing achieves some of its most stunning effects by ruthless elimination of cliches. . . . It is not the easiest work to apprehend, even in two hearings. But it contains much feeling, much material to ponder, and every inducement for further listening." In a later performance of the work in 1962 in New York City with the Juilliard Orchestra, with Jean Morel conducting and Rose as soloist, Francis Perkins of the *New York Herald Tribune* remarked, "This is imaginative music which calls upon the cello for instrumental song. . . . and its persuasive lyricism is expressed in terms of the present without retrospective derivation; both ideas and hues contribute to an absorbing poetic atmosphere."

Almost ten years after the premiere of *A Song of Orpheus*, Joseph Machlis, a distinguished author and faculty member at both Queens College and the Juilliard School, wrote a playful and perceptive letter to Schuman in 1971:

> Permit me to tell you how much I enjoyed your piece [*A Song of Orpheus*] last night. It had a dark lyricism that not only made fine use of the instrument but also persuaded the ear. Some of the dramatic measures put me in mind of your ballet *Undertow* but since I don't have the scores, I cannot say if this was just a subjective impression or had any basis in fact.

Schuman responded:

> Frankie was particularly delighted with what you had to say about the connection of *A Song of Orpheus* and *Undertow*, since she has often made the same observation.

The Machlis letter ends with a jocular and profane paragraph showing the easy interplay between the two men:

> Also let me congratulate you on reaching the seventh decade. What with the world being as fucked up as it is, this is quite an achievement. I commend you for it.

See the appendix for further discussion of *A Song of Orpheus*.

As the first day of January 1962 approached and his duties as president of Lincoln Center began, Schuman closed the door on a remarkably productive and creative period. As he set out to change Lincoln Center from an assemblage of impressive buildings to an environment that nourished the performing arts as never before in the history of America, he would soon learn that the camaraderie and good will he had enjoyed at Juilliard would be in limited supply in his new position.

CHAPTER 9

At Least at Juilliard There Was Music

With the final details of his departure from Juilliard addressed, Schuman left the school he had led for sixteen years and assumed his new position as Lincoln Center's president on January 1, 1962.

In a letter dated September 12, 1961, one day before the official announcement, and sent to each member of the Juilliard faculty, Schuman wrote that he would be resigning his position at Juilliard to take on the leadership of Lincoln Center:

> It is my conviction that Lincoln Center can be and must be a dynamic and constructive force for music, drama, and the dance not only in the New York City area but for the entire nation, and internationally as well. . . . It can lead to a vastly increased interest in and support for the performing arts. . . . We owe a duty to make its highest promise a reality.

Schuman was asked by the Juilliard presidential search committee, composed of David M. Keiser (chairman), Franklin B. Benkard, and Edward R. Wardwell, to recommend names of potential successors. Schuman sent letters to Keiser in early 1962 suggesting such candidates as Richard Franko Goldman, Norman Lloyd, Vincent Persichetti, and Hugo Weisgall. Schuman's eventual successor, Peter Mennin, was not recommended.

> Peter Mennin was interviewed very early on, in the fall of 1961. . . . He was not offered the appointment, but he was not turned down either. By spring he must have known that he wasn't a hot item. I felt that Mennin had done very well as an administrator at Peabody, but I was amazed that he was taken on because at Juilliard he was always late for class, and he didn't seem to have the attributes you think of in an administrator. . . . There was a great deal of resistance to

appointing him, but there was more resistance to appointing anybody else. At the end it was felt, and I concurred, that he was the best candidate, but nobody was excited about it.

Schuman had been both an innovative and effective administrator as well as a successful composer during his presidency of Juilliard. As satisfying as his work as a composer was, he realized that he needed to make a living to support his family, and he could not do that by composing alone. Therefore he immersed himself in his Juilliard duties with typical energy: "To me, running the school with all the very difficult problems that are always attendant . . . to a large institution . . . problems of personality . . . budget . . . directors . . . physical plant . . . I enjoyed all that. That wasn't a chore for me." In later life Schuman wondered whether he should have stayed at Juilliard longer, for he remembered genuinely wonderful years at the school. With his energetic personality, he had no interest in a sinecure at either Sarah Lawrence or Juilliard, something he certainly could have had. Rather, Schuman saw himself as "an innovator in the things I have done as an administrator and as a teacher." His move to Lincoln Center was part of the natural trajectory of his career.

A celebratory meeting of Juilliard's faculty and staff was held on December 19, 1961, to honor Schuman. His colleagues contributed $1,000 to "endow a seat in the Juilliard Theatre at Lincoln Center" and gave him a handsome book signed by the entire faculty and staff. A citation was also presented, which read:

The faculty and staff deeply regret your resignation from the presidency of the Juilliard School of Music.

In the sixteen years you have been our President your vision and your outstanding qualities of leadership have won our admiration; your artistic ideals and integrity our highest respect; your kindness, consideration, and warm humanity our affection.

We are happy that your achievements have received yet further recognition; we congratulate the Board of Directors of Lincoln Center for the Performing Arts on their election of you as President. The great influence that Lincoln Center will have on the artistic life of our nation tempers to a degree the regret we feel at your departure.

Our congratulations, our complete confidence in you, our enthusiastic support and our warmest best wishes go out to you and will be with you in the years ahead.

Perhaps the most succinct and compelling encomium came from Juilliard's chairman of the board (and the person who had initially invited Schuman to consider the Juilliard presidency), James P. Warburg: "Bill Schuman's greatest gift is his ability to integrate art with life."

The professional environment that William Schuman entered on January 1, 1962, was light-years away from the genteel and hierarchal climate he had enjoyed at Juilliard for the previous sixteen years. Schuman had administered Juilliard more as an arts performance institution than a traditional academic environment. The Juilliard faculty was clearly—though, as it happened, contentedly—subordinate in Schuman's administrative structure. They had various responsibilities in developing curriculum, choosing repertoire, and many other day-to-day tasks, but ultimate authority came from the president's office.

In addition, the Juilliard School of Music's small board of trustees was quite comfortable with Schuman's leadership style and his fiscal management of the School. Owing to the Juilliard Musical Foundation and a rather lean budget in the major financial areas of faculty and administrative salaries and production costs, Juilliard remained a remarkably solvent and stable institution in the eyes of Schuman's board members.

Finally, Schuman's professional schedule was largely determined by his own artistic and personal needs. Schuman's Juilliard years were his most productive ones as a composer, thanks in large part to the liberal amount of time he was able to devote to developing new compositions on a schedule that often involved arriving at Juilliard after noon, a significant time away from the School in the summer months, and the comparatively stress-free environment of an educational institution with a strong administrative staff, a quiescent faculty, and a respectful student body.

The work environment at the fledgling Lincoln Center for the Performing Arts could not have been more different. Schuyler Chapin, Schuman's vice president for programming, described the work environment in the Center's early years as "poisonous." The original Lincoln Center concept had been much more benign. Spearheaded by John D. Rockefeller 3rd and a group of civic-minded businessmen, it began officially with the creation of an Exploratory Committee for a Musical Arts Center in November 1955. The work of this committee closely paralleled the plans of the imperious and brilliant Robert Moses, chairman of New York City's Committee on

Slum Clearance, to initiate the Lincoln Square Urban Renewal Project, which included a seventeen-block area on Manhattan's West Side between 62nd and 70th Streets, the largest project of its type in the city's history.

The distinguished architect Wallace K. Harrison had been working closely with Moses on a plan to move the Metropolitan Opera from its old home on Broadway and 39th Street and make it the linchpin of the new Lincoln Square project. Harrison was also a close associate of John D. Rockefeller 3rd through his work on the design of Rockefeller Center in the 1930s and the United Nations after World War II. Another major player in this landscape was Charles M. Spofford, a respected and well-connected lawyer and retired brigadier general, and an important force in the formation of NATO. Spofford spoke with Rockefeller at a Council of Foreign Relations meeting in the Poconos on September 8 or 9, 1955, about the New York Philharmonic's desire to leave Carnegie Hall owing to problems with the owners. The Philharmonic was committed to moving to Lincoln Square. Spofford asked Rockefeller if he would be "willing to meet with leaders of the Met and the Philharmonic to consider what, if anything more than an opera house and a concert hall might be feasible and desirable." According to Edgar Young, who was at one time chairman of the Lincoln Center Building Committee, for a time acting president of Lincoln Center, and ultimately its executive vice president, Rockefeller "was aware that something potentially important in the life of the city was under consideration, and he was willing to consider it quite seriously."

As work by the exploratory committee progressed, there were numerous conversations with professionals in the fields of dance, drama, and music, as well as professional consultants in the area of institutional planning and organization. The plan for Lincoln Center that evolved out of these meetings included not only institutions representing opera and symphonic music but also spoken drama, ballet and possibly modern dance, an educational center for the training of professional artists, a library and museum for reference and research, and an institution to present operetta and musical theater.

The founding members of the exploratory committee were Spofford and Anthony A. Bliss of the Metropolitan Opera, Floyd Blair and Arthur A. Houghton Jr., of the New York Philharmonic-Symphony Society, Harrison, and Rockefeller. Rockefeller quickly expanded the group to include Devereux C. Josephs, chairman of the New York Life Insurance Company and a civic leader; Robert E. Blum, a vice president of Abraham & Strauss department store and a prominent leader in Brooklyn; and Lincoln Kirstein, the brilliant arts innovator and author who was general director of the New York City Ballet.

Importantly, the exploratory committee argued that the Lincoln Center member organizations, later referred to as constituents, would retain their

> artistic and financial autonomy . . . that the new organization [Lincoln Center] would accept responsibility for raising the funds required . . . the capital funds of the new center . . . [but] the new organization would not subsidize the ordinary ongoing operations of the constituent organizations. Their financial autonomy would be complete. Very quickly it was established that Lincoln Center would own all the buildings.

The fundamental concept of having the new constituents maintain their institutional autonomy while being handed sparkling new buildings within which to further their missions meant that this was an opportunity no arts institution could turn down. However, the need to coordinate fund-raising with the constituents for the new structures at Lincoln Center and the future role of the Center as an arts producer eventually caused numerous problems for all participants in this mammoth cultural enterprise. Furthermore, Rockefeller stated plainly that "he was not interested merely in a real estate operation. If the Center could not be a constructive force in the arts beyond a physical place, he had no interest in it." Recalled Edgar Young:

> I think it's fair to say the other members of the Exploratory Committee accepted in varying degrees of enthusiasm the role of the new center in maintaining standards in the arts and in encouraging education and, the term was "artistic advancement." The early concept, which was retained until at least 1959, was that it was not expected that Lincoln Center Incorporated would be a producing organization [but rather a] coordinating organization, that free time in the halls would be booked by outside producing agencies such as Sol Hurok or Columbia Concerts.

Arthur Houghton, one of the members of the exploratory committee, put it more poetically: "Lincoln Center would be a trilogy of the heritage of the past, the preeminence of the present, and the promise of the future."

Rockefeller also had a political and social agenda for the new venture he headed, believing that Lincoln Center would bring the arts to larger segments of the public, often at "popular" prices. This seemingly benign concept, however, would eventually cause friction between Lincoln Center and the constituents, not only because of the high cost of presenting productions in the new theaters, but because of individuals such as Kirstein, who had little interest in compromising on artistic standards for the sake of Rockefeller's plans.

Rockefeller's extra-artistic agenda mirrored the social aspirations that were in full flower at the time in Washington. A burgeoning sense of social consciousness, which developed after 1945 and reached a peak during the Kennedy and early Johnson administrations, created a groundswell for providing more services to disadvantaged Americans through a series of federal initiatives, culminating in Lyndon Johnson's Great Society programs. Along with this benevolent government effort came programs reflecting a populist view of the arts—a philosophical approach manifested in the creation of Lincoln Center.

Schuman used his considerable diplomatic skills to persuade the embryonic leadership of Lincoln Center for the Performing Arts, headed by Rockefeller, to make the Juilliard School of Music the educational wing of the new venture. His working relationship with Rockefeller regarding Juilliard helped create the foundation for Schuman to become the president of the fledgling performing arts center.

Schuman first met Rockefeller in the mid-1950s while he was president of Juilliard. Schuman wrote in his unpublished memoirs:

> One day, some time in the mid-1950s, I was sitting in my office at Juilliard with Mark Schubart, who was dean, when my secretary announced that Mr. John D. Rockefeller 3rd was on the phone. "John D. Rockefeller 3rd is on the phone!" I said to Mark, "I don't know him. Do you think I should talk to him?" Mark said, "Ask him how he spells his name."

Rockefeller told Schuman that he was part of a group charged with planning a performing arts center in New York City, and that the group believed this new organization should have an educational constituent. Schuman quickly accepted Rockefeller's invitation to discuss this initiative with a few of the new center's leaders.

At the luncheon meeting, Schuman, Schubart, Rockefeller, and Edgar Young explored the educational plans for the new performing arts center.

The discussion included expectations about participation of the Metropolitan Opera and the New York Philharmonic, as well as the redevelopment envisioned by Robert Moses for the Lincoln Square area (approximately bordered by 62nd to 66th Streets, between Broadway and Amsterdam Avenue). Schuman saw Rockefeller several times in the ensuing months, and intensively worked to persuade not only him, but also the members of the Juilliard board, to make the School a constituent of the arts center:

> I stepped up my lobbying efforts. . . . I spoke to the members of my board who were connected to Lincoln Center, and said, if this were a university, where you wanted an academic institution, I wouldn't be recommending Juilliard. But this is the big, naughty, tough, jungle world of performing arts, and Juilliard's the greatest school in the world. I didn't make it so; it was before I came. I tried to keep it up and make it an even better school, and I think it's a big mistake for Lincoln Center not to take us seriously.

The professional association that grew between Schuman and Rockefeller, beginning in the mid-1950s and culminating in Schuman's departure from Lincoln Center on January 1, 1969, represented a juxtaposition of two distinct socioeconomic worlds: Schuman, the born-and-bred New Yorker from a German Jewish family who made his way from simple beginnings to becoming one of the most respected American composers and administrators of his day; and Rockefeller, philanthropist par excellence and quintessential American royalty, whose patrician manner and lack of any real working knowledge of the performing arts made him a frequent source of frustration for Schuman when Rockefeller was chairman of the board of directors of Lincoln Center (1961–70) and Schuman was its president (1962–68).

Significantly, the relationship presaged the leadership hierarchy in America's art world that would exist at the beginning of the twenty-first century: artistic professionals on one side, and on the other, individuals whose business acumen and practices determine the level of financial support provided to artistic endeavors. Schuman once commented regarding the members of Lincoln Center's board, "Those business relationships were always at the backs of their minds, and the conflicts that came up did not necessarily produce the best results for Lincoln Center." Schuman often said that in the arts "our goal was not the usual bottom line; our goal was to lose money wisely." From Rockefeller and his Lincoln Center board, Schuman was to learn how naive that attitude really was.

Rockefeller grew to know Schuman quite well through their discussions of and negotiations over Lincoln Center in the late 1950s. In addition to advocating for Juilliard, Schuman also presented Rockefeller with a philosophical overview for the new arts endeavor, dwelling on the synergy that would be generated by having so many distinguished arts institutions in one locale. It was therefore not surprising, except perhaps to Schuman himself, that Rockefeller would look to him to provide leadership of this new venture after the precipitous resignation of Maxwell Taylor as the Center's first president. Taylor had been appointed president on January 1, 1961, but was called back to Washington, D.C., by President John F. Kennedy after the Bay of Pigs disaster in April 1961 to investigate the failed invasion. He eventually was appointed Chairman of the Joint Chiefs of Staff and became a principal architect of the United States' Vietnam strategy.

The plans for the Juilliard building at Lincoln Center were underway when, in August 1961, Rockefeller invited Schuman to a luncheon meeting. Schuman had a clear sense that they would be discussing the vacant Lincoln Center presidency, although he told his wife, Frankie, that he would arrive armed with a list of candidates, conspicuously not including himself. At the luncheon Rockefeller did indeed explain that Lincoln Center was looking for a new president. Schuman replied that he was aware of that and had come prepared with some ideas. In telling the story, he said that Rockefeller then surprised him: "The board of directors wants me to sound you out and see if you would be interested in coming here. I would personally be delighted." Schuman said he was greatly flattered, and "Rockefeller, ever charming and insecure said, 'Didn't I do that well!'"

Schuman's surprise at Rockefeller's invitation was surely disingenuous. He had been president of Juilliard for sixteen years by 1961 and understood well the artistic power and potential of the new endeavor at Lincoln Center. In addition, he was well known to members of the Lincoln Center board. He asked Rockefeller for time to consider the offer, but he was so excited over the prospect of leading Lincoln Center that he called Frankie from Grand Central Station to tell her the news. By the time he got off the train at New Rochelle—a half-hour ride—he had decided to accept the offer:

I'm going to call Rockefeller this afternoon and tell him I would like to meet with him and any members of his executive committee, or any members of the board he wants, and outline what I think Lincoln Center can be. If they are interested in my views, we can pursue the discussion. If they are not, they have my word as a gentleman that no one will ever know of our meeting. I could think for days but that's just not my style. I called Rockefeller, and he agreed to set up the meeting.

Schuman's recollection of his agenda with members of the Lincoln Center committee is strongly reminiscent of his first encounter with members of the Juilliard board in 1945.

Schuman's haste was perhaps ill-advised. His closest friends counseled against such a career change. Schuman recalled:

In the meantime, I discussed the idea with some of the people closest to me: James P. Warburg, who was then chairman of the Juilliard board, Leonard Bernstein, Mark Schubart, and Goddard Lieberson, the record producer. Everyone was horrified. Warburg said, "Don't do it, don't get involved with these people. The school is where you belong, you're very successful in it." Frankie said, "That's no job for you, it's going to be tough being a composer and doing that." Bernstein said, "Don't do it, stay at the school," and Goddard Lieberson warned me, "You're going to meet some of the worst people in the world, people you could never imagine existed." . . . Frank Loesser wrote to me in horror from California when he found out I had taken the job. "At least at Juilliard there was music," he said. . . . But I told them all, "I'm not going to take your advice."

As it turned out, Schuman's friends were particularly prophetic. Aside from the hardball financial dealings that Schuman experienced with the members of the Lincoln Center board, the personal and professional relationship between Schuman and Rockefeller seems to have been seriously flawed from the onset.

The unsteady foundation between these two powerful men was based on Schuman's equivocal view of his chairman. In his unpublished memoirs, written toward the end of his life, Schuman wrote:

It's very difficult for me to describe Rockefeller. There was so much about him I admired, and quite a bit that I didn't, but that simply reflected the protected life he had led. I would not describe him as a bright man, though I wouldn't call him dull. He certainly didn't have much wit. He was very different from his brothers David and

Nelson. . . . I don't think he ever really knew what he wanted to be in the world. Tragic is too strong a word for his life, yet that lack of self-knowledge was very sad. He was certainly not lazy, and he didn't shirk his responsibilities at all. And Rockefeller had gifts. He was a professional philanthropist, and he did it very well. . . .

Rockefeller gave away millions, yet in his day-to-day dealings with money he was so careful it was humorous. He would agonize what tip to leave in a restaurant, on those rare occasions when he would pay the bill. . . .

He understood nothing about the practicalities of life, I suppose because he never earned anything. Laurance was the business man, and David was the banker, but John had no business experience at all. He and his wife were perfectly charming and unpretentious, but were so used to wealth that they couldn't envision a world without it.

Other ways of the world were mysteries to him too. He once asked me where I went swimming. I said that as I was an honorary alumnus of Dartmouth, I could swim in the Yale "plunge." "Why don't you swim at the University Club," he wanted to know. "Aren't you a member?" I said, "No, don't you know they don't take Jews at the University Club?" He said, "I didn't know that. I'd be glad to propose you." I don't know how he felt privately on the subject, but I never found him prejudiced about young people, women, blacks, Jews, or other minorities. . . .

I got along with him well, although we were such opposites, because I had to. I suppose I would have gotten along with any chairman, but he didn't make it difficult for me. We certainly never had any open breaks, though we had some differing views, though he rarely had strong views about anything. . . . I don't know if he ever made a first draft on anything. He was serviced up to the hilt. I can't think of a single, original idea that he presented in the twelve years that I worked with him.

When Schuman was officially invited to become the president of Lincoln Center in September 1961, it was with Rockefeller's written confirmation that "we have every expectation and intention that it will continue until the normal retirement date" (i.e., 1975, when Schuman would turn sixty-five). In the press release formally announcing Schuman's appointment, Rockefeller commented that Lincoln Center faced "major financing problems, and the great task of building has only begun. . . . William Schuman, an administrator of proven ability, has pre-eminent gifts for such a leadership role."

Schuman's remarks in the release exuded optimism and vision: "Lincoln Center . . . can lead to a vastly increased interest in and support for the performing arts. It deserves . . . widespread support from all segments of our society." And in a later interview he declared tellingly: "I didn't take this job to be a landlord."

Their relationship continued on this positive note into 1965, when Schuman was given a $10,000 raise over his original $50,000 salary. Regarding an earlier meeting, Rockefeller commented to Schuman:

> I said that at this point all of us realized the job was a rougher and tougher one than we had imagined in the beginning, and I wanted to be sure that your belief in the Center's objectives and your enthusiasm for your job continue to be real and meaningful. You assured me that this was the case and that you had no thought other than to stay on indefinitely as the chief executive officer, provided that was the wish of the board.

Rockefeller had great faith in Schuman, as can be seen in a confidential letter written in December 1965 to Charles M. Spofford, chairman of Lincoln Center's executive committee. In it he pledges a further $5 million to Lincoln Center to assist in completing the then $160.7 million campaign goal "as a tangible expression of my confidence not only in Bill Schuman's leadership as President, but also in the continuing interest and support of the members of the Board." The chairman of Juilliard's board, James P. Warburg, had also voiced strong support of Schuman's appointment: "I can think of no other man who so uniquely combines creative imagination with executive ability."

Frenetic, problematic, and fascinating, Lincoln Center became William Schuman's new workplace. Rockefeller added financial conditions to the contract that were to apply if Schuman terminated his employment before 1975 and concluded:

> We have every confidence that under your leadership as President the Center will not only be financed and built but will attain the objectives we envision for it, namely that it will become a creative force in the artistic and educational world which will be of

significance in New York City and nationally and internationally as well. It is a pleasure and a satisfaction to write this letter.

At the time of Schuman's appointment, Rockefeller told the press that Schuman "brings to Lincoln Center a thorough and professional awareness of the artistic opportunities that lie before us as well as an understanding of the difficult business problems that must be surmounted."

Schuman himself also made it clear to Rockefeller and the Lincoln Center board that he would continue to compose, stating bluntly, "You want an artist, I presume, not an ex-artist." The board could not fail to notice their new president was something of a maverick. On the eve of his first day on the job, Schuman said to the *New York Times*: "Lincoln Center has to work by projects. That is the only way it can be organized. But I am not necessarily a believer in the chain-of-command concept. I have always jumped channels, and will continue to do so. . . . I am a pragmatist."

There were three basic goals that needed to be addressed by the new president: completion of the design and construction of the new Center's buildings; development of a productive working relationship with the new constituents; and the creation of artistic programs to fill the various Lincoln Center halls when constituents were not using them. All of these activities, of course, created a complex matrix of financial and logistical challenges that ultimately had to be resolved by Schuman and his board.

After Maxwell Taylor returned to Washington, the Lincoln Center board expressed the belief that they needed a president who possessed a different set of abilities from those of a decorated army officer. Edgar Young later recalled, "Bill Schuman was brought in as president at a point in time when they wanted the Center to begin to assert its role beyond just buildings and real estate. And that was his forte. That was what he knew and what he was able to do very effectively." One of Schuman's friends who lived in Washington, D.C., joked to the new appointee: "I could understand that you could succeed General Taylor as president of Lincoln Center, but if you ever succeed him as military advisor in the White House, we are moving to the Soviet Union."

Schuman addressed his new assignment with his customary passion and an agenda for change that took his directors—and the Lincoln Center constituents—by storm. By early 1962 Schuman had begun initial inquiries into or implementation of such projects as a summer arts festival in the Lincoln Center halls, the creation of the Lincoln Center Teachers Institute, the development of a plan to have summer events in the air-conditioned Philharmonic Hall (initially called "Promenade Concerts"), the creation of a constituent dedicated to musical theater, a film festival, and the development of a modern-dance constituent.

In addition, Schuman had to help oversee the completion of the New York State Theater in time for the opening of the World's Fair in 1964, try to resolve the ongoing problem of the acoustics of Philharmonic Hall, negotiate the relationship of City Center to Lincoln Center, strategize as to the best fund-raising initiatives to complete the construction of the Center, and find funds to support new artistic endeavors, as well as serve as the ambassador for Lincoln Center in the city, the nation, and around the world. It is no wonder the number of works Schuman was able to compose fell off significantly during this period, nor that his health was also affected by these multiple demands.

The *New Yorker* magazine published a blithely self-aggrandizing interview with Schuman in the winter of 1962 in which he was described as a man who gave "a strong impression of sincerity and diligence and hail-fellow-well-met." Schuman provided a self-satisfied description of a typical day in his new position at Lincoln Center:

"The work at Lincoln Center is extremely demanding, but I like it," he said, at a good clip. "The more work the better; that is, if you have my feeling for *organization*. Take my organization of this day. I sprang out of bed at six-thirty, rushed down to the swimming pool in the basement of my house, in New Rochelle (in summer I swim in an open-air pool in my back yard), swam a hundred yards in tepid water, went back upstairs, shaved, took a hot shower, finished it off with an icy spray, read the *Times* from beginning to end—editorials, obituaries, personal ads, real-estate ads, everything—and then drove to the office, in exactly fifty minutes, composing a little along the way. I arrived here at eight-fifteen, and after you"—he glanced at his desk pad—"I'll be seeing Robert Whitehead and Elia Kazan, co-producers of our repertory theatre, who are bringing in Robert Lewis, the Broadway director, for a talk. After them there will be Louis B. Ames, from the New York World's Fair, and Reginald Allen, our executive director for operations. Then I must attend a reception at the Met, following which, with luck, I may be able to stop in at a small apartment I've just taken across the street from the office and freshen up a bit and rest before going on to a concert or something, which my wife is sure to have planned. Somewhere along the line, I will have to slip in a couple of hours of composing; I never let a year pass without spending six hundred hours composing. You see, you are seeing my public self, but this couldn't exist without composing—my private self. . . . My mind seethes with ideas and projects . . . I can see them flowing past in my mind."

The *New York Post* also sized up the new executive, describing Schuman as "a tall man (a fraction under 6-foot) who has aged handsomely, metamorphosing from a bland faced juvenile into an executive of distinction, bright-eyed, quick-smiling, ready-witted. His competence is cloaked in spontaneity." In a strikingly egotistical aside, Schuman also brags about his physique: "'See how slim I am?' he boasts, slapping at his flat stomach. 'You think that's by accident? All I do is sacrifice everything I like to eat!'"

Schuman did not suffer fools gladly, as was evident during his Lincoln Center years. A micromanager to extremes on occasions when he needed to resolve thorny problems, he never hesitated to go straight to the top. When he was issued a parking ticket in 1953, he immediately wrote the chief magistrate of the Court of the City of New York protesting his citation: "I do not believe that it is fair to penalize honest citizens who do not violate parking regulations because a patrolman's watch may be slow. . . . May I respectfully request that this irresponsible patrolman be called to task for his carelessness." Schuman even had his dentist corroborate in writing his contention that he had arrived at 10:05 A.M. for his appointment, proving that the time on the ticket was incorrect. Another time Schuman wrote the chairman of the board of General Motors, Frederic G. Donner, to complain that his Oldsmobile dealership had not put antifreeze into his car's radiator for the winter, thus causing the Olds to overheat. Even the president of Ballantine Beer received a letter of complaint:

The very best ale that I think I have ever had is yours, called Pale India Ale. It is a matter of enormous regret to me, as it must be to other weight-watchers, to receive word that no longer are your little bottles of this ale to be continued. Those little bottles enabled one to have his most modest glass every evening. . . . I can only hope that your company might reconsider its decision.

Ballantine sent Schuman a case of the small bottles but then discontinued their production.

Rather than viewing these complaints to corporate America as arrogant, Andie Schuman explained that her father (and her brother) saw the letters as playful ways to tweak giant enterprises: "He [Bill] and Tony had a competition in this. . . . Tony wrote to Lifesavers when they discontinued his favorite flavor, and got a box of rolls in return—the 'Imagine my dismay . . .' tone was part of the game and getting the freebies a source of glee."

On the eve of Schuman's ascendancy to the most powerful arts position in America, a playful and revealing article by Harold C. Schonberg was published in the *New York Times Magazine* about him as both a man and a composer. Schonberg began by describing the new Lincoln Center president as

> an organization man and also an organized man who has come pretty close to making the best of two worlds, like a cherubim in good standing being voted into a floating crap game with the blessings of both sides. . . . [He] happily hobnobs with nabobs, and shakes big ideas out of his sleeve with the nonchalance of The Great Trimetragon producing elephant after elephant from his silk hat.

Schonberg dwelled on Schuman's activities as both administrator and composer, describing him sequentially as "an unusual combination," a "practical visionary," "an artist who gets things done," and commenting that "those who respect him but do not like him call him a super-salesman of a politician with Madison Avenue in his blood." Schonberg also praised Schuman for his exceptional public speaking ability, especially when he delivered his talks extemporaneously: "The man can speak with the fervor, hypnotism and eloquence of Gielgud on one of his better days. . . . When he talks off the cuff . . . he is witty, brilliant and inspirational. . . . Schuman knows he is good, and there is something of a ham in him."

Schonberg then touched upon the important role that Frankie plays in her husband's life: "Close friends of the Schumans are intrigued by the way his wife keeps him in line when his natural exuberance runs away with him. 'When he gets too ebullient or too hammy,' an intimate says, 'she quietly puts him back in the box. I admire her for that.'"

Overall, Schuman must have been pleased by the tone of the article. The section that had to be painful, however, concerned his place as a composer. Describing both his music and his personal beliefs as representative of a person who is "a radical with conservative ideas," Schonberg saw Schuman's music as complex and "not easy to assimilate. . . . [His scores] tend toward rhythmic complexity and a good deal of dissonance, and on the whole are more respected by his fellow musicians than by the public." The cruelest barb flew when an unidentified composer stated, "Let's face it, if he was a great composer, then he would have been Stravinsky and not president of Lincoln Center."

Schuman became such a public personality that he was a "mystery guest" on the popular television game show *What's My Line?* on September 30, 1962, just after the opening of Philharmonic Hall. He was ultimately identified by Bennett Cerf.

The Lincoln Center board of directors and its executive committee each met once a month during Schuman's presidency. The businessmen who made up these groups were driven by a civic-mindedness and fiscal discipline that were not always congruent with Schuman's management style. Schuman was an energetic leader who gained a reputation as a brilliant public speaker, a creative mind, and a president who often acted precipitously on certain matters, frequently causing his directors to question the fiscal feasibility of his many suggested initiatives.

Schuman was not always comfortable with the lines of reporting he encountered at Lincoln Center. At Juilliard, he had enjoyed a comparatively free hand in implementing his ideas; no consistent checks and balances were placed on his fertile administrative mind by a rigid board or a militant faculty. At Lincoln Center, Schuman encountered quite a different context within which to work, with his board trying to watch every penny spent on new initiatives and the Lincoln Center constituents needing to be persuaded, cajoled, or even forced to comply with Schuman's wishes.

Initially Schuman's relationship with John D. Rockefeller 3rd and the other board members was quite harmonious. In late November 1961, before Schuman even officially took office, he proposed what was described in executive committee minutes as Lincoln Center Project No. 1: the creation of summer festivals starting in June 1966. The idea was unanimously adopted by the executive committee and subsequently by the full Lincoln Center board. The first festival was slated to last four weeks and to include not only Lincoln Center constituents, but also artists and performing arts companies from around the world.

Schuman also had to begin the elaborate plans for the official opening of Lincoln Center and Philharmonic Hall on September 23, 1962. In addition to the opening concert by the New York Philharmonic, Schuman embraced Rockefeller's philosophy of bringing the arts to more people, especially the young, by developing plans for a Saturday noon student concert of the New York Philharmonic, "a Friday evening vocal and instrumental concert using largely Juilliard talent; and an organ concert on Sunday afternoon." The invited audience would be students for the Saturday New York Philharmonic concert and music teachers from the metropolitan area for the Juilliard presentation on Friday, and the organ program would be "conceived as an interfaith concert with an invited audience to be arranged through Catholic, Jewish and Protestant channels."

Importantly, these would be the first Lincoln Center events to be subsidized through a special and significant fund—the Lincoln Center Fund for Education and Creative Artistic Advancement. It would subsequently provide major grants in support of many artistic initiatives at the Center.

The opening of Philharmonic Hall as Lincoln Center's first functioning concert venue was a uniquely glittery event. The *New York Times* devoted about a quarter of its front page on September 24, 1962, the morning after the opening, to the event, as well as two full pages in the body of the paper. The distinguished architecture critic Ada Louise Huxtable analyzed the architectural aesthetics of the new building; a "Man in the News" column was devoted to the hall's architect, Max Abramovitz; and articles addressed a series of issues, from the hall's acoustics (a very mixed reaction) and ticket prices (ranging from $1 to $250) to the disastrous traffic jam caused by the opening (with police reportedly directing traffic in tuxedos). The cultural critic and editor Arthur Gelb trumpeted the opening as something that "will be chronicled as a symbol of the cultural coming of age of the United States."

In John D. Rockefeller 3rd's remarks from the stage, over which "acoustical clouds" hung (sound deflectors suspended over the stage), he spoke of moving away from planning and "into the world of performance. Now and in the years ahead, only the artist and his art can fulfill the aspirations of the planners and exalt the labors of the builders." Without mentioning Schuman's name, Rockefeller also spoke appreciatively of his presence as president: "it is gratifying indeed that we have as our president a distinguished composer and educator."

The arrival of the first lady, Jacqueline Kennedy, was the high point of the evening. A member of the crew who was completing the last-minute cleanup of the hall opined that "she's even more beautiful than she's supposed to be." Mrs. Kennedy stayed for only the first half of the concert because she had to be in Newport, Rhode Island, the next day, when President Kennedy was planning to host a visit by Field Marshal Ayub Khan, the president of Pakistan. Worsening weather in New York threatened her departure from LaGuardia Airport, so the first lady's concert stay was cut short, but not before she greeted Bernstein backstage at intermission, telling him that he looked ten pounds lighter. The maestro responded that "he had sweat[ed] it off during the first half of the concert."

The musical program consisted of the Gloria from Beethoven's *Missa solemnis*, the premiere of Aaron Copland's *Connotations*, the *Serenade to Music* of Vaughan Williams, and the first movement of Mahler's Symphony No. 8, presented by the New York Philharmonic, with Bernstein conducting. It included such vocal artists as Eileen Farrell, Shirley Verrett, Jennie Tourel, Jon Vickers, Richard Tucker, and George London. The Schola Cantorum of New York, the Columbus Boychoir, and the Juilliard Chorus also participated.

The *Times*'s chief music critic, Harold C. Schonberg, wrote that "the New York Philharmonic sounded in brilliant form; and that Mr. Bernstein, buoyed by the occasion and by a program so admirably suited to his uninhibited personality, led the orchestra as an extension of himself." However, most of Schonberg's review dealt with the acoustics and ambience of the new hall:

Philharmonic Hall probably will be too conservative to please most of the avant-garde, and too modern to please most of the conservatives. . . . For at present Philharmonic Hall is an inconsistent hall. . . . From Row R on the orchestra floor the sound was clear, a little dry, with not much reverberation and a decided lack of bass. It was good sound, but one had hoped for a more mellow quality.

The "lack of bass" criticism would dog the hall's acoustics into the twenty-first century.

At the opening concert Frankie and Bill were seated in a box with Governor Nelson Rockefeller; his stepmother, Martha Baird Rockefeller; and August Heckscher, cultural advisor to President Kennedy, and his wife. A protocol officer seated Frankie next to the governor. Nelson Rockefeller had divorced his wife, Mary Todd Hunter Clark, in March 1962 and was courting Happy Murphy, whom he eventually married in May 1963. Schuman remembered that "everybody in the audience and on home television around the country thought that Frankie was Mrs. Murphy, and even described her dress. We really loved that." The governor also committed the faux pas of starting to applaud after "The Star-Spangled Banner," then "stopped and looked terribly embarrassed," Schuman said. Schuman remembered, too, that the audience "just hated Copland's *Connotations*. . . . They absolutely hated it, and the program didn't go well. Altogether it was a rather disastrous evening, I thought."

One reason for the lack of enthusiasm for Copland's work may have been that *Connotations* was the composer's first public effort in twelve-tone composition for orchestra. The result was a sound quite different from that of Copland's beloved earlier works. In addition, the composition's rhythmic stasis at the beginning and overall lugubriousness made it a particularly charmless work for the audience.

After the excitement of opening night, the new president quickly initiated other projects, both large and small. One of the most lasting elements of Schuman's tenure was created at the very beginning of his term with the authorization in February 1962 to establish the Lincoln Center Teachers Institute (eventually the Lincoln Center Institute), intended "to offer teachers of the performing arts the opportunity of advancing their own professional performing skills by studying in the summer months with leading artists in their fields."

With the unanimous support of the Lincoln Center board, Schuman also addressed the creation of a Lincoln Center logo, which he undertook with the well-known graphic design firm of Chermayeff & Geismar Associates; the development of a commissioning program of new works for Festival '66; the initiation of a study to find "the proper place in the Center's program for motion pictures [as well as] the extent of the Center's participation in the presentation of a film series"; and the creation and staffing of an administrative structure that would take on the Center's tasks of artistic production, construction and maintenance, education, public relations, and fund-raising.

Schuman's first public challenge as president came about because of the problematic acoustics of Philharmonic Hall. Initial reports on the acoustic quality of the Hall were actually positive. Schuman reported to his board in June 1962 that the results of the "tuning period" were good: "most of the specialists believe that the Hall has basically fine acoustics. Problems exist which have to be solved, but he [Schuman] is most optimistic about their eventual solution." The minutes also indicate that both Leopold Stokowski and Leonard Bernstein had been "favorably impressed with the Hall's acoustical properties."

The acoustics of the first performance hall to open at Lincoln Center were of paramount importance to all parties in the venture. Max Abramovitz, the hall's architect, worked with the acoustical firm of Bolt, Beranek & Newman in developing the interior structure. Leo Beranek was the lead acoustician in the project. The architectural and acoustical team focused on Symphony Hall in Boston, the Concertgebouw in Amsterdam, and the Musikverein in Vienna in the hopes of replicating the acoustics of those great halls.

Edgar Young remembered that in the opening week of Philharmonic Hall in September 1962, the initial reaction was that

the hall had remarkable and unusual clarity of sound . . . [but] what they [critics and musicians] quickly realized was that they were hearing a stridency of emphasis of high frequency notes and a diminution of the bass notes, and then of course there quickly emerged complaints from the orchestra players that they couldn't hear each other . . . confidence in Beranek . . . was being lost, both on the part of the musicians and the lay people that were responsible.

The board authorized an outlay of $250,000 on June 28, 1962, to make changes in Philharmonic Hall before the official opening. However, the results were never acceptable to either critics or musicians. The prevailing attitude toward the hall's acoustics is illustrated by a famous anecdote: when George Szell and the Cleveland Orchestra had a dress rehearsal in the new hall, they played for just fifteen minutes before Szell turned to Lincoln Center officials awaiting his opinion and said simply, "Tear it down." The well-known German acoustician Heinrich Keilholz was brought in to address the problems, but as the years passed it was eventually decided that a major rebuilding would be necessary. It would take place under the guidance of the architect Philip Johnson and the acoustician Cyril Harris in the summer of 1976.

The acoustical problem in Philharmonic Hall was an ongoing irritant to Schuman throughout his presidency because the hall quickly developed a negative reputation that was keeping away major American orchestras, who eventually gravitated back to Carnegie Hall. Rental fees dipped below budgeted levels, and the cachet of a new hall to attract new audiences to the

Center was diminished considerably. Schuman found himself having to defend in public the questionable acoustics, a frequent source of frustration. His favorite line in these matters was, "Actually acoustics is only hearsay."

Although Schuman was firmly ensconced at Lincoln Center by the spring of 1962, he still had to deal with a matter relating to his beloved Juilliard. The School was eventually moving to Lincoln Center and needed to sell its building, and to generate sales money that could be put toward the move. A willing buyer was found in the Manhattan School of Music, then on the Upper East Side.

Not only was the transfer of real estate in play, but a merger was being discussed between the Manhattan School and the Mannes College of Music, also located on Manhattan's East Side in cramped quarters. In addition, a proposal was floated to merge the preparatory departments of both Manhattan and Juilliard, to be housed at Claremont Avenue when Manhattan took over the property.

Schuman had been quite concerned about the elimination of Juilliard's Preparatory Department as a condition of moving to Lincoln Center. In a letter of October 1962 to Peter Mennin, Juilliard's president-designate, Schuman wrote:

> Through the acquisition of the Juilliard plant by Manhattan, the Juilliard Preparatory Division has indeed been "saved." There has been much adverse criticism on the Juilliard move in connection with the dropping of the Preparatory Division. The preservation of the Preparatory Division under other than Juilliard auspices was a project on which I have spent more hours than I could possibly recall during the last four years. . . . Manhattan buying Juilliard will ease your problem of transition to Lincoln Center. There will be teachers not to be brought to Lincoln Center who will be kept on by Manhattan.

However, neither the Manhattan/Mannes nor the Manhattan/Juilliard Preparatory merger was ever realized.

In Lincoln Center's early days, Schuman had to act as both an impresario, creating new artistic programs and organizations for the times when the buildings were not presenting constituents' presentations, and also an emissary, cajoling existing arts organizations to join the Lincoln Center family. Schuman's greatest challenge in this area was negotiating the agreement that would have the various artistic components of the New York City Center of Music and Drama, located at 55th Street just east of Seventh Avenue, move uptown to Lincoln Center.

In the early 1960s City Center was the home of not only the New York City Ballet, but also the New York City Opera, dubbed the "people's opera" by Mayor LaGuardia for its reasonable prices and a clientele that differed markedly from the high-society patrons of the Metropolitan Opera. In addition, a drama and light opera company under the leadership of Jean Dalrymple performed at the Center.

Because Lincoln Kirstein was a charter member of the Lincoln Center exploratory committee and was also the general director of the New York City Ballet, whose artistic head was George Balanchine, the City Ballet was on the ground floor of the move to the new arts center. The auditorium, located on the Center's southeasternmost corner and eventually known as the New York State Theater—in early planning it was even called "the Theater for the Dance"—was specifically designed to support ballet and modern dance. The architect Philip Johnson conferred frequently with Balanchine and Kirstein on design, and Schuman expected to place new constituents in musical theater, operetta, and modern dance in the theater when the City Ballet was not performing.

Funding for the new theater was supported to a significant extent by a complex financial agreement involving both the State of New York and New York City. It totaled approximately $30 million, through funds that were being allocated for construction of facilities in Flushing Meadows, Queens, relating to the 1964–65 World's Fair. Robert Moses, president of the New York World's Fair, and Governor Nelson Rockefeller required that the new theater be ready to present attractions when the fair opened in April 1964, since Lincoln Center was seen "as the performing arts angle, the performing arts expression of the World's Fair." Under the terms of this agreement, the State Theater would be owned by New York City at the conclusion of the World's Fair.

Schuman faced two daunting problems in late 1962, both of which had to be successfully resolved in less than two years' time: completing the construction of the State Theater, and stocking it with attractions that would make it a viable performing arts venue. Although the construction schedule was eventually met, the mix of personalities involved and the complexity of having the City of New York as an important player in the negotiations made them arduous for Schuman.

In mid- to late 1962 the chairman of City Center, Newbold Morris (a founder of City Center in 1943 along with Mayor LaGuardia and Morton Baum), who was also the New York City parks commissioner, proposed to John D. Rockefeller 3rd that thought be given to having the whole of City Center (i.e., New York City Ballet, New York City Opera, and the drama and light opera program) come to Lincoln Center. This proposal was backed by the powerful chairman of City Center's finance committee, Morton Baum, with the added condition that the property at 55th Street could be sold to offset construction costs.

Baum was a seasoned fighter in the bare-knuckles arena of New York City politics. A graduate of Columbia College and Harvard Law School, he served as an assistant United States attorney in the early 1930s, was elected alderman, and was Mayor LaGuardia's tax counsel from 1935 to 1938, when he helped create the city's first sales tax. An aggressive and hard-edged negotiator, he had honed his political skills by running for office frequently during his career. In 1965 he stated, "It's [running for office] the greatest education a man can have. I would not have had a moment's chance for success at the City Center if I had not learned the rules of political in-fighting right on the battlefield." It was Baum who would be Schuman's, and Lincoln Center's, nemesis in the negotiations between City Center and Lincoln Center.

The proposal to bring all the performing companies of City Center north triggered a predictable response from the venerable Metropolitan Opera, which had no interest in having another opera company on campus. City Opera's presence violated the exclusivity provision the Metropolitan Opera had signed in its constituent agreement stipulating that the Met would be the only entity on campus to present professional opera productions. Kirstein, for his part, held firm that the City Ballet would not move to Lincoln Center unless all of the City Center entities went together.

Baum then confronted Schuman with another proviso to the agreement, and this one brought negotiations to a standstill. Baum proposed that City Center should be a direct tenant of the City of New York in the State Theater, as it had been at 55th Street. This was in direct conflict with one of the basic tenets of the Lincoln Center concept, which clearly stated that each constituent would be dealing with Lincoln Center, and not the city, in their residencies in the Center's various halls. City Center saw this approach as a way of maintaining its autonomy and not having to be beholden to Lincoln Center on any matters of importance. However, the Met and the Philharmonic also had such aspirations of autonomy. To agree to the City Center proposal would have torn the unity of the fledgling arts center to shreds.

Proposals and counter-proposals flew back and forth as the new year of 1963 was celebrated. Although City Center had been invited to become a constituent of Lincoln Center in December 1962, the City Center board had numerous rebuttals to the circumstances of constituent status having to do with percentage distribution of box-office receipts—in which City Center was to receive 75 percent and Lincoln Center, 25 percent—and in particular the inclusion of the New York City Opera in the move to Lincoln Center.

Schuman was put in the unenviable position of negotiating not only with the iron-fisted Baum, but also with the brilliant and wily Kirstein, who was closely allied to the interests of City Center. Schuman was not alone in having to deal with the tension-fraught environment. Schuman's lieutenant, Schuyler Chapin, recalled that Kirstein became so angry during a telephone conversation that "he ripped the entire telephone off the wall, wires, everything. . . . Lincoln was a madman at times." Kirstein also held sway over the design and construction of the State Theater, perhaps his boldest move being the installation of four enormous and corpulent female statues created by the Polish-born American abstract sculptor Elie Nadelman and entitled *Circus Women* and *Two Nudes*. According to the New York City Ballet, the statues

> recreate smaller, 4-foot versions made of plaster and paper that were made by Nadelman decades before. The name of the actual Italian sculptor [who created the oversize versions of the originals] is lost to history. Overhearing construction workmen remarking on the naked "goils," Kirstein arranged to have the immense artworks brought into the Theater just before the fourth and final wall was closed up and before the Lincoln Center leadership could order their removal, which, in fact they did; but the statues could no longer be removed. They were here to stay.

Schuman celebrated his first anniversary in office by making decisions that would result in having the City Ballet open the New York State Theater in April 1964, a specific request of Governor Rockefeller. In addition, he had already made a commitment to create the New York Music Theater, headed by no less a figure than Richard Rodgers and slated to perform musicals and operettas in the New York State Theater when the City Ballet was not performing. An obvious challenge was how to squeeze City Opera into the

State Theater's schedule, as well as how to eliminate entirely City Center's drama and light opera component.

Schuman also had almost no option concerning the City Ballet's move to the State Theater. Clearly, no other ballet company in America had City Ballet's reputation at the time. The Ballet Theater had serious financial and artistic problems, and the work of modern choreographers such as Graham and Limón was considered too esoteric to fill the State Theater on a regular basis. Forming a new ballet company was rejected as impractical.

A lengthy and well-researched memo to Lincoln Center's executive committee from both Schuman and Edgar B. Young, who was now the Center's executive vice president, reveals that it was ultimately decided to concede to most of City Center's demands, with two exceptions: the State Theater would not be run by the government of the City of New York, and the drama and light opera company would be eliminated. City Center would agree to keep its top ticket price at $4.95, take responsibility for all of its performing organizations when they arrived at Lincoln Center in both financial and artistic matters, and, at the end of the World's Fair in the fall of 1965, begin the process of becoming a constituent of Lincoln Center. In turn, Lincoln Center would make available to City Center $200,000 from the Lincoln Center Fund for Education and Creative Artistic Advancement to commission new works for the City Ballet and to subsidize student tickets.

The negotiating process between Schuman and Baum was a significant watershed in the history of the fledgling arts center. For the first time the affairs of Lincoln Center were wrenched from the genteel boardrooms and private clubs of the exploratory committee meetings chaired by Rockefeller and dragged into the fierce and rancorous world of the New York City streets. The acrid negotiations also presaged the contentious relationship developing between Schuman and the Center's constituents, who began to see Schuman more as an adversary than as an ally.

Even Rockefeller was exposed to Baum's continuing wrath as the agreement was set in place. Four years later, Baum had still not embraced the Lincoln Center concept. In a *New York Times* article of September 23, 1967, Baum continued his contrarian rhetoric: "The Rockefellers have a great possessive quality. Mr. Rockefeller [John D. Rockefeller 3rd] is the iceberg of which you only see a tenth. He is the power. Nobody on the board will cross him. They'll never get reconciled to our independence. There will always be resentment toward them on the part of the constituents."

CHAPTER 10

Schuman versus
Everybody Else

In the midst of the disruptive City Center negotiations, Schuman continued to pursue his mandate of providing arts activities for the new buildings opening on campus. Inviting the City Ballet and Balanchine to Lincoln Center had been a logical decision; but in the view of the Lincoln Center board there was no comparable theater company in New York City that had City Ballet's reputation and cachet. Therefore Schuman set out to create a brand-new drama constituent for Lincoln Center.

The creation of a drama constituent was discussed by a specially formed exploratory committee chaired by George Stoddard, then chancellor of New York University, and including the director Elia Kazan, the producer Robert Whitehead, and the critics Brooks Atkinson and Walter Kerr. Among a number of New York theater luminaries, Lee Strasberg, representing his Actor's Studio, suggested that he himself take over drama responsibilities, both presenting and teaching at Lincoln Center, but the Lincoln Center board believed it would be best simply to start a new theater company.

Before Philharmonic Hall had even opened in September 1962, a Repertory Theater of Lincoln Center had already been formed through the exploratory committee's efforts, with George Woods as president of the board, and artistic leadership shared by Robert Whitehead and Elia Kazan. Unfortunately, the opening of the Vivian Beaumont Theater was delayed until 1965, two years past its proposed opening date of 1963, owing to construction problems. So Whitehead and Kazan developed a plan whereby a temporary theater would be created downtown, near Washington Square, in a partnership with the American National Theatre and Academy (ANTA) and New York University. Woods himself expressed grave concerns about the long-term financial feasibility of the initiative, and the Lincoln Center board reconfirmed that it would not provide funds to construct such a building.

Nevertheless, Whitehead was determined to proceed with ANTA and NYU. According to Edgar Young, "By mid-February 1963, [Woods] told the

Lincoln Center Executive Committee that he had lost confidence in Whitehead." But five months later contracts were signed, and the temporary building began to take shape on Washington Square. Whitehead and Kazan continued to work artistically as well, supported by a $500,000 grant from Lincoln Center's Fund for Education and Creative Artistic Advancement. Eventually, on January 13, 1964, Arthur Miller's play *After the Fall* opened at the ANTA Washington Square Theater at 40 West 4th Street.

Despite acceptable advance sales on the play, the Repertory Theater immediately found itself in severe financial distress. The theater requested and received a loan of $100,000 from Lincoln Center's New Projects Underwriting Fund to stay afloat. However, the loan was only a stopgap, and by the end of its first year the Repertory Theater had a deficit of $350,000. George Woods stepped down from the presidency of the theater and was replaced by Robert L. Hoguet Jr., the executive vice president of the First National City Bank of New York.

The 1964 season opened downtown with Elia Kazan directing the Jacobean tragedy *The Changeling* by Middleton and Rowley—to such poor reviews that its scheduled run was shortened. Both members of the theater board and the Lincoln Center board began to question the quality of the leadership provided by the Whitehead-Kazan team. In a gesture that would come back to haunt Hoguet and Schuman, the former reached out to the latter in November 1964 to see if Schuman could help find a new managing director for the Repertory Theater. Schuman had already been giving serious thought to the theater's management problems. In a lunch with Charles Spofford, Schuman suggested that "if they [LCT] could divide that job in two and get a first-class artistic director and have an overall theater impresario, Herman Krawitz would do a fabulous job because he is very gifted at these things. I don't necessarily trust his artistic judgment, but he is certainly gifted in the other way." Spofford was enthusiastic about the idea and suggested that Schuman speak to Rockefeller.

Although in practice the president of Lincoln Center was not supposed to become involved in the internal decisions of a constituent, Schuman contacted Krawitz, the assistant manager of the Metropolitan Opera, to inquire whether he would be interested in the position at the Repertory Theater.

This seemingly benign move ignited a firestorm of public controversy in the press regarding the sensitive interactions between Lincoln Center and its constituents. Hoguet had not helped matters: he had given no indication to Whitehead or Kazan that a change in administration was in the offing. For their part, neither the president of the Metropolitan Opera, Anthony Bliss, nor its general manager, Rudolf Bing, had any idea that Krawitz, a key administrator in the construction of the new opera house and the move to Lincoln Center, had been approached by Lincoln Center's president until Schuman himself told Bliss during a lunch at the Plaza Hotel Oak Room on November 27. According to Schuman, Bliss responded emphatically: "Please don't do that because Krawitz is so enormously valuable, and you mustn't do it. You absolutely can't do it." He then made clear in an offhand remark that he considered the leadership of the Metropolitan Opera more important than the presidency of Lincoln Center: "Anyway, you know, we sort of thought that when you might leave Lincoln Center you might step into Bing's job." Bing became furious when he found out what Schuman had done and set out to attack him in a very public way. As Schuyler Chapin described the situation, "It was Bing at his insect-biting best."

On December 4, 1964, the Schumans gave a large, elaborate dinner party at their new apartment at 1120 Fifth Avenue following the opening of Arthur Miller's play *Incident at Vichy*, which was produced at the ANTA Theater on Washington Square by the Repertory Theater of Lincoln Center. Guests included Miller, Leonard Bernstein, Kazan, Whitehead, and numerous Lincoln Center trustees, including Bliss and Hoguet. According to Schuman, "That night Mr. Hoguet and Mr. Bliss had [a] fairly heated discussion for a social occasion and, in general, the plotting against the president of Lincoln Center was going on in his own home, with Mr. Bliss saying to me that there would be more in the papers the next day than a review of the play."

The controversy indeed became public on December 5, when the *New York Times* published a front-page article outlining the details of the brouhaha. What should have been an internal personnel shift was now being touted as a major flaw in the governance of Lincoln Center, with the imperious Bing throwing fuel on the fire by claiming that Lincoln Center was "apparently deteriorating to a free-for-all jungle where constituents can raid each other at will." Bing also said that he planned to resign from the Lincoln Center Council, the group composed of all the CEOs of the Lincoln Center constituents—a threat on which he never made good.

Newspaper accounts incorrectly reported that Schuman had actually offered Krawitz the position at the Repertory Theater, something Schuman was simply incapable of doing—only the theater board could issue such an invitation. Bing continued in the article: "I am deeply disturbed over the matter . . . because I see in the way it's been handled the breakdown of the Lincoln Center concept, that is, a group of constituents, of sister organizations who, under the umbrella of Lincoln Center, work toward a higher goal of artistic achievement."

The *New York Times* article also reported that there was intense friction between the Whitehead-Kazan team and Schuman over the Repertory Theater's artistic mission. Schuman had suggested publicly in September 1963 that he hoped the play chosen to open the Beaumont Theater would be Shaw's *Caesar and Cleopatra*, starring Rex Harrison, one of the leading men of the time on both stage and screen. Whitehead and Kazan had countered that such a suggestion showed a lack of understanding on Schuman's part as to what the mission of the Repertory Theater was. Clearly, Schuman's suggestion of casting Harrison was seen as catering to the popular trends of the day. The Harrison idea was eventually dropped, but the harm had already been done.

The *New York Times* article presented Schuman as an interloper who was exceeding his authority in artistic and administrative matters on the Center's campus: "Cultural observers have recently said that Mr. Schuman is seeking to assume a greater degree of artistic control over the Lincoln Center constituents, which are autonomous, and that this is being resented." The reporter quoted from an article written by Schuman at the time of the opening of Philharmonic Hall in September 1962: "The role of Lincoln Center is not that of a passive landlord and housekeeper for its distinguished tenants. . . . Lincoln Center is conceived as a creative and dynamic force." To add insult to injury, the article concluded with a description of the ongoing acrimonious negotiations between Lincoln Center and City Center over which entity actually controlled the use of the New York State Theater.

On the following day another *New York Times* front-page article appeared that reviewed the issues revealed the previous day and included more quotes from the principals in the imbroglio. Hoguet, Schuman, and Charles M. Spofford, a Lincoln Center vice chairman and board member of the Repertory Theater, as well as chairman of the Metropolitan Opera's executive committee, gave an interview at the Links Club on East 62nd Street in which Spofford maintained that "Mr. Hoguet and Mr. Schuman had acted properly in seeking to hire Mr. Krawitz." As it turned out, Krawitz backed away from the offer, and the Metropolitan Opera made it clear that it would not release Krawitz from his contract with the opera company.

In perhaps the most outrageous article generated by the contretemps, the Broadway trade journal *Variety*, known for its punchy headlines, printed a notorious one: "Samson in Longhair Temple: Schuman versus Everybody Else." Presenting the situation as a "three-front war," *Variety* listed the "casualties" as the New York City Ballet, which was going to vacate the New

York State Theater (it did not), and the Lincoln Center Theater, in total upheaval and on the brink of a total reorganization (partially true); furthermore, "Resignations and statements of protest and denunciation are breaking almost daily, with no end in sight of the public washing of culture's dirty linen and power-grab politics" (essentially correct).

By December 27, 1964, it was reported that the team of Whitehead and Kazan had resigned. Such theatrical luminaries as Arthur Miller and Maureen Stapleton vowed never to work at the Repertory Theater again. Edgar Young summed up the situation:

> By the end of 1964, the Repertory Theater was left without professional leadership, but with a handsome, new theater nearing completion. Lincoln Center's public image had been badly tarnished. But within Lincoln Center, Schuman's position was secure despite the criticism that had been heaped on him in the press.

Schuman was badly bruised by the publicly embarrassing and disparaging remarks made by Bing and by the firestorm of criticism directed at him by the press and individuals in the profession, including leading constituent administrators. In all his years at Juilliard, he had never been exposed to the vitriol that came his way in December.

Schuman believed that he had been hung out to dry by the members of the Lincoln Center board, who did not rally to his side as he had expected. A regularly scheduled meeting of the Center's board of directors took place at the Century Association on December 14, 1964, at 12:30 P.M. Schuman had prepared carefully for the meeting and he gave a highly detailed report on the discussions and meetings leading up to the public announcement of *l'affaire Krawitz* on December 5. Before the meeting began, Schuman saw Bliss and said, "Tony, we have to rebuild this thing, and as a symbol of it, let's sit together at the board meeting."

Schuman's notes for the meeting indicate, in fact, that several Repertory Theater and Lincoln Center directors were involved in ongoing conversations regarding Krawitz's candidacy, including Hoguet, Spofford, and John D. Rockefeller 3rd, and that Schuman had even attended a full board meeting of the Repertory Theater on November 20, 1964, at which he was invited to find artistic leadership for the theater. It was also revealed that during Schuman's luncheon meeting with Bliss on November 27, Schuman had told Bliss that Krawitz's name would be forwarded to Hoguet and Schuman would step away from the process. In addition, Schuman made it clear that Krawitz was not an innocent pawn in the process but was genuinely interested in taking on the new position at the Repertory Theater, since he had no hope of becoming general manager of the Met anytime soon. Schuyler Chapin said bluntly that "to be quite candid, Herman was salivating at the idea of it."

Schuman said at the board meeting that he had inherited two major problems when he began his tenure as Lincoln Center's president: the Repertory Theater and City Center. His hope was always to heal breaches, not widen them, and this was a "time for silence with [the] press [and] full discussion with [the] Board." The reasons he had decided not to talk to the press at any length were that he did not wish to respond to personal slander (presumably from Bing, which Schuman called "reprehensible and inexcusable") and that he had nothing to defend. He also explained that there was a need for "institutional solidarity of Lincoln Center [and] loyalty to [the] Met and all constituents."

Schuman then revealed in dramatic tones that he had been told by Howard Taubman, chief drama critic of the *New York Times*, that administrators of the Metropolitan Opera and City Center Ballet had said he "was on the way out and they were proposing other names [for a successor]. Bing did not himself propose names," but these discussions were revealed "to give [the] extent of [the] machinations." Schuman then concluded the presentation by saying that Lincoln Center and its president had been pushed "out on a limb—high and dry—we have run out of no comments" and that "full support [was] needed." Anthony Bliss was reported to have said that the situation "had attracted an unfortunate amount of adverse criticism and he echoed Dr. Schuman's statement that the main objective at this time should be to rebuild. Mr. Hoguet briefly stated that all Dr. Schuman had done was to respond to a request for help from the Repertory Theater."* Also according to the minutes of the meeting, the "Board of Directors expressed their complete confidence in Dr. Schuman and his actions by a unanimous standing vote with applause for all his efforts." Ironically, the minutes also record a request that the Lincoln Center Council draft some "informal rules for processing the hiring of employees of one constituent by another."

For Schuman the entire episode was deeply troubling. Although his musical compositions had been lambasted at times in the press, his personal integrity and honesty had never been questioned publicly. Much as he had done with the National Association of Schools of Music in 1958–59, Schuman

---

* Although Schuman never earned a doctoral degree, he was first referred to as "Dr. Schuman" during his Juilliard years. He received a total of twenty-seven honorary doctorates during his lifetime.

vigorously defended his position on the Krawitz problem. Now, however, he was not able to make his case without being portrayed in the press as petty or defensive. Looking back on the matter in 1969, Schuman commented, "I did not want Bing's apology because I would not reduce institutional issues to a personal level." As to the lack of public support Schuman believed he was receiving from his board, one can only surmise that the board members saw Schuman as the appropriate person to represent them. In all likelihood, the board may have been reluctant to exacerbate the problem by entering into the public dispute. Ultimately it is the paid professionals, and not the volunteer board members, who must face the press on controversial matters.

Nevertheless, Schuman was not accustomed to the public backbiting generated by Bing, in particular, whom he thought sanctimonious and rude. Frankie derided the standing ovation from the board as too little, too late—"in the meantime you've been hung up on butcher hooks . . . all those weeks," she said. The Krawitz affair was the first indication to the public that all was not well with Schuman's presidency of Lincoln Center. Schuyler Chapin summarized the situation succinctly: "The Krawitz thing blew higher than a kite. . . . No Whitehead, no leadership, the Beaumont getting ready to open with a company almost bankrupt by virtue of the first season."

Schuman was scarred by the incident and quite bitter about the actions of his board of directors. Years later he remarked:

> That's the kind of thing that would get me in the gut. It was very unpleasant. However inept I may have been in the procedures, I should never have been attacked. I should have been protected by all the people that I was protecting. That's when I saw that their conduct was something less than honorable, because it should have been up to them to come out and say: "We [the board] were well aware as the leaders of this organization what was taking place, and we encouraged our president to do so as long as he went." They never did that. So that told me something about them in no uncertain terms.

While representatives of the constituents were battling each other, construction continued on the various buildings in the Center. Philharmonic Hall had opened on September 23, 1962, and the next hall that would be opened to the public was the New York State Theater. The theater's opening was directly linked to the beginning of the New York World's Fair in April 1964: the new hall served as the performing arts arm of the fair, and the architect, Philip Johnson, worked closely with George Balanchine on the details of the construction. The State Theater opened on the evening of April 23, 1964. The Music Theater of Lincoln Center presented a scene from Rodgers and Hammerstein's *Carousel* featuring John Raitt and Joan Weldon. The New York City Ballet presented Balanchine's *Allegro brillante*, with Maria Tallchief and André Prokovsky, and *Stars and Stripes*, starring Patricia McBride and Jacques d'Amboise. In general the hall was praised for its elegance and fine acoustics, especially by Lincoln Kirstein, who considered it the finest hall for the presentation of dance in the world, with the dancers' footfalls hardly audible.

Perceptions of the new theater changed dramatically in May when the Royal Shakespeare Company presented *King Lear*, directed by Peter Brook and starring Paul Scofield. Brook had been told by Schuyler Chapin that his company should have a dress rehearsal before opening night to accustom the actors to the sound amplification system. Brook, "arrogantly indifferent," retorted, "Our actors know how to deal with any condition; we won't have any problem."

Regrettably, the acoustical problems were significant for the British actors, and audience members complained that they could not understand a word coming from the stage. Not only had the State Theater stage been a sound trap for the actors, but the theater's amplification system could not be used because *Lear*'s raised set completely "covered all the microphone outlets for the sound system, so it was not possible to put the sound system into use." Schuman had sent Chapin, as his vice president for programming, to attempt to deal with Brook. In subsequent performances the actors slowed the pace of their words and the lines were finally understandable, but the performance merely highlighted another of Lincoln Center's acoustical problems. Although Brook exploded in an "angry public outburst that revived the public's preoccupation with acoustics [at Lincoln Center]," the issue dissipated as time passed and did not have the sticking power of the acoustical issues at Philharmonic Hall.

The acoustic problems shadowing the City Opera's residency at the New York State Theater, however, were to be a constant source of dispute in succeeding decades, leading to numerous attempts at remediation, including the installation of a "sound reinforcement" system in the 1990s.

The Lincoln Center Theater was dedicated before an invited audience on October 14, 1965. The theater was designed by Eero Saarinen and Associates, with Jo Mielziner as a collaborating designer. The Library-Museum, by the architect Gordon Bunshaft, officially opened on November 30, 1965.

Although the architectural centerpiece of Lincoln Center, the Wallace Harrison–designed Metropolitan Opera House, was also to be completed in 1965, construction setbacks and cost overruns delayed the opening and brought the cost to $45.7 million, approximately $9.5 million higher than the 1962 budget estimate. The problems with the Met put considerable pressure on Edgar Young, Lincoln Center's executive vice president in charge of construction, and on Schuman. They not only had to complete the buildings on time, but the Lincoln Center board also saw an ever-expanding construction budget that was depleting the financial resources Schuman needed in order to develop the Center's artistic programming.

The situation became so bad that "there was very serious consideration on the part given by Rockefeller and Spofford and Dev Josephs and Young to the possibility of changing the architect [Harrison]—and Tony Bliss was in on it— . . . of the Metropolitan Opera." The main source of the frustration was "Harrison's own lack of conviction and confidence at his then stage of design." However, he was kept on, in no small part because of his close working relationship with Robert Moses, and the Metropolitan Opera House eventually opened on September 16, 1966, with the world premiere of Samuel Barber's commissioned opera *Antony and Cleopatra.* Justino Díaz and Leontyne Price were in the title roles, with Rosalind Elias as Charmian and Jess Thomas as Caesar. Thomas Schippers conducted, Franco Zeffirelli was both director and designer, and Alvin Ailey provided the choreography in his Met debut.

Schuman and Barber had been friends for many years, and in 1964 Schuman had written him a letter congratulating him on the Met commission:

I am simply overjoyed that you will be doing an opera for the opening of the new Met. You know how long I have been plugging for precisely this. It has always seemed to me that the new house simply must open with a new opera by an American composer and, by all odds, you are the logical choice for the Metropolitan. They have confidence in you, as do all the rest of us, to produce a magnificent singing score.

Barber wrote back:

It is always good when embarking on such an undertaking to have good wishes from one's friends, but such a message as yours meant particularly much to me: Extra special!

The opening of the Metropolitan Opera House at Lincoln Center was indeed a glittery and gala event, the most elaborate opening of any building at the arts complex. The first lady, Lady Bird Johnson, was the guest of honor, and she was joined by another first lady in the person of Imelda Marcos, who was there with her husband, the president of the Philippines, Ferdinand Marcos. The *New York Times* crowed that the audience included

> virtually every member of New York's predictably elegant diamond brigade. . . . Hundreds of formally dressed tycoons, aristocrats, nabobs, bankers, moguls, diplomats, potentates, fashion plates, grande dames and other assorted Great Society over-achievers were among the 3,800 persons who produced a record $400,000 gross—more than 12 times what the Met usually gets for a sellout—and the kind of glamour the nation has come to associate with New York on a good day.

Greeting arriving guests, Rudolf Bing met Leontyne Price's mother, who commented, "Mr. Bing . . . I've always envisioned you as a heavier man." "Until a week ago I was," responded Bing.

The general manager was referring to a problem he had been wrestling with for several months. The Met orchestra had planned to strike immediately after the opening-night performance, putting the remainder of the season in jeopardy. The orchestra members had been working without a contract for the prior two years, and their union, Local 802 of the American Federation of Musicians, obviously saw the historic opening of the new Met as the perfect instrument for pressuring the opera company to settle on a new contractual agreement. The Met's management and the union negotiators came to an agreement only at 8 P.M. on opening night, with the musicians voting in favor of the contract during the second intermission. As a result, Bing stepped onstage at the beginning of the third act and announced, "I'm sure you'll be happy as I am that the dispute with our musicians is settled. . . . The strike is over and . . . the season is secured. . . . I welcome this fine orchestra back as friends." The news was greeted by the audience with cheers and applause.

Unfortunately, the critics of the *New York Times* did not share in the evening's ebullient spirit. The architecture critic, Ada Louise Huxtable, wrote, "The architecture sets no high-water mark for the city . . . it is average rather than adventurous or avant-garde." Harold C. Schonberg, the chief music critic, reported that the new Barber opera was "a bit lost in [the] shuffle" of the opening festivities, sarcastically writing that the opera was a big, complicated package: big, grand, impressive and vulgar; a Swinburnian mélange of sad, bad, mad, glad; rich and also nouveau-riche; desperately aiming for the bigger and the better. Not many will deny that the Metropolitan Opera at least came up with the bigger. . . . Sets nobly and ponderously arrived from the rear, slowly and majestically, like a Sherman tank passing over a wheat field. . . .

It was all very technological. It also was all so naive, so innocent, so delightfully childish, so unself-consciously exhibitionistic. And, it must be confessed, sometimes so vulgar: artifice masquerading with a great flourish as art. . . . Almost everything about the evening, artistically speaking, failed in total impact.

Included in the general failure was a highly touted stage turntable designed to make scene changes as fluid and effortless as possible.

The exciting opening of the Met could not alleviate the challenges Schuman continued to face at Lincoln Center. Throughout Schuman's volatile first few years as president, the Center's overall financial picture became more and more bleak. Construction costs for the completion of the campus's buildings were spiraling out of control, and deficits appeared not only through the artistic activities of the Lincoln Center Theater and the musical theater productions, but also in the film festivals and the summer festivals Schuman created. Lincoln Center even lost money through the campus's guided tour program for the public, which in May 1965 declared a deficit of $150,000.

John D. Rockefeller 3rd worked tirelessly to support the growing costs of the Center, aided by major grants from the Ford and Rockefeller Foundations. Rockefeller was always concerned that his wealth would be perceived as the ultimate financial safety net for the overall project. In particular, he believed that Robert Moses certainly felt that way. Rockefeller therefore worked hard to persuade both the state and the city to make major contributions to the construction of the Lincoln Center buildings, especially through the vehicle of New York's World's Fair. A development committee of the board was created in 1965 to replace the original campaign committee, and in June 1965 Henry Bessire was hired as vice president for development.

Although Schuman was involved in fund-raising for the Center, Rockefeller and his board colleagues took on the lion's share of the duties in this area. Schuman, charming and persuasive as he was, was hardly enamored of hobnobbing with New York City's elite:

> The society part was so boring, and getting involved in upper-crust society, once I understood how it worked . . . the whole ritual of it: you know, sitting down at a formal dinner, the separation of the men and women, talking to the one-on-one side for X minutes, watching the host turning the other way—it was like Victorian England.

Early in Schuman's tenure, he was one of the very few Jews on the Lincoln Center board, and certainly the only artist. He commented:

> Way down deep, it [Lincoln Center] was WASP-controlled, society controlled, money controlled. Yet I would not say for a minute that these were not dedicated men. . . . But they had political axes to grind . . . and they had financial obligations that could not suddenly be put on the shelf because they were on a certain Board. In other words . . . there was an interweaving of personal, professional, financial lives with their views as volunteer directors.

The relationship between Rockefeller and Schuman deteriorated badly throughout 1966, as can be clearly seen in a letter from Rockefeller to Schuman dated December 30, 1966. Rockefeller regularly wrote end-of-the-year "shape-up letters," as his staff called them, to the heads of all the philanthropic organizations he chaired. Rockefeller divided his five-page letter to Schuman into six parts: "Fund-Raising," "Management of the Property" (Lincoln Center), "The Impresario Function," "The Constituents," "Living Within Our Means," and "Confidence." It would form the blueprint for the dissolution of the relationship between the two men, and Rockefeller would refer to it frequently over the next two years.

Although Rockefeller urged Schuman to consider more involvement in fund-raising and in shoring up relations with the Lincoln Center constituents, his greatest concerns surfaced in the "Impresario Function" section of the letter. It is here that Rockefeller first raised the issue of the cost and pace of Schuman's artistic programming at Lincoln Center:

From the beginning we all recognized you have made a particularly important contribution to Lincoln Center in this connection. The development of imaginative and high quality programs is important not only to keeping the halls filled but also in terms of attaining the Center's full potential. All of us agree on this without any question but did have three concerns: (1) the rate of progress, (2) the case as to whether others on the outside might not well carry more of the load in this connection and (3) the feeling among the constituents that Lincoln Center was a competitor.

Rockefeller restated his deepening concern regarding the mounting costs of Schuman's proposed programs and suggested that the creation of new programs should be curtailed until the Center's long-range fund-raising could be firmly established.

In "Living Within Our Means" Rockefeller's tone changed from matter-of-fact to that of a troubled supervisor:

There is still the feeling in Lincoln Center as well as among the constituents that somehow we have relatively unlimited funds available; that in a showdown funds will be forthcoming. This is unfortunate indeed as it makes it harder from your point of view keeping our budget at a level that will be raisable [*sic*] on an annual basis. Also it is unfortunate as it makes our dealings with the constituents infinitely more difficult. Furthermore, if the idea gets around generally it makes it harder to raise substantial amounts of money, particularly from the city. . . .

In connection with the foregoing I found your talk at Princeton somewhat disturbing as it seemed to me it is subject to misinterpretation. You emphasized the desirability of larger deficits if art institutions are to attain artistic heights without equally emphasizing that such deficits must be within the bounds of obtainable contributions if the project is to survive. This kind of deficit philosophy can be the downfall of Lincoln Center or any other artistic institution unless as much attention is given to sound financial planning and effective fund-raising as to the creation and development of programs.

Rockefeller then bluntly (for such a patrician) admonishes Schuman in the final section:

This [confidence] of course underlies all human relations. In the Center today I believe that we have a job to do in this respect if we are to move forward at the pace and with the effectiveness, which are desirable. With the constituents as within our own group we must speak frankly and forthrightly putting all the cards on the table. All must feel that they are in your confidence and likewise you must have, or seek, theirs. All of us can be helpful, but the primary effort and initiative must be yours. The unfortunate experiences of the past in which we all were involved will be forgotten with the passage of time so that the job can be done, but it will require a strong and conscious effort. As Dev Josephs has said "cultural leadership must be earned."

Rockefeller ends with a clear challenge to Schuman:

The months ahead are crucial ones. It is your leadership that will be the determining factor. You can count on the support of your fellow trustees. The stakes are high but the time is short.

The tone of the letter came as a shock to Schuman. There is a distinct possibility that it was actually drafted by Edgar Young, who during Schuman's tenure not only assisted Rockefeller in various Lincoln Center matters but also was directly involved in the budget and construction elements of the still-incomplete building project. In a confidential memorandum to his files dated January 9, 1967, Schuman characterizes Rockefeller's letter as "unfriendly" and "out of balance" compared to the "enormous progress the Center had made." Although Rockefeller's demeanor during a meeting on January 4, 1967, was gracious and occasionally "apologetic," Schuman concluded the memo with a complaint: "But I cannot in all candor say, even in a confidential memorandum to the files, that I was completely satisfied."

The Princeton speech to which Rockefeller referred represented a watershed for Schuman and Rockefeller. Schuman was invited to be a principal speaker at the Princeton University Conference on the Performing Arts: Their Economic Problems, held at Princeton University on December 8 and 9, 1966. The gathering's organizers included William Bowen, a professor of economics and future president of Princeton. Schuman was at the height of his powers in late 1966, and his administrative staff had emphasized to him in a series of internal memos that the speech would be an important opportunity for his views to be heard beyond Lincoln Center and New York City. A provocative presentation would clearly have an impact on a wide audience. The conference's participants were high-level representatives of industry and philanthropy. One of the conference's principal topics was to address the issue of the rising deficits most non-profit performing groups had been incurring since World War II.

Schuman entitled his speech "The New Establishment," referring to the recently created phenomenon of the performing arts center, with Lincoln Center leading the way in this area. In retrospect, it was an aggressive, courageous, and perhaps foolhardy presentation on Schuman's part, in which he argued for placing the quality and production of art above the economic factors that supported that art. Considering that his audience consisted of businesspersons and academic economists, Schuman must have felt very secure in his position at Lincoln Center to present such a forceful statement of his beliefs. As it turned out, the speech was a fundamental miscalculation on Schuman's part. He believed he would be able to persuade his listeners that artistic imperatives could take precedence over financial solvency. Schuman was so proud of the talk that he distributed copies of it to the entire Lincoln Center board. Rockefeller first learned of the contents of the presentation after receiving the printed speech, and it was then that he began to realize just how far apart were his and Schuman's views.

In his speech, Schuman immediately went on the offensive by referring to the "New Establishment" in less than glowing terms:

Despite the important advances that have taken place in the construction of new facilities and the increased awareness of economic needs, the fundamental stodginess of most performing arts institutions and of most educational endeavors remain just that: stodgy. There is little evidence of real understanding; of distinguishing means from ends; or realizing that progress can be measured only by creative, artistic and educational programming, and by enhancing the place of the performing arts in the fabric of American society as a whole.

Unfortunately, Schuman placed his audience in the "stodgy" camp, putting some of his listeners (and readers, particularly Rockefeller and other

Lincoln Center board members) on the defensive. This characterization was then extended to board members:

> Public spirited citizens who understand the nature of the trustees' role increasingly populate the boards of the performing arts centers: the trustees of experience who help form policies, but never attempt to direct professional operation; the trustees who assume the responsibility of choosing the professional leaders, through that strange alchemy in which bodies of men and women who may be comparatively ignorant of the specific field under their jurisdiction somehow manage to choose appropriate leaders; and, the trustees who are ready to prove their sense of true involvement by raising the money.

The heart of Schuman's thesis lay in what he called "Schuman's Law and Postulates," which gently tweaked the academically oriented tone of the gathering:

> Nonprofit institutions in the performing arts compromise their reason for being in direct proportion to the programs and policies which are adopted for fiscal reasons extrinsic to artistic purpose. This law has two postulates. First: Timidity in programming concept tends to increase in direct proportion to:
>
> > The degree of catering to the social and esthetic predilections of those who buy the tickets.
> > The percentage of the budget which must be met by voluntary contributions, and
> > The size of the enterprise.

> Second: Imagination in programming concept tends to increase in direct proportion to:
>
> > The clarity of institutional mission.
> > The sophistication of the trustees, and
> > The convictions of the professional leadership.

Earlier I stated that all of us in the performing arts swam in the same sea: the sea of deficit. This sea is obviously a red sea, and only a p-r-o-f-i-t profit can part it. Now, as deep as that red sea is, I think it should be deeper. Basic to our problem is not that our deficits are too large, but that they are too small.

Such a thesis from the administrative and artistic leader of Lincoln Center must have made Rockefeller particularly uncomfortable, considering the daunting financial problems the Center was facing in late 1966. Schuman ended his presentation with a passionate defense of the supremacy of the integrity of the arts over the dictates of the financial ledger:

> But I believe, as a matter of life-long conviction, that the only road to practicality in the world of the arts is for responsible leadership to be Simon-pure. I believe that compromise with artistic standards is totally impractical. The only way that the performing arts can begin to approach the level of support to which their inherent value entitles them in a civilized society, is to state clearly and purely what the problems are, what the mission is, and what the process to their realization must be.
>
> If we reject the anti-democratic political doctrine that the ends justify the means, we must be equally on guard against the inverse: that the means justify the ends. Always we must evaluate means in terms of their adequacy to do the job and not rationalize by confusing the possible with the ideal. We are often so accustomed to the necessity of accommodating to the means at hand that we lose sight of the compromises; a most dangerous form of self-deception. And, if we who find ourselves in the new establishment solve our economic problems by cowardice in esthetic and social doctrine, we have solved nothing at all.
>
> The success or failure of our enterprise cannot be measured in the plusses and minuses of ledgers, but in philosophy and mission, and in the clarity and conviction with which they are given life in our theaters, in our concert halls and in our classrooms.

The speech sounded like a direct assault on Rockefeller's leadership. Schuman's manifesto challenged in public all the initiatives Rockefeller wished to undertake: the scaling back of new artistic ventures at the Center, general reductions of future operating budgets, and the presentation of Lincoln Center as an operation that did not live beyond its means.

Schuman, undaunted, continued to push forward with significant new artistic initiatives, including the creation of a chamber music constituent.

Rockefeller's increasing anxiety about Schuman can be seen in a letter of February 22, 1967, in which Rockefeller expressed grave concern about the financial feasibility of creating a Chamber Music Society at Lincoln Center:

> What specific action you have in mind asking for at this time regarding the proposed Chamber Music Society, I do not know. I am sympathetic to moving forward with the development of the project, but I am unsympathetic to Lincoln Center's making any further financial commitments in relations to it. I feel in this instance as I did in connection with the motion picture equipment for Tully Hall; that is, we just do not have the money. Such limited funds as we do have, in my judgment, must be conserved for already existing responsibilities and commitments. Until we have proven that we have a substantial fund-raising potential for ongoing annual needs, I believe we must not take on added responsibilities that have ongoing financial obligations. . . .
>
> What would appear to be proposed in connection with the Chamber Music Society is a good illustration of the concerns in the minds of those who met with you at lunch just before the New Year. It is not a question of merit, not a question of importance, but rather the future of Lincoln Center as a whole. You will remember that Winston Churchill once said that he did not wish to preside over the liquidation of the British Empire. Neither you nor I want to preside over the liquidation of Lincoln Center. My belief is that we are moving in that direction unless we stop now the making of new commitments for programs involving substantial amounts of money. This is, of course, particularly true whether the commitment has an implied open-endedness because we are in the position of parent and thus cannot see the baby die.

Rockefeller's intensity in the letter was unprecedented. Schuman responded with a highly detailed three-page letter on March 2, 1967. For Schuman, it was unthinkable that Lincoln Center should back away from its basic mission. His letter clearly expressed some of his strongest feelings about what he saw as the true mission of Lincoln Center and reiterated the basic points of his Princeton speech:

> However regrettable these [capital] overages are, in my view we cannot afford at this moment to be diverted from our course, from

the very sound programs that have been accepted and, in truth, the programs that give Lincoln Center its position of leadership. To be frank, your letter gives me the impression that you are questioning the timing of our ongoing program because of the capital overages. If so, this is indeed a major issue, going far beyond the question of chamber music alone. . . .

One of the principal arguments advanced in all our fund-raising efforts was our repeated assertions that Lincoln Center was to be more than buildings. I know that you have stressed that you are not questioning the merit or importance of our proposals. The fact that we have to meet building overages should not lead us into the trap of tacitly reasoning that educational and artistic programs are, after all, postponable.

The buildings of Lincoln Center stand, but each day their justification must be proved anew by what goes on the stages. And each day we must prove anew our dedication to educate the young and to bring to an ever widening segment of the public the finest offerings of the performing arts as conceived by our member institutions and as aided, encouraged and complemented by the programming and educational projects we have designed so far, and those that may be developed in the future. As you have always agreed, this is the dynamic of Lincoln Center.

Your letter and the end-of-the-year one which preceded it have cast some doubts. I look forward to the meeting, which I ask you to call soon, so that we may discuss these critical matters fully.

Unfortunately, during the next two years those discussions would take a direction that neither Schuman nor Rockefeller ever envisioned.

CHAPTER 11

An Intense Inner Life

Schuman's problems as president of Lincoln Center were accumulating at an alarming rate, and the acrimonious atmosphere began to affect both his artistic and his personal life. A prolific composer heretofore, the period between 1962 and 1968 was Schuman's leanest time in terms of new compositions. Of the ten works premiered in this period, his Eighth Symphony (1962) was mostly composed before he began his work at Lincoln Center; *The Orchestra Song* (1964) and *Variations on "America"* (1964) were light arrangements of other material; and a choral work, *Deo Ac Veritati* (1963), and two fanfares, *Philharmonic Fanfare* (1965; withdrawn) and *Dedication Fanfare* (1968), were short *pièces d'occasion*. Finally, his last ballet for Martha Graham, *The Witch of Endor* (1965), was a failure. The three remaining works in this period, *Amaryllis: Variations for String Trio* (1964), *To Thee Old Cause* (1968), and the Symphony No. 9, "Le Fosse Ardeatine" (premiered in January 1969), all display a strident melodic and harmonic vocabulary that seems to express the tension in his life at the time.

The Schuman family was confronting its own challenges as well. In the 1960s parents and children clashed over the Vietnam War, women's rights, free love, drugs, and hair. Both Tony and Andie looked back at the Lincoln Center years as "horrible for the household. Our parents were concerned with appearances." Andie was caught smoking pot in ninth grade, and Tony grew a large head of hair that led his parents to fear that they would be embarrassed or, worse, disgraced by their children.

During these years the Schumans hosted a weekly dinner party for eight to twelve guests at their elegant apartment at 1120 Fifth Avenue. By this time Tony was already away at college at Wesleyan University, so Andie was obliged to chat with her parents' guests over cocktails before returning to her room. On evenings when they had no social or artistic engagements, Bill and Frankie would sit in their cozy library and work on each other's letters, reviewing content and wording: "They were a real team. Whenever there was conflict within the family, the two of them were always an inseparable unit. Mom would be the negotiator, but would always support Dad. On the big questions, however, Dad was fine supporting the explorations of both children," Tony said.

In 1966 Frankie's breast cancer and subsequent mastectomy added to stress throughout the family. Bill's love and admiration for his wife was intense and enduring:

> I've been blessed with the opposite of a composer's wife. Composers' wives are basically Helen Carter, Elliott's wife—somebody who is completely immersed in her husband's music and takes an active role in his music. Frankie is just the opposite, and it's been wonderful for me. If I had someone as my "soul-mate," who said, "Oh, what you're doing is just wonderful," it would have been my ruination. I have to have somebody who is objective about it—encouraging and loving and understanding, but objective about it, to a high degree.

Tony's issues with his father focused primarily on the length of his hair and the Vietnam War:

> My conflict with Dad was ephemeral. When I became radicalized, I looked the part, and Dad would say, "There's a premiere of mine coming up, and I want you there, but you have to get a haircut." I did get a haircut, but it was a mistake. . . . Although Dad opposed the Vietnam War his position on anything was to keep a low profile, which goes back to friends that were hurt by the McCarthy hearings. His belief was that people shouldn't sign petitions.

Although Frankie was inclined toward political activism—she was seen by her children as a proto-feminist—Bill never was, even though he read widely and had strong opinions on domestic and international issues. According to Tony, his father preferred, as he said, to "'fight my fights in my own field.' He wanted to stay politically neutral." One rare exception was when he agreed to serve on a local New Rochelle committee to raise funds for the Stevenson-Kefauver ticket of 1956. Andie added, "Dad had an organic patriotism and had a great respect for the office of the president. He felt that our vehement opposition to the war was wrongheaded."

After Tony received his bachelor of arts from Wesleyan in 1965, he moved on to the quintessential hotbed of student radicalism, Columbia University, where he earned a master's degree in French in 1966 and another master's in architecture in 1970. Andie missed her brother terribly. Frankie urged her to attend the Brearley School in Manhattan "and participate in cotillions," but she eventually enrolled in the still distinguished but slightly less socially conscious Dalton School. A rebellious but talented student, she went to Sarah Lawrence College at the end of her junior year of high school, with the support of her parents. After one year of study, she took a leave of absence and joined her brother on the Columbia campus as an administrative assistant in the registrar's office, where she decided "not to report male students to their draft boards if they fell below a certain grade point average." At the same time, she fell in love with Donald Weiss, a graduate student in philosophy at Princeton. They were married two years later, on May 30, 1968. Bill suffered a major heart attack just before the wedding, which was a small gathering in the Schuman apartment, with Bill seated through the ceremony. The marriage produced a son, Joshua, born in 1974, but Andie and Donald divorced four years later. Andie said that one of the very few times her father showed any violence was when her husband told Frankie to "shut up" and Bill slapped him across the face: "They were ferociously protective of each other."

Bill and Frankie were distraught over Andie's divorce. Tony recalled that "one or both of my parents were crying, they were so worried about Andie's future." However, Andie believed that her divorce enabled her to establish a mature adult relationship with her parents. She went on to earn a master's degree in early childhood education (special education) at SUNY–Binghamton and a Ph.D. from Brandeis.

Despite the sometimes intense family frictions during the 1960s, the Schumans' combination of business acumen and thrift afforded them a very good life. Aside from a generous compensation package from Lincoln Center—approximately $60,000 in 1965—Bill and Frankie were fortunate always to be able to stay on the crest of the New York City housing market after selling their home in New Rochelle at 241 Elk Avenue in August 1963 and moving to 1120 Fifth Avenue. In 1963–64 they built a home on a four-acre plot in "back-country" Greenwich, Connecticut, at 88 Richmond Hill Road, not far from the Westchester (New York) airport. According to Tony, the home

was an adaptation of a model house from the builders to which Mom added the porch room which itself was modeled on the great room in the Charak house on North Road on Martha's Vineyard. . . . They were always "buying up" in real estate and they were thrifty. Their main luxury was food. But there was never anything we felt we couldn't do. Dad saw himself as being financially savvy.

Andie added that "planning and thrift were part of the ethos of the house."

The Connecticut land was sold to the Schumans by their friend, James Warburg, who wanted to surround his own home in the area with congenial companions for himself and his wife, Joan. Three other lots were sold to Norman Lloyd, Schuman's Juilliard colleague; Max Abramovitz, the architect of Philharmonic Hall; and Robert Mann, the first violinist of the Juilliard String Quartet. In the summer Schuman would compose in a small studio detached from the house, and Frankie would tend her vegetable and flower gardens. The Greenwich home became a pleasant retreat for the Schumans where they could escape the stress of New York City. Frankie wisely designed the house on one floor so that in later years she and Bill would not have to negotiate any stairs.

Dinner parties with the Schumans in "the country" were relaxed and stimulating affairs. The porch room included a seating area near an inviting fireplace where cocktails were served before dinner. A twelve-foot-long French farm table occupied the opposite side of the room overlooking the outdoor pool. There Gilda Celini, the Schumans' cook and housekeeper, served homemade pasta and delectable meat courses, while animated conversations touched upon every topic from international affairs to the most recent Lincoln Center gossip.

Despite the intrigues and confrontations that swirled around him at Lincoln Center, William Schuman was determined to continue composing. The Eighth Symphony was his first work to be premiered, as part of the inaugural concerts of Philharmonic Hall on October 4, 1962, during his tenure as president of Lincoln Center. The program began with Beethoven's overture *The Consecration of the House*; Irving Fine's Adagio from *Notturno for Strings and Harp*, performed in commemoration of the composer's death the previous August 23; and the Schuman Symphony No. 8. After intermission came the Brahms Symphony No. 4.

Edward Downes had been asked to write the program notes for the concert and requested Schuman's comments on the new symphony. In a somewhat condescending and testy letter of August 21, 1962—reproduced in its entirety by Downes in the notes—the composer made absolutely clear how pointless he thought program notes were:

Frankly I have become increasingly resistant about issuing play-by-play accounts of my own music. . . . Complicated polemics for particular aesthetic creeds or compositional procedures may be of value to scholars, but they confuse laymen. Techniques, after all, are work methods, which, in the mature artist, cannot be isolated from his creative process. Preoccupation with description of techniques bears a direct relationship to the rather absurd length we go to in placing composers in categories and often pre-judging their work accordingly as though musical vocabulary itself had something to do with excellence.

Schuman concluded in a more benign tone: "Having divested myself of these gratuitous comments, I had better stop before I write the kind of essay I am complaining about." He went on to explain that the work had been commissioned by the New York Philharmonic in 1960, before he became president of Lincoln Center, to celebrate its opening, which was then planned for the 1961–62 season. Composition of the symphony was interrupted so that Schuman could compose *A Song of Orpheus*, but the symphony was finally completed on June 14, 1962.

The thirty-minute work is composed in three movements: Lento sostenuto–Pressante vigoroso–Lento, Largo–Tempi più mosso–Largo, and Presto–Prestissimo. The first movement begins with a distinctive bell-like chord, followed by an extended French horn solo reminiscent of the beginning of Schuman's *Night Journey*. Much of the first two movements is pensive in character, presaging Schuman's approach to his Ninth Symphony, which he would compose six years later, at the end of his Lincoln Center presidency. The second movement is based on musical materials found in the third movement of Schuman's Fourth String Quartet. The final movement has the perkiness and quick tempi so strongly associated with Schuman's scherzolike movements.

Critical opinion of the new symphony was uniformly positive, a remarkable response considering its cragginess, mournfulness, and complexity. The *New York Times* depicted the symphony as "tragic and intense . . . Indeed the whole work hangs together remarkably well and one gets the sense of a piece dominated by a single broad-arched, rather mournful melody." Schuman was also congratulated on having maintained his artistic abilities despite his administrative responsibilities: "And in its concentration and mastery it [the symphony] showed no sign of being the work of a busy executive."

Paul Henry Lang in the *New York Herald Tribune* was even more effusive in his praise:

Mr. Schuman's is a genuine symphony. . . . There are no tricks, no cliches, and none of the schematized peculiarities one constantly encounters in both post-romantic and serial composers. . . . The core of the work is the middle movement, an extended dirge with long, flowing melodies, steadily mounting in intensity. . . . It is comforting to know that the president of Lincoln Center not only remains a composer while assuming an important executive position, but is growing in stature.

The *New York World-Telegram and Sun* summed up Schuman's status: "The symphony shaped up, section by section, into a rousing complex of animated sound. Between passages of broad, haunting lyricism came buildups of sharp crisis. Schuman must live an intense inner life, to judge by his music."

He ought to have been on top of the world, but Schuman's "intense inner life" would only become more complex throughout his tenure as president of Lincoln Center.

Owing to the increasingly difficult demands of the early years of his presidency, Schuman tended to compose miniatures and lighter works, although one would become his most often performed composition. The short choral work, *Deo Ac Veritati* ("For God and for truth"), the motto of Colgate University, was described by Schuman as a canon with coda for three-part a cappella men's chorus (tenor I, tenor II, and bass). It was commissioned by Colgate for the inauguration of its president, Vincent Barnett, and premiered on April 19, 1963. The text of the three-minute work uses only the words of the motto. Schuman's masterful contrapuntal texture begins with an extended two-line canon of sixty-five measures at the stately tempo of quarter note = c. 72, marked "Full voice, with dignity and strength." At the coda the chorus is divided into two tenor parts and bass, then comes together in rhythmic unison until the conclusion, marked "Molto sonoro al fine." A classic *pièce d'occasion*, the work is also the only choral piece that Schuman would compose during his Lincoln Center years, and the first work for voices since the premiere of his *Carols of Death* in 1959.

Schuman continued working in simple miniatures with his approximately four-minute arrangement for orchestra of *The Orchestra Song* (also arranged for concert band as *The Band Song*), premiered on April 11, 1964, by the Minneapolis Symphony Orchestra conducted by Andre Kostelanetz. The work is based on a "series of traditional Austrian melodies . . . [with] the first two melodies . . . played in succession and then together. . . . Each succeeding melody is heard alone and then combined with all the melodies that have preceded it."

In 1939 Schuman had written *The Orchestra Song*, with English text by his friend Marion Farquhar, for a cappella chorus, and it quickly became a bestseller for G. Schirmer. He decided that an orchestral arrangement would sell as well, especially to the school orchestra market. One might wonder why a composer of Schuman's depth would undertake such a simply wrought project. But Schuman often expressed a desire to provide quality music for school-age children, and *The Orchestra Song* filled the bill perfectly.

The next arrangement by Schuman was more complex and became his most popular work. During the dedication of the four-manual, 5,500 pipe Aeolian Skinner organ in Philharmonic Hall on December 15, 1962, the well-known organ virtuoso E. Power Biggs performed Charles Ives's *Variations on "America,"* written in 1891. Schuman, who was present at the performance, had never heard the work before. Excitedly turning to the person next to him, the composer Henry Cowell, he announced that the composition was perfectly suited for an orchestral arrangement. Cowell agreed. The next day Schuman called his publisher to inquire about getting the rights to arrange the Ives work but was told that, judging from past experience, permission would be difficult to realize: he had to obtain the authorization of Ives's artistic executor. When he inquired to whom he should address his request, the answer was none other than Henry Cowell.

The arrangement, commissioned by BMI for its twentieth anniversary, has been an audience favorite ever since it premiered with the New York Philharmonic, Andre Kostelanetz conducting, on May 20, 1964. A subsequent arrangement for band based on Schuman's orchestra arrangement was completed in 1968 by William E. Rhoads. The work's popularity clearly stems from the familiarity of the theme "America" and Ives's playful permutations of it. Schuman changed nothing in the original work, except to add the prominent percussion parts throughout.

In Schuman's program notes for the May premiere he quoted from Henry and Sidney Cowell's biography of Charles Ives:

[Ives composed] an organ fantasia entitled *Variations on "America"* [that] was played in organ recitals in Danbury [Connecticut] and Brewster, New York in 1891. This work contained pages his father would not let him play at the Brewster concert because they had canons in two and three keys at once that proved to be unsuited to performance in church: they "made the boys laugh out loud and get noisy." . . . This is the earliest surviving piece using polytonality.

The stentorian fortissimo statement of a variant of the theme followed by the ludicrous four horns soli played with bells in the air sets the stage for a raucous romp with this patriotic melody, but then Schuman arrives at a very reverent statement of the theme that shows it appropriate respect, even if it will eventually be turned on its head. The ensuing five variations, separated by interludes and meno mosso sections, run the stylistic gauntlet, from contrapuntal accompaniments to Spanish-style castanet and tambourine flourishes to solo trumpet obbligati straight from the nineteenth-century cornet solos of Herbert L. Clarke. Little wonder that this charming eight-minute work has been a crowd pleaser ever since its premiere.

The arrangement also engages audience members because the faster metronome markings and individual instrumental voices Schuman calls for have greater aural clarity and color than does the organ version. In addition, contrapuntal lines are realized in a lighter texture than in the original organ part. Especially in the sections that involved the organ pedals, Schuman could ask a trumpet or a flute to play at a markedly faster pace, enlivening the entire work:

> I took all the liberties that a transcriber must take to make the thing come out, plus the fun of [seeing] if you could do it without changing anything, and I did. . . . I tried to orchestrate it in a manner that I thought might have appealed to him [Ives] . . . you can't say that it's typical Ives, and certainly it's not important Ives, but I think it's interesting because it shows where he was heading: that whole bitonal section . . . it shows his original mind at work. And you don't have to justify it any more than just the fact that it pleases audiences. It's just that kind of piece.

Cowell was quite pleased with the arrangement: "The Ives is delightful—the scoring strong, but witty and deft as Ives would have liked. I thought as it went on how glad that you gave it a sense of fun—Ives did not make it for Queen Victoria, nor did you make it for Queen Elizabeth. I liked the instrumentation better than anything on the program."

It is tempting to hypothesize that the hostility by which Schuman was surrounded at Lincoln Center influenced his compositional language. A work that could not have been more stylistically distant from *Variations on "America,"* although it too was a set of variations on a theme dear to his heart, is a case in point. *Amaryllis: Variations for String Trio* (based on an old English round) was first performed in Washington, D.C., by the New York String Trio on October 31, 1964, having been "commissioned for The Thirteenth Festival of Chamber Music by the Elizabeth Sprague Coolidge Foundation in the Library of Congress on the occasion of the one hundredth anniversary of the birth of its founder." The Coolidge Foundation had also commissioned Schuman's Fourth String Quartet in 1950. The work is dedicated "to the memory of Elizabeth Sprague Coolidge . . . and to the Music Division of the Library of Congress, Harold Spivacke, Chief, in tribute to its distinguished and imaginative realization of the purposes for which the Foundation was established." Schuman had, of course, known Spivacke since late 1941, when he had asked for Spivacke's support in enlisting in the armed forces.

The three-day festival encompassed four programs involving the music of twelve living composers including, in addition to Schuman, such luminaries as Luigi Dallapiccola, Alberto Ginastera, Howard Hanson, Gian Francesco Malipiero, Darius Milhaud, Walter Piston, Virgil Thomson, and Aurelio de la Vega. The festival programs included Bartók's String Quartet No. 5, Copland's *Appalachian Spring*, Paul Hindemith's *Hérodiade*, and Prokofiev's String Quartet No. 1, as well as birthday pieces by Henry Purcell, Mozart, Beethoven, and Schubert.

Amaryllis is a profoundly complex and somber work, about twenty-five minutes in length, for string trio (violin, viola, and cello) and voices. It stands as one of Schuman's most expressively intense and harmonically challenging compositions, with an introduction, four variations, and conclusion played without pause. The words to the round are:

Turn Amaryllis to thy swain,
thy damon calls thee back again.
I know a pretty pretty pretty arbor nigh,
where Apollo, where Apollo dare not hide.
Come to me and whilst I play,
sing to my love a rondelet.

Schuman used "Amaryllis" as well as three other rounds in his *Concerto on Old English Rounds*, written in 1973. Commented Schuman about borrowing from earlier works: "Composers do this all the time. The whole idea of reworking materials is as old as composition itself."

Amaryllis has the words to the round printed under the string parts, as was done with the solo cello part in *A Song of Orpheus*, to "enable the performer to project the melody with the clarity of a singer." The work commences with muted strings, slow (half note = c. 50), somber, and eerily dissonant. In a nod to the distant origins of the round, there are moments that replicate harmonies heard in musical compositions of the Renaissance, but by the beginning of Variation I the listener is brought into the mid-twentieth century with extremely dissonant harmonies and frequently changing meters; its ethereal and elusive tonal center challenges even the sophisticated listener. Although Variation II is marked "light—playful" in the syncopated cello and violin, the music is more jagged and pointillistic than jocular. Schuman writes a biting and emotional viola melody against transparent accompanying lines in the violin and cello. In Variation III the work takes on characteristics of the string quartets of Bartók, with heavy, accented triple-forte chords of surprising brutality and marked at one point "savagely." Schuman's remarkable understanding of both counterpoint and idiosyncratic string writing produces many stunning melodic, rhythmic, and harmonic textures as the work progresses. In Variation IV Schuman puts all three instruments in rhythmic unison, includes his characteristic flourishes, and creates some remarkable pizzicato passages for the ensemble in complex rhythmic patterns.

It is toward the end of the work, however, that Schuman pulls off a *coup de théâtre* when three sopranos come onstage and sing the round itself, each voice entering successively at the fifth measure of the melody and accompanied only by a low A drone in the cello. The strings eventually are incorporated with the voices to provide particularly piquant dissonant harmonies to the sweet melodic clarity of the voices. As the voices complete their round on the word "rondelet," the sound of the strings slowly dies away on the last chord.

Robert Evett, writing in the *Musical Quarterly*, found "the juxtaposition of tonal and non-tonal materials . . . unsettling, and the obscurity of the theme in the variations was confusing." Evett also saw the surprise appearance of the vocal trio as "disconcerting." Day Thorpe, however, commented that Schuman had taken the sixteenth-century English round and "worked [it] in conservative, severe style. The writing for strings is extraordinarily sensitive, the whole piece is very moving, and Mr. Schuman has provided ambitious string trios with what they have heretofore lacked—a companion piece for the Mozart Divertimento in E flat." Thorpe viewed the arrival of the vocal trio as "an unusual and sophisticated surprise."

Amaryllis is one of Schuman's most musically adventurous compositions. Its intellectual depth and emotional intensity give it a unique place in his most important works for chamber ensemble.

Owing to his workload at Lincoln Center, after *Amaryllis* Schuman had only three new works premiered between late 1964 and late 1968, and two were brief fanfares: *Philharmonic Fanfare*, premiered on August 10, 1965, in New York City for the New York Philharmonic's annual parks concerts and eventually withdrawn by the composer; and *Dedication Fanfare*, premiered on July 4, 1968, to celebrate the opening of Eero Saarinen's Gateway to the West Arch in St. Louis, and performed by the LaClede Band. In between the fanfares was Schuman's music for Graham's ballet *The Witch of Endor*, which was premiered on November 2, 1965, in New York. The ballet received poor reviews and faded from the scene as both a choreographic and a musical work.

The travails of family life, the challenges of a career as a working composer, and the internecine battles at Lincoln Center never distracted Schuman from what he believed was Lincoln Center's mission as an arts institution. Schuman's senior staff of late 1965 included Mark Schubart, vice president of the Lincoln Center Fund; Schuyler Chapin, vice president for programming; Edgar B. Young, executive vice president and chairman of the building committee; Colonel William F. Powers, vice president for engineering; Arno C. Zeyn, controller; and Henry Bessire, vice president for development. Young recalled that the prevailing view of this group was that Lincoln Center's

> artistic position and prestige ... was going to depend on what it, the corporation, did. Now in the course of time it became clear that this was a different philosophy from the philosophy of Lincoln Center aiding and abetting and coordinating the constituents. . . . This tendency had the result of making Lincoln Center ... a competitor of the other constituents.

The tension between the point of view of the center's staff and that of its constituents would cause considerable problems for Schuman for the remainder of his presidency.

The harsh financial climate at Lincoln Center and Rockefeller's admonitions did not put a damper on Schuman's determination to develop artistic activities for the campus. Earlier he had created the foundation upon which his initiatives would be based, and now he persuaded his board to create a fund that could be used to finance his artistic initiatives and subsidize potential losses. The New Projects Underwriting Fund was created in January 1963 with a fund-raising goal of $2.5 million. The original idea of having Schuman create artistic projects when the halls were empty in the summer, which led to the Promenade Concerts in Philharmonic Hall, a film festival in September 1963, and various visiting international opera, dance, and drama companies in summer festivals, was supplemented by Schuman's initiatives in launching new performing arts ensembles and creating future constituents that would eventually fill all of the campus's halls.

In his President's Report to the Lincoln Center board at its annual meeting on May 10, 1965, Schuman announced his plans to develop four separate organizations that would support new artistic initiatives at the Center:

(1) a chamber music group . . . in an attempt to develop an organization; (2) a film institute . . . ; (3) a modern dance constituent which could be housed in the Recital Hall [eventually Alice Tully Hall], and (4) the teacher's institute [eventually the Lincoln Center Institute], long an established goal, will be a summer activity at the Center.

This initiative was planned to begin in the summer of 1968. The board indicated no dissatisfaction with the Schuman projects, even voting him a raise of $12,100 in deferred compensation at its executive meeting of June 29, 1965.

Schuman's first summer program was called August Fanfare and was presented in Philharmonic Hall. It was "a twelve-week summer series held only once in 1963 [that] included chamber music, dance, jazz and piano recitals." Although it ran a small deficit, the program proved that there was a concertgoing public in New York City in the summer. His film festivals also were popular with the public, but by 1965 earlier modest deficits had ballooned to $170,000. Schuman met with serious opposition over the appropriateness of film festivals and an eventual film constituent at the center. When Anthony Bliss complained that it was "not a live art," Schuman retorted, "It's a hell of a lot livelier than that Metropolitan Opera." Schuman was always a great devotee of film. Even though he had refused to follow his friend Frank Loesser to Hollywood in the 1930s to find his fortune writing film music, Schuman did write two film scores, one for the 1944 documentary *Steeltown* and one for a 1959 film called *The Earth Is Born*, that was sponsored by Time-Life. Unfortunately, according to Schuman,

> there was some disagreement between Time's publisher, Henry Luce, and the producer of the movie as to how the earth was born, one taking an ecclesiastical and the other a scientific approach, so the film was never released. . . . I was able . . . to put some of the music from *The Earth is Born* in my Seventh Symphony. And I remember taking music that went with a blast furnace in *Steeltown* and using it for the rape scene in *Undertow*. The same music did very well for both subjects!

Schuman believed that film was the "only really new form of art in the twentieth century, and if Lincoln Center weren't open to them [sic] it would be a kind of anachronism—we might as well have founded it a hundred years ago." Unfortunately, he told a journalist during what he believed to be an off-the-record interview that film at the center was "a cultural necessity." The article shocked John D. Rockefeller 3rd, who had no idea that was what Schuman planned to do; and, of course, Schuman had no authority to proceed with film without full board approval. In addition, the Museum of Modern Art, which had an active film program and had been supported by the Rockefeller family since its founding, was surprised that it now had a potential rival.

Schuman was able to calm the waters by opting for the creation of a film festival before acquiring a full film constituent. He traveled to London to ascertain how that city's annual film festival functioned and there hired Richard Roud, who was working for the British Film Institute, as a co-director, along with Amos Vogel, to create the Lincoln Center Film Festival.

Schuman then called his friend Martin E. Segal to help create the organizational and financial structure of the new film venture. Schuman's favorite social outing was to go with Segal and their wives "to a late-afternoon flick, about a 5:30 show, then have a leisurely dinner in some little bistro, and we're home by ten o'clock."

It was Segal who recruited William F. May, chairman of the American Can Company, to be the chairman of the film festival. Schuman was a great admirer of Segal: "Marty was so successful with the Film Society that it was only a matter of time before Lincoln Center tapped him. He eventually became chairman of Lincoln Center itself. . . . A remarkable man—I always tell him he's my best 'placement.'" The Film Society eventually became a full Lincoln Center constituent in 1969.

With his longtime friend Richard Rodgers, Schuman created a new constituent, the Music Theater of Lincoln Center, dedicated to presenting revivals of established American musicals as well as developing new works. Hoyt Ammidon, the chairman of United States Trust Company, agreed to chair the new organization, which would perform in the New York State Theater. The financial assumption was that the musical revivals would essentially break even and that subsequent national tours of the musicals would generate a profit. A loan of $65,000 from the New Projects Underwriting Fund was given to the Music Theater to assist in planning for a 1964 summer season.

However, the venture was short-lived. According to Edgar Young,

> the Music Theater brought revivals of American musical shows to the New York State Theater each summer through 1970. The productions met a strong public interest, but operated at a deficit. Its sponsoring group was unable to generate sufficient recurring financial support, and its board with the concurrence of Richard Rodgers terminated the Music Theater operation and liquidated the corporation [in 1970].

The Repertory Theater of Lincoln Center was the worst offender of all the constituents when it came to creating deficits. In 1963 the theater received a grant of $500,000 from the center's Fund for Education and Creative Artistic Advancement, but that was quickly absorbed in the production of Arthur Miller's *After the Fall* at the ANTA Theater downtown. In late 1963 the theater's chairman, George Woods, was forced to appeal to the Lincoln Center board for a loan of $100,000 from the New Projects Underwriting Fund to stay afloat. The new theater ended the season with a deficit of $350,000 and an outstanding loan of $100,000.

In the aftermath of the Krawitz affair, both Elia Kazan and Robert Whitehead left the Repertory Theater in late 1964. They were replaced in

January 1965 by two theater professionals, Herbert Blau and Jules Irving, the co-producers of the San Francisco Actor's Workshop. In the brief interim, without any professional leadership, Lincoln Center provided another $300,000 to the theater in December 1964 as a "'last resort' call on the Rockefeller special gift fund." That "last resort" was nullified in late 1965 by two more $100,000 loans.

In addition to the financial friction at the center, the constituents continued to be uneasy with Schuman's aggressive impresario initiatives. The New York Philharmonic felt threatened by the Chamber Music Society Schuman envisioned, and the Metropolitan Opera was distressed by the Hamburg Opera's participation in the summer festival of 1967 and the planned presence of the Rome Opera in Festival '68. According to Young, by early 1966 "these frictions in the constituent relationships became a subject of great concern to Rockefeller. He felt they indicated a lack of trust and confidence in Lincoln Center and its officers, and a lack of consensus on where and how Lincoln Center should be moving."

Young also posits that fund-raising was becoming increasingly difficult for Lincoln Center because the center's needs were "no longer at the top of . . . philanthropic list[s]" and "they [donors] were concerned about racial strife and riots in the streets, and their whole focus in the late '60s was turning to the social upheaval."

In the midst of the increasing construction and artistic deficits and the tension between Lincoln Center and the constituents, Schuman moved boldly forward in late 1965 with a major new artistic initiative: the creation of the Chamber Music Society of Lincoln Center. This idea was, in fact, endorsed by John D. Rockefeller 3rd in a handwritten note to Schuman of October 28, 1965, in which he responded to the creation of a chamber music organization through the potential assistance of Alice Tully: "Your idea here outlined intrigues me. Why don't you try it on Arthur Houghton [the chairman of the New York Philharmonic, a Lincoln Center vice chair, the president of Steuben Glass, and one of Tully's cousins] through a telephone call, as he was most helpful to me in my approach to Miss Tully."

In late 1964 Lincoln Center leaders realized that their earlier plan of constructing a 500–600 seat chamber music hall in the Juilliard building was neither economically nor artistically feasible and opted to enlarge the seating to 1,000 and to use the space for performances of both music and dance.

Because the Houghton family, which included Alice Tully, Mr. and Mrs. Arthur Houghton Jr., Mr. and Mrs. Amory Houghton, and the Houghton Family Foundation, had already contributed about $850,000, it was initially proposed that the new space be named Houghton Hall.

Schuman wrote Arthur Houghton a letter on November 12, 1965, about the creation of a chamber music constituent at Lincoln Center, its venue the "Chamber Music Hall" in the new Juilliard building. Schuman went on to write that the new constituent would be a "creative artistic enterprise . . . [and the new hall would] not simply [be] a booking operation to be rented on an ad hoc basis to other institutions." It was Schuman's hope that Alice Tully would agree to exploratory conversations on the topic.

Houghton acted quickly in contacting Tully, and Schuman was able to meet her for the first time in early December 1965. The meeting, as mentioned in a letter from Schuman to Tully on December 6, 1965, seems to have gone exceedingly well: "But I was more than delighted—I was encouraged. The spirit of dedication and genuine involvement which was apparent in everything that you said about *our* chamber music project was deeply appreciated" (emphasis added).

Schuman began to develop programming for the new venture by inviting David Amram to create a proposed series of six chamber music and jazz concerts for the 1966–67 season to be presented at the Vivian Beaumont Theater, with Amram as the music director. Amram's approach was to include at least two contemporary works on each program along with "not too-often performed works of the old masters." In a letter to Amram in mid-January 1966, Schuman praises Amram's programming but also indicates that without a real chamber music hall he feels considerable hesitancy in starting the chamber music series. Amram never again appears in the planning process of the Chamber Music Society.

Tully became more and more enthusiastic about the chamber music constituent. In February 1966 she wrote to Schuman that "my own especial joy is the thought that each day that passes brings our cherished dream of a Chamber Music Center nearer to realization." Schuman responded by setting up a meeting in March with her, Mark Schubart (whose title at that time was vice president and executive director of the Lincoln Center Fund for Education and Creative Artistic Advancement), and Charles Wadsworth, American pianist and artistic director for chamber music at the Festival of Two Worlds in Spoleto, Italy, who appears for the first time in the planning process and who would become the first and longtime artistic director of the Chamber Music Society of Lincoln Center.

Events moved quickly from those important meetings of late winter 1966, and on May 10, 1966, Lincoln Center triumphantly announced that "the chamber music recital hall which will open in late 1968 [it actually opened in late 1969] at Lincoln Center for the Performing Arts, will be named for Alice Tully"—not the entire Houghton family. In a letter from Rockefeller to the Juilliard building architect, Pietro Belluschi, who at the time was the dean of the MIT School of Architecture and Planning, Rockefeller writes that Tully "seems to be quite touched at our desire to name it after her." It was also reported in the press that Charles Wadsworth would be retained as a consultant for programming in chamber music at Lincoln Center.

Rockefeller Archive Center documents indicate that the Tully naming gift amounted to $1.3 million, donated in two separate tranches of $500,000 in 1958 and $800,000 in 1964. The delay of the announcement of the naming until 1966 was due to Tully's wish that nothing be announced until the entire $800,000 pledge was paid; furthermore, her 1958 gift was to be categorized as coming from an anonymous donor. It was also Tully's understanding that the $1.3 million gift "[would] amount to one-half of the estimated $2,600,000 cost of the substantially enlarged Chamber Music Hall presently planned at the Center." To put the project in historical perspective, the very first plans for a "chamber music hall" in 1958 envisioned a space seating 500–600 people, to be located in Philharmonic Hall, and to cost about $1 million.

As construction of the hall, within the Juilliard building but to be administered solely by Lincoln Center, moved haltingly forward, with construction delays and cost overruns, in February 1967 Lincoln Center's Executive Committee gave official recognition to create an exploratory committee for chamber music at Lincoln Center with Alice Tully as chairman. Other members of the committee included Edward Wardwell, Sampson R. Field, the Lincoln Center administrators Schuman, Schubart, and Chapin, and Wadsworth as the resident professional who would implement the plan. The committee was charged with developing "a plan to utilize Alice Tully Hall for the furtherance of the art of chamber music on the highest level of performance and the broadest availability to the public." In Schuman's own terms, he wished to create "a repertory theater of chamber music."

Schuman asked Tully for a three-year grant totaling $300,000 to assure that planning for the creation of the Chamber Music Society could be realized until the beginning of the first season in 1969–70. Tully quickly agreed, eventually giving $100,000 in each of the calendar years 1967, 1968, and 1969. In rapid succession new board members joined the exploratory committee, including Mary Rosenwald and Frank Taplin as president to Tully's chairmanship. Commissions for the opening season were suggested by Wadsworth and included such composers as Samuel Barber, Pierre Boulez, Carlos Chávez, Alberto Ginastera, Olivier Messiaen, and Darius Milhaud, as well as a younger group that included John Corigliano. Schuman was pleased with the composers on the list but reduced most of the suggested commissioning fees by $500.

By late 1967 the exploratory committee had begun to grapple with an issue that would hover over the fledgling chamber music venture for a great while: should the nucleus of the new group be composed of eight or so musicians employed full-time by the society, or should established chamber groups be hired to perform during the first season? Frank Taplin, in particular, was not sure that a full-time group was best for the society. Schuman agreed with Taplin that this was a valid issue for discussion but then countered in a letter on December 22, 1967, that after thorough review,

> I was convinced that in the excellent artistic plan [of Wadsworth] . . .
> the resident group is basic for reasons of quality, continuity and
> breadth of repertory. It seems to me that these artistic considerations
> must come first. . . . I hope that the concern about the establishment
> of the Chamber Music Society which some of our Lincoln Center
> friends have expressed is not also an issue. It seems to me that we are
> a free and independent group, with an obligation centered solely in
> our determination to make the best possible Chamber Music Society
> that this troubled earth of ours has ever seen.

Schuman was clearly passionate about the creation of the society, and he was chafing at complaints from the New York Philharmonic about its creation and the concomitant budgetary demands it would have to face in the near term. He seemingly took on this endeavor as a way of strengthening his artistic leadership of Lincoln Center. But the line in the sand that he drew with his insistence on the existence of the society began to focus the ire of his directors on the Lincoln Center board.

CHAPTER 12

Knocked Out of the Box

Beginning in 1968, the Chamber Music Society's status at Lincoln Center could be clearly linked to Schuman's deteriorating position as the Center's president. Frank Taplin, the Society's president, continued to study the question of whether a full-time resident ensemble should be created just as they were beginning to understand what the operating costs of Alice Tully Hall entailed. Schuman proposed that the Chamber Music Society, once declared a constituent, could either manage the hall on its own, therefore benefiting from any profits and conversely absorbing any deficits, or allow Lincoln Center to manage the hall and split operational costs based on use by the Society—the formula used by the New York Philharmonic and Lincoln Center for Philharmonic Hall.

On May 10, 1968, in the midst of these protracted explorations and negotiations, Schuman suffered a major heart attack. He was not able to return to his desk at Lincoln Center until September 4. During his absence, John Mazzola was designated chief executive officer of Lincoln Center and worked with the Center's board to reduce the projected next fiscal year's budget. Soon after his return in the early autumn, Schuman instructed his vice president for development, Henry Bessire, to draw up a prospectus on raising endowment funds for the Chamber Music Society, but the effort was viewed by both the Lincoln Center board and the constituents as having a dampening effect on their own annual fund-raising. Schuman's absence from Lincoln Center and his weakened physical state upon his return made his position as the Center's leader less and less tenable.

Remarkably, during this period of ill health and difficulties at Lincoln Center, Schuman continued to compose. The next to last work that he created during his Lincoln Center tenure was, in fact, written while he was recovering. *To Thee Old Cause: Evocation for Oboe, Brass, Timpani, Piano and Strings,* was composed between June 11 and August 17, 1968, while Schuman was in residence at his country home in Greenwich. It was commissioned by the New

York Philharmonic in celebration of its 125th anniversary and first performed in New York with Leonard Bernstein conducting and the orchestra's principal oboist, Harold Gomberg, as soloist on October 3, 1968. Originally Schuman had planned to write a divertimento based on Bernstein's "New York, New York," from his show *On the Town*. Schuman envisioned his work as upbeat and fun filled. However, with the assassinations of both Martin Luther King (April 4, 1968) and Robert F. Kennedy (June 5, 1968), Schuman, along with the rest of the nation, fell into a somber mood. (Schuman did eventually contribute a short musical birthday greeting to Bernstein based on "New York, New York" during a seventieth-birthday celebration for Bernstein presented by the Boston Symphony Orchestra on August 28, 1988.)

In an effort to find comfort in poetry, Schuman began to read one of his favorite poets, Walt Whitman, and came upon "To Thee, Old Cause!":

To thee, old Cause!
Thou peerless, passionate, good cause!
Thou stern, remorseless, sweet Idea!
Deathless throughout the ages, races, lands!
After a strange, sad war—great war for thee,
(I think all war through time was really fought, and ever will be really fought, for thee;)
These chants for thee—the eternal march of thee.
Thou orb of many orbs!
Thou seething principle! Thou well-kept, latent germ! Thou centre!
Around the idea of thee the strange sad war revolving,
With all its angry and vehement play of causes,
(With yet unknown results to come, for thrice a thousand years,)
These recitatives for thee—my Book and the War are one,
Merged in its spirit I and mine—as the contest hinged on thee,
As a wheel on its axis turns, this Book, unwitting to itself,
Around the Idea of thee.

Schuman had an abbreviated version of the Whitman poem printed in the score as a guide to the meaning of the orchestral work. The poetry is not part of the performed composition.

At the world premiere the work was dedicated to the memory of both King and Kennedy. It is a lament, with dissonant harmonies and glacial tempi, although Schuman varied each section's tempo by doubling the metronome marking, moving from quarter note = c. 40 to quarter note = c. 80 in Tempo II to quarter note = c. 160 in Tempo III.

Schuman treated the oboe line more as a coloristic addition than as a concerto solo, providing little musical material for the instrument. In many ways it is not a gratifying part for the oboist, who is asked to sustain single notes at exceedingly slow tempi or to play staccato sixteenth-note passages on practically the lowest note of the instrument.

There are typical Schumanesque musical characteristics in the composition such as triple-forte chords, flourishes, a section reminiscent of the Symphony for Strings in Tempo III at measure 72, juxtapositions of brass choirs against strings, brutish-sounding chords in the brass and piano, the inclusion of the words of the poem in the score so as to have the "melodic line played clearly, as though the words were sung," and the final mournful unison F-sharp. Regrettably, the work is not awash in new musical ideas.

Schuman commented:

> But that piece [*To Thee Old Cause*] people even that are sympathetic to my music...find...a difficult piece to listen to. It's quite strange. I don't know why, but they do.... I would say that generally, according to my wife, I write some very sad music.... Poignant. But I always feel that as you get older you have the ability to give more of yourself, to give more of your true emotions.

To add to his woes, by 1967–68 Schuman and the Lincoln Center board had to grapple with the festering issue of how to fund the new drama division of the Juilliard School when it completed its move to the Lincoln Center campus. For several years while he was still president of the School, Schuman had invested considerable time and resources into bringing drama to Juilliard. In addition to Juilliard officials' expectations that the drama division would be fully funded by outside grants, the continuing issue of cost overruns in the construction of the Juilliard building caused the Lincoln Center board no end of financial problems.

Schuman had proposed that funds from some of the larger grants, in particular from the Carnegie Corporation, could be used to offset construction costs. Juilliard's president, Peter Mennin, was no longer on good terms with Schuman, and both institutions' boards clashed continually well into 1968. In 1969, as Schuman ended his tenure as Lincoln Center's president, the task of negotiating this issue was handed to Amyas Ames, chairman of the Center's executive committee.

In a frosty letter dated January 8, 1969, to John W. Drye Jr., of the Juilliard board, Ames wrote that it was time for the negotiations to end, saying that "we have, with considerable reluctance, decided to accept your offer" to distribute funds to Juilliard—approximately $1.5 million—in support of the drama division during a period stretching from 1969 to 1975. Ames ended the letter with a twinge of anger: "Lincoln Center cannot subsidize Juilliard, either directly or indirectly."

Since his return to Lincoln Center in September 1968, Schuman must have realized that he could no longer have the freedom he had enjoyed earlier in his tenure in the creation of new artistic endeavors at the Center. Facing deficits, the diminution of artistic programming, and the ongoing battles with the constituents, in addition to his deteriorating health, a reasonable approach would have been to step back from his earlier combative stance and allow time to heal some of the deep wounds of the period. However, Schuman refused to compromise and on December 17, 1968, even tried to push through a press announcement of a complete Chamber Music Society season, over the protests of the leadership of the Lincoln Center board. The announcement included news of the creation of a resident ensemble of eight musicians, as well as the appointment of Charles Wadsworth as artistic director and Irwin Scherzer, Alice Tully's confidant and frequent escort, as business manager. Rockefeller himself had to call Arthur Ochs Sulzberger, publisher of the *New York Times*, to stop the press release.

Another factor that should have alerted Schuman to the need to back off a bit had been Rockefeller's decision in late 1965 to relieve Edgar Young from oversight of the Center's financial dealings and place it squarely on Schuman's shoulders. Although Young would continue to chair the building committee in order to realize the completion of the Juilliard building and Alice Tully Hall, his exit from financial planning for the Center would leave Schuman as the principal figure in charge of Lincoln Center's current fiscal crisis. Young had

been on a full-time loan to Lincoln Center since the emergency in 1961 [Taylor's resignation]. [He resumed his former position as an associate in Rockefeller's office in 1966 and] in addition to his need to have Young back at his own office, Rockefeller felt that the time had come for Schuman to assume complete executive responsibility for all facets of Lincoln Center. He was particularly concerned that Schuman carry the full responsibility for the financial planning for the future.

Young recalled that Rockefeller, Devereux Josephs, and he believed "that if I [Young] no longer was there on a full time basis, if I was no longer pulling the financial threads together, . . . Schuman and his own staff would have to do this and he would have to face up, more than he had, to the reality of his ambitions and the rate at which things could be done." Rockefeller and his colleagues on the Lincoln Center board desperately wanted their president to defer some of his projects, but Schuman would not agree to that. He continued to pursue the creation of a full season of chamber music and his parallel thrust to create summer festivals and a film society, which the Center's executive committee insisted had to be self-supporting in order to gain constituency status.

At the time of his heart attack in May 1968, Schuman had already lost the support of one of his greatest advocates in the person of Charles M. Spofford, chairman of the Center's executive committee, who had strongly supported his appointment in 1962. Spofford resigned as executive committee chair in a letter to Rockefeller dated September 30, 1968, in which he suggested that Amyas Ames's expertise in addressing the Center's budgetary woes during the summer would lead to "the assumption of the chairmanship of the Committee by Amyas Ames, at least during the period of the financial crisis and the implementation of the budgetary plan of which he was largely the author." According to Young,

> John Rockefeller was still trying very hard to help Schuman succeed. John didn't want to see a change occur if it could be avoided, but as the end of 1968 approached, John prevailed on Amyas Ames to take the chairmanship of the Executive Committee. . . . [Spofford's health was failing at this time from a second stroke.] Ames did agree to come on and we had the situation, while Schuman was ill, that [John] Mazzola was functioning as chief executive officer, and Ames was chairman of the Executive Committee, and they embarked on a rigorous program of retrenchment.

Elsewhere Young wrote:

A major objective was a reduction in the costs of the central administration from $1.4 million to $600,000, a target to be reached in one year. . . . A strong day-by-day executive control was needed during this important period [of Schuman's illness and financial retrenchment] and [John] Mazzola was designated chief executive officer of Lincoln Center, with direct responsibility to the Executive Committee and with authority to carry out its mandates.

Festival '68 was held in the summer, and it generated even greater deficits than anticipated:

Additional deficits occurred later in the summer from the August Serenades and the Film Festival. By mid-October the undesignated fund reserve had dropped to nearly $500,000. Weekly expenditures were running at a rate of $125,000 per week, and technical bankruptcy of Lincoln Center operations could occur before the end of the year.

Schuman's working notes for his President's Report of the October 7, 1968, board meeting give a telling sense of Schuman's view of the artistic worth of Lincoln Center's summer programs in 1968 versus the mammoth deficits generated by these ventures. Far from taking a defensive posture, Schuman's report pointed to the artistic successes of the summer that should have offset, in his view, the financial problems of the fall:

Festival '68 was the most ambitious undertaking of its kind ever held in this country. As you may remember, the Festival included visits from the Rome Opera, the American Ballet Theatre, the New York Philharmonic, the Pittsburgh Symphony, the Royal Philharmonic, the Boston Symphony, the English Chamber Orchestra, special Koussevitzky Chamber Music concerts, the Preser[v]ation Hall Jazz Band, the Theatre de la Cite from Lyons, the Atalje 212 Theatre from Belgrade, the Dublin Gate Theatre from Ireland, poetry readings and a Greta Garbo retrospective done in association with the Museum of Modern Art.

Schuman then explained that the deficit from the Festival was a whopping $595,977, close to $100,000 higher than budgeted. He added that the Midsummer Serenades, which eventually became the Mostly Mozart

Festival, generated another deficit of $105,515 but the Sixth New York Film Festival of the early fall was mostly on budget. He acknowledged that

> there have been mixed feelings on the part of the board with regards to Lincoln Center's film activity, but I hope that even those who don't favor film will realize that the New York Film Festival has now taken its place as a leader in this activity throughout the world. . . . All of us on the Lincoln Center staff are united in our feeling about the importance of continuing this work.

Schuman reported that $786,576 had been paid by Lincoln Center to the Metropolitan Opera, the Vivian Beaumont Theater, and Philharmonic Hall from June 22 to September 28 for rental of these venues to accommodate the summer's activities. All in all, the report is hardly a paean to the budgetary retrenchment that the Center's leadership had undertaken during its president's absence.

By November 1968 the die had been cast for Schuman when Mazzola issued a memorandum to be discussed at the November 12 board meeting menacingly entitled "Analysis of the Disappearing Net Worth of Lincoln Center Fund." At the meeting, the board passed a series of motions intended to address the problem, such as authorizing the investment committee to convert long-term securities to short-term securities or cash and establishing a line of credit not to exceed $1 million to cover projected Lincoln Center deficits. Of greatest import for Schuman were resolutions that prohibited any further programming unless funds were in hand, pledged, or guaranteed. The minutes indicated that

> the Executive Committee re[s]cinded its action of June 18, 1968, authorizing the administration to enter into contracts for Lincoln Center Festival '69 and agreed not to proceed with the Mid-Summer Serenades during August 1969, because there is not enough time to raise the money to complete the arrangements for the Festival or for the Mid-Summer Serenades.

Although Schuman voted to discontinue the Serenades, he also "asked that his abstention in voting for cancelling Lincoln Center Festival '69 be noted." His abstention was a defiant signal to the board that he recognized neither its artistic nor its financial prerogatives.

Weakened by his illness and essentially outmaneuvered by his board, Schuman finally realized in the late fall of 1968 that whatever artistic dreams he had held for Lincoln Center could not be realized under the circumstances. On November 25, 1968, Schuman submitted his letter of resignation to Rockefeller, effective January 1, 1969. In typical fashion, Rockefeller sent a draft of his reply to Schuman for approval. In reply, Schuman suggested that he not begin the letter with the words "thank you for your letter tendering your letter of resignation" and commented in a handwritten note in the margin, "called to say how sorry he was. He always began letters with 'thank you' and forgot . . . Freudian?" Rockefeller then changed the wording to "I received with regret. . . ."

It was announced at the time that Schuman would be available to Lincoln Center for consultation if needed and that he would also chair a study of the Lincoln Center educational program that was funded by a Carnegie Corporation grant. Schuman was given a severance package which paid him $30,000 in 1969 and $15,000 in each of the ensuing two years. He was also granted the honorary title of President Emeritus. According to the Lincoln Center archives, there are no minutes extant for the December 16, 1968, board meeting which addressed Schuman's resignation.

On December 5, 1968, Schuman released a public announcement of his resignation from the presidency of Lincoln Center, ostensibly so that he could find more time to compose. His decision to resign was a painful one for all parties at Lincoln Center. Young contended, however, that it was necessary "to bring financial reality and to create a situation where they could start almost afresh to raise money for the ongoing operations and purposes."

As news of Schuman's resignation spread, his absence became a source of great concern for the Chamber Music Society. By December 26, 1968, Taplin had to write a disturbing memo to the members of the chamber music exploratory committee. He first explained that Lincoln Center and the other constituent organizations "view with alarm our plan for a general endowment campaign at this time. . . . We therefore find ourselves in an embarrassing position . . . [because] contract terms with the eight resident artists have been agreed upon, and the contracts have in some cases been signed by the artists or their representatives."

A meeting had taken place on December 20, 1968, with Tully, Wardwell, and Taplin representing the Society and Rockefeller, Josephs, and Mazzola representing Lincoln Center, to address the many weighty issues facing chamber music at Lincoln Center. The results of the meeting were that the general endowment campaign was to be abandoned for the moment, the 1969–70 season could not be sustained, and the contracts with the eight resident musicians would not be honored. The Society would open Alice Tully Hall on September 17–24, 1969, but would then become inactive until the opening of the first regular season in 1970.

Taplin's memo laid the blame for this fiasco on Schuman: "Mr. Rockefeller made clear that the fault in this matter was not ours, but rather a failure of communication between Mr. Schuman and the Lincoln Center Trustees. Both he and Mr. Josephs apologized for putting us in a very difficult position, particularly with respect to the artists whom we have engaged."

Although the Chamber Music Society eventually became a constituent in February 1969 and flourished artistically, the legacy left by Schuman in this last endeavor of his Lincoln Center presidency was a bitter one.

The fundamental breach between Rockefeller and Schuman, between sound business practices and artistic imperatives, was irreparable. In the ensuing months, financial pressures on the Lincoln Center board caused by the completion of construction of the Center's physical plant, as well as the constituents' increasing "feelings of mistrust, fear, competition and even bitterness," were the greatest challenges Schuman had to face as president of the Center. The last straw was his budget proposal for the 1969 fiscal year, which recommended an increase of nearly $640,000 in expenditures. Rockefeller wrote to Schuman: "It would have been my thought or hope that there should have been a decrease of something like this amount." This budget proposal was what precipitated Schuman's resignation.

The constant bickering between constituents and Lincoln Center, Inc., the financial exigencies of the final stages of the Center's construction, the dwindling support of Rockefeller and the other members of the Lincoln Center board, and the lack of time for composing—to say nothing of his second heart attack in early 1968 (he had suffered a mild, and initially misdiagnosed, heart attack in 1966)—combined to create an untenable situation for Schuman. In the final analysis, he was much more comfortable with his artistic peers than with the trustees of Lincoln Center.

In later years Schuman benignly said that the Lincoln Center presidency was an experience that allowed him to grow professionally:

I can't possibly describe to you what a rich experience that was. I never would have met this whole group of men. I never would have known about the whole operation of the big financial and business powers. And I also had some great satisfactions there, and I would not want to lose sight of the satisfactions by my major disappointment.

The "major disappointment" to which he referred was the cutback of his artistic initiatives owing to budget constraints.

Schuman also admitted that if he had not been so intransigent about slowing the pace in creating new artistic projects, he would have been able to stay as Lincoln Center's president: "And from the point of view of the directors, I think they would argue there would have been no reason for my disillusionment if I had been a good boy and said: 'All right, I'll cut out all these departments.' I could have stayed there for the rest of my life."

Schuman was not the only Lincoln Center administrator whose health was stricken by the intense work environment. Schuyler Chapin suffered as well: "I had a nervous breakdown from it, to be quite candid. . . . I got sick. The buildup of the pressures and the constant, hateful business really just got to me."

After his resignation Schuman undertook several writing projects, one of which was a book, never published, entitled "Letters I Never Sent." Included in these "letters" was a remarkable one to John D. Rockefeller 3rd expressing the veiled disdain with which Schuman had regarded Rockefeller throughout their professional relationship, as well as Rockefeller's lack of understanding, as Schuman saw it, of his feelings and reputation.

Schuman began the "letter" in the most respectful tone imaginable, reminiscent of eighteenth-century correspondences between great personages. He emphasized his continuing respect for Rockefeller and reinforced his belief in Rockefeller as the "key person in the Lincoln Center scene" and as the Center's "greatest asset." However, Schuman soon began to give vent to thoughts and feelings he had been suppressing for years:

But no man lacks the defects of his virtues, and you are certainly no exception, for I think your remarkable dedication to the Center has been insufficiently realized. The other side of the coin is something that I also want to discuss because I feel, and will say in these letters, that you must bear the major responsibility for the virtual abandonment of the Lincoln Center concept, a concept of which I will remind you and to which I will contrast the present Lincoln Center housekeeping operation.

The "housekeeping operation" pointed to an area of disagreement that had surfaced in their correspondence in early 1967. As the 1960s drew to a close, it was clear to the Lincoln Center board members that the initial gargantuan push to construct the Center and placate the new constituent organizations would soon be replaced by the altogether different task of developing annual programming. Schuman saw himself at the center of that programming, while Rockefeller thought it was a responsibility the constituents ought to take on.

Although Schuman was acknowledged as a creative force in the development of performing arts programming at Lincoln Center, the financial solvency, or lack thereof, of several of his projects was a problem for the Lincoln Center directors. Hence Schuman's comment that Rockefeller had "abandoned" the basic artistic principles upon which the Lincoln Center concept was created, a stance Schuman had taken with Rockefeller in a letter to him dated March 2, 1967.

Schuman then turned in his "letter" to a recent incident that capsulized Rockefeller's condescension toward his past president. Schuman recounted that Rockefeller had telephoned and wished to speak to him, an opportunity that Schuman welcomed because they had spoken to each other only intermittently in the recent past. Expecting to begin the call with the usual exchange of pleasantries, Schuman was surprised when Rockefeller dispensed with small talk and immediately began to explain that the opening celebration of the Juilliard School would take place on October 26, 1969, and that he needed advice on the speakers for the evening. Because Schuman saw himself, with good reason, as the driving force behind Juilliard's presence at Lincoln Center, he expected an invitation from his former boss to be one of the speakers at this important occasion. Schuman had already decided to decline the invitation but, he wrote, the conversation took an unexpected turn:

You said the speakers would be Peter Mennin as President of Juilliard, yourself as Chairman of Lincoln Center, and President Nixon. [Nixon never appeared.] And then you said, "Bill, I would like you to write my speech for me." I was really taken aback because there was no sensitivity on your part whatsoever on what you were asking in the first place, and in the second, no consideration as to whether I would wish to write such a speech or would have time to. (There is a Hebrew—Yiddish?—expression, "hutzpah," which means much more than the English word "nerve." It is classically defined by the story of the boy who killed his parents and asked clemency of the court because he was an orphan.) What was astonishing to me— though it shouldn't have been after our long association—was that your request was absolutely natural and you were in no way departing from your customary gentlemanly demeanor.

The deep sense of surprise and hurt that jumps out from Schuman's "letter" opened a wound that had been festering for over a decade. In light of Schuman's vulnerable position at the time after his resignation, to say nothing of his justifiable sense of pride in what he had accomplished in earlier years, Rockefeller's request must have stung him deeply. Schuman continued:

I told you quite candidly how busy I was with my own plans and that I really did not think it would be a good idea for me to become involved again with Lincoln Center. Your reply to that I shall never forget. You complimented me on my speaking ability and said that I did these things so easily that I could dream the remarks up in the shower. In reply, I told you that the shower is the place they send pitchers when they are knocked out of the box. You of course hadn't the remotest idea of what I was talking about, and certainly your request of me was not viewed by you as being the least bit unusual. But I did not go beyond saying that I would give the matter some thought, which is precisely what I did; and on September 16[, 1969] I wrote to you in part as follows:

"It was like old times talking with you last week and I was happy that you felt free to call me. Always I would want to be of help to you and to Lincoln Center. It is therefore with genuine regret that, for reasons both institutional and personal, it will not be possible for me to accede to your request for help in the presentation of your remarks for the opening of Juilliard next month. If you wish, I will be happy to explain more fully when next we meet."

For anyone who knew Schuman and his knowledgeable love of baseball, his reference to pitchers being "knocked out of the box" and to Rockefeller's not having "the remotest idea of what I was talking about" was a clear indication of Schuman's contempt for Rockefeller. The patrician Rockefeller's inability to understand baseball terminology was in Schuman's mind supercilious and un-American. Nor did Schuman have much regard for Rockefeller's ability as a public speaker: "Anything that came out of his mouth sounded platitudinous, whether or not it was, and if you used any adjective that was warm, he would quite properly excise it as not being a natural thing for him to say. Oh, it was so hard for him to speak in public. He really suffered terribly because he didn't do it well, and he knew it."

In defense of Rockefeller's request, Schuman was one of the great orators of his day, especially when speaking extemporaneously. In the past Schuman had been the ghostwriter for many of Rockefeller's speeches having to do with the arts. In addition, the relationship between Schuman and Juilliard's president at the time, Peter Mennin, was at best icy and strained owing to Schuman's equivocal support of Mennin's appointment as Juilliard president in 1962 and to the many financial conflicts Schuman and Mennin had during Juilliard's move to Lincoln Center in the late 1960s. Schuman's presence onstage with Mennin, although appropriate in one sense, was perhaps not the best choice for a function focused on Mennin as Juilliard's president.

The official opening ceremony of the Juilliard School on October 26, 1969, was a very grand affair. The celebration took place in Alice Tully Hall and was broadcast live by CBS. The program began with the Juilliard Orchestra playing "The Star-Spangled Banner," followed by the Preludes to Acts I and III of Richard Wagner's *Lohengrin*, with the venerable Leopold Stokowski, decked out in elegant afternoon formal attire, conducting. After remarks by Rockefeller and Mennin, the program went on to feature Juilliard alumni as soloists: Itzhak Perlman, only one year out of Juilliard, playing the first movement of Paganini's Violin Concerto No. 1; the distinguished mezzo-soprano Shirley Verrett singing the "Alleluia" from Mozart's *Exsultate, jubilate*, and arias from Donizetti's *Anna Bolena* and Saint-Saëns's *Samson et Dalila*; and, to end the program, Van Cliburn performing the Liszt Piano Concerto No. 1. Jean Morel conducted the orchestra for all of the soloists, and also for the "Danse générale" from Maurice Ravel's *Daphnis et Chloé Suite No. 2*.

Audience members included the first lady, Pat Nixon; her daughter, Julie, and son-in-law, David Eisenhower; New York's governor, Nelson Rockefeller, and his wife, Happy; Mr. and Mrs. John D. Rockefeller 3rd; Alice Tully; Martha Graham; Sol Hurok; Isaac Stern; and many other luminaries. The evening was hosted by Leonard Bernstein, who was ensconced in the house-right box of the hall along with a television camera and bright lights.

William Schuman was present but did not speak from the stage. According to Schuman, Bernstein, in his television script, planned to praise Schuman's role in bringing Juilliard to Lincoln Center, but Mennin would have none of that. In Mennin's opening remarks "he simply said words to the effect that 'my distinguished predecessor William Schuman couldn't have done anything else [but] accept the offer to come down here,' knowing perfectly well what a long and arduous fight I had had, but anyway he's an ungenerous person."

Mennin's exact words were, "Thirteen years ago, when the idea was first presented by Lincoln Center to my distinguished predecessor, William Schuman, and the Juilliard board, it was an invitation they could hardly resist." Mennin was surely still smarting from a very lengthy letter to the editor Schuman had written that had appeared in the *New York Times* that very morning (October 26, 1969); it refuted many points made in a September 28 *Times* article by Martin Mayer in which Mayer had publicly discussed the ongoing feud between Schuman and Mennin relating to Juilliard's move to Lincoln Center.

As the evening came to a conclusion, Bernstein ignored Mennin's prohibition, went off script, and spoke glowingly and dramatically of his friend:

> And ultimately, I suppose the most rewarding result [of Juilliard's presence at Lincoln Center] can be the attainment of the Socratic ideal, where teachers learn and students teach, where wisdom is acquired by all from all in an endless, free-flowing exchange of ideas and knowledge. And that's the real meaning and the promise of today's event. . . . I would like to say a word of tribute to a man without whom none of this might have happened. William Schuman, one of America's most celebrated composers, has been within the past quarter of the century president of *both* the Juilliard School and of Lincoln Center itself. Through his unique combination of intellect and spirit, he has lent an originality and grandeur of concept to the whole project that it could easily have lacked without him. William Schuman should be a very proud man this Sunday evening.

In the enthusiastic applause that followed this speech Schuman had to take two bows. Later he told Bernstein how much he appreciated the mention and thanked him for his friendship. Bernstein replied, "It was not a matter of friendship but principle."

Schuman never stopped feeling that he had been abandoned by Rockefeller and his board regarding the artistic leadership of Lincoln Center. He had burst on the scene as a creative and energized leader who saw the new arts center not as a collection of buildings, but as a vibrant, dynamic institution that could justify its existence only through the development and presentation of dance, drama, music, and film at the highest possible level. In many ways his efforts were pioneering initiatives in a new land. Fiscal limitations were meaningless to him. Edgar Young posited that Schuman wanted Lincoln Center to have

> its own place in the sun in the artistic firmament. The constituent leadership and, indeed, a considerable portion of the board leadership of Lincoln Center, wanting a continuation of the concept that Lincoln Center was principally dependent for its artistic greatness on the continued success and high standards of the constituents. So you had this conflict between Schuman wanting to create something that he, personally, was the head of, and the less conspicuous role of a leader of Lincoln Center who would be the coordinator and the one who would pull together the efforts of these independent institutions. . . . One can say that Schuman came in at a time when his kind of leadership was needed. He worked too hard and too fast for what he wanted.

To put Young's comments in context, there was little love lost between him and Schuman. Although they worked together for almost all of Schuman's tenure at Lincoln Center, Schuman had no respect for Young:

> There is a man [Young] who didn't earn a position on the Lincoln Center board either because he came from a source which should be represented on the board or by his own achievements, but only because he was Rockefeller's lieutenant. I found him very destructive because he had the imagination of a boy scout leader when it came to the arts, and what so often happens with people who are not in the arts

and they are exposed to them suddenly in great depth is they think—
they begin to form opinions, and this happens time and time again.

Furthermore, Schuman believed that the constituents did not really wish
to embrace the Lincoln Center concept, in which the whole would be greater
than the sum of its parts: "All they wanted to get was beautiful buildings . . .
but they never had any idea that Lincoln Center should have a role of its own."
According to him, "The only way you could make Lincoln Center work in
terms of my ideas was to risk incurring the enmity of the constituent heads,
which is exactly what I did, especially the Metropolitan Opera."

Schuman deeply resented Rockefeller's lack of leadership, as he saw it.
Several years after his resignation, Rockefeller called him and complained:
"You know, it's [Lincoln Center] turning out to be a real estate operation. . . .
I never wanted it to be that." Schuman recalled, "And I felt like saying: 'It's
a hell of a time to tell me. Why didn't you speak up then?' He is not the
brightest man in the world."

Fundamentally, though, Schuman believed that it was not Lincoln
Center's fiscal problems that doomed his presidency but rather

> the fact that the constituents didn't like my independence, didn't like
> my building Lincoln Center into its own "constituency." . . . The
> center is a success because of the symbol that it's become, and some
> of the things that it still does, and it may do more. . . . But to me, it
> is a sellout in terms of what it might have been, success though it is.

In Schuman's view,

> if you compromise on a major commitment and you don't know you
> are compromising, that is something terrible. It's even worse than
> hypocrisy. You are doing something that as far as I am concerned is
> amoral. That's what I believed they did, despite all the pleasant
> things that were said when I left.

Schuyler Chapin analyzed the aftermath of the Schuman years from a
slightly different perspective:

> Those people who serve on Boards of great organizations for the most
> part are all amateur lovers of what they're supporting. But with the

[performing] arts they seem to feel a greater liberty to put forth their desires, on the theory that they're paying the bills. They wouldn't do that at a hospital. . . . I think that time has proven the validity of Bill's point of view, but oh, boy, it was at quite a cost. . . . It was a rough ride.

Toward the end of his life Schuman often said that the ultimate goal of a leader is survival. He obviously did not take his own advice in 1968. No doubt Rockefeller would have supported Schuman as president if only he had lessened the intensity of his initiatives and put less pressure on the Center's budget. In turn, one cannot help but conclude that Schuman, with his private scorn for Rockefeller and his colleagues' lack of artistic understanding, saw himself as taking the high road, with art trumping the ubiquitous power of money.

Schuman once remarked that he was "not a political animal," defining the term as "somebody who worries more about what the effects will be on someone else by his actions. . . . It's implied that if a person is as successful as I have been in an administrative capacity he must also be political." No matter how one defines the term "political," Schuman's position in 1968 perhaps would be better described as "self-righteous." His belief that he could prevail in an arena of budget deficits, construction overruns, and enormous egos could also be fairly called naive.

The relationship between Schuman and Rockefeller was an early example of the growing battle in the 1970s and early 1980s between those who produce art and those who fund it. Although prudent business practices and balanced ledger sheets became essential elements of arts organizations at the end of the twentieth century, the influence of the businessperson or trustee on artistic programming was in its nascent stage in the formative years of Lincoln Center. Schuman, as an artist-administrator, was caught between the conflicting forces of business and the arts, and it eventually forced him out of public life. Rockefeller and Schuman never again interacted professionally after January 1, 1969, although they and their wives would occasionally see each other socially until Rockefeller's fatal automobile accident on July 10, 1978.

If one examines Schuman's legacy during his tenure of only six years as Lincoln Center president, his list of accomplishments is impressive by any measure: the creation of the (albeit short-lived) Music Theater of Lincoln Center, the Chamber Music Society, the Film Society, the Lincoln Center Institute, summer festivals, Mostly Mozart, the Great Performers series, and Lincoln Center Out of Doors, along with all of the initiatives involved in bringing the original constituents together in the first place.

The press announcements and interviews at the time of his resignation reported that Schuman was stepping down because he wanted to return to composing. There is no question that there was a grain of truth in this face-saving maneuver, but Schuman, for the first time in his life at the age of fifty-eight, would now have to admit defeat in an endeavor that had become an integral part of his persona.

CHAPTER 13

A Composer Now Free
of the Shackles

From 1935, when he became a faculty member of Sarah Lawrence College, to the last day of 1968, when he resigned as president of Lincoln Center, William Schuman worked within an institutional context that supported his teaching, his composing, and his exceptional imagination. On January 1, 1969, Schuman left the supportive confines that he had known for the past thirty-three years and ventured out as a free agent, taking with him the experience, prestige, and psychological bruises that he had garnered along the way.

As a composer, he was at the height of his powers. He had begun to explore a new compositional language that he used to create complex and often profoundly emotional works. Schuman's administrative imagination stayed active as well, with new projects having to do with education and technology already percolating in his fertile mind. Not even his heart attack stopped him. Although he had occasional chest pains, especially at times of stress or during exercise, he was managing his illness well, and he developed a schedule that would not exacerbate his heart disease. Most important—and remarkably—Schuman's spirit was not broken by the bruising battles of the autumn of 1968 at Lincoln Center, which ultimately resulted in his resignation.

Throughout his adult life he experienced almost continuous professional success. True, not all of his compositions met with critical or audience acclaim, but Schuman was quite secure in his compositional journey and was able to disregard reviewers' barbs or see them as misplaced interpretations.

There is also no question that the presence of Frankie in his life was the foundation upon which all of Schuman's happiness and self-assurance were based. Bill and Frankie worked as a team, with Frankie protecting Bill from the noise and distractions of family life so that his compositions could be created unimpeded. She was also Bill's political and social partner, who understood which individuals needed to be cultivated and which would not be allowed to enter the Schuman inner circle. Frankie was a person of great intellect, determination, and strength. Over cocktails at a dinner party she could look around, a cigarette held elegantly in her hand, and evaluate every guest with a knowing eye and a calculating mind. When Schuman was left without institutional support, it was Frankie who provided the structure and encouragement that her husband needed to move forward with his compositional and administrative plans.

As a practical person and someone who had lived through the Great Depression, Schuman was mainly concerned at the beginning of 1969 with how he could support his family financially. Through his affiliation with his performing rights company, BMI, and a long-term contract with his publisher, Theodore Presser, Schuman was assured a healthy flow of royalties from the works in his catalog, as well as commissioning fees. After he left Lincoln Center, he no longer had medical insurance and knew that, owing to both his and Frankie's health problems, it would be difficult and expensive to obtain it privately. Fortunately, BMI and its new president, Edward M. Cramer, solved the problem by appointing Schuman a consultant to the president and an employee of the company, making him eligible for the company's medical insurance benefits. By 1977 Schuman would be happily concluding that "I've made so much more money than I ever made while I was at Lincoln Center because I have so much more time."

However, Schuman admitted that there was even a larger issue than finance troubling him. He wrote in his unpublished autobiography, "But none of these problems were as important to me as my astonished psyche. Suddenly, after years of public leadership in my field, I was a private person, a composer now free of the shackles from which I wanted to be free and yet through force of habit greatly missing certain aspects that they supplied."

Schuman had considered teaching, if only briefly, and had actually received an invitation from UCLA to be appointed a full professor. The idea of living in Los Angeles did not sit well with the native New Yorker: "I think I considered this offer for 10 seconds." He was also approached by New York University to develop a course in arts administration. But the classroom no longer beckoned to the worldly administrator and composer.

Only a few days after his official departure from Lincoln Center, Schuman gave a lengthy interview to Daniel Webster of the *Philadelphia Inquirer* linked to the world premiere on January 10, 1969, of his Ninth Symphony by the Philadelphia Orchestra, Eugene Ormandy conducting. In the interview,

Schuman discussed the programmatic elements of the symphony and explained his reasons for resigning and his plans for the future:

> For the first time in 33 years, I will not have administrative chores. I know it is true, but I just can't believe that I don't have to prepare the January directors' meeting. But since I made the decision to leave, I have felt nothing but happiness. I know it is the right thing. . . . The first [reason for leaving Lincoln Center] was institutional. We had reached a point where the administration needed a fiscal expert, not an artistic president. I was spending more and more of my time going to Wall Street to talk to bankers and I must say they were glad to help. But when the chips are down . . . they react in the only way they know how. They cut back. That's what has happened at Lincoln Center. We had to cancel the summer festival, and a project very near to my heart, the Film Festival. These people can raise money for a building and equip it, but not for a program. That sort of thing is outside their experience and training.
>
> The second reason is personal. I suppose it's no secret that I had a heart attack last summer and I had four months in which to think and to ask myself: "What do you really want to do with the time you have left?"
>
> Look, I'm a composer, and I knew I didn't want to be a fund raiser. I think an arts administrator must be strongly motivated and full of ideas he wants to try. I think we have Lincoln Center's artistic and educational goals clearly defined and on the way to achievement. . . . I am thinking about several things, but what I really want to do is write—both music and prose. . . . I look on composition as a moral issue: I want to write the best way I can. More, none of us can do, but that is my obligation.

Schuman's continuing animosity toward his former Lincoln Center directors was obvious, and his rock-solid belief that the development of Lincoln Center's artistic initiatives should have continued regardless of the Center's current financial situation remained very much in his mind. Nor was his wry wit diminished when he explained that he had no wish to be a "24-hour-a-day composer." When offered a composer-in-residence position at a university where he "could have all the time I wanted to write . . . they said I could get away from the rat race. I wrote back that if I couldn't make a rat race out of that in two weeks I'd be ashamed of myself." He said that he would remain on the boards of several organizations and work as a consultant to various institutions.

In an interview around this time with the *New York Times*, Schuman expressed guarded interest in experimenting in the medium of electronic music, although he quickly added that "trying to be fashionable is the quickest way to go out of fashion. I try to write as I want to write. And I am willing to explore what is new with as much zest as when I was 25 and writing my First Symphony." Schuman was quick to acknowledge that he was no longer considered a radical composer, explaining that he had recently described to a group of young composers his own view of how his music was categorized: "'they used to call me radical, then middle-of-the-road. Before I die I would like to be on the right,' at which point one of the young composers said, 'You already are, sir.'"

Whether or not his music was considered avant-garde or cutting-edge, the last work Schuman composed while he was Lincoln Center's president, his Ninth Symphony, was imbued with new levels of intensity and poignancy.

Schuman first mentioned creating a Ninth Symphony in June 1967 in a letter to his good friends Nathalie and Hugo Weisgall. Hugo was in the latter months of a one-year stay at the American Academy in Rome, and he and his wife had recommended that when Bill and Frankie came to Rome in June, they visit the monument commemorating the slaughter of 335 Italians by the Nazis on March 24, 1944, in retaliation for the killing of 32 German soldiers on the previous day by Italian partisans. After their visit Schuman wrote to the Weisgalls:

> Never in my life have I been so affected by a monument as I was [b]y the Nervi [the artist whom Schuman believed to be the designer of the monument]. I keep thinking about it all the time. At the moment, it is leading me to write a symphony with a programmatic starting point. This I have never done before, but it appears to be happening to me now. The work will not be any attempt at a realistic musical summary of those horrible events, but it will certainly reflect my feelings as they have evolved from the experience of visiting the memorial.

Nathalie Weisgall responded in August with an informative and knowledgeable account of the details surrounding the massacre. She explained in a quote taken from a guide to Rome and Central Italy by Muirhead that the

335 Italian victims "had no connection to the killing of the Germans [and] included priests, officials, professional men, 100 Jews, dozens of foreigners and a boy of 14. After the incident the Germans buried the bodies under an avalanche of sand artificially caused by the exploding of mines." She went on to explain that her Italian watch repairman, Alberto Misini, was one of the individuals rounded up in the local Gestapo prison from which most of the victims came. Misini was able to escape and to tell the horrible tale to Nathalie many years later. Since practically all of the victims came from the Gestapo prison, this would explain "the disproportionate number of Jews, and also the impression that most were very prominent and influential intellectuals who were thrown in the German prison for their anti-Nazi activities and their possible alliance with the resistance."

Nathalie wrote that the members of the resistance planned on ambushing the German troops after observing them on their daily march by the Via Rasella, and

> one day, throwing a bomb in their midst, killing them all. It is said that orders came directly from Hitler to kill 10 Italians for every German soldier killed, and so the easiest place to get enough Italians was at the nearby Gestapo prison. In their haste they got more than the number they needed. . . . It seems that the monks at the adjacent Catacombs of Callixtus heard the mine explosions and traced the sound, thereby discovering the bodies . . . the actual title of the monument is "Fosse Ardeatina." Ardeatina is a section of Rome. Fosse (the plural of fossa) means pitch, ditch, or grave.

Weisgall ended her remarkable letter with a poignant thought:

> I feel so strongly that those days should never be forgotten . . . much less forgiven. Histories, documents, etc. . . . are there for the facts . . . which are too horrible and too numerous to be comprehensible. It is only through a work of art that one can feel the impact of the madness of those days.

The story proved to be the impetus Schuman needed to complete his symphony. He threw himself into the project in the summer of 1967, corresponding with Nathalie Weisgall about the correct Italian phrasing of a programmatic subtitle for his Ninth Symphony, eventually settling on "Le Fosse

Ardeatine." The work was commissioned by friends of Alexander Hilsberg in his memory and divided into three parts, played without pause—Anteludium, Offertorium, and Postludium. Schuman intended that it eventually be performed by the Philadelphia Orchestra under the direction of Eugene Ormandy. Hilsberg had joined the violin section of the Philadelphia Orchestra in 1926, becoming concertmaster in 1942 and associate conductor as well in 1945. He resigned as concertmaster during the 1950–51 season and died in August 1961.

Ormandy was anxious to study the completed score. He wrote to Schuman in October 1967 that he had over thirty new works to learn and he could only do it during the few weeks he had free in July of next year. Schuman promised to deliver the score at the end of the orchestra's season in early June.

In March 1968 Ormandy recounted to Schuman a humorous story that surfaced during the Philadelphia Orchestra's recent concerts featuring Schuman's Seventh Symphony. According to Ormandy, "An elderly lady turned to her husband after Maazel finished your Symphony and said: 'Darling, that didn't sound like *Schumann* [emphasis added] to me,' to which her husband replied: 'but darling, he wrote this Symphony just before he went insane.' Everyone has a wonderful time when they hear this story and they know it will reach you sooner or later."

In a *New York Times* article of April 1968, Schuman proclaimed that he had completed his Ninth Symphony, dedicating to it 306 hours and 25 minutes of composing since he began the work in July 1967:

> I never write at the office. . . . I've never even had a musical thought at the office. I only think of music when I drive. But my life is spent working in the arts through composing, teaching and administration. . . . I don't consider administration one whit less creative than composing. It all has to do with proportions, priorities and balances.

Clearly Schuman was not acknowledging, at least in public, the downturn in his dealings with the Lincoln Center board that he would experience in the second half of 1968. He did admit, however, that the Lincoln Center presidency had cut into his composition time considerably: "When I was head of Juilliard, I used to do about 400 to 600 hours of composition a year. . . . Here [at Lincoln Center], the most I've done is about 300 hours. I write fast but, remember, I'm talking about thinking."

Even before Schuman sent Ormandy the score of his Ninth Symphony, he was lobbying the recording executives at RCA Victor, Roger Hall and Jack

Pfeiffer, to record the work. Ormandy expressed concern to Schuman that it was premature to pressure RCA Victor to record a symphony he, Ormandy, had not even seen. He complained that Schuman should not have shared a copy of a letter from Ormandy to Schuman about a potential recording:

> Roger Hall and Jack Pfeiffer were here yesterday and we talked about repertoire. Suddenly Roger told me that you sent him a copy of my letter to you. This was *not* really my idea. What I had in mind was that you, from your end, and I from this end could push the Victor Company to record your Symphony. I hope by sending him my letter you did not defeat our purpose. (Emphasis in original)

Ormandy's concern was prescient, as Schuman would see in 1969. RCA Victor was investing a good deal of resources in selling recordings of Ormandy's orchestra at the time using the key marketing phrase "Those Fabulous Philadelphians."

On May 13, 1968, shortly after Schuman's heart attack, he downplayed his illness to Ormandy: "It seems that I have been working too hard and have gotten myself a fine case of fatigue. Nothing of any concern, but the doctors are not permitting me out all week." The heart attack was not severe enough to diminish Schuman's playful style: in a letter to the Philadelphia Orchestra's manager, Boris Sokoloff, he wrote, "If you want to make me feel better, please remit as soon as possible the remainder due on my commission."

As the premiere of the symphony approached in January 1969, preparations for rehearsals and ancillary activities were in full swing. Schuman, invited to speak before an open rehearsal of the symphony, admitted that he became very nervous before a performance of a new work. He wrote to Ormandy:

> It must sound silly to the performer who carries the entire burden that the composer, whose work is finished, should be nervous. Maybe it's because the composer—no matter how many times he's been through it—is being "revealed." However many toothaches you have, a new one is nonetheless painful because of prior experiences.

After news of Schuman's resignation from the Lincoln Center presidency became public in December, the focus on the Ninth Symphony premiere intensified, but it provided a welcome diversion from his problems in New York City. Ormandy had taken the somber mood of Schuman's symphony to heart and programmed Krzysztof Penderecki's gripping *Threnody to the Victims of Hiroshima* in its Philadelphia premiere to begin the concert, followed by the Schuman symphony. After intermission, in an esoteric twist, the Beethoven Concerto in D Major for Piano and Orchestra, Op. 61, which is arranged from his Violin Concerto, was performed by the twenty-one-year-old Peter Serkin.

Although Schuman remarked that his Ninth Symphony was not programmatic in content, the entire work exudes the terror and remorse embodied in the tragedy of the Ardeatine caves. The composition's overall somber tone and the striking moments of bombast provided by the brass and percussion point explicitly to the horrors of this incident. No other work in Schuman's catalog depicts more vividly the twentieth century's legacy of cruelty and inhumanity.

Press response to the Ninth Symphony was in general extremely favorable, especially given the somber quality of the entire work and its complex harmonic and melodic structure. Daniel Webster of the *Philadelphia Inquirer* wrote:

Its structure is firm, its statement direct and its somber mood pervading . . . there are subtle colors, powerful, even thunderous climactic moments, highly innovative use of usually inarticulate instruments like the cymbals. . . . By any measurement, it is a big, aspiring piece whose continuity of mood makes acceptable the hammer stroke at the end, rather in the manner of Mahler, as a summation of the score. Eugene Ormandy's direction was incisive.

The *Philadelphia Evening Bulletin* reviewer was a bit confused by the work's complexity but concluded, "It seemed that Mr. Schuman's piece has a sincerity and an involvement in its grisly subject that cannot be questioned. It has the ring of an important composition."

The same program was brought to Philharmonic Hall by the Philadelphia Orchestra on January 14, 1969. The *Newsday* reviewer wrote that Schuman

has been considered mainly a cerebral composer who could touch only remotely and fleetingly the emotions of his listeners. The new symphony, however, is fruit of a different vintage and it speaks far more directly and passionately to the listener than anything that went before it. . . . The music has a warmth, born of anger, tenderness, outrage and simple humanity, which could fit any programmatic design.

The pianocentric Harold C. Schonberg of the *New York Times* was more concerned about the fact that Gunnar Johansen had replaced the indisposed Peter Serkin at the Philharmonic Hall concert and had learned the esoteric Beethoven work in twenty-four hours, a feat that, for Schonberg, blotted out the rest of the program. In the final two paragraphs of his review, though, Schonberg wrote that

> Mr. Schuman's newest symphony is a serious work written in his sharp, clear, busy style. . . . Everything is skillfully put together, but the melodic impulse flickers low, and the symphony sounds more like a professional paste job than anything that stems from a deep impulse. . . . Certainly the audience received it warmly enough to drown out a few boos.

The premiere performances of Schuman's Ninth Symphony did not end the extended saga of this profoundly dark work. In what must have been a casual comment in the context of a very busy time of interviews and presentations, Schuman told a reporter that the performance of his Ninth Symphony had "a satisfactory reading enough, at least, to get an idea of how the music sounds." Eugene Ormandy was incensed by the quote and sent Schuman a handwritten letter reminding him

> how elated you were after the premier[e] and again on Saturday night and it is difficult for me to believe that one as honest and articulate in expressing himself as I have known you to be over the years would give two such contradictory statements. . . . I wish you would take the trouble of telling me whether you really made the statement you are quoted to have made and why?

Schuman did not want any conflict with Ormandy: their friendship was of long standing, and the symphony had yet to be recorded. He replied, "I gave no interviews about the Symphony subsequent to the first performance." He immediately wrote a letter to the music editor of the *Philadelphia Inquirer* for publication, which read in part, "To correct any impression to the contrary, I want to say that the results achieved by Mr. Ormandy and the brilliant artists he leads were nothing short of phenomenal." The publication of this letter on March 16 seemed to quell the impending storm.

Schuman was later genuinely grateful to Ormandy because the conductor had programmed the Ninth Symphony during his guest appearances with the

Concertgebouw Orchestra in Amsterdam in late 1969. Unfortunately, Ormandy reported to Schuman on December 2, 1969

> of the shock I had when I wanted to rehearse your Ninth last Thursday only to learn that a) the wrong material; b) the wrong score; and c) not the extra parts were sent here, contrary to my original orders. . . . When I started to rehearse different groups I found that they had absolutely no idea what the work was all about . . . they were unable to play together. Unless I had 8 rehearsals I knew it could be a disaster, and these they couldn't give. So, regretfully, I had to take the symphony off the performance.

Schuman had an exceedingly difficult time as well with recording the work soon after its premiere. He had already worked very hard to ensure that it would be recorded and had succeeded in obtaining $7,500 from the Alexander Hilsberg Fund to support the Philadelphia Orchestra's recording. Unfortunately, Schuman was a bit too far ahead of the executives at RCA Victor, who were not overly enthusiastic about including the Ninth Symphony in their upcoming releases; nor were they confident that the $7,500 would cover the personnel costs of the recording. In a letter to Sol Schoenbach, former principal bassoonist of the Philadelphia Orchestra, Schuman bitterly denounced the RCA executives for their hesitancy, echoing his earlier criticism of his former bosses at Lincoln Center: "The profits keep rising, the dividends get larger, but the paucity of funds for artistic enterprises of a non-commercial nature remains."

As Schuman feared, the Philadelphia Orchestra's manager, Boris Sokoloff, in a letter of March 13, 1969, returned the $7,500 check to the Hilsberg Fund with a note that

> it was very possible that the costs of recording this work would far exceed the amount contributed. . . . Therefore, since neither RCA nor The Philadelphia Orchestra Association is in a financial position to augment the amount contributed for the purpose of recording the work, we feel the only possible course to take now is to cancel the recording.

Schuman fired off a letter to Sokoloff in which he gave vent to all of his considerable moral outrage:

the quickest and most accurate way for me to describe my reaction to your letter is the word "incredible." It is incredible to me that one of our greatest cultural institutions and one of our most distinguished corporations should so cavalierly go back on their word and their obligation. . . . After seven years as President of Lincoln Center and more than seventeen as President of The Juilliard School, I hardly need to be instructed on the rising costs in the profession of music. But we are talking more than economics. . . . What is involved here is a pure and simple case of basic ethics.

He sent a copy of his letter to Roger Hall, accompanied by a one-sentence missive: "This situation I find truly shocking." It is interesting to note that although only a few months removed from his Lincoln Center resignation, Schuman seemed not at all to have been personally diminished by his debacle of late 1968.

By early April Schuman wrote in a memorandum to his files that he had "refused to budge from my position that what had taken place was a breach of ethics. Apparently my stand has finally shamed them into sticking to the original concept." In quick succession, Ormandy persuaded first his manager and then his board that the recording had to proceed, the officials of the Hilsberg Fund reinstated the original $7,500 grant and also agreed to make available another grant not to exceed $2,500 for any extra costs of the recording, and RCA agreed to record and release the symphony. However, Hall sent Schuman a stinging letter in late May 1969 enumerating their misunderstandings regarding the recording and laying the responsibility for them squarely at Schuman's feet. In an ironic twist, when the final accounting for the May 28 recording was made in late October, the total personnel costs exceeded the original $7,500 grant by only $937.45.

Once again, Schuman proved he was not above accusing others of ethical lapses that he would not tolerate. That he was able to summon the physical energy and moral certitude to address the issue as forcefully as he did so soon after his Lincoln Center departure speaks volumes as to the inner strength and determination of this driven man.

See the appendix for further discussion of the Symphony No. 9, "Le Fosse Ardeatine."

In the spring of 1969, while Schuman was in the throes of realizing the completion of a recording of the Ninth Symphony, he was approached by Lawrence A. Fleischman of the Kennedy Galleries in New York City to compose a work in honor of Ben Shahn, who had died on March 14. The commission would be funded by several of Shahn's friends. Shahn had immigrated with his family to the United States in 1906 from Lithuania and later became a well-known artist and photographer.

Although Schuman and Shahn had met on only a few social occasions and did not know each other well, their lives had to some extent run on parallel tracks: Schuman and Shahn shared a strong belief in American democracy, and both had liberal leanings in their early lives, although Shahn's politics were much more deeply tinged with socialism than were Schuman's. They also shared a friend in Carl Mydans, the distinguished photographer, who had worked with Shahn in the mid-1930s at the federally sponsored Farm Security Administration, where they photographed the rural poor in America.

Schuman remarked that at one dinner party where he and Shahn were together, "I was struck immediately by the artist's ebullience, far-ranging social interests and insights, and most of all by his optimistic embrace of life." Schuman was touched when Shahn's friend and neighbor of some thirty years in Roosevelt, New Jersey, Morris (Moishe) Bressler, sent the composer a handwritten note accompanying an audio tape of Bressler singing Eastern European and Jewish folk songs that he had sung to Shahn over the years. Bressler wrote of one of the songs, "The Hallelujah Song—the 150th psalm—the Shahn funeral lament . . . [that] you would probably feel the lonesomeness, fear and despair of the drowning, helpless man, who calls for help, and knows that none is forthcoming." Schuman wrote back, "The more I struggle to find ideas for the Shahn piece, the more I realize that I will not be able to use any traditional music."

The work was entitled *In Praise of Shahn: Canticle for Orchestra* and was premiered by the New York Philharmonic under Leonard Bernstein on January 29, 1970, at Philharmonic Hall. The "clarion call" that Schuman writes for the first 145 measures of the work is actually a verbatim statement, with the inclusion of woodwinds toward the end of the section, of Schuman's *Anniversary Fanfare*, premiered on April 13, 1970, to celebrate the centennial of the Metropolitan Museum of Art. The composer must have assumed that the clangorous acoustics of the museum galleries would obscure the aural memories of those audience members who were at both the museum and earlier at Philharmonic Hall.

The entrance of the strings after the fanfare on a G major chord following a G-flat major triad in the winds and brass creates an unexpected and effective musical touch that Schuman found intriguing: "One of the things I love about the piece is where the strings come in because that's a great surprise—they come in as a body—and the tonality is very fresh when it comes in. . . . I was beside myself, I liked it so much." After a languorous slow section for strings, a lento marked "Tenderly, warmly expressive" weaves a theme reminiscent of the "Requiem" melody at the end of *The Mighty Casey*. Schuman moves the melody through various "different pitch levels with developing contrapuntal embellishments," continuing to create a more complex rhythmic and harmonic texture that arrives at an allegro reminiscent of some of the energy of the beginning fanfare but with a more pointillistic approach. Schuman concludes by introducing extended flourishes in the woodwinds and having the brass carry both fanfare and earlier melodic elements while the string choir develops a counterpoint to the winds and brass. In Schuman's typical fashion, the work comes to an energetic, bombastic conclusion: "All lead to a final acceleration, a spirit of celebration which alone seems apposite for any statement honoring Ben Shahn's memory."

Schuman's love of writing for chorus was a leitmotif of his compositional life, and although he always believed that his choral music was consciously written in a less complex style than his orchestral or chamber music, his wit and pathos were always present in these works. In 1971 Schuman created two choral works that premiered in March and April of 1972.

As with his jocular treatment of words beginning with the letter "s" in *Esses*, which would be composed in 1982, Schuman ventured into a witty treatment of advertisements that were found in a Sears, Roebuck catalog of 1897 in a work he entitled *Mail Order Madrigals*. Commissioned for the Iowa State Singers by the Department of Music at Iowa State University, the work was first performed on March 12, 1972, in Ames, Iowa.

The four movements are based on Schuman's free adaptation of the contents of the catalog, which targets the female consumer: "Attention, Ladies!," which urges the female readers of the catalog to buy "Maison Rivieres Preparations" to maintain a beautiful complexion; "Superfluous Hair," which points out that the same elixir mentioned in the first madrigal also removes unwanted facial hair in women; "Sweet Refreshing Sleep," which peddles a cure for insomnia and throws in a way to counteract overindulgence in alcohol as well; and "Dr. Worden's Pills," which purify blood and cure a host of other maladies. These a cappella works are a charming divertissement for any audience.

Schuman's next work, again for a cappella chorus, is completely different in character and embraces the words of Schuman's favorite poet, Walt Whitman. Entitled *Declaration Chorale*, it was commissioned by Lincoln Center for the Third International University Choral Festival and premiered on April 30, 1972, in Philharmonic Hall "by the Combined Choruses of the Sixteen Participating Countries under the direction of Robert Shaw." This choral festival was, in fact, founded by Schuman while he was president of Lincoln Center.

The Whitman poem was "freely adapted and arranged" by Schuman. The words are a paean to the idealism of the young:

> Youth full of force, full of fascination.
> Day, day of the immense sun, action, ambition, laughter.

And they urge future generations to work toward freedom:

> 'Till men and women of all races, in ages to come,
> will be free the world over
> And brethren and lovers as are we.
> We, we of different lands.
> We of all continents.
> We of all castes.
> We, we of all theologies.
> Peace. Peace over all lands and over all the seas.
> Peace. Peace. Peace.

Particularly appropriate for international youth choruses, the text also shows Schuman's continuing idealism during the depths of the Vietnam War. Much of the music for the work is in rhythmic unison for the four voice types, creating an emotional fervor that drives the work to a pianissimo *morendo* conclusion on the word "Peace."

Schuman was able to combine his love of chorus and orchestra in a highly individual and innovative work, the *Concerto on Old English Rounds*. The development of this piece was exceptional in that, unlike most of his commissions, it was driven by the tenacity of an accomplished instrumentalist, the violist Donald McInnes. McInnes was a recipient of a grant from the Ford Foundation in 1972 through which various individuals could choose the composer they wished to commission in the creation of a new work. (Schuman had composed the *Song of Orpheus* for Leonard Rose under a similar Ford Foundation program.) Schuman was initially cool to the idea of writing a work for solo viola, but McInnes persevered, asking Schuman if he would at least listen to tapes of his playing. Schuman agreed, with the idea that he would find another composer for the entrepreneurial violist.

When the tapes arrived, Schuman was quite taken with McInnes's artistry. In 1973 McInnes became a member of the music faculty at the University of Washington. Schuman was flattered to be asked for a piece from such a fine musician but stated that McInnes should find a younger composer, and that he was not free to undertake another commission. McInnes responded, "No, I'll wait. I'll wait ten or fifteen years. I'll wait as long as I have to wait if you will do it."

McInnes gave as references two musicians whom Schuman knew quite well: his old friend Morton Gould and the conductor Michael Tilson Thomas. Gould, who had a remarkable wit, responded to Schuman's query by saying, "I can only tell you what my wife Shirley says. We went back after hearing him play and she said, 'With a name like McInnes, how can you be Jewish?'" Schuman explained that "virtually all the great string players of the world have been Jews of Eastern European extraction." Tilson Thomas said simply, "Bill, you've got to write for him, and you have to promise me the world premiere."

McInnes visited Schuman in Greenwich, where he played for him and won the composer over to the idea of the project. Said Schuman, "By the end of the afternoon, I fell in love with the viola as a solo instrument."

The complexity of the project increased when Schuman told McInnes that he did not hear in his mind's ear a conventional viola concerto, but rather one that also included a women's chorus: "I hear the viola moving up above the chorus and below the chorus and through it, and it's [an] absolutely stunning sound together, and I can't get it out of my imagination. And who A) is going to hire . . . an unknown violist, and on top of that engage a chorus?" [and] "he [McInnes] said: 'Ha! Just great!'"

As for the words, after rejecting texts by Sylvia Plath—"I wasn't *that* depressed, just because I intended to write for viola!"—Schuman remembered old English rounds that had been shown to him by his good friend Marion

Farquhar. McInnes and Schuman quickly developed a close friendship over discussions of the parameters of the work. Schuman said, "I say to people that he [McInnes] plays like an angel and talks like an insurance salesman."

The detail and specificity of their communications during the evolution of the work were unique in Schuman's non-dramatic compositional history, with McInnes frequently making precise suggestions as to how to improve the writing for the solo viola. Only in his work with Tudor and Graham in dance, with Jeremy Gury and J. D. McClatchy as librettists of his two operas, and with Richard Wilbur for the text of *On Freedom's Ground* did Schuman work so closely with a collaborator in creating a work. But no colleague had actually made the extensive *musical* suggestions that McInnes made. Schuman remembered that when he composed *A Song of Orpheus* for Leonard Rose, "he didn't criticize one passage; he was no help to me at all, although he is a fine performer, in one sense he doesn't know anything about music. He knows about performing, about cello. . . . He doesn't know music structurally the way a composer does, and that's the way Don knows it."

The specificity of McInnes's suggestions was remarkable. In a letter to Schuman in May 1974 he wrote, "meas. 160—Can we drop the lower D sharp on the half note? Measure 161 becomes much more effective without the double-stop in meas. 160," or "meas. 279—How about making octaves out of the three G's. That is, the note you have plus the octave below it. Much stronger!"

The concerto caused a serious breach between Schuman and his trusted copyist, Anthony Strilko, who first became associated with Schuman when he functioned as the liaison between the Juilliard Orchestra and the Schuman family during the 1958 European tour. It seems that the length of the work grew exponentially from its inception to its final form. Strilko had agreed to a top fee of $2,000 for preparing the work, planned to be about 140 pages. In fact, the concerto logged in at approximately 250 pages, and Strilko requested another $1,000 in copying costs. Strilko wrote Schuman that "our business relationship cannot sustain another situation like the present one," primarily because McInnes had inserted himself into the proofreading of the score, accusing Strilko of missing a number of errors that the copyist had in fact already found and corrected. "The only purpose his [McInnes's] comments have served has been to create a state of anxiety in our relationship," Strilko wrote Schuman.

In a testy letter from Strilko to McInnes in February 1974, the copyist accused the violist of rupturing a twenty-year relationship with Schuman: "After all, six pages of single spaced typewritten 'errors' would be enough to shake even a 200 year confidence." Another $500 was provided for Strilko, but the working relationship between him and Schuman was seriously damaged and ultimately ended owing to Schuman's belief that Strilko's copying fees were too high. Strilko was eventually replaced as Schuman's copyist by Ken Godel.

After Schuman's death, Strilko assisted Frankie in sorting Schuman's manuscripts for submittal to the Library of Congress. However, at the time of Frankie's death, Strilko, according to Tony Schuman, "tried to back bill [the Schuman estate] for the work as if there had been an agreement to do the work for hire. It led to the end of a long friendship between the Schuman family and a quite endearing, if eccentric, man whom we had known since 1958."

The first performance of *Concerto on Old English Rounds* took place on November 29, 1974, with McInnes as soloist and Michael Tilson Thomas conducting the Boston Symphony Orchestra and the Radcliffe Choral Society. Leonard Bernstein conducted the first New York performance on April 15, 1976, once again with McInnes as soloist, and the New York Philharmonic and the Camerata Singers. The forty-minute work is one of Schuman's most profoundly complex and moving compositions. Leonard Bernstein said to Schuman that "this piece is all about your love of music. . . . It's also about your former life at Sarah Lawrence, where you conducted the chorus."

In an interview with Phillip Ramey, program editor of the New York Philharmonic, that appeared on the back of the album cover of the work's first recording with Bernstein and the New York Philharmonic in 1978, Schuman said he chose a women's chorus as an integral part of the work because it "would be a stunning sound, and I think it is." He also said it used some beloved rounds that "were taught to me, by rote, by the late Marian Jones Farquhar"—"Amaryllis" (origin and date unknown), "Great Tom is Cast" (Henry Aldrich, 1646–1710), "Who'll Buy Mi Roses" (ca. 1700, composer unknown), and "Come, Follow Me" (John Hilton, 1599–1657).

When asked how he made these "monotonous" rounds interesting, Schuman said, "They're not that interesting in themselves. . . . You have to keep doing things to them, . . . rhythmically, melodically, harmonically, and making all kinds of juxtapositions. I had the most marvelous time!" Schuman had taken the same approach earlier with the Billings melodies of the *New England Triptych* and with his song "Orpheus with His Lute," used as the musical foundation of his cello fantasy *A Song of Orpheus.*

Ramey quoted the reviewer Andrew Porter's description of the work as "'at once a viola concerto in five movements and a suite-cum-fantasia' on the rounds." Schuman's enthusiastic response was, "I like that. He's right: It is a fantasy as well as a concerto." Unfortunately, owing to the length of the work, the lack of public interest in a composition for solo viola, and the logistical complexity of providing a women's chorus for performances, Schuman's sense that the work might not be frequently performed was indeed accurate.

Schuman did not give up on the creative possibilities of old English rounds, however. *To Thy Love: Choral Fantasy On Old English Rounds* for a cappella women's chorus uses all four rounds used in the concerto, with an emphasis on Schuman's favorite round, "Amaryllis." The work was finished on June 29, 1973, about six months before the completion of the concerto on December 4, 1973. In 1976 he composed an eight-minute work for string orchestra entitled *Amaryllis: Variants for Strings on an Old English Song*, the score of which notes that the work is "adapted from the opening and closing sections of *Concerto on Old English Rounds*." Schuman explained that in this approach to "Amaryllis," "the variants consist of the melody set forth in various harmonic guises and with a variety of contrapuntal embellishments as it travels its brief, tranquil course." The work was premiered in Philadelphia by Andre Kostelanetz and the Philadelphia Orchestra on July 27, 1976. Of course, the impact of Marion Farquhar and her haunting presentation of "Amaryllis" to Bill and Frankie many years earlier was also manifested in the striking String Trio of 1964, *Amaryllis: Variations for String Trio*. The performance of the round by three female voices at the end of this work presaged the unconventional way the voice was used in the *Concerto on Old English Rounds* and in Schuman's 1978 chamber work *In Sweet Music*.

Not long after he left Lincoln Center, Schuman focused his considerable energies on a new endeavor that would merge his passion for education with the new technology of the early 1970s. At the time, many American and foreign companies were undertaking extensive experimentation on how video recordings could be brought into the home consumer market. Schuman had read about the invention of the videorecord or videodisc and was impressed with its potential as an educational tool. He had also noticed that CBS was one of the companies in the race to create a product in this area and decided to telephone his good friend Goddard Lieberson, the well-known and highly regarded record executive at CBS, to learn more about the project.

Over lunch, Schuman told Lieberson that he had long believed that the record companies were not using their product effectively as an educational tool. He thought, however, that a new video device, which would bring high-quality video as well as sound to the home or the classroom, could be "one of *the* most extraordinary teaching devices yet known, and that I really thought it could be almost as important as the invention of the printing press."

The development of content for the new videorecording device was not in Lieberson's area of responsibility at CBS, so he referred Schuman to Robert Brockway, a CBS executive who was overseeing the development of the CBS prototype. Brockway was intrigued with Schuman's ideas and invited him to see the secret machine in operation, "which [was] not only under lock and key but ... under an armed guard." The development of the CBS machine was overseen by Peter Goldmark, a leader in the development of the long-playing record.

Schuman was invited by Brockway to function as a paid consultant investigating the development of educational programs for the new invention. He traveled to America's larger cities and interviewed academics and performers about potential programming. Schuman's report to CBS suggested that the company concentrate on the programming part of the venture because no one was sure as to the eventual format of the most widely accepted machine.

Schuman also requested that his report be developed with other consultants who could examine the new product: "I needed the principal consultants because I was well aware that one of my greatest assets and strengths could also be one of my greatest liabilities; i.e., I am an enthusiast."

Brockway, in turn, reacted to the report by saying to Schuman, "What you have given me is a philosophy, but you haven't told me whether it's a business." Schuman responded by saying that his problem was "not finding the answers. My problem is the more difficult one of not knowing the questions." He set about learning those questions by conferring with CBS officers and business executive friends such as Martin E. Segal, who worked with Schuman in creating the Film Society of Lincoln Center, and the marketing executive William Bernbach, chairman of the board of the highly successful advertising agency Doyle Dane Bernbach.

It was Bernbach who moved Schuman in a different direction in his technology exploration by telling him that he wanted Schuman to meet some people involved in a similar venture in which Bernbach and others had invested: "Why don't you forget about answering all those business questions? Why don't you simply meet the principals of the new enterprise and join forces with us and concentrate on those things that interest you and leave the solution of the specific business problems to those for whom they are a normal concern?" At a subsequent luncheon Schuman met with Bernbach; Stafford L. Hopwood Jr., president of Videorecord Corporation of America; and Eli Jacobs, a partner in the investment firm of White, Weld & Company. Hopwood explained that he had formed a company to do exactly what Schuman was recommending to CBS—create content for the new home video machine. Schuman recalled "that they wanted me to forget my association with CBS and to line up with them," explaining that "there is no contract that you can't get out of. All you have to do is talk to them."

When Brockway learned of Schuman's request, he immediately conferred with CBS's powerful chairman, William Paley, who purportedly told him: "Look Brockway, your plate is already full. We have twenty million dollars involved in the hardware. Don't get involved with the software." CBS then released Schuman from his contract, freeing him to join Hopwood's new venture. Schuman also recalled that "about two or three years later, they [CBS] dropped their whole project and lost something like sixty million dollars because they determined they should not be in the hardware business."

Videorecord Corporation of America (VRA) was founded in 1970 by Hopwood, who had an earlier CBS connection as their vice president for business development and professional products. VRA was presented as a company that would

> create, produce and distribute software—pre-recorded video program packages which can be played over any ordinary television set for viewing at any time and location by an individual or group. The video recordings for education, medicine, industry, home entertainment and other fields represent a new communications dimension made possible by recent technological developments.

The board that Hopwood put together was a distinguished one and included Schuman; Bernbach; Jacobs; Beardsley Graham, co-founder of Communications Satellite; Alan R. Novak, former executive director of the President's Task Force on Communications Policy; and Eugene V. Rostow, Sterling Professor at the Yale Law School and former Undersecretary of State for Political Affairs. In this rarified climate Schuman was elevated to chairman of the Westport, Connecticut–based firm on March 2, 1970, bringing prestige, credibility, and an articulate spokesperson to the enterprise, with Hopwood as president and chief executive officer.

A laudatory article in the *Washington Post* on Schuman's venture into the business world portrayed the composer's initiative as an exciting new chapter in his life:

> It may seem to the casual observer as if the limelight has passed over
> William Schuman. . . . But those who know the man—his creativity
> and gumption, his phenomenal energy, undimmed at 60, the quality
> of his vision and his appetite for risk—realize that reticence is not his
> destiny, that his aura is apt to rekindle itself at any moment, more
> brightly than ever.

And the way Schuman had addressed his new journey, according to the article, was "Nothing less than paving the way for the future of the arts. What looks like grass under his feet turns out to be the mint green of a bold new idea."

Although the article was thoroughly saturated with hyperbole, it clearly makes the point that what Schuman and others were undertaking actually explored a new paradigm for the information age of the twenty-first century. The article ends with a prediction that the author characterizes as "delirious . . . speculat[ion]": "any item [will be] available upon a dialed request from the customer . . . a choice from every film ever released, every human or instrumental sound ever recorded, any page from any book in the Library of Congress." Not even in 2008 could there be a better description of the iPod or Google.

Sadly, the vaunted expectations of Videorecord were primarily smoke and mirrors. By May 1972 Schuman had already stepped down as chairman of VRA. Hopwood had turned out to be quite unreliable. Said Schuman: "Instead of husbanding the resources that were raised—which were maybe a couple of million dollars in private capital to start this—instead of doing it very slowly, he suddenly assembled a staff of sixty people for a business that didn't exist."

Hopwood also began to turn against the board members, each in his turn. Schuman believed that Hopwood had experienced some kind of "psychotic" episode: he was "obviously emotionally very, very disturbed, so he would take out his problems on each person on that board—one after another." Schuman recalled that "Bernbach and I and several of the others just became disillusioned with him [Hopwood], so we decided to accept our losses. . . . To me, it was no loss at all because I had a wonderful time. I learned more than I could possibly tell you about the workings of business." It seems unlikely that Schuman had put a great deal of his own money into the venture, but he would never again lend his name or become personally involved in any other for-profit venture.

However, Schuman frequently acted as a consultant to organizations large and small. One of his more extensive undertakings as an advisor in his post–Lincoln Center years involved his work in Puerto Rico as a consultant to evaluate the Conservatory of Music of Puerto Rico and the Puerto Rico Symphony Orchestra in the winter of 1971. Since he was still chairman of VRA, he requested and received formal permission from Hopwood to undertake the Puerto Rico project, which took up about two months of Schuman's time.

Schuman's charge from the sponsors of the consultancy, the Puerto Rico Industrial Development Company and Festival Casals, was extraordinary in its far-reaching goals, which included a comprehensive evaluation of the conservatory, including its

> policies and objectives, educational and artistic practices, organizational structure, depth and scope of technical and educational programs including curriculums, faculty and student relations . . . physical plant . . . budgetary and financial needs, and any other matters that Festival Casals, Inc. and/or The [Industrial Development] Company sees fit to require your evaluation.

In addition, Schuman was contracted to make the same comprehensive evaluation of the Puerto Rico Symphony Orchestra as an "artistic, cultural and educational institution" within Puerto Rico. All this was to be accomplished, including a written report, between January 22 and April 15, 1971, for the generous sum of around $10,000, plus all expenses, including those for Frankie.

Bill and Frankie traveled to Puerto Rico on February 22 and stayed only until March 3. The cost of an administrative assistant was also included in the expenses for the project. Although Schuman was paid handsomely, it seems difficult to believe that in the short time frame allocated for the project he would be able to realize anything but a superficial treatment of the issues, a conclusion supported by the lengthy agenda with which the conservatory presented Schuman. It included most of the school's physical plant, a significant increase in its scholarship support to students, expansion of programs in the library, the hiring of new full-time and visiting faculty, and the enhancement of so-called cultural activities that would bring "outstanding artists" to the island.

In a section of the briefing document entitled "Second Decade," the conservatory proposed new initiatives, including the creation of graduate, preparatory, and dance divisions; new support services for faculty such as sabbaticals and retirement; and a breakaway board of directors for the conservatory, which was overseen at the time by the Festival Casals board.

Remarkably, Schuman finished the report by mid-March 1971, one month before the April 15 deadline, although he admitted that "it turned out . . . to be a bigger job than we had anticipated." He stated that the report was not marked "draft" because "I do not believe that any changes that will be suggested will require altering the report. . . . If I receive any suggestions that I wish to incorporate in my final findings, *I* shall prepare an appropriate addendum" (emphasis added). The time allowed for his commissioners to respond to the report was also truncated when Schuman reported to José A. Franceschini, executive director of Festival Casals, that he and Frankie would be leaving for Europe on March 28 and not returning until April 18. Although addresses for his hotels in Paris and Rome were provided, one senses that Schuman had little interest in spending any more time revising the report; he could be contacted "if it is essential to do so." Schuman used the next four pages of the five-page letter to present in extraordinary detail the expenses—for taxis, copying, and meals—for which he needed to be reimbursed, just as he had done for the minor expenses the Schumans incurred during their European tour in 1958.

Although the report—entitled "Music in Puerto Rico: The Next Decade (1972–1982)" and dated March 15, 1971—includes forty-seven pages of analyses and recommendations, it does not stand as one of Schuman's stronger analytical efforts, for it contains recommendations that would be difficult for even a fully developed, appropriately funded, and well-staffed conservatory to realize. The Conservatory of Music of Puerto Rico was none of these. It had just completed its first decade and had meager resources in all areas. Why Schuman would make such aggressive recommendations for the fledgling school is puzzling. In addition, the presence of the revered Pablo Casals as the spiritual leader of all things in classical music in Puerto Rico makes the Schuman report either a subtle slap at what had already been achieved by Casals or a call to arms that could never be realized by the elderly maestro.

The long list of recommendations included the creation of a crash program to train string players; enlarging the orchestra and eventually extending the length of its season to fifty-two weeks; significantly upgrading the conservatory's physical plant and integrating it into a newly proposed arts center; doubling the conservatory's scholarship budget; continuing the school's tuition-free policy; creating preparatory, dance, and opera departments; and reorganizing the teaching of theory to embrace the approach of the Juilliard Literature and Materials of Music program. In a more practical vein, Schuman also suggested separating the boards of the conservatory and the symphony orchestra into two autonomous boards, but with the inclusion of representatives "from the funding agencies, thus creating inter-locking directorates." Also proposed was an achievable initiative: creating a Puerto Rico Arts Council so that the island could receive funds from the National Endowment for the Arts.

Schuman ended his report with a bit of personal merchandising, recommending that Puerto Rico become involved in

> new emerging technologies such as videorecording, with which I happen to be particularly familiar . . . an extraordinary new opportunity which has been compared in importance to the invention of the printing press. Here again, it is not too soon to begin special studies of these new techniques as they can [a]ffect education (and, indeed, industry) in Puerto Rico.

The research and writing that went into the report do not reflect well on Schuman's motives. He seems uncharacteristically disingenuous, and many of the proposed solutions were plucked from Juilliard initiatives he had seen realized at least two decades earlier. Few of the recommendations in the study were ever fully implemented.

Schuman continued to be affiliated with several not-for-profit organizations through membership on boards, of which he was often chairman. One such organization was especially dear to his heart: the Walter W. Naumburg Foundation. It was founded in 1926 by the eponymous chairman of the group and was dedicated to identifying, through competitions, some of the finest young musicians of the day. The award provided a debut recital and, as time went on, other career benefits, from professional management to performances with the New York Philharmonic to recording contracts. Such distinguished musicians as the pianists Jorge Bolet, Abbey Simon, and William Kapell; the singers Shirley Verrett and Dawn Upshaw; and the violinists Robert Mann and Joseph Silverstein were all Naumburg winners. Schuman, along with Aaron Copland, had been appointed to the board in 1946. By 1948 Schuman was chairing a committee to explore new initiatives for the foundation. The committee eventually concluded that there was a need for more recordings of American music, and this led to an annual award for a major American work to be recorded.

After Naumburg's death in 1959, Schuman was elected president of the board, and he set about in his usual entrepreneurial fashion to expand the programs of the foundation. Specifically, the winner of the annual competition would now

> receive a substantial cash prize for use in furthering a career, a two-year contract with a professional management, a solo recording, and an appearance with the New York Philharmonic on a Naumburg-sponsored concert; to add to the synergy—that concert would also feature a young conductor of special promise selected by the Foundation, and would program the latest winner of the Recording Award.

Soon after Schuman moved to Lincoln Center from Juilliard he decided to step down from the Naumburg presidency. He was succeeded by Leopold Mannes, the well-known New York music educator. Mannes's tenure as president ended when he died suddenly in August 1964. He was succeeded by the president of Juilliard, Peter Mennin, who also added to the awards menu by developing programs in conducting and chamber music.

Schuman and Mennin had never been close friends or colleagues, most probably because Schuman had not supported Mennin to succeed him at Juilliard, and also because of the bruising battles the two engaged in during Juilliard's move to Lincoln Center in the mid-1960s. So it comes as no surprise that Schuman would be involved in unseating Mennin as the foundation's president in 1971.

In September 1969 Schuman sent a letter to Mennin that bluntly began, "There is increasing restiveness on the Naumburg front. . . . I have taken steps to quiet questioning voices with the assurance that after Juilliard opens [which was only a few weeks away] you will give some thought to the Naumburg Foundation."

Two months later Schuman pulled out all the stops. Perhaps this was due to the fact that he had essentially been snubbed by Mennin during the inauguration ceremonies of the new Juilliard building on October 26, 1969. Schuman sent a fiery memo to the Naumburg Foundation directors that he said was motivated by "increasing concern over the inactivity and consequent default of the Naumburg Foundation in carrying out the mandate of its

Founder over the last several years." Schuman pointed out what he saw as three severe deficiencies. First, the foundation was not using its income in the manner for which it was designated and had in fact accrued $100,000 in unused income. Second, Congress was now more carefully investigating not-for-profits, meaning that the foundation could be liable for penalties imposed on account of non-performance. And third, "our president clearly does not have the time to devote to the affairs of the Foundation. In my opinion it is unfair of us to ask him to continue in office."

The memo also asked any available board members to join Schuman for a luncheon rump meeting at the Century Association on December 8 to discuss the matter further. Schuman's power play concluded:

> I feel a deep sense of personal obligation towards the Foundation. Unfortunately, due to other commitments, I could not at this time, even if the Board so wished, assume the presidency. I would be happy, however, to chair a nominating committee to find a qualified person. If this is agreeable to the Board, *I would want to choose the members of the committee.* (Emphasis added.)

Schuman's move triggered an immediate reaction from Mennin. Schuman then sent the board another memo on November 21:

> My memorandum to you had the exhilarating effect of prompting the immediate calling of an official meeting by our president [Mennin] for Tuesday, December 2nd. This action encourages me to believe that our president may now be in a position to give the Foundation the time and leadership it requires. If he assures us that this is indeed the case, he will have my full backing.

Schuman also cancelled his rump gathering.

However, time did not improve the situation. On May 5, 1971, the executive committee of the Naumburg Foundation met at the Century Association prior to a dinner meeting of the full board. According to Robert Mann, the first violinist of the Juilliard String Quartet, who was present at both meetings, the meeting began in a matter-of-fact manner with Mennin as chairman presenting a synopsis of the board agenda and an outline of the foundation's budgetary issues. As the meeting was drawing to a close, Schuman looked at Mennin and said, referring to Mennin's budget presentation, "Pete, that's actually amateursville."

According to Mann, Mennin and the other members of the executive committee, which included Aaron Copland, seemed shocked by Schuman's insult, yet no one spoke another word. Instead, they moved to the dining room, where the rest of the board awaited the beginning of the general meeting. There Mennin called the meeting to order, resigned on the spot, and left the room.

As the shock of the moment permeated the atmosphere, Schuman broke the silence by announcing that nominations for a new Naumburg president should now take place. In what must have been an atmosphere of awkwardness and tension, Aaron Copland and Robert Mann were both nominated for the position. Copland immediately demurred, leaving Mann as the only nominee. He eventually agreed to be president beginning in the fall of 1971.

In a letter of late June 1971 to Francis Thorne, the foundation's executive secretary, Schuman affirmed his continuing and deep interest in the foundation's affairs:

> Had this not been the case, I would have not gone through the anguished sessions that led to the resignation of our president [Mennin]. However, when I stated that I would not stand for re-election as president of the Foundation, it was because I wanted to make it absolutely clear to the other Directors that my motives were not personal but institutional.

Schuman was pleased when Mann was voted the new president in the fall of 1971. However, he counseled Mann against appointing his wife, Lucy Rowan Mann, as the new executive secretary. In a handwritten letter to Schuman dated December 1971, Mann rejected Schuman's concerns about the perception of nepotism, explaining that "the simple fact is that her assistance would be what I think we need and I would feel a great empathy in having her doing it rather than someone else." Mann and his wife continued to serve as president and executive secretary of the foundation for several decades. Schuman's relationship with Mennin became even chillier after this incident. The two had a rapprochement of sorts in the spring of 1983, not long before Mennin's death.

In the 1970s Schuman continued to seek out consulting and board activities to complement his composing activities. He was a member of the Joint U.S.–Japan Committee on Cultural and Educational Cooperation in 1970–71

and traveled to Tokyo to participate in a conference for that initiative. In April 1975 he became the chairman of the board of the Norlin Foundation, which was funded by the Norlin Corporation. At the time Norlin was America's largest musical instrument company, selling Gibson guitars, Lowrey organs, Moog synthesizers, and Olds and Reynolds band instruments.

The mission of the new foundation was to "help people discover, develop and enjoy their capacities to the fullest and specifically to recognize, encourage and reward achievement in music." Norlin initially funded the foundation with a grant of $100,000. In addition to Schuman, the founding trustees of the foundation were Norton Stevens and Arnold Berlin, respectively president and chairman of the Norlin Corporation.

Schuman received a retainer to serve as chairman of the foundation and quickly set out to reward projects that were related to his ongoing interests, including a grant to the MacDowell Colony to create fellowships in perpetuity in honor of Aaron Copland on his seventy-fifth birthday. Funding was also provided to research the development of a festival of the arts in New York City.

Schuman readdressed the issue of education and technology by suggesting to Norton Stevens that Norlin possibly become involved in a "Music Learning System" developed by Peter Goldmark. Goldmark's Music Learning System used audio cassettes to make "music learning and practice fun . . . while providing the versatility to record alone, play an instrument or sing along and compare with professional artists." In addition, Schuman advised Stevens on the relationship between education and a proposed Norlin television music series, suggesting questions for the film on conducting, such as "what does a conductor do" and "what is meant by tempo," as well as providing other questions for films on jazz, amateur music making, and chamber music. Neither project had the significant impact on music education in America for which Schuman had hoped.

In the mid-1970s Schuman served on the board of trustees that organized the National Humanities Center. In fact, he was the only representative of the arts on the board, which was composed of distinguished scholars in such areas as English, philosophy, history, engineering, and religious studies. It included John Chancellor of NBC News, Sol M. Linowitz of the law firm Coudert Brothers, and a young William J. Bennett, who was assistant director of the nascent center and who would eventually become Secretary of Education in Ronald Reagan's administration. The center, located in the Research Triangle Park in Durham County, North Carolina, is dedicated to the support of advanced studies in the humanities and each year appoints approximately forty fellows who undertake various research projects in the humanities. Schuman's appointment to this prestigious board as the only representative of the arts reflected the high esteem in which he was held at the time by America's intellectual community. However, Schuman's time on the board was brief. He resigned in September 1977, writing to the center's president, Charles Frankel, that he was forced to leave owing to the pressure of other commitments. Frankel told Schuman that the center's executive committee wished for him to serve for at least another year: "It will be helpful to us—to our morale, to our public position, and to our power to use your advice effectively—if you remain officially with us." Schuman reluctantly agreed to stay but left the board in 1978.

Given Schuman's superb entrepreneurial abilities as well as his lifelong patriotism, it is no surprise that he began planning a compositional project of considerable proportions ten years before the actual date of America's bicentennial. In June 1966 Schuman sent a detailed letter to his publisher at Theodore Presser, Arthur A. Hauser, outlining an ambitious compositional project with which Schuman planned to be engaged for several years. Schuman envisioned

> music for soloists, mixed chorus (children's chorus may also be used) and orchestra. The length of the work will be the normal running time of a concert [a full evening]. . . . It will be my intention to give the feeling and spirit of some of the facets of "The American Dream.". . . It is my ambition, in this work, to give expression through words and music to some of the feelings that are so deep within me. If I can succeed in expressing these feelings to my own satisfaction, then I have no doubt that the work will have meaning for others. . . . Over the course of the next ten years, I hope to write two or three sections of the work which might be separately performed.

Schuman presented his own analysis of his American roots:

> I seem to have been drawn to Americana. . . . The choral music uses texts of Whitman ("Pioneers!", "A Free Song," "Carols of Death"), Sandburg, Cullen, Millay ("Canonic Choruses"), Benjamin Franklin (one of the "Rounds on Famous Words"), Genevieve Taggard

("Holiday Song" and the cantata "This is Our Time"), Thomas Wolfe ("Prelude for Voices"), not to mention "The Mighty Casey." . . . In addition, other Americana would be "The New England Triptych," "Circus Overture," and "American Festival Overture."

Schuman proposed using the words of Emerson, Dreiser, Paul Engle, and others and even suggested that one movement based on Dreiser would be "a dramatic scena for soprano and orchestra. This will probably be the drowning scene from *An American Tragedy*," an idea that Schuman had first considered in the early 1950s when he attempted to obtain, through correspondence with Dreiser's widow, the rights to *An American Tragedy*, on which he planned to base an opera. The project was never realized.

Schuman's active mind continued to explore this grand design, and by the fall of 1971 he had put together a carefully written proposal entitled "Project 1976" that included some of the ideas of his seminal 1966 letter as well as an encomium Copland delivered when Schuman received the MacDowell Colony Medal in the summer of 1971. Speaking of Schuman's "Musical Americanism," Copland said:

> And the music itself! Whenever I think of it, I think of it as being the work of a man who has an enormous zest for life . . . and that zest informs all his music. . . . His music represents big emotions. In Schuman's pieces you have the feeling that only an American could have written them. . . . You hear it in his orchestration, which is full of snap and brilliance. You hear it in the kind of American optimism which is at the basis of his music.

The proposal also outlined a princely commissioning fee of $125,000, with Schuman receiving $100,000 and the remainder going to support a research assistant and copying costs.

By 1972 Schuman had set out to find a funder or funders to provide the commission. The National Symphony Orchestra agreed to provide $20,000 toward the grand scheme, but no more. Through the good offices of his close friend Martin E. Segal, Schuman applied to the Helena Rubinstein Foundation, asking for a $50,000 grant and dropping his fee to $70,000. In Schuman's application letter he wrote passionately about the project: "I regard this as a culminating effort of a life's work." The foundation rejected the application.

As 1976 loomed Schuman lowered his sights still further, but he nevertheless kept intact his concept of an entire evening dedicated to his music during the bicentennial year. With the enthusiastic support of Antal Doráti, who had worked with Schuman on the premiere performance of the Sixth Symphony in Dallas in 1949 and who was now music director of the National Symphony Orchestra in Washington, D.C., the idea was developed of having two new works performed in April 1976 as well as a reworking of *The Mighty Casey* in a "cantata version" for orchestra, chorus and a limited number of vocal soloists. The three works that resulted were *The Young Dead Soldiers*, the Tenth Symphony, and *Casey at the Bat*. The entire program was called simply "The Music of William Schuman."

Of the three works, the Tenth Symphony was the composition that embodied most of the lofty ideas Schuman had described in "Project 1976." Schuman wrote to Doráti in April 1974:

> It seems to me that the remarkable development of American artists in all media—music, visual arts, letters—has been truly remarkable. I want to dedicate my symphony to America's artists because I believe that they have been a complete success. They have been as diverse as the democracy that gave them birth, and their achievements have found world acceptance. At this time, when there is so much reason for doubt and re-evaluation, it is good to be reminded of positive achievements. . . . For these reasons I am subtitling my Symphony No. 10 American Muse.*

Schuman later told Doráti, "I regard your forthcoming performances of my music for the Bicentennial celebration as one of the most exciting artistic events of my career."

The Tenth Symphony was finished in late March of 1975, more than a year before its premiere. The composer told Doráti in 1974 that

> when I decided to do a more extended piece for Hirshhorn [*Prelude for a Great Occasion* for brass and percussion, premiered on October 1, 1974, as part of the opening ceremonies for the Hirshhorn Museum and Sculpture Garden of the Smithsonian Institution], I used

* The comment "At this time, there is so much reason for doubt and re-evaluation" is a reference to the Watergate scandal, which had been brewing for two years and was to bring down the administration of President Richard Nixon that next August.

materials that will be in the first movement of Symphony No. 10, although treated quite differently. For this reason, the Hirshhorn piece should not be on the W. S. program you are planning.

In fact, *Prelude for a Great Occasion*, which was completed on June 24, 1974, presents only a few musical elements heard in the first movement of the Tenth Symphony. It is not even close to the total replication of musical material in the *Anniversary Fanfare* that appears at the beginning of *In Praise of Shahn*, both works premiered in 1970.

Doráti was exuberant in his praise of the new symphony as the premiere approached, writing in the winter of 1976 that it was

> a stupendous work: a great musical contribution to America's third century. What struck me to "my core" is its second movement. Probably the most beautiful (hauntingly so), the most concentrated, the most "giving" and most "taking" slow movement in American music I have ever read. . . . The third movement is exquisite, brilliant in its conception as well as in its realization.

However, it was with the first movement that Doráti expressed his ongoing concerns: "With the first movement I have still problems. It is a good and solid piece, perhaps somewhat 'too good and solid';—I have, so far, difficulties in imagining it as a beginning—it is so 'final,' so monolithic in material execution." Drawing a triangle, Doráti suggested that "I hope to be able to show this work in a sort of Renaissance triangle-shape with the 2nd movement on the top."

Schuman replied immediately: "Did any composer ever receive a letter as encouraging as the one I have just received from you?" He went on to address Doráti's only substantive concern:

> Of course I think the first movement will work very well despite the finality of the ending. (When Symphony No. 3 was first played, the same comment was made to me about the brilliant close of the first part.) . . . I believe that the fanfarish nature of the concluding section gives a feeling of something more to come. Further, since a principal theme of the first movement is introduced in the last movement, I think there will be a convincing sense of wholeness to the entire work. But the performance will tell us.

The Tenth Symphony, "American Muse," calls for a large orchestra, including four flutes, six horns, four trumpets, harp, and a large percussion section. A major work of about thirty minutes, it was premiered on April 6, 1976, in Washington, D.C., at the Kennedy Center with the National Symphony Orchestra, conducted by Doráti. The program opened with the premiere of *The Young Dead Soldiers*, with poetry by Archibald MacLeish, and concluded after intermission with Schuman's cantata arrangement, *Casey at the Bat*, of his opera *The Mighty Casey*.

Rehearsal time was limited owing to the pressure of premiering three works, and Schuman was not pleased with the performance of the Tenth Symphony: "The second movement was very well done, but the other movements certainly weren't done to his [Doráti's] satisfaction or to mine. . . . The second movement is a very melodic movement that obviously the audience liked—they didn't like the other two."

In Schuman's Symphony No. 10 the composer returns to the exuberant style of his early days. The first movement, which is close to six minutes in length, is a full-bodied "fanfare extraordinaire" of constant energy, using offbeats, triplets, percussion with the obligatory rim shots, all working together to create an intense drive to the end of the movement.

It is clear why Doráti saw the long (about thirteen minutes), intense second movement as the center of the symphony. In typically slow Schumanesque tempo (half note = c. 30), the movement introduces string glissandi that give the music an eerie, otherworldly quality, reinforced later by duo flute and trumpet passages. There are characteristic flourishes in piccolo, flutes, and oboes over long melodies in the strings, superseded by hefty brass chords reminiscent of the texture of the first movement. Overall the movement shows off Schuman's musical complexity at its most mature, and the final morendo to an E-flat major chord sets the stage for the perky last movement.

The final movement, Presto (half note = c. 160), includes much of Schuman's compositional vocabulary, with flourishes, triplet figures in the winds over long string melodies, and then the whole orchestra moving from eighths to triplets to rapid sixteenth notes in a written accelerando with accompanying brass chords. One unique element of orchestration appears in the first third of the movement when Schuman writes for a combination of celesta, harp, vibraphone, chimes, crotales, glockenspiel, piano, and muted strings. Schuman was quite pleased with the sound, which is unique in his compositional output. As would be expected, he ends his last symphony in typically bombastic fashion with crashing cymbals, an animated timpani part, and full brass chords marked triple forte, with all the brass players instructed to put their "bells in air al fine."

Tim Page, writing in 1985, commented about the Tenth Symphony:

It begins with a celebratory and virtuosic proclamation. For this listener, Mr. Schuman is at his weakest in such moments. Everything seemed busy and overstated, as if a writer, asked to make a paragraph stronger, were to add an exclamation point to the end of each sentence. The second movement, however, is masterly; a long, haunted nocturnal procession, superbly orchestrated and deeply compelling.

Like so many of Schuman's works, the Symphony No. 10 is not easily accessible to the uninitiated listener but requires an introduction in order to comprehend the intricacies of the score.

In May 1979, after a performance of Schuman's Symphony No. 10 by the Minnesota Orchestra conducted by Stanislaw Skrowaczewski in April at Carnegie Hall, the author Joseph Machlis wrote Schuman a perceptive and witty letter, reproduced here in full:

Dear Bill,

Let me tell you how much I enjoyed your Symphony X the other night. The first movement had a wonderful tensile strength about it, the sense of power I associate with your music, projected through the building up of those massive dissonances, one on top of the other. In fine contrast was the lyrical second movement, that had a—the word must never be used since women's lib, so don[']t tell anybody [I] used it—fine manly feeling about it, a lyricism that ran deep yet never became mawkish. And I thought it was so astute of you, after those two intensely expressive movements, to make the finale lighter in weight and content, thereby achieving a fine formal balance.

The idiot who passes for a critic on the Times was sure you wrote the way you did because you had not heard what's being done these days. Did it never occur to him that you wrote the way you did precisely because you HAD heard what people are doing nowadays?

Anyway, my congratulations, and I eagerly await your XIth. This one certainly takes its place among your strongest works.
Best,
Joe

Van Cliburn *(left)* with New York City Mayor Robert F. Wagner Jr. and Schuman, May 20, 1958. (Juilliard School Archives.)

Schuman plays host to the committee of American composers assembled at Juilliard to judge works of young composers for the National Institute of Arts and Letters, January 1959. *Left to right, seated:* Douglas Moore and Roger Sessions; *standing:* Aaron Copland, Elliott Carter, Wallingford Riegger, Schuman, and Walter Piston. (Photo by Maria Metzger. Juilliard School Archives.)

Schuman, October 1959.
(Photo by Carl Mydans.
Schuman Family Archives.)

Visiting delegation of composers from the Soviet Union to Juilliard, November 17, 1959.
Left to right: Schuman, interpreter Daniel Wolkonsky, Kostyantyn Dan'kevych, Tikhon
Khrennikov, Dmitri Shostakovich, and George Safirov of the Soviet Embassy.
(Impact Photos, Inc. Juilliard School Archives.)

John D. Rockefeller 3rd *(left)* and Schuman on the first day of Schuman's Lincoln Center presidency, January 1, 1962. (Photo by Bob Serating. Archives of Lincoln Center for the Performing Arts, Inc.)

Martha Graham receiving the Ninth Annual Capezio Dance Award from Schuman, January 10, 1960. (Photo from Jean Graf/Galbraith-Hoffman. Juilliard School Archives.)

Peter Mennin *(left)* and Schuman at a reception at the Lotos Club, November 5, 1962, on the occasion of Mennin's appointment as president of Juilliard. (Impact Photos, Inc. Juilliard School Archives.)

An assemblage of artists and administrators associated with the yet-to-be-completed Lincoln Center for the Performing Arts in a *Look* magazine photo of January 19, 1960. Grouped on the construction site around an early model of the Center are *(left to right)* prima ballerina Alicia Markova, Martha Graham, Schuman, Juilliard violin student Dorothy Pixley, American soprano Lucine Amara, Rudolf Bing, executive director of operations for the Center Reginald Allen, New York Philharmonic managing director George E. Judd Jr., Leonard Bernstein, Julie Harris, and theatrical producer Robert Whitehead. (Photo by Arnold Newman. By permission of Getty Images.)

Schuman *(left)* with Leontyne Price and Robert Merrill at the topping out of the Metropolitan Opera House, January 20, 1964. (Photo by Bob Serating. Juilliard School Archives.)

Schuman *(left)* and Rudolf Bing, April 11, 1966.
(Photo by Bob Serating. Juilliard School Archives.)

Bill and Frankie Schuman at the opening of the Metropolitan
Opera House, September 16, 1966. (Photo by Bob Serating.
Juilliard School Archives.)

Schuman with
Princess Grace of
Monaco on Lincoln
Center Plaza, fall
1966. (Juilliard
School Archives.)

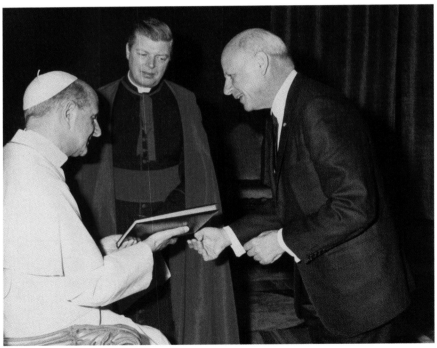

Schuman presents a gift to Pope Paul VI, April 5, 1967.
(Pontificia Foto, Felici. Juilliard School Archives.)

Andie, Bill, Frankie, and Tony, March 12, 1967. (Whitestone Photo. Schuman Family Archives.)

Leonard Bernstein *(left)* and Schuman, c. 1972. (Schuman Family Archives.)

At a celebration of Schuman's sixty-fifth birthday, 1975. *Left to right:* Schuman, Aaron Copland, and Leonard Bernstein. (Schuman Family Archives.)

Schuman *(left)* with
Elliott Carter at a
MacDowell Colony
benefit, December 7,
1985. (Schuman
Family Archives.)

Schuman in his study at 888 Park Avenue, 1991.
(Photo by Nancy Lea Katz. Juilliard School Archives.)

The "idiot" in question was John Rockwell, who had written: "[The Tenth Symphony] is also determinedly, blissfully old-fashioned; Mr. Schuman writes his music in calm contradiction of nearly every avant-garde musical fashion of the last 40 years. . . . Right now . . . his anachronistic qualities sound as if he simply hasn't been listening to the music of his time."

Knowing of the celebratory bicentennial theme of the all-Schuman program, it seems strange that he would compose for the opening piece one of his most somber works, the fifteen-minute *The Young Dead Soldiers: Lamentation for Soprano, French Horn, Eight Woodwinds and Nine Strings*. In the first performance, Rosalind Rees was the soprano soloist and Edwin C. Thayer, the French horn soloist (no relation to Ernest Lawrence Thayer, author of "Casey at the Bat").

The text, by the poet Archibald MacLeish, was taken from his 1948 collection *Act Five and Other Poems*. In this somber lament the dead soldiers whose lives were cut so short wonder whether their deaths were justified:

Our deaths are not ours;
They are yours;
They will mean what you make them.

Schuman had been asked to compose a relatively short piece for the opening of the program but was having trouble coming up with an idea. He told his friend Clare Rosenstein "that I was stuck, fed up with reading the same things all the time and not finding a text. . . . [She] came up with "The Young Dead Soldiers." Schuman was so moved by the poem that he choked up when he later attempted to read it to Rosalind Rees over the phone.

Schuman wrote to MacLeish in July 1975: "Last week I finished the music for 'The Young Dead Soldiers.' What wonderful and moving words you have written. I have been living with them for over a year, and I can only hope that my setting translates to another medium something of your intentions." Schuman would use MacLeish's poetry again in his composition for voice and piano *Time to the Old*.

Schuman's wish to create a somber work seems a far cry from the plans laid out in his "Project 1976" document. But the United States was just extricating itself from the debacle of the Vietnam War when Schuman set to work on this composition, and the many fallen soldiers in all of the country's wars since the Revolution certainly were a part of Schuman's thinking at that time. He noted that "the instrumentation is a very dark instrumentation:

eight woodwinds but no flutes—just oboes, clarinets, bassoons, and only violas, cellos, and one double bass. It has a very stark sound. And that I think works very, very well. I am very happy about that."

The soprano and horn begin the piece alone. Then, in the twenty-ninth measure, all the instruments enter on a surprising chord of which Schuman was particularly enamored:

> the whole trick of that chord is the scoring, because it uses all the notes, but all the instruments are in thirds, and so they all sound consonant with each other within families of instruments, which is something that's always intrigued me . . . on the piano it'd be a rather ugly and muddy sound, but it's absolutely clear when you have it on other instruments.

To listen to it, one would likely conclude that it was a work written for a memorial service, not a concert intended to celebrate the bicentennial and one of America's most respected living composers. Remarkably, the piece moves at the glacial pace of quarter note = c. 40, never wavering from that tempo. The solo horn part is distinctively non-heroic and presages the role Schuman would choose for the same instrument in his *Three Colloquies* of 1980. The soprano line, an extended lament, reaches a dramatic height when the voice literally cries out the word "young" on a high C. The soprano, horn, and ensemble end the work on a diminuendo chord marked "morendo." Christopher Rouse wrote of the piece:

> It is austere and unremittingly bleak, not unlike *To Thee Old Cause* [Evocation for Oboe, Brass, Timpani, Piano, and Strings (1968)] in its muted despair, and may best be described as a single fifteen-minute melody over a dissonant chordal accompaniment. The textures remain simple, and except for occasional two-part writing for the soprano and horn, the work contains virtually no counterpoint. There is an asceticism in *The Young Dead Soldiers* unusual to Schuman, and in this regard it is unique, standing apart from his other scores.

After the somberness of *The Young Dead Soldiers* and the complexity of Symphony No. 10, the comparatively carefree quality of Schuman's cantata arrangement of *The Mighty Casey* must have been the perfect antidote to the darkness of the first half of the program. Entitled *Casey at the Bat: A Baseball*

Cantata, for baritone-reciter, soprano, chorus, and orchestra, it featured as soloists in the first performance Rosalind Rees as Merry and the great operatic baritone and baseball fan Robert Merrill as the narrator. The composer received for it a commission fee of $25,000 from the Norlin Corporation; at the time, Schuman was also chairman of the Norlin Foundation. The work is dedicated to the composer's son, Anthony William Schuman.

Admitted Schuman, "I love that work [*Casey*] more than anybody else does. . . . I still believe that one day that work is going to find its mark. . . . There are some weaknesses. . . . So it's what I would call a flawed work, but I think its strengths should be able to carry it through." For the cantata Schuman cut about forty minutes—half its length—from the opera. Although Schuman was very pleased with the work of Rees and the Westminster Choir, Merrill was a disappointment:

I didn't know then that he has some block about learning. . . . He can't remember anything. And so I would rehearse and rehearse. . . . He is a charming and lovely man, and he wanted to do well . . . but he didn't understand what it was. . . . And he had it a year ahead to study it. You rehearsed for an hour—I didn't want to stay for ten hours—and then it would be over, and nothing happened.

The entire program of three Schuman works was viewed by Robert Paris of *High Fidelity/Musical America* as a major miscalculation:

Composers writing for the Bicentennial should be properly aware of the danger involved in constricting their musical focus and losing their self-critical faculty. Patriotism may indeed be the last refuge for a composer whose spirit is grounded. . . .

The Young Dead Soldiers . . . had a lovely air about it; quiet, cool, elegant, but like most of Schuman, distant and unmoving. . . . [The Tenth Symphony] seems to me an effort almost totally invested in harmonic sonority and orchestral color which unsuccessfully camouflage a stultifying bone-dryness.

. . . Watching Dorati conducting this boring monument to the clichés of Broadway [*Casey at the Bat*] was like those surreal juxtapositions of the incongruent that occur in dreams from which we wake up laughing. . . . Robert Merrill, who had little to sing and lots to declaim . . . seemed to be reading at sight what little there was.

Although Schuman had received less-than-enthusiastic reviews of his compositions dating back to his Second Symphony of 1938, the negative response to this all-Schuman program during the bicentennial celebrations was a great disappointment to the aging composer. Ultimately, however, Schuman believed that he had to continue composing—unlike his friend Copland, who abandoned composition in his later years. Schuman's determination permitted the creation of at least one work that would reinforce his reputation as one of America's most important composers.

In Sweet Music

As William Schuman left his administrative duties behind in his later life, he was able to concentrate more on his musical composition. Yet, with a few exceptions, the works belonging to this last period in his life did not always reach the creative heights he had conquered as a younger composer.

One exception was a remarkable chamber work entitled *In Sweet Music*. When Schuman set out to create a new work on a commission from his beloved Chamber Music Society of Lincoln Center, he came upon an instrumentation that he had never used before and would never use again: a beguiling ensemble of flute (doubling alto flute and piccolo), viola, voice, and harp. Despite the unique instrumentation, the composition harked back to *Amaryllis: Variations for String Trio* of 1964 in its complex harmonic structures and to *A Song of Orpheus* of 1962 for cello and orchestra in its choice of text: the song Schuman had written for Billy Rose in 1944 for *Henry VIII*. Finally, Schuman still had the sound of a solo viola in his mind's ear from the 1974 *Concerto on Old English Rounds*. Schuman remarked that the new work "may [be] said to be an outgrowth of both the Song ["Orpheus with His Lute"] and the Fantasy [*A Song of Orpheus* for cello], but naturally the chamber music setting renders the new work a complete departure."

All of these experiences came together in one of Schuman's most masterful and moving chamber works. He clearly saw the composition in dramatic terms, providing instructions in the score as to how the players should be seated onstage and instructing the singer to stand until measure 7 and then stay seated until measure 397, at which point she remains standing until the end. Thus the soprano was less a soloist than a member of the ensemble, a status Schuman emphasized in a wonderfully creative way by asking the soprano to sing the text, "In sweet music," in the first six measures and then to hum or to vocalize for most of the rest of the piece, until the full text is sung at the very end of the work. This was an approach to text-setting of which Schuman was quite fond. He recalled that "I won a prize for a piece called *Choral Etude* [1938] which was a wordless phonetic text. . . . It's a bit like 'scat' singing—I love 'scat' singing, when it's wonderfully done." Schuman also has the flutist switch back and forth from alto flute to regular flute to piccolo throughout the work. The composer worked with the American harpist Pearl Chertok in writing the harp part, which almost continually provides the harmonic foundation for the work.

In Sweet Music was premiered in Alice Tully Hall on October 29, 1978, in commemoration of the tenth anniversary of the Chamber Music Society of Lincoln Center. The performers were Jan DeGaetani, mezzo-soprano; Paula Robison, flute; Walter Trampler, viola; and Osian Ellis, harp. Regrettably, the chief music critic of the *New York Times*, Harold C. Schonberg, did not consider the work at all exceptional:

> There were some sweet, lyrical things in the piece, but there also was a good deal of mechanical padding. Schuman never has been a distinguished melodist, and his inspiration seemed to give out after a short while. At least De Gaetani, using her voice as another instrument in the ensemble, made a personal tour de force out of the piece.

Calling Schuman "never . . . a distinguished melodist" overlooks numerous works of his which present compelling and mellifluous melodies. In addition, Schuman's compositional process was to a great extent structured horizontally, in the sense that he intertwined several melodies at one time to create unique and innovative harmonies. Despite Schonberg's criticism, *In Sweet Music* has become one of Schuman's most admired and frequently performed chamber works.

See the appendix for further discussion of *In Sweet Music*.

Schuman's relationship with the Metropolitan Opera Association stretched back to his Juilliard years, when he was a member of its national association and of the board of directors. He resigned from the national association upon his departure from Lincoln Center but stayed on the main governing board until his resignation in 1977. It seems that the august opera company was experiencing severe financial problems in the mid-1970s and the president of the association, William Rockefeller, was asking all board members to help raise $12.4 million—almost $4 million more than the previous year—by July 31, 1977. Without it, there would be no 1977–78 season.

Schuman had neither the resources nor the desire to donate a significant sum to the association, and he resigned in February 1977. However, in 1978 he was approached to compose a short work to honor Eleanor Robson Belmont, one of the most generous patrons of the Met, on the occasion of her one hundredth birthday. What Schuman created was a clever pastiche of twenty-five themes from several famous operas, appropriately entitled *XXV Opera Snatches*, for unaccompanied trumpet in B-flat. It was premiered on January 10, 1979, during a celebration for Belmont, with Melvyn Broiles, principal trumpet of the Metropolitan Opera Orchestra, and Frank Hosticka, an extra trumpet player in the Met Orchestra, switching off on the continuous "snatches."

A version for solo flute was created for a seventy-fifth birthday celebration for Schuman given by the Chamber Music Society of Lincoln Center on October 1, 1985, with Paula Robison as the soloist. Schuman wrote on the title page of the solo flute score, "Experience has demonstrated that audience enjoyment is enhanced if the performer explains informally that the humor of the composition lies in the unexpected sequences of disparate operatic melodies and by challenging the listeners to see how many of the 25 they recognize." In the span of only about five minutes, Schuman flies through operatic themes from *Pagliacci* to *Die Meistersinger* to *Der Rosenkavalier* to *William Tell*, always presenting just enough of a well-known melody to allow it to be recognized before he runs off to the next. An engaging work for audiences, *XXV Opera Snatches* makes significant demands in both technique and endurance on the very busy soloist.

As a distinguished composer identified with both Americana and bombastic brass interludes, Schuman naturally was approached to compose short works or fanfares for special celebratory occasions. He would do several during his long career, but perhaps his greatest organizational challenge in this area was his *Anniversary Fanfare* of 1970. Commissioned by the Metropolitan Museum of Art in New York City to celebrate its centennial between the fall of 1969 and early 1971, the events around the celebration focused on five principal exhibitions stretching from "The Year 1200" to "Before Cortés: Sculpture of Middle America" to "New York Painting and Sculpture: 1940–1970."

Schuman was asked not only to compose a fanfare, but also to invite four other leading American composers to write short works. He chose

Leonard Bernstein, Aaron Copland, Virgil Thomson, and Walter Piston. Schuman's work opened the "19th Century America" exhibition on April 13, 1970, with Frederik Prausnitz, Schuman's former Juilliard colleague, conducting. The exhibition displayed about "200 paintings and 30 pieces of sculpture in typical period settings. In addition there [were] six completely reconstructed 19th century rooms, a garden court, and 22 vignettes." As noted earlier, Schuman's contribution was taken entirely from the beginning of his work *In Praise of Shahn*, which had been premiered just two and a half months earlier.

At roughly the same time, Schuman was approached to write a short variation on "Happy Birthday to You" that would commemorate not only the seventieth anniversary of the Philadelphia Orchestra but also the seventieth birthday of Schuman's good friend, Eugene Ormandy, who had premiered Schuman's Ninth Symphony a year earlier. Originally the tiny work was to be for piano, and the manuscript would be included in a memento gift book to Ormandy. However, plans became more complex, with three of the variations—supposedly chosen at random—to be orchestrated. As fortune and good musical taste would have it, the three composers chosen were Schuman, Copland, and Bernstein.

Schuman described the variation as "in the form of a brief two part invention. The upper line (right hand) is a combination of the Star Spangled Banner and Happy Birthday. The lower line (left hand) is Rosenkavalier plus the opening phrase of the Haffner Symphony." Schuman was even asked to conduct the orchestra in the variation on January 24, 1970, but a previously scheduled board meeting of National Educational Television in Dallas prevented him from being present for the performance, which was attended by President Nixon and the first lady. The variation was never published.

Schuman's next fanfare of this period, *Prelude for a Great Occasion*, was written for the opening ceremonies of the Hirshhorn Museum and Sculpture Garden of the Smithsonian Institution in Washington, D.C., on October 1, 1974. It was performed by members of the National Symphony Orchestra conducted by Antal Doráti. As had his earlier fanfare for the Metropolitan Museum, this work did double duty for Schuman: the beginning of his Tenth Symphony, premiered in 1976, used the same musical material as the Hirshhorn work. Schuman was a friend of the museum's benefactor, Joseph H. Hirshhorn, and the fanfare was a great success for the generous donor. "[The fanfare] was a joy to listen to and it was more than was anticipated. We wish they would play it from time to time—like every day at five so that all those thousands of visitors could hear it. The composition goes with the Hirshhorn Museum—both so contemporary—so alive," Hirshhorn wrote.

One of Schuman's most pressing volunteer responsibilities in the mid-1970s, which he embraced with typical intensity, was as chairman of the MacDowell Colony in Peterborough, New Hampshire. Founded in 1907, this artists' retreat in the New Hampshire woods had awarded Schuman its Gold Medal, MacDowell's highest honor, in 1971. He was the chairman of MacDowell's board from 1974 to 1977 and again from 1980 to 1983. In 1984 he was named an honorary chairman. Schuman became the principal volunteer fund-raiser for the Colony, zealously soliciting musical luminaries and others.

The extensive list of potential donors solicited by Schuman reads like a who's who of the American music business in the second half of the 1970s. The resulting correspondence also indicated how hard Schuman "tracked" his prey. The distinguished recording executive Goddard Lieberson wrote in 1975: "Dear Bill—(Dear Irresistible Bill): Of course, I will be glad to be a sponsor to anything you are chairman of, except I haven't got a thousand dollars. Can I be something else for $100 or $50? Or, make me an offer."

In 1978 the Colony announced that it needed to raise $3 million in endowment funds to be able to survive beyond the next ten years. Frankie Schuman took on the position of chairman of the development committee. The pairing of Bill and Frankie as fund-raisers made any campaign a sure success. Schuman had no qualms about pressing his old friend Aaron Copland to commit to the sizable sum of $250,000, paid over a period of years or in his will to match the same amount awarded earlier to the Colony in Copland's name by the Norlin Foundation. Schuman closed his solicitation letter to Copland with a less-than-discreet reminder: "I should tell you that the involvement of the Schumans is entirely due to you. When you awarded me the MacDowell Medal in 1971 our feelings about the Colony were cordial but uncommitted. You changed all that and both Frankie and I are determined to help the Colony achieve a sounder financial base."

Although Copland responded that he would attempt to provide a gift to the Colony through a bequest, Schuman did not lessen his grip on him, suggesting that he also provide a yearly gift equivalent to the annual interest earned on a bequest of $250,000. The suggestion was then thrust further forward by a Schumanesque hard sell of wry wit and chutzpah:

Since you have now become such a world famous conductor, it is obvious that, like all your confreres in that profession, you will live for decades and with this hope and expectation you can understand why we trust that, in the interim years, you will consider the above proposal. . . . You have only yourself to blame for bringing us and the organization together

Copland sent in a check for $2,500.

In 1979 Schuman sent solicitation letters to a diverse list of artistic luminaries, including Louise Talma, Mrs. Goddard Lieberson, Jerome Robbins, and another old friend, Leonard Bernstein. He wrote to Harry Kraut, Bernstein's manager, that "it is my hope that a reply can be forthcoming quickly so that the magic Bernstein name can be included among the leaders on the invitation and in the program book [of the Colony's benefit dinner/dance]."

Schuman had long been known as one of the great public speakers of his day, especially when he spoke extemporaneously. The many honorary doctorates conferred upon him often came with a request to be the commencement's main speaker. He had toyed with the idea of going out on the professional speaking circuit, which was quite lively in universities and colleges in the 1970s, but he eventually soured on the idea because of travel demands and due to the need to speak in abstract terms instead of actually addressing concrete initiatives he wished to act upon. The well-known concert manager Herbert Barrett in fact tried to persuade Schuman to undertake an intensive schedule of lectures in the early 1970s. Schuman considered the idea but eventually demurred: "Instinctively I felt that somehow they [lectures] would represent fragmentation of my activities and would not supply the answer I was seeking."

Schuman's wit was a signal part of his public speaking style, as demonstrated in this brief quip from his speech accepting the Gold Medal from the American Academy and Institute of Arts and Letters in 1982:

This winter . . . I was sent a book on composers in what was described as historic photographs. The first thing I did was to determine whether or not it was a worthy publication. This is done through a quick process of objective analysis. If you are included and the listing under your name is favorable, it's a splendid work! Well, there was my picture all right, and under it "1910," followed by that nasty little dash. But, lo and behold, a second date was there, too—"1981." Since we are said to have memory lapses as we get older, I naturally concluded that my death was simply something that had slipped my mind. You can understand how reassured I feel today.

One of his ad hoc speaking engagements in the 1970s involved his being a featured participant in the dedication of the Mary Duke Biddle Music Building on the campus of Duke University in October 1974. Once again Schuman was joined by other distinguished participants in the three-day opening celebration, including Nancy Hanks, chairman of the National Endowment for the Arts; Carlos Moseley, president of the New York Philharmonic; Isaac Stern; and Dizzy Gillespie.

Schuman also was writing prose at this time and submitted an article entitled "The Great American Music Snub of '76" to the *New York Times*. In it he contended that the nation's bicentennial would not include an adequate number of performances of contemporary American music by the nation's orchestras. In his rather blunt rejection of the piece, William H. Honan, the newspaper's arts and leisure editor, wrote in June 1975 that the article "just doesn't go anywhere. You state your theme and then it gets repeated again and again. To make a successful article for our pages, the case would have to be made in a more ingenious or interesting way."

Schuman accepted the criticism and persevered. His revision reflected his love of baseball: he suggested that an "American Bicentennial Box Score" be calculated and printed which would list some seventeen to twenty major American orchestras, the number of programs they presented, and the number of those programs that contained American music. This would result in a batting average of sorts; the more American music performed, the higher the average. Once again the *Times* declined to follow up on Schuman's suggestion.

In a more serious vein, Schuman was invited to present the twentieth Charles C. Moskowitz Memorial Lecture on March 14, 1979, on the topic "Economic Pressures and the Future of the Arts." The lectures were established at New York University's School of Business and Public Administration "to contribute to the understanding of the function of business and its underlying disciplines in society by providing a public forum for the dissemination of enlightened business theories and practices." Schuman was joined as a lecturer by Roger L. Stevens, chairman of the board of trustees of the John F. Kennedy Center for the Performing Arts. In past years such distinguished public figures as Jacob Javits, Hubert Humphrey, George Shultz, and Paul Volcker had been invited to speak, so this was a particularly prominent venue through which Schuman could present his views.

Schuman entitled his talk "The Esthetic Imperative" and set out to reinforce and elaborate on a philosophical position that harked back to his Lincoln Center presidency:

> To state the matter succinctly, the balancing of financial intake and outgo—a balanced budget—does not necessarily mean that art is being well served. . . . The balancing of a budget does not insure that an artistic purpose has been realized. . . . A central theme of this paper is that there can be no dichotomy between economics and esthetics: they are interdependent.

The paper echoed the way he had approached his presidency of Lincoln Center, which had ended ten years earlier. He barreled ahead:

> The functioning of art in our contemporary American capitalistic structure is profit centered, rather than, if you will forgive the pun, prophet centered. In the performing arts quality can be both profitable and unprofitable. . . . For art, or for that matter, anything that doesn't pay its way, is a special problem in a profit oriented economy.

Schuman diverged from his principal argument by proclaiming that America's recent achievements in the arts had been extraordinary: "America . . . has emerged as an export nation in music, with its artists in demand throughout the entire world, and an import nation for education in the arts." He noted, however, that arts education in America had suffered considerably in the recent past and that the reasons for education in the arts in "heightening perception, in sharpening intellect and in strengthening conviction" had been undervalued in American educational circles.

It was when he addressed how he believed America was perceived by the world in 1979 that Schuman used some of his strongest language:

> The critics of American society claim that we are exclusively materialistic. . . . In our own country, as well as abroad, America is most often pictured as a land of violence, vulgarity, racism and urban decay. . . . All our debits are listed in the daily ledger of world

opinion but virtually none of our assets. Among these, the one I feel about most strongly is America's unquestionable identity as a land of the arts. . . .

This country, as I have noted, has proven that it is capable of producing and appreciating great art. It is, alas, also capable of neurotic self-effacement in this regard. It has a lingering penchant for self-criticism and self-doubt that in artistic matters concedes us to be the barbarous country cousins of our European relatives.

Here Schuman turned to a concept he had embraced at Lincoln Center, contending that when one considers art and money, "there is the unalterable fact that we must, in the performing arts, operate at a deficit." Schuman explained to his audience that it is the "technology of the performing arts" that creates these deficits (i.e., productions, performers' fees, etc.). He playfully argued that if the performing arts had kept pace with technological advancement in other fields, a "Schubert quartet should now be capable of being performed by three-quarters of one man. The symphony that 60 years ago required 100 in the orchestra would now only need 40 men. And the corps de ballet would be down to one dying swan." One sees behind the wit something quite prescient in Schuman's words, considering the frequent use in the twenty-first century of synthesizers to create instrumental sounds by one keyboardist that would ordinarily require an ensemble of forty players or more.

Schuman contended that the reason society must support the inefficient and expensive act of creating art is that it is "basic to our physical, spiritual and intellectual needs." And the artist must be supported as well.

Artistic standards, after all, must of necessity be elitist, or if you prefer aristocratic. Only the artist can create standards. . . . Committees do not write plays or paint pictures. The artist at work is engaged in the most aristocratic and exclusive of pursuits—and, one might add—one of the loneliest. In contrast, the democratic element, far from being lonely and exclusive, is inclusive and gregarious. . . . Our challenge and invitation is to make the arts available to the many without compromising the standards set by the few.

The remainder of the paper dwelled on a lengthy and detailed description of the structural and economic challenges of being a professional classical or "concert" composer such as Schuman himself. Finally, Schuman recycled verbatim his 1966 Princeton speech on the topic of the New Establishment, which so incensed John D. Rockefeller 3rd and which included "Schuman's Law and Postulates."

His concluding remarks, however, looked back to the powerful concepts introduced in the beginning:

> If we solve our economic problems [in the arts] by cowardice in esthetic and social doctrine, we have solved nothing at all.
>
> Success or failure in art cannot be measured in the plusses and minuses of ledgers, but in philosophy and mission, and in the clarity and conviction with which they are given life in our theaters, in our concert halls and in our classrooms.

Schuman, at the age of sixty-eight, had not lost any of his fire, nor had his idealism dimmed concerning the importance of the arts in American society. His talk reiterated the need for elitism, or even aristocracy, to be part of the fabric of the American arts scene, as he saw it, reflecting his sense of entitlement as someone who was above the fray in all his endeavors. It was this perceived condescension and adherence to exclusivity that made Schuman both resented and revered in the profession he helped to form.

In testimony before Congress in 1981, Schuman echoed the major theme of his NYU talk. Speaking out passionately before the House Interim Appropriations Subcommittee against cutting federal funding to the arts, he dwelled on the need for elitism in art's producers and populism in its consumers:

> To decrease expenditures for the arts at the very moment when we see such an astonishing increase in public demand and participation goes against the very concept of democracy. Without government subsidy, the arts can be available only to the few. But the many have the right of exposure to the best of art if we are serious when we speak of equal opportunity. . . .
>
> Taking away any government support now from its present extremely modest, hard-won funding level will be a totally destructive act. It will sharpen not only our own, but the world perception of the official United States attitude toward the arts—*no priority*. Will the Congress itself accept the responsibility for

obstructing the continuity of America's emergence as a world leader in this exalted sphere of human endeavor?

In 1979 Schuman was invited by the New York Philharmonic to compose a work for solo French horn to be performed by their newly appointed principal hornist, Philip Myers. Entitled *Three Colloquies* for French horn and orchestra, it is divided into three movements—Rumination, Renewal, and Remembrance—played without pause. Schuman had used a solo horn in his doleful work *The Young Dead Soldiers,* and he continued his dark view of the instrument in his new work: "I knew that it was not a concerto I would compose, for my goal was not a priori to exploit all the technical resources of the instrument as a display piece. Rather, I hoped to create music which required a solo French horn to realize its intentions."

What Schuman produced was a work that did not embrace the usual attributes of the French horn, but rather created a solo line that asked for frequent trills, glissandi, large melodic leaps, and frequent shifts from stopped to open horn, providing a less than gratifying role for the soloist. Most of the work is introspective in character, reflecting in part the titles of the three movements. Certainly the heroic quality of the French horn heard in the concertos of Richard Strauss or the symphonies of Gustav Mahler is not heard here. The beauty and complexity of Schuman's earlier and extraordinary *In Sweet Music* is also lacking.

Schuman's next work, *Time to the Old,* was a composition for voice and piano dedicated to Rosalind Rees, who had premiered Schuman's *Young Dead Soldiers* and had sung Merry in *Casey at the Bat* at the special Schuman program in Washington, D.C., in April 1976. It used the poetry of Archibald MacLeish, who also provided the text for *The Young Dead Soldiers.*

Schuman showed a true affinity for and understanding of MacLeish's poetry and suggested in 1977 that they collaborate on a song cycle that could be made, he wrote, "from Conway Burying Ground, The Old Gray Couple, both I and II, and possibly one or two others, such as Dozing on the Lawn. . . . For example, in The Old Gray Couple, II, I am not clear yet in my mind how to handle the She/He antiphonal effect since we cannot sing each time She and He. . . . My tentative title for the song cycle is MacLeish."

MacLeish responded quickly in a handwritten letter, first commenting on recent reviews of *The Young Dead Soldiers*: "Marvellous the difference in critical vocabularies between music and letters. In letters 'magnificent' means 'not too bad': in music 'not too bad' means 'magnificent'. Once that simple fact of life is recognized everything makes sense." Turning to the matter at hand, MacLeish then wrote, "I think a setting of some of the late poems, done by you, would be wonderful if you were moved to undertake it. The theme of most of them is old age, or the losses of old age."

In February 1978 Schuman wrote MacLeish that the work was going slowly. That was a bit of an understatement: in November 1979 Schuman wrote to the poet, "I am still with the songs and hope that my settings will do justice to your magnificent words. I am using three in the following order: Dozing on the Lawn, Conway Burying Ground and The Old Grey [sic] Couple (1). This three-song set is to be performed as a unit without pause between songs." In the final published version, the order of the songs was reversed, starting with "The Old Gray Couple."

The delay in writing the songs was a curious one. The work was not commissioned, however, so no deadline had been established. But Schuman didn't have many commissions before him. *In Sweet Music* was completed in January 1978 and the *Three Colloquies*, close to two years later, in September 1979. So he may have been experiencing a rare case of writer's block. The work was eventually completed in late December 1979, with the original title discarded in favor of *Time to the Old*, with the enthusiastic support of the poet.

The three poems Schuman chose for the cycle were telling ones, likely reflecting the composer's mood as he moved toward his seventieth year. "The Old Gray Couple" tells the story of a couple at the end of their lives:

Everything they know they know together— . . .
their deaths they think of in the nights alone.

The second poem, "Conway Burying Ground," talks of a cemetery and of time passing:

They set up stones to show where time has ended . . .
Only the old know time: they feel it flow
like water through their fingers when the light
ebbs from the pasture and they wade in night.
It frightens them.
Time to the old is world, is will,

turning world, unswerving will,
interval

until

And the third poem, "Dozing on the Lawn," talks of coming death:

I fall asleep these days too easily— . . .
. . . It was dark in the dream where I was laid:
It is dark in the earth where I will lie.

The mood of the song cycle is unrelentingly somber, not unlike that of *The Young Dead Soldiers*. The designated tempi of the three songs are quite slow, and the rolled chords in the piano impart a certain eerie quality to the work, which presents a continuous view of lives at the end of their time. Perhaps the poet's view of the profound inevitability of death was too much for Schuman to overcome as he thought of his own mortality. The work was premiered by Rosalind Rees, soprano, and Thomas Muraco, piano, on May 19, 1980.

As Schuman approached his seventieth year in 1980, the intensity of musical creativity he had enjoyed since the mid-1930s began to dissipate. With the exception of his 1983 work for a cappella mixed chorus entitled *Perceptions*, Schuman produced no memorable work in the 1980s until 1986, when his "American Cantata" *On Freedom's Ground* was premiered. However, that is not to say that he had stopped composing. Between 1980 and 1982 Schuman produced three versions of compositions based on an original hymn that he had composed in 1957 on the Langston Hughes poem "The Lord Has a Child." *American Hymn: Variations on an Original Melody* for concert band, commissioned by the American Bandmasters Association and the United States Air Force Band for the fiftieth anniversary of the American Bandmasters Association, was premiered on March 5, 1980, by the United States Marine Band; *American Hymn* for brass quintet was premiered by the American Brass Quintet in New York City on March 30, 1981; and finally, *American Hymn: Orchestral Variations on an Original Melody*, commissioned by the Saint Louis Symphony Orchestra for its centennial celebration, was premiered by that orchestra, Leonard Slatkin conducting, on September 24, 1982.

The version for brass quintet had a curious performance history. In its earliest form, which was eventually withdrawn, it was premiered, under the title *Three Pieces for Five Brasses*, at the Conference on Contemporary Music of the Aspen Music Festival on August 4, 1980, by the American Brass Quintet (ABQ).

The movements were "Ladies and Gentlemen!," "The Lord Has a Child," and "Look Before You Leap!" The revised version premiered by the ABQ in 1981 was viewed as impractical to perform because Schuman had all five brass instruments playing continually throughout the composition. Without any rest for the players, the quintet was simply too physically taxing to program, according to Raymond Mase, senior trumpet of the American Brass Quintet. Subsequently a double brass quintet version was arranged by the ABQ trumpeter Kevin Cobb and premiered at the Aspen Music Festival in the summer of 2000.

The orchestral version of *American Hymn* is by far the longest at about twenty-five minutes. The work consists of an introduction and six variations, played without pause. It is for the most part a somber piece that simply lacks the imagination, rhythmic energy, and pathos typical of Schuman's earlier work. The long, elaborate Schumanesque melodies are there, but they never reach the complex textures and intricacies of prior compositions. The fourth section is based almost entirely on repeated eighth-note patterns throughout the orchestra that never seem to come to a logical conclusion. Even the orchestration is surprisingly colorless. The drive to the conclusion, a Schuman hallmark, offers no engaging harmonizations, aimlessly resolving on an F major chord. The music seems the product of a diminished man. Schuman was probably feeling the effects of his heart disease; he would undergo heart bypass surgery in 1983.

Also included in Schuman's compositions of this period are the 1981 reworking of his score for *Night Journey*, now subtitled *Choreographic Poem for Fifteen Instruments*; *Esses* (1982), a charming twelve-minute work for a cappella mixed chorus on words that begin with the letter "s" (the last movement, "Singaling," includes the text "Saratoga, Seattle, Savannah, Susquehanna, Sebago, Sierra, Santiago, Santa Barbara, Salt Lake City, . . ."); *Dances* (1985; revised in 1986), a light work for woodwind quintet and percussion made up of various dances, from a jig to a polka to the Charleston, that would be used as the basis for the fourth movement of *On Freedom's Ground* of 1986 and was premiered at a special celebration honoring Schuman by the Chamber Music Society of Lincoln Center on October 1, 1985; and an adaptation of "When Jesus Wept" from the second movement of the *New England Triptych* for pipe organ, realized by Samuel Adler.

See the appendix for further discussion of *Night Journey: Choreographic Poem for Fifteen Instruments*.

Another work of this period, *Perceptions*, was commissioned by the National Endowment for the Arts for a consortium of chamber choirs led by the Gregg Smith Singers, a favorite choral ensemble of Schuman's. The work, for mixed a cappella chorus, is based on eight poems by Walt Whitman. Although it is only about twelve and a half minutes long, Schuman weaves an intense aural texture that gives the work more energy and imagination than his contemporaneous instrumental works. All of the movements, with the exception of the last, "To You," are written for the most part in rhythmic unison for the four voice types and reflect the character of the text. The first movement, "Thought," has the chorus holding long notes on one syllable, initially to great effect, but then the ensemble curtly ends the section on the quickly sung words "as if it harm'd me." The next two movements, "Beautiful Women" and "To Old Age," are sung without pause, so that the meaning of the first poem's "the old are more beautiful than the young" segues seamlessly to thoughts of death, including some masterful harmonic movement on the last word, "sea," in "To Old Age." The fourth movement, "Each of Us," contains some of the harmonic flavor heard in the previous movement. However, where the third movement ends on a crescendo to a triple forte, the fourth concludes with a wondrous triple piano, each voice slowly filling in the pitches to create a B major triad. In the final sixteen measures Schuman sets the line "Each of us here as divinely as any is here" with great sensitivity.

The fifth movement, "To the States," marked "With conviction and force," is only for men's voices, repeating with tension the words "resist much, obey little"; the sixth, "A Farm Picture," is for female voices and is marked "Tranquillo." The penultimate seventh movement, "Whoever You Are," is perhaps the most compelling of all, utilizing a distinctive triplet figure throughout to give motion to the words, "Whoever you are!" Schuman marks the second half of the movement "expansively" and brings out a fresh and full-voiced sound from the ensemble. The final movement, "To You," is scored for soprano solo and chorus. This is the most melodically and harmonically challenging movement of the piece, and in it the soprano solo is provided with sonic underpinning from a humming chorus.

The work was premiered at a concert in Greenwich, Connecticut, on January 9, 1983, with the Gregg Smith Singers conducted by Gregg Smith, but it was given a preview in New York City at the home of Mr. and Mrs. William R. Mayer on December 15, 1982. Overall, Schuman created an exceptional musical environment for Whitman's words and showed that when motivated by a project, the traditional Schuman musical imagination was still fresh and alive.

In his early seventies Schuman became intensively involved with a curious fixation related to a charitable contribution tax plan which he named "Advance Bequest Certified Deposit" (ABCD). Schuman described the ABCD "as a new instrumentality for voluntary support of not-for-profit institutions. . . . The aim of ABCD is to bring into being a new category of contributor. The economic incentives of ABCD will make it more attractive and feasible for people of middle income to contribute regularly to not-for-profit causes."

Schuman explained in extraordinary detail how the ABCD plan worked, although any opportunity for implementation hinged on Congress's passing enabling legislation to adjust the tax code to accommodate the plan. In many ways ABCD was similar to a charitable remainder trust, whereby the donor contributes an amount of money to a not-for-profit organization through a binding contract. The organization then pays the donor a set rate of return on the corpus of the gift until the donor dies, at which point the corpus is absorbed by the not-for-profit.

What was remarkable about the ABCD was not its novel approach to eleemosynary initiatives, but rather Schuman's determination and downright doggedness in trying to get an article about his plan published in a distinguished publication. From about September 1981 to January 1985, Schuman corresponded with numerous individuals in an attempt to get his idea accepted as a viable approach to philanthropy.

Included in this lengthy and distinguished list were Leonard Silk, Max Frankel, and Robert B. Semple Jr., of the *New York Times*; Lester Bernstein of *Newsweek*; Paul Hume of the *Washington Post*; Robert L. Bartley of the *Wall Street Journal*; and Henry C. Suhrke of the *Philanthropy Monthly*. In addition, Schuman communicated with David Rockefeller; Eli Evans, president of the Revson Foundation; John Casey, of the investment firm of Scudder, Stevens & Clark; high-level officials from the public relations firm Brakeley, John Price Jones; the Columbia Broadcasting System; TIAA-CREF; and the Independent Sector, a Washington, D.C.–based organization established to encourage not-for-profit initiatives. Schuman's good friend Martin E. Segal, who became Lincoln Center's chairman in the 1980s, often acted as the go-between in trying to move ABCD forward by referring Schuman to more and more knowledgeable sources or publication options. The most patient player in this four-year drama was a Washington attorney by the name of Thomas A. Troyer, who received and graciously answered, at no fee, numerous inquisitive letters from Schuman on what turned out to be arcane interpretations of the federal tax code.

Why Schuman was so determined to have his plan adopted by Congress or at the very least to appear in a national publication is intriguing. At no previous time had rejection come in such consistent waves. *Newsweek*'s editor, Lester Bernstein, wrote to Schuman that "your idea for tax legislation is so complex and technical that I doubt we could tempt many readers to venture very far into the piece," adding that he had asked other editors to read it "but, like me, they have great difficulty in penetrating it." His Washington lawyer correspondent Tom Troyer wrote, "I must confess to a sense that, though the proposal is an imaginative one, it simply is not finally going anywhere." The deputy editorial-page editor of the *Washington Post* wrote to Schuman that he'd be happy to consider a piece from the composer, "but it should be a piece from a man of the arts informing the political community of your crisis. . . . Your piece sounds as though it came from an accountant."

Amazingly, Schuman persevered in his quixotic quest even after undergoing cardiac bypass surgery. In his letters he maintained his sunny view of the situation after numerous rejections, writing to potential publishers, "My final version has passed muster on all technical counts," and "It is now time, I am advised, to publish my plan, and your distinguished publication has been suggested to me as the appropriate medium."

Schuman ultimately prevailed when his plan was printed in *Philanthropy Monthly* in May 1983, and he sent offprints to some of the publications that had originally rejected his work. His friend Leonard Feist wrote that he was

> deeply impressed to have a friend who has contributed to *The Philanthropy Monthly*. I have friends . . . who have written for The Animal Husbandry Quarterly Review, The Journal of the American Acne Foundation [and] . . . Creak, the Journal of Geriatrics, but never anything as high-minded . . . as the aforementioned . . . Philanthropy Review.

Clearly, Feist was one of the few actors in this lengthy drama who could see the humor in Schuman's quest to make ABCD a reality. Over the next eighteen months Schuman continued to attempt to get his idea reviewed by Congress, telling Charles T. Clotfelter, Duke University's vice provost and a professor of public policy studies and economics, in a letter of January 1985, "I have been encouraged by a number of leading professionals who think my proposal has merit," but finally admitting that "obviously in the present climate of tax reform there seems little chance of its being adopted." After amazing determination and effort, resulting in a voluminous correspondence, by 1985 Schuman finally admitted defeat on a plan that he contended was as simple as ABCD.

In his later years, until around the time of his death in 1992, Schuman was involved with varying degrees of intensity in several other board memberships: founding director of the Charles Ives Society, chairman of the BMI Awards, a member of the boards of the Koussevitzky Foundation and National Educational Television, and treasurer of the American Academy and Institute of Arts and Letters. It was through his leadership role in the American Academy that a poignant request for money came from his fellow composer, David Diamond. Diamond had decided in 1982 to take a year off from his teaching responsibilities at Juilliard to orchestrate a long-evolving opera—which, in fact, was never performed—and he needed funds to replace his lost compensation from the school, for Juilliard did not have paid sabbaticals.

Diamond advised Schuman that in order to survive, he would have to sell his beloved Picasso and Tanguy etchings, which he had bought in Paris in 1938. In asking for $15,000 from the Academy, he wrote Schuman:

> Please avoid the group among the avant-garde and even [Jacob] Druckman who resent me strongly. . . . Some have suggested I sell my house [in Rochester, New York]. After one heart attack, with vascular problems I do not plan to die in an apartment or hole in NYC. I am selling much valued music and books. That is enough. Please whatever you do, keep the issue one of leave-of-absence to get the opera orchestrated and not poor little David without funds again which annoys Lenny [Bernstein]. . . . At 67 I must not beg. And never will.

A memo to Schuman's personal file dated March 16, 1982, states that Diamond was given a $2,500 grant from the Academy "and later called Diamond to so inform him. Diamond was appreciative, but, true to his usual form, said it was just a drop in the bucket."

Throughout his professional life Schuman advocated consistently for the recording of American music. For most of his career he lobbied successfully with orchestras and recording companies to produce recordings of his own work, but in his seventh decade he broadened his efforts for all American composers by spearheading the creation of the American Music Recording Institute (AMRI). Formed in 1982, it was funded by the Koussevitzky Music Foundation and the National Endowment for the Arts.

As chairman of AMRI, Schuman issued a statement not only about the new organization, but about his view of America within the artistic continuum of the time:

> The true measure of a nation's achievements in music is not fully to be found in its wonderful performers and institutions of higher education but in the literature of music created by its own cit[i]zens. We have American music in abundance and our best composers take second place to no other national school. Yet, without recordings, the extraordinary development of our native creative musical art remains inaccessible both to present and succeeding generations.
>
> Unless we can glory in the achievements of our most accomplished composers, we are guilty, as we have been before, of that inverse chauvinism in which we think of ourselves somehow inferior to our European cousins. If we do not wish to preserve and disseminate our own art, perhaps we deserve the view, which some have of us, that we are a purely materialistic people. We know this is not true, yet even for the music of our best composers we set an example of shameful neglect and deny our listeners the opportunity made possible by modern technology.
>
> The American Music Recording Institute is dedicated to help preserve our great musical heritage. The seriousness of our concern and effort is shown in the strength of our Board of Directors and, after reviewing this proposal, I hope you will join with us in this most important endeavor.

AMRI was created to provide funds for the recording of American music never before released and to reissue recordings of the past that were judged to be of importance but were no longer available. It would be a service organization that would not itself produce or manufacture records. An early prospectus on the AMRI activities outlined an ambitious agenda in which thirty-four recordings would be issued in the first two years of operation, based on a budget of slightly over $1 million. In the summer of 1984 the directors of the new venture included the composers Jacob Druckman, Fred Lerdahl, Ezra Laderman, Gunther Schuller, and Schuman; an attorney, Ellis J. Freedman; the oboist and conductor Adrian Gnam; and the music commentator Martin Bookspan.

The ambitious plan found few significant backers. By February 1985 Schuman approached the author, who had recently become the president of Juilliard, to put AMRI under the school's institutional umbrella. Schuman saw the Juilliard American Music Recording Institute (JAMRI) as an independent entity within the school that would use Juilliard student performers to record the designated works.

One of the first JAMRI fund-raising efforts was a rather amusing meeting between the author, Schuman, and Gordon Getty, the philanthropist and part-time composer, in Getty's suite in the Sherry-Netherland Hotel on Fifth Avenue across from the Plaza Hotel. Schuman could not have been more charming to Getty, engaging him in discussions about orchestration and symphonic structure. Getty never seemed humbled by being in the presence of a composer of Schuman's stature and freely gave his own, often unorthodox, responses to various technical musical questions. Getty eventually gave the first grant in support of JAMRI's activities, but Schuman would always be bemused and amused by Getty's self-assurance in the realm of musical composition.

JAMRI eventually developed three multi-composer discs. The first included works by Copland, Schuman, and Sessions, and was produced by New World Records. After Schuman's death in 1992, JAMRI was dissolved, but Juilliard continues to produce commercially distributed recordings of American music.

In his later years, Schuman gave his greatest attention to two organizations he had helped found when he was Lincoln Center president: the Film Society of Lincoln Center and the Chamber Music Society of Lincoln Center. Schuman was not one to suffer fools gladly, nor was he reluctant to put his ideas forward. Often he would express his concerns with a philosophical bent, dwelling on issues of mission and long-term planning. In 1980 Schuman was disturbed as to how the Film Society board was polled in choosing the society's annual honoree, which in this case was the movie star Barbara Stanwyck. Finding the polling process "disorderly," he expressed even greater concern with "the direction the Film Society was taking with regard to the type of person being honored," asserting that "we should not lend our name to honoring any successful actor or actress just for the purpose of fundraising, and if we can't find someone who has truly made an outstanding contribution to film then perhaps we should change our sights." Schuman's close friend and the chairman of the Film Society, Martin E. Segal, was usually of like mind on governance issues at the Film Society, and therefore Schuman was not always the lead person in board-related concerns with this organization.

Such was not the case with the Chamber Music Society of Lincoln Center (CMS). Schuman had invested considerable psychological capital in the CMS from his days as Lincoln Center president and had essentially relinquished his presidency over the issue of when the CMS should become operational and how it should support itself. So it is no surprise that Schuman would focus his still considerable energies, as he approached the age of seventy-five in 1985, on what he believed was the best course of action for the organization.

By 1984 the CMS was experiencing artistic and financial challenges that reflected poorly on the entire organization. Andrew Porter, writing in the New Yorker, had disparagingly referred to the CMS in a review as the "Sight-Reading Society of Lincoln Center," complaining that the chamber concerts "have seldom in my experience maintained a consistently high level. . . . On the whole, the fare has been agreeable and unexacting, offered to an unexigent audience by expert players functioning at reduced voltage."

The CMS was led at the time by Charles Wadsworth as artistic director and Joanne Cossa as executive director. Wadsworth had been placed in his artistic directorship by Schuman just before he left the Lincoln Center presidency in late 1968. Schuman clearly felt an intense responsibility to ensure that the CMS continued to flourish as a presenting organization, based on the precepts he had created with the support of Alice Tully and others in the mid-1960s.

Therefore Schuman, as the CMS's vice chairman, felt enfranchised on September 19, 1983, to write a candid and often scathing memorandum to the CMS's president, Henry S. Ziegler, and two other board members, Sally Ganz and Isaac Shapiro (a board vice president), stating that he had no problem having Wadsworth and Cossa also see the document. This document was curiously reminiscent of the tone and intent of Schuman's memo to the Naumburg Foundation board of 1969, in which he was severely critical of Peter Mennin. Schuman began with typical forthrightness by stating that "my concern with the CMS is centered in the gradual but unmistakable shift from the original concepts which gave birth to the Society."

Schuman briefly reviewed the basic tenets of the CMS, pointing out that the organization was to serve the art of chamber music as symphony orchestras served their specific repertoire, and that a wide range of repertoire would be performed, with special attention paid to American music of the past and present. Although he admitted that early on this mission was addressed adequately, Schuman lamented that "one must observe the distance we have wandered in certain fundamental respects," citing the large number of guest artists who had been brought in by the CMS, therefore abrogating, in Schuman's view, the artistically cohesive concept for the CMS that was based on a solid core of artists who would perform together on a regular basis, just as a world-class string quartet would do.

Schuman put the blame for the CMS's philosophical drift squarely on Wadsworth's shoulders: "Our Artistic Director should either be requested to carry out the Board's mandate or the Board itself will have to reconsider its position. We can't have a policy that is ignored." Schuman then slightly softened his approach by stating that "the strong criticism of his lacks is in no way intended to overlook his achievements." However, he soon returned to a highly critical tone, focusing on the fact that

> he [Wadsworth] seems unwilling to take the advice of others (such as his Advisory Committee on Contemporary Music, whose members inform me that they have received nothing but lip-service—an obvious truth when one examines the programming). . . . It is especially in the realm of American music that CMS is failing in its responsibility. . . . As far as founding principles, the Society now has Wadsworth's astonishing proposal for increasing the resident artists from 14 to 21 or 22. This move would be disastrous and would exacerbate all our present problems. . . . In fact, Artist Members in such profusion would preclude the "repertory company" concept, and CMS would in effect become a booker of artists.

Schuman went on to deprecate the reasons for needing to engage so many "artists of the Society," characterizing Wadsworth's and Cossa's thinking as a "litany of whines."

Schuman then questioned Wadsworth's planning abilities:

> We have on more than one occasion asked Charles Wadsworth for future plans. We get none . . . there is no great itch present. We are not being led, inspired or, in short, being made to realize the grand opportunity for the future flowering of CMS.

In concluding, Schuman threw down the gauntlet before his board and Wadsworth:

> As the person who chose Charles Wadsworth in the first place, I am enormously grateful for his past achievements and for the general effectiveness of his public persona. Now, however, I am truly concerned whether he is the man to lead us into the future. . . . My hope is that the Directors will agree with me that we need a confrontation. If I use a provocative term, it is not through carelessness. Does our Board have the spine?

One would think that this blazing condemnation of Wadsworth and the course of the CMS under his leadership would have made Wadsworth start thinking about packing his bags, but that was not the case. Schuman finally sent a much softened version of the memorandum to the CMS board on January 26, 1984. In it he dwelled on the basic points of the September memo concerning repertoire, planning, and personnel, but his attack on Wadsworth was not so virulent. Schuman's ire had obviously been raised by Wadsworth's leadership; however, proverbial cooler heads came to prevail as time passed. A board resolution at the June 5, 1984, meeting established guidelines and goals relating to an emphasis on the engagement of resident artists and minimizing the use of outside artists, and stating that artist members could be added only with the consent of the board. Ultimately, Wadsworth stayed on as the CMS's artistic director until 1989. Yet Schuman's lifelong fire and self-righteousness had clearly not ebbed with the years.

The CMS put aside all hostilities and honored Schuman during his seventy-fifth year with a gala concert and dinner on October 1, 1985, at Alice Tully Hall. Hosted by Wadsworth, the all-Schuman program featured mostly lighter fare, including his *Quartettino for Four Bassoons* (1939); *XXV Opera Snatches* (1979) in a first performance of the flute version; *Time to the Old* (1980), a three-song set on words of Archibald MacLeish; and the world premiere of *Dances*, a work for woodwind quintet and percussion that was completed on August 12, 1985, and was based on various nineteenth- and twentieth-century tunes such as reels, jigs and the Charleston. Wrote Schuman: "All the tunes are treated freely, often in a manner far removed from their original habitat. The *Finale* recalls the *Dances* through juxtapositions and alterations which lead to a brief coda." He would use his *Dances* one more time in what would be a significant work for the aging composer.

CHAPTER 15

Your Devoted Icarus

Schuman wrote in a 1979 letter, "I have just completed my tenth year without an overriding and demanding administrative post. . . . This has been one of the richest and most rewarding decades of my professional life." As is often the case with individuals who exhibit excellence and who live long lives, Schuman's later years included many awards that celebrated his legacy and his exceptional vision. He remarked whimsically:

> I've received many honors and awards, and in the last decade [1980s], they seem to have come more frequently. I suppose that has to do with reaching elder statesman age. When I was elected to the American Academy of Arts and Letters, I recognized it was partly a reward for reasonable health: If you're around long enough, they have to do something.

In total, Schuman received twenty-seven honorary degrees, including an honorary doctorate from the Juilliard School in 1987, the first year that the School ever conferred honorary degrees. Schuman had advised the author not to become enmeshed in the business of conferring honorary degrees at Juilliard because so many accomplished alumni would feel snubbed when they were not chosen. Juilliard went ahead anyway, and Schuman was joined in the first year by Martha Hill, founder of the School's dance division; John Houseman, co-founder of Juilliard's drama division; Blanchette Hooker Rockefeller, Juilliard trustee and the widow of John D. Rockefeller 3rd; the soprano Leontyne Price; and the violinist Itzhak Perlman. Schuman was the commencement speaker. Bill and Frankie had started the charming tradition, many years earlier, of sewing together the various doctoral hoods that came along with the degrees, creating a multicolored quilt that eventually grew large enough to drape over a couch.

Schuman's non-academic awards in his later life included being named the first recipient of, appropriately, the William Schuman Award. Created by

Columbia University in 1981, the award celebrated the lifetime achievement of an American composer and came with a $50,000 prize. The award, to be granted approximately every two years, was established through a gift of $250,000 from the Bydale Foundation, an organization created by Schuman's good friend James P. Warburg.

In 1985 Schuman was the recipient of a Pulitzer Prize Special Citation "for more than half a century of contribution to American music as composer and educational leader"; the first annual Alfred I. du Pont Award for Outstanding American Composers and Conductors; and the Gold Baton Award from the American Symphony Orchestra League. However, the honor Schuman treasured most had been bestowed on him three years earlier, in May 1982, when he received the prestigious Gold Medal from the American Academy and Institute of Arts and Letters. He was one of only fifty members of the academy. The presenter was Schuman's old and now distinguished friend, Leonard Bernstein. Bernstein was in particularly articulate form and in making his presentation borrowed from Greek mythology and Shakespeare. Beginning with Falstaff's so-called Honors Speech from *Henry IV, Part I*, Bernstein queried, "What is honor? . . . Air. . . . who hath it? He who died o' Wednesday. . . . therefore I'll none of it." This was followed by a level of hyperbole rarely heard in any award ceremony, with Bernstein declaring that Schuman

is an incarnation of honor, both personal and public. He is an intersection of the coordinates music and humanity, of pragmatic reason and high art. . . . He exists on a loftier level than us mere mortals. . . . He is my living model of Icarus; he flies joyous and confident into the sun, and for over four decades, with each beat of his wings, has been turning my recurrent pessimism into an almost Panglossian optimism. . . . For Bill, being Icarus, is also the son of Daedalus, to a degree James Joyce himself might well envy. . . . Thank you, Bill, for so consistently re-kindling in us the sense of hope, of faith and of future. Take this extremely valuable gold medallion, attach it to the side of your flying Pontiac [Bernstein and Schuman had first met in a rented Pontiac that Schuman drove to Symphony Hall in Boston for a rehearsal of his Second Symphony] (which will entitle you to be a very special and prosperous taxi-driver) and take us all flying with you, for many golden years to come.

Schuman responded to this glorious encomium with a rare handwritten note to Bernstein:

> Our relationship is for me absolutely special—unlike any other—a loving friend and artist champion all in one. Your consistent belief in me and my work is a lifetime blessing. Until the sun has its way, your devoted Icarus.

Schuman also returned the favor by being the presenter when Bernstein was awarded the same Gold Medal in Music in 1985. Although not able or willing to match the rhetorical heights of his friend, Schuman nonetheless was his articulate self:

> *West Side Story* could have been composed only by a populist rooted in the classical traditions of his art—and a *Candide*, only by a classicist with the voice of a populist . . . [his music] brilliantly combine[s] those often disparate worlds [of opera, symphony, and Broadway] into a single cohesive language.

An exchange of letters between Bernstein and Schuman encapsulates the playful friendship they enjoyed. In 1967 Bernstein sent a handwritten note to Schuman apologizing for his assistant's mistake in not sending a telegram of congratulations to be read at an awards ceremony for Schuman: "It's bad enough I couldn't be there myself to cheer you, but that I was unrepresented even by the printed word is unbearable. Forgive, forget, and fuck-all. I love you, always have, always will. Lenny"

Schuman responded a week later:

> Dear Lenny,
>   The whole dinner was worth it just to get your marvellous letter. It is being framed and will soon be placed in Macy's window. The reason: My mother told me never to write anything in a letter that couldn't be placed in Macy's window.
> Always in warm friendship.
> Yours,
> William Schuman

Of all the great artists and personalities whom Schuman knew during his lifetime, it was Bernstein and Martha Graham for whom he had the greatest respect and admiration. Not even Schuman's close friend Aaron Copland received the praise that Schuman reserved for Bernstein and Graham. Schuman once wrote about Graham:

> She has created an original vocabulary of dance movement that has added a new dimension to the expressivity of the choreographic art. . . . She has achieved a position which is not adequately to be described solely as one of pre-eminence in her field. For whether we speak of the world of Dance, of Music, of Literature, or of the Graphic Arts, Martha Graham is one of the greatest artists America has ever produced.

Schuman had little patience for composers whom he found dogmatic and doctrinaire. He had particular disdain for Pierre Boulez, the French intellectual, composer, and conductor. Discussing the desire of composers to influence others, Schuman said:

> But if you talk about influence, who is there who wishes to influence more than Boulez? He wishes to influence absolutely through the dictatorial method of his own convictions. He absolutely believes in what he believes and without the slightest trace of doubt. Now, that's fine, but I don't see people flocking to follow him as a composer, and if they do, in my judgment they won't for very long.

On the other hand, Schuman was a great admirer of the music of Paul Hindemith: "I think Hindemith is terribly underrated. I think he is a marvelous composer. . . . I think Mathis der Maler, the opera as well as the symphonic suite, is one of the towering achievements of this century."
Schuman once listed for an interviewer his most admired composers:

> If I had to name favorites, I would pick out Lassus and Bach, and would underline Beethoven. I'd minimize Wagner and Liszt, but would include Berlioz, Ravel, and Debussy for orchestration. I'm a great Tchaikovsky fan. And I'm still crazy about the Americans of my youth, Harris and Copland particularly.

In his later years Schuman was circumspect regarding his views on minimalist music, quipping to an interviewer, "'I would be a very difficult person to hypnotize' and 'I like music of development.' As for serialism, he recognizes its importance . . . but believes that 'those who have used it as a religion have failed.'"

In the non-musical realm, of special importance to Schuman was the creation of an oil painting commemorating his presidency of Juilliard. By 1987 the Juilliard boardroom had paintings of Frank Damrosch and Peter Mennin and a bust of John Erskine, but nothing of Schuman.*

Frankie and Bill requested of the author that the great American portrait artist Aaron Shikler paint the portrait. After conferring with Juilliard's director of finance, the author called Shikler, who knew and admired Schuman and was enthusiastic to paint "someone of substance," as he said. When the subject of the fee was brought up, Shikler gave a figure of $75,000, $65,000 more than Juilliard budgeted for the painting. Shikler was understanding and said that he would try to recommend a younger, less expensive artist.

Only fifteen minutes after the conclusion of the telephone call, Shikler called the author and asked, "Well, how much do you have for the portrait?" When the embarrassingly low fee of $10,000 was meekly proposed, there was a long silence and then an excited response from Shikler: he would paint the portrait without a detailed background and would therefore undertake the commission.

The painting was unveiled on February 11, 1987, at a luncheon in the Juilliard boardroom attended by trustees, faculty, family, and friends. The portrait was considered remarkable by all for capturing Schuman's likeness and his enthusiastic personality, shown particularly in Shikler's depiction of the subject's eyes. Shikler's detailed treatment of Schuman's hands was also viewed as exceptional.

During a quiet moment before the unveiling, the author asked Shikler why he had signed his painting "Aaron Annie Shikler." The artist explained that Annie was the name of his mother—the person who most encouraged him to be an artist. All of his paintings have this distinctive signature in honor of his mother's faith in him.

Another representation of Schuman would eventually be placed in Alice Tully Hall. Soon after Schuman's death, his memory was honored by the

---

* The portrait of Frank Damrosch (founder and director of the Institute of Musical Art in 1905) is by Frederick S. Beaumont; the portrait of Peter Mennin (president, 1962–83) is by Aubrey C. Davidson-Houston; and the bust of John Erskine (president, 1928–37) is by Jo Davidson. There is no portrait of Ernest Hutcheson (president, 1937–45).

Chamber Music Society of Lincoln Center with a brass bas-relief of his visage created by the American sculptor, Leonard Baskin. It was placed in Alice Tully Hall, facing east, just around the corner from a full-length oil painting of Tully.

The grandest and certainly most public award that Schuman received in his later life (with the National Medal of Arts running a close second in 1987) was his 1989 Kennedy Center Honor "for an extraordinary lifetime of contributions to American culture through the performing arts." The Kennedy Center Honors had become familiar to the American public through the gala taped television broadcast every Christmas season that excerpted the evening's festivities, usually dwelling on those recipients who were well-known through their involvement in movies or pop music. Schuman recalled receiving a newspaper clipping about the broadcast, which, he said, reported that

> "most of these people are unknown. Who knows Claudette Colbert? As for Schuman, nobody's ever heard of him." Somebody thought I was the composer of the music for *Dragnet*; that was Walter Schumann. . . . The Kennedy Center Award is set up for people in the performing arts. For the most part, the people chosen have been performers, not creators. . . . When they chose me it must have been a very difficult thing for them to do. They were quite worried about what music they could perform on the show. . . . They got me down from a three-movement work (*New England Triptych*) to a two-movement work [the first and third movements], from which one movement was cut out by the time it got on the air [so that only the third movement was broadcast].

The honorees in 1987, in addition to Schuman and Claudette Colbert, were Mary Martin, Alexandra Danilova, and Harry Belafonte. "Only in America could you mix all these things," Schuman remarked. He enjoyed the elaborate celebratory weekend, which included a black-tie dinner on Saturday evening at the State Department, hosted by Gregory Peck. Leontyne Price gave the dinner toast in Schuman's honor, singing an operatic version of "For He's a Jolly Good Fellow," "which brought down the house." Schuman was surrounded by family and close friends, including

Andie's fifteen-year-old son, Josh, who was in his first tuxedo and went from refusing wine with dinner on Friday to inquiring of his grandmother by the end of the weekend whether he should drink white or red.

Barbara Bush was the host at the White House on Sunday afternoon. Schuman found her quite charming, although he had little admiration for Marilyn Quayle, Vice President Dan Quayle's wife, who he thought was "difficult to talk to, and never initiated any conversation at all." The official presentation and gala took place in the Kennedy Center Opera House on December 3, 1989. Van Cliburn spoke about Schuman in an amusingly awkward analysis of the hemispheres of the brain, but the actress Kelly McGillis, a graduate of Juilliard's drama division, was brief and charming. Leonard Slatkin conducted the Juilliard Orchestra in the first and third movements of *New England Triptych* and spoke from the stage perhaps the most moving words of the evening for Schuman. As Schuman recalled,

> [Slatkin] said twenty or twenty-five years ago, when he made his conducting debut, he performed this work called *New England Triptych* and that the orchestra he conducted then consisted mostly of Juilliard students who could be considered my [Schuman's] children. On this occasion, he said, they were all my grandchildren, who had come to play. They were absolutely marvelous.

A concluding dinner was held in the entire length of the Kennedy Center, reminding Schuman of prints of the Congress of Vienna. The members of the Juilliard Orchestra, all of whom had been invited, surrounded Schuman and asked for his autograph during dinner.

Schuman summed up the celebration, the last great honor that he would experience: "It feels great to be honored. To have somebody pat you on the back is a lovely thing to have happen. The only problem with it is that it's so pleasant that you could easily choose it as a way of life and begin to believe what was said, instead of getting back to work, which is what you have to do."

In 1984 Schuman was approached by Albert K. (Nick) Webster, executive vice president and managing director of the New York Philharmonic, to compose a work for the commemoration of the Statue of Liberty Centennial in 1986, the fourth commission presented to Schuman by the New York

Philharmonic.* The composer expressed a desire to write a choral work with orchestra; he had wanted to write such a work for the American bicentennial in 1976, but it was never realized. Schuman also suggested that it be a consortium commission, based on the rationale that it would produce more money for the composer and less cost for each of the commissioning organizations, and the work would have several guaranteed performances around the country. Webster agreed to the idea and also said that he would find the consortium participants.

Several days later Webster called Schuman to ask if he knew anything about the Crane School of Music of the State University of New York at Potsdam in upstate New York. Schuman was aware of the strong choral tradition at Potsdam. By coincidence, the School would be celebrating its one hundredth anniversary in 1986. Ultimately the consortium consisted of the New York Philharmonic in association with the Crane School of Music, the Albany Symphony Orchestra, the Atlanta Symphony Orchestra, the Chicago Symphony Orchestra, the National Symphony Orchestra, the Oregon Symphony, the Pittsburgh Symphony Orchestra, and the St. Louis Symphony Orchestra, with the New York Philharmonic and the Crane School having the honor of the premiere. The total commission to Schuman was $75,000; obviously Schuman's entrepreneurial skills were still in fine shape. In a very personal gesture, the work was dedicated "to my family: my wife, son, daughter, grandson, sister, and to the memory of my parents and brother." The dedication is particularly significant because it marks the first time Schuman publicly acknowledged the existence of his brother, Robert.

In finding a source for the text, Schuman focused on the work of the distinguished poet, teacher, and French translator Richard Wilbur, who would eventually become the poet laureate of the United States from 1987 to 1988. Schuman approached Wilbur initially through a phone call, but then sent a highly detailed and persuasive letter to the poet in February 1984 that had many of the characteristics of letters Schuman had received from Antony Tudor and Martha Graham in the second half of the 1940s during the development of their ballets. This began an exceptional correspondence between two older artists (Wilbur was sixty-three in 1984 and Schuman was about to turn seventy-four) that would show the perceptive views of both men regarding the relationship of verse to music.

* The other three commissions were the Eighth Symphony (1962), *To Thee Old Cause* (1968), and *Three Colloquies for French Horn and Orchestra* (1980).

Schuman began the letter by referring to the creation of *Judith* with Martha Graham in 1949–50 and the give-and-take between the composer and choreographer. He then explained that the new work would be based on the centennial of the Statue of Liberty. Rejecting all the potential disasters inherent in the "utter banality in trying to sing about 'Liberty's torch,'" Schuman then explained that "despite the dangers of the hortatory, that there was no subject of essential nobility that could not be treated handsomely by a poet of your accomplishments and distinction." Resurrecting the tone of Antony Tudor, Schuman continued, "I hope that you can supply words that will create in me a burning desire to set them in a convincing manner for the panoply of singers and players that will be at our disposal," adding that it was "the essence of the meaning of the Statue and of immigration that matters, rather than any specific facts which might well resist suitable treatment." Sketching the basic structure of the work, which initially was viewed in four sections but ultimately evolved to five, Schuman referred to MacLeish's "The Young Dead Soldiers" as the type of text that would be appropriate for the third section, which he saw as the

> centerpiece of the work and is the one that I described to you as a Requiescat [eventually titled "Like a Great Statue"]. . . . What I would hope you could supply for this movement would be the most moving lines imaginable, relating to all the moments of despair which the subject matter suggests and yet somehow leads to a serene ending.

After suggesting that Emma Lazarus's "Give me your tired, your poor" could be sung in several languages if it would not be too "corny," Schuman wrote, still channeling Tudor, "Where does this leave you—probably much more confused than before I started! But it is your juices that I am counting on." Schuman even provided a postscript à la Tudor: "Take heart. My letters are usually very, very short!"

Wilbur responded two weeks later: "I am reeling a bit still from your suggestion that, instead of providing some closing lines for the Lady Liberty, I try my hand at making a text for the whole. One reason for reeling is that your suggestion is a great honor for me." Wilbur agreed to provide the entire text in this letter and even concurred with Schuman that a "multilingual treatment of 'Give me your tired, your poor' is . . . *not* a corny idea and might be very powerful," though the idea was eventually rejected by both poet and composer.

Schuman quickly confirmed the partnership, writing enthusiastically: "For reasons of intuition which, if I were up to date, I would call my gut reaction, I am absolutely convinced that your text will flow, that it will inspire me and that our offspring will flourish! There is nothing I can do at this end until I get your first page, for which I yearn without being anxious."

Wilbur sent the first fruits of his efforts to Schuman in April 1984—two stanzas—noting, "I have a calm ego and am not touchy. If you are discouraged by these drafts, don't hesitate to dissolve our partnership; or if you don't want to go so far just yet, do be downright about what doesn't please you." As it turned out, in the final work the initial texts were used almost in their entirety.

The interplay between composer and poet over the next year or so was a wonderful example of how two senior artists could use their experience and sophistication to develop a work of breadth and passion. Schuman, for example, extolled the virtues of the text but then questioned other directions of the poet:

Your thought of freedoms, shores, waves, gulls, et al. seems absolutely marvelous to me. In the first stanza I love your third line ["When Bedloe's Island had no English name"], but I will question for later on the use of proper names. It seems to me that the more we are down to earth in expository terms, the more difficult it will be for us to soar.

He ended, "Your letter makes me want to begin to work, and that feeling has been a long time in coming since the miserable last year with its health problems"—a reference to his coronary bypass surgery in 1983.

Over the course of 1984 Schuman made several decisions about the work, including a fourth movement that should be "light and swift, of a 3 to 4 minute duration (not many verses) [and eventually based on his chamber work *Dances* of 1985]. The word, 'Dance,' occurs to me. American ethnic groups have almost all kept their traditional dances. Is it worth a thought?" He also decided that the third movement would definitely not have a female solo, "but either a baritone or possibly—a fleeting thought—a narrator." In addition, the title of the work bounced from "Centennial: An American Cantata" to "The Wind Is With Us: An American Cantata" to the final title, *On Freedom's Ground: An American Cantata for Baritone, Chorus, and Orchestra.*

Wilbur conceived of the text as one poem in five sections, which corresponded to the movements of the work:

Back Then
Our Risen States
Like a Great Statue

Come Dance
Immigrants Still

It was a mixture of history:

> It was an English thought
> That there is no just government
> Unless by free consent,
> And in that English cause we fought.
> > (from "Our Risen States")

and laudatory verse:

> Where was the thought of freedom then?
> It came ashore within the minds of men.
> > (from "Back Then")

and a celebration of the diversity of America:

> Now in our lady's honor
> Come dance on freedom's ground,
> And do the waltz or polka,
> Whatever spins around.
> > (from "Come Dance")

The emotional heart of the work, which Schuman referred to earlier in its gestation as a Requiescat, is the third movement. Wilbur took Schuman's advice seriously about referring to "The Young Dead Soldiers." There is much in the movement which deals with the death of those whose reason for giving their lives in war is questioned by future generations. Also included are the human abuses that mar the country's history:

> Mourn for the dead who died for this country,
> Whose minds went dark at the edge of a field,
> In the muck of a trench, on the beachhead sand,
> In a blast amid ships, a burst in the air. . . .
> Grieve for the ways in which we betrayed them,
> How we robbed their graves of a reason to die:

The tribes pushed west, and the treaties broken,
The image of God on the auction block,
The immigrant scorned, and the striker beaten,
The vote denied to liberty's daughters.
            (from "Like a Great Statue")

Although Schuman's collaboration with Wilbur was an enjoyable and productive one, his own compositional process was hampered by a visual impairment caused by cataracts. He wrote to Wilbur in February 1985 in Cassis, France, where the poet was translating Racine's play *Phaedra*:

> It has been very difficult writing these days because I have no sight in my right eye at all. I asked the doctor if the operation could be postponed until I finished the work. I doubled my efforts which really meant I quadrupled them because of the handicap, and I can report that the work is completed. . . . I very much hope I can complete the first batch of proofreading by April 15, when I go into the hospital.

With the work completed, Schuman set about choosing the baritone soloist. He was specific in his requirements: "The last thing I want is an opera star. The singer must first of all have the ability to project the Wilbur text [in the third and fifth movements] with clarity and understanding. . . . A young John Reardon might describe what I have in mind." Therefore it is surprising that one of the best-known operatic baritones of the time, Sherrill Milnes, was chosen as the soloist. The work was premiered by the New York Philharmonic and the Crane Chorus, Zubin Mehta conducting, on October 28, 1986, one hundred years to the day after the Statue of Liberty was dedicated. The day before the premiere Wilbur, Mehta, and Schuman received honorary doctorates from the State University of New York at Potsdam at a special convocation in New York City coinciding with the culmination of the centennial.

The first performance was a bit disconcerting for Schuman. Mehta had returned from conducting in Israel just two days before the premiere and had needed to charter a plane to hear the chorus in Potsdam. The peripatetic maestro stayed for only about thirty or forty minutes, declaring to Schuman, "The chorus is fine, it needs twenty more men." Sherrill Milnes turned out to be the perfect soloist for the work, according to Schuman, and Mehta expressed his delight with the jauntiness of the fourth-movement waltz, especially once Schuman told him that the tune came from the "opera"

Schuman had written decades earlier with Frank Loesser on the life of Leonardo da Vinci.

On Freedom's Ground is an uneven work. Its central dramatic moment clearly arrives in the third movement ("Like a Great Statue"), as Schuman had planned. In fact, the clarity of the text for the baritone brings great strength to the overall musical content. Of interest is Schuman's somewhat abstract but nonetheless evident use of the melody from the Requiem chorus that ends *The Mighty Casey* in the work's first movement ("Back Then") and then periodically throughout the composition.

Schuman seemed to have been challenged by Wilbur's text, deciding to repeat several times the words "It was an English thought" in the second movement ("Our Risen States") for no evident dramatic reason. The effective and emotional third movement then segues into the ultra-light fourth movement ("Come Dance"), which jars the listener after the pathos of what had come before, breaking a meaningful and emotionally intense mood. As the last movement ("Immigrants Still") begins, the baritone solo returns as the chorus reinforces his line. At the end of the work the chorus brings the piece to an emotional height:

We are immigrants still, who travel in time,
Bound where the thought of America beckons;
But we hold our course, and the wind is with us.

Schuman takes the last phrase, "and the wind is with us," and has the baritone and chorus repeat the words while the orchestra moves forward in a gradual accelerando that culminates in the typical Schumanesque conclusion at the dynamic level of triple forte. One cannot help but feel that it is *On Freedom's Ground* that actually fulfilled Schuman's hope to write a work that would reflect the American dream, the kind of work he outlined in his "Project 1976" document. This view is substantiated by the handwritten postscript of a letter from Wilbur to Schuman by Wilbur's wife, Charlee, in 1987:

I can't imagine a more sensitive or faithful interpretation of Dick's text, but you have done so much more. The music is so full of both serious, witty and moving statements straight from your own American gut that, without question, it will stand as long as this country does as an expression of one man's dignity and loyalty.

Like other recent works of Schuman, *On Freedom's Ground* did not fare well with the *New York Times*'s reviewer, John Rockwell:

> Richard Wilbur, Mr. Schuman's poet, suggests in his text that Americans derived their idea of liberty from the English. Mr. Schuman's 40-minute score struck this writer as similarly English, akin to those grand, empty, ceremonial pieces with which English composers of this century have favored us. Most of the time, Mr. Schuman sets a massed chorus . . . to thick, tuneless proclamations. . . .
>
> The score is at its most successful in its instrumental interludes, especially the quiet patter of percussion at the end of the third part and the witty dance music at the outset of the fourth. But for most of the time, this is a work more noble in its patriotic intentions than its esthetic realization.

As uneven as the piece may be, the sense of passion for America and the pathos created by both text and music in remembering the struggles of immigrants who had arrived on America's shores since the erection of the Statue of Liberty in 1886 make *On Freedom's Ground* an affecting reflection of a composer's patriotism at the end of a rich and fulfilling life.

While creating the massive *On Freedom's Ground* Schuman continued to accept small commissions, including *Showcase: A Short Display for Orchestra*, commissioned by the Houston Symphony to commemorate the Texas Sesquicentennial. It premiered in Houston on September 26, 1986, but then had a life of its own, so to speak, with performances in San Francisco, Minneapolis, and Chicago in the early 1990s.

In August 1986 Schuman completed what seemed to be a simple assignment: a duo for clarinet and violin commissioned by an organization he knew well, the Walter W. Naumburg Foundation. The work was to be performed by the virtuoso clarinetist Charles Neidich, who was a Naumburg winner. The composition, *Awake Thou Wintry Earth*, was premiered in Alice Tully Hall on March 10, 1987, by Neidich and the distinguished violinist Curtis Macomber.

What might have been a perfunctory exercise on Schuman's part for such simple forces turned out to be a thoughtful work that would also influence the composition of his Fifth String Quartet, completed in August 1987. The duo was written in two movements. The first, "Reverie," according to the composer, "as the name suggests, is basically contemplative although there are some contrasting moments of a more animated nature. The two instruments wend their separate ways but always each complements the other."

In typical fashion, Schuman marks this movement "Tranquillo" at the very slow tempo of quarter note = c. 40. What is distinctive about this tempo is not only its exceedingly calm feeling but also the fact that the composer asks the clarinet to hold a low E for five full measures, allowing for a breath at the end of the third measure "only if necessary." Neidich's clarinet technique extended to circular breathing, so he met the challenge easily. Schuman occasionally adds some slow short flourishes, but for the most part the entire movement has a static quality.

The second movement, "Variations," is based on a seventeenth-century Dutch carol, "Awake Thou Wintry Earth," that Schuman had known since his Sarah Lawrence years. Wrote the composer: "The Variations are mostly continuous rather than sectional. In one way or another all the music derives from the carol melody, sometimes identifiably so and sometimes far removed from the simplicity of the original." Schuman uses harmonic and rhythmic variants to playfully and originally derive music from the Dutch melody, but he quietly ends the work at the slow tempo of quarter note = c. 52. He would also arrange this duo for flute and bassoon.

Schuman was inspired by this work—or, more precisely, the carol tune—when composing his fifth and last string quartet. This commission was realized by his good friend Martin E. Segal, who was then the head of the first New York International Festival of the Arts, a short-lived summer festival that began in 1988. The funding for the commission came from the Chase Manhattan Bank. It was premiered by the Orford Quartet at the 92nd Street YMHA on June 21, 1988.

Although Schuman's physical and creative energies were waning in 1987, he still had the wherewithal to compose a work of great complexity and emotional depth with his String Quartet No. 5. In it Schuman's lifelong feel for string writing is evident. Like the duo, the quartet is in two movements, and the second movement also uses the Dutch carol "Awake Thou Wintry Earth" as the theme. Although Schuman borrows generously from the second movement of the duo in writing the second movement of the Fifth String Quartet, the latter work is a tableau of many musical ideas not encountered in the work for clarinet and violin.

The composer marks the first movement of the quartet "Introduction—Monody—Coda." The wonderfully idiosyncratic writing for all four instruments adds intensity throughout this achingly slow movement. The monody is a solo violin melody, first presented stepwise but then becoming more expressive with the introduction of wider interval leaps. Schuman, in typical fashion, expertly juxtaposes a soulful cello line against rapid figures in the first violin, but the somber and emotionally intense coda slowly and calmly brings the movement to a conclusion on an E-flat major chord.

The second movement, "Variations—Epilogue," presents the familiar Dutch carol, with sections of the movement borrowing liberally from the duo. However, Schuman expands upon the theme in so many ways that one sees his original musical thoughts in the duo evolving to far more extended and complex treatments of the theme. The movement ends with a section marked "Epilogue," in which we hear a mix of impassioned forte chords and very slow evocative variants on the melody. Gratifyingly, Schuman, at the age of seventy-seven, was able to realize a masterful work that would easily stand comparison with his earlier compositions.

CHAPTER 16

Carols of Death

Given Schuman's deteriorating health and flagging mental energy, it seems remarkable that he would decide to tackle the composition of a new opera, but that is exactly what he did in 1987. A year earlier he had been pleased with a production of *The Mighty Casey* at Glimmerglass Opera in Cooperstown, New York, in a double bill with Puccini's comic opera *Gianni Schicchi*. Hearing and seeing *Casey* at the home of major league baseball's Hall of Fame was an exhilarating experience for the aging composer. Schuman had also contributed a one-minute fanfare for two trumpets and two trombones that was premiered on June 27, 1987, at the opening of Glimmerglass Opera's Alice Busch Opera Theater. Appropriately titled "Cooperstown Fanfare," it was subsequently played during future seasons of the opera company on an outdoor balcony of the theater to advise the audience that the opera was to begin and to call patrons back from intermission.

Schuman was proud of his baseball opera. Not only that, but from the time of its premiere in Hartford in 1953 he always believed it deserved more and better productions than had been accorded it. Another one-act opera would be able to fill out a complete evening for a producing company, providing a double bill with each work reinforcing the other. Therefore, when Glimmerglass Opera offered Schuman a commission, funded for $75,000 by the Eugene V. and Clare E. Thaw Charitable Trust, for a new one-act opera to be paired with *The Mighty Casey* in a new production, the composer readily accepted.

Earlier in his career Schuman had thought of topics that might evolve into operas, Dreiser's *An American Tragedy* being the most prominent. He had no ready ideas, however, for his new work until Frankie suggested that he look at Roald Dahl's short story "Taste," first published in the *New Yorker* in 1951. The story deals with a wager concerning the naming of an unidentified wine between two gentlemen of means. Schuman read the story and agreed with his wife that it would definitely work as an opera. But who would write the libretto?

Schuman first turned in April 1987 to his recent collaborator for *On Freedom's Ground*, Richard Wilbur, who that same month was named poet laureate of the United States. Wilbur responded:

"Taste" seems to me an amusing story which rather telegraphs its ending. My sense of what might adapt to music is not a keen one, but I *think* I see that this tale might make for a very light short opera . . . but I don't think I'm the one to do it, and in any case I am . . . very anxious at present to concentrate on recovering the habit of writing my own poems.

In the letter Wilbur recommended as an alternative John Hollander, a well-known poet and critic who over the years had collaborated with the composers Milton Babbitt, George Perle, and Hugo Weisgall.

Another potential librettist who was recommended to Schuman by mutual friends was the respected young poet J. D. (Sandy) McClatchy. He was invited to Schuman's home at 888 Park Avenue on April 20, 1987, to discuss the project, but in the course of their meeting the composer sprang a surprise on his potential collaborator. McClatchy recalled:

In a way that parallels the contest of wits at the center of the story ["Taste"], so too did Bill . . . announce that he'd already asked two other potential librettists to submit proposals, from which he would choose one to collaborate with. [Wilbur had already declined by this time. There is a letter in the New York Public Library Archives to Schuman on May 2, 1987, from the poet and translator Michael Bawtree that provides text for an aria for the female love interest in the story, Louise.] I was a little taken aback but could sympathize with his position, not wanting a pig in a poke.

McClatchy agreed to write the first scene of the opera, and by late May he had been chosen as Schuman's collaborator on what would turn out to be the composer's last original work.

While Schuman was writing his new opera, he also adapted his 1957 chorale *The Lord Has a Child*, with words by Langston Hughes, for brass quintet and chorus. Dedicated to Schuman's good friend and Greenwich neighbor Joan Warburg, widow of Juilliard's former chairman, James P. Warburg, and to the Greenwich Choral Society, directed by Richard Vogt, it was premiered on June 16, 1990, in Greenwich, Connecticut, to commemorate the 350th anniversary of the city's founding in 1640.

Although hobbled by a number of health problems from arthritis to spinal stenosis and the onset of Parkinson's disease, Schuman approached his work with McClatchy with the same intensity he had shown with Wilbur on the text of *On Freedom's Ground*, parsing words and challenging rhymes or story lines that the poet provided in numerous drafts of the libretto.

McClatchy kept a diary of his work with Schuman that was published in part in *Opera News* in 1994. At one point McClatchy recorded a conversation in which Schuman discussed the reasons for taking on the demanding project of composing an opera. Schuman said:

> Basically I've been a symphonist. But then when *The Mighty Casey* was done last summer [1986], I realized my love of writing for the stage again because it was the first time I ever heard it produced [properly]. I saw it was just wonderful with audiences . . . so when they [Glimmerglass Opera] asked me if I'd think of doing a companion piece I thought, "How wonderful." It has nothing to do with *Casey*. We're not trying to complement *Casey*. I didn't want to write another choral piece. I wanted to write for solo voices. . . . I love the collaborative process—it's less lonely!

The new work was *A Question of Taste*, a fifty-five-minute one-act opera with six singing roles. It was premiered on June 24, 1989, by Glimmerglass Opera in a double bill with *The Mighty Casey*. The story is a simple one: the setting is a small dinner party in a well-appointed New York brownstone in 1910 (not by coincidence the year of Schuman's birth). Mr. and Mrs. Schofield have invited a successful businessman and wine connoisseur, Phillisto Pratt, to dinner and to experience one of Mr. Schofield's most prized wines. The dinner will also be attended by the Schofield daughter, Louise, and her beau, Tom, and it will be overseen by the family's maid, Mrs. Hudson. Mr. Pratt clearly is interested primarily in Louise, not the cuisine, but Mr. Schofield attracts his attention by asking if he would like to participate in a wager to guess the name of the evening's prize wine. Mr. Pratt not only agrees to the wager but ups the ante by asking for Louise's hand in marriage if he wins, adding to the pot a check for half a million dollars that Louise may keep whether she marries Pratt or not.

Because Schofield believes that there is no possibility that Pratt can guess the name of the wine, he agrees to the wager, much to the chagrin of his wife and daughter, to say nothing of Tom. In an extended aria Pratt analyzes the wine in question, moving closer to the source of the bottle from Bordeaux to Médoc to Saint-Julien to a "fourth growth." Tension rises when he declares the wine a Château Talbot, only to retract his answer. Finally he decides on an 1875 Château Branaire-Ducru—the correct answer.

Fortunately, a *deus ex machina* of sorts arrives in the person of Mrs. Hudson, who points out that Mr. Pratt has cheated—he spied the wine in an upstairs room while ostensibly removing a stain created by a spilled aperitif. It turns out that Pratt had left his eyeglasses where the wine was stored. Mrs. Hudson triumphantly flaunts the forgotten spectacles for all to see, and the opera ends in an exuberant quintet.

Reaction to the opera was muted. Paul Kellogg, Glimmerglass's general director, and Stewart Robertson, the music director, initially expressed concern about the work during a workshop production of the opera in late August 1988. McClatchy recalled that, at first hearing, the Glimmerglass officials found the score "Knotty, clotted, dour . . . Where I'd anticipated Mozart or Puccini, my un-trained ear heard Schoenberg. ('Bi-tonal' was the term the rehearsal pianist used.)" Because the vast majority of Schuman's works after the mid-1940s incorporated bitonal or polychordal harmonic devices, it is a mystery that anyone would be surprised by Schuman's harmonic language in 1988. However, as is the case with so many of Schuman's works, after further hearings the harmonies become less harsh and more compelling, which is exactly what happened with the Glimmerglass artistic team.

In the midst of creating *A Question of Taste*, the 1989 Eighth Van Cliburn International Piano Competition, a quadrennial event held in Fort Worth, Texas, asked Schuman for a short piano work that all semifinalists would be required to perform. He obliged with *Chester: Variations for Piano*. Derived from the last movement of the *New England Triptych* and his band overture *Chester*, it is a slight work, no more than six minutes in length, wherein the familiar *Chester* theme is introduced and then varied in comparatively static forms. Schuman had known Cliburn since the pianist was a student at Juilliard in the mid-1950s. Because the composer was deep into completing his second opera and his energies were therefore somewhat divided, the *morceau imposé* for the competition resulted in a comparatively tepid set of variations for the piano.

As the opera evolved, numerous suggestions for changes were presented to Schuman, who resisted revisiting the score, admitting to McClatchy that "he just didn't want to go back to the score, that he felt 'written out.'" McClatchy also commented that he saw Schuman at a concert in December 1988, "and he seems much frailer. As Frankie said, just referring to their schedule though she may as well have had more in mind, 'Everything's slowing down.'"

Although *A Question of Taste* realized modest success and was buoyed by the exuberance of *The Mighty Casey*, the work was not an audience hit owing to the exceedingly light and unlikely story line, as well as the fact that much of the opera is written in a *parlando* style, in which the characters sing the text in a way that resembles speaking. Furthermore, the melodies and harmonies are tonally abstract. The double bill was produced again at the Juilliard School in December 1990, and both *The Mighty Casey* and *A Question of Taste* were recorded live by Delos International.

The reviewer for the *New York Times*, Bernard Holland, articulated the negative reception of the new Schuman opera:

> After a few minutes . . . comes the depressing evidence that "A Question of Taste" is going to be the kind of period melodrama that these 1910 diners might have seen in the theater the night before. There is villainy and virtue, love and contempt—but no people. Rather we are given characters who wear their one-idea identities like name tags at an auto dealer's convention.

As Schuman approached his eightieth birthday in 1990, the toll of a long life that was made physically challenging by his long-term muscular weakness, his heart problems (in addition to the heart attack in 1968 and cardiac bypass in 1983, he would have a pacemaker implanted in 1991), cataract surgery in 1985, and constant insomnia began to limit his mobility and his energy. Schuman, who had seemed to possess unlimited determination and discipline, noticed that his powers were waning.

Nevertheless, he enjoyed the liberty of being a free agent in his later years. In 1977 he commented on his lifestyle: "I find that my luxury now is an easy beginning of the day, a leisurely coffee with Frankie, a leisurely reading of the paper, riding my silly stationary bike to keep my hips from doing whatever hips shouldn't do but often do, and getting to work maybe at ten o'clock instead of eight." He added, "I have no hobbies, absolutely no hobbies."

In discussing his 1959 work *Carols of Death*, Schuman remarked about the composition's title and the larger implications of the work: "'Carols of Death' is my own title. I thought it was a wonderful title. I don't mean it in an ironical sense at all; they are simply songs about death, and I am not and have never been morbid about death. I always think that death is one branch of life."

In his oral history of 1990–92, written with Heidi Waleson, Schuman spoke of a new work for solo violin to be written for Robert McDuffie, whom the composer admired for McDuffie's performance of Schuman's Violin Concerto. However, in his first acknowledgment of his failing energy, he admitted:

> I don't know what'll happen [with the solo violin piece]. If I can write again, the project excites me. But I also recognize that I'm not writing much. . . . I wouldn't dignify it by calling it a writer's block; it's such a cliché term. It just means that I'm not functioning as a composer very well. . . . I get tired a lot. But I'll get to it. I'll get my discipline back.

Schuman had great difficulty walking by the time he turned eighty, exhibiting symptoms which were ultimately diagnosed as Parkinson's disease. He spent many hours in his study at 888 Park Avenue looking at the photographs of his many musical friends that covered the walls: "I've always claimed that Aaron Copland's picture will talk to you if you look at it long enough." He also continued to read voraciously, focusing on "serious literature and articles" primarily about government, politics, and economics. He admitted he did not listen to much music, except for the recordings sent to him by young composers who asked for a supportive comment from the maestro: "I find very little of the music the young composers send me to be of much interest, but almost all of *them* are of great interest, so I find I can contribute to their thinking in an indirect way."

Schuman once mused:

> I remember the way I used to think about older composers. Any young composer who at some point in his career doesn't want to kick over the traces is probably not a very interesting young composer. This is part of growing up. I feel that as people mature, if they really mature, they are likely to have a broader appreciation of a wide variety of music. . . . Now, my pleasure in being old is that I am exploring *their* method of speech.

Schuman took great pride in being chairman for over two decades of the BMI Student Composer Awards.

At the time of his seventy-fifth birthday he commented on the advice he often gave to young composers: "First I tell them not to die young. Second, I tell them to write what moves them without thinking about its practicality. The only practical thing about being a composer is the dream."

Schuman was intrigued by the decision of Copland, who died in 1990, to stop composing. He said to Schuman, "Bill, appetites change." For Schuman, it seemed that it was his personal health, declining energy, and high standards that slowed his compositional output.

> The primary goal and obligation of a composer, as I see it, is to write the best music he or she can write . . . You have to decide what you are willing to put out under your signature. . . . I get inquiries about when I'm going to write my eleventh symphony. People call and want big works, but it doesn't occur to me to write one because I don't have the appetite now. I don't have the stomach to take on a big work. . . . For me to write a large work, just the physical aspect is a very serious one, and a limiting one. I have trouble with my fingers and my hand, and it's extremely difficult to sit at a desk for long periods of time.

In 1967 Schuman gave a candid and enlightening interview to Robert S. Hines that provided a focused look into how he viewed the compositional process as a seasoned composer. In the interview (not published until 1995), Schuman explained that he still had great faith that composers of the future would write for the symphony orchestra with the same intensity that he did, as had the composers before him: "It is hard to imagine that composers will not continue to be born who will wish to express themselves using large forces of instrumentalists. . . . I think that the form of the symphony is no more invalid than that of the novel."

Schuman also explained his compositional approach in the context of his desire to create a particular environment through the music: "The pervading element of any piece that I begin is my own desire to come to some conclusion with myself as to the emotional climate that I am striving for." Emphasizing that he had always seen himself as a melodist, he explained that he found the appropriate emotional climate by singing: "Everything is singing; however I have never consciously in my whole life 'assigned' a melody to an instrument. I always think of the melody in terms of the instrument, never separately."

Simplicity is something a composer must master, yet this does not always come across to listeners. . . . So when I say simple, it has to be simple to me as the composer in that the architecture is clear. If I were to choose one word to describe my preoccupation . . . it is the word clarity—clarity of architecture. At any single moment, I must know, and I hope the listener knows too, the forces at work.

Consistent with his desire for simplicity in musical structure, Schuman also explained his seminal approach to harmonic structure: "I do not use harmony as a device for musical progression, but as an environmental factor for the kind of horizontal sounds that I am interested in at that particular moment."

Unlike composers who see a tonal work evolve through vertical assemblages of notes to create harmonic milestones in a composition, Schuman saw his compositional style as paralleling that of Renaissance composers, who created harmonies through the intertwining of melodic lines:

I do not think of the bass line as being a line of production. I do not use harmony that way and have not since student days. . . . The harmonic texture is to give a tonal palette to a particular section. That is its purpose—rhythm, melody, form and the orchestra carry the weight. I do not use harmony in that other sense at all.

Theorists and others who have commented on my music are always analyzing the harmonic element, and I think quite falsely. Maybe these people are analyzing it correctly. It is hard to know . . . I got one [article] the other day, a doctoral thesis on my choral music, and I was astounded to read about some of the things I was doing as a composer. Maybe he was right, and maybe not, but he was objectifying things which were not part of an objective process.

After World War II composers were deeply committed to championing the twelve-tone system of composition, which had been suppressed by the regimes of Hitler and Stalin. Even the supremely celebrated Igor Stravinsky embraced serialism in the early 1950s in such works as the Septet and *Agon*. The Summer Courses for New Music in Darmstadt, Germany, led by such passionate composers and modernist zealots as Pierre Boulez and Karlheinz Stockhausen, preached a type of artistic revolution that broke from traditional compositional approaches and sought out "freedom" in all that was new. According to Stockhausen, "Schoenberg's great achievement . . .

was to claim freedom for composers: freedom *from* the prevailing taste of society and its media; freedom *for* music to evolve without interference." This compositional "freedom" also addressed the new technologies of sound synthesis and computer-generated sounds that, in the 1950s, were in their infancy. In addition, as Alex Ross notes in his highly perceptive book *The Rest Is Noise*, "neoclassical lingo—Sonatine, Scherzo . . . dropped from sight, replaced by phrases with a cerebral tinge: *Music in Two Dimensions, Syntaxis, Anepigraphe.*"

This cultural sea change in Europe spread to the United States, where the nation's best universities became the twentieth-century equivalent of the Esterházys, Haydn's royal patrons, providing a financial base and the comparative freedom to explore new compositional approaches not influenced by commerce or tradition. The twelve-tone technique of composition became the prevalent compositional approach in the academy. In this compositional system each pitch of the chromatic scale is given equal importance, so that the listener experiences no tonal center, no key, such as C major or F minor. The American critic Kurt List wrote: "The [American] composer will finally have to shoulder the burden of the less popular, aesthetically more honest, style of atonal polyphony . . . if music is to exist as an artistic expression of modern America, atonal polyphony is really the only valid guide."

American composers such as Roger Sessions, and particularly Elliott Carter and Milton Babbitt, became some of the most prominent representatives of this new musical aesthetic, although they realized their musical goals differently: "Carter renounced Copland-style populism and embraced the aesthetic of density and difficulty." Carter said, after composing his First String Quartet, "I decided for once to write a work very interesting to myself, and so say to hell with the public and with the performers too." Babbitt echoed Carter's thought in a much-quoted article of 1958:

I dare suggest that the composer would do himself and his music an immediate and eventual service by total, resolute and voluntary withdrawal from this public world to one of private performance and electronic media, with its very real possibility of complete elimination of the public and social aspects of musical composition . . . the composer would be free to pursue a private life of professional achievement, as opposed to a public life of unprofessional compromise and exhibitionism.

Such was the intellectual and artistic environment that Schuman knew from after World War II until the vehemence of this aesthetic waned in the early to mid-1980s. It was during the ascendancy of serialist (twelve-tone) and aleatory (chance) compositional styles in the 1950s that Schuman composed *The Mighty Casey* and *New England Triptych*—works that in no way would ingratiate him to the American musical intelligentsia of the time.

Although Schuman's music would become more dissonant and tonally obscure as he aged (take, for example, his Ninth Symphony, which frequently uses twelve-note chords throughout), he never embraced the twelve-tone system as the basis of his compositional approach. Rather, throughout his later works he often juxtaposed disparate tonalities in polychords that obscured but did not entirely erase the tonal center. Perhaps of even greater importance to Schuman were the European intellectual roots that were embodied in the twelve-tone system. To adopt the system, as Copland did in his later years, was a rejection of the American ethos that was so much a fundamental element of Schuman's music, whether in colonial hymns, popular rounds, or the patriotic sound of a brass band with its "muscular" musical presence. The Eurocentric orientation of America's musical intelligentsia at mid-twentieth century was anathema to everything in which Schuman believed.

Schuman was troubled in the latter part of his life by the rejection of American themes and styles in the music of the younger generation:

> Many young American composers have given up their heritage and are looking again to Europe for devices—electronic devices—and systems. Systems do not create composers, composers create systems. . . . The result of American composers turning away from their national heritage, or not even being aware of it, is that there is a great deal of grey music being written without real composers of profile emerging.

Schuman saw this issue as a fundamentally important one, and he would return to it during the remaining years of his life. In a speech to the American Symphony Orchestra League in 1980, he said, "It is difficult to imagine any other country in the world in which orchestras would not rise to the riches of their own literature; it is really only in America that we have this kind of inverse chauvinism in which we are so often guilty of profligate neglect."

For a composer who was so clearly dedicated to the ethos of America, it is curious that Schuman rejected an idiom that was perhaps his country's greatest contribution to musical expression: jazz. Considering the fact that

Schuman's introduction to composition, albeit at a rudimentary level, was through his own jazz band and his popular songs with Frank Loesser and Eddie Marks, it is striking to note that, for the most part, Schuman rejected his jazz roots when he decided to become a "serious" composer.

Schuman said on numerous public occasions that jazz was, in his view, "mating music," a remark that usually evoked gasps and angry retorts from his audience. In fact, it seems clear that Schuman consciously and emphatically rejected his earliest musical roots, believing that the worlds of jazz and classical music were separated by an intellectual divide that could not be breached. In conversations with the author, Schuman expressed the belief that jazz should not be offered in a conservatory because its structures and performance traditions were anathema to how classical music was approached and practiced. Although some commentators have noted that elements of the jazz idiom, such as syncopation, scat singing, prominent percussion parts, among others, do appear in Schuman's compositions, his works do not embrace the characteristics of jazz that one hears in the music of such non-Americans as Ravel or Stravinsky.

In his later years, Schuman discussed the relationship of his work as a composer to the administrative and teaching duties he undertook simultaneously, work he needed as the head of a family and its principal wage earner. Commenting that both Copland and Barber lived different lives than his—a pointed reference to their homosexuality—Schuman said, "Composers who are not family men have a very different attitude toward the practicalities of life which their station makes possible. It doesn't mean that they aren't as serious or they aren't as ambitious. It does have to do with the amount of latitude they can permit themselves if they are living by the pen." What Schuman meant precisely by this quote can be debated, but clearly, on some level he resented the fact that his compositional colleagues who did not have to support a family were given the luxury of being able to decide when they wished to compose. However, Schuman went on to explain that, independent of sexual preferences and family responsibilities, he actually enjoyed the administrative life: "True to my bourgeois background, I liked working with groups of people, I liked to share responsibilities."

By the end of his life, Schuman had accumulated adequate financial resources to live quite comfortably. For tax purposes, in the mid-1980s he created a New York State–registered corporation called William Schuman Associates, which received revenue from his publishers and BMI and which dispensed monthly income to him, as well as providing tax deductions for medical insurance and paying pharmacy costs, utilities, and related expenses having to do with his work as a composer.

All of his musical manuscripts were gradually donated to the Library of Congress starting in the 1950s, and close to the time of his death Schuman sold his collected papers to the New York Public Library for $50,000. He was also able to sign a five-year contract with BMI, beginning on January 1, 1992, that guaranteed him an annual payment of $60,000, a $10,000 increase from an earlier contract. With various pensions and annuities, plus his royalties and guarantees, Schuman was able to reap significant financial benefit from his many years of composing and arts administration.

Bill and Frankie's desire to be socially involved with friends and acquaintances continued until the ends of their lives. The Schumans would often invite a diverse group of guests to 888 Park Avenue to enjoy good food and drink and intelligent conversation. Friends from the business and arts worlds interacted under Frankie's elegant and watchful eye in a large central room that held both a sitting and a dining area; often a beautiful amaryllis would grace a table. In particular, the Schumans cultivated younger friends, to whom they referred as "our kiddies group," who would visit them in New York City or their gracious home in back-country Greenwich, at 88 Richmond Hill Road. Two of these special younger friends were Kenneth S. Davidson and his wife, Marya Martin, the distinguished flutist. Ken Davidson had known the Schumans when they lived in New Rochelle in the 1950s and early 1960s; they became reacquainted in the 1980s. A successful hedge fund director, Davidson was very solicitous of the elderly Schumans' needs, providing a car to drive them to doctors' appointments and acting as a sounding board for various personal and professional questions. It was during these friendly gatherings that Schuman's many friends noticed that his strong walk had become a tentative shuffle and that his razor-sharp mind and speech no longer had their usual acuity. He was also hospitalized briefly in late 1991 with what was diagnosed as a heart irregularity.

The last public celebration for Schuman before his death was on October 25, 1991, given by the music division of the New York Public Library for the Performing Arts at Lincoln Center, where all of Schuman's personal and professional papers are housed. The concert that evening celebrated the opening of an exhibit at the library entitled "An American Triptych: The Dynamic Worlds of William Schuman." The program announced that "the works on this evening's program are a vivid example of his assimilation of the many components comprising this American experience—the language, poetry, and axioms of popular culture as well as the musical integration of vernacular and concert music idioms." The compositions performed were the String Quartet No. 5, *In Sweet Music, Prelude for Voices, Five Rounds on Famous Words, Carols of Death,* "Dr. Worden's Pills" from *Mail Order Madrigals,* and "Singaling" from *Esses.*

The opening of the exhibition and the ensuing concert were a great physical challenge for the failing Schuman. Arriving by wheelchair, he gallantly left it aside to greet the many well-wishers present, but he was clearly exhausted by the activity.

On February 14, 1992, Schuman complained of angina early in the morning. Sometime later he fell while using his walker in his New York apartment. He was taken to the emergency room of Lenox Hill Hospital, just across Park Avenue from his apartment, where he was diagnosed with a broken left hip and left hand. An electrocardiogram also indicated a blockage on the left side of the heart.

His doctors decided that hip surgery was necessary, and he was administered spinal anesthesia because of his advanced cardiac disease and angina. Schuman survived the surgery and was judged by his physicians to be stable on the morning of February 15. However, at 10:40 A.M. hospital personnel called a code blue, requiring a full ACLS (Advanced Cardiac Life Support) protocol. They were unable to resuscitate him. William Schuman was pronounced dead at 11:43 A.M. of a massive pulmonary embolism.

Word of Schuman's sudden death rapidly spread through the New York arts community. A lengthy obituary appeared the next day in the Sunday *New York Times,* with a short bullet announcement on the front page. The bulletin of the MacDowell Colony mourned their honorary chairman's passing: "He set the highest standards for those around him, and lived up to them himself. He gave valuable advice whenever it was sought—advice that was thoughtful, tough minded, and always in the best interest of the [MacDowell] Colony." Daniel Webster of the *Philadelphia Inquirer* wrote that Schuman "showed composers that social activism is part of their responsibility."

Frankie had no religious service for her husband of almost fifty-six years. Before his cremation, she authorized an autopsy, which was done twenty-four hours after his death. The examination found significant atherosclerotic cardiovascular disease, as well as signs of Parkinson's, Alzheimer's, and Paget's (a deteriorative disease of the bones) diseases.

A memorial tribute was held on April 1, 1992, in the Juilliard Theater in celebration of both the man and his music. The ninety-minute program included the Juilliard Orchestra conducted by Leonard Slatkin performing *American Festival Overture*, *George Washington Bridge*, and the second movement of the Symphony for Strings. Harold Rosenbaum, a favorite choral conductor of Schuman's, and his New York Virtuoso Singers performed *Carols of Death*. Speakers included the author, Tony Schuman, Martin E. Segal, Christopher Rouse, Mr. Slatkin, and Morton Gould. The tribute ended with a poignant *coup de théâtre* during which an enlarged 1971 portrait of Schuman done by Carl Mydans was spotlighted while the orchestra and chorus performed the last pages of *The Mighty Casey* as the light gradually dimmed to complete darkness. It was clear to all in the Juilliard Theater that an era had indeed ended.

Epilogue

Almost a month after William Schuman's death a thoughtful column appeared in the *New York Times* dealing with Schuman's legacy. The piece, entitled "A Composer with Many Public Faces," was written by Edward Rothstein, the chief music critic of the *Times*.

Rothstein began by referring to Schuman's sometime nemesis, Virgil Thomson, who wrote in 1939 that

> every composition's style is influenced by the source of the composer's income. A composer who earns a living outside music writes pieces marked by a naïve quality that can give "a useful kick to the profession," the way Mussorgsky, Satie and Ives did. Composers who depend on commissions display an "international" style good for "prestige value." A teaching composer combines the bossiness and pomposity of a schoolmaster with timidity and overscrupulousness.

Rothstein openly pondered in what category Thomson would place Schuman, who "earned his living as the most important musical administrator of the 20th century. His impact on our musical life stemmed more from the way he treated music than from the way he wrote it. At one time, he was probably the most powerful figure in the world of art music."

Rothstein went on to emphasize his point by referring to Schuman's many visionary innovations at Juilliard and his leadership of Lincoln Center. He wrote of Schuman's skills as a "proselytizer" who often fought for stronger educational initiatives in the arts in America "emphasizing sophisticated achievements [in the arts] rather than mass appeal. . . . Not since the last century has a composer shown such institutional prowess and such a consistent practical vision."

Returning to the original premise voiced in Thomson's words, Rothstein became less than enthusiastic about the substance of Schuman's music:

Had he been a greater composer, he might never have been as great an administrator. . . . The music is handsome, honest, well-managed. . . . It is music of a fluent public speaker. It is easy to follow; it is declamatory; it contains much variety. But often, I am afraid, it is not that interesting. It has passions within it, but it is not music of passion; it contains elements of sentiment, but not of deep feeling. It is never less than professional, but it rarely seems much more. . . . Schuman's music served, without pandering or posturing, to make him a composer. That gave him the vision to play a more influential role as a leader of the art, its public statesman. Accomplished composers are a rarity, but Schuman's accomplishments are rarer still. His public role will not soon be filled.

Schuman himself wrote that it was exactly the rich mix of artistic creation and administrative leadership that made his life so worthwhile:

There are many composers who have known more composers, administrators who have spent their lives just in administration and who know more, with ditto for educators, editors, public speakers and what not. The fact of my life that might be worth recording is the fantastic variety of my experience. I think it is safe to say that there isn't anyone else in my day who has had quite the intense experience that I have had in such myriad fields. . . . The associations range from the most bourgeois to the most avant-garde. . . . To me this enormous variety of experience as composer, teacher, editor, administrator, speaker, etc., is significant not, curiously, in terms of its diversity, but its unity. To me it is all one, and I view my life as a whole. All these parts form a single, unified embrace.

Rothstein's respectful and generally positive view of Schuman's legacy echoed the conventional wisdom of the time, which held that Schuman's lack of total focus as a composer made him a lesser creator. It is an approach to Schuman's music that undervalues an extraordinary catalog of work. His more accessible and popular works, such as *American Festival Overture*, *New England Triptych*, and *Variations on "America"* exude an energy and a truly American spirit that weave these compositions into the fabric of the twentieth-century American musical scene. His eight extant symphonies present an extraordinary array of compositional approaches, from the straightforwardness of the Third

Symphony and the Symphony for Strings to the more complex structures and harmonic explorations of the Seventh, Eighth, and Ninth Symphonies.

If one seeks passion in Schuman's music, it will be found in the pathos and intensity of the Ninth Symphony or the amazing driven melodies of *Night Journey* and *Judith*, focused by the psychologically motivated concepts of Martha Graham. Schuman's solo works for both violin and violoncello create deeply moving and intense aural experiences that expertly utilize the specific attributes of each instrument. Even his logistically challenged *Concerto on Old English Rounds* for solo viola has an engaging charm as Schuman juxtaposes the complex viola line with the simplicity of the rounds sung by a women's chorus.

In Schuman's string chamber music he exhibits a profound understanding of the sonorities of each instrument. The Fourth Quartet challenges the very concept of the volume and intensity of sound that can be produced by only four players. Schuman's string trio *Amaryllis* presents some of the most challenging music to appear in his entire oeuvre, with harmonies and rhythmic structures that reflect an amazingly sophisticated musical palette.

Schuman's choral music, which he produced constantly throughout his life, embodies a wide variety of moods, from the mischievous *Mail Order Madrigals* and *Esses* to the deeply moving *Carols of Death*. Finally, his two operas, *The Mighty Casey* and *A Question of Taste*, although not written in the European tradition, present a charming view of America at a simpler time. In addition, echoes of themes from *Casey* appear in many of Schuman's other works, raising the intriguing question of whether or not he consciously used melodies from the opera as a leitmotif, sprinkling them in various compositions to reflect his reverence for all that *Casey* stood for in American folklore. Any baseball aficionado cannot help but be moved by the final chorus of *Casey*, even though we all know that our hero did not succeed on that fateful day.

William Schuman, on the other hand, had a great batting average throughout his life. Many of his compositions deserve careful study and performances from today's artists. Schuman's works were not enthusiastically embraced by the intelligentsia of the dodecaphonic world during his lifetime, but as more and more young composers of the twenty-first century readdress the many intricacies of tonal music, it is the music of William Schuman that should stand as the foundation upon which they can develop their own work.

Schuman once said about the compositional process:

If you have to worry about originality or think about it, you're not original. And if you're a composer you are original in the sense that you're writing what you are, you're writing your personal profile, and if you don't have a personal profile, you're not a composer. You're someone who's merely schooled in the techniques of composition.

Schuman was never comfortable with being referred to as someone who personified an unusual combination of being an administrator and a creative artist: "I got [in]to administration because I was so often dissatisfied with the way things were being managed, and I just sort of fell into it . . . to me it's just as natural as being a composer." Referring to his many years overseeing Juilliard and Lincoln Center, Schuman said, "I wouldn't have missed that experience for anything . . . and I would do it all again. It was extreme and there were problems, but those were nothing compared with the enriching facet of it to me personally in my own life. . . . I would find a void in my life if I didn't have something in addition to composing."

Frankie died on December 19, 1994, just two years after her husband. A lifelong smoker, she suffered from emphysema and eventually lung cancer. A memorial service was held on March 1, 1995, at the Lotos Club, where *In Sweet Music*, one of her favorite works, was performed, along with *Five Rounds on Famous Words* and "Kiss Me Not Goodbye" from *The Mighty Casey*. Her son, Tony, spoke, as did her close friends Mark Schubart, Inge Heckel, Mary Carswell, and Mary Rodgers Guettel. The William Schuman Music Trust was established from the proceeds of the Schuman estate to create programs that would support the performance and recording of his music. Chaired by Tony and Andie Schuman, the trust's advisory board includes many of the most important American composers, conductors, and performers of the twenty-first century.

Schuman's legacy in 2008 is alive and functioning at the Juilliard School and at Lincoln Center. Remarkably, Schuman's initiatives at both institutions—the Juilliard String Quartet, the Juilliard dance and drama divisions, the Literature and Materials of Music program, Juilliard's move to Lincoln Center, the Chamber Music Society and Film Society of Lincoln Center, Mostly Mozart, the Lincoln Center Institute, the Lincoln Center Council, and many others—are so well established that few actually remember who the progenitor of those ventures was.

But it is Schuman's music that is at the heart of his legacy. His music deserves to be reassessed and performed with greater frequency, with the caveat that much of his work requires more than one listening in order for audiences to fully engage with and understand it.

Even as he neared death, William Schuman continued to exhibit the optimism and self-assurance that had marked his entire life:

> If someone asked me whether I believed or hoped my music would last beyond my lifetime, I would have no hesitation whatsoever in saying, "Yes, I believe that it will and certainly I hope that it will. I don't mean it has to be played all the time, but if there were not some contribution of continuity, I would feel I hadn't succeeded. . . ." When I made all these statements to my father and others recognizing what a wretched profession the writing of music was and what a glorious pursuit it was, that there is one wonderful thing about it that I have always appreciated but never really focused on in so many words: there are not many professions where the young are dependent on the old, and the old relate to the young. In the writing of music, you are part of a continuum of people . . . you are part of a world which depends on . . . continuity. If you have succeeded in your life, you have made some contribution to that continuity. It's really that simple.

Appendix: Ten Compositions of William Schuman

This appendix includes descriptive analyses of ten of Schuman's compositions, with musical examples. It is designed to give the reader a better understanding of the remarkable craft and depth contained in Schuman's compositions and includes works from as early as 1939 (*American Festival Overture*) to 1981 (*Night Journey: Choreographic Poem for Fifteen Instruments*).

Although an ability to read music is not necessary to comprehend the analyses of the works, numerous musical examples have been provided to further illustrate theoretical and structural elements of the ten compositions, reinforcing descriptions or analyses in the text. Occasionally these excerpts will not include all instrumental parts found in the score. Musical examples begin on page 405.

The word "flourishes," a term coined by the author that appears frequently both in the text and in these analyses, refers to bursts of rapid sixteenth notes irregularly interrupted by sixteenth rests. In these short passages the most typical melodic interval is the second, although larger intervals are also employed. The flourish is one of Schuman's most distinctive compositional signatures and appears in his works consistently throughout his long life.

Descriptive Analyses

American Festival Overture

Premiere: October 6, 1939, Boston Symphony Hall (Boston, Massachusetts); Boston Symphony Orchestra, cond. Serge Koussevitzky

Duration: approximately 9 minutes 30 seconds

The "call to play" of Schuman's boyhood days in New York City created by the syllables "Wee-Awk-Eee" is melodically based on descending and ascending minor thirds. The muscularity and great energy of Schuman's music in his early years are much on display as the overture begins, with most of the instruments of the orchestra proclaiming the call to play. Suspended cymbal, snare drum, and xylophone add an edge to the opening section (see example 1).

Schuman then varies the rhythm of the theme and presents it sequentially in triplets and offbeats; intersperses the theme between woodwinds, brass, and strings; and develops it further by adding woodwind flourishes.

This opening section concludes with triplets exchanged between woodwinds and strings, leading to a meno mosso section of serenity and melodic beauty. It begins with a melody in the flute, oboe, and English horn and adds a distinctive horn solo that quietly intones the call motive at the end of the meno mosso (see example 2).

This serene section is short-lived, however. It is followed by an extended contrapuntal section for strings alone, marked "leggiermente" and "piano sempre," in which the rhythmic structure builds from eighth notes to eighth-note triplets to rapid sixteenth notes, finally developing into a fully composed accelerando. Schuman also writes at m. 163 a major/minor pentachord that he will use in one form or another throughout the remainder of the overture, creating one of the distinctive sonorities identified with the composer during this period (see example 3).

This part segues into a section for woodwinds alone using much of the same melodic and rhythmic material heard earlier in the strings. The strings are reintroduced with a soulful melody marked "cantabile dolce" that offsets the sharp staccatos in the woodwinds.

Schuman then adds piquancy to the overall texture of the overture by introducing his playful sixteenth-note flourishes in the woodwinds as the string line becomes more frenetic. Finally the work arrives at a new section with eighth notes in the strings supported by an extended chord of open fourths in the woodwinds (see example 4).

The full brass choir blasts out the call theme with variants at triple forte leading to a bombastic chord, followed by a melody in the first violins, marked "un poco presto," reminiscent of a Scottish gigue. This melody soon forms a contrapuntal background to the announcement of the theme in the horns, with a subtle stylistic replication of Ferde Grofé's 1931 *Grand Canyon Suite* (see example 5).

The overture finally shifts to a Tempo I in which inventive interplay is developed between the strings, woodwinds, and brass, with the call theme distributed throughout the orchestra. Vigorous string triplets then lead to the return of an earlier theme in the horns and trumpets (see example 6).

Toward the conclusion of the work, a driving sixteenth-note figure in the strings (minus the double bass) is introduced. The call theme is then heard in a brass choir while the strings continue their rapid sixteenth-note figures, resulting in a push to a final triple-forte pentachord on E-flat (see example 7).

The *American Festival Overture* is a signature piece for Schuman and reflects his youthful vigor as well as his immense imagination and orchestration skills in a composition that has become one of his most popular works.

Symphony No. 3

Part I: a. Passacaglia; b. Fugue
Part II: c. Chorale; d. Toccata
Premiere: October 17, 1941, Boston Symphony Hall (Boston, Massachusetts);
Boston Symphony Orchestra, cond. Serge Koussevitzky
Duration: approximately 29 minutes

Schuman's Third Symphony represents a brilliant burst of compositional creativity from a thirty-one-year-old who, only eleven years earlier, was asking a receptionist at a small music school how he could become a composer. Considering Schuman's youth and inexperience as a composer, the complexity of the Third Symphony and its compositional focus are that much more remarkable. The work exhibits the energy and muscularity that were hallmarks of the Schuman aesthetic.

The Third Symphony is organized into two large parts: Part I, Passacaglia and Fugue; and Part II, Chorale and Toccata. Said Schuman, "I soon found that normal, conventional four-movement symphonic structure wasn't any good for this piece; I was really thinking of two huge chunks of music." He commented that he did not view the baroque compositional forms that he used as strict structures to adhere to slavishly. Rather, all four forms were simply springboards for his musical imagination:

I was amazed when reviewer after reviewer talked about my use of "these baroque forms," speaking of them as though they were something that was set. Now to me, a "passacaglia" . . . is basically a stately theme in three-time, which the composer reiterates with variations. In my terms, it was not a set form, but merely a principle of composition and approach. The same is true of fugue. . . . When I began to write the Symphony, I found that with each successive entry of the theme [of which there are seven], my imagination took the tonal center a half a step higher. . . . Then when I came to the Fugue, I made it a variation on the Passacaglia.

Clearly his counterpoint studies with Charles Haubiel had a major influence on Schuman's approach to this composition. It is written for a very large orchestra, and the composer even asks for extra wind instruments as "optional but very desirable"— additions that swell the horn section, for example, to eight players.

The opening of the symphony, with its quiet introduction of the Passacaglia theme, is in its tempo and overall feeling briefly reminiscent of the Third Symphony of Schuman's mentor Roy Harris. In fact, Schuman stated that he was taken with the Passacaglia theme in Harris's Quintet for Piano and Strings and that he too wanted to work with the form. Schuman introduces the Passacaglia theme in the bass but extends it much farther than the traditional eight-measure pattern. This theme, which will reappear in various forms and variations throughout the symphony, is notable for its large, expressive intervals of the seventh and octave (see example 8).

As new instruments take up the theme, the contrapuntal texture that Schuman weaves becomes progressively more complex. Schuman continues to increase the intensity of the movement through the introduction of triplet figures, which soon culminate in a classic Schumanesque series of brass chords in the horn, trumpet, and trombone. This eventually leads to a vigoroso section of great rhythmic vitality. In this section Schuman introduces a rapid sixteenth-note figure in the cellos that provides a dizzying undercurrent beneath sustained chords in the French horns and upper strings (see example 9). This combination of figures is a manifestation of Schuman's comments that he heard conflicting bits of music in his head as he composed, often in juxtaposition with other themes.

Eventually all the lower strings join in this agitato pattern, which ends with stentorian brass chords played triple forte that lead into a final presentation of the Passacaglia theme in four-part harmony for trombones. This last section, in 6/4, leads immediately into the Fugue, with lively trills on all six beats in the violins, violas, and cellos.

The unconventional Fugue subject begins with an intervallic profile similar to that of the Passacaglia theme in an approximate inversion (e.g., an ascending octave turns into a descending octave; a descending third turns into an ascending sixth; etc.) but then moves to a different melodic structure (see example 10). Later comes a virtuosic variation of the theme for four trumpets (see example 11). This approach to brass writing—exuberant and technically demanding—is heard in many subsequent Schuman works.

The composer then inserts a tranquillo section, introduced by a plaintive English horn solo stating a variation on the Fugue subject. Additional woodwind and string parts enter and eventually the woodwinds move to frenetic triplets against the string choir. The section culminates in a dramatic timpani solo, quite similar in character to the "Tribal Dance" movement of *Newsreel* for band. The Fugue movement roars to a furious conclusion that uses many rhythmic variations in both the strings and winds, including the typical Schuman flourishes he had employed earlier in *American Festival Overture* and would utilize in many other future works (see example 12). A crescendo to triple forte closes the Fugue and Part I emphatically, much like the style he would use in the first movement of the *New England Triptych* of 1956.

Part II begins with a contemplative chorale theme reminiscent of the final chorale melody eventually to be found in Schuman's 1953 opera *The Mighty Casey*. Schuman was always intrigued with exceedingly slow tempi, as demonstrated by the beginning of his Second Symphony, and this fascination increased as he matured. The distinctive American quality of the trumpet solo, which states the theme's scalar passages and wistful wide leaps, is comparable to Ives's *Unanswered Question* and much of Copland's writing for trumpet up to that time. The beautiful, mellifluous quality of the flute and trumpet against the homophonic texture of the string choir is quite arresting, presenting a musical aesthetic reminiscent of orchestral interludes from the romantic period (see example 13). Schuman was not at all offended by descriptions of his work as "romantic": "I don't find any satisfaction in music that intrigues me intellectually but doesn't reach me [emotionally]."

In the poco più mosso section of this movement one hears again the introspective inner voices of the second violin and viola, a phenomenon that harks back to Schuman's experience of many musical themes running through his imagination at the same time. The movement eventually brings together the entire orchestra in a full-bodied statement of the chorale theme and concludes with the eerie sound of four stopped horns and muted trumpets against muted strings. Into this serene setting Schuman introduces a dramatic element by writing pizzicati for cellos and basses marked "triple sforzando," which decrescendo to piano as the bassoons and contrabassoon, on a low B-flat, seamlessly segue into the Toccata movement.

The Toccata begins with the snare drum, which quietly sets the rhythmic pattern for the entire movement, establishing the Toccata as it has historically been known in the baroque period as a display or virtuoso work. The rhythmic figure has a bouncy melody added to it through a bass clarinet solo, which has become a standard bass clarinet excerpt for orchestral auditions (see example 14). Schuman had discussed the feasibility of the solo with the bass clarinetist of the Boston Symphony, Rosario Mazzeo. Mazzeo learned it, proclaimed it unlike anything anyone had ever written for the instrument, and played it flawlessly at the first rehearsal, to much applause from his colleagues.

Through rhythmic and canonic variations and virtuoso writing for the entire orchestra, the movement continues to build to an arresting and strong-voiced recitative or cadenza of sorts for divisi cellos. They are finally joined by all strings, and the passage culminates in dramatic pizzicato chords before the return to Tempo I (see example 15).

With rim shots in the snare drum, intensification of the Toccata rhythm, and brassy calls from trumpets, trombones, horns, and tuba creating a musical tempest quite similar to the conclusion of *American Festival Overture* (even including a remnant of the "Wee-Awk-Eee" call), the symphony comes to a spectacular close on a triple-forte E-flat major/minor pentachord (see example 16).

The sophistication and complexity of the Third Symphony, as well as its youthful vigor and brashness, ensured Schuman's place as one of America's great symphonists. It offers brilliant and dramatic evidence of his singular craft and creativity.

Symphony for Strings (Symphony No. 5)

I. Molto agitato ed energico (♩. = 76)
II. Larghissimo (♩ = 40)
III. Presto (♩ = 184)
Premiere: November 12, 1943, Boston Symphony Hall (Boston, Massachusetts);
Boston Symphony Orchestra, cond. Serge Koussevitzky
Duration: approximately 17 minutes

This compact and intense work hinges on rhythmic complexity and a pervasive contrapuntal texture that grips performers and audience members alike. Eschewing the historical baggage linked to a Fifth Symphony, Schuman titled the work, which displays the composer's strong understanding of idiomatic string writing, *Symphony for Strings*. It was commissioned by the Koussevitzky Music Foundation and is dedicated to the memory of Natalie Koussevitzky, who died in 1942.

The first movement, in 12/8, is marked "Molto agitato ed energico, ♩. = 76." First and second violins present the first theme in a bold fortissimo and introduce the distinctive quadruplet eighth-note figure heard throughout the movement. Violas and cellos soon join the violins, providing an accented harmonic underpinning to the violin melody when all strings, with the exception of double basses, come together in rhythmic unison to maintain the movement's stentorian quality (see example 17).

Schuman soon gives the violas a quadruplet quarter-note figure that reinforces the importance of this rhythmic unit in the movement and, when they are joined by the first violins, showcases the work's rhythmic complexity. The quadruplet figure is subsequently taken up by the second violins, cellos, and basses, after which Schuman creates a brilliant contrapuntal texture culminating in a "sonoro molto" section of divisi strings exuding great fervor, with interlocking E major and A minor triads at mm. 77–78 and similarly with interlocking D-flat major and A-flat minor triads at mm. 86–87 (see example 18).

Next comes a variation of the earlier melodic and rhythmic materials, which leads to an extended contrapuntal section of repeated eighth-note quadruplets, again emphasizing the power of this rhythmic unit. This section culminates in a repetition of the earlier interlocking E major and A minor triads, and at m. 148 a passage begins that is reminiscent of Schuman's opening to *American Festival Overture* and the signature "Wee-Awk-Eee" cry. The movement maintains its energy to the end, with four repeated G major chords moving to an intense, sustained crescendo on a unison A-flat (see example 19).

The second movement, marked "Larghissimo ♩ = 40," is set at an exceedingly slow tempo that the composer often favored. Schuman divides the muted string choir into eight parts, including solo parts for cello and bass, to create a sweet sotto voce quality. This leads to an extended melody of fifteen measures for first and second violins. Divisi violas and cellos meanwhile provide a soulful harmonic underpinning for the violin melody that leads into a section marked "tenderly" (see example 20). Pizzicato cellos provide a strumming heartbeat that anchors the expressive melody played by the first violins, which are eventually joined in counterpoint by the second violins and violas (see example 21).

This plaintive, serene texture changes at m. 58 with first violins and cellos— marked "molto legato"—playing an octave apart while the second violins and violas present a highly animated sixteenth-note motive that eventually brings all strings together in rhythmic unison at mm. 72–73. This entire passage presents a masterly example of Schuman's ability to effectively juxtapose rhythmic textures to bring a diverse yet homogeneous quality to this plaintive section (see example 22).

Schuman concludes the movement imaginatively, using sustained chords as in the first movement but, in this case, as a calming element. The movement ends with a mystical quality, with divisi muted strings ascending to a triple-piano F-sharp major chord.

The final movement is a Presto with an exceedingly fast tempo marking of ♩ = 184. All strings are in an animated rhythmic unison for the first seventeen measures of the movement, which includes the familiar Schuman flourishes so typical of his up-tempo movements as well as his signature moving quarter-note passage in mm. 16–17 (see example 23).

The ensuing eighth-note upbeats provide a spirited rhythmic sensibility reflecting the liveliness of the first movement. Schuman then adds an engaging pizzicato passage for all strings that culminates in a multi-accented section of great wit and vigor divided between pizzicato and arco strings. The composer also plants his tongue firmly in cheek with a passage reminiscent of the famous pizzicato third movement of Tchaikovsky's Sixth Symphony (see example 24).

A playful melody for first violins marked "Leggieramente" continues the jaunty character of the movement. (The first-violin melody reappears in Schuman's 1953 opera *The Mighty Casey*, when the Watchman sings to Merry.) Schuman then creates an entirely new texture, expertly using imitative counterpoint to weave a beguiling section for divisi strings that culminates in a highly expressive passage beginning at m. 210 (see example 25).

Schuman prepares the conclusion of the symphony with rapid stentorian chords marked triple forte for all strings and introduces in rhythmic unison another brilliant rhythmic figure reminiscent of the first movement (see example 26), including a repetition of the characteristic Schuman flourishes (see examples 27 and 28) and masterly use of syncopated figures and contrapuntal writing, as well as the reintroduction in m. 284, at half tempo, of the Watchman's theme from *The Mighty Casey* (see example 29). This leads to a driving triplet figure, initially in the violins, that draws the movement to a rousing conclusion on a series of sustained and crescendoing fortissimo D major chords (see example 30).

The *Symphony for Strings* stands as a testament to Schuman's skill in writing for strings and to his continuing youthful energy, as well as his musical tenderness, which balances the more rhythmically driven parts of the work.

Concerto for Violin and Orchestra

I. Allegro risoluto—Molto tranquillo—Tempo primo—Cadenza—
Agitato fervente
II. Introduzione (Adagio—Quasi cadenza)—Presto leggiero—Allegretto—
Adagietto—Poco a poco accelerando al allegro vivo

First premiere: February 10, 1950, Boston Symphony Hall (Boston, Massachusetts);
Boston Symphony Orchestra, cond. Charles Munch, with Isaac Stern, violinist

Revised version premiere: February 24, 1956, Juilliard School of Music
(New York); Juilliard Orchestra, cond. Jean Morel, with Isaac Stern, violinist

Final version premiere: August 9, 1959, Aspen, Colorado; Aspen Festival
Orchestra, cond. Izler Solomon, with Roman Totenberg, violinist

Duration: approximately 31 minutes

Schuman's Concerto for Violin and Orchestra is the composer's most publicly revised piece. First written for a commission from the violinist Samuel Dushkin in 1945, it did not reach its final version until 1959. Despite its fourteen-year gestation period, it clearly benefited from the composer's constant reworking: this extraordinary work stands as one of Schuman's most focused and highly structured compositions. Divided into two strongly varied parts or movements, the composition reveals Schuman's very sophisticated understanding of the violin and shows how he combined his expert knowledge of the orchestra with idiosyncratic writing for the solo instrument.

The concerto begins with a section marked "Allegro risoluto ($\downarrow$ = c. 76)," with the violin asked to present its robust theme "with full, broad strokes of the bow." The theme is accompanied by an insistent eighth-note figure, played staccato in the winds and *col legno* (struck with the wood of the bow) in the strings (see example 31); this driving rhythm is one of Schuman's compositional signatures and will be heard again in various forms throughout the movement.

The resolute violin theme becomes more and more rhythmically complex, while the orchestra accompaniment grows in volume and strength, building to a fortissimo high A in the solo violin. A cadenza-like passage is answered by descending and then ascending sixteenth-note passages in the winds.

The ensuing meno mosso (♩ = c. 69; ♩ = c. 138) presents another of Schuman's compositional signatures: rapid eighth notes, in this case played in rhythmic unison by violins and violas (see example 32).

This section, only thirteen measures long, eventually slows the pace of the beginning of the movement and acts as a bridge to the più mosso (Tempo I, ♩ = c. 76). Here the solo violin introduces a melodic motive that evolves until it is taken over by the strings in a comedic version accompanied in circus-band "oom-pah" fashion by horns, trombones, and percussion, like one of Shostakovich's caustically sarcastic melodic motives (see example 33).

This motive continues to grow in power without the solo violin until the music is calmed with a solo flute and clarinet playing in unison to create an intricate and haunting intertwining of sound (see example 34). Schuman then presents an ethereal solo for English horn reminiscent of the solo violin melody at the very beginning of the concerto but now with the accompaniment in the clarinets and bassoons at half the tempo of the beginning. A muted trumpet solo marked "dolce cantabile" brings this section to a slow, soft conclusion.

In the second section, marked "Molto tranquillo (♩ = c. 60)," the muted solo violin returns playing an expressive melody at a dynamic level no louder than mezzo-piano, accompanied by a string choir of sustained chords. The solo violin is soon joined by a solo clarinet over the strings (see example 35), similar to the approach Schuman would eventually use for the bassoon and oboe lines in the second movement of *New England Triptych*.

A solo flute then joins the clarinet and solo violin, and the eventual addition of piccolo, horn, and timpani creates an extraordinarily delicate and moving orchestral texture.

At the end of this section the violin accelerandos to the Tempo primo section, which functions as an elaborate and insistent bridge to the prodigious Cadenza section for the solo violin.

Schuman expressed great pride in the fact that throughout the many revisions of the concerto not a note of the Cadenza was ever changed. In addition, violinists who played the solo part were enthusiastic in their praise of how well the Cadenza was shaped. Its virtuoso turns and introspective measures prove the composer's intimate knowledge of the violin, and it stands as one of Schuman's finest compositional achievements (see example 36).

As the Cadenza ends on a diminuendo marked "morendo" to a pianissimo, muted strings enter at the same dynamic level in varied patterns of sixteenth notes and eighth notes reminiscent of the accompanying string figure heard under the solo violin at the beginning of the concerto. This secco accompaniment, marked "clear," using muted strings, underpins what is actually a continuation of the Cadenza material, marked "Agitato fervente." A tense and persistent sense of driving toward the end of the movement is provided by the recapitulation of the circus-style accompaniment heard earlier and a poco più mosso section that has the solo violin playing rapid sixteenth-note double stops accompanied by a brass choir of horns and trumpets.

Schuman reinforces the conclusion by marking it "con moto," with the orchestra taking over the sixteenth-note motive of the solo violin, and adding descending intervals of diminished octaves and octaves in the winds and strings. Just when the movement seems about to come to a crashing conclusion, Schuman adds a codetta of sorts at m. 382

with the secco string accompaniment heard earlier (see example 37), quickly followed by the orchestra and soloist driving to a brilliant triple-forte conclusion (see example 38).

Unlike the first movement, with its highly structured sections, the second movement moves quixotically, presenting rapid mood, tempo, and rhythmic changes for a musical—and emotional—roller-coaster ride. Schuman relies heavily on a rather beefy brass presence, which is heard throughout the movement and may be perceived as sonically out of balance with the delicacy of the violin. Nevertheless, Schuman's use of brass choirs, such as that heard at the very beginning of the movement at triple forte, supplies the foundation for much of the movement. Also prominent in these introductory measures is the timpani, which eventually leads to the entry of the solo violin over sustained string chords.

It should be noted that this sonorous brass introduction appeared only in the final version of the concerto, which premiered in 1959. It is Schuman's most prominent change to the concerto. However, he made many other changes in the second movement as well, including completely new material for the solo violin. For example, in the final version the concerto ends with an animated rapid eighth-note passage in the solo violin that does not appear in earlier versions. This new passagework brings the concerto to a rousing conclusion, matching the overall forcefulness of the entire second movement.

Schuman marks the solo violin part, which does not enter until m. 33, "sempre espr., ma semplice" (always expressive, but simple). The accompaniment of the solo violin by three trumpets, three trombones, and strings at the dynamic level of piano provides a somber and less forceful setting for the solo violin line than did the triple-forte introduction of the movement. As the solo violin melody evolves, an accented chord in the brass propels it into a rhythmically eccentric Quasi cadenza section, where it skittishly jumps from one pitch to another in an improvisatory fashion (see example 39).

The ensuing Presto subito section continues in this free-form and cadenza-like vein. Next, in the Presto leggiero (♩ = c. 160) section, Schuman presents playful imitative counterpoint in the orchestral strings and eventually the woodwinds as well.

Schuman brings back the soloist after triple-forte stentorian accented eighth notes and a sustained chord by a trio of trumpets, but now the solo violin becomes quite skittish again, presenting accented three-sixteenth patterns that buzz over sustained trumpet chords marked piano. The solo violin continues the rapid sixteenth-note passages, which are eventually embellished in typical Schumanesque fashion by sixteenth-note flourishes in the woodwinds, creating an infectiously playful texture (see example 40).

The movement progresses to another cadenza-like section marked "In tempo," which segues to a section marked "Meno mosso, a la recitativo." A deliberate "Allegretto" in 6/8 quickly follows, accelerating to a contrapuntal section in which the familiar group of three trumpets, eventually replaced by two clarinets and a bass clarinet, accompanies the solo violin. Schuman varies the rhythm by shifting from complex to simple meters and gradually links the solo violin and the first violins in a dialogue that continues for a little more than twenty measures (see example 41). The solo violin takes up a light, playful motive cleverly accompanied by three trombones. It then moves to a highly filigreed solo line over string chords marked piano, with winds and brass eventually added to the accompaniment (see example 42). Schuman then brings the concerto to one of its most energized moments, with an accelerando leading to a "molto ritard" including triple-forte chords, rim shots, and horn, trumpet, and woodwind lines marked "wild" and "sonoro," reminiscent of a Hollywood score for a chariot race.

This fervid orchestral section continues without solo violin, but eventually is calmed with a meno mosso that brings the movement to its adagietto section (♩ = c. 56–60). Here the solo violin presents a surprisingly relaxed cantabile section accompanied by elongated chords in the orchestra. Throughout this section the moving, emotional solo melody is periodically interrupted by cadenza-like flourishes (see example 43).

Schuman progresses to the conclusion by introducing a section marked "pressing forward" where the orchestra and soloist answer each other in melodic triplet bursts. Schuman marks an accelerando from ♩ = c. 92 to a breakneck ♩ = c. 160 over eleven measures. The rapid eighth-note passage in the solo violin is eventually picked up by the orchestral strings, then transitions to an insistent accelerando triplet figure and a three-against-two rhythm in the brass that concludes the work with massed chords and an active timpani part marked triple forte (see example 44).

In his Violin Concerto Schuman combines his skills as a symphonist and his knowledge of the violin to create a work of pathos, passion, and drive that showcases the virtuosic and expressive qualities of the violin. In particular, Schuman liberates the solo violin line from the harmonic underpinnings in the orchestra, allowing the principal melodic elements of the concerto, as heard in the solo violin, to float above the accompaniment, reminiscent of the texture of some Renaissance works. Schuman's extensive editing of the concerto's second movement gave the entire work a focus and passion that merits consideration of the Violin Concerto as one of his most successful and masterfully composed works.

New England Triptych:
Three Pieces for Orchestra after William Billings

Be Glad Then, America (♩. = c. 126–132)
When Jesus Wept (♩ = c. 60)
Chester (♩ = c. 84; ♩ = 160)
Premiere: October 28, 1956, Miami, Florida; Miami University Symphony
Orchestra, cond. Andre Kostelanetz

Duration: approximately 15 minutes 30 seconds

Schuman's own description of *New England Triptych* is in the program note that appears just before the title page of the score. *New England Triptych* is Schuman's most popular wholly original work. The author has provided musical examples and amplified Schuman's comments for the second and third movements.

Program Notes

Because of the special nature of this composition, the composer requests that the following be printed in the program book and, if this is not possible, it be read or paraphrased for the audience:

WILLIAM BILLINGS (1746–1800) is a major figure in the history of American music. The works of this dynamic composer capture the spirit of sinewy ruggedness, deep religiosity and patriotic fervor that we associate with the Revolutionary period. Despite the undeniable crudities and technical shortcomings of his music, its appeal, even today, is forceful and moving. I am not alone among American composers who feel an identity with Billings and it is this sense of identity which accounts for my use of his music as a point of departure. These pieces do not constitute a "fantasy" on themes of Billings, nor "variations" on his themes, but rather a fusion of styles and musical language.

I. Be Glad Then, America

Billings' text for this anthem includes the following lines:

"Yea, the Lord will answer
And say unto his people—behold!
I will send you corn and wine and oil
And ye shall be satisfied therewith.
"Be glad then, America,
Shout and rejoice.
Fear not O land,
Be glad and rejoice.
Hallelujah!"

A timpani solo begins the short introduction which is developed predominantly in the strings. This music is suggestive of the "Hallelujah" heard at the end of the piece [see example 45]. Trombones and trumpets begin the main section, a free and varied setting of the words "Be Glad Then, America, Shout and Rejoice" [see example 46]. The timpani, again solo, leads to a middle fugal section stemming from the words "And Ye Shall Be Satisfied" [see example 47]. The music gains momentum and combined themes lead to a climax. There follows a free adaptation of the "Hallelujah" music with which Billings concludes his original choral piece and a final reference to the "Shout and Rejoice" music [see examples 48 and 49].

II. When Jesus Wept
"When Jesus wept the falling tear
In mercy flowed beyond all bound;
When Jesus groaned, a trembling fear
Seized all the guilty world around."

The setting of the above text is in the form of a round. Here, Billings' music is used in its original form, as well as in new settings with contrapuntal embellishments and melodic extensions.

The use of a low-pitched tenor drum and the juxtaposition of the bassoon and oboe lines at the beginning of the movement introduce the hymn tune in a somber texture. Schuman then transforms the tune to develop a much more contemporary harmonic setting (see example 50).

Schuman writes only for one oboe, one bassoon, tenor drum, and strings in this movement. The string section is primarily responsible for the various treatments of the theme throughout the movement, often written divisi and always muted.

The reintroduction of the bassoon and oboe with dotted whole-note string accompaniment once again changes the texture of the movement and eventually brings the movement to a somber end with a diminuendo in the tenor drum (see examples 51 and 52).

III. Chester

This music, composed as a church hymn, was subsequently adopted by the Continental Army as a marching song and enjoyed great popularity [see example 53]. The orchestral piece derives from the spirit both of the hymn and the marching song. The original words, with one of the verses especially written for its use by the Continental Army, follow:

"Let tyrants shake their iron rods,
And slavery clank her galling chains,
We fear them not, we trust in God,
New England's God forever reigns.
"The foe comes on with haughty stride,
Our troops advance with martial noise,
Their vet'rans flee before our youth,
And gen'rals yield to beardless boys."

This dignified presentation of the hymn theme quickly is transformed at the Allegro vivo (♩ = 160), where the melody is played at twice the earlier tempo by flutes, oboes, and clarinets, with militant and incessant downbeats played by brass and strings (see example 54).

Schuman then introduces his distinctive flourishes as melodic material for only the woodwinds, with the strings eventually taking up the theme on tremolo eighth notes (see example 55). A distinctive quasi-fanfare in flutes and piccolo, horns, and trumpets further adds to the movement's playful vivacity (see example 56). The military quality of this Revolutionary War marching song is enhanced by the addition of a stately snare and bass drum figure to a brass choir. Schuman indicates in the score that "if available, 2 or 3 snare drums or field drums would be an effective addition in the 3rd movement, from measure 106 to end." Schuman then positions the music for its conclusion by bringing in first the brass, then the woodwind and string choirs with eighth-note triplets that drive the composition to a new level of energy. Flourishes, snare drum solos, triumphant brass chords, and a roaring timpani part all arrive finally at a triple-forte E-flat major chord (see example 57).

The imagination with which the Billings tunes inspired Schuman makes *New England Triptych* his most accessible and beloved original work. The popular style of this composition was rarely duplicated in subsequent pieces.

String Quartet No. 4

I. Adagio ($\quarternote$ = c. 50)
II. Allegro con fuoco ($\halfnote$ = c. 126)
III. Andante ($\quarternote$ = c. 66)
IV. Presto ($\halfnote$ = c. 168)
Premiere: October 28, 1950, Library of Congress (Washington, D.C.);
Hungarian Quartet
Duration: approximately 28 minutes

Written while the composer was recuperating from a ruptured blood vessel in his leg realized in a pick-up baseball game, Schuman's Fourth String Quartet was composed very rapidly, from June 26 to August 3, 1950, while he was staying at Menemsha, Martha's Vineyard. It is his most profound and compelling work for this genre.

The first movement, Adagio, has a typically slow and Schumanesque tempo marking of $\quarternote$ = c. 50. This ponderous tempo pervades the movement, the only relief a short più mosso $\quarternote$ = c. 60 in the middle of the movement. The dynamic level of the initial freely chromatic and contrapuntal lines between first violin and viola, marked "calm and relaxed," rarely goes beyond triple-piano, creating a deeply moving and quietly passionate musical experience (see example 58).

Gradually Schuman incorporates the second violin and cello in a gently moving motive that integrates all four instruments, until at m. 25 he returns to the chromatic counterpoint of the beginning of the movement, developing a rhythmic and harmonic interplay between the two violins that leads into a solo viola line reminiscent of m. 1 (see example 59).

Schuman's signature major/minor tetrachord, based on major and minor thirds, appears in m. 47, ushers in a più mosso at m. 48, and is repeated in transposed form at m. 56. All four instruments take part in a contrapuntal passage that quickly returns to the earlier slow tempo, presenting a simple, transparent interplay between the instruments (see example 60). The final measures, marked "delicamente" and triple piano, end in a morendo. This masterly movement, lasting just short of seven minutes, stands as a remarkable study of the use of hushed dynamics and slow tempos to create a mournful and introspective mood.

Although typical of earlier Schuman slow movements in its tempo markings and dynamics, this first movement also has a sonic power that is rare in Schuman's oeuvre at this time, beautifully complemented by the quartet's ensuing third movement. The intertwining of the four instrumental lines creates a melodic and harmonic interplay of great complexity and beauty.

Placid and introspective as the first movement is, the second movement, Allegro con fuoco $\halfnote$ = c. 126, forms a strong contrast to it, with jagged rhythms and fortissimo passages. Schuman utilizes triplet configurations throughout the second movement to create a skittish feeling that propels the music forward, along with meter changes from cut time to 3/2 and eventually to 4/2 (see example 61).

In addition, Schuman changes the forward-moving mood of the movement with occasional cantabile parts, inserting a "tenero un poco più mosso" section that provides some expressive contrapuntal writing for the instruments (see example 62). He also writes consecutive measures where all four instruments are in rhythmic unison accented on the offbeat, as in mm. 99–101 (see example 63). The familiar major/minor tetrachords heard in the first movement are also frequently present, as in mm. 37 and 39–42 (see examples 64 and 65).

As the movement progresses, Schuman skillfully blends the instruments at triple piano to create an eerie and highly effective contrast to the earlier driven elements and segues to a resonant chordal section, bringing the quartet together with a marvelously rich sonority. There is also a juxtaposition of fortes and pianos and upbeat sixteenth notes, offbeat passages in rhythmic unison for all instruments, and a final agitato section that increases the intensity still further. This sparkling, playful, and rhythmically complex movement ends on a major/minor tetrachord (see example 66).

The third movement, Andante with warmth ♩ = c. 66, is the musical and emotional heart of the quartet. At close to ten minutes, it is almost twice as long as any of the other movements. The initial distinctive double stops, marked "molto legato," create a polychordal harmonic texture, once again based on major/minor tetrachords, that is both complex and beguiling (see example 67). This polychordal chorale builds over twenty-one measures to a triple-forte chord that quickly dissipates dynamically, then rushes back to another triple forte, eventually transitioning to a slightly faster tempo.

Schuman subsequently uses the steady pizzicato of the cello to anchor an extraordinary contrapuntal section between the three upper strings (see example 68) that culminates in a new section of "mounting intensity" and a considerably faster tempo (♩ = c. 112; see example 69). This faster section features the two violins and viola interacting in imitative rhythmic figures that create an aural freedom not previously heard in the work. It culminates in a furious rhythmic unison of sixteenth-note triplets marked triple forte that returns to the slow tempo primo, but the rhythm remains the same, with crescendi and decrescendi throughout. The established rhythmic motive then begins to break up in the violins, and eventually the movement grows to a grand, ardent apotheosis at m. 117 based mainly on major triads built on A-flat and A-natural (see example 70).

Schuman calms the environment and slowly brings the movement to a quiet repose over fifteen emotional measures, blending the four instruments in a harmonic structure reminiscent of the first measure of this extraordinary movement, which reflects Schuman's fascination in this work with the sonority of the major/minor tetrachord.

The fourth movement, Presto, set at the breakneck tempo of ♩ = c. 168, is a wild rush to the end of this grand composition, mixing quick shifts of pizzicato and arco sections, marked "agilmente," and highly innovative uses of the instruments, as in the wonderful effect Schuman creates for pizzicato quartet (see example 71). His rhythmic juxtapositions for the instruments are both playful and powerful, and the offbeat and triplet figures heard throughout the quartet bring the work to a new level of excitement. However, by using the viola and eventually the cello to introduce a flowing melody surrounded by frenetic accompaniment in the other strings, he also changes the character of the movement, making it slightly more lyrical (see examples 72 and 73). In the midst of his rapid tempo, Schuman also creates clarity of sound through pizzicato and dynamics that are truly transparent in texture (see example 74).

The exceedingly quick tempo, a technical challenge for any quartet, drives the work to its conclusion, and Schuman ups the ante by writing an accelerando presaged by rhythmically unison triplet eighth note–quarter note figures in all strings to an even faster tempo (Prestissimo ♩ = c. 184) that brings the work to a series of polychords (mainly interlocking major triads alternating between pentachords and hexachords), creating a remarkable sonic effect (see example 75). The work concludes with triple-forte accented G major first-inversion chords, followed by a final root-position chord in the same tonality (see example 76).

Schuman's Fourth Quartet stands as a masterpiece of quartet writing. It also represents another breakthrough in Schuman's compositional growth. His fascination with the sonority of the major/minor tetrachord throughout the work provides the work with a particularly distinctive sonic environment.

A Song of Orpheus: Fantasy for Cello and Orchestra

Premiere: February 17, 1962, Indianapolis, Indiana; Indianapolis Symphony
Orchestra, cond. Izler Solomon, with Leonard Rose, soloist

Duration: approximately 23 minutes

This soulful work for solo cello and orchestra uses Schuman's song "Orpheus with His Lute" as melodic material transmuted by the composer into a work of beguiling simplicity and pathos. The solo cello presents numerous musical moods that vary from deeply introspective to jocular, although the overall tone of the work is somber. The subtitle, *Fantasy for Cello and Orchestra*, points to the many "personalities" realized in the solo line, with particular emphasis on the three cadenza-like sections for solo cello, reminiscent of his earlier violin concerto.

Curiously, Schuman not only requests that the text of the original song, taken from Shakespeare's *Henry VIII*, be printed in the program book of each performance, but he also includes the text under the solo cello line at the beginning of the composition, indicating in the score, "The words are given to enable the soloist to perform the melody with the clarity of a singer's projection." This is an approach he would use frequently in other works based on song texts or rounds. As in the song, the cello line sings out with the memorable concluding theme of the song on the words "In sweet music is such art, / Killing care and grief of heart, / Fall asleep, or hearing die," marked "Delicatamente" by the composer.

The work is written in one movement of continuous contrasting sections beginning in the very slow tempo of ♩ = c. 50. The solo cello line begins the work with no accompaniment, playing a variation of the original song material, with brightly textured accompaniment eventually appearing in the woodwinds and strings. The distinctive song melody that defines the text begins on an upbeat to m. 24 (see example 77).

Schuman then begins to modify the structure of the melody and creates a beautiful interplay between oboe and solo cello, interspersed with a series of pentachords providing both consonant and dissonant textures. The melody continues to vary until a brief cadenza-like part is presented by the solo cello that segues to a section for oboe, harp, and solo cello, with divisi strings sustaining chords that produce some extraordinary juxtapositions of polychordal lines. As the solo cello line intensifies, unison pizzicati in the orchestral strings lead to the first full cadenza for cello. Schuman's writing in the cadenza is masterly: he utilizes multiple stops and brusque, forceful chords to create an agitated monologue for the cello (see example 78).

The cadenza moves seamlessly to the most extended fast section of the composition, marked "Leggiero," ♩ = c. 138. This playful section soon introduces

Schumanesque flourishes in the woodwinds, with the cello playing rapid sixteenth-note figures accented both off and on the beat. As this section progresses, Schuman creates a jocular interplay between the solo cello and woodwinds, juxtaposing meters from five to four to five to three, eventually leading to a charming duo between harp and cello. The intricacies of the harp part were clarified through the advice of the great harp virtuoso and teacher Marcel Grandjany, who edited the part for Schuman. Finally, while the solo cello continues its headlong flight in the upper register, Schuman provides a distinctive accompaniment in the winds and strings of a three-against-four rhythmic configuration that adds to the power of this section (see example 79).

The ensuing "Più mosso ♩ = c. 144" is an orchestral interlude that dispenses with the solo cello, providing a robust aural texture, including the flourishes and muscular, brassy chords for which Schuman is so well known. In this case, however, the chords do not include the usual trumpets and trombones because the only brass for which the work is scored is French horns.

When the solo cello returns at the end of this section, the accompaniment becomes much less dense, and soon there is a segue into the second cadenza section of the work. As opposed to the pensive quality of the first cadenza, the second is more frenetic and set at a much quicker tempo (♩ = c. 144), with fits and starts for the soloist enhanced by triple- and quadruple-stop pizzicati, accelerandi, and the fascinating device of having the cello play a pedal D-natural over rapid sixteenth notes (see example 80).

When the orchestral accompaniment returns, it is initially played only by bass clarinet and two bassoons in triplet eighths, followed by an exceedingly short presto of only ten measures that leads into the third and final cadenza for cello, marked "Presto possibile" and "sotto voce" (see example 81).

This cadenza segues to the final section of the work, which is reminiscent of the plaintive and introspective quality at the beginning of the composition. Here one hears a very quiet pizzicato accompaniment for muted strings with a melancholy solo cello line emerging above. The prominent harp part also reappears, and the tempo gradually slows through the introduction of successive meno mossos, to eventually arrive at the work's original tempo of ♩ = c. 50.

At the beginning of the concluding section the solo cello plays a variant of the song melody, but the English horn presents a melodic line much closer to the original song, creating a remarkable counterpoint (see example 82). The cello then plays harmonics that move to a statement of the song melody, providing a gripping juxtaposition of dissonant and consonant textures, enhanced by the tuneful familiarity of the original song melody (see examples 83 and 84).

Moving through various keys, the soulful, contemplative music ends with a "heavenly choir" of muted violins and harp, while the solo cello insistently repeats a B-natural that eventually dies away to silence (see example 85).

A Song of Orpheus is a work of deep feeling in which Schuman once again shows his mastery of string writing. The dialogue that he creates between cello and orchestra is both profound and multifaceted and shows the cello in its most plaintive and conversational light.

Symphony No. 9, "*Le Fosse Ardeatine*"

Anteludium—Offertorium—Postludium (played without pause)
Premiere: January 10, 1969, Academy of Music (Philadelphia); Philadelphia
Orchestra, cond. Eugene Ormandy
Duration: approximately 28 minutes

Schuman wrote brief explanatory notes, dated November 19, 1968, about the music of his Ninth Symphony at the beginning of the printed score of the work and requested that the analysis be reprinted in program notes whenever the work was performed. The quotations that appear below are from that source.

Descriptive words or terms that surface continually when one hears Schuman's Ninth Symphony include "ominous," "dark," "tormented," and "profoundly troubling." Schuman exposed through his music the horror of the 1944 massacre of 335 Italians at the Ardeatine Caves:

> The mood of my symphony, especially in its opening and closing sections, is directly related to emotions engendered by this visit [to the Caves]. But the entire middle section, too, with its various moods of fast music, much of it far from somber, stems from the fantasies I had of the variety, promise and aborted lives of the martyrs. . . . The work does not attempt to depict the event realistically. . . . My reason for using the title is not then, musical, but philosophical. One must come to terms with the past in order to build a future. But in this exercise I am a foe of forgetting. Whatever future my symphony may have, whenever it is performed, audiences will remember.

Schuman saw the symphony as a "continuum," the three parts played without pause. It is curious to note that the composer does not even indicate in the score where one section ends and the next one begins, although the change of musical mood is evident:

> The Anteludium begins quietly, with a single melodic line separated by two octaves, played by the muted violins and cellos. The first section of this melody, which is 11 bars in length, continues its development over a span of 33 bars. At the 12th bar, however, the same melody appears in the second violins and violas, one-half step higher in pitch [A-sharp to B], and at the 23rd bar the same melody begins again one-half step higher still [B to B-sharp] in the strings and the pitch is raised one-half step in each of the succeeding entrances during the first section of the work.

In addition, Schuman uses the expressive ascending and descending sixth to add tension to the melodic line, and the extreme harmonic dissonance at the entrance of the second violins and violas at m. 12 creates a growing sense of intensity in the work, as does the dissonant counterpoint heard in the strings throughout the early part of the movement. The musical texture at the beginning of the work is densely chromatic and contrapuntal, with dissonances that are clearly intended to create a disturbing and unsettling aural environment (see example 86).

Within the context of the dissonant string lines Schuman introduces his characteristic flourishes in the flute, oboe, and bassoon, but here, played against a long line in the strings at triple piano, the flourishes sound ominous. The woodwind figure becomes more elaborate as the section progresses and the strings inexorably rise in pitch, creating greater tension. The jagged triplet and offbeat rhythms in the second violins and violas add further to the taut quality of the work (mm. 65–68; see example 87), as does a highly dramatic and ominous timpani part, all of it leading to a definitive whole-note chord marked triple forte, piano subito that crescendos to two accented eighth notes of dramatic finality (m. 84; see example 88).

Although Schuman never used serial technique in his works, the composer Robert Beaser has mused that the presence of twelve-note chords in the Symphony No. 9 may indicate a recognition of the technique at a time when American composers were under considerable pressure to include it in their compositional process. Certainly the level of harmonic dissonance obscures tonal centers throughout the work.

Wrote Schuman:

> The music of the Anteludium leads without pause, but with identifiable transition, to the Offertorium, which section forms the bulk of the work. The moods are varied and range from the playful to the dramatic. This music is fast with the exception of several short contrasting interludes which always return to the fast tempo. The climax of the Offertorium is reached with an even faster tempo and a sonorous climax for full orchestra, with three pairs of struck cymbals employed in rhythmic patterns.

The beginning of the Offertorium is playful, with shifting meters of 2/4, 5/8, 4/4, and 3/4 in the first five measures. This creates a jagged, syncopated effect in the strings and piano at the very fast tempo of ♩ = c. 160, which develops much energy as the movement progresses.

In typical fashion, the orchestra choirs are divided. Schuman inventively writes a jocular woodwind line against syncopated pizzicato strings (see example 89) and then provides a variant of his flourishes, marked "playfully," for piccolo, flutes, and eventually clarinets (see example 90).

This is soon punctuated by dissonant chords, first in the brass (mm. 148–50; see example 91), then in the full orchestra (mm. 170 and 177; see examples 92 and 93), which create powerful dissonances throughout this section.

Schuman then begins a section for only woodwinds that stretches for a remarkable forty-seven measures, beginning with a bass clarinet solo reminiscent of that in his Third Symphony. This section culminates with all woodwinds in sixteenth-note rhythmic unison at the exceedingly fast tempo of ♩ = c. 160, creating a whirlwind of sound.

Strings and piano then continue, soon joined by harsh, accented rhythmic figures in the lower woodwinds, brass, and strings that grow in tension as the accented lines in the brass are placed against a jagged rhythmic line in the violins, increasing the tension in this section (see example 94). In quick succession Schuman presents a long melody in the strings, marked "cantabile," juxtaposed against a frenetic timpani line—and eventually woodwinds and brass—that further increases the tension (see example 95).

Once again Schuman shifts into a calming string melody. This then quickly moves to triple-forte dissonant chords in the entire orchestra, followed by an ominous timpani figure (see example 96). A kaleidoscope of musical moods ensues—long string lines paralleling contrapuntal touches in the winds, ominous rhythmic bass figures, brass figurations in jagged rhythms, woodwinds in triplets that sound like buzzing bees (mm.

435–40; see example 97), a brass chorale played over frightening snare and bass drums, and timpani parts embellished by flourishes in the woodwinds. Schuman brings this part to a close at a section marked "Presto, breathlessly," ♩ = c. 208, in which triple-forte chords reinforced by xylophone and timpani, and eventually three pairs of struck cymbals, create a consuming, horrific aural environment that diminuendos into the symphony's final section. In this longest section of the symphony, Schuman allows his musical imagination to blossom, taking a blank musical canvas and splashing it with aural episodes that conjure up the horrors of the massacre.

Schuman writes of the final section:

> The music of the Postludium at first echoes, in slow tempo, some elements of the climax just heard. Finally the opening theme of the symphony is again stated, but in an even slower tempo than at first. The setting is different and the melody, although again played by the strings, is harmonized in the trombones and tuba. New figurations are introduced and reference is made to the music of the Offertorium. The symphony draws to a close with a long, freely composed quiet ending characterized by an emotional climate which sums up the work and eventually leads to a final concluding outburst.

In this final section Schuman continues the work's ominous quality by presenting a foreboding twelve-note chord in woodwinds and brass followed by the use of three cymbals and tam-tam, creating a chilling effect over sustained, divisi muted strings (see example 98). The ensuing snare, tenor, and bass drum solos create a distinctly military effect but are interrupted by a beautiful yet eerie chorale for strings in the extremely slow tempo of ♩ = 36.

At m. 575 we hear a suggestion of the opening theme in collaboration with the low brass (see example 99)—a soulful and beautiful dissonance with echoes of harmonies from *The Mighty Casey*. Soon the string line is embellished by flourish-like passages in the bass clarinet and piccolo, with solos in the xylophone that add to the poignancy of this section (see example 100). Schuman breaks this peaceful mood by presenting a triple-forte chord played by four muted trumpets, timpani, and bass drum that brings the listener back to the underlying horror of the symphony, followed immediately by the sudden quiet entrance of the strings (marked "entrance of strings should be inaudible"), woodwind lines marked "plaintively," and ominous timpani beats along with a snare drum and bass drum reminding us of the ultimate fate of the victims.

The work ends with a continuous string chord over wailing woodwinds and the frightening peal of a tubular bell at m. 623 that leads to a triple-forte crescendoing twelve-note chord at the conclusion of the work, aurally depicting the horror of the massacre in a musical portrayal of a human scream (see example 101).

A tormented and poignant quality permeates this work, which manifests the profoundly somber character of the composer's later compositions. Perhaps more than any other Schuman orchestral work, the Ninth Symphony expresses the many conflicting emotions experienced by the composer owing to the deeply troubling theme of the Ardeatine Caves and also the traumatic events he had just realized in his professional life.

In Sweet Music: Serenade on a Setting of Shakespeare for Flute, Viola, Voice, and Harp

Premiere: October 29, 1978, Alice Tully Hall (New York City);
Chamber Music Society of Lincoln Center

Duration: approximately 25 minutes

From the first chord played by the harp, it is evident that William Schuman created with *In Sweet Music* an aural environment that looks at once to both the past and the present. In this work, one experiences the textures of the music of the Renaissance, with a haunting vocal part sung over sustained harp chords echoing the sound of a lute. At the same time, a dissonant counterpoint in the alto flute and viola brings the listener squarely into the twentieth century.

As he had done in the *Song of Orpheus* and *Amaryllis: Variations for String Trio*, Schuman sets the words to the original song he composed in 1943, "Orpheus with His Lute," below an instrumental line (the alto flute), "to enable the flutist to perform the melody with the clarity of a singer's projection." In a fascinating juxtaposition, Schuman has the singer announce the words "In sweet music," but most of the remainder of the work is a textless vocalise.

The arpeggiated harp chords that follow, which accompany the alto flute line, return to the Renaissance in character, but the entrance of the muted viola adds a piquant counterpoint, arresting, disturbing, and contemporary (see example 102).

Soon the distinctive core melody of the original song is introduced for the first time with harp accompaniment, reminiscent of Schuman's use of the "Amaryllis" melody in works based on that song. However, the subsequent introduction of the dissonant viola part accompanies the voice humming a melody to create a remarkable mixture of aural textures (see example 103).

Throughout the work, Schuman is quite masterly in juxtaposing instrumental colors by having the flutist switch from alto flute to regular flute to piccolo. With the introduction of the regular flute, the sultry tones of the alto flute are replaced by a more rhythmically animated and tonally abstract line against the humming in the voice and the accompanying harp. This section is then enhanced by the counterpoint in the viola and harp, creating a beguiling, almost otherworldly effect (see example 104).

After another brief interlude between harp and humming voice on the syllable "loo," a "quasi cadenza a due" occurs between flute and viola that changes the basic nature of the work from a rather dreamy statement of the melody to a much more animated and dissonant treatment for flute and viola, very much in late twentieth-century style (see example 105).

The quasi cadenza leads to an animated section ($\downarrow$ = c. 138) in which all four performers have a lively rhythmic interchange accented by a kind of scat singing on the syllables "la-lee" (see example 106) and eventually "bee-de-baa" (see example 107).

Schuman's understanding of the viola, which he gained from his work on the *Concerto on Old English Rounds,* is evident in the next section, where the flute and viola participate in a complex counterpoint accompanied by the harp. It is the harp that throughout the work provides the harmonic underpinning for the composition.

The work continues to build in force and liveliness, with excited scat singing and rapid passages in the three instruments, culminating in the introduction of the piccolo. This leads to an accelerando and then to a più mosso at $\downarrow$ = c. 144. The piccolo plays flourishes, and frenzied passages in the harp create an animated environment that contrasts strongly with the calm experienced at the beginning of the work. The voice now forcefully declaims the melody on the syllables "lee," "la," "bee," and "baa" (see examples 108 and 109). What seemed to be a rather sedate treatment of a beguiling melody has now turned into a musical experience of wild abandon.

This feeling of abandon is reinforced by the ensuing technically demanding piccolo solo with harp accompaniment, marked "Presto ♩ = c. 160," that once again changes the texture of the work. But Schuman cleverly moves the composition forward by first writing a languorous viola solo (♩ = c. 60) primarily in double stops (see example 110), followed by a brief and animated Presto possible section for harp and viola (see example 111).

As Schuman develops the conclusion of the work, the four players are brought back together with the voice still humming variations on the original song melody, often in rhythmic unison with the instruments. The alto flute is reintroduced, and the three instruments then prepare the way for the eventual entrance of the voice with a particularly unique treatment of the theme in harmonics on the viola. Schuman does not present the melody conventionally, but rather as a transformation of the song.

The work ultimately begins to settle into the song melody in its original form, so that the melody is recognizable in the voice and the accompanying instruments on the words "Orpheus with his lute" (see example 112).

This final section culminates in the dramatic core of the song on the words "In sweet music," etc., marked "with utmost beauty and purity of tone," presenting the song in a simple and uncomplicated harmonic setting (see example 113). The voice continues to repeat "or hearing, die," accompanied by flute and viola, as the work ends with a morendo on the syllable "ah" (see example 114).

In Sweet Music shows how Schuman's remarkable compositional imagination brings together the voice with a disparate group of instruments to create a compelling and moving chamber work. Of profound depth and beauty, it stands out as one of his most creative and skillful combinations of complex counterpoint and polychords with a simple melodic line.

Night Journey: Choreographic Poem for Fifteen Instruments

Premiere: February 27, 1981, Empire State Performing Arts Center (Albany, New York); Endymion Ensemble, cond. Jon Goldberg

Duration: approximately 21 minutes 30 seconds

The original 1947 version of *Night Journey* was adapted by Schuman for an ensemble of fifteen instruments and entitled *Night Journey: Choreographic Poem for Fifteen Instruments*. The later version is about seven to eight minutes shorter than the original, thanks to the deletion of certain repeats and bridge sections that were required for the staged version of the ballet.

In the music of *Night Journey* one hears a different quality from that in his 1945 ballet score for Antony Tudor, *Undertow*. *Night Journey* is more introspective, pensive, jagged, and dissonant. Its beginning is similar to the beginning of *Undertow*, with its static chords in the lower strings, but the initial horn melody has more color than do the wind lines in *Undertow*. The horn theme presents a series of whole-tone relationships, which are heard throughout the work. In the first two measures almost all twelve tones are presented, creating a chromatic texture. Descending chromatic lines are also frequently used, and there are more intervallic relationships rather than the triadic structures heard in *Undertow* (see example 115).

The subsequent piano figure sets a new and unsettled mood, and the dissonant motive, in rhythmic unison, is heightened by the eerie sul ponticello figure in the strings (see example 116).

The characteristic slow tempo of ♩ = 48–52 sets the context for the introduction of the principal melodic motive, which is presented by the oboe and will be reintroduced frequently. The ensuing cadence is approached by a descending line, now landing on E minor, with the flute solo purposely clashing on F, a half step off. Then Schuman presents an F major chord. The flute clashes again by half step (now G-flat). A "furioso" section begins with the jagged piano figure heard earlier, extending for many measures until an accelerando molto occurs in a rhythmically strident section, presenting first strings, and then piano and winds, arriving at the exceedingly fast tempo of ♩ = 184 (see example 117).

Soon another variant of the Schuman flourishes appears, involving rapidly ascending sixteenth notes. The violins and violas then introduce a passionate melody with large expressive intervals—a hallmark of Schuman's later melodic writing (see example 118).

In this section, Schuman writes triplet figures that eventually become sextuplets in a written accelerando—another typical Schumanesque compositional signature—adding even more tension to the music (see example 119).

As the piece progresses the musical context becomes more and more violent, with a distinctive dissonance that could be characterized as a tone cluster functioning as a diminished or half-diminished chord. The tonality is purposely ambiguous. In a typical gesture, Schuman juxtaposes the wind choir against the strings in this section (see example 120).

On an extended trill at the end of this section, Schuman once again creates a diminished sound that is a cluster as well. No specific tonality is implied, and the conclusion of the trill pushes upward by ending a half step higher than it began (see example 121).

The work comes to a quiet conclusion. The tonality remains ambiguous, but the D pedal in the left hand of the piano and the basses with the horn (on an F-natural) imply D minor. However, the upper voices keep the tonal center unclear. As the work concludes, the continuing D pedal keeps the tonal center at least on D to the end, but the chromatic treatment of the instruments above keeps the modality amorphous (see example 122).

Through his initial harmonic experimentation in *Undertow* and the more audacious results in *Night Journey*, Schuman transitioned from an earlier compositional style to a newer, more dissonant and introspective approach that would be a component of his compositions for the rest of his life. The intertwining melodic lines in this fifteen-instrument version have a clarity and focus that are not found in the original orchestration and that create an astringency appropriate to the somber story line of the original Martha Graham ballet.

Musical Examples

Example 1. *American Festival Overture*, mm. 1–12.

Example 1 (*continued*).

Example 2. *American Festival Overture*, mm. 60–84.

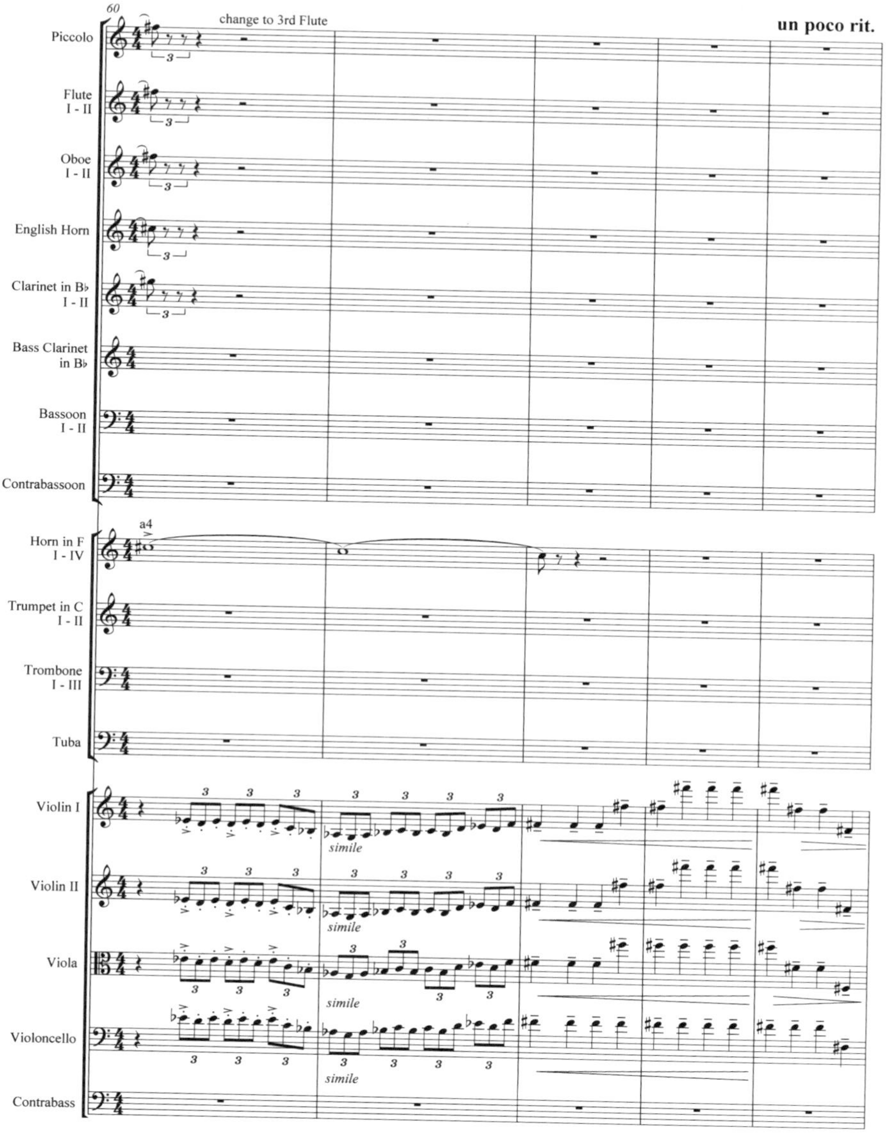

Example 2 (*continued*).

Example 2 (*continued*).

Example 2 (*continued*).

Example 3. *American Festival Overture*, mm. 150–65.

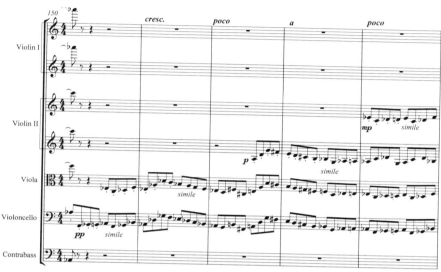

Example 3 (*continued*).

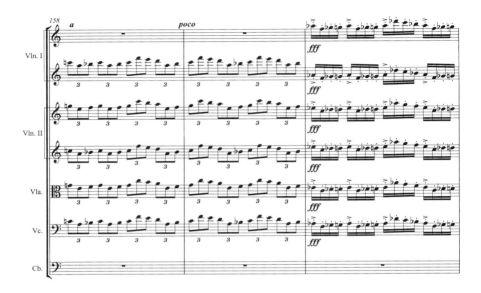

Example 3 (*continued*).

Example 4. *American Festival Overture*, mm. 205–12

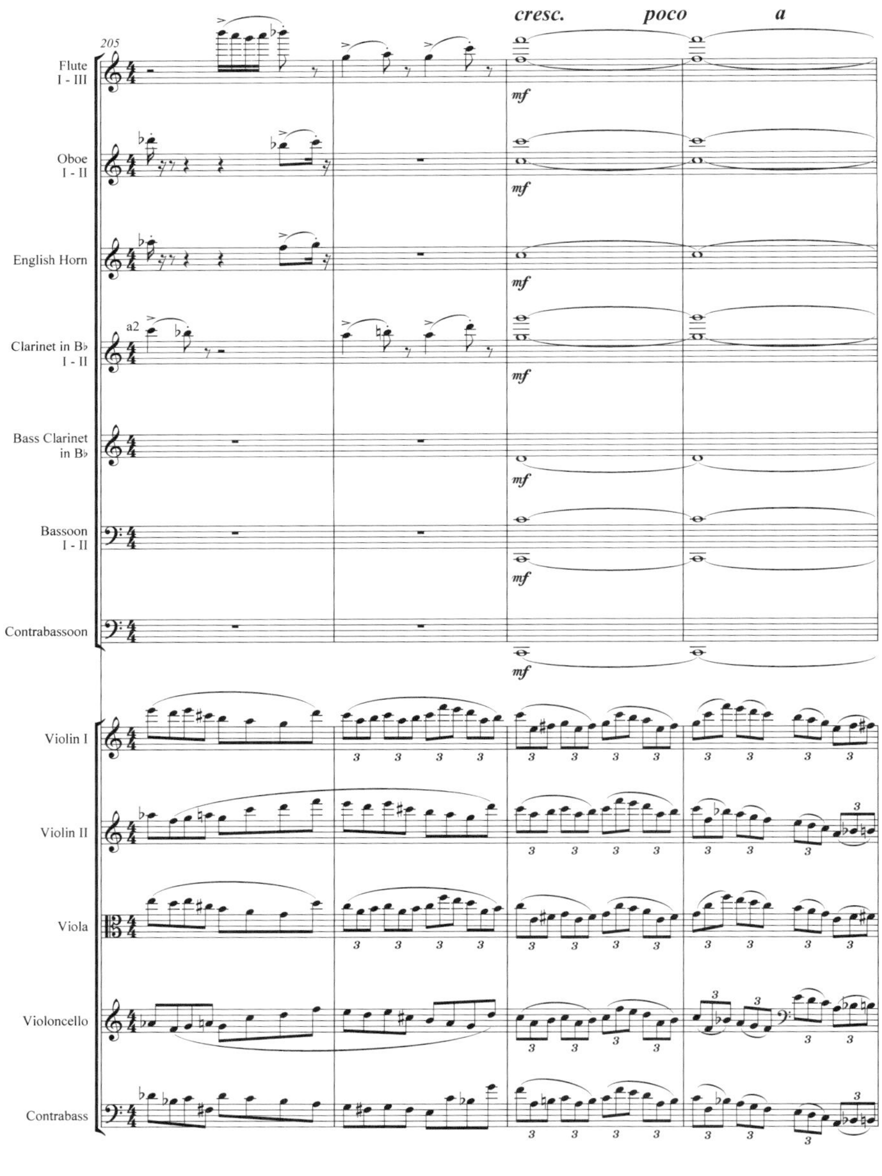

Example 4 (*continued*).

Example 5. *American Festival Overture*, mm. 254–60.

Example 6. *American Festival Overture*, mm. 310–20.

Example 6 (*continued*).

Example 6 (*continued*).

Example 7. *American Festival Overture*, mm. 350–end.

Example 7 (*continued*).

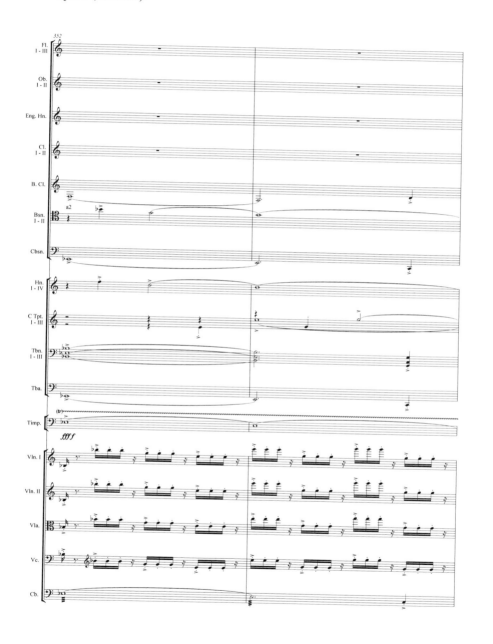

Example 7 (*continued*).

Example 7 (*continued*).

Example 8. Symphony No. 3, Part I, mm. 1–7.

Example 9. Symphony No. 3, Part I, mm. 87–93.

Example 10. Symphony No. 3, Part I, mm. 146–50.

b. Fugue

Example 11. Symphony No. 3, Part I, mm. 195–200.

Example 12. Symphony No. 3, Part I, m. 320.

Example 13. Symphony No. 3, Part II, mm. 21–31.

Example 14. Symphony No. 3, Part II, mm. 157–71.

Example 15. Symphony No. 3, Part II, mm. 249–85.

Example 16. Symphony No. 3, Part II, mm. 422–end.

Example 17. Symphony for Strings, first movement, mm. 26–31.

Example 18. Symphony for Strings, first movement, mm. 65–87.

Example 18 (*continued*).

Example 19. Symphony for Strings, first movement, mm. 146–end.

Example 20. Symphony for Strings, second movement, mm. 5–20.

Example 21. Symphony for Strings, second movement, mm. 40–50.

Example 22. Symphony for Strings, second movement, mm. 58–73.

Example 22 (*continued*).

Example 23. Symphony for Strings, third movement, mm. 16–18.

Example 24. Symphony for Strings, third movement, mm. 78–84.

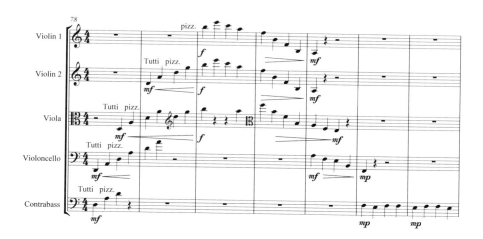

Example 25. Symphony for Strings, third movement, mm. 210–15.

Example 26. Symphony for Strings, third movement, mm. 232–33.

Example 27. Symphony for Strings, third movement, mm. 253–57.

Example 28. Symphony for Strings, third movement, mm. 270–71.

Example 29. Symphony for Strings, third movement, mm. 280–92.

Example 30. Symphony for Strings, third movement, mm. 374–end.

July 31, 1943
New Rochelle, N.Y.

Example 31. Concerto for Violin and Orchestra, first movement, mm. 1–7.

Example 32. Concerto for Violin and Orchestra, first movement, mm. 61–63.

Example 33. Concerto for Violin and Orchestra, first movement, mm. 83–86.

Example 34. Concerto for Violin and Orchestra, first movement, m. 105.

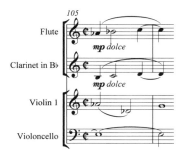

Example 35. Concerto for Violin and Orchestra, first movement, mm. 152–60.

Example 36. Concerto for Violin and Orchestra, first movement, mm. 240–98.

Example 36 (*continued*).

Example 37. Concerto for Violin and Orchestra, first movement, mm. 382–84.

Example 38. Concerto for Violin and Orchestra, first movement, mm. 398–end.

Example 38 (*continued*).

Example 39. Concerto for Violin and Orchestra, second movement, mm. 59–69.

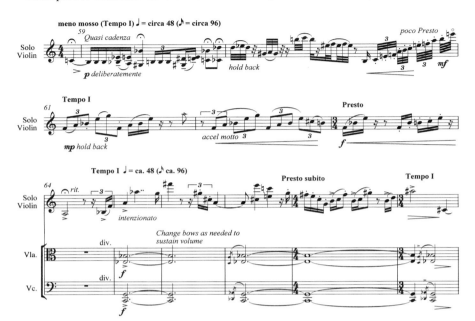

Example 40. Concerto for Violin and Orchestra, second movement, mm. 149–53.

Example 41. Concerto for Violin and Orchestra, second movement, mm. 239–45.

Example 42. Concerto for Violin and Orchestra, second movement, mm. 302–5.

Example 43. Concerto for Violin and Orchestra, second movement, mm. 387–95.

Example 43 (*continued*).

Example 44. Concerto for Violin and Orchestra, second movement, mm. 437–end.

Example 44 (*continued*).

Example 45. *New England Triptych*, "Be Glad Then, America," mm. 7–20.

Example 46. *New England Triptych*, "Be Glad Then, America," mm. 40–45.

Example 47. *New England Triptych*, "Be Glad Then, America," mm. 135–72.

Example 48. *New England Triptych*, "Be Glad Then, America," mm. 286–90.

Example 49. *New England Triptych*, "Be Glad Then, America," mm. 322–end.

Example 50. *New England Triptych*, "When Jesus Wept," mm. 34–43.

Example 51. *New England Triptych*, "When Jesus Wept," mm. 75–80.

Example 52. *New England Triptych*, "When Jesus Wept," mm. 105–end.

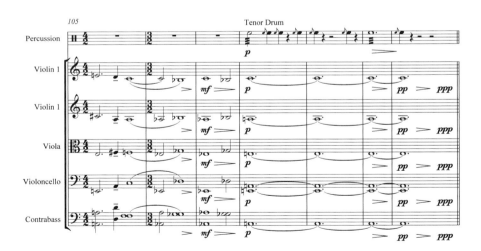

Example 53. *New England Triptych*, "Chester," mm. 1–18.

Example 54. *New England Triptych*, "Chester," mm. 22–30.

Example 55. *New England Triptych*, "Chester," mm. 55–61.

Example 56. *New England Triptych*, "Chester," mm. 91–93.

Example 57. *New England Triptych*, "Chester," mm. 159–end.

Example 57 (*continued*).

New Rochelle June 12, 1956

Example 58. String Quartet No. 4, first movement, mm. 1–7.

Example 59. String Quartet No. 4, first movement, mm. 28–33.

Example 60. String Quartet No. 4, first movement, mm. 45–56.

Example 61. String Quartet No. 4, second movement, mm. 1–5.

II

Example 62. String Quartet No. 4, second movement, mm. 68–75.

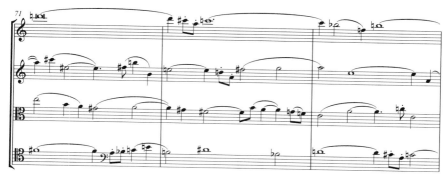

Example 63. String Quartet No. 4, second movement, mm. 99–101.

Example 64. String Quartet No. 4, second movement, m. 37.

Example 65. String Quartet No. 4, second movement, mm. 39–42.

Example 66. String Quartet No. 4, second movement, mm. 225–end.

Example 67. String Quartet No. 4, third movement, mm. 1–5.

Example 68. String Quartet No. 4, third movement, mm. 54–57.

Example 69. String Quartet No. 4, third movement, mm. 70–74.

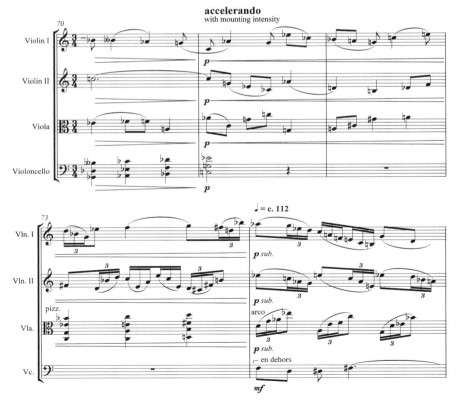

Example 70. String Quartet No. 4, third movement, mm. 115–20.

Example 71. String Quartet No. 4, fourth movement, mm. 40–45.

Example 72. String Quartet No. 4, fourth movement, mm. 75–80.

Example 73. String Quartet No. 4, fourth movement, mm. 102–5.

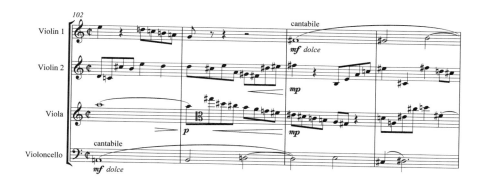

Example 74. String Quartet No. 4, fourth movement, mm. 162–65.

Example 75. String Quartet No. 4, fourth movement, mm. 337–40.

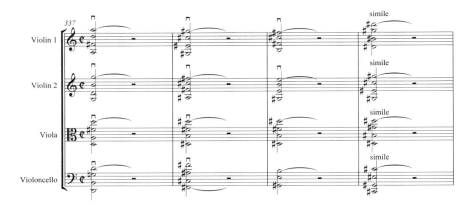

Example 76. String Quartet No. 4, fourth movement, mm. 381–end.

Menemsha, Marth's Vineyard, Mass. June 26-August 3, 1950.

Example 77. *A Song of Orpheus*, mm. 1–31.

*) The words are given to enable the soloist to perform the melody with the clarity of a singer's projection.

Example 77 (*continued*).

Example 78. *A Song of Orpheus*, mm. 67–90.

Example. 79. *A Song of Orpheus*, mm. 168–71.

Example 80. *A Song of Orpheus,* mm. 258–80.

Example 81. *A Song of Orpheus*, mm. 307–24.

Example 82. *A Song of Orpheus*, mm. 361–65.

*) English Horn Solo (bars 361 - 365 and 371 - 375); dynamics are relative depending on soloist,
but the melodic line carried by the English Horn should always be clearly audible.

Example 83. *A Song of Orpheus*, mm. 368–71.

Example 84. *A Song of Orpheus*, mm. 375–80.

Example 85. *A Song of Orpheus*, mm. 403–end.

*) Change bows to sustain sound.

Example 86. Symphony No. 9, mm. 1–25.

Example 86 (*continued*).

Example 87. Symphony No. 9, mm. 65–68.

Example 87 (*continued*).

Example 88. Symphony No. 9, mm. 83–84.

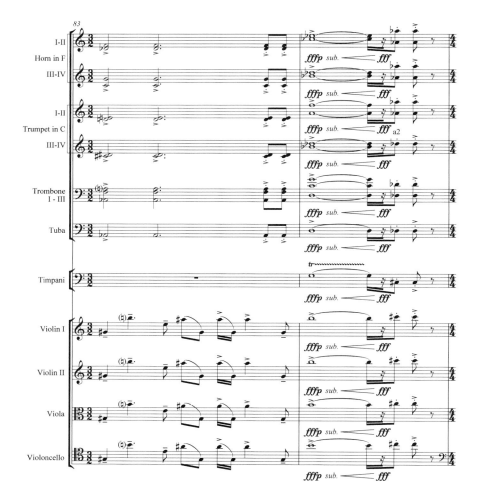

Example 89. Symphony No. 9, mm. 127–30.

Example 90. Symphony No. 9, mm. 139–45.

Example 91. Symphony No. 9, mm. 147–50.

Example 92. Symphony No. 9, m. 170.   Example 93. Symphony No. 9, m. 177.

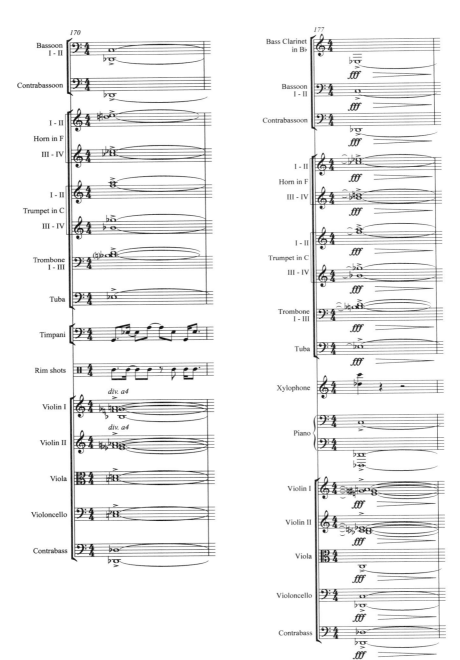

Example 94. Symphony No. 9, mm. 255–61.

Example 95. Symphony No. 9, mm. 263–70.

Example 96. Symphony No. 9, mm. 289–302.

Example 96 (*continued*).

Example 97. Symphony No. 9, mm. 435–40.

Example 97 (*continued*).

Example 98. Symphony No. 9, mm. 545–55.

Example 98 (*continued*).

Example 99. Symphony No. 9, mm. 575–78.

Example 100. Symphony No. 9, mm. 591–94.

Example 100 (*continued*).

Example 101. Symphony No. 9, mm. 623–end.

Example 101 (*continued*).

Example 102. *In Sweet Music*, mm. 1–16.

IN SWEET MUSIC

Serenade on a Setting of Shakespeare
for Flute, Viola, Voice and Harp

WILLIAM SCHUMAN

* N.B. The words are given to enable the flutist to perform the melody with the clarity of a singer's projection.

Example 103. *In Sweet Music*, mm. 46–51.

Example 104. *In Sweet Music*, mm. 53–56.

Example 105. *In Sweet Music*, mm. 87–95.

Example 106. *In Sweet Music*, mm. 108–12.

Example 107. *In Sweet Music*, mm. 190–94.

Example 108. *In Sweet Music*, mm. 250–54.

Example 109. *In Sweet Music*, mm. 275–77.

Example 110. *In Sweet Music*, mm. 301–5.

Example 111. *In Sweet Music*, mm. 314–18.

Example 112. *In Sweet Music,* mm. 415–20.

Example 113. *In Sweet Music*, mm. 439–48.

Example 114. *In Sweet Music*, mm. 457–end.

Example 115. *Night Journey*, mm. 1–10.

Night Journey
Choreographic Poem for Fifteen Instruments

WILLIAM SCHUMAN

Example 116. *Night Journey*, mm. 20–29.

Example 117. *Night Journey*, mm. 130–38.

Example 118. *Night Journey*, mm. 184–88.

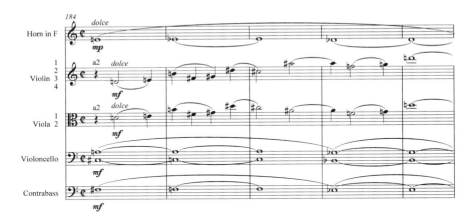

Example 119. *Night Journey*, mm. 204–6.

Example 120. *Night Journey*, mm. 362–70.

Example 121. *Night Journey*, mm. 407–11.

Example 122. *Night Journey*, mm. 500–end.

** no bow change E to D

Notes

Prologue

xvi "*never achieved the kind of name recognition*": Joseph McLellan, "Appreciation: Schuman's American Song; Remembering the Composer & His Musical Lives," *Washington Post*, Feb. 18, 1992.

xvi "*Whatever meaning my life has*": Karl F. Miller, "William Schuman, 1910–1992," *American Record Guide* 55, no. 4 (July–Aug. 1992): p. 30.

xvi "*a radical with conservative ideas*": Harold C. Schonberg, "Man to Orchestrate Lincoln Center," *New York Times Magazine*, Dec. 31, 1961, p. 30.

xvii "*It seems to me*": William Schuman, letter to Antal Doráti, Apr. 16, 1974; New York Public Library for the Performing Arts (hereafter cited as NYPL of the Performing Arts), Box 147, Folder 10.

xvii "*I have rarely met*": Leonard Bernstein, introductory note, in Christopher Rouse, *William Schuman Documentary* (Bryn Mawr, PA: Theodore Presser; New York: G. Schirmer, 1980), p. vi.

Chapter 1

2 *More than a third of all Americans*: Oliver E. Allen, New York, New York (New York: Atheneum, 1990), p. 250.

2 *By 1879 elevated train tracks*: ibid., p. 235.

2 "*The building was so far out of town*": ibid.

2 *By 1910 New York City's population*: statistical and historical information in this section is taken from James Trager, *The New York Chronology: The Ultimate Compendium of Events, People, and Anecdotes from the Dutch to the Present* (New York: HarperCollins, 2003), and from Gorton Carruth, *The Encyclopedia of American Facts and Dates*, 10th ed. (New York: Harper Collins, 1997).

2 *That fall Gimbels opened*: Allen, p. 323.

2 *From 1880 to 1914*: Selma C. Berrol, "In Their Image: German Jews and the Americanization of the *Ost Juden* in New York City," *New York History* 63 (Oct. 1982): p. 417.

2 *After 1840 German Jews predominated*: Naomi W. Cohen, *Encounter with Emancipation: The German Jews in the United States, 1830–1914* (Philadelphia: Jewish Publication Society of America, 1984), p. xi.

3 *Of these, the 200,000 or so German Jews*: ibid., p. 12.

3 *Although the number of German Jewish immigrants*: ibid.

3 *Of these, about 1 million*: Herman Eliassof, *German-American Jews* (Chicago: German-American Historical Society of Illinois, 1915), p. 14.

3 *Most, and the poorest*: Berrol, p. 420.

3 *In the United States they were able*: Cohen, p. 13.

3 "*Jews labored*": ibid., pp. 110–11.

3 "*These newcomers must*": Berrol, p. 424.

4 *the college had an enrollment*: Allen, p. 244.

4 "*believed in education*": William Schuman and Heidi Waleson, "William Schuman Memoirs, 1990–92, New York" [unpublished manuscript] (hereafter cited as Schuman and Waleson), chap. 1, p. 1; Schuman Family Archives.

4 *According to family lore*: unless otherwise noted, all genealogical information presented in this chapter is based on the research of Henry Heilbrunn, the great-grandson of Louis Heilbrunn and the first cousin once removed of William Schuman.

4 *a large German-speaking community*: Cohen, p. 21.

4 *Billy's older sister, Audrey, remembered*: interview by Deborah Gutmann with Audrey (Schuman) Gerstner, June 30, 1994, Larchmont, NY.

4 *Sam's granddaughter . . . described him*: telephone interview by the author with Judith Israel Gutmann, Mar. 5, 2007.

5 "*He always said*": transcript of interview by Vivian Perlis with William Schuman, no. 46 a–hh, Feb. 2–Nov. 16, 1977, New York City and Greenwich, CT [unpublished manuscript] (hereafter cited as Perlis), p. 4; American Music Series.

5 *In contrast to the outgoing*: telephone interview by the author with Judith Israel Gutmann, Mar. 5, 2007.

5 *A native of Alsace-Lorraine*: interview by Deborah Gutmann with Audrey (Schuman) Gerstner, June 30, 1994, Larchmont, NY.

5 *Schuman recalled hearing her described*: Perlis, p. 6.

5 "*a combination of Walt Whitman*": William Schuman and William Zinsser, "Dialogue between William Schuman and William Zinsser, April 4, 1989–July 11, 1989, New York and Greenwich, Connecticut" [unpublished manuscript] (hereafter cited as Schuman and Zinsser), Apr. 10, 1989, p. 4; Schuman Family Archives.

5 *He promised his new wife*: Schuman and Waleson, chap. 1, p. 3.

7 "*That boy is only interested*": Perlis, p. 5.

7 *It was there that Billy first saw*: ibid., p. 6.

7 "*Temple in the morning*": Henry Heilbrunn, Schuman Family History, p. 16.

7 Schuman retained vivid memories: William Schuman, "Autobiography" [unpublished manuscript] (hereafter cited as Schuman, "Autobiography"), chap. IV, p. 2; Schuman Family Archives.

7 "*We put on shows*": ibid., p. 4.

8 *The Heilbrunn stable*: ibid., p. 5.

8 "*We lived in Far Rockaway*": Schuman and Waleson, chap. 1, p. 5.

8 *Schuman later recalled having "sings"*: transcript of interviews by Sharon Zane with William Schuman, July 10–Oct. 18, 1990, New York City and Greenwich, CT (hereafter cited as Zane, Schuman Oral History), p. 6, Lincoln Center for the Performing Arts Oral History Project; Schuman Family Archives.

9 "*As the years have passed*": Ruth [Wertheim] Bruckner, letter to Samuel Schuman, Sept. 3, 1947; NYPL for the Performing Arts, Box 150, Folder 13.

9 *Her mellifluous German*: Schuman and Waleson, chap. 1, p. 6.

9 "*The fantastic sounds*": Schuman, "Autobiography," chap. IV, p. 7.

9 *The Schumans (who in their politics)*: Perlis, p. 31.

9 "*a part of many different worlds*": ibid., p. 35.

9 *Both Sam and Ray had gone*: Zane, Schuman Oral History, p. 3.

9 *Almost every Friday night*: ibid.

10 "*condition was not discussed*": Schuman and Waleson, chap. 1, p. 7.

10 *Robert left the household earlier*: Judith Gutmann, e-mail to the author, May 9, 2008.

10 *Robert often behaved*: interview by Deborah Gutmann with Audrey (Schuman) Gerstner, June 30, 1994, Larchmont, NY.

10 *After doctors advised*: Schuman and Waleson, chap. 1, p. 7.
10 *Yet Schuman visited*: Schuman, "Autobiography," chap. IV, p. 12.
10 *"Both my parents and my sister"*: ibid, p. 13.
10 *"My mother actually went"*: Andrea Schuman, e-mail to the author, Apr. 27, 2005.
11 *"[The] attitude within the family"*: Anthony Schuman, e-mail to the author, Apr. 27, 2005.
11 *was told of Robert's existence*: telephone interview by the author with Judith Israel Gutmann, Mar. 5, 2007.
11 *"[Audrey and Bill] distanced themselves"*: ibid.
12 *Sam had the charming practice*: Perlis, p. 4.
12 *"later on, with my newfound musical erudition"*: ibid, p. 5.
12 *Records on the Victrola*: Schuman and Waleson, chap. 1, p. 8.
12 *"That boy is going to be something"*: interview by Deborah Gutmann with Audrey (Schuman) Gerstner, June 30, 1994, Larchmont, NY.
12 *"South Field and watch[ing]"*: Zane, Schuman Oral History, p. 16.
12 *"the wonderful experience"*: Schuman, "Autobiography," chap. IV, p. 13.
13 *The camp allowed Billy*: Zane, Schuman Oral History, p. 19.
13 *"I loved camp"*: ibid., p. 17.
13 *"Billy Schuman yesterday accomplished"*: Schuman, "Autobiography," chap. IV, pp. 18–19.
13 *"The music reflected"*: William Schuman, memorandum to M. B. and L. K., Jan. 27, 1970, p. 6; Schuman Family Archives.
13 *"the entire spirit"*: William Schuman, letter to Abraham Friedman, Jan. 6, 1965; Schuman Family Archives.
13 *"the sadism of fraternity initiations"*: ibid.
13 *"In 1924, I was awarded"*: Schuman and Waleson, chap. 1, p. 10.
14 *At P.S. 165*: William Schuman, memorandum to M. B. and L. K., Jan. 27, 1970, p. 4; Schuman Family Archives.
14 *Schuman's academic work*: Schuman and Waleson, chap. 1, p. 12.
14 *He was suspended*: Zane, Schuman Oral History, p. 22.
14 *Entitled College Chums*: Schreiber, in Flora Rheta Schreiber and Vincent Persichetti, *William Schuman* (New York: G. Schirmer, 1954), p. 4.
14 *"The basic moral"*: Schuman, "Autobiography," chap. IV, p. 15.
14 *"Anything done to an excess"*: William H. Schuman, *College Chums*, Schuman Family Archives.
15 *he was voted "Best Orator"*: Schuman and Waleson, chap. 1, p. 12.
15 *"At the contest"*: William Schuman, memorandum to M. B. and L. K., Jan. 27, 1970, p. 5; Schuman Family Archives.
15 *He finally prevailed*: Schreiber, in Schreiber and Persichetti, p. 5.
15 *"either beer or bathtub gin"*: William Schuman, letter to Abraham Friedman, Jan. 6, 1965; Schuman Family Archives.
15 *"The Boys' Educational Tour of France"*: Zane, Schuman Oral History, p. 19.
16 *"No one could ever be the same"*: Perlis, p. 48.
16 *"it certainly would be a shame"*: Folder, Letters from Cobbossee & Paris (1925); Schuman Family Archives.
16 *"at the time"*: Schuman and Waleson, chap. 1, p. 14.
16 *"not one of [the band's] members"*: Perlis, p. 28.
17 *he readily acknowledged*: Perlis, pp. 24, 28.
17 *"For C— sake"*: William Schuman, letter to Edward B. Marks Jr., Oct. 31, 1928; Schuman Family Archives.
17 *"See you [at] Thanksgiving"*: ibid.
18 *"Frank didn't play"*: Schuman and Waleson, chap. 1, p. 18.
18 *"When I first met Bill"*: Frank Loesser, letter to Vincent Persichetti, Apr. 10, 1948; Schuman Family Archives.
18 *"Once when we were about twelve"*: ibid.

18 *"musical illiterate"*: Schuman and Waleson, chap. 1, p. 19.
18 *"straight out of Damon Runyon"*: ibid.
19 *"As far as I know"*: William Schuman, letter to Abraham Friedman, Jan. 6, 1965; Schuman Family Archives.
19 *"I'll have one for you"*: Schuman and Waleson, chap. 1, p. 20.
19 *"Frank's idea"*: ibid., p. 21.
19 *"Do you know"*: ibid.
19 *"You'll never make a living"*: ibid., p. 22.
19 *"Over the years"*: William Schuman, memorandum to L. K. and M. B., Jan. 19, 1970, p. 7; Schuman Family Archives.
20 *"drank too much at night"*: Perlis, p. 41.
20 *"mother-in-law used to say"*: ibid.
20 *Schuman often said that although*: ibid.
20 *The program*: Schreiber, in Schreiber and Persichetti, p. 7.
21 *"I decided on the spot"*: Schuman and Waleson, chap. 1, p. 23.
21 *He also quit his part-time job*: Schreiber, in Schreiber and Persichetti, p. 8.
21 *"I want to be a composer"*: Schuman and Waleson, chap. 1, p. 23.
21 *"He is almost twenty"*: Schreiber, in Schreiber and Persichetti, pp. 8–9.
22 *"is dedicated to the establishment"*: New York Public Library of the Performing Arts, Uncatalogued Material "MBD," in Special Collections, Malkin Conservatory of Music, Catalogue 1927–28.
22 *"was sort of a fly-by-night conservatory"*: Schuman and Zinsser, Apr. 4, 1989, p. 4.
23 *"Mr. Persin's courses"*: Uncatalogued Material "MBD," in Special Collections, Malkin Conservatory of Music, Catalogue 1927–28, p. 7; NYPL of the Performing Arts.
23 *A champion of American music*: Charles Haubiel Papers, 1916–78; Washington State University Libraries, Manuscripts, Archives, and Special Collections, Cage 482. http://nwda-db.wsulibs.wsu.edu/findaid/ark:/80444/xv92684, accessed Apr. 22, 2008.
23 *"that he could trace his teachers"*: Perlis, p. 449.
23 *"at the end of his [Schuman's] first summer"*: Schreiber, in Schreiber and Persichetti, p. 15.
24 *"I was not a literate musician"*: Schuman and Waleson, chap. 1, p. 28.
24 *"I hear[d] sounds in my head"*: Schuman and Zinsser, Apr. 24, 1989, pp. 3–4.
24 *"to lead a perfectly normal social life"*: ibid.
25 *"Schuman is relatively free"*: Schreiber, in Schreiber and Persichetti, 37. 25 "The problem is": Perlis, pp. 46–47.

Chapter 2

27 *Sometime that evening*: Schuman and Waleson, chap. 1, p. 29.
27 *"instantaneous and mutual"*: ibid.
27 *She had studied piano*: Perlis, p. 50.
27 *"worldly and sophisticated"*: Schuman and Waleson, chap. 1, p. 29.
28 *Leonard and Frankie's mother*: ibid., p. 30.
28 "amused by his [Leonard's] failed business ventures": Anthony Schuman, e-mail to the author, May 11, 2008.
28 *Frankie continued to live with her parents*: ibid.
28 *Throughout his lifetime he felt*: Perlis, p. 52.
28 *"high and low points"*: Schuman and Waleson, chap. 1, p. 31.
29 *"the ability to teach"*: Schuman, "Autobiography," chap. V, p. 11.
29 *One of the guest speakers*: Schuman and Zinsser, Apr. 4, 1989, p. 24.
29 *"I just love what you said"*: Schuman and Waleson, chap. 1, pp. 31–32.

30 *"Hebrew is scarcely more"*: William H. Schuman, "Richard Wagner Alias 'K. Freigedank,'" pp. 3–4. William Schuman, biographical files; Juilliard School Archives, Box 2, Folder Essay on Wagner & Judaism, 1933.

30 *"In conclusion, I can only repeat"*: ibid., p. 6.

30 *"the inadequacy of using our Major and Minor System"*: William H. Schuman, "On the Increased Use of Modes," Music Ed. 214H; May 26, 1934; Schuman Family Archives.

31 *"If the music of this modern giant"*: William H. Schuman, "'Prometheus' as Experience," for T.C. Music 169, Aesthetics of Music, Prof. Dykema, n.d., p. 2; Schuman Family Archives.

31 *"I saw that education"*: Schuman and Waleson, chap. 1, p. 32.

32 *"a specialist in Mozart and women"*: ibid., p. 35.

32 *"The score should be in the head"*: Perlis, p. 60.

32 *"Frankie, if I ever had"*: William Schuman, letter to Frances Prince, August 14–17, 1935; Schuman Family Archives.

33 *Schuman and another American*: Schuman, "Autobiography," chap. V, p. 25.

33 *Schuman had been warned*: Schuman and Waleson, chap. 1, p. 37.

33 *"One of the men on my right"*: Perlis, p. 60.

33 *Schuman's inherent charm*: Schuman and Waleson, chap. 1, p. 37.

33 *German soldiers were everywhere*: ibid., p. 38.

34 *"set him on fire"*: Perlis, p. 55.

34 *"education [would be] geared"*: Schuman and Waleson, chap. 2, p. 40.

34 *"great concern [given]"*: Schuman, "Autobiography," chap. V, p. 13.

34 *"I can tell you now"*: Perlis, p. 55.

34 *"very much the old New England schoolmarm"*: Schuman and Waleson, chap. 2, p. 41.

34 *Fortunately, he wasn't offered*: Perlis, p. 57.

35 *"After dining at the School"*: William Schuman, letter to Abraham Friedman, Jan. 6, 1965; Schuman Family Archives.

35 *"I said I definitely was not"*: Perlis, p. 58.

35 *"Nobody can possibly claim"*: Schuman and Waleson, chap. 2, pp. 42–43.

35 *"must have known"*: Schuman and Waleson, chap. 4, p. 3.

36 *"included talk of the Jews"*: William Schuman, letter to Sam and Ray Schuman, June 24, 1937; Schuman Family Archives.

36 *"My work schedule calls"*: William Schuman, letter to Sam and Ray Schuman, July 3, 1937; Schuman Family Archives.

36 *"The thing I like best about France"*: ibid.

36 *"If one carried over"*: ibid.

37 *"Sarah Lawrence students were a breed apart"*: Schuman and Waleson, chap. 2, p. 43.

37 *"should drop its quota"*: ibid., p. 44.

37 *"everyone was a professional"*: ibid.

37 *"wasteful of time"*: Perlis, p. 63.

38 *They included Edmund Ezra Day*: Schuman, "Autobiography," chap. V, p. 28.

38 *"The music studio was in an old stable"*: Schuman and Waleson, chap. 2, p. 45.

38 *"See if you can find"*: Perlis, p. 64.

38 *"penetrative listening"*: ibid.

38 *"could read scores"*: ibid.

39 *"William, I hear [that] you have a chorus"*: Schuman and Waleson, chap. 2, p. 52.

39 *"Well, I do"*: Perlis, p. 68.

39 *In addition to conducting*: ibid., p. 73.

39 *"I was always conscious"*: ibid., p. 74.

39 *"loved six of the ten unequivocally"*: Schuman and Waleson, chap. 2, p. 58.

39 *"realized that one could become"*: Perlis, p. 71.

39 *"I wanted to teach teachers"*: ibid., p. 72.

Chapter 3

41 *"I remember playing it"*: Schuman and Waleson, chap. 13, p. 1.

41 *The year 1932*: K. Gary Adams, *William Schuman: A Bio-Bibliography* (Westport, CT: Greenwood Press, 1998), p. 25.

41 *"how wonderful it was"*: Schuman and Waleson, chap. 3, p. 2.

42 *flawed "experiment"*: ibid., chap. 3, p. 3.

42 *"overly modernistic"*: ibid.

42 *"Roy Harris was born"*: ibid.

43 *"You're not going to be happy"*: ibid, chap. 3, p. 5.

43 *Schuman's early settings*: ibid., chap. 3, p. 6.

43 *"spent more time promoting"*: ibid., chap. 3, pp. 4–5.

43 *"In his 'Third Symphony'"*: ibid., chap. 3, p. 5.

44 *Born Beulah Duffy*: Dan Stehman, *Roy Harris: A Bio-Bibliography* (Westport, CT: Greenwood Press, 1991), p. 6.

44 *Harris's influence over her*: Schuman and Waleson, chap. 3, p. 6.

44 *"'nothing will ever happen'"*: ibid.

44 *This curious right-wing position*: Stehman, p. 13.

44 *"emphasis on the importance"*: Schuman and Waleson, chap. 3, p. 8.

44 *Throughout their compositional careers*: Stehman, p. 17.

44 *"Mr. Schuman's music recalls Harris's"*: John Rockwell, "William Schuman—'The Continuum Has Been Composition': A Talk with William Schuman," *New York Times*, Aug. 3, 1980.

45 *"The names [of the winners]"*: Chalmers Clifton, letter to William Schuman, Jan. 25, 1938; Schuman Family Archives.

45 *"In my mind, Roy Harris"*: Robert S. Hines, "William Schuman Interview," *College Music Symposium* 35 (1995): p. 144.

46 *Schuman was deeply hurt*: Perlis, p. 102.

46 *"In those early days"*: Schuman and Waleson, chap. 3, p. 12.

46 *Early in their marriage*: "War Damage Corporation" document; NYPL for the Performing Arts, Box 149, Folder 15. The document lists Ray as the first mortgagee.

46 *a "just man"*: Schuman and Waleson, chap. 3, p. 12.

46 *"I was never part"*: ibid.

47 *"The remarkable thing"*: ibid., chap. 3, p. 13.

47 *"cut the crap"*: ibid., chap. 5, p. 103.

47 *"Stassevitch says you're the only composer"*: ibid., chap. 5, p. 104.

47 *"horrific sounds"*: ibid.

48 *"Mais, je suis pauvre"*: ibid., chap. 5, p. 105.

48 *The prize was awarded*: Adams, p. 27.

48 *"a few excellent"*: Schuman, "Autobiography," chap. III, p. 2.

49 *"Schuman is, so far as I am concerned"*: Aaron Copland, "Scores and Records," *Modern Music* 15, no. 4 (1937–38): pp. 245–46; see also Adams, p. 207.

49 *To his amazement*: Schuman and Waleson, chap. 3, p. 16.

49 *it was so surprising*: Goddard Lieberson, "Over the Air," *Modern Music* 16, no. 1 (1938–39): pp. 65–69.

49 *In 1938 CBS radio*: Stehman, p. 9.

50 *"My intellectual idea"*: Schuman, "Autobiography," chap. III, p. 8.

50 *"melody or harmonic design"*: Stehman, p. 19.

50 *"What I didn't know"*: Schuman and Waleson, chap. 3, p. 17.

50 *"To exacerbate the problem"*: ibid.

50 *After the broadcast*: Adams, p. 27.

51 *"That so-called symphony"*: Schuman and Waleson, chap. 3, p. 17.

51 *"When we went backstage afterwards"*: Perlis, p. 101.

51 *"Lenny was 20"*: ibid., pp. 19–20.
52 *"What now is wise"*: William Schuman, statement for television broadcast of Leonard Bernstein's sixtieth birthday celebration, Washington, D.C., 1978; NYPL for the Performing Arts, Box 125, Folder 3A.
52 *"concerning the opening of 'tomorrow's door'"*: Noel Straus, "Composers' Forum Opens Music Week," New York Times, May 8, 1939.
52 *"he was very excited"*: David Wright, "Koussevitzky and Notoriety," sample chapter, p. 12, in "Composer in America: William Schuman Talks about His Life and Works" [unpublished manuscript, 1987]; Juilliard Archives, Box 3, Folder: Schuman, William: Chapter drafts from proposed memoir with David Wright; correspondence, 1986–87.
52 *"only inferior Harris"*: Leonard Bernstein, "Young American: William Schuman," *Modern Music* 19, no. 2 (1941–42): p. 97.
53 *Koussevitzky greeted the young composer*: Wright, "Koussevitzky and Notoriety," p. 14.
53 *"say anything critical"*: Schuman and Waleson, chap. 3, p. 21.
53 *"This work with the "pooblic""*: ibid., chap. 3, p. 22.
53 *At the conclusion of the work*: ibid., chap. 3, p. 23.
53 *"I walked up"*: ibid.
54 *"a hotel called the Hemenway"*: Wright, "Koussevitzky and Notoriety," p. 16.
54 *"is technically unconventional"*: C. W. D., "Music, Symphony Hall, Boston Symphony Orchestra" [review], Boston Globe, Feb. 18, 1939.
54 *"When in the course of the single movement"*: Warren Storey Smith, "Myra Hess Soloist at Symphony: Work by Schuman Is Received Rather Coldly," *Boston Post*, Feb. 18, 1939.
54 *"The young composer clearly knew"*: Adams, p. 7.
54 *"the Schuman Symphony"*: Leonard Bernstein, "The Latest from Boston," *Modern Music* 16, no. 3 (1938–39): p. 183.
55 *"connectivity of the melodic line"*: ibid.
55 *"marked development"*: Lieberson, p. 67.
55 *"'Now, wait a minute, Dad'"*: Schuman and Waleson, chap. 3, p. 24.
55 *"that the music was a great study"*: Schuman, "Autobiography," chap. III, p. 15.

Chapter 4

57 *"two special concerts"*: program page, Boston Symphony Orchestra program, Oct. 4, 1939; Boston Symphony Orchestra Archives.
57 *The Boston event seems*: "Boston Symphony, Barred from Music Festival in New York, Stages Its Own," Lewiston (Maine) Sun, Oct. 5, 1939.
57 *The Boston concerts were presented*: Knickerbocker News (Albany, NY), Oct. 5, 1939; Boston Symphony Orchestra Archives, Pres 56, V. 66, p. 38.
57 *"Koussevitzky is never going to agree"*: Schuman and Waleson, chap. 5, p. 108.
57 *"unlike Aaron, he [Harris] never showed"*: ibid.
58 *"I want to open this overture"*: ibid., chap. 5, p. 109.
58 *"Great, that's a wonderful theme"*: ibid.
58 *Schuman composed most of the overture*: Schreiber, in Schreiber and Persichetti, p. 19.
58 *"was very hospitable"*: Schuman and Waleson, chap. 5, p. 109.
58 *"pages that were filled"*: Perlis, p. 114.
58 *Although the work was considered a success*: Schuman and Waleson, chap. 5, p. 111.
59 *"the quite extraordinary coda"*: ibid.
59 *"Koussevitzky had great instincts"*: ibid., chap. 5, p. 112.
59 *"The first three notes"*: Boston Symphony Orchestra, program note for program of Friday, Oct. 6, 1939, Boston Symphony Hall, Boston, MA, p. 12; Boston Symphony Orchestra Archives.

59 *"has vitality and conviction"*: Elliott Carter, "Forecast and Review: American Music in the New York Scene," *Modern Music* 17, no. 2 (1939–40): p. 96.

60 *"This overture is a lusty piece"*: Olin Downes, "American Music Applauded Again," *New York Times*, Nov. 26, 1939.

60 *"[There is] an energetic drive"*: Bernstein, "Young American," p. 97.

60 *The Symphony No. 2*: Adams, p. 29.

60 *"[The quartet] . . . revealed"*: Paul Rosenfeld, "Current Chronicle: Copland–Harris–Schuman," *Musical Quarterly* 25 (July 1939): p. 380.

61 *"In the Second Symphony"*: ibid.

61 *"Olin Downes found energy"*: Schreiber, in Schreiber and Persichetti, p. 19.

61 *"[Schuman's] new quartet is marked"*: Francis D. Perkins, "Introducing an American Work," *New York Herald Tribune*, Feb. 29, 1940.

61 *"the fugue . . . was abstruse"*: Irving Kolodin, "Quartet Gives Work by Schuman," *New York Sun*, Feb. 28, 1940.

61 *Schuman eventually used*: Schuman and Waleson, chap. 13, p. 18.

62 *"You have to learn"*: Perlis, p. 99.

62 *"[Because] I had"*: ibid., p. 113.

62 *"In some respects"*: Schuman and Waleson, chap. 6, pp. 108–9.

63 *"This has nothing to do with money"*: ibid., chap. 6, p. 109.

63 *Schuman did not compose at the piano*: ibid., chap. 6, p. 111.

63 *"he frequently banged out . . . chords"*: Anthony Schuman, e-mail to the author, May 11, 2008.

63 *"When I go to the piano"*: ibid.

63 *"made up of iron workers"*: Schreiber, in Schreiber and Persichetti, pp. 19–20.

64 *"In writing the symphony"*: Schuman and Waleson, chap. 6, pp. 131–32.

64 *"as the Passacaglia was drawing to a close"*: William Schuman, letter to Frankie Schuman, Oct. 14, 1941; Schuman Family Archives.

64 *"Yesterday with you"*: ibid., pp. 1–2.

65 *"my symphony"*: Schuman and Waleson, chap. 6, p. 133.

65 *"Young man . . . tell me"*: ibid., chap. 6, p. 135.

65 *"It is a symphony"*: Schreiber, in Schreiber and Persichetti, p. 20.

65 *"young Mr. Schuman"*: ibid.

65 *"This Third Symphony"*: Winthrop Sargeant, "Musical Events," *New Yorker*, Mar. 30, 1963; p. 149.

65 *"Now, look boys"*: Perlis, pp. 137–38.

65 *"All right, remember"*: ibid., p. 138.

66 *Schuman's rhetoric quickly cooled*: ibid., pp. 137–38.

66 *"new talent"*: Schuman and Waleson, chap. 7, p. 12.

66 *"The Symphony is the work"*: R. L. F. McCombs, program notes, Philadelphia Orchestra program, Apr. 4, 1942.

66 *"It wasn't personal"*: Schuman and Waleson, chap. 7, p. 15.

67 *"My audiences can't take"*: ibid.

67 *"'Well, Mr. Ormandy'"*: ibid.

67 *"Ormandy was not pleased"*: ibid., chap. 7, p. 16.

67 *"audiences [liked] the music"*: ibid.

67 *"disappointing"*: Olin Downes, "Ormandy Offers New Composition," *New York Times*, Apr. 8, 1942.

67 *"I found it [the Fourth Symphony] vague"*: Virgil Thomson, "Music," *New York Herald Tribune*, Apr. 8, 1942.

68 *"I think it's quite a different work"*: Perlis, p. 154.

68 *"I wanted to write music"*: ibid., pp. 158–59.

68 *"it makes you feel"*: Schuman and Waleson, chap. 13, p. 24.

68 *"[I] thought how amusing"*: ibid., chap. 13, pp. 22–23.

69 *Newsreel was premiered*: Adams, p. 31.
69 *"form of dystrophy"*: Schuman and Waleson, chap. 7, p. 1.
69 *"In most people"*: http://www.merck.com/mmhe/sec06/ch095/ch095b.html, accessed Mar. 13, 2007.
69 *"atypical ALS"*: Andrea Schuman, e-mail to the author, Apr. 7, 2005.
70 *"Our medical department regrets"*: Harry I. Kapp, letter to William Schuman, Mar. 30, 1942; NYPL for the Performing Arts, Box 149, Folder 15.
70 *"music advisers to the service commands"*: Harold Spivacke, letter to William Schuman, Aug. 12, 1942; NYPL for the Performing Arts, Box 21, Folder 7.
70 *"must be ineligible for drafting"*: "Specialist Corps Is Set Up for Army," *New York Times*, June 12, 1942; cited in Steve Swayne, "William Schuman, World War II, and the Pulitzer Prize," *Musical Quarterly* 89, no. 2–3 (Summer–Fall 2006): p. 291.
70 *"only accept 4F men from the first draft"*: William Schuman, letter to Harold Spivacke, July 5, 1942; NYPL for the Performing Arts, Box 21, Folder 7.
70 *"I feel that part"*: William Schuman, letter to Harold Spivacke, July 5, 1942; NYPL for the Performing Arts, Box 21, Folder 7.
71 *"that we are now prepared"*: Harold Spivacke, letter to William Schuman, Aug. 12, 1942; NYPL for the Performing Arts, Box 21, Folder 7.
71 *"it is with considerable regret"*: Lt. Col. Theodore P. Bank, letter to William Schuman, Oct. 17, 1942; NYPL for the Performing Arts, Box 21, Folder 7.
71 *"The regulations drawn up"*: "Army Specialist Corps Regulations (Tentative; 42. Physical examination and standards; c. *Physical Standards*," [United States] War Department, Washington, Mar. 24. 1942, 20, in Swayne, p. 292.
71 *"Since I cannot serve"*: William Schuman, letter to Harold Spivacke, Oct. 17, 1942; NYPL for the Performing Arts, Box 21, Folder 7.
71 *"I was surprised to hear"*: Harold Spivacke, letter to William Schuman, Oct. 20, 1942; NYPL for the Performing Arts, Box 21, Folder 7.
71 *"Write a piece of music"*: Schuman and Waleson, chap. 7, p. 3.
72 *The composer later borrowed*: Perlis, p. 185.
72 *The eventual performance*: ibid., p. 196.
72 *"When I walked out on stage"*: Schuman and Waleson, chap. 7, p. 4.
72 *The works became known*: Howard Pollack, *Aaron Copland: The Life and Work of an Uncommon Man* (New York: Henry Holt, 1999), p. 137.
73 *"Don't you agree"*: William Schuman, letter to Mrs. Robert A. Schmid, Feb. 16, 1942; NYPL for the Performing Arts, Box 11, Folder 6.
73 *"I thought your replique admirable"*: Aaron Copland, letter to William Schuman, cited in Pollack, p. 593 n. 37.
73 *During the war Schuman also composed*: Adams, p. 37.
73 *Schuman needed a particularly thick skin*: Ronald F. Eyer, "William Schuman Is First Subject of Music Forum," *Musical America* (Jan. 25, 1943), p. 19.
73 *"have a fellow like Bach"*: ibid.
74 *"sought out resemblances"*: ibid.
74 *"wanted to know why"*: ibid.
74 *"any succession of notes"*: ibid.
74 *"whether or not anything of value"*: ibid.
74 *"Isn't there some new chorus"*: Schuman and Waleson, chap. 7, p. 19.
74 *"a fellow who conducted"*: ibid.
74 *"Number one, the chorus is marvelous"*: ibid., chap. 7, p. 21.
75 *"As the Eroica started unfolding"*: ibid.; see also Perlis, pp. 185–86.
75 *"Shaw lasted four lessons"*: Schuman and Waleson, chap. 7, p. 22.
75 *"Rose was a vulgarian"*: ibid., chap. 7, p. 24.
75 *"That's an advance"*: ibid., chap. 7, pp. 24–25.
75 *"too rich"*: ibid., chap. 7, p. 25.

76 *"You're going to earn another thousand bucks"*: Schuman and Waleson, chap. 7, p. 27.

76 *"That settles it"*: ibid.

76 *"Do you think I would have"*: ibid., chap. 7, p. 28.

76 *"Your ballet colossal success"*: ibid. For a detailed analysis of the trials of the Rose revue, see John Schuster-Craig, "Stravinsky's *Scènes de Ballet* and Billy Rose's *The Seven Lively Arts*: The Abravanel Account," in *Music in the Theatre, Church and Villa: Essays in Honor of Robert Lamar Weaver and Norma Wright Weaver*, ed. Susan Parisi (Sterling Heights, MI: Harmonie Park Press, 2000), 285–89.

76 *"changed the 'I's' to 'we's'"*: Schuman and Waleson, chap. 13, p. 4.

77 *"pour softly down"*: William Schuman, A Free Song (*Secular Cantata* No. 2), text adapted from poems by Walt Whitman (New York: G. Schirmer, 1943), pp. 10–11, 13–17, and 25–30.

77 *"I was so surprised"*: Perlis, pp. 146–47.

78 *"he [Schuman] first learned of the honor"*: "Pulitzer Prize in Music Won by William Schuman," *Campus*, May 5, 1943, p. 1.

78 *"had a great desire"*: Schuman and Waleson, chap. 7, p. 17.

79 *"I became sufficiently intrigued"*: Perlis, p. 189.

79 *It was premiered*: Adams, p. 37.

79 *"I am asking you"*: Eugene Goossens, letter to William Schuman, Aug. 9, 1944; Schuman Family Archives.

79 *"always wanted a family"*: Perlis, p. 110.

80 *"Well, I don't know"*: Schuman and Zinsser, July 11, 1989, p. 19.

80 *"After a while"*: Schuman and Waleson, chap. 7, p. 32.

80 *"I am not sure I understand"*: Schreiber, in Schreiber and Persichetti, p. 25.

80 *"There was music we thought we could sell"*: Schuman, "Autobiography," chap. VIII, p. 1.

80 *"In my mind"*: ibid.

81 *"Your music isn't being published"*: Schuman and Waleson, chap. 7, p. 34.

81 *"Mr. Gustave Schirmer knew nothing"*: Schuman, "Autobiography," chap. VIII, p. 3.

81 *Three hundred at maximum*: ibid., chap. VIII, p. 4.

81 *"At Schirmer's I not only left"*: ibid., chap. VIII, p. 6.

81 *"trapped"*: Schuman and Zinsser, July 11, 1989, p. 22.

Chapter 5

84 *"I have such mixed feelings"*: Schuman and Waleson, chap. 8, p. 2.

84 *"Don't be so tough"*: Schuman, "Autobiography," chap. IX, p. 1.

84 *"I would do so if"*: ibid., p. 2.

84 *One can imagine*: "Juilliard Musical Foundation: Report on Examination," June 30, 1945, Arthur Young & Company; Juilliard School Financial Office files.

85 *"To my great surprise"*: Schuman, "Autobiography," chap. IX, p. 3.

85 *"The first was that"*: ibid., p. 4.

85 *"except that of music"*: ibid.

85 *"I loved the way"*: ibid., p. 5.

85 *"You must do something"*: ibid.

86 *"incompetent and without any relationship"*: ibid.

86 *He also told Warburg*: Perlis, pp. 252–53.

86 *"Now that it is all settled"*: Schuman, "Autobiography," chap. IX, p. 7.

86 *In 1945 the board*: Schreiber, in Schreiber and Persichetti, p. 29.

87 *"It's like Westbrook Pegler"*: "Ventilation for Juilliard," *Time*, Oct. 22, 1945. See also http://geocities.com/westbrook_pegler/, accessed Nov. 26, 2006; and Philip Nel, "About the Newspaper PM," http://www.k-state.edu/english/nelp/purple/miscellaneous/pm.html, accessed Nov. 26, 2006.

87 *"make responsible adults"*: "Ventilation for Juilliard," *Time*, Oct. 22, 1945.
87 *"Our large music centers suffer"*: "Wants Music Expansion: Schuman, President of Juilliard, Stresses Need for Development," *New York Times*, Oct. 10, 1945.
87 *"Unlike his distinguished and dignified predecessors"*: "Maestro in Play Clothes," *Newsweek*, Aug. 13, 1945, p. 100.
88 *"resent . . . strongly"*: Schreiber, in Schreiber and Persichetti, p. 39.
88 *"do some useful work"*: Schuman, "Autobiography," chap. IX, p. 8.
88 *"I am 43 years old"*: Mark Schubart, letter to William Schuman, Feb. 14, 1962; NYPL for the Performing Arts, Box 21, Folder 9.
88 *"It is . . . painful for me"*: William Schuman, letter to Martin Rapp, Feb. 18, 1984; Schuman Family Archives.
89 *"I explained to the Juilliard Board"*: Schuman, "Autobiography," chap. IX, p. 9.
89 *"Hutcheson was always the gentleman"*: Perlis, p. 254.
90 *"that this was an extraordinary request"*: Schuman, "Autobiography," chap. IX, p. 12.
90 *"very elegant"*: Zane, Schuman Oral History, p. 113.
90 *"Since the President assumed office"*: Office of the President (1928–36; 1945–77), President's Report to the Board of Trustees, Dec. 15, 1961, pp. 4–5, Juilliard School, New York; Juilliard School Archives.
92 *However, although they shared*: Jeni Dahmus, "Time Capsule," Augustus Juilliard Society Newsletter, Fall 2006.
92 *In the fiscal year ending June 30*: Arthur Young & Company, "Juilliard School of Music, Report on Examination," June 30, 1945; Juilliard School Financial Office files.
92 *"The end of the war"*: President's Report, Nov. 13, 1945, p. 1.
93 *"this report assumes"*: ibid., p. 2.
93 *"one of the most difficult things"*: Schuman and Waleson, chap. 8, p. 5.
93 *"Practically anyone could go"*: ibid.
93 *"I pointed out"*: Perlis, p. 258.
93 *"exceptionally gifted students"*: President's Report, Nov. 13, 1945, p. 4.
93 *"a nucleus of fifteen"*: ibid., p. 6.
94 *He promised the directors*: Zane, Schuman Oral History, p. 96.
94 *"I don't mean to imply"*: Perlis, p. 258.
95 *"It was a very small Board"*: Zane, Schuman Oral History, p. 100.
95 *The enrollment statistics*: President's Report, May 14, 1946, p. 10.
95 *"While it is true"*: President's Report, Oct. 5, 1948, p. 1.
96 *"enabled students to represent themselves"*: President's Report, Dec. 5, 1952, p. 5.
97 *"constructive self-evaluation"*: President's Report, May 14, 1946, p. 1.
97 *"a realistic relationship"*: ibid.
97 *"Music education must certainly bear"*: ibid., p. 2.
97 *"In the years ahead"*: ibid.
98 *"I have a request"*: Schuman and Waleson, chap. 8. p. 7.
98 *Schuman noted that deleting*: ibid.
98 *"worked like demons"*: ibid., chap. 8, p. 9.
98 *"The outstanding impression"*: President's Report, Feb. 17, 1948, p. 2.
99 *"It is essential"*: William Schuman, "On Teaching the Literature and Materials of Music," Musical Quarterly 34, no. 2 (Apr. 1948): p. 156.
99 *The curriculum would be taught*: ibid., p. 159.
99 *"Most of them said"*: Schuman and Waleson, chap. 8, p. 9.
99 *"he thought might enlarge"*: ibid.
100 *"organized flexibility"*: Schuman, "On Teaching the Literature," p. 156.
100 *"He [the student] must assume"*: ibid., pp. 162–63.
100 *Schuman's predilection*: William Schuman, "Unconventional Case History," *Modern Music* 15, no. 4 (May–June 1938): pp. 222–27.
100 *"he described how a student"*: Schreiber, in Schreiber and Persichetti, p. 24.

100 *"There are many reasons"*: Schuman, "Unconventional Case History," p. 222.

100 *"the arts play"*: ibid.

100 *"trained in the technic"*: ibid., p. 223.

100 *"Theoretical subjects"*: ibid.

100 *"Why wasn't she using"*: ibid., p. 226.

100 *"the situation was definitely experimental"*: ibid.

100 *"If we are to raise"*: Schuman, "On Teaching the Literature," p. 167.

100 *"If what we are doing"*: ibid., p. 168.

101 *"Study of the Literature and Materials"*: Juilliard School of Music catalog, 1952–53, p. 14.

101 *"has aroused great interest"*: President's Report, Feb. 6, 1951, p. 2.

102 *"[the] Literature and Materials instructor"*: ibid., pp. 9–10.

102 *"when it worked"*: Schuman and Waleson, chap. 8, p. 11.

103 *"The program is courageous"*: H. Wiley Hitchcock, review of *The Juilliard Report on Teaching the Literature and Materials of Music, Notes* 11 (2nd ser.), no. 2 (Mar. 1954): p. 299.

103 *"the L. and M. curriculum"*: John H. Lowell, review of *The Juilliard Report on Teaching the Literature and Materials of Music, Musical Quarterly* 40, no. 2 (Apr. 1954): p. 249.

103 *"In the final analysis"*: ibid., p. 250.

104 *"over the last seven years"*: President's Report, May 2, 1952, p. 2.

104 *"There was opposition"*: Schreiber, in Schreiber and Persichetti, p. 32.

105 *"We had a long train ride"*: Perlis, p. 221.

105 *The Schumans had two domestic employees*: Anthony Schuman, e-mail to the author, May 11, 2008.

105 *"We didn't seem"*: Perlis, p. 320.

106 *"Frankie and I have often wondered"*: Perlis, p. 325.

106 *In 1978 Andie set out*: interview by the author with Anthony Schuman and Andrea Schuman, Apr. 27, 2007, Juilliard School.

106 *"The study was off-limits"*: ibid.

106 *Andie recalled that the most*: ibid.

106 *"my first move"*: Nina Jones, "Beautiful and Organized Apt for Frances Schuman," *New Rochelle* (NY) *Standard Star*, April 14, 1962.

106 *"Mom was mostly involved"*: ibid.

107 *"Tell me what you did"*: ibid.

107 *"Dad wouldn't talk"*: ibid.

108 *"This was one of the great sadnesses"*: ibid.

108 *"believed that religion was the source"*: ibid.

108 *"secular in the extreme"*: ibid.

108 *"Dad was not Semitic"*: ibid.

108 *"derive[d] its name"*: Schuman, "Performance" [fragment], in "Autobiography," p. 32. Schuman Family Archives.

108 *"referred obliquely"*: ibid., p. 33.

108 *Then, on October 11*: William Schuman, letter to Mrs. W. Leipold, Jan. 24, 1950; NYPL for the Performing Arts, Box 150, Folder 13.

109 *Although he recovered*: William Schuman, letter to Dr. Madison Brown, Dec. 4, 1950; NYPL for the Performing Arts, Box 150, Folder 12.

109 *"I remember it because"*: Perlis, p. 322.

109 *"he had had a good day"*: interview by the author with Anthony Schuman and Andrea Schuman, Apr. 27, 2007, Juilliard School.

Chapter 6

111 *"I have to tell you"*: Schuman and Waleson, chap. 8, p. 5.
111 *"Not everyone can have"*: ibid., chap. 8, p. 6.
111 *"But you haven't heard"*: ibid.
112 *"His repertory was so limited"*: ibid., chap. 8, pp. 6–7.
112 *"was a poor conductor"*: Perlis, p. 270.
112 *"that would stand for something specific"*: Schuman and Waleson, chap. 8, p. 12.
112 *"an American string quartet"*: ibid.
112 *"I've got a wonderful cellist"*: ibid., p. 13.
112 *"Then we'll change the personnel"*: ibid., p. 15.
113 *"Although the Quartet played"*: ibid., p. 14.
113 *"Dear Bobby"*: Perlis, p. 273.
113 *For example, in 1948–49*: President's Report, Feb. 1, 1949, p. 6.
114 *"The audience yelled"*: "Bartok & Juilliard," *Time*, Oct. 13, 1958; quoted in President's Report, Oct. 24, 1958, p. 13.
114 *"a School of Theatre and Dance"*: President's Report, Nov. 13, 1945, p. 6.
114 *"also served as a means"*: President's Report, May 2, 1950, p. 5.
114 *"Dance . . . uses more music"*: President's Report, Feb. 6, 1951, pp. 4–5.
115 *"train[ing] students to become"*: Juilliard School of Music, Department of Dance Bulletin, 1951–1952; Juilliard Archives, Box 1, Folder: Schuman, William, 1951–1952.
115 *"You want them all together"*: Perlis, p. 289.
115 *"'Can I bring the two of you'"*: ibid., p. 290.
116 *The first program included*: President's Report, May 2, 1952, p. 3.
116 *"Once again"*: Robert Sabin, "José Limón Introduces Six Works in His Juilliard Dance Concerts," *Musical America* (Jan. 1953): pp. 5, 16; cited in President's Report, Feb. 6, 1953, p. 3.
116 *"the quality of the young dancers"*: President's Report, May 13, 1955, p. 7.
117 *"the Division of Dance would have to be"*: President's Report, May 28, 1959, p. 5.
117 *"I must say"*: William Schuman, letter to Edgar B. Young, June 20, 1961; NYPL for the Performing Arts, Box 21, Folder 9.
117 *"the problem for support"*: President's Report, Dec. 15, 1961, p. 3.
118 *The saga of Juilliard dance*: see Joseph Polisi, "An Unsettled Marriage: The Merger of SAB and Juilliard," *Ballet Review* 34, no. 1 (Spring 2006): pp. 72–82.
118 *These included special festivals*: President's Report, Oct. 7, 1947, p. 4.
118 *"Music has a stake"*: Alice Eversman, "News of Music: Shepherds of Young Talent Concerned with Their Future in Ideology," *Washington (DC) Sunday Star*, Nov. 12, 1950.
119 *The committee included*: News Release, U.S. Information Agency, SR-604—11-10, undated; Juilliard Archives, Box 1, Folder: Schuman, William, 1960–1961.
119 *"We must look to them"*: Albert Goldberg, "Schuman Calls for Review of U.S. Arts Program," *Los Angeles Times*, June 22, 1958.
119 *"a single Government agency"*: "Confusion in Federal Arts Program Cited by Schuman," Juilliard Press Release, May 31, 1958, Juilliard Archives, Box 1, Folder: Schuman, William, 1957–1958.
119 *As early as 1947*: President's Reports, Oct. 7, 1947, pp. 3–4, and Oct. 5, 1948, pp. 4–5.
119 *Schuman negotiated*: President's Report, Feb. 6, 1951, p. 8.
119 *He established a program*: President's Report, June 9, 1961, p. 9, and Vice President's Report, Apr. 25, 1962, p. 7.
120 *Perhaps not coincidentally*: Elizabeth McPherson, The Contributions of Martha Hill to American Dance and Dance Education, 1900–1995 (Lewiston, NY: Edwin Mellen Press, 2008), p. 65.
120 *As of one month before*: President's Report, May 23, 1958, p. 3.

120 *"manufactured [the clothes]"*: William Schuman, "Juilliard Goes on Tour," *Juilliard Review* 5, no. 3 (Fall 1958): p. 4.

121 *"Mal de Kodak"*: interview by the author with Anthony Schuman and Andrea Schuman, Apr. 27, 2007, Juilliard School.

121 *"I am also terribly let-down"*: Frankie Schuman, letter to Leonard Bernstein, July 31, 1952, Schuman Family Archives.

122 *JUILLIARD ORCHESTRA TOUR*: "Juilliard Orchestra Tour—1958: Repertory," *Juilliard Review* 5, no. 3 (Fall 1958): p. 8.

123 *London's* Evening Standard *trumpeted*: President's Report, Oct. 24, 1958, p. 9.

123 *"and should prompt"*: ibid., p. 9.

123 *"a world reputation"*: ibid., p. 9.

123 *"Freshness, optimism and vitality"*: ibid., p. 10.

123 *"These musical messengers"*: ibid., p. 11.

123 *"who were invited"*: President's Report, Oct. 24, 1958, p. 6.

123 *"which states unequivocally"*: Memorandum of Feb. 1958 from William Schuman to the Executive Committee of the Commission of the Middle States Association of Colleges and Secondary Schools, Nov. 13, 1959, p. 9; NYPL for the Performing Arts, Box 21, Folder 9.

124 In *an extraordinary moment*: Anthony Tommasini, "Cold War, Hot Pianist: Now Add 50 Years," *New York Times*, Mar. 9, 2008.

124 *Cliburn's beloved teacher*: William Schuman, letter to Mark Schubart, Apr. 17, 1958; NYPL for the Performing Arts, Box 21, Folder 8.

124 *"Dear Mark"*: ibid.

126 *"Because I recognize"*: William Schuman, "The Responsibility of Music Education to Music" [address to the biennial meeting of the Music Educators National Conference, Apr. 17, 1956, St. Louis, MO], *Music Educators Journal* 42, no. 6 (June–July 1956): p. 17.

126 *"cheap and tawdry materials"*: ibid., p. 19.

126 *"My purpose in bringing"*: ibid.

126 *"attributed to Johannes Brahms"*: ibid.

126 *"What, in terms of public education"*: Theodore F. Normann, "The Responsibility of Music to Education," *Music Educators Journal* 43, no. 1 (Sept.–Oct. 1956): p. 20.

126 *"everything that is worth doing"*: ibid.

127 *"is at once"*: ibid.

127 *"stirred up so much"*: Parker LaBach, "Why We Are Criticized: A Music Educator's Analysis," *Music Educators Journal* 43, no. 2 (Nov.–Dec. 1956): p. 18.

127 *"If school administrators"*: Hope Stoddard, "William Schuman Discusses Problems in the Field of Music Education," *International Musician* (Mar. 1961): p. 22.

127 *"musical training"*: President's Report, Oct. 7, 1955, p. 2.

127 *"I brought the idea"*: Zane, Schuman Oral History, p. 111.

128 *"the scythe of progress"*: Hilary Ballon and Kenneth T. Jackson, eds., *Robert Moses and the Modern City: The Transformation of New York* (New York: W. W. Norton, 2007), p. 279.

128 *"It was New York City's biggest"*: ibid. See also http://pbskids.org/bigapplehistory/building/topic27.html, accessed Nov. 8, 2007.

128 *"educational facilities included"*: President's Report, March 20, 1956, p. 1.

128 It *was to be termed*: President's Report, Mar. 20, 1956, p. 1.

128 *Therefore, Schuman proposed*: ibid., p. 3.

129 *"It is the President's conviction"*: ibid., p. 7.

129 *"There does not exist"*: President's Report, Mar. 20, 1956, p. 7.

129 *"They [the board] didn't quite see it"*: Zane, Schuman Oral History, p. 114.

129 In *subsequent meetings with Rockefeller*: President's Report, Dec. 7, 1956, p. 3.

130 *"reduce present expenditures"*: ibid., p. 4.

130 *"Rockefeller spoke to Douglas Moore"*: telephone conversation with Jack Beeson, July 26, 2005.

130 *"Juilliard was the second choice"*: ibid.
130 *"I am sorry"*: Perlis, p. 287.
131 *"no student [would be] denied"*: Juilliard Faculty Meeting, William Schuman presiding, Feb. 5, 1957, Juilliard School of Music, New York; CD recording, The Juilliard School.
132 *"can help the arts in America"*: ibid.
132 *"By backing the horses"*: ibid.
132 *"milestone of major importance"*: President's Report, Feb. 1, 1957, p. 4.
132 *"The interrelated activities"*: ibid., pp. 5–6.
133 *The trustees of the Juilliard Musical Foundation*: Juilliard School of Music Catalog, 1956–1957, p. 4.
133 *The School would now be known*: President's Report, Feb. 26, 1960, p. 6.
133 *"provide scholarships and other assistance"*: Florence Anderson, letter to John D. Rockefeller 3rd, Nov. 24, 1958; NYPL for the Performing Arts, Box 21, Folder 8.
134 *"If they can do this"*: Performing Arts, May 22, 1959.
134 *"but in the end"*: Zane, Schuman Oral History, p. 124.
134 *The Rockefeller Foundation provided a grant*: President's Report, Feb. 7, 1958, p. 8.
135 *"Anything you can say"*: Zane, Schuman Oral History, p. 125.
135 *"the Lincoln Center did not wish"*: President's Report, Nov. 20, 1958, p. 3.
136 *"It is of utmost importance"*: President's Report, May 17, 1960, p. 6.
136 *Kazan and Whitehead represented*: Lincoln Center Theater Web site, http://www.lct.org/history.html, "History," p. 2 of printout, accessed Nov. 26, 2006.
136 *"in other words"*: President's Report, May 17, 1960, p. 6.
136 *"My purpose in reviewing"*: President's Report, May 17, 1960, p. 7.
137 *"DRAMA AND DANCE"*: President's Report, Dec. 7, 1956, pp. 4–5.
137 *In a letter to Maxwell D. Taylor*: William Schuman, letter to General Maxwell D. Taylor, Feb. 27, 1961; NYPL for the Performing Arts, Box 21, Folder 9.
138 *"At one time they"*: Zane, Schuman Oral History, p. 136.
138 *"Adoption of your proposals"*: William Schuman, letter to Robert Whitehead, Mar. 9, 1961; NYPL for the Performing Arts, Box 21, Folder 9.
138 *"maximum obligation of Lincoln Center"*: President's Report, June 9, 1961, p. 2.
138 *"to provide a reasonable basis"*: ibid.
139 *"there is the possibility"*: ibid., p. 4.
139 *An associate director*: President's Report, Dec. 15, 1961, p. 5.
139 *Instead, he accepted*: Vice President's Report, Mar. 2, 1962, p. 7.
139 *"Giving that artist"*: Zane, Schuman Oral History, p. 122.
139 *"some of whom will be selected"*: Vice President's Report, Apr. 25, 1962, p. 4.
139 *"My successor, Peter Mennin"*: Zane, Schuman Oral History, p. 125.

Chapter 7

141 *"I had determined"*: Schuman and Waleson, chap. 11, p. 1.
141 *"it's always easier"*: Perlis, p. 267.
142 *"Don't you sometimes"*: Schuman and Waleson, chap. 11, p. 1.
142 *Referring to Paul Hindemith and Darius Milhaud*: ibid., chap. 6, pp. 117–18.
142 *"I would say that 50%"*: ibid.
142 *"quantitatively . . . it was not"*: ibid., chap. 6, p. 118.
142 *"I write consecutively"*: Perlis, p. 224.
142 *"The work proceeds"*: Schuman and Waleson, chap. 6, pp. 119–20.
142 *"I am terribly conscious"*: Perlis, p. 226.
143 *"He [Schuman] does not write down"*: Nathan Broder, "The Music of William Schuman," *Musical Quarterly* 31, no. 1 (Jan. 1945): p. 22.
143 *"I think the closest analogy"*: Schuman and Waleson, chap. 6, p. 122.

144 *"gymnasium music"*: telephone conversation with Jack Beeson, July 26, 2005.
144 *"In some recent performances"*: Schuman and Waleson, chap. 6, p. 125.
144 *"A composer has both"*: ibid., chap. 6, pp. 129–30.
145 *"The evidence is accumulating"*: Alfred Frankenstein, "American Composers, XXII: William Schuman," *Modern Music* 22, no. 1 (Nov.–Dec. 1944): p. 23.
145 *"Schuman's choral music"*: ibid., p. 26.
145 *"'Enthusiasm' is the word"*: ibid., p. 27.
145 *"despite its frequent irregularity"*: Broder, p. 17.
146 *"Schuman's music is predominantly"*: ibid., pp. 18–19.
146 *"boldness, originality, freshness"*: ibid., p. 22.
146 *"But what strikes the unbiased listener"*: ibid., pp. 23–24.
146 *"His almost complete freedom"*: ibid., p. 25.
147 *"I knew relatively little"*: Schuman and Waleson, chap. 9, p. 1.
147 *"psychological choreographer"*: see Alistair Macaulay, "Under Analysis: The Psychology of Tudor's Ballets," *New York Times*, May 11, 2008.
147 *"'I need music'"*: ibid., chap. 9, p. 2.
147 *At the time Tudor was touring*: Perlis, p. 241.
148 *"It suddenly seems to me"*: Antony Tudor, letter to William Schuman, Aug. 31, 1944; NYPL for the Performing Arts, Box 41, Folder 14.
148 *"the emotional instability"*: ibid.
148 *"It is impossible to write"*: ibid.
148 *"The other interpolated motifs"*: ibid.
149 *"After the melody"*: Antony Tudor, letter to William Schuman, Nov. 8, 1944; NYPL for the Performing Arts, Box 41, Folder 14.
149 *"I was very excited"*: ibid., p. 2.
149 *"chill in the air"*: ibid.
149 *"little moments of disquiet"*: Antony Tudor, letter to William Schuman, Jan. 7, 1945; NYPL for the Performing Arts, Box 41, Folder 14.
150 *"Then when we get to 2b."*: ibid.
150 *"She is the kind"*: ibid.
150 *"Your letter has been quite a shock"*: William Schuman, letter to Antony Tudor, Jan. 13, 1945; NYPL for the Performing Arts, Box 41, Folder 14.
150 *"You promised me"*: Antony Tudor, letter to William Schuman, Feb. 21, 1945; NYPL for the Performing Arts, Box 41, Folder 14.
151 *"I expect to see you"*: ibid.
151 *"Tudor had a diabolical"*: Judith Chazin-Bennahum, *The Ballets of Antony Tudor: Studies in Psyche and Satire* (New York: Oxford University Press, 1994), p. 153.
151 *"wouldn't have ever liked"*: Schuman and Waleson, chap. 9, p. 5.
151 *"American composers wrote for them"*: ibid., chap. 9, p. 6.
151 *"but he made ballet"*: ibid.
151 *"He was terribly clever"*: ibid., chap. 9, p. 2.
152 *"concerns itself"*: program notes, Nov. 29, 1945; NYPL for the Performing Arts, Box 146, Folder 12.
152 *"The hero is seen"*: ibid.
152 *"The characters in* Undertow": Chazin-Bennahum, p. 142.
153 *"It's a dance audience"*: Schuman and Waleson, chap. 9, p. 4.
153 *"who was seven months pregnant"*: ibid.
153 *"I must regard it"*: William Schuman letter to A. J. Pischl, Aug. 13, 1963; NYPL for the Performing Arts, Box 146, Folder 12.
153 *"their most striking work"*: Virgil Thomson, "Schuman's 'Undertow,'" *New York Herald Tribune*, Apr. 29, 1945.
153 *"weak in specific expressivity"*: ibid.
153 *"a pure product"*: ibid.

153 *"His workmanship is skillful"*: ibid.
154 *"Schuman turns out to be"*: ibid.
155 *"'Mr. Schuman, your music'"*: Schuman and Waleson, chap. 9, p. 8.
155 *"Agnes de Mille used to say"*: ibid., chap. 9, p. 9.
155 *"astonishing woman"*: ibid., chap. 9, p. 22.
155 *"a curious mix"*: ibid., chap. 9, p. 21.
155 *"I was influenced tonally"*: ibid., chap. 9, pp. 22–23.
155 *"beautiful singing voice"*: http://beinecke.library.yale.edu/cvvpw/gallery/reeds1.html, accessed Oct. 25, 2006.
155 *"at that instant"*: Schuman and Waleson, chap. 9, pp. 9–10.
156 *"I wanted to know"*: ibid., chap. 9, p. 10.
156 *"She would be backstage"*: ibid., chap. 9, p. 12.
156 *"I can hear your power"*: Martha Graham, letter to William Schuman, Aug. 30, 1946; NYPL for the Performing Arts, Box 18, Folder 10.
156 *"It [the music] will have such a life"*: Martha Graham, letter to William Schuman, Oct. 28, 1946; NYPL for the Performing Arts, Box 18, Folder 10.
156 "I do know that it is serious": ibid.
157 *"DANCE FOR JOCASTA"*: Martha Graham, script (p. 5) accompanying letter to William Schuman, Oct. 28, 1946; NYPL for the Performing Arts, Box 18, Folder 10.
157 *"a metal bed"*: Don McDonagh, *Martha Graham: A Biography* (New York: Praeger, 1973), p. 200.
157 *An earlier symposium concert*: John Martin, "Graham Dancers in Harvard Event," *New York Times*, May 5, 1947.
158 *who was also romantically linked*: McDonagh, p. 31.
158 *"screamed at them"*: Perlis, p. 249.
158 *"In* Night Journey": William Schuman, *Night Journey: Choreographic Poem for Fifteen Instruments*, full score (Bryn Mawr, PA: Merion Music, 1978).
158 *"not one of Miss Graham's more inspired"*: John Martin, "Graham Dancers in Harvard Event," *New York Times*, May 5, 1947.
159 *Graham was reading the Apocrypha*: Schuman and Waleson, chap. 9, p. 16.
159 *"and went forth up the mountain"*: William Schuman, Judith: Choreographic Poem for Orchestra, full score (New York: G. Schirmer, 1950), p. [i].
159 *"this has been the most difficult"*: Martha Graham, letter to William Schuman, June 14, 1949; NYPL for the Performing Arts, Box 18, Folder 10.
159 *"The thing which has been so difficult"*: ibid.
160 *"I know that I am trying"*: ibid.
160 *"is still a legend of re-birth"*: Martha Graham, letter to William Schuman, June 24, 1949; NYPL for the Performing Arts, Box 18, Folder 10.
160 *"sensational, electric"*: Schuman and Waleson, chap. 9, p. 16.
161 "Judith *was a vivid and striking*": John Martin, "The Dance: 'Judith'—Martha Graham Creates a Major Solo Work," *New York Times*, Jan. 7, 1951.
161 *"his mastery of somber orchestral color"*: Albert Goldberg, "'Judith' Arresting Orchestral Novelty," *Los Angeles Times*, Feb. 15, 1952.
161 *"Is this din and discord"*: Julia S. Novak, letter to Juilliard School of Music, Apr. 26, 1952; NYPL for the Performing Arts, Box 144, Folder 14.
161 *"Through a curious twist of fate"*: William Schuman, letter to Julia S. Novak, June 12, 1952; NYPL for the Performing Arts, Box 144, Folder 14.
162 "Judith *is going to be remembered*": Schuman and Waleson, chap. 9, p. 17.
162 *"'Judith' was done in another period"*: Martha Graham, letter to William Schuman, Nov. 10, 1984; NYPL for the Performing Arts, Box 130, Folder 8A.
162 *"I hold you in great esteem"*: Martha Graham, letter to William Schuman, July 13, 1984; NYPL for the Performing Arts, Box 130, Folder 8A.
163 *"an erotic frolic"*: McDonagh, p. 223.

163 *"the three men"*: ibid.
163 *"Martha gave me"*: Schuman and Waleson, chap. 9, p. 18.
163 *"By chance"*: ibid., chap. 9, p. 19.
164 *"I'm going to ask Bill"*: ibid.
164 *"'but you'll really go down'"*: ibid., chap. 9, pp. 19–20.
164 *"when summoned"*: Martha Graham, précis of work attached to letter to William Schuman, June 8, 1965; NYPL for the Performing Arts, Box 59, Folder 12.
164 *"probably will not be considered"*: Rosalyn Krokover, "Martha Graham: Indomitable" [review], *High Fidelity/Musical America* (Jan. 1966): p. 142.
165 *"a work of great psychological complexity"*: Clive Barnes, "Dance: Martha Graham, 'The Witch of Endor' Is Opener of Season—Story of Saul Is Made Universal," *New York Times*, Nov. 3, 1965.
165 *"Judith works better"*: Schuman and Waleson, chap. 9, p. 23.
165 *"So out of our four ballets"*: ibid., chap. 9, p. 20.

Chapter 8

167 *It was the product*: Adams, p. 38.
167 *Although the official premiere*: Mary E. Rice, letter to Gertrude Martin, Sept. 6, 1949; NYPL for the Performing Arts, Box 144, Folder 4.
167 *Schuman admired her enormously*: Perlis, p. 300.
167 *"in the sense that she was the first 'lady'"*: ibid., p. 301.
168 *"'Marion, this is Bill'"*: ibid., p. 302.
168 *"The first and last parts"*: Antal Doráti, "William Schuman—Symphony No. VI, in One Movement," program notes, Dallas Symphony Orchestra, Feb. 27, 1949; NYPL for the Performing Arts, Box 146, Folder 5.
169 *"the work did not receive"*: William Schuman, untitled statement, Nov. 14, 1951, p. 1; NYPL for the Performing Arts, Box 146, Folder 5.
169 *"found the Symphony"*: ibid.
169 *"deeply shaken"*: ibid., p. 3.
169 *"I firmly believe"*: William Schuman, "To the Audience," pp. 1–2; NYPL for the Performing Arts, Box 146, Folder 5.
170 *"The Symphony is beautifully written"*: Edwin H. Schloss, "Cliburn Lives Up to Expectations," *Philadelphia Inquirer*, Jan. 12, 1963.
170 *"Here is a sincere"*: Elliott W. Galkin, "Music Notes: Cliburn, Ormandy," *Baltimore Sun*, Mar. 28, 1963; p. 17.
170 *"one of the most profound"*: Karl F. Miller, "William Schuman, 1910–1992," *American Record Guide* 55, no. 4 (July–Aug. 1992): p. 30.
170 *"the Sixth Symphony . . . is the one"*: Schuman and Waleson, chap. 11, pp. 7–8.
171 *"I think it does make"*: Perlis, p. 305.
171 *"The Sixth Symphony could hardly"*: Christopher Chapman Rouse III, "Expansion of Material in the Seventh Symphony of William Schuman" (master's thesis, Cornell University, 1977), part 2, p. 69.
171 *"I just thought"*: Christopher "Chip" Rouse, letter to William Schuman, June 18, 1969; NYPL for the Performing Arts, Box 146, Folder 15.
172 *"During April and May"*: ibid.
172 *"I vill play"*: Schuman and Waleson, chap. 11, p. 15.
172 *"I don't care"*: ibid., chap. 11, pp. 15–16.
173 *"Listen, Sam"*: Perlis, p. 315.
173 *"just terrible"*: ibid.
173 *"I thought about you"*: William Schuman, letter to Samuel Dushkin, Sept. 29, 1959; NYPL for the Performing Arts, Box 13, Folder 8.

173 *"Munch loved the work"*: Perlis, p. 315.
173 *"the inability of certain performers"*: ibid., p. 316.
173 *"fiendishly difficult"*: Jules Wolffers, "Bostonians Premiere New Schuman Violin Concerto," *Music Courier*, Mar. 1, 1950.
174 *"a study of the individual"*: R. P., "Stern the Soloist in Schuman Work," *New York Times*, Mar. 16, 1950.
174 *"horribly difficult"*: "Bread & Butter," *Time*, Feb. 20, 1950.
174 *"very unusual"*: Perlis, p. 318.
175 *"most unreliable"*: ibid., p. 497.
175 *"bringing to Carnegie Hall"*: Andre Kostelanetz, letter to William Schuman, Feb. 25, 1954; NYPL for the Performing Arts, Box 23, Folder 7.
175 *"1. The rehearsal time for these concerts"*: ibid.
176 *He was bedridden*: William Schuman, letter to Andre Kostelanetz, July 16, 1954; NYPL for the Performing Arts, Box 23, Folder 7.
176 *"at present it is my intention"*: William Schuman, letter to Andre Kostelanetz, Aug. 2, 1955; NYPL for the Performing Arts, Box 23, Folder 7.
176 *Schuman had also suggested*: Schuman and Waleson, chap. 11, p. 2.
176 *Upon Schuman's request*: http://www.loc.gov/performingarts/encyclopedia/collections/spivacke.html, accessed Dec. 28, 2006.
176 *Schuman finally said*: William Schuman, letter to Andre Kostelanetz, Aug. 2, 1955; NYPL for the Performing Arts, Box 23, Folder 7.
176 *"Regarding your idea"*: Andre Kostelanetz, letter to William Schuman, Aug. 19, 1955; NYPL for the Performing Arts, Box 23, Folder 7.
177 *"Every [sic] since you decided"*: William Schuman, letter to Andre Kostelanetz, Dec. 14, 1955; NYPL for the Performing Arts, Box 23, Folder 7.
178 *"I'm too nervous"*: Schuman and Waleson, chap. 11, p. 2.
178 *"Billings and Schuman are both"*: Alfred Frankenstein, review, *San Francisco Chronicle*.
178 *"New England Triptych . . . impressed"*: Albert Goldberg, "Solti, Pennario Team Brilliantly," *Los Angeles Times*, Feb. 27, 1960.
178 *The second movement*: Judith Ilika (Theodore Presser Co.), e-mail to Anthony Schuman and Andrea Schuman.
179 *However, Schuman eventually resented*: Perlis, p. 192.
179 *"Why don't you write another"*: Schuman and Waleson, chap. 11, pp. 4–5.
179 *"this Prelude is intended"*: William Schuman, *When Jesus Wept: Prelude for Band*, full score (Bryn Mawr, PA: Merion Music, 1957), p. 1.
179 *It was the first time*: William Schuman, "Credendum"; NYPL for the Performing Arts, Box 144, Folder 9.
180 *In 1952 the department had appointed*: BMI, brochure on William Schuman; NYPL for the Performing Arts, Box 144, Folder 9.
180 *"Suffice it to say"*: William Schuman, letter to Frances Schuman, Sept. 21–23, 1952; Schuman Family Archives.
181 *"They planned to appoint him"*: David S. Cooper, letter to William Schuman, Oct. 10, 1959; NYPL for the Performing Arts, Box 11, Folder 5.
181 *"The first movement, Declaration"*: William Schuman, "Credendum"; NYPL for the Performing Arts, Box 144, Folder 9.
181 *After the performance in Cincinnati*: Sheet listing performances of *Credendum*; NYPL for the Performing Arts, Box 144, Folder 9.
182 *"I wasn't trying"*: Schuman and Waleson, chap. 11, p. 11.
182 *"It does not have"*: Robert S. Hines, "William Schuman Interview," *College Music Symposium* 35 (1995): p. 139.
182 *"I was so enamored"*: Schuman and Waleson, chap. 11, p. 12.
182 *"extramusical idea"*: Hines, p. 139.

182 *"the work is important"*: Oliver Daniel, "An American Approach to the Grand Manner," *Saturday Review*, Nov. 9, 1957.

182 *"Last night's concert"*: Paul Henry Lang, review, *New York Herald Tribune*, Mar. 14, 1956.

182 *"music of immense beauty"*: Paul Hume, "Schuman's Credendum Given Here," *Washington Post*, March 21, 1956.

183 *"lack of paper"*: Nathan Broder, letter to William Schuman, Oct. 23, 1946; NYPL for the Performing Arts, Box 180, Folder 4.

183 *"As one not wholly unfamiliar"*: William Schuman, letter to Nathan Broder, Oct. 24, 1946; NYPL for the Performing Arts, Box 180, Folder 4.

184 *"matters affecting our general program"*: Robert J. Burton, letter to William Schuman, Aug. 26, 1952; NYPL for the Performing Arts, Box 8, Folder 1.

184 *"Today I stopped in"*: William Schuman, letter to Robert Burton, Sept. 11, 1952; NYPL for the Performing Arts, Box 8, Folder 1.

184 *"for the publication"*: Abraham Friedman, letter to William Schuman, Sept. 25, 1953; NYPL for the Performing Arts, Box 180, Folder 2.

185 *"There is no use"*: William Schuman, letter to H. W. Heinsheimer, Sept. 14, 1954; NYPL for the Performing Arts, Box 180, Folder 5.

185 *"Why have a publisher"*: ibid.

185 *"I have a realistic understanding"*: ibid.

185 *"I wish a peaceful"*: ibid.

186 *"had had enough"*: William Schuman, memo to file, Feb. 10, 1955; NYPL for the Performing Arts, Box 180, Folder 5.

186 *"Now Heinsheimer is being"*: William Schuman, memo to file, Sept. 17, 1955; NYPL for the Performing Arts, Box 180, Folder 5.

187 *"use its best efforts"*: Agreement between William Schuman and Theodore Presser Company, Jan. 1, 1956, p. 16; NYPL for the Performing Arts, Box 178, Folder 1.

187 *"Your avaricious publisher"*: Herbert E. Marks, letter to William Schuman, Sept. 12, 1958; NYPL for the Performing Arts, Box 180, Folder 3.

187 *"Giving you an advance"*: Herbert E. Marks, letter to William Schuman, Apr. 2, 1959; NYPL for the Performing Arts, Box 180, Folder 3.

187 *"make a successful piece"*: William Schuman, letter to Herbert E. Marks, Apr. 18, 1959; NYPL for the Performing Arts, Box 180, Folder 3.

187 *"I must confess"*: Herbert E. Marks, letter to William Schuman, Feb. 24, 1960; NYPL for the Performing Arts, Box 180, Folder 3.

188 *"I am amused"*: William Schuman, letter to Herbert E. Marks, Feb. 29, 1960; NYPL for the Performing Arts, Box 180, Folder 3.

188 *"Come, come, come lovely and soothing death"*: "To All, to Each," from *Carols of Death* (Bryn Mawr, PA: Merion Music, 1959).

189 *"haunted me for years"*: Schuman and Waleson, chap. 13, pp. 5–6.

189 *"If one were asked"*: Robert Sabin, "Twentieth-Century Americans," in *Choral Music*, ed. Arthur Jacobs (Baltimore: Penguin Books, 1963), p. 379.

189 *During this time Schuman*: Adams, pp. 41–49.

189 *"drove past the George Washington Bridge"*: Schuman and Waleson, chap. 13, pp. 23–24.

189 *"Later I did a choral version"*: Schuman and Waleson, chap. 13, pp. 19–20.

190 *"is one of Schuman's most mature works"*: "William Schuman (1951)," in Aaron Copland, *Copland on Music* (New York: Doubleday, 1960), pp. 233–36.

191 *"ultra-modern and . . . presents"*: Olin Downes, "Annual Music Fete Starts in Capital," *New York Times*, Oct. 29, 1950.

192 *"There always is a chance"*: Walter Simmons, explanatory notes, in "Casey at the Bat," Educational Audio Visual Music Appreciation Series, 1980; Schuman Family Archives.

192 *"perhaps the notion"*: ibid.

192 *"I had a wonderful time"*: Schuman and Waleson, chap. 12, p. 32.
193 *"We can permit ourselves"*: Jeremy Gury, letter to William Schuman, May 23, 1951; NYPL for the Performing Arts, Box 145, Folder 2.
193 *It was also hoped*: Robert Whitney, letter to William Schuman, July 6, 1951; NYPL for the Performing Arts, Box 145, Folder 2.
193 *"Frankly, this whole thing"*: Hans Heinsheimer, letter to William Schuman, July 12, 1951; NYPL for the Performing Arts, Box 145, Folder 2.
194 *"At this point"*: Jeremy Gury, letter to William Schuman, Aug. 1, 1951; NYPL for the Performing Arts, Box 145, Folder 2.
194 *"new* musical": Hans Heinsheimer, letter to Alfred de Liagre, Nov. 8, 1951; NYPL for the Performing Arts, Box 145, Folder 2.
194 *"The news from NBC"*: Hans Heinsheimer, letter to William Schuman, May 19, 1952; NYPL for the Performing Arts, Box 145, Folder 2.
194 *Indiana University also*: Wilfred C. Bain, letter to Hans Heinsheimer, June 23, 1952; NYPL for the Performing Arts, Box 145, Folder 2.
194 *"I still think"*: William Schuman, letter to Alfred de Liagre, Feb. 25, 1955; NYPL for the Performing Arts, Box 145, Folder 2.
194 *The production included*: "The Mighty Casey," *Broadcasting-Telecasting*, Mar. 14, 1955; Juilliard Archives, Box 1, Folder: Schuman, William, 1951–1960.
195 *wrote a playful questionnaire*: questionnaire for distribution at television party at New Rochelle home of William Schuman; Schuman Family Archives.
195 *"My dear Bill"*: Alfred de Liagre Jr., letter to William Schuman, Mar. 7, 1955; NYPL for the Performing Arts, Box 145, Folder 2.
195 *"is essentially unfitting"*: Harold Schonberg, "There Is No Joy in 'Casey' Opera," *New York Times*, Mar. 7, 1955.
195 *"downright annoying"*: John Rockwell, "Juilliard Demonstrates Its Up-to-Dateness," *New York Times*, Dec. 16, 1990.
196 *"I wasn't looking"*: Schuman and Waleson, chap. 12, p. 32.
196 *Schuman had obtained*: William Schuman, letter to Lincoln Kirstein, July 15, 1953; NYPL for the Performing Arts, Box 23, Folder 6.
196 *Kirstein expressed interest*: Lincoln Kirstein, letter to William Schuman, July 23, 1953; NYPL for the Performing Arts, Box 23, Folder 6.
197 *"Especially noteworthy"*: Program note, undated; NYPL for the Performing Arts, Box 146, Folder 6.
198 *"the Seventh Symphony of William Schuman"*: Paul Hume, "Bostonians Present New Schuman Work," *Washington Post*, Dec. 2, 1960.
199 *"Mr. Schuman has his own style"*: Harold C. Schonberg, "Music: Diamond Jubilee," *New York Times*, Dec. 1, 1960.
199 *"The ceremony was familiar"*: Winthrop Sargeant, quoted in Robert Sabin, "The Dangers of Being a Destructive Reactionary," *Musical America* (Feb. 1961): p. 8.
199 *"was particularly stung"*: Anthony Schuman, e-mail to the author, May 11, 2008.
200 *"His suggestion came to mind"*: Program notes by the composer for *A Song of Orpheus*; NYPL for the Performing Arts, Box 146, Folder 1.
200 *"He is writing allusively"*: Henry Butler, review, *Indianapolis Times*, Feb. 18, 1962.
201 *"This is imaginative music"*: Francis D. Perkins, "Juilliard Doubleheader At the New Philharmonic: The Orchestra," *New York Herald Tribune*, Sept. 29, 1962.
201 *"Permit me to tell you"*: Joseph Machlis, letter to William Schuman, undated; NYPL for the Performing Arts, Box 146, Folder 15.
201 *"Frankie was particularly delighted"*: William Schuman, letter to Joseph Machlis, Jan. 7, 1971; NYPL for the Performing Arts, Box 146, Folder 15.
201 *"Also let me congratulate you"*: Joseph Machlis, letter to William Schuman, undated; NYPL for the Performing Arts, Box 146, Folder 15.

META

META

META

META

META

Chapter 9

203 *"It is my conviction"*: William Schuman, letter to Juilliard School faculty and staff, Sept. 12, 1961; NYPL for the Performing Arts, Box 21, Folder 9.

203 *"Peter Mennin was interviewed"*: Schuman and Waleson, chap. 10, pp. 30–31.

204 *"To me, running the school"*: Perlis, p. 297.

204 *With his energetic personality*: ibid., p. 298.

204 *"an innovator"*: ibid.

204 *"The faculty and staff deeply regret"*: Vice President's Report, Mar. 2, 1962, p. 1.

204 *"Bill Schuman's greatest gift"*: "William Schuman Elected President of Lincoln Center," *Juilliard Review* 8, no. 3 (Fall 1961): p. 4.

205 *"poisonous"*: Transcript of interviews by Sharon Zane with Schuyler Chapin, Jan. 7, 1991–Jan. 22, 1992, New York City (hereafter cited as Zane, Chapin Oral History), p. 38; Lincoln Center for the Performing Arts Oral History Project (Lincoln Center for the Performing Arts, 1992); Archives of the Lincoln Center for the Performing Arts. (hereafter cited as LCPA Archives).

206 *"willing to meet"*: Transcript of interviews by Sharon Zane with Edgar Young, June 11–Nov. 13, 1990, New York City (hereafter cited as Zane, Young Oral History), p. 10; Lincoln Center for the Performing Arts Oral History Project (Lincoln Center for the Performing Arts, 1990); LCPA Archives.

206 *"was aware that something"*: Zane, Young Oral History, p. 11.

206 *The founding members*: Edgar B. Young, *Lincoln Center: The Building of an Institution* (New York: New York University Press, 1980), p. 20.

207 *"artistic and financial autonomy"*: ibid., p. 35.

207 *"he was not interested"*: Zane, Young Oral History, p. 36.

207 *"I think it's fair"*: ibid.

207 *"Lincoln Center would be a trilogy"*: ibid., p. 68.

208 *"One day, some time in the mid-1950s"*: Schuman and Waleson, chap. 8, p. 15.

209 *"I stepped up"*: ibid., chap. 8, p. 18.

209 *"Those business relationships"*: Schuman and Waleson, chap. 10, p. 26.

209 *"our goal was not"*: ibid., chap. 10, p. 18.

210 *"The board of directors want me"*: ibid., chap. 10, p. 1.

210 *"I'm going to call Rockefeller"*: ibid., chap. 10, pp. 1–2.

211 *"In the meantime"*: ibid., chap. 10, pp. 2–4 passim.

211 *"It's very difficult"*: ibid., chap. 10, pp. 5–7; Schuman and Waleson, chap. 10, pp. 8–9.

212 *"we have every expectation"*: John D. Rockefeller 3rd, letter to William Schuman, Sept. 14, 1961; Schuman Family Archives.

212 *"major financing problems"*: Lincoln Center press release, Sept. 13, 1961; Juilliard Archives, Box 1, Folder: Schuman, William, 1961–1968.

213 *"Lincoln Center . . . can lead"*: ibid., p. 2.

213 *"I didn't take this job"*: Ronald Eyer, "William Schuman," *Musical America* (Sept. 1962): p. 26.

213 *"I said that at this point"*: John D. Rockefeller 3rd, letter to William Schuman, July 1, 1965; Schuman Family Archives.

213 *"as a tangible expression"*: John D. Rockefeller 3rd, letter to Charles M. Spofford, Dec. 16, 1965; Schuman Family Archives.

213 *"I can think of no other man"*: Philip Benjamin, "Composer to Head Lincoln Art Center," *New York Times*, Sept. 13, 1961.

213 *"We have every confidence"*: John D. Rockefeller 3rd, letter to William Schuman, Sept. 14, 1961; LCPA Archives.

214 *"brings to Lincoln Center"*: Benjamin, "Composer."

214 *"You want an artist"*: Schonberg, "Man to Orchestrate," p. 29.

214 *"Lincoln Center has to work"*: ibid.

214 *"Bill Schuman was brought in"*: Zane, Young Oral History, p. 225.

214 *"I could understand"*: Perlis, p. 333.

215 *"a strong impression"*: Ved Mehta, "An Enclave," *New Yorker*, Feb. 17, 1962, p. 26.

215 *"'The work at Lincoln Center'"*: ibid., pp. 26–27.

216 *"a tall man"*: Fern Marja Eckman, "Lincoln Center's Practical Artist-in-Charge," *New York Post Sunday Magazine*, Sept. 17, 1961, p. 2.

216 *"I do not believe"*: William Schuman, letter to the Honorable John M. Murtagh, Nov. 24, 1953; NYPL for the Performing Arts, Box 149, Folder 2.

216 *Another time Schuman wrote*: William Schuman, letter to Frederic G. Donner, Jan. 6, 1961; NYPL for the Performing Arts, Box 149, Folder 2.

216 *"The very best ale"*: William Schuman, letter to John E. Farrell, Dec. 12, 1967; NYPL for the Performing Arts, Box 48, Folder 4.

217 *"He [Bill] and Tony had a competition"*: Andrea Schuman, e-mail to the author, Apr. 23, 2008.

217 *"an organization man"*: Schonberg, "Man to Orchestrate," p. 8.

217 *"an unusual combination"*: ibid.

217 *"Close friends of the Schumans"*: ibid. p. 29.

218 *"a radical with conservative ideas"*: ibid., p. 30.

219 *"a Friday evening vocal and instrumental concert"*: Lincoln Center for the Performing Arts, Minutes of the Meeting of the Executive Committee, Jan. 29, 1962, p; 2, LCPA Archives.

219 *"will be chronicled as a symbol"*: Arthur Gelb, "A Deeper Significance," *New York Times*, Sept. 24, 1962.

219 *"acoustical clouds"*: "The Welcoming Address," *New York Times*, Sept. 24, 1962.

220 *"she's even more beautiful"*: Alan Rich, "First Lady Pays Bernstein a Visit," *New York Times*, Sept. 24, 1962.

220 *"he had sweat[ed] it off"*: ibid.

220 *"the New York Philharmonic sounded"*: Harold C. Schonberg, "Music: The Occasion," *New York Times*, Sept. 24, 1962.

220 *"Philharmonic Hall probably will be"*: ibid.

221 *"everybody in the audience"*: Perlis, p. 454.

221 *"stopped and looked terribly embarrassed"*: ibid.

221 *"just hated Copland's* Connotations": ibid., p. 455.

221 *"to offer teachers"*: Teachers Institute Resolution Passed at Board of Directors Meeting, Feb. 19, 1962; LCPA Archives.

221 *"the proper place"*: Lincoln Center for the Performing Arts, Minutes of Meeting of Board of Directors and Members, Apr. 9, 1962, p. 5; LCPA Archives.

221 *"most of the specialists"*: Lincoln Center for the Performing Arts, Minutes of Meeting of Board of Directors and Members, June 11, 1962, p. 4; LCPA Archives.

222 *"favorably impressed"*: ibid.

222 *"the hall had remarkable"*: Zane, Young Oral History, p. 112.

223 *"Through the acquisition"*: William Schuman, letter to Peter Mennin, Oct. 11, 1962; NYPL for the Performing Arts, Box 28, Folder 3.

224 *"the Theater for the Dance"*: Zane, Young Oral History, p. 50.

224 *"as the performing arts angle"*: ibid., p. 52.

225 *In mid- to late 1962 the chairman*: ibid., p. 58.

225 *"It's [running for office] the greatest education"*: obituary of Morton Baum, *New York Times*, Feb. 8, 1968.

226 *"he ripped the entire telephone off"*: Zane, Chapin Oral History, p. 48.

226 *"recreate smaller, 4-foot versions"*: http://www.nycballet.com/nyst/fun.html, accessed Apr. 13, 2007.

227 *"The Rockefellers have"*: Murray Schumach, "Lincoln Center: Hub of Arts; Lincoln Center, 5 Years Old Today, Wields a Major Influence in Nation's Arts," *New York Times*, Sept. 23, 1967.

Chapter 10

229 *"By mid-February 1963"*: Young, *Lincoln Center*, p. 243.
230 *George Woods stepped down*: ibid., p. 244.
230 *"if they [LCT] could divide"*: Perlis, p. 356.
231 *"Please don't do that"*: ibid., p. 357.
231 *"It was Bing at his insect-biting best"*: Zane, Chapin Oral History, p. 61.
231 *"That night Mr. Hoguet and Mr. Bliss"*: William Schuman, letter to Abraham Friedman, Jan. 6, 1965; Schuman Family Archives.
231 *"apparently deteriorating"*: Milton Esterow, "Bing Attack Airs Dispute on Theater of Lincoln Center," *New York Times*, Dec. 5, 1964.
231 *"I am deeply disturbed"*: ibid.
232 *"Cultural observers have recently said"*: ibid.
232 *"The role of Lincoln Center"*: ibid.
232 *"Mr. Hoguet and Mr. Schuman had acted properly"*: Milton Esterow, "Lincoln Center Will Continue Seeking Director from Met," *New York Times*, Dec. 6, 1964.
232 *"Samson in Longhair Temple"*: Robert J. Landry, "Samson in Longhair Temple," *Variety*, Dec. 16, 1964, p. 1.
233 *"By the end of 1964"*: Young, *Lincoln Center*, p. 246.
233 *"Tony, we have to rebuild"*: Perlis, p. 358.
234 *"to be quite candid"*: Zane, Chapin Oral History, p. 61.
234 *"time for silence"*: William Schuman, notes for board meeting, Dec. 14, 1964; LCPA Archives.
234 *"was on the way out"*: ibid.
234 *"Board of Directors then expressed"*: Lincoln Center for the Performing Arts, Minutes of Meeting of Board of Directors and Members, Dec. 14, 1964, pp. 4–5; LCPA Archives.
235 *"I did not want"*: William Schuman, letter to Abraham Friedman, Jan. 6, 1965, p. 3; Schuman Family Archives.
235 *"in the meantime"*: Perlis, p. 359.
235 *"The Krawitz thing blew higher"*: Zane, Chapin Oral History, pp. 61–62.
235 *"That's the kind of thing"*: Perlis, p. 359.
236 *"arrogantly indifferent"*: Zane, Young Oral History, p. 117.
236 *"covered all the microphone outlets"*: ibid., p. 119.
236 *"angry public outburst"*: Young, *Lincoln Center*, p. 186.
237 *"there was very serious consideration"*: Zane, Young Oral History, pp. 147–48.
237 *"I am simply overjoyed"*: William Schuman, letter to Samuel Barber, June 1, 1964; Schuman Family Archives.
237 *"It is always good"*: Samuel Barber, letter to William Schuman, June 13, 1964; Schuman Family Archives.
238 *"virtually every member"*: Charlotte Curtis, "First Lady Adds to Glitter; Musicians' Strike Is Settled," *New York Times*, Sept. 17, 1966.
238 *"Mr. Bing . . . I've always envisioned"*: ibid.
238 *"I'm sure you'll be happy"*: Raymond Ericson, "Rudolf Bing Announces Settlement of the Musicians' Strike from Stage of the Met," *New York Times*, Sept. 17, 1966.
238 *"The architecture sets"*: "Sweet and Sour Notes on the Met," *New York Times*, Sept. 18, 1966.
238 *"a bit lost"*: Harold C. Schonberg, "Onstage, It Was 'Antony and Cleopatra,'" *New York Times*, Sept. 17, 1966.
239 *"was a big, complicated package"*: ibid.
240 *"The society part was so boring"*: Perlis, p. 360.
240 *"Way down deep"*: ibid., pp. 349–50.
240 *"Fund-raising"*: John D. Rockefeller 3rd, letter to William Schuman, Dec. 30, 1966; Schuman Family Archives.

241 *"From the beginning"*: ibid.
241 *"There is still the feeling"*: ibid.
242 *"This [confidence] of course underlies"*: ibid.
242 *"The months ahead"*: ibid.
242 *"But I cannot in all candor"*: William Schuman, confidential memorandum re: Rockefeller letter, Jan. 9, 1967; Schuman Family Archives.
243 *"Despite the important advances"*: William Schuman, "The New Establishment," speech delivered at the Princeton University Conference on the Performing Arts, Dec. 8–9, 1966, Princeton, NJ; NYPL for the Performing Arts, Box 79, Folder 1, 2–3.
244 *"Public spirited citizens"*: ibid., Folder 1, 5.
244 *"Nonprofit institutions in the performing arts"*: ibid., Folder 1, 6.
245 *"But I believe"*: ibid., Folder 1, 15–16.
246 *"What specific action"*: John D. Rockefeller 3rd, letter to William Schuman, Feb. 22, 1967; Schuman Family Archives.
246 *"However regrettable these [capital] overages"*: William Schuman, letter to John D. Rockefeller 3rd, Mar. 2, 1967; Schuman Family Archives.

Chapter 11

249 *"horrible for the household"*: interview by the author with Anthony Schuman and Andrea Schuman, Apr. 27, 2007, Juilliard School.
250 *"They were a real team"*: ibid.
250 *In 1966 Frankie's breast cancer*: Schuman and Waleson, chap. 13, pp. 7–8.
250 *"I've been blessed"*: ibid.
250 *"My conflict with Dad"*: interview by the author with Anthony Schuman and Andrea Schuman, Apr. 27, 2007, Juilliard School.
250 *"'fight my fights'"*: ibid.
250 *One rare exception*: "Funds Sought for Adlai," *New Rochelle* (NY) *Standard Star*, Oct. 15, 1956.
250 *"Dad had an organic patriotism"*: interview by the author with Anthony Schuman and Andrea Schuman, Apr. 27, 2007, Juilliard School.
251 *"and participate in cotillions"*: ibid.
251 *"not to report male students"*: ibid.
251 *"They were ferociously protective"*: ibid.
251 *"one or both of my parents"*: ibid.
251 *"was an adaptation"*: Anthony Schuman, e-mail to the author, Dec. 18, 2007; and interview by the author with Anthony Schuman and Andrea Schuman, Apr. 27, 2007, Juilliard School.
252 *"planning and thrift"*: interview by the author with Anthony Schuman and Andrea Schuman, Apr. 27, 2007, Juilliard School.
253 *"Frankly I have become"*: Edward Downes, program notes for New York Philharmonic concerts, Oct. 4–7, 1962, p. 38; NYPL for the Performing Arts, Box 146, Folder 7.
253 *The thirty-minute work*: ibid., p. 39.
253 *"tragic and intense"*: "Season Is Opened by Philharmonic," New York Times, Oct. 5, 1962.
253 *"And in its concentration"*: ibid.
253 *"Mr. Schuman's is a genuine symphony"*: Paul Henry Lang, "New York Philharmonic," *New York Herald Tribune*, Oct. 5, 1962.
254 *"The symphony shaped up"*: Louis Biancolli, "Bernstein Plays New Symphony," *New York World-Telegram and Sun*, Oct. 5, 1962.
255 *"series of traditional Austrian melodies"*: William Schuman, *The Orchestra Song* (Bryn Mawr, PA: Merion Music, 1964).

255 *"[Ives composed] an organ fantasia"*: William Schuman, program notes for *Variations on "America,"* Apr. 1964, p. 2; NYPL for the Performing Arts, Box 146, Folder 13.

255 *"I took all the liberties"*: Perlis, pp. 464–65.

256 *"The Ives is delightful"*: Henry Cowell, letter to William Schuman, May 22, 1964; NYPL for the Performing Arts, Box 146, Folder 13.

257 *"commissioned for The Thirteenth Festival of Chamber Music"*: William Schuman, *Amaryllis: Variations for String Trio* (Bryn Mawr, PA: Merion Music, 1966).

257 *"to the memory of Elizabeth Sprague Coolidge"*: ibid.

257 *The three-day festival*: Day Thorpe, "Washington, D.C./Coolidge Festival," *Musical America* 84 (Dec. 1964): p. 64.

258 *"Composers do this all the time"*: Schuman and Waleson, chap. 13, pp. 17–18.

258 *"enable the performer to project"*: Schuman, *Amaryllis*, p. 1.

258 *"the juxtaposition of tonal and non-tonal"*: Robert Evett, "Current Chronicle: Washington, D.C.," *Musical Quarterly* 51, no. 2 (Apr. 1965): p. 408.

258 *"worked [it] in conservative"*: Thorpe, p. 64.

258 *Owing to his workload*: Adams, p. 52.

259 *"artistic position and prestige"*: Zane, Young Oral History, p. 178.

260 *"(1) a chamber music group"*: Lincoln Center for the Performing Arts, Minutes of Meeting of Board of Directors and Members, May 10, 1965, pp. 8–9; LCPA Archives.

260 *"a twelve-week summer series"*: Judith Johnson (director, Information Resources, Lincoln Center for the Performing Arts), e-mail to the author, Mar. 17, 2008.

260 *His film festivals also were popular*: Young, *Lincoln Center*, p. 230.

260 *"not a live art"*: Perlis, p. 376.

261 *"there was some disagreement"*: David Wright, "Film and Lincoln Center," chap. B, p. 7, in "Composer in America: William Schuman Talks about His Life and Works" [unpublished manuscript, 1987]; Juilliard Archives, Box 3, Folder: Schuman, William: Chapter drafts from proposed memoir with David Wright; correspondence, 1986–87.

261 *"only really new form of art"*: ibid., p. 8.

261 *"a cultural necessity"*: ibid., p. 9.

261 *"to a late-afternoon flick"*: ibid., p. 16.

261 *"Marty was so successful"*: ibid., p. 17.

262 *"the Music Theater brought revivals"*: Young, *Lincoln Center*, p. 307.

262 *In late 1963 the theater's chairman*: ibid., p. 244.

262 *The new theater ended the season*: ibid.

263 *"'last resort' call"*: ibid., p. 247.

263 *"these frictions"*: ibid., p. 249.

263 *"no longer at the top"*: Zane, Young Oral History, p. 175.

263 *"Your idea here outlined"*: John D. Rockefeller 3rd, letter to William Schuman, Oct. 28, 1965; NYPL for the Performing Arts, Box 51, Folder 7.

264 *Because the Houghton family*: Memo from John W. McNulty to John D. Rockefeller 3rd, Dec. 14, 1964; Rockefeller Family Archives, Record Group 5 (JDR3rd Papers), Series 1 (Office of the Messrs. Rockefeller), Subseries 4 (Lincoln Center), Box 69, Folder 603.

264 *"creative artistic enterprise"*: William Schuman, letter to Arthur A. Houghton Jr., Nov. 12, 1965; NYPL for the Performing Arts, Box 51, Folder 7.

264 *"But I was more than delighted"*: William Schuman, letter to Alice Tully, Dec. 6, 1965; NYPL for the Performing Arts, Box 51, Folder 7.

264 *"not too-often performed works"*: David Amram, letter to William Schuman, Dec. 23, 1965; NYPL for the Performing Arts, Box 51, Folder 7.

264 *"my own especial joy"*: Alice Tully, letter to William Schuman, Feb. 2, 1966 NYPL for the Performing Arts, Box 51, Folder 7.

265 *"the chamber music recital hall"*: Press release, May 10, 1966; NYPL for the Performing Arts, Box 51, Folder 7.

265 *"seems to be quite touched"*: John D. Rockefeller 3rd, letter to Pietro Belluschi, May 13, 1965; Rockefeller Family Archives, Record Group 5 (JDR3rd Papers), Series 1 (Office of the Messrs. Rockefeller), Subseries 4 (Lincoln Center), Box 69, Folder 603.

265 *"[would] amount to one-half"*: Alice Tully, letter to John W. Mazzola, May 27, 1965; Rockefeller Family Archives, Record Group 5 (JDR3rd Papers), Series 1 (Office of the Messrs. Rockefeller), Subseries 4 (Lincoln Center), Box 69, Folder 603.

265 *"a plan to utilize Alice Tully Hall"*: William Schuman, letter to Alice Tully, Feb. 28, 1967; NYPL for the Performing Arts, Box 51, Folder 7.

265 *"a repertory theater of chamber music"*: Perlis, p. 378.

266 *"I was convinced"*: William Schuman, letter to Frank E. Taplin, Dec. 22, 1967; NYPL for the Performing Arts, Box 51, Folder 7.

Chapter 12

268 *"To thee, old Cause!"*: Walt Whitman, "To Thee, Old Cause!," in *Leaves of Grass* (Philadelphia: David McKay, [1900]); www.bartleby.com/142/, accessed Jan. 8, 2008.

269 *"melodic line played clearly"*: William Schuman, *To Thee Old Cause* (Bryn Mawr, PA: Merion Music, 1971), p. 38.

269 *"But that piece"*: Perlis, pp. 457–59 passim.

270 *"we have, with considerable reluctance"*: Amyas Ames, letter to John W. Drye Jr., Jan. 8, 1969; LCPA Archives.

270 *"been on a full-time loan"*: Young, *Lincoln Center*, p. 238.

270 *"that if I [Young] no longer"*: Zane, Young Oral History, p. 181.

271 *"the assumption of the chairmanship"*: Charles M. Spofford, letter to John D. Rockefeller 3rd, Sept. 30, 1968; LCPA Archives.

271 *"John Rockefeller was still trying"*: Zane, Young Oral History, p. 186.

272 *"A major objective"*: Young, *Lincoln Center*, p. 296.

272 "Additional deficits": ibid.

272 *"Festival '68 was the most ambitious"*: William Schuman, notes for Oct. 7, 1968, Board Meeting; LCPA Archives.

273 *"there have been mixed feelings"*: ibid.

273 *"the Executive Committee re[s]cinded"*: Lincoln Center for the Performing Arts, Minutes of the Executive Committee Meeting, Nov. 12, 1968, p. 5; LCPA Archives.

273 *"asked that his abstention"*: ibid.

274 *In reply, Schuman suggested*: draft of letter from John D. Rockefeller 3rd to William Schuman, Dec. 17, 1968; Schuman Family Archives.

274 *"to bring financial reality"*: Zane, Young Oral History, p. 187.

274 *"view with alarm"*: Frank E. Taplin, memo to Exploratory Committee, Chamber Music Society, Dec. 26, 1968, p. 1; NYPL for the Performing Arts, Box 51, Folder 8.

275 *"Mr. Rockefeller made clear"*: ibid., p. 2.

275 *"feelings of mistrust"*: John D. Rockefeller 3rd, letter to William Schuman, Apr. 4, 1968; Schuman Family Archives.

275 *"It would have been my thought or hope"*: John D. Rockefeller 3rd, letter to William Schuman, Apr. 9, 1968; Schuman Family Archives.

276 *"I can't possibly describe"*: Perlis, p. 340.

276 *"And from the point of view"*: ibid., p. 346.

276 *"I had a nervous breakdown"*: Zane, Chapin Oral History, p. 81.

276 *"key person"*: William Schuman, "Some Thoughts on the Second Letter—to John D. Rockefeller 3rd," in "Letters I Never Sent," pp. 10–11; Schuman Family Archives.

276 *"But no man lacks"*: ibid., p. 11.

276 *"You said the speakers"*: ibid., pp. 12–14.

278 *"I told you quite candidly"*: ibid., pp. 14–15.

279 *"Anything that came out of his mouth"*: Perlis, p. 455.
280 *"he simply said words"*: ibid., p. 528.
280 *"Thirteen years ago"*: "Juilliard Comes to Lincoln Center: A Dedication Concert," CBS Broadcast, Oct. 26, 1969; Juilliard Library Audio-Visual Collection.
280 *"And ultimately, I suppose"*: ibid.
281 *"It was not a matter of friendship"*: William Schuman, memo to L. K. and M. B., Jan. 19, 1970, p. 9; Schuman Family Archives.
281 *"its own place in the sun"*: Zane, Young Oral History, pp. 211–27 passim.
281 *"There is a man"*: Perlis, p. 367.
282 *"All they wanted"*: ibid., p. 362.
282 *"The only way"*: ibid., p. 356.
282 *"You know, it's [Lincoln Center] turning out"*: ibid., p. 363.
282 *"the fact that the constituents"*: ibid., p. 366.
282 *"if you compromise"*: ibid., pp. 352–53.
282 *"Those people who serve"*: Zane, Chapin Oral History, p. 92.
283 *"not a political animal"*: Perlis, pp. 486–88 passim.

Chapter 13

286 *"I've made so much more"*: Perlis, p. 532.
286 *"But none of these problems"*: Schuman, "Post Lincoln Center" (fragment), in "Autobiography," p. 3; Juilliard Archives, Box 3, Folder: Post Lincoln Center.
286 *"I think I considered"*: ibid.," p. 5.
287 *"For the first time"*: Daniel Webster, "Executive Rat Race Returns Schuman to Composing Field," *Philadelphia Inquirer*, Jan. 5, 1969.
287 *"24-hour-a-day composer"*: ibid.
288 *"trying to be fashionable"*: Raymond Ericson, "Schuman: No Pessimist He," *New York Times*, Jan. 19, 1969.
288 *"'they used to call me radical'"*: ibid.
288 *"Never in my life"*: William Schuman, letter to Nathalie and Hugo Weisgall, June 16, 1967; NYPL for the Performing Arts, Box 146, Folder 8.
289 *"had no connection"*: Nathalie Weisgall, letter to William and Frankie Schuman, Aug. 3, 1967; NYPL for the Performing Arts, Box 146, Folder 8.
289 *"one day, throwing a bomb"*: ibid.
289 *"I feel so strongly"*: ibid.
290 *"Hilsberg had joined"*: Program for the Philadelphia Orchestra, Jan. 10–11, 1969, p. 17; NYPL for the Performing Arts, Box 146, Folder 9.
290 *He wrote to Schuman*: Eugene Ormandy, letter to William Schuman, Oct. 20, 1967; NYPL for the Performing Arts, Box 146, Folder 8.
290 *"An elderly lady"*: Eugene Ormandy, letter to William Schuman, Mar. 8, 1968; NYPL for the Performing Arts, Box 146, Folder 8.
290 *"I never write at the office"*: Richard F. Shepard, "Schuman Finishes His 9th Symphony," *New York Times*, Apr. 9, 1968; NYPL for the Performing Arts, Box 146, Folder 8.
290 *"When I was head of Juilliard"*: ibid.
291 *"Roger Hall and Jack Pfeiffer were here"*: Eugene Ormandy, letter to William Schuman, Mar. 8, 1968; NYPL for the Performing Arts, Box 146, Folder 8.
291 *"It seems that I have been working"*: William Schuman, letter to Eugene Ormandy, May 13, 1968; NYPL for the Performing Arts, Box 146, Folder 8.
291 *"If you want to make me feel better"*: William Schuman, letter to Boris Sokoloff, May 29, 1968; NYPL for the Performing Arts, Box 146, Folder 8.
291 *"It must sound silly"*: William Schuman, letter to Eugene Ormandy, Oct. 11, 1968; NYPL for the Performing Arts, Box 146, Folder 8.

292 *"Its structure is firm"*: Daniel Webster, "Orchestra Presents Premiere of Work by William Schuman," *Philadelphia Inquirer*, Jan. 11, 1969.
292 *"It seemed that Mr. Schuman's piece"*: Max de Schauensee, "Threnody to Hiroshima Victims Penetrates Horrors of Holocaust," *Philadelphia Evening Bulletin*, Jan. 11, 1969.
292 *"has been considered mainly"*: Ron Eyer, "Ormandy Concert Is a Novelty," *Newsday*, Jan. 15, 1969.
293 *"Mr. Schuman's newest symphony"*: Harold C. Schonberg, "Music: Philadelphia with Johansen," *New York Times*, Jan. 15, 1969.
293 *"a satisfactory reading enough"*: *Philadelphia Inquirer*, Feb. 9, 1969.
293 *"how elated you were"*: Eugene Ormandy, letter to William Schuman; NYPL for the Performing Arts, Box 146, Folder 10.
293 *"I gave no interviews"*: William Schuman, letter to Eugene Ormandy, Feb. 13, 1969; NYPL for the Performing Arts, Box 146, Folder 10.
293 *"To correct any impression"*: William Schuman, letter to music editor, *Philadelphia Inquirer*, Mar. 6, 1969.
294 *"of the shock I had"*: Eugene Ormandy, letter to William Schuman, Dec. 2, 1969; NYPL for the Performing Arts, Box 145, Folder 9.
294 *"The profits keep rising"*: William Schuman, letter to Sol Schoenbach, Jan. 22, 1969; NYPL for the Performing Arts, Box 146, Folder 9.
294 *"it was very possible"*: Boris Sokoloff, letter to Sidney N. Repplier, Mar. 13, 1969; NYPL for the Performing Arts, Box 146, Folder 10.
295 *"the quickest and most accurate way"*: William Schuman, letter to Boris Sokoloff, Mar. 18, 1969; NYPL for the Performing Arts, Box 146, Folder 10.
295 *"This situation I find"*: William Schuman, letter to Roger G. Hall, Mar. 18, 1969; NYPL for the Performing Arts, Box 146, Folder 10.
295 *"refused to budge"*: William Schuman, "Subject: Ninth Symphony," memorandum to file, Apr. 1, 1969; NYPL for the Performing Arts, Box 146, Folder 10.
296 *"I was struck immediately"*: Program note, New York Philharmonic, Jan. 29, 1970, p. F; NYPL for the Performing Arts, Box 144, Folder 13.
296 *Schuman was touched*: Frances K. Pohl, *Ben Shahn* (New York: Chameleon Books, 1993).
296 *"The Hallelujah Song"*: Moishe Bressler, letter to William Schuman, [c. Aug. 1–6?, 1969]; NYPL for the Performing Arts, Box 144, Folder 13.
296 *"The more I struggle"*: William Schuman, letter to Morris Bressler, Aug. 7, 1969; NYPL for the Performing Arts, Box 144, Folder 13.
297 *"One of the things I love"*: Perlis, p. 461.
297 *"different pitch levels"*: Program note, New York Philharmonic, Jan. 29, 1970, p. F; NYPL for the Performing Arts, Box 144, Folder 13.
297 *"All lead to a final acceleration"*: Program note, New York Philharmonic, Jan. 29, 1970, p. H; NYPL for the Performing Arts, Box 144, Folder 13.
298 *"by the Combined Choruses"*: William Schuman, *Declaration Chorale* (Bryn Mawr, PA: Merion Music, 1971), title page.
298 *"freely adapted and arranged"*: ibid., p. 2.
298 *"Youth full of force"*: ibid., pp. 3-4.
298 *"Till men and women of all races"*: ibid., pp. 8–12.
299 *"No, I'll wait"*: Perlis, p. 502.
299 *"I can only tell you"*: ibid., p. 503.
299 *"By the end of the afternoon"*: ibid., p. 504.
299 *"I hear the viola moving"*: ibid., p. 505.
299 *"I wasn't that depressed"*: Philip Ramey, interview of William Schuman, back cover of *Concerto on Old English Rounds*, New York Philharmonic/Camerata Singers; Leonard Bernstein, conductor; Donald McInnes, viola (Columbia M35101, 1978).
300 *"I say to people"*: Perlis, p. 505.
300 *"he didn't criticize"*: ibid., p. 514.

300 *"meas. 160—Can we drop"*: Donald McInnes, letter to William Schuman, May 7, 1974; NYPL for the Performing Arts, Box 144, Folder 8.

300 *"our business relationship"*: Anthony Strilko, letter to William Schuman, Jan. 15, 1974; NYPL for the Performing Arts, Box 144, Folder 8.

300 *"The only purpose his [McInnes's] comments"*: Anthony Strilko, letter to William Schuman, Feb. 9, 1974; NYPL for the Performing Arts, Box 144, Folder 8.

300 *"After all, six pages"*: Anthony Strilko, letter to Donald McInnes, Feb. 9, 1974; NYPL for the Performing Arts, Box 144, Folder 8.

301 *"tried to back bill"*: Anthony Schuman, e-mail to the author, July 20, 2007.

301 *"this piece is all about"*: Perlis, p. 510.

301 *"would be a stunning sound"*: Philip Ramey, interview of William Schuman, back cover of *Concerto on Old English Rounds*, New York Philharmonic/Camerata Singers; Leonard Bernstein, conductor; Donald McInnes, viola (Columbia M35101, 1978).

301 *"They're not that interesting"*: ibid.

301 *"'at once a viola concerto'"*: ibid.

302 *"adapted from the opening and closing"*: William Schuman, *Amaryllis: Variants for Strings on an Old English Song* (Bryn Mawr, PA: Merion Music, 1975), p. 3.

302 *"the variants consist"*: William Schuman, "Amaryllis: Variants for Strings on an Old English Song"; NYPL for the Performing Arts, Box 148, Folder 5.

303 *"one of the most extraordinary"*: Perlis, p. 471.

303 *"which [was] not only"*: ibid., p. 472.

303 *"I needed the principal consultants"*: Schuman, "Post Lincoln Center," p. 19.

303 *"What you have given me"*: Perlis, p. 474.

303 *"Why don't you forget about"*: Schuman, "Post Lincoln Center," p. 27.

304 *"that they wanted me to forget"*: Perlis, p. 475.

304 *"Look Brockway"*: ibid.

304 *"about two or three years later"*: ibid., p. 476.

304 *"create, produce and distribute"*: David E. Moore, "Videorecord's Dr. Hopwood Calls for Innovation in Marketing and Programming the New Television," *Southern Connecticut Business Journal*, Oct. 27, 1970, p. 20.

305 *"It may seem"*: Alan M. Kriegsman, "From Lincoln Center to Video Tape Cassettes—With Gusto," *Washington Post*, Oct. 25, 1970.

305 *"Nothing less than paving the way"*: ibid.

305 *"delirious . . . speculat[ion]"*: ibid.

305 *"Instead of husbanding"*: Perlis, p. 477.

305 *"obviously emotionally very, very disturbed"*: Perlis, pp. 478–79 passim.

306 "policies and objectives": "Contract for Services" between William Schuman and the Puerto Rico Industrial Development Company and Festival Casals, Inc., pp. 1–2; NYPL for the Performing Arts, Box 95, Folder 12.

306 *"artistic, cultural and educational institution"*: ibid., p. 2.

306 *All this was to be accomplished*: Abraham Friedman, of Bernays & Eisner, letter to William Schuman, Jan. 29, 1971, and José A. Franceschini, letter to Chemical Bank, Apr. 6, 1971; NYPL for the Performing Arts, Box 95, Folder 12.

306 *It included most*: Document, Conservatory of Music of Puerto Rico, undated; NYPL for the Performing Arts, Box 95, Folder 12.

307 *"it turned out"*: William Schuman, letter to José A. Franceschini, executive director of Festival Casals, Mar. 1971.

308 *"from the funding agencies"*: William Schuman, "Music in Puerto Rico: The Next Decade (1972–1982)," Mar. 15, 1971, p. 41; NYPL for the Performing Arts, Box 95, Folder 12.

308 *"new emerging technologies"*: ibid., p. 44.

309 *"receive a substantial cash prize"*: http://www.naumburg.org/about.php, p. 4 of printout, accessed June 19, 2007.

309 *"There is increasing restiveness"*: William Schuman, letter to Peter Mennin, Sept. 26,

1969; Schuman Family Archives.

309 *"increasing concern"*: William Schuman, memo to the directors of the Walter W. Naumburg Foundation, Nov. 12, 1969, p. 1; Schuman Family Archives.

310 *"our president clearly"*: ibid.

310 *"I feel a deep sense"*: ibid., p. 2.

310 *"My memorandum to you"*: William Schuman, memo to the directors of the Walter W. Naumburg Foundation, Nov. 21, 1969; Schuman Family Archives.

310 *"Pete, that's actually amateursville"*: Telephone interview by the author with Robert Mann, Jan. 8, 2008.

311 *As the shock of the moment*: ibid.

311 *"Had this not been the case"*: William Schuman, letter to Francis Thorne, June 25, 1971; NYPL for the Performing Arts, Box 109, Folder 5.

311 *"the simple fact is"*: Robert Mann, letter to William Schuman, Dec. 3, 1971; NYPL for the Performing Arts, Box 109, Folder 5.

312 *At the time Norlin was*: Norlin Foundation press release, Apr. 15, 1975; NYPL for the Performing Arts, Box 110, Folder 2.

312 *"help people discover"*: ibid., p. 1.

312 *Funding was also provided*: Perlis, pp. 536–37.

312 *"music learning and practice fun"*: Warner Bros. Publications and Goldmark Communications, "The New Music Learning System" [brochure]; NYPL for the Performing Arts, Box 110, Folder 2.

312 *"what does a conductor do"*: William Schuman, memorandum to Norton Stevens, n.d.; NYPL for the Performing Arts, Box 110, Folder 2.

313 *"It will be helpful"*: Charles Frankel, letter to William Schuman, Sept. 13, 1977; NYPL for the Performing Arts, Box 109, Folder 1.

313 *"music for soloists"*: William Schuman, letter to Arthur A. Hauser, June 3, 1966; NYPL for the Performing Arts, Box 147, Folder 10.

313 *"I seem to have been drawn"*: ibid.

314 *"a dramatic scena"*: ibid.

314 *"And the music itself!"*: "Project 1976," n.d., p. 3; NYPL for the Performing Arts, Box 147, Folder 10.

314 *The proposal also outlined*: ibid., p. 4.

314 *"I regard this"*: William Schuman, letter to Harold Weill, Nov. 25, 1972; NYPL for the Performing Arts, Box 147, Folder 10.

315 *"It seems to me"*: William Schuman, letter to Antal Doráti, Apr. 16, 1974; NYPL for the Performing Arts, Box 147, Folder 10.

315 *"I regard your forthcoming performances"*: William Schuman, letter to Antal Doráti, Aug. 5, 1974; NYPL for the Performing Arts, Box 147, Folder 10.

315 *"when I decided"*: William Schuman, letter to Antal Doráti, Aug. 5, 1974; NYPL for the Performing Arts, Box 147, Folder 10.

316 *"a stupendous work"*: Antal Doráti, letter to William Schuman, n.d. [mid–late Feb. 1976?]; NYPL for the Performing Arts, Box 99, Folder 4.

316 *"With the first movement"*: ibid.

316 *"Did any composer ever receive"*: William Schuman, letter to Antal Doráti, Feb. 28, 1976; NYPL for the Performing Arts, Box 99, Folder 4.

316 *"Of course I think"*: ibid.

317 *"The second movement was very well done"*: Perlis, pp. 496–519 passim.

318 *"bells in air al fine"*: William Schuman, *Symphony No. 10: American Muse* (Bryn Mawr, PA: Merion Music, 1977), p. 198.

318 *"It begins with a celebratory"*: Tim Page, "Music: Schuman Concerto and 10th Symphony," *New York Times*, Dec. 16, 1985.

318 *"Dear Bill"*: Joseph Machlis, letter to William Schuman, n.d. [May 1979]; NYPL for the Performing Arts, Box 107, Folder 6.

319 "*[The Tenth Symphony] is also*": John Rockwell, "Music: Schuman by Skrowaczewski," *New York Times*, Apr. 22, 1979.
319 "*Our deaths*": William Schuman, *The Young Dead Soldiers* (Bryn Mawr, PA: Merion Music, 1976), pp. 20–21.
319 "*that I was stuck*": Schuman and Waleson, chap. 13, p. 2.
319 "*Last week I finished*": William Schuman, letter to Archibald MacLeish, July 24, 1975; NYPL for the Performing Arts, Box 107, Folder 7.
319 "*the instrumentation*": Perlis, p. 495.
320 "*the whole trick*": ibid., p. 528.
320 "*It is austere*": Christopher Rouse, *William Schuman Documentary* (Bryn Mawr, PA: Theodore Presser; and New York: G. Schirmer, 1980), p. 25.
321 "*I love that work*": Perlis, pp. 520–21.
321 "*I didn't know then*": Perlis, p. 520.
321 "*Composers writing for the Bicentennial*": Robert Paris, "Washington, National Sym: Schuman Prems," *High Fidelity/Musical America* (Aug. 1976), p. MA-30.

Chapter 14

323 "*may [be] said to be*": William Schuman, undated notes for *In Sweet Music*; NYPL for the Performing Arts, Box 148, Folder 5.
323 *He clearly saw*: William Schuman, *In Sweet Music*, full score (Bryn Mawr, PA: Merion Music, 1978), p. 4.
323 "*I won a prize*": Schuman and Waleson, chap. 13, pp. 16–17.
324 "*There were some sweet, lyrical things*": Harold C. Schonberg, "Music: Chamber Music Society," *New York Times*, Nov. 6, 1978.
325 "*Experience has demonstrated*": William Schuman, *XXV Opera Snatches for Unaccompanied Flute* (Bryn Mawr, PA: Merion Music, 1979).
326 "*200 paintings*": Description of the Metropolitan Museum of Art's centennial exhibitions; NYPL for the Performing Arts, Box 144, Folder 15.
326 "*in the form*": William Schuman, letter to Stuart F. Louchheim, Oct. 17, 1969; NYPL for the Performing Arts, Box 145, Folder 9.
326 "*[The fanfare] was a joy*": Joseph H. Hirshhorn, letter to William Schuman, Oct. 19, 1974; NYPL for the Performing Arts, Box 147, Folder 5.
327 "*Dear Bill—(Dear Irresistible Bill)*": Goddard Lieberson, letter to William Schuman, Sept. 16, 1975; NYPL for the Performing Arts, Box 107, Folder 1.
327 "*I should tell you*": William Schuman, letter to Aaron Copland, Sept. 20, 1978; NYPL for the Performing Arts, Box 107, Folder 4.
328 "*Since you have now become*": William Schuman, letter to Aaron Copland, Dec. 14, 1978; NYPL for the Performing Arts, Box 107, Folder 4.
328 "*it is my hope*": William Schuman, letter to Harry Kraut, Sept. 27, 1979; NYPL for the Performing Arts, Box 107, Folder 5.
328 "*Instinctively I felt*": Schuman, "Post Lincoln Center," p. 10.
328 "*This winter*": William Schuman, Response—The Gold Medal Award [of the American Academy and Institute of Arts and Letters], May 19, 1982; NYPL for the Performing Arts, Box 123, Folder 8.
329 "*just doesn't go anywhere*": William H. Honan, letter to William Schuman, June 18, 1975; NYPL for the Performing Arts, Box 109, Folder 11.
329 "*to contribute to the understanding*": Program of the Twentieth Charles C. Moskowitz Memorial Lecture, New York University College of Business and Public Administration, Mar. 14, 1979; NYPL for the Performing Arts, Box 110, Folder 1.
330 "*To state the matter succinctly*": William Schuman, "The Esthetic Imperative," paper presented Mar. 14, 1979, at the New York University College of Business and

Public Administration, p. 2; NYPL for the Performing Arts, Box 110, Folder 1.
330 *"The functioning of art"*: ibid., pp. 5–7 passim.
330 *"America . . . has emerged"*: ibid., pp. 8–10 passim.
330 *"The critics of American society"*: ibid., p. 10.
331 *"there is the unalterable fact"*: ibid., pp. 11–13 passim.
331 *"basic to our physical"*: ibid., p. 14.
331 *"Artistic standards, after all"*: ibid., pp. 14–15.
332 *"If we solve"*: ibid., p. 28.
332 *"To decrease expenditures"*: Statement by William Schuman before the House Interim Appropriations Subcommittee of the House Appropriations Committee, Mar. 25, 1981, pp. 1–3; Juilliard Archives, Box 2, Folder: Schuman, William: Misc. Speeches & Articles, 1963, 1979–82.
333 *"I knew that it was not"*: composer's materials for New York Philharmonic program book, Jan. 24, 1980; NYPL for the Performing Arts, Box 148, Folder 5.
333 *"from Conway Burying Ground"*: William Schuman, letter to Archibald MacLeish, Nov. 14, 1977 (dictated Nov. 8); NYPL for the Performing Arts, Box 107, Folder 7.
333 *"Marvellous the difference"*: Archibald MacLeish, letter to William Schuman, Nov. 16, 1977; NYPL for the Performing Arts, Box 107, Folder 7.
334 *"I am still with the songs"*: William Schuman, letter to Archibald MacLeish, Nov. 28, 1979; NYPL for the Performing Arts, Box 107, Folder 7.
334 *"Everything they know"*: William Schuman, *Time to the Old: Three Song Set on Words of Archibald MacLeish* (Bryn Mawr, PA: Merion Music, 1980), p. 2.
336 *Without any rest for the players*: interview by the author with Raymond Mase, Feb. 29, 2008, Juilliard School.
337 *In the final sixteen measures*: William Schuman, *Perceptions* (Bryn Mawr, PA: Merion Music, 1983), pp. 8–9.
338 *"as a new instrumentality"*: William Schuman, "ABCD—A New Plan," Feb. 1982; NYPL for the Performing Arts, Box 123, Folder 3.
339 *"your idea for tax legislation"*: Lester Bernstein, letter to William Schuman, Apr. 1, 1982; NYPL for the Performing Arts, Box 123, Folder 3.
339 *"I must confess"*: Thomas A. Troyer, letter to William Schuman, July 13, 1982; NYPL for the Performing Arts, Box 123, Folder 3.
339 *"but it should be a piece"*: Stephen S. Rosenfeld, letter to William Schuman, Apr. 8, 1983; NYPL for the Performing Arts, Box 123, Folder 4.
339 *"My final version"*: William Schuman, letter to Robert L. Bartley [editor of the *Wall Street Journal*], Apr. 18, 1983.
339 *"It is now time"*: William Schuman, letter to Henry C. Suhrke [editor of *Philanthropy Monthly*], May 29, 1983; NYPL for the Performing Arts, Box 123, Folder 4.
339 *"deeply impressed"*: Leonard Feist, letter to William Schuman, Aug. 16, 1983; NYPL for the Performing Arts, Box 123, Folder 4.
339 *"I have been encouraged"*: William Schuman, letter to Charles T. Clotfelter, Jan. 10, 1985; NYPL for the Performing Arts, Box 123, Folder 4.
340 *"Please avoid the group"*: David Diamond, letter to William Schuman, Mar. 6, 1982; NYPL for the Performing Arts, Box 128, Folder 12.
340 *"and later called Diamond"*: memo to William Schuman personal file, Mar. 16, 1982; NYPL for the Performing Arts, Box 128, Folder 12.
341 *"The true measure"*: "Statement by William Schuman, Chairman of AMRI," AMRI Proposal (n.d., unpaginated); NYPL for the Performing Arts, Box 132, Folder 10.
341 *An early prospectus*: "Proposed Two Year Budget for AMRI," AMRI Proposal (n.d., unpaginated); NYPL for the Performing Arts, Box 132, Folder 10.
342 *"the direction the Film Society"*: Minutes of the meeting of the Board of Directors of the Film Society of Lincoln Center, Sept. 16, 1980, p. 3; NYPL for the Performing Arts, Box 129, Folder 11.

343 *"Sight-Reading Society"*: Andrew Porter, "Voices of Rome," *New Yorker*, May 21, 1984.

343 *"my concern with the CMS"*: William Schuman, memorandum to Henry S. Ziegler, Mrs. Victor W. Ganz, and Isaac Shapiro, Sept. 18, 1983, p. 1; NYPL for the Performing Arts, Box 127, Folder 2.

344 *"one must observe"*: ibid.

344 *"Our Artistic Director should either"*: ibid., p. 2.

344 *"artists of the Society"*: ibid., p. 2.

344 *"We have on more than one occasion"*: ibid., p. 3.

345 *"As the person who chose"*: ibid., pp. 3–4.

345 *A board resolution*: Chamber Music Society of Lincoln Center, Minutes of Executive Committee meeting, June 5, 1984, pp. 4–5; NYPL for the Performing Arts, Box 127, Folder 2.

345 *"All the tunes"*: William Schuman, program notes, Chamber Music Society of Lincoln Center, Oct. 1, 1985; NYPL for the Performing Arts, Box 127, Folder 2.

Chapter 15

347 *"I have just completed"*: William Schuman, letter to David Ewen, Jan. 5, 1979; NYPL for the Performing Arts, Box 99, Folder 12.

347 *"I've received many honors"*: Schuman and Waleson, chap. 14, p. 12.

348 *"What is honor?"*: Leonard Bernstein, presentation speech, American Academy and Institute of Arts and Letters, May 19, 1982, p. 1; NYPL for the Performing Arts, Box 125, Folder 3A.

348 *"is an incarnation of honor"*: ibid., pp. 1–4.

349 *"Our relationship is for me"*: William Schuman, letter to Leonard Bernstein, May 21, 1982; NYPL for the Performing Arts, Box 125, Folder 3A.

349 "West Side Story *could have been*": William Schuman, presentation speech, American Academy and Institute of Arts and Letters, May 15, 1985, p. 1; NYPL for the Performing Arts, Box 123, Folder 8.

349 *"It's bad enough"*: Leonard Bernstein, letter to William Schuman, Mar. 13, 1967; NYPL for the Performing Arts, Box 49, Folder 5A.

349 *"Dear Lenny, the whole dinner"*: William Schuman, letter to Leonard Bernstein, Mar. 20, 1967; NYPL for the Performing Arts, Box 49, Folder 5A.

350 *"She has created"*: quoted from Agnes de Mille Prude, letter to William Schuman, Mar. 28, 1980; NYPL for the Performing Arts, Box 128, Folder 8.

350 *"But if you talk about influence"*: Perlis, p. 451.

350 *"I think Hindemith"*: Perlis, p. 544.

350 *"If I had to name"*: Sheila Keats, "William Schuman," *Stereo Review*, June 1974, p. 77.

350 *"'I would be a very difficult person'"*: Harlow Robinson, "William Schuman," *High Fidelity/Musical America* (Aug. 1985): pp. MA-5, 9.

352 *"for an extraordinary lifetime"*: http://www.williamschuman.org/awards/index.htm, accessed July 6, 2007.

352 *"'most of these people'"*: Schuman and Waleson, chap. 14, pp. 13–14 passim.

352 *"Only in America"*: ibid., chap. 14, pp. 15.

352 *"which brought down the house"*: ibid., chap. 14, p. 16.

353 *"difficult to talk to"*: ibid., chap. 14, p. 18.

353 *"[Slatkin] said"*: ibid., chap. 14, p. 21.

353 *A concluding dinner*: ibid.

353 *"It feels great"*: ibid., chap. 14, p. 22.

354 *"to my family"*: William Schuman, *On Freedom's Ground*, text by Richard Wilbur (Bryn Mawr, PA: Merion Music, 1986), title page.

355 *"utter banality"*: William Schuman, letter to Richard Wilbur, Feb. 2, 1984; NYPL

for the Performing Arts, Box 145, Folder 7.

355 *"centerpiece of the work"*: ibid.
355 *"Where does this leave you"*: ibid., p. 3.
355 *"I am reeling"*: Richard Wilbur, letter to William Schuman, Feb. 17, 1984; NYPL for the Performing Arts, Box 145, Folder 7.
355 *"For reasons of intuition"*: William Schuman, letter to Richard Wilbur, Feb. 26, 1984; NYPL for the Performing Arts, Box 145, Folder 7.
356 *"I have a calm ego"*: Richard Wilbur, letter to William Schuman, Apr. 5, 1984; NYPL for the Performing Arts, Box 145, Folder 7.
356 *"Your thought of freedoms"*: William Schuman, letter to Richard Wilbur, Apr. 12, 1984; NYPL for the Performing Arts, Box 145, Folder 7.
356 *"Your letter makes me want"*: ibid.
356 *"light and swift"*: William Schuman, letter to Richard Wilbur, July 23, 1984; NYPL for the Performing Arts, Box 145, Folder 7.
356 *"Back Then / Our Risen States"*: all quotes from Schuman, *On Freedom's Ground.*
357 *"Mourn for the dead"*: Quoted in ibid.
358 *"It has been very difficult"*: William Schuman, letter to Mr. and Mrs. Richard Wilbur, Feb. 21, 1985; NYPL for the Performing Arts, Box 145, Folder 7.
358 *"The last thing I want"*: William Schuman, letter to Albert K. Webster, Oct. 18, 1984; NYPL for the Performing Arts, Box 145, Folder 7.
358 *"The chorus is fine"*: Schuman and Waleson, chap. 13, p. 10.
359 *"I can't imagine"*: Charlee Wilbur, in Richard Wilbur, letter to William Schuman, Apr. 6, 1987; NYPL for the Performing Arts, Box 145, Folder 10.
360 *"Richard Wilbur, Mr. Schuman's poet"*: John Rockwell, "Music: Liberty Potpourri," *New York Times*, Nov. 2, 1986.
361 *"as the name suggests"*: William Schuman, *Awake Thou Wintry Earth* (Bryn Mawr, PA: Merion Music, 1987), p. 2.
361 *"only if necessary"*: ibid., p. 3.
361 *"The Variations are mostly continuous"*: ibid., p. 2.

Chapter 16

364 *"'Taste' seems to me'"*: Richard Wilbur, letter to William Schuman, Apr. 6, 1987; NYPL for the Performing Arts, Box 145, Folder 10.
364 *"In a way that parallels"*: J. D. McClatchy, "William Schuman: A Reminiscence," *Opera News* 10, no. 4 (1994): p. 23. See also Michael Bawtree, letter to William Schuman, May 2, 1987; NYPL for the Performing Arts, Box 145, Folder 10.
365 *"Basically I've been a symphonist"*: McClatchy, p. 26.
366 *"Knotty, clotted, dour"*: ibid., p. 29.
366 *"he just didn't want"*: ibid., pp. 31–32.
367 *"After a few minutes"*: Bernard Holland, "Review/Opera; 'Casey,' New Schuman Work, as Glimmerglass Opens," *New York Times*, June 26, 1989.
367 *"I find that my luxury"*: Perlis, p. 546.
367 *"'Carols of Death' is my own title"*: Schuman and Waleson, chap. 13, pp. 5–6.
367 *"I don't know what'll happen"*: ibid., chap. 14, p. 24.
368 *"I've always claimed"*: ibid.
368 *He spent many hours*: The photographs would eventually be donated to the Juilliard School, where they were remounted in a fifth-floor lounge area and dedicated as "The William Schuman Photograph Collection" on March 13, 2001.
368 *"serious literature and articles"*: ibid.
368 *"I find very little of the music"*: ibid., chap. 14, p. 25.
368 *"I remember the way"*: Perlis, p. 491.

369 *"First I tell them"*: Harlow Robinson, "William Schuman," *High Fidelity/Musical America* (Aug. 1985): p. MA-9.

369 *"Bill, appetites change"*: Schuman and Waleson, chap. 14, p. 27.

369 *"The primary goal and obligation"*: Schuman and Waleson, chap. 14, pp. 27–29 passim.

369 *"It is hard to imagine"*: Robert S. Hines, "William Schuman Interview," *College Music Symposium* 35 (fall 1995): p. 134.

369 *"The pervading element"*: ibid., p. 135.

370 *"Simplicity is something"*: ibid., p. 136.

370 *"I do not use harmony"*: ibid., p. 140.

370 *"I do not think of the bass line"*: ibid.

370 *"Schoenberg's great achievement"*: Anders Beyer, *The Voice of Music: Conversations with Composers of Our Time*, ed. and trans. Jean Christensen and Anders Beyer (Ashgate, 2000), p. 178, quoted in Alex Ross, *The Rest Is Noise: Listening to the Twentieth Century* (New York: Farrar, Straus and Giroux, 2007), p. 392.

371 *"neoclassical lingo"*: Alex Ross, *The Rest Is Noise: Listening to the Twentieth Century* (New York: Farrar, Straus and Giroux, 2007), p. 392.

371 *"The [American] composer"*: Kurt List, "Music Chronicle: The State of American Music," *Partisan Review*, Jan. 1948, p. 90, quoted in Ross, p. 401.

371 *"Carter renounced"*: Ross, p. 404.

371 *"I decided for once"*: David Schiff, *The Music of Elliott Carter*, 2nd ed. (Cornell University Press, 1998), p. 55; quoted in Ross, p. 404.

371 *"I dare suggest"*: Milton Babbitt, "Who Cares If You Listen?," *High Fidelity* 8, no. 2 (Feb. 1958): p. 126; quoted in Ross, p. 406.

372 *"Many young American composers"*: Hines, p. 143.

372 *"It is difficult to imagine"*: William Schuman, "The Purpose of a Symphony Orchestra," address delivered before the American Symphony Orchestra League, Carnegie Hall, New York City, June 19, 1980, p. 13; Juilliard Archives, Box 2, Folder: Schuman, William: Misc. Speeches & Articles, 1963, 1979–82.

373 *"Composers who are not"*: Schuman and Waleson, chap. 14, pp. 31–32 passim.

374 *"The works on this evening's program"*: "In Praise of William Schuman" [program notes], Oct. 25, 1991, Bruno Walter Auditorium, New York Public Library for the Performing Arts; NYPL for the Performing Arts, Box 177, Folder 2.

375 *"He set the highest standards"*: *MacDowell Colony [Peterborough, NH] News* (Spring–Summer 1992), p. 12.

375 *"showed composers that social activism"*: Daniel Webster, "An Appreciation. Schuman: Activist, Composer," *Philadelphia Inquirer*, Feb. 18, 1992.

Epilogue

377 *"every composition's style"*: Virgil Thomson, in Edward Rothstein, "A Composer with Many Public Faces," *New York Times*, Mar. 8, 1992.

377 *"earned his living"*: Rothstein, "Composer."

377 *"emphasizing sophisticated achievements"*: ibid.

378 *"Had he been a greater composer"*: ibid.

378 *"There are many composers"*: William Schuman, letter to Abraham Friedman, Jan. 6, 1965; Schuman Family Archives.

379 *"If you have to worry"*: Schuman and Waleson, chap. 13, p. 21.

379 *"I got [in]to administration"*: Perlis, p. 484.

380 *"I wouldn't have missed"*: ibid., p. 485.

381 *"If someone asked me"*: Schuman and Waleson, chap. 14, p. 34.

Appendix

385 *"I soon found"*: Schuman and Waleson, chap. 5, p. 124.
385 *"I was amazed"*: ibid., pp. 114–15.
385 *"optional but very desirable"*: William Schuman, *Symphony No. III* (New York: G. Schirmer, 1942), n.p.
385 *In fact, Schuman stated*: Schuman and Waleson, chap. 5, p. 123.
386 *"I don't find any satisfaction"*: ibid., pp. 119–20.
392 *Schuman's own description*: William Schuman, *New England Triptych: Three Pieces for Orchestra after William Billings* (Bryn Mawr, PA: Merion Music, 1957).
394 *"if available, 2 or 3 snare drums"*: ibid., p. 39.
397 *"The words are given"*: William Schuman, *A Song of Orpheus: Fantasy for Cello and Orchestra* (Bryn Mawr, PA: Merion Music, 1963).
399 *The quotations that appear below*: William Schuman, *Symphony No. IX: Le Fosse Ardeatine* (Bryn Mawr, PA: Merion Music, 1971).
402 *"to enable the flutist"*: Schuman, *In Sweet Music*, p. 5.

Selected Bibliography

Adams, K. Gary. *William Schuman: A Bio-Bibliography*. Westport, CT: Greenwood Press, 1998.

Allen, Oliver E. *New York, New York*. New York: Atheneum, 1990.

Ballon, Hilary, and Kenneth T. Jackson, eds. *Robert Moses and the Modern City: The Transformation of New York*. New York: W.W. Norton, 2007.

Bernstein, Leonard. "The Latest from Boston." *Modern Music* 16, no. 3 (1938–39): pp. 182–84.

———. "Young American: William Schuman." *Modern Music* 19, no. 2 (1941–42): pp. 97–99.

Berrol, Selma C. "In their Image: German Jews and the Americanization of the *Ost Juden* in New York City." *New York History* 63 (Oct. 1982): pp. 417–433.

Birmingham, Stephen. *"Our Crowd": The Great Jewish Families of New York*. New York: Harper & Row, 1967.

"Bread & Butter." *Time*, Feb. 20, 1950.

Broder, Nathan. "The Music of William Schuman." *Musical Quarterly* 31, no. 1 (Jan. 1945): pp. 17–28.

Caro, Robert A. *The Power Broker: Robert Moses and the Fall of New York*. New York: Alfred A. Knopf, 1974.

Carruth, Gorton. *The Encyclopedia of American Facts and Dates*. 10th ed. New York: Harper Collins, 1997.

Carter, Elliott. "Forecast and Review: American Music in the New York Scene." *Modern Music* 17, no. 2 (1939–40): pp. 93–101.

Chazin-Bennahum, Judith. *The Ballets of Antony Tudor*. New York: Oxford University Press, 1994.

Cohen, Naomi W. *Encounter with Emancipation: The German Jews in the United States, 1830–1914*. Philadelphia: Jewish Publication Society of America, 1984.

Copland, Aaron. *Copland on Music*. Garden City, NY: Doubleday, 1960.

———. "Scores and Records." *Modern Music* 15, no. 4 (1937–38): pp. 244–48.

Daniel, Oliver. "An American Approach to the Grand Manner." *Saturday Review*, Nov. 9, 1957.

Dolkart, Andrew S. *Morningside Heights: A History of Its Architecture & Development*. New York: Columbia University Press, 1998.

Duberman, Martin. *The Worlds of Lincoln Kirstein*. New York: Alfred A. Knopf, 2007.

Eliassof, Herman. *German-American Jews*. Chicago: German-American Historical Society of Illinois, 1915.

Evett, Robert. "Current Chronicle: Washington, D.C." *Musical Quarterly* 51, no. 2 (Apr. 1965): pp. 406–9.

Eyer, Ronald. "William Schuman." *Musical America* (Sept. 1962): pp. 26, 76.

Eyer, Ronald F. "William Schuman Is First Subject of Music Forum." *Musical America* (Jan. 25, 1943): pp. 19.

Frankenstein, Alfred. "American Composers, XXII: William Schuman." *Modern Music* 22, no. 1 (Nov.–Dec. 1944): pp. 23–29.

Graham, Martha. *Blood Memory*. New York: Doubleday, 1991.

Hines, Robert S. "William Schuman Interview." *College Music Symposium* 35 (1995): pp. 132–44.

Hitchcock, H. Wiley. Review of *The Juilliard Report on Teaching the Literature and Materials of Music*. *Notes* 11 (2nd ser.), no. 2 (Mar. 1954): pp. 299–300.

Jacobs, Arthur, ed. *Choral Music*. Baltimore: Penguin Books, 1963.

The Juilliard Report on Teaching the Literature and Materials of Music. New York: W.W. Norton, 1953.

Keats, Sheila. "William Schuman." *Stereo Review* (June 1974): pp. 68–77.

Kouwenhoven, John A. *The Columbia Historical Portrait of New York: An Essay in Graphic History*. New York: Harper & Row, 1972.

Krokover, Rosalyn. "Martha Graham: Indomitable" [review]. *High Fidelity/Musical America* (Jan. 1966): p. 142.

LaBach, Parker. "Why We Are Criticized: A Music Educator's Analysis." *Music Educators Journal* 43, no. 2 (Nov.–Dec. 1956): pp. 18–19.

Lieberson, Goddard. "Over the Air." *Modern Music* 16, no. 1 (1938–39): pp. 65–69.

Lowell, John H. Review of *The Juilliard Report on Teaching the Literature and Materials of Music*. *Musical Quarterly* 40, no. 2 (Apr. 1954): pp. 248–50.

Macaulay, Alastair. "Under Analysis: The Psychology of Tudor's Ballets." *New York Times*, May 11, 2008.

"Maestro in Play Clothes." *Newsweek*, Aug. 13, 1945.

Mayer, Grace M. *Once upon a City: New York from 1890–1910 as Photographed by Byron*. New York: Macmillan, 1958.

McClatchy, J. D. "William Schuman: A Reminiscence." *Opera News* 10, no. 4 (1994): pp. 21–37.

McDonagh, Don. *Martha Graham: A Biography*. New York: Praeger, 1973.

McPherson, Elizabeth. *The Contributions of Martha Hill to American Dance and Dance Education, 1900–1995*. Lewiston, NY: Edwin Mellen Press, 2008.

Mehta, Ved. "An Enclave." *New Yorker*, Feb. 17, 1962.

Miller, Karl F. "William Schuman, 1910–1992." *American Record Guide* 55, no. 4 (July–Aug. 1992): pp. 29–31.

Moore, David E. "Videorecord's Dr. Hopwood Calls for Innovation in Marketing and Programming the New Television." *Southern Connecticut Business Journal*, Oct. 27, 1970.

Normann, Theodore F. "The Responsibility of Music to Education." *Music Educators Journal* 43, no. 1 (Sept.–Oct. 1956): pp. 20–23.

Paris, Robert. "Washington. National Sym: Schuman Prems." *High Fidelity/Musical America* (Aug. 1976): p. MA-30.

Perlis, Vivian. Transcript of interview with William Schuman, no. 46 a–hh, Feb. 2–Nov. 16, 1977, New York City and Greenwich, CT [unpublished manuscript]. American Music Series.

Perlis, Vivian, and Libby Van Cleve. *Composers' Voices from Ives to Ellington: An Oral History of American Music*. New Haven, CT: Yale University Press, 2005.

Pohl, Frances K. *Ben Shahn*. New York: Chameleon Books, 1993.

Pollack, Howard. *Aaron Copland: The Life and Work of an Uncommon Man*. New York: Henry Holt, 1999.

Robinson, Harlow. "William Schuman." *High Fidelity/Musical America* (Aug. 1985): pp. MA 4–5, 9.

Rockefeller Family Archives. John D. Rockefeller 3rd Papers, 1906–1978. Series 1, Office of the Messrs. Rockefeller Files. Subseries 4: Lincoln Center.

Rosenfeld, Paul. "Current Chronicle: Copland–Harris–Schuman." *Musical Quarterly* 25 (July 1939): pp. 372–81.

Ross, Alex. *The Rest Is Noise: Listening to the Twentieth Century*. New York: Farrar, Straus & Giroux, 2007.

Rouse, Christopher. *William Schuman Documentary: Biographical Essay, Catalogue of Works, Discography, and Bibliography*. Bryn Mawr, PA: Theodore Presser and G. Schirmer, 1980.

Rouse, Christopher Chapman III. "Expansion of Material in the Seventh Symphony of William Schuman." Part 2. Master's thesis, Cornell University, 1977.

Sabin, Robert. "The Dangers of Being a Destructive Reactionary." *Musical America* (Feb. 1961): pp. 8, 60.

Sargeant, Winthrop. "Musical Events." *New Yorker*, Mar. 30, 1963.

Schonberg, Harold C. "Man to Orchestrate Lincoln Center." *New York Times Magazine*, Dec. 31, 1961.

Schreiber, Flora Rheta, and Vincent Persichetti. *William Schuman*. New York: G. Schirmer, 1954.

Schuman, William. "Autobiography" [unpublished manuscript]. Schuman Family Archives.

——. *Biographical Files*. Juilliard School Archives. The Juilliard School, New York.

——. "Juilliard Goes on Tour." *Juilliard Review* 5, no. 3 (Fall 1958): pp. 3–4.

——. "On Teaching the Literature and Materials of Music." *Musical Quarterly* 34, no. 2 (Apr. 1948): pp. 155–68.

——. Papers. Music Division. New York Public Library for the Performing Arts. Astor, Lenox, and Tilden Foundations.

——. "The Responsibility of Music Education to Music" [address to the biennial meeting of the Music Educators National Conference, Apr. 17, 1956, St. Louis, MO], *Music Educators Journal* 42, no. 6 (June–July 1956): pp. 17–19.

——. "Unconventional Case History." *Modern Music* 15, no. 4 (May–June 1938): pp. 222–27.

Schuman, William, and Heidi Waleson. "William Schuman Memoirs, 1990–1992, New York" [unpublished manuscript]. Schuman Family Archives.

Schuman, William, and William Zinsser. "Dialogue between William Schuman and William Zinsser, April 4, 1989–July 11, 1989, New York and Greenwich, Connecticut" [unpublished manuscript]. Schuman Family Archives.

Schuster-Craig, John. "Stravinsky's *Scènes de Ballet* and Billy Rose's *The Seven Lively Arts: The Abravanel Account.*" In *Music in the Theatre, Church and Villa: Essays in Honor of Robert Lamar Weaver and Norma Wright Weaver*, ed. Susan Parisi. Sterling Heights, MI: Harmonie Park Press, 2000. pp. 285–89.

Stedman, Preston. *The Symphony*. 2nd ed. Englewood Cliffs, NJ: Prentice Hall, 1992.

Stehman, Dan. *Roy Harris: A Bio-Bibliography*. Westport, CT: Greenwood Press, 1991.

Stewart, Louis C. *Music Composed for Martha Graham: A Discussion of Musical and Choreographic Collaboratives*. Ann Arbor, MI: UMI, 1991.

Stoddard, Hope. "William Schuman Discusses Problems in the Field of Music Education." *International Musician* (Mar. 1961): pp. 22–23.

Swayne, Steve. "William Schuman, World War II, and the Pulitzer Prize." *Musical Quarterly* 89, no. 2–3 (Summer–Fall 2006): pp. 273–320.

Thorpe, Day. "Washington, D.C./Coolidge Festival." *Musical America* 84 (Dec. 1964): p. 64.

Trager, James. *The New York Chronology: The Ultimate Compendium of Events, People, and Anecdotes from the Dutch to the Present*. New York: HarperCollins, 2003.

Trow General Directory of New York City, 1922–23. New York: R. L. Polk, 1923.

"Ventilation for Juilliard." *Time*, Oct. 22, 1945.

Wedge, George A. *Advanced Ear-Training and Sight-Singing as Applied to the Study of Harmony*. New York: G. Schirmer, 1922.

Wright, David. "Composer in America: William Schuman Talks about His Life and Works" [unpublished manuscript, 1987]. Juilliard Archives, Box 3, Folder: Schuman, William: Chapter Drafts from Proposed Memoir with David Wright; Correspondence, 1986–87.

Young, Edgar B. *Lincoln Center: The Building of an Institution*. New York: New York University Press, 1980.

Zane, Sharon. Transcript of interviews with Schuyler Chapin, Jan. 7, 1991–Jan. 22, 1992, New York City. Lincoln Center for the Performing Arts Oral History Project. Lincoln Center for the Performing Arts, 1992. Lincoln Center for the Performing Arts Archives.

——. Transcript of interviews with William Schuman, July 10–Oct. 18, 1990, New York City and Greenwich, CT. Lincoln Center for the Performing Arts Oral History Project. Schuman Family Archives.

——. Transcript of interviews with Edgar Young, June 11–Nov. 13, 1990, New York City. Lincoln Center for the Performing Arts Oral History Project. Lincoln Center for the Performing Arts, 1990. Lincoln Center for the Performing Arts Archives.

Zuck, Barbara A. *A History of Musical Americanism*. Ann Arbor, MI: UMI Research Press, 1980.

Index

synthesizers, 331
timpani, 249, 267, 269, 320, 401
trumpet, 387, 391, 401
viola, 302, 323–24, 375, 402–3, 516–24
violin, 12, 16, 18, 41, 58, 111, 172–75, 279,
 379, 389–91, 446–61
woodwinds, 315, 317, 319–21, 333, 384
xylophone, 383
*In Sweet Music: Serenade on a Setting of
 Shakespeare for Flute, Viola, Voice and
 Harp* (Schuman), 302, 323, 375
 descriptive analysis, 402–3
 musical examples, 516–24
 premiere, 324, 402
International Conference of Creative Artists,
 180
International Cultural Exchange Service, 120
International Musician, 127
International Tchaikovsky Competition, 124
Iowa State University, 297
Iron Curtain, 125
Irving, Jules, 263
Irving, Washington, 176
Isabella, Queen, 19

Jacobs, Eli, 304
JAMRI. *See* Juilliard American Music
 Recording Institute
Jardin aux lilas (Tudor), 146
jazz, 372–73
JDT. *See* Juilliard Dance Theater
Jeu de cartes (Stravinsky), 47–48
Jews, 44. *See also* anti-Semitism; German Jews;
 Judaism; religion; Sephardic Jews
JMF. *See* Juilliard Musical Foundation
Johnson, Lady Bird, 238
Johnson, Philip, 222, 224, 236
Johnson, Thor, 181
Johnson administration, 208
Josephs, Devereux C., 206
Joyce, James, 348
JSM. *See* Juilliard School of Music
Judaism, 8, 37, 108
Judd, George, 65, 134
Judith (Schuman), 114, 116, 165, 188, 379
 development of, 160
 story of, 159–60
Juilliard American Music Recording Institute
 (JAMRI), 342
Juilliard Dance Theater (JDT), 116
Juilliard Graduate Institute, 23
Juilliard Musical Foundation (JMF), 84, 92,
 130, 133

Juilliard Orchestra, 174
 European tour, 119–20
 repertory for tour, 121–22
 reviews of tour, 123
*The Juilliard Report on Teaching the Literature
 and Materials of Music* (Goldman), 101
Juilliard Review, 118
The Juilliard School (at Lincoln Center), 279
Juilliard School of Music (JSM), 31, 62, 83,
 111, 351
 Academic Division of, 104
 board of directors response to downsizing
  plan, 129
 branding of, through Juilliard Quartet, 113
 controversy with NASM, 123
 dance division of, 114–17
 degrees offered by, 93
 discontinuation of summer school, 96
 distribution of instrumentalists in, 96
 downsizing of, 128–29, 131, 132
 drama, 134, 136–39
 faculty changes in, 89
 financial issues of, 95
 history of, 92
 honorary doctorate from, 347
 leadership style at, 205
 Lincoln Center and, 127–31, 135, 137–39,
  209, 270
 Literature and Materials of Music, 103
 Preparatory Department, 223
 presidential search committee, 203
 prevailing attitude of, 102
 resignation as president, 203–4
 Schuman's educational philosophy at, 84,
  99–101
 Schuman years at, 84–86, 89, 90–91, 97
 Wedge as director of summer school, 86
Juilliard String Quartet, 380
 finances of, 113
 foundation of, 112–13
 legendary rise of, 114
J. & W. Chester, 183

Katherine Cornell Foundation, 163
Kazan, Elia, 136, 138, 215, 229, 230
 friction with Schuman, 232
 Saint-Denis relationship strained with, 139
Keilholz, Heinrich, 222
Keiser, David, 130
Kellogg, Paul, 366
Kennedy Center Honor, 352–53
Kennedy, Jacqueline, 220
Kennedy, John F., 208, 220

Music Credits

Grateful acknowledgment is made to the following
for permission to reproduce musical examples:

G. SCHIRMER, INC.

American Festival Overture: Copyright, 1941, by G. Schirmer, Inc. International copyright secured.

Symphony No. 3: Copyright, 1942, by G. Schirmer, Inc. International copyright secured.

Symphony for Strings: Copyright, 1943, by G. Schirmer, Inc. International copyright secured.

String Quartet No. IV: Copyright, MCMLI, MCMLIII, by G. Schirmer, Inc. International copyright secured.

THEODORE PRESSER COMPANY

Concerto for Violin and Orchestra: © Copyright 1960 by Merion Music, Inc. All rights reserved. International copyright secured.

New England Triptyke: © Copyright 1957 by Merion Music, Inc. International copyright secured. All rights reserved.

A Song of Orpheus: © Copyright 1963 by Merion Music, Inc. 446-41006-29. All rights reserved. International copyright secured.

Symphony No. IX: © 1971 Merion Music, Inc., Bryn Mawr, Pa. Theodore Presser Co., Sole Representative. 446-41016. All rights reserved. International copyright secured.

In Sweet Music: © 1978 by Merion Music, Inc., Bryn Mawr, Pa. Theodore Presser Co., Sole Representative. 144-40072. All rights reserved. International copyright secured.

Night Journey: © 1978 by Merion Music, Inc., Bryn Mawr, Pa. Theodore Presser Co., Sole Representative. 444-41011. All rights reserved. International copyright secured. This edition published 1982.